AUTHOR	CLASS
	599·8i5
TITLE	No.
Comparative Ecology and Behaviour of primates	470073292

Comparative Ecology
and
Behaviour of Primates

Conference held at the Zoological Society
London, November 1971

Sponsored by

PRIMATE SOCIETY OF GREAT BRITAIN
President: Richard P. Michael

and

ASSOCIATION FOR THE STUDY OF ANIMAL BEHAVIOUR
President: Robert A. Hinde

Comparative Ecology
and
Behaviour of Primates

Proceedings of a Conference held at the Zoological Society
London, November 1971

Edited by

RICHARD P. MICHAEL
JOHN H. CROOK

1973

Academic Press: London and New York

A Subsidiary of Harcourt Brace Jovanovich, Publishers

ACADEMIC PRESS INC. (LONDON) LTD.
24/28 Oval Road,
London NW1

United States Edition published by
ACADEMIC PRESS INC.
111 Fifth Avenue
New York, New York 10003

47007329

Library of Congress Catalog Card Number: 73–2289
ISBN: 0–12–493450–1

Printed in Great Britain
by Unwin Brothers Limited
The Gresham Press, Old Woking, Surrey, England

N. G. Blurton-Jones, Institute of Child Health,
University of London

N. R. Chalmers, The Open University, Bletchley

D. J. Chivers, Veterinary Anatomy, University
of Cambridge

J. H. Crook, Department of Psychology,
University of Bristol

J. M. Deag, Department of Zoology, University
of Edinburgh

PARTICIPANTS   A. Gautier-Hion, Station biologique de Paimpont,
University of Rennes

J. P. Hess, Department of Zoology,
University of Basel

C. Hutt, Department of Psychology, University
of Reading

A. Kendon, Bronx State Hospital, New York

R. D. Martin, Department of Anthropology,
University College London

R. P. Michael, Institute of Psychiatry,
University of London

D. Ploog, Max-Planck-Institute for Psychiatry,
Munich

P. S. Rodman, Department of Anthropology,
Harvard University

M. J. A. Simpson, Sub-department of Animal
Behaviour, University of Cambridge

P. K. Smith, Department of Psychology,
University of Sheffield

Y. Sugiyama, Primate Research Institute,
Kyoto University

M. J. Waterhouse, Department of Sociology,
University of Reading

Contemporary Developments in Primate Behaviour

This book, the outcome of a joint conference held in London arranged by the Primate Society of Great Britain and the Association for the Study of Animal Behaviour, provides a wide-ranging conspectus of current trends in the study of both human and non-human primate behaviour. There is now a realization that anatomical, physiological, sociological and ecological studies of particular species should no longer be pursued in isolation from each other but that, whatever the details of the specialized topics under consideration, each provides an insight into what is a larger system of organization. The clear task for social ethologists, whether primarily physiologically or behaviourally oriented, is now to work out in detail the relations involved.

The articles in this volume fall into four main categories: (i) Socio-ecological studies of a range of non-human primates from lemurs to great apes, (ii) Studies of the inter- and intra-group dynamics and their spatial characteristics, (iii) Physiological, especially endocrine and neural, analyses of social interactions, (iv) Studies of human behaviour based largely on ethological methods and premises. All the papers presented reveal a consistent trend towards greater precision in the statement of problems and greater sophistication in attempts to find answers.

We owe a great debt to former generations of primate field workers on whose painstaking observations these new developments are founded. While their work originally focussed attention on displays, it has gradually become apparent that the social organization of a given population of a species might be better understood in terms of the

operation of various selection pressures, primarily in relation to the
acquisition of food and other resources, to mating and rearing success
and to risks from predation: these views have been provocative of
lively discussion and fresh experimentation (Crook, 1965, 1970, 1972;
Crook and Gartlan, 1966; Eisenberg, 1966; Eisenberg, Muckenhirn and
Rudran, 1972). Attempts to interpret correlations between the behavioural organization of a species and the features of its ecological niche
represent the new discipline of socio-ecological ethology which is now
importantly influencing the study of primate behaviour.

The contributions by Martin, Gautier-Hion, Rodman, Sugiyama
and Chivers in this volume illustrate these trends in varying degrees
and provide invaluable new findings on the chosen species. Sugiyama
provides an important overview of the Japanese researches on the
chimpanzee in East Africa that need careful consideration in relation to
the better known studies based on the Gombe Stream Reserve. By
studying the chimpanzee in a range of contrasting conditions,the Japanese
and others have broadened our understanding of the social structure of a
species taxonomically very close to our own. Rodman's study of the
orangutan makes an interesting comparison with the chimpanzee work
by revealing a quite different type of social structure and contrasting
patterns of behaviour. Chivers' survey reveals the extraordinary
research potential of the Malayan forests for primatology - one that we
hope will be developed successfully. Deag's paper is a quantified account
of attempts to analyze inter-group, in contrast to intra-group, relations;
an analysis that seems likely to be influential in future studies on
this topic. Chalmers shows the value of examining the behavioural
characteristics of a species both in the laboratory and in the field, and
demonstrates the striking way in which laboratory testing can be used

to supplement field material in understanding sources of adaptation.
The papers by Simpson and Hess, on wild chimpanzees and captive
gorillas respectively, examine detailed aspects of the personal interactions in these animals that can be related to other studies on hominoid
species, notably our own. Simpson not only establishes relations
between social grooming and hierarchical organization among adult male
chimpanzees but the methodological problems posed in this type of
analysis are fully detailed.

    The ethological approach to analyzing the communication and
social organization of animals, first applied to the study of fishes and
birds, has now been developed further in higher mammals and sub-
human primates. Latterly, these methods have been employed to study
non-verbal communication in man and to such intractable psychiatric
problems as infantile autism and schizophrenia. Ploog in his deeply
thoughtful introduction to the ethology section touches on these matters.
Comparative studies of an increasing number of species enable us to
gain insight into which behavioural mechanisms are phylogenetically
old, namely, those that correlate most closely with structure, in contrast to those that are more readily adapted by extrinsic ecological or
even social factors. Thus, as Chalmers points out in comparing the
behaviour of different primate species, one must take into account both
taxonomic position and ecology. Recent thinking supports the view that
communicative interactions in sexual and agonistic situations, that is,
display behaviour generally, are more intimately related to taxonomy
than to the immediate environment. The mechanism, for example,
whereby aggressive tendencies associated with pair bonding are
rendered harmless in fishes and birds by redirection away from the
partner also operates in the rhesus monkey (Zumpe and Michael, 1970)

and probably in the human; an extraordinarily widely generalized behavioural mechanism.

As one ascends the comparative scale there is increasing flexibility in the expression of behaviour and richness in the communicatory repertoire. Nevertheless there remains considerable reliance on phylogenetically old mechanisms: olfactory pheromones, for instance, have now been shown to be important for communication in prosimians, in New and Old World monkeys (Michael et al., 1972), and Hess' data suggest that this is also the case for the gorilla although we still await the proper documentation of evidence for man. The gorilla study reveals the importance of genital contact, manipulation and touching throughout life, views for which Freud was earlier much criticized. The mother touches the offspring's genitals in such widely varying contexts as sexual arousal, punishment or rejection, and in forms of social training. The increasing flexibility of behavioural patterns is illustrated by the progression from the somewhat stereotyped, rodent-like copulatory lordosis posture of tree-shrews and some prosimians to the rich variety of postures, soliciting gestures and facial expressions that characterize the sexual interactions of hominoid primates. It will help assuage the guilt of many of us to be made aware that, for instance, oro-genital sex is quite acceptable to gorillas, and it might even seem paradoxical that cultural constraints should operate to rigidify the richness and flexibility of the behaviour of our own species in the sexual sphere. Insofar as sexual difficulties constitute a major component of human social pathology, these comparative studies must have special interest for both psychiatrists and social scientists.

There is a quite different area of research to which the comparative approach is bringing fresh insight and to which reference

should briefly be made, namely, steroid biochemistry. While the bio-
synthesis and metabolism of the major steroid hormones are well
documented in man, data for sub-human primates are only now becoming
available and are restricted to three genera, Macaca, Papio and Pan.
The relative paucity of information makes it difficult to develop arguments
about the evolution of biosynthetic mechanisms but certain examples merit
attention. In man, progesterone is catabolized largely by a process of
reduction, and pregnanediol is the main urinary metabolite, there being
little cleavage of the side chain at C-17. In the macaque, however, a
desmolase system appears to be active which results in the urinary
excretion of C-19 steroids, particularly androsterone (Plant, James and
Michael, 1971). Conversion of progesterone to urinary androsterone
also occurs in baboons although quantitatively pregnanediol is an important metabolite. In contrast, in the chimpanzee progesterone catabolism
is quite similar to that in man, and it is therefore tempting to speculate
that differences in the extent of cleavage between C-17 and C-20 in
macaque, baboon, chimpanzee and man represents an evolutionary trend
in a protein molecule responsible for the catabolism of the corpus
luteum hormone in primates. The behavioural implications of these
differences in steroid metabolism await investigation.

The ethological approach to human group processes is very
much in its infancy and poses problems of methodology and inference
making of even greater complexity than those concerned with signalling.
The papers by Smith, by Blurton Jones and Konner, and by Brindley
et al. show clearly the analytical sophistication that is required. This
approach has focussed primarily on interactional rituals and the details
of facial and gestural kinesics. Kendon and Ferber emphasize that in
communicative behaviour lie some of the best opportunities for

insightful comparisons between human and animal behaviour. They point out, as does Eibl-Eibesfeldt (1968), that while some components of greeting behaviour are apparently universal in man, others show great and culturally influenced diversity. The range of variation in close salutations is greater than when greetings are made from a distance. Clearly these contrasts relate to interpersonal situations carrying vastly different information loads - those requiring least recognition of informational content being, not surprisingly, the most stereotyped. Their detailed description based on film analysis has emphasized fascinating regularities in human behaviour some of which remain very puzzling to understand. It is clear that other social rituals in man need studies of equal depth, and that efforts should be made to understand analogous, if not homologous, rituals in other hominoids. The exploration of this research area seems necessary for an adequate social psychology of man.

The two papers concerned with sex differences are of special contemporary significance and perhaps foreshadow ways out of an unusually tangled controversy. Ever since J.S. Mill attributed the female "subservience" of his time to sociological factors and especially to domineering male mores there has been a tendency to regard women as in some sense captive to and conditioned by men - especially those of Victorian persuasions. The work of Malinowski and of Mead has also stressed the important cultural basis of gender roles in man. By contrast, Darwin stressed that behavioural and psychological differences might be associated with naturally selected structural divergencies between the sexes and thus possessed a biological basis which we would now consider genetic. Needless to say the somewhat shrill altercations between protagonists of these different viewpoints are based on stressing the dichotomies. As has been pointed out (Crook, 1972, 1973), any

Preface

examination of the gender differences in human behaviour from the standpoint of an out-dated nature-nurture controversy is doomed to failure, unless conceived merely as an after-dinner diversion. The need now is for exact empirical investigations of the developmental processes, both before and after birth, that underlie the emergence of gender identity in men and women - a formidable task indeed. The papers by Brindley et al. and by Blurton Jones and Konner attempt to set this garden in order. Despite the undoubted importance of cultural factors there can remain little doubt that neuroendocrine mechanisms are basic to many of the behavioural differences between the sexes, and this view is strongly supported by comparative studies on the sexual ethology of vertebrates as a whole. The implications of these findings for the "sexual politics" of human beings may well be considerable, and an effective understanding of them will not only give a deeper historical and evolutionary perspective to the controversy but will also enhance our ability to comprehend the needs of men and women in the rapidly shifting conditions of modern society. Not least in terms of interpersonal stresses and mental health generally, a greater understanding between the sexes seems crucial for a happier social environment than patterns of contemporary living commonly allow.

Throughout this book the emphasis on the ethological approach as well as an evolutionary perspective on primate and human biology and behaviour will be clearly apparent. We trust that such studies will continue to gain the recognition they truly deserve and will help to provide modern psychology with a more adequate biological foundation.

Richard P. Michael and John H. Crook

May 1973

Preface

REFERENCES

Crook, J.H. (1965). The adaptive significance of avian social
organisations. Symp. zool. Soc. London, 14, 181-218.

Crook, J.H. (1970). The Socio-ecology of Primates. In: Social
Behaviour in Birds and Mammals (J.H. Crook, Ed.). Academic
Press.

Crook, J.H. (1972). Sexual selection, dimorphism and social organisation in primates. In: (B. Campbell, Ed.). Sexual
Selection and the Descent of Man. Chicago: Aldive.

Crook, J.H. (1973). Darwinism and the Sexual Politics of Primates.
In: "L'Origine dell 'Uomo". Academia Nazionale Linaei. Rome.

Crook. J.H. and Gartlan, J.S. (1966). Evolution of primate societies.
Nature, 210, 1200-1203.

Eibl-Eibesfeldt, I. (1968). Zur Ethologie des menschlichen Grussverhaltens. I. Beobachtungen an Balinesen, Papuas und Samoanern
nebst vergleichenden Bemerkungen. Z. Tierpsychol., 25,
727-744.

Eisenberg, J. (1966). The social organisation of mammals. Handb.
der Zoologie, 10, 1-92.

Michael, R.P., Zumpe, D., Keverne, E.B. and Bonsall, R.W. (1972).
Neuroendocrine factors in the control of primate behavior. Rec.
Progr. Hormone Research, 28, 665-706.

Plant, T.M., James, V.H.T. and Michael, R.P. (1971). Conversion
of $[4 \, {}^{-14}C]$ progesterone to androsterone by female rhesus
monkeys (Macaca mulatta). J. Endocr., 51, 751-761.

Zumpe, D. and Michael, R.P. (1970). Redirected aggression and
gonadal hormones in captive rhesus monkeys (Macaca mulatta).
Anim. Behav., 18, 11-19.

CONTENTS

Contents

A REVIEW OF THE BEHAVIOUR AND ECOLOGY

OF THE LESSER MOUSE LEMUR

(Microcebus murinus J. F. Miller 1777)

R. D. Martin

Department of Anthropology
University College
Gower Street
London W C 1

INTRODUCTION

This paper summarises data currently available from a continuing study of the behaviour and ecology of the Lesser Mouse Lemur, Microcebus murinus. A previous publication covers the results of a field-study conducted in Madagascar during July - December 1968 (Martin 1972a). Since November 1969, a laboratory colony of Mouse Lemurs has been maintained in London in order to study certain aspects of reproduction, general behaviour and morphology. Preliminary results of the breeding programme have already been reported (Martin 1972b). In 1970, the author was able to extend certain observations made during the 1968 field study, and the main results are presented here[1].

The Mouse Lemur is a particularly suitable subject to investigate for several reasons. Seventy-five per cent of prosimian species are nocturnal in habits, and the Mouse Lemur was originally selected for study because of the pressing need to obtain information about nocturnal prosimians. Since 1968, however, there have been several other publications on the behaviour and ecology of nocturnal lemurs and lorises (Charles-Dominique 1971, 1972; Charles-Dominique and Hladik 1971; Petter & Hladik 1970; Petter, Schilling and Pariente 1971),

[1]Thanks to an invitation to attend the International Conference on the Conservation of Natural Resources held in Tananarive (October 1970), the month of September 1970 was spent in the Mandena forestry reserve, south-east Madagascar, which was the main study area visited in 1968. This particular month was selected because the onset of the mating season occurred in September in 1968, and it was hoped that more detailed information could be obtained about Mouse Lemur reproduction and social organisation.

and there is now a considerable pool of information about this category
of primates. Nevertheless, the Mouse Lemur is of special interest
among the nocturnal prosimians because there are striking morphological and behavioural similarities between members of the Malagasy
Mouse Lemur group (Subfamily Cheirogaleinae) and African Bush-babies
(Subfamily Galaginae) - see Charles-Dominique and Martin 1970 for
summary. Such similarities may be due to retention of characters from
the early Tertiary ancestral stock which originally gave rise to the
Afro-Asian bush-babies and lorises and the Malagasy lemurs. Alternatively, there may have been a later separation between the Cheirogaleinae and the Galaginae, or there may have been considerable convergence between these two groups, occurring some time after their derivation from the common lemur/loris stock. Detailed studies now in
progress (e.g. see Martin 1972c) indicate that the shared similarities
are, in fact, largely based on retention of ancestral characteristics.
Thus, careful study of the Cheirogaleinae (e.g. Microcebus murinus)
and the Galaginae (e.g. Galago demidovii) should eventually provide
valuable information about the early radiation of the lorisoids and
lemuroids (Strepsirhini of Hill, 1953) and of the primates in general.
Figure 1 gives a good indication of the general degree of resemblance
between Demidoff's Bush-baby (Galago demidovii - A) and the Lesser
Mouse Lemur (Microcebus murinus - B).

The taxonomy of the Mouse Lemurs at the species level has yet
to be resolved. It is usually stated (e.g. Hill 1953; Petter 1962) that
there is a single, island-wide species of the Lesser Mouse Lemur
(Microcebus murinus) with a brown, small-eared subspecies in the
East Coast rain-forest (M. m. rufus) and a grey, large-eared subspecies
in the drier forest areas (M. m. murinus). However, field information

Fig. 1.   Photographs of <u>Galago</u> <u>Demidovii</u> (A) and <u>Microcebus</u> <u>murinus</u> (B) taken with flash.

Fig. 2.   Plan of the Fort Dauphin area (S.E. Madagascar) adapted
           from File 62, Service Géographique de Madagascar and
           aerial photographs obtained from the Institut National
           Géographique de Madagascar. (Area shown = approx.
           20 km x 20 km)

F.D. = Fort Dauphin   P.L. = Pic St. Louis
A.M. = Aerodrome de Marrilac   L.A. = Lac Ambavarano
B   = Bezavena   M.A. = Lac Mananivo
A   = Ampasy   L.   = Lac Lanirano
M   = Mandena   P.E. = Pointe Evatra

Dense stippling indicates littoral forest (habitat of Grey Mouse Lemur);
spaced stippling = rain forest (habitat of Brown Mouse Lemur). Black
triangles indicate hilly areas; marshy areas are indicated by horizontal bars with radiating lines.

collected in 1968 and 1970 indicates that these two main "subspecies" may actually be separate species. For example, populations of the two types of Lesser Mouse Lemur live within a few hundred yards of one another in the Fort Dauphin area (See Fig. 2) without showing any indications of interbreeding (no mixed groups; no intermediate types). In addition, all specimens in the collection at the British Museum of Natural History (London) can be clearly separated into the two categories on the basis of several external and cranial characters which show little or no intergrading (Martin: in prep.). However, this present communication is exclusively concerned with the Grey Mouse Lemur, which can be correctly referred to as Microcebus murinus in any any event. Where reference is made to the East Coast form, it will simply be called the Brown Mouse Lemur.

STUDY AREA AND METHODS

1. Study Area

Observations were conducted in the forestry reserve area of Mandena (Fig. 2: M). This forestry reserve includes a block of reconstituted endemic littoral forest lying northwards of Fort Dauphin, 8 km along the Route Nationale 7. The forest lying to the west of this road is situated on the flanks of prominent hills, and it is characterised by a flora generally typical of the East Coast rain-forest. In this latter humid forest zone, the Brown Mouse Lemur occurs to the exclusion of the Grey form. The littoral forest to the east of the road has a much lower rainfall, and the humidity is kept at a low level because of rapid water run-off through the sandy soil. The Grey Mouse Lemur occurs in this littoral forest zone and in secondary vegetation bordering the roads and other pathways. Fig. 3 shows the general layout of the central part of the forestry reserve, with the house (B) used as a base-camp and the area in which observations were conducted. The study area (MS) lies in a block of reconstituting endemic forest, which is characterised by a large number of small-diameter, short vertical trunks and relatively dense foliage in the range 1m - 10m. There are very few trees that are more than 15m in height in this selected area, though other areas of the reconstituting endemic forest do include larger trees. The two blocks of endemic forest shown in Fig. 3 are bounded by areas of introduced trees (Eucalyptus and Indo-Chinese pine). Personal observations showed that the endemic forest areas as a whole are inhabited by the Grey Mouse Lemur (Microcebus murinus), the Fat-tailed Dwarf Lemur (Cheirogaleus medius), an unidentified species of Hapalemur, and the Avahi (Avahi laniger). All but the Gentle Lemur (Hapalemur sp.) are nocturnal in habits. Although the area is protected by law, a certain amount of clandestine tree-felling and hunting occurs, and this constitutes a serious threat to the survival of lemur species in the area.

2. Methods

The methods used for studying the Mouse Lemurs have already been described in detail (Martin 1972a) and need only be summarised here. The work was divided into night-time (usually sunset to midnight) observations of the active animals and daytime searches for nests. Mouse Lemurs can easily be located at night, since there is a reflecting layer (tapetum) behind the retina of each eye, which will reflect light from a headlamp back to the eyes of the observer (Fig. 4). Individual animals in the forest can be spotted up to 30m

Fig. 3.   Detailed map of the region containing the Mandena Study area (MS).

IR = Iaridrano River   FV = Forestry village
B = House used as base   E = Entrance to Mandena Forestry Reserve

open circles = Eucalyptus plantation   black triangles = introduced pine plantations
fine stippling = reconstituted endemic forest

The study area is part of a block of endemic forest covering 12 hectares on the left of the River
Iarindrano. To the right of the river, there is a further block of 80 hectares.

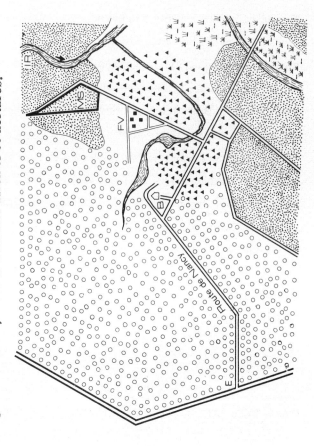

Fig. 4. Photograph of a tail-marked female Grey Mouse Lemur taken
at night with flash in the Mandena study area. (The white
arrow indicates the removal of fur from the tip of the tail for
easy recognition.) Note the reflection from the tapetum of
each eye. The Mouse Lemur is photographed on a <u>Vaccinium</u>
<u>emirnense</u> shrub, which seemed to represent one of the main
sources of food in the Mandena study area in 1970 (September).

away with a headlamp powered by 3 U-2 dry batteries and they can often be approached to within 10m once located. The animals can be
examined with binoculars in the light of the headlamp, and it proved
possible to identify the sex in about 72% of cases (70% in 1968; 74% in
1970). In many cases, the animal will continue its activities (e.g.
feeding) and will not flee even if approached to within 5m. In the course
of this study, night-time observations were limited to animals within
the study area, in order to establish their general movements and activities. The author was already thoroughly familiar with the Mandena
study area and it was possible to confirm and extend observations carried out in 1968. In 1968, it appeared that the Mouse Lemurs were
primarily active alongside the pathways; but this impression was only
supported by rather haphazard excursions into the centre of the study
area. In 1970, four old pathways through the core of the area were
cleared of ground-level vegetation, so that movements of the animals
through this core could be followed (p. 46). As can be seen from the
pattern of sightings based on equivalent patrols around and through the
study area (p. 40), it has been established that the Mouse Lemurs were
still primarily sighted near the periphery of the forest.

As in 1968, repeated nightly patrols of the study area were
made in order to record the positions of Mouse Lemurs when sighted.
In addition, the 1968 technique was extended by noting the distance and
direction travelled by each animal after sighting in order to obtain
extra information about possible home ranges. Animals which had
been trapped in 1968 had been marked only by clipping of the tail fur.
This is effective only for a few months, and there was therefore no
possibility of recognising individuals two years later. Attempts were
again made to trap animals in 1970 in order to examine, mark and

release them, and this time they were marked both on the tail (removal of hair in specific patterns - Fig. 4) and on the ears (notches in various combinations). In the short time available in 1970, it was not possible to trap more than a few individuals. Three were captured on separate occasions with a flexible plastic-coated wire noose on the end of a long cane (technique developed with P. Charles-Dominique and M. Hladik), and two were captured in a mist-net set around a tree-hollow nest. Because of the brief duration of the study period, only three of the marked animals were re-sighted after release.

During the daytime, the study area was investigated in order to find nests, measure precise distances and identify food-plants. It was soon discovered that the Mouse Lemurs seemed to be feeding primarily upon two plant species (also recognised as important in 1968) and a final survey was made in order to map the occurrence of these two types of food-plant.

Local villagers were employed, as in 1968, in order to obtain a large body of data on Mouse Lemurs living in a quite separate area of the littoral rain-forest. The villagers live extensively on the proceeds of tree-felling, and they frequently find Mouse Lemur nests in the course of their work. Maximum payment was given for any nests which were brought back apparently intact, with the occupants blocked inside and with a leaf sample taken from the foliage of the nest-tree. The Mouse Lemurs in each nest thus obtained were sexed, weighed and examined, and they were then released in the forest 5-10 km from the area of origin. Forty-seven apparently intact nests containing a total of 166 Mouse Lemurs (134 females; 32 males) were examined. Four additional nests were of little value, since the occupants (5 females; 5 males) had already been removed from the nests and placed together in a box by the villagers. In addition, a total of 32 female Mouse Lemurs were brought in without nests, mainly by some helpers who failed to follow instructions early on. In these latter cases, the animals were weighed and examined and (with the four empty nests) the nest dimensions were taken, but no details of nest groupings could be obtained.

GENERAL OBSERVATIONS

1. Body-Weights

As in 1968, the average body-weight for the Lesser Mouse Lemur proved to be about 60 g. A total of 37 males weighed between 6th and 29th September (Fig. 5) had an average body-weight of 59 g, and 126 females weighed between 6th and 18th September (i.e. generally prior to gestation - Fig. 6) had an average weight of 63 g. The extremes of body weight found in the period 6th to 29th September were 39 g and 98 g. Since all of the animals examined were adults (see p. 55), this wide range of variation is striking. It is also noteworthy (cf. Figs. 5 and 6) that only one male over 70 g was found, whereas almost 25% of the females weighed between 6th and 18th September (i.e. prior to gestation) were heavier than 70 g.

These results are generally very close to those obtained in 1968, except that 33% of a small sample of males (N = 17) weighed more than 70 g in that year. The average body-weights of the non-gestating females were also somewhat higher (N = 65; average = 66 g). This may indicate that food availability was greater in 1968 than in 1970 towards the end of the dry season (May-October), and that the males were more affected by the relative shortage of food in 1970.

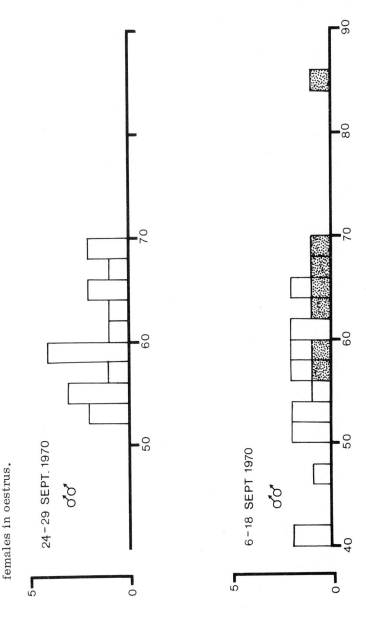

Fig. 5. Histograms showing the weights of individual males found in tree-hollow nests during the peak of mating activity (6–18th September) and soon afterwards (24th–29th September). Note that there is no obvious difference between the two samples. The stippled boxes in the lower histograms indicate males which were found in nests with females exhibiting recently opened, or as yet unopened, pink vulval swellings. This may indicate that the heaviest males have preferential access to females in oestrus.

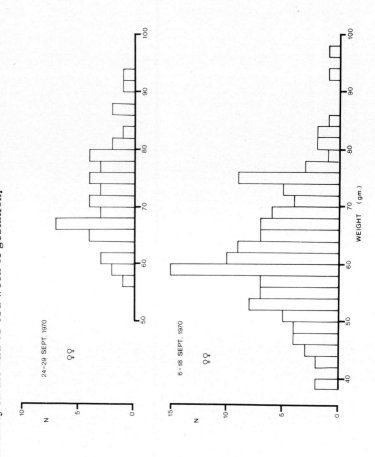

Fig. 6.   Histograms showing the weights of individual females found in tree-hollow nests during the peak of mating activity (6th–18th September) and soon afterwards (24th–29th September). Note that the average weight of the first batch of females is about 10 gm below that of the second batch, and that there is a marked difference in minimum weights. The majority of the second batch of females were probably in the 2nd or 3rd week of gestation.

Charles-Dominique and Hladik (1971), who were working in the South
of Madagascar in September 1970, have already reported that the dry
season was more severe in 1970 than at any time during the previous
decade. However, there is also the possibility that tree-felling in the
area is having an adverse effect on foraging behaviour of the Mouse
Lemur population.

2. Habits

As reported previously (Martin 1972a) the Lesser Mouse Lemur exhibits extremely versatile locomotion, and it is generally active
in what can be called the fine branch niche (e.g. see Fig. 1). The
height at which Mouse Lemurs are active in any forest area depends
upon the height at which fine branches, lianes and associated dense foliage are present. Accordingly, Mouse Lemurs are commonly encoun--
tered at heights of 0 - 10m in secondary forest and pathside vegetation,
whereas they tend to occur up in the canopy at heights of 15 - 30m inside dense primary forest. In general, it can be said that the Lesser
Mouse Lemur is far more common in secondary forest than in primary
forest. Indeed, in the Fort Dauphin area it was fairly easy to find
Mouse Lemurs in the bushes of gardens and patches of waste land
around the port.

No systematic data were collected in 1968 to establish the typical height at which Mouse Lemurs were active in vegetation of the
Mandena study area. This omission was rectified in 1970. It can be
seen from Fig. 7 that the animals were most active at heights of 2-4m,
though they were sighted at all levels between the ground and 10m. The
heights of the animals were recorded both for the initial point of sighting and for the point at which they eventually disappeared from view, in

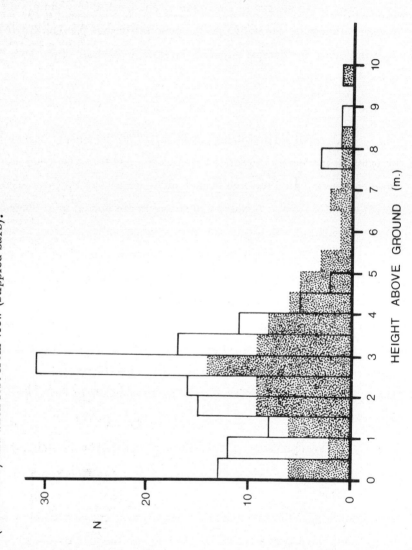

<u>Fig. 7.</u>   Histogram showing the heights at which individual Mouse Lemurs were seen when first sighted (white bars) and when lost from view (stippled bars).

order to see whether response to the presence of the observer had any effect upon vertical distribution. Fig. 7 shows that the observer had very little influence on vertical occurrence, though there was perhaps a slight tendency for the animals to move higher in the trees. This is just one indication of the relatively limited influence exerted by the observer on the animals' behaviour.

It is, at first sight, surprising to see that the animals were so frequently seen low down in the forest (0 - 1m). However, two factors help to explain this. Firstly, it was found that the Mouse Lemurs would often descend to the ground in order to cross a pathway, especially where it would have been necessary to leap further than 3m if a purely arboreal route had been used. Secondly, as reported previously, Mouse Lemurs often descend to the ground in order to hunt for terrestrial beetles in the leaf-litter on the forest-floor. When sighted at these low levels, the Mouse Lemurs either persisted in attempts to move across the ground or moved up higher into the vegetation (see Fig. 7).

When crossing the ground, the Mouse Lemurs moved in a frog-like hopping fashion. Locomotion was achieved largely by thrusts with the hind-legs, but the hopping was not bipedal.

Mouse Lemurs are completely nocturnal in habits. At least some are seen active at all times throughout the night. The animals were first sighted at sunset and some were still seen moving around in the forest when dawn was so far advanced that the reflections from the animals' eyes were barely visible. However, Mouse Lemurs which were seen so late in the morning always seemed to be returning to their nests.

3. Diet

    The Lesser Mouse Lemur can best be described as omnivo-
rous. Its diet includes fruits, flowers, leaves, insects, arachnids,
probably small vertebrates (e.g tree-frogs and chamaeleons) and possibly molluscs. It has also been found that the Grey Mouse Lemur
(Microcebus murinus) feeds upon sap in various regions. In 1968, the
author had observed sap-feeding in the Analabe study area (near
Morondava; west Madagascar); but the significance of this was only
realised during subsequent discussions with Dr. Pierre Charles-
Dominique. A male had been seen "chewing" fine branches during one
night patrol in 1968, and other Mouse Lemurs were frequently seen in
association with, and occasionally feeding upon, groups of sap-eating
Fulgorid bugs (Phromnia sp.). In the course of his study of Lepilemur
in South Madagascar in 1970 (see Charles-Dominique and Hladik 1971),
Charles-Dominique observed a Mouse Lemur scoring lianes by rotating
the anterior teeth around the bark. The animal was seen to return to
the same liane on several nights, each time licking the exuded sap. In
retrospect, it would seem that the branch-chewing male Microcebus
murinus observed in the Analabe study area in 1968 was engaged in the
same activity, and that Mouse Lemurs seen in association with Fulgor-
ids may have been attracted both by the sap exudation and by the possibility of preying upon the insects. (Similar behaviour has since been
reported for Phaner furcifer by Petter, Schilling and Pariente, 1971).
In 1970, the author again observed single Mouse Lemurs in association
with Phromnia groups (this time in the Fort Dauphin area), though no
feeding behaviour was observed. In the Mandena study area, a male
Mouse Lemur was also observed making scraping movements over an
area of bark which was covered with small insects. The animal was

using its tooth-scraper with movements similar to those seen during self-grooming, and it seemed likely that some of the insects were ingested along with small quantities of sap. At a later stage, the author saw a male Grey Mouse Lemur using characteristic tooth-scraper and tongue movements to eat sap from a Euphorbia tree in the semi-arid bush zone studied by Charles-Dominique and Hladik (Berenty; South Madagascar). It can therefore be regarded as established that Lesser Mouse Lemurs, at least occasionally, include sap in their diet, and that the anterior dentition (particularly the tooth-scraper) is probably instrumental in sap-collection.

It should be emphasised that observation of active animals in the present study was largely restricted to rapid patrols of the study area conducted in order to obtain data about the occurrence and movements of a large number of Mouse Lemurs. Therefore, direct observations of feeding behaviour were rare, and in many cases it was only possible to draw inferences from repeated association with certain known food-plants. From the study conducted in Mandena in 1968, it was known that the Grey Mouse Lemurs frequently fed upon the flowers and fruits of a pathside shrub, Vaccinium emirnense (see Fig. 4), on the leaves and fruits of Uapaca trees, and on various other small fruits, flowers, and leaves. In 1970, the author again observed a few cases of feeding upon Vaccinium emirnense flowers and fruits and Uapaca fruits; but no further direct observations of feeding on Uapaca leaves were made. Isolated cases of feeding on the fruits of Scolopia sp., Memecyclon sp. and Canthium sp. were observed. Thus, although Mouse Lemurs were frequently seen on various identified food-plants it could only be presumed in many cases that those plants had been visited for feeding purposes. In 63% of cases where animals were first

sighted, a note was made of the associated vegetation. Analysis of
these sightings (N = 135) gives the pattern shown in Table I.

Table I.　Sightings (N=135) of Mouse Lemurs on Various Plant Types
in the Mandena Study Area.

Nature of sighting	% of observations
On vegetation with no known relationship to feeding	50
On Vaccinium emirnense[1]	31
On Uapaca sp.[1]	12
On Scolopia sp.[1]	2
On Memecyclon sp.[1]	1
On Canthium sp.[1]	1
Eating insects on vegetation	2
Eating sap and small insects on the trunk of a tree	1

[1]Mouse Lemurs were seen feeding on all of these plants at some time
during the 1970 field study.

This tabulation could give the impression that the Mouse Lemurs spent
much more time on food-plants than eating insects; but it must be remembered that insect catching and eating is rapidly accomplished, and
that it is very difficult to observe what an animal is doing if sighted at
a distance of 8m or more inside the forest. However, the fact remains
that the Mouse Lemurs were observed in 43% of cases on the two main
known food-plants, despite their relative rarity in the study area (see
p. 45). This confirms the suggestion made previously (Martin, 1972a)

that Mouse Lemurs are probably heavily dependent upon plant food derived mainly from a small number of plant species, and that animal
prey are taken in an opportunistic fashion (see fig. 8). The clear association with the same two main food-plants in 1968 and 1970 supports
the suggestion that there is marked local specialisation on particular
food-sources. However, detailed long-term observations on feeding
behaviour and diet will be necessary to establish the validity of these
preliminary conclusions.

NEST OCCUPANCY AND SOCIAL INTERACTIONS

1. Nests

Mouse Lemurs can be found in spherical leaf nests, or in tree-
hollow nests lined with a small number of leaves. In 1968, several
nests of both kinds were found in various areas of Madagascar; but in
1970 only tree-hollow nests were found in the Mandena study area,
partly because it is extremely time-consuming to trace leaf-nests in
dense vegetation. In addition, most information on nests was obtained
through the help of villagers who concentrated on the collection of tree-
hollow nests.

The vast majority of the tree-hollow nests examined in 1970
(N = 51) were brought in by local villagers, though 5 were located and
superficially examined in the Mandena study area (MS of Fig. 3). Unfortunately, it is usually necessary to destroy a tree-hollow nest in
order to examine it closely, so detailed examination was restricted to
nests which were brought in by villagers from the tree-felling area.

As with the 1968 tree-hollow nests, measurements were taken

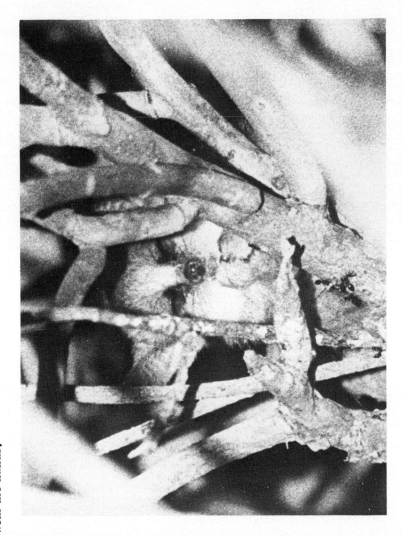

Fig. 8. Grey Mouse Lemur photographed in the act of eating a spider in a Euphorbia bush in the semi-arid forest near Amboasary. Note the closure of the eyes as the prey is brought to the mouth with the hands.

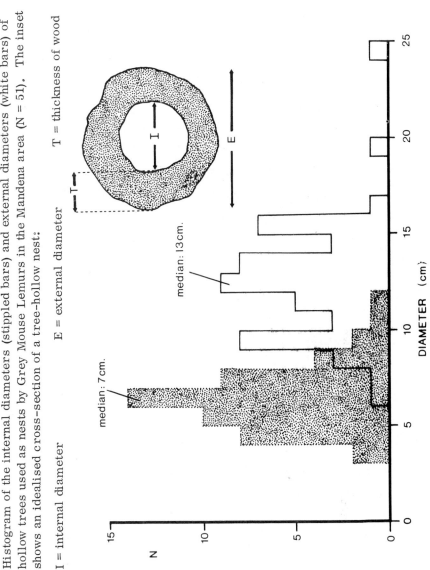

Fig. 9. Histogram of the internal diameters (stippled bars) and external diameters (white bars) of hollow trees used as nests by Grey Mouse Lemurs in the Mandena area (N = 51). The inset shows an idealised cross-section of a tree-hollow nest:

I = internal diameter   E = external diameter   T = thickness of wood

of the diameter of the trunk, the diameter of the cavity, the length of
the cavity (where possible) and the dimensions of any lateral apertures
used as entrances to the tree-hollow. The histograms in Fig. 9 show
the distributions of the internal diameters (I) and external diameters
(E) of the 51 tree-hollows examined. In both cases, the medians and
the means are identical: I = 7 cm; E = 13 cm. Using these typical
dimensions, it is possible to establish an idealised tree-hollow section
(Fig. 9: inset), in which the average thickness of the cavity wall (T) is
3 cm. These figures generally resemble those recorded in 1968; but
the 1968 dimensions are larger in every case (see Table II).

Table II. Main Dimensions of Tree Hollow Nests in 1968 and 1970

	1968 cm	1970 cm
E (median)	17	13
I (median)	9	6
T (median)	3.5	3.0

This difference may be due to a sampling effect or to differences in
tree-felling patterns between 1968 and 1970; but there is a possibility
that tree-felling in the Mandena area is gradually altering the range of
available nest-hollows. If the 1968 figures more closely reflect the true
preferences of Grey Mouse Lemurs, it is vital for any conservation
policy to take account of the fact that trees of a certain age and size,
containing hollows with the appropriate dimensions, may be necessary

for the long-term maintenance of a thriving Grey Mouse Lemur population.

In many cases, the nests brought back by villagers had been cut
in such a way that the nest-entrance had been damaged or omitted, and
it was only possibly to measure the size of entrance apertures in 21 out
of 51 cases (Fig. 10). These entrances were usually in the lateral wall
of the trunk, though some were almost horizontal apertures produced
by the loss of one vertical ramus of a subdivided trunk. The average
dimensions of these apertures were: height - 10.4 cm; width - 4 cm.
These figures agree well with the averages for the natural tree-hollow
apertures measured in 1968 (height - 7 cm; width - 3 cm), but this
time the dimensions are slightly larger. Once again, it is possible
that tree-felling in the Mandena area is forcing the resident Mouse
Lemurs to occupy tree-hollows with different characteristics. In view
of the fact that there may be heavy predation on young Mouse Lemurs
left in tree-hollows by their mothers (Martin 1972a, pp. 80-81) the
selection of tree-hollows with optimal dimensions could well be a critical factor.

Wood samples and foliage samples were taken from 17 of the 51
trees containing nest-hollows in order to gain some information on the
range of choice of tree cavities available to Mouse Lemurs. It was
found that these 17 samples came from 12 different genera representing
12 different plant families (see Table III).

It is therefore apparent that any area of secondary littoral forest
of reasonable age would probably contain a fairly large number of suitable nest-hollows. One of the striking features of the littoral forest of
the Mandena area is the high frequency of hollow trees of relatively

Fig. 10. Graph showing dimensions of apertures of individual tree-
          hollow nests (N = 21).

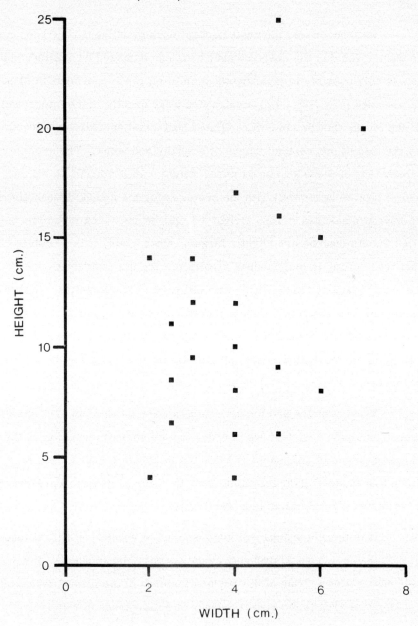

Table III.   Genera and Families of 17 Trees Containing Mouse
Lemur Nests.

Sample No.	Genus	Family
1	Asteropeia	Theaceae
2	Scolopia	Flacourtiaceae
3	Brachylaena	Compositae
4	Diospyros	Ebenaceae
5	?	Tiliaceae
6	Ficus	Moraceae
7	Cabucala	Apocynaceae
8	Diospyros	Ebenaceae
9	Eugenia	Myrtaceae
10	Eugenia	Myrtaceae
11	Xylopia	Anonaceae
12	Scolopia	Flacourtiaceae
13	Vepris	Rutaceae
14	Erythroxylon	Erythroxylaceae
15	Asteropeia	Theaceae
16	Erythroxylon	Erythroxylaceae
17	Potomeia	Lauraceae

small size. In virtually all of the nest-hollows studied, the surrounding
wood was apparently still alive and growing. It is not clear whether
these hollows are produced as a natural feature in the growth of such
trees, or whether the hollows appear through the action of fungi, insects
and other agents. Nevertheless, it is certain that such hollows appear
with great regularity in at least some forest areas of Madagascar, and
that Mouse Lemurs are thus provided with a wide range of nesting opportunities.

2. Nest-groups

One of the most important features observed in 1968 (Martin
1972a), was the occurrence of nesting groups in the Grey Mouse Lemur.
Although such nesting groups had previously been loosely identified by
various authors as "family groups", detailed examination of nest occupancy showed that there was clear-cut segretation of males and females,
and that the larger groups were almost always composed exclusively of
females. Males were found nesting singly or in pairs, and females
were found in groups of 1-15, with a median of 4 per nest. However,
most of the data collected in 1968 came from nests located some time
after the first phase of mating activity, and in 1970 the opportunity was
taken to see whether mating activity had any effect on typical nesting
group composition. For the 47 nests which were examined with the
occupants still inside, the following groups were found (Table IV).

It can be seen that the median group size for nests containing
only females is 3, whilst only two nests were found with males alone
(2 males in each case). Thus, the typical group-size for females was
lower than in 1968. Examination of the remaining nest-groups, in
which males and females occurred together, shows that such groups

Table IV. Combinations of Males and Females (Total N = 134) in 47 Tree Hollow Nests examined in 1970 (1968 figures in brackets).

Number of MALES	Number of FEMALES										
	0	1	2	3	4	5	6	7	8	9	15
0	– (–)	– (4)	6 (6)	12 (4)	5 (6)	– (3)	– (2)	1 (2)	– (2)	– (1)	– (1)
1	– (–)	4 (–)	– (–)	6 (1)	– (–)	3 (1)	1 (–)	1 (1)	– (–)	– (–)	– (–)
2	2 (–)	3 (–)	1 (–)	1 (–)	– (–)	– (–)	– (–)	– (–)	– (–)	– (–)	– (–)
3	– (–)	1 (–)	– (–)	– (–)	– (–)	– (–)	– (–)	– (–)	– (–)	– (–)	– (–)

contained a median of one male and three females. The average size
of female groups without males (3.1) is only slightly larger than the
average size (2.8) of female groups with males, and actually slightly
smaller than the average size of female groups with only one male
(3.3). One interpretation of these figures would be that there are many
cases in which single males nest with established female groups (11
single males with groups of 3-7 females), but that there are also cases
where single females may nest with one or more males (8 single females in nests with 1-3 males). If this interpretation is correct, one
might expect to find that the occurrence of male/female nest-sharing
would be higher when the females are in oestrus than when they are in
post-oestrus. A sample of nests examined in the period 6.9.70 -
18.9.70 contained many females in various stages of oestrous activity,
whilst a later sample examined in the period 24.9.70 - 29.9.70 largely
consisted of post-oestrous females (see section on reproduction). Fig.
11 shows the compositions of the nesting groups for these two periods,
showing that there is indeed a striking difference. During the period
when many females were in oestrus, it would appear that most of the
nests containing both males and females represented cases of single
males nesting with female groups. At this time, only 9.7% of the Mouse
Lemurs found in the nests were males. During the period just after
oestrus, however, the mixed nests seemed to be largely represented
by instances where small numbers of males were sharing nests with
single females. In addition, the proportion of males found in all nests
examined had risen to 30.5%, indicating a change in male nesting behaviour. In the first sample, it was found that there was at least one
female with some stage of vulval swelling in every nest containing a
male, whereas this was not true of a single case in the second sample.

Fig. 11. Histograms of numbers of females contained in individual
tree-hollow nests collected at the peak of mating activity
(6th to 18th September) and soon afterwards (24th to 29th
September). Note that the female groups in the second
sample tended to be smaller. The black dots in each box
indicate the numbers of males found with each female group.

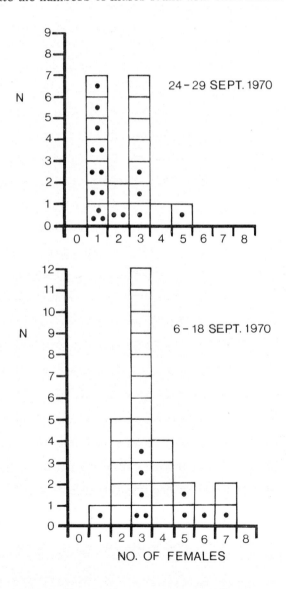

In the second sample, the female groups of 3 (N = 3) and 5 (N = 1) found in a nest with a single male contained at least one female showing signs of recent vulval closure, whilst those females found singly (N = 7) or in pairs (N = 1) with one or more males exhibited no trace whatsoever of vulval activity.

It is possible that the data shown in Fig. 11 simply reflect a sampling effect, since the nests were brought in by tree-fellers and were not collected in a closely controlled fashion; but it is also possible that there is a phase in which a small number of males share nests with females in oestrus, followed by a phase in which a larger number of males share nests with already fecundated females. Whatever the explanation, it is clear that post-oestrous females may share nests with males, indicating that males and females may associate other than for actual mating. In 1968, when a large number of nests were examined in the latter half of the first gestation phase, only 2 out of 42 nests contained both males and females, and the histogram of female group size was quite similar to that seen with the first 1970 sample of oestrous females. Therefore, if there is a phase in which single females typically occur with one or more males in nests after oestrus, it is probably of brief duration.

It is noteworthy that the maximum size of female groups found in 1968 was 15, whilst that found in 1970 was 7. This could be interpreted in various ways (e.g. as a result of different times of sampling or as a further sign of gradual degradation of the Mouse Lemur habitat in the Mandena area, brought about by tree-felling).

As with the 1968 study, the procedure of investigating nests brought in by villagers did not provide any information on the stability

of nesting groups of Mouse Lemurs. The only direct indication of continuous inhabitation of the tree-hollow nests was the presence in some
cases (N = 4) of horizontal leaf platforms. In all such cases, there
were fresh leaves on the top of the platform and layers of successively
older and more fragmented leaves from the top to the bottom. These
findings indicate that a particular tree-hollow may be used frequently
over a given period of time, but they do not show that the hollow is used
every day by the same group of Mouse Lemurs. Marking of animals in
the Mandena study area in 1968 showed that there are probably restricted home ranges which are maintained at least for a period of several
weeks, and this would mean that each group of Mouse Lemurs in a given
area would have a restri ted choice of nesting facilities, and perhaps be
constrained to utilise a small number of nests continuously. However,
a detailed and long-term field study would be necessary to investigate
the stability of female and male groups, and the degree of attachment
to nests.

In the course of the 1970 study in Mandena, some information
was obtained about the persistence of nest-utilisation. Two females
were trapped from a tree-hollow nest using a mist-net set around the
nest entrance just before sunset. Despite the fact that the females
were probably greatly disturbed by their experience in the mist-net,
they were both re-sighted in the same area within the following week,
and the nest was found to be occupied every day of that week. (A fine
twig was inserted into the tree-hollow, and this invariably elicited a
snorting vocalisation.) However, an interesting observation was made
on the morning (prior to sunrise) when the females were originally followed back to their nest. The nest was located when one Mouse Lemur
was spotted with its head projecting from the nest entrance, and ano-

ther (identified as a female) was seen on a thin vertical trunk nearby.
The animal already in the nest withdrew into the trunk cavity, but the
one still outside was apparently very disturbed by the presence of a
human observer. It ran down the vertical trunk and extended itself
horizontally, with the grasp maintained by the hind-feet, to sniff at the
nest entrance. The Mouse Lemur then abruptly ran back up the thin
vertical trunk and began leaping into the forest to the right. At this
point, two more Mouse Lemurs were seen approaching rapidly through
the forest, and all three animals subsequently disappeared into another
tree-hollow nearby. (The two nest-trees concerned are indicated towards the bottom left of Fig. 13a.) This observation suggests that the
first female was acquainted with at least one other nest-tree in the
area, since she headed directly towards it when surprised near the
first hollow tree, and it also indicates that the nest-groupings may be
somewhat labile within a given area. There is good reason to believe
that the occupants of the two nests concerned were already familiar
with one another, since the first female and the other two entered the
second nest without exchanging any aggressive vocalisations.

As in the 1968 study, some evidence was found for the use of
"resting nests" during the night, as distinct from the nests used for
sleeping during the daytime. On two separate occasions, individual
females were seen entering tree-hollows (upper two hollows indicated
in Fig. 13a) that were never found occupied during the daytime. This
reinforces the suspicion that each Mouse Lemur is familiar with a range
of possible retreats within its normal radius of activity, and that there
may be some localised lability in nest-use according to circumstances.

Some evidence was also obtained in the Mandena study area to
support the suspicion that the males may be more versatile in their

use of nests than the females. Just before sunrise, one male was
found returning to sleep in a small, cup-like hollow on the top of a tree-
stump (hollow indicated on extreme left of Fig. 13a). The hollow was
scarcely big enough to contain the animal and certainly represented an
extremely rudimentary nest-site. On subsequent days, in which the two
known female sleeping nests were always found to be occupied, this
male "nest" was never again found to be occupied.

Therefore, although the techniques of study do not permit any
firm conclusions about temporal patterns of nest-use, it would appear
that the female Grey Mouse Lemurs (at least) form relatively stable
nesting groups with some localised lability in nest-use. The observations on oestrus synchronisation within nesting groups (p. 55) would
tend to confirm that there are fairly close associations between females
belonging to a nesting group, and the fact that females will rear their
offspring in such groups without apparent animosity both in the field
(Martin, 1972a) and in the laboratory (Martin, in prep.) supports this
interpretation.

Social Interactions and Home Ranges

As with the 1968 study, most of the information obtained about
areas of activity ("home ranges") of resident Mouse Lemurs in the
Mandena study area was indirect. Only 5 animals were marked by the
end of the study, and only 3 of these were re-sighted. However, in no
case were the marked individuals seen at a distance greater than 30m
from the area of the original sighting. This agrees well with the 1968
observation (Martin, 1972a) that no known individual was seen to range
over an area greater than 50 m in diameter.

With the additional evidence provided above, it would seem to be quite certain that Grey Mouse Lemurs generally nest in groups, with the females forming larger groups than the males, and with a general tendency towards segregation of the sexes. It can be assumed that these groups are relatively stable, because of the necessity for any individual to remain in a small area with which it is well acquainted. However, the males would have less need to remain resident in a given area since they do not have the additional constraint of parental care.

It has already been reported (Martin 1972a) that Mouse Lemurs generally occur as localised "population nuclei", and that the cores of such nuclei contain far more females than males. In 1968, there were only 7 males found in nests from the Mandena area in a period during which 113 females were found; but it is likely that the males are more difficult to locate through daytime searches for hollow trees because of their apparent tendency to make use of more rudimentary nests. In September 1970, when a far higher proportion of male/female nest-sharing was found, 32 males were found with 134 females in the 47 intact nests examined (see p. 28). This gives an overall ratio of just over 4 females for every male found in the area samples, whereas in 1968 the observed ratio was 16 females for every male. This difference between the figures for the two years, which is related to differences in timing relative to mating, confirms the assumption (p. 30 and Fig. 11) that most of the males found in nests with females - particularly those found with more than one female - were nesting with well-established female groups. If these nests had been examined 1-2 months later in 1970, it is likely that a greater proportion of females would have been found, and that the males would have returned to the more typical pattern of sleeping alone or in pairs in rudimentary nests.

When the 1968 and 1970 data on night sightings of animals of identified sex in the Mandena study area are compared, there is remarkably good agreement (Table V).

Table V. Sex Identification in Mouse Lemur Sightings (Mandena Study Area; 1968 and 1970).

Year	Identified males		Identified females		Sex unidentified	
	No.	% of identified sightings	No.	% of identified sightings	No.	% of sightings
1968	23	27.4	51	72.6	32	30
1970	50	31.1	111	68.9	56	26

These data indicate, for both years, that just over two females are sighted for every male. However, most or all of the animals of un-identified sex were likly to have been females, since it often happened that when two or more animals were sighted close together only one could be sexed, and the other was lost to sight. Fig. 12b shows that most sex-unidentified sightings occurred in areas where females were common. Since the females nest in groups, it is likely that they would frequently be sighted in close proximity. If all of the individuals of unidentified sex listed in the table are counted as females, the ratio of females to males sighted at night would be about 3 : 1. Thus, the ratio of females to males in the population nucleus core of the Grey Mouse Lemurs in the Mandena study area would seem to be between 4 : 1 (1970 data from nest occupancy) and 3 : 1 (1970 data from night sight-

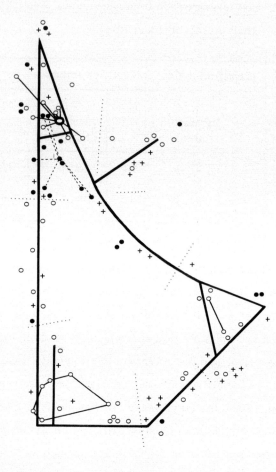

Fig. 12.   Detailed maps of the Mandena study area (approx. surface area = 1.5 hectares; for scale see Fig. 13). These show "scatter diagrams" indicating observations of active Mouse Lemurs at night.

o = definite females   ● = definite males   + = sex not identified

Lines linking separate points indicate observations of marked animals or movements of individual animals under surveillance.

12a: Observations from 1968 (weak dotted lines indicate possible borders between separate groups)

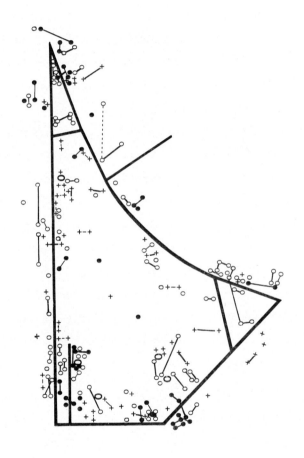

12b: Observations from 1970 (nests indicated by large circles)

ings). This correlates well with the estimate of 4 : 1 made from the 1968 study.

The sightings of Mouse Lemurs at night in the Mandena study area were plotted on a "scatter diagram", as for the 1968 study (Fig. 12). Far more observation points were obtained in 1970, and recording of the movements of animals after sighting provided yet more information about possible home ranges. It can be seen from Fig. 12b that there is clear-cut clustering in the 1970 "scatter diagram', and that the sightings of males - in particular - are quite well segregated. As with the 1968 study (Fig. 12a), this scatter diagram can be interpreted in the light of the facts already established (above) with regard to Mouse Lemur activity range size, segregation of the sexes, and typical sizes of male and female nest-groupings (Fig. 13). It can be seen that the observations and interpretations for the two years are quite similar in terms of the positioning and extent of probable male and female areas of activity. In 1968, it was estimated that there were between 20 and 40 Grey Mouse Lemurs in the Mandena study area. The 1970 data indicate that there were probably about the same number, though it was impossible to make any direct estimate because of the paucity of data on marked animals.

Since none of the animals trapped in 1968 had been marked for long-term recognition, no reliable extrapolation to the 1970 study can be made. It is certain that one female had disappeared from the population, since the partially blind female repeatedly seen in area C in 1968 (Fig. 13a) was not seen in 1970 (Fig. 13b). In 1968, two males were often seen moving, and even grooming, together in area 1 of Fig. 13a; but in 1970 no contact was seen between males in that area. This suggests that one or both of the original males in that area may have died, or moved elsewhere. However, there were indications of some degree of continuity. In 1968, three females were often seen moving close together in area B of Fig. 13a, although females in other areas tended to move and feed separately. In 1970, exactly the same applied, and the three females concerned seemed to occupy approximately the same range as in 1968. There were a number of other similarities of a less precise kind between the activities of animals observed in 1968 and 1970, and it can be tentatively assumed that there was at least some continuity in activity range, and possibly group composition, from 1968 to 1970. This is not unexpected, since Lesser Mouse Lemurs may live for up to 15 years in captivity. Over and above this, comparison of the two diagrams in Fig. 13 indicates that there were also several general changes over the course of the two years. In particular, the area C of 1968 (Fig. 13a) seemed to have become split into two quite distinct female group ranges (C_1/C_2) by 1970. There were other weak indications of minor changes in range location and boundaries; but no definite conclusions can be drawn without a detailed long-term study involving marking, release and recapture.

Since it had been inferred that the Mouse Lemurs were probably feeding primarily on two sources of plant food (flowers and berries of Vaccinium emirnense; fruits and possibly leaves of Uapaca sp.), an attempt was made to determine whether the distribution of the two plant species showed any correlation with the apparent pattern of activity ranges in the Mandena study area. A careful survey was made of the study area in order to plot, as far as possible, the locations and approximate maximum foliage diameters of every Vaccinium shrub and every Uapaca tree. This survey was hampered by the fact that there

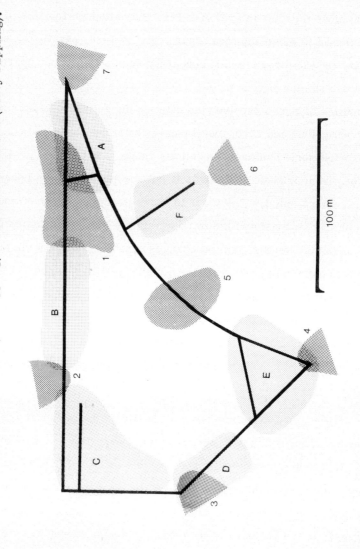

Fig. 13. Detailed maps of the Mandena study area indicating interpretations of areas of activity of female groups of average size 4 (fine stippling) and of resident males (heavy stippling).

13a: Observations from 1968 (note scale)

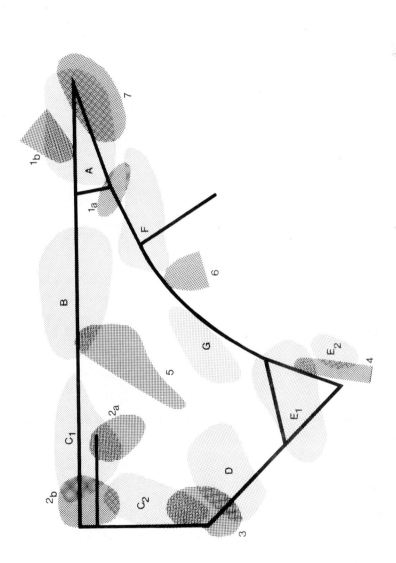

13b: Observations from 1970; the pattern of female groups and resident males is roughly the same as in 1968, and there is some indication of fragmentation and alteration of groups during the intervening 2-year period.

were extensive forest-fires in the area at the end of the study. As a result, the survey had to be conducted hurriedly after fire had swept past the study area (luckily leaving the endemic forest virtually untouched), and whilst there was a constant threat of a renewed outbreak of fire from the smouldering plantations alongside. Nevertheless, it proved possible to make a fairly accurate map of the distribution of the two plant species in the study area (Fig. 14). This map emphasises the fact that Vaccinium emirnense generally occurs alongside clearings or broad pathways (such as those bordering the study area), as has been reported previously (Martin 1972a). Uapaca trees can occur in the forest; but in the study area many of them were located on or near broad pathways. Despite careful searching, no Vaccinium shrubs were found in the centre of the area.

If Fig. 14 is compared with Fig. 13b, it can be seen that the tentatively identified female groups generally coincided with aggregations of one or both of the major inferred plant food sources. Some (e.g. "A", "E_1" and "E_2") seemed to have access only to Vaccinium shrubs whilst others (e.g "B") apparently had access only to Uapaca trees. In the remaining cases (e.g. "D" and "G") access to both food plants was possible. However, it is particularly striking that the tentatively identified male home ranges did not generally coincide with aggregations of one or both of these plant species. In general, it would seem that the inferred female group ranges covered areas of aggregation of the two plant species, whilst the inferred (but perhaps incomplete) male home ranges were outside these area. In some cases, individual males were sighted in areas overlapping with only one recorded Vaccinium shrub (e.g. "2a", "4", "5"). It should be emphasised that the area covered by the foliage of all identified Vaccimium shrubs and Uapaca

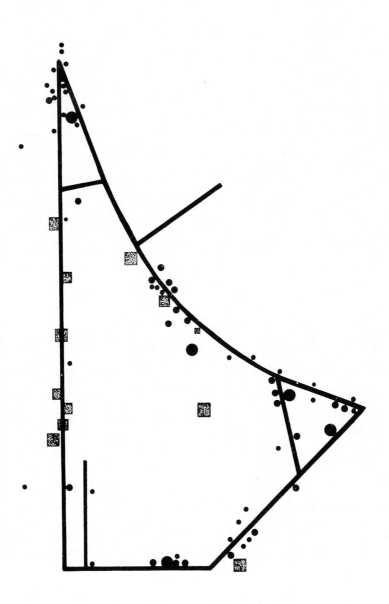

Fig. 14. Detailed map of the Mandena study area showing the recorded occurrence of the two major food-plants: <u>Vaccinium emirnense</u> (black circles) and <u>Uapaca</u> sp. (stippled squares). The sizes of the symbols indicate the maximum estimated foliage diameter of each shrub or tree.

trees represented less than 5% of the total surface of the study area. Therefore, frequent occurrence of Mouse Lemurs on these two plants was not due to random association (see Table I).

It is obvious from Fig. 12 that Mouse Lemurs are generally sighted near fairly wide pathways and clearings. However, it is possible that Mouse Lemurs do occur more frequently inside the forest and are simply far more difficult to spot with a headlamp. It was for this reason that 4 existing narrow pathways were cleared through the study area in 1970. These pathways ran parallel to the main path shown at the top of Fig. 12b, and provided visual access with torchlight to virtually all zones within the study area. Control surveys conducted along these pathways at night showed that far fewer Mouse Lemurs were sighted per metre of pathways travelled by the observer than was the case along the main paths bordering the study area.

However, it could still be objected that it is easier to spot Mouse Lemurs with a headlamp when walking along a wide path bordering the study area than when walking along a narrow path with little freedom of movement inside the area. In order to examine this possibility, the distances of Mouse Lemurs from main pathways were noted and plotted (Fig. 15). Since the penetration of the light-beam into the forest is affected by the density of the intervening vegetation, it is to be expected that with a moderately dense forest like that in Mandena it would be difficult to see animals inside the forest beyond a certain distance. The density of the vegetation, rather than the attenuation of the light-beam, is likely to be the limiting factor. Since the likelihood of spotting an animal probably depends simply on obtaining a minimal reflection from the tapetum, and not upon the intensity of that reflection, it can therefore be expected that the likelihood of <u>not</u> spotting an animal

Fig. 15. Histogram showing the numbers of Mouse Lemurs sighted
at various distances from the main paths of the study area
in 1970. Note the pronounced peak between 0 and 2 metres.

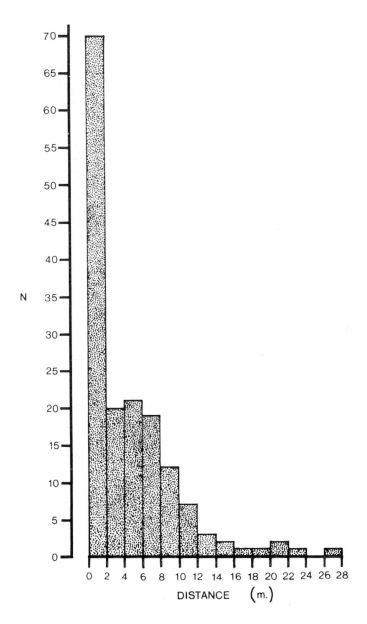

would depend primarily upon the number of trees (etc.) between the animal and the observer, and thus upon the distance between them. Accordingly, if the Mouse Lemurs occurred homogeneously throughout the study area, the observer would probably spot a standard proportion of animals up to given distance into the forest, (beyond which there was an increasing probability that an animal would be effectively surrounded by vegetation and thus concealed from view) throughout the visual sweep made by the observer. Animals fairly close to the edge of the forest should all, at some point, become accessible to the observer's head-lamp and thus susceptible to identification. Given these considerations, nocturnal observation data from a homogeneously distributed population of nocturnal lemurs should show sighting of equal numbers of animals per metre up to a certain distance, followed by gradual decline in the numbers spotted beyond that distance. This is virtually the situation found by Charles-Dominique and Hladik (1971), with Lepilemur muste-linus in semi-arid bush. Such vegetation is much less dense than that in Mandena, and the fall-off point in observation frequency occurred at about 16m. In the histogram of the Mandena data on Mouse Lemurs, a comparable fall-off point occurred at about 8 m. However, there is a distinct difference from the Lepilemur observation histogram in that there are vastly more sightings at 0-2 metres from the main paths than at distances between 2 m and the 8 m fall-off point. This provides strong evidence in favour of the assumption that the Mouse Lemurs really were more active at night alongside paths than in the core of the study area. The clearing of pre-existing pathways through the core area might have modified the animals' behaviour to some extent, but would surely not have driven them to the very fringe of the study area.

It is not clear, however, whether the Mouse Lemurs were

mainly active on the forest fringes because they have a behavioural preference for clearings, or because the major food-sources in Mandena were primarily located along the paths. But since Mouse Lemurs have also been observed chasing beetles in leaf-litter in relatively clear areas (Martin 1972a), and since observations in 1970 showed that Mouse Lemurs frequently cross the ground to move from one patch of vegetation to another, it is highly probable that Lesser Mouse Lemurs are adapted for life on the fringes of forests, rather than in their centres. The forest fringes probably provide greater access to small shrubs bearing edible fruit, a more suitable cover of intertwined fine branches, and more frequent possibilities for preying on small arthropods and vertebrates betrayed by their movements through leaf-litter. The Mouse Lemur has extremely mobile, large ear pinnae which are moved in a characteristic way when animal prey is moving through leaf litter. The characteristic patterns of locomotion (p. 36) are obviously well adapted to an existence requiring rapid quadrupedal running through finely tangled branches, short leaps between relatively fine supports, and occasional (fairly rapid) sorties to the ground.

REPRODUCTION

It is a striking feature of all Malagasy lemur species so far studied that they exhibit a strictly seasonal pattern of breeding, regardless of local climatic zonation- see Martin 1972c for a review. In all cases, it would appear that a major factor in the timing of the breeding season for each species is the requirement that the infants should be weaned at a time of maximum food availability. This ensures that the infants - the most vulnerable members of the species - are able to accu-

mulate sufficient tissue nutrient reserves to survive the subsequent
period of poor food availability. Nevertheless, it is remarkable that
lemurs inhabiting the East Coast rain-forest areas (e.g. the Brown
Mouse Lemur) exhibit almost the same strict seasonality of breeding as
those inhabiting the drier forest areas (e.g. the Grey Mouse Lemur),
despite the fact that the rain forest exhibits relatively little annual variation in rainfall and probably much less marked variation in food availability.

With the Lesser Mouse Lemur, the gestation period is so short
(approximately 60 days) that the entire breeding season can be virtually
confined to the rainy season, which generally covers the period November-
April. In Mandena, mating typically begins in mid-September, and the
first births occur in mid-November when the rainy season is already
under way (Martin 1972a). In fact, the gestation period is so short that
it is theoretically possible for each adult female to produce and rear two
successive litters in the period September-April, as was suggested by
Kaudern (1914). There is some circumstantial evidence (Martin 1972a)
suggesting that two successive litters may indeed be produced in the
Mandena area. This would be an important demographic factor with a
small mammal which has a typical litter-size of only 2-3 and exhibits
restriction of reproduction to a particular season of the year.

1. Female Cycles:

It has been established in the laboratory (Petter-Rousseaux
1962; Martin 1972b) that female Mouse Lemurs exhibit a typical pattern
of vulval activity during the breeding season. The vulva is completely
closed and quiescent during the non-breeding season, and the first signs
of activity appear with reddening and swelling of the vulval area prior to

the first oestrus. Laboratory data (Martin, in prep.) indicate that this initial swelling phase persists for an average of 5 days, at the end of which the swelling has reached a maximum size (an oval mound measuring approximately 6.5 x 4.0 mm at its base). At this point, the vulval area ruptures and mating becomes possible, though preliminary observations (Petter-Rousseaux, pers. comm.) indicate that ovulation, and probable peak mating activity do not occur until 2-3 days after vulval opening. The red colouration then disappears fairly rapidly, and the swelling collapses, leaving the vulval area flat but still open. Personal laboratory observations indicate that the period from opening to closure is typically about 9 days. Thus, the entire range of vulval activity usually lasts no more than 14 days.

It is assumed that mating typically occurs 2-3 days after rupture of the vulval swelling. Females examined just after mating may exhibit one of two conditions: in the majority of cases, the ruptured swelling seems to close off temporarily by approximation of the two lateral lips. This effectively closes the vulva, but the two lips do not fuse; the vulval opening typically reappears, and true closure (by transverse fusion of the vulval skin) does not occur until about a week later. In a few cases, however, such temporary approximation of the lateral walls of the swelling does not occur. Instead, the vulval opening is filled with a large, white vaginal plug of conical form. This was only found with one female from Mandena; but it has since been observed with two females in the laboratory, so the formation of a vaginal plug is probably a regular, if relatively uncommon, feature. In both cases, however, the net result is temporary closure of the vaginal aperture after mating. Where a vaginal plug is formed, it seems to be retained for only a few days at the most, after which it falls away.

In Mandena in 1970, as in 1968, extensive signs of mating activity were found in mid-September, and there was again clear evidence
of general synchronisation of all the females examined. Data on females
collected in the period 6-18 September were lumped and compared with
data for females examined in the period 24-29 September (Fig. 16). It
can be seen clearly that the majority of the females collected in mid-
September exhibited some stage of vulval activity, whilst those collected
towards the end of September exhibited either the terminal stages of
vulval activity or vulval inactivity. When the vulva is sealed off, it is
somewhat difficult to distinguish between pre-oestrous and post-oestrous
females. However, in many cases it was possible to identify a white
scar marking recent vulval fusion, and it seems likely that most - if not
all - of the anoestrous females collected in late September had recently
passed through an oestrous phase.

About 30 of the females collected in late September were kept
in captivity for about 10 days, and palpation at the end of this period indicated that at least 75% of them were gestating. This figure compares
well with that of 75-85% obtained in 1968 (Martin 1972a). One of these
females was subsequently taken to London, where she gave birth to two
infants on 2nd November 1970, indicating that she was impregnated on
about 2nd September.

The body-weights of females weighed towards the end of
September (Fig. 6) provide further evidence that a large proportion of
them had commenced gestation at about the same time. The average
weights of the females had increased by about 10 g in about two weeks,
and the minimum weight of females at the end of September (55 g) was
greater by double this margin than the minimum weight of females in
mid-September (45 g). It is, of course, possible that the females had

increased in body-weight largely or entirely as a result of increased food intake. However, the body-weights of males (Fig. 5) showed no comparable increase, so there is no evidence for a general increase of food availability. The extensive synchronisation evident in the patterns of vulval activity (Fig. 16) and of the shift in average weight (Fig. 6) strongly suggests that most or all of the females were fertilized, and commenced gestation, within a period of about 3-4 weeks during the month of September. It is, of course, possible that females automatically increase in weight after oestrus; but at least 75% of them were probably pregnant. This synchronisation of breeding with a high fertilization rate exactly replicates the pattern found in 1968, and seems to be typical of the Grey Mouse Lemur in several parts of its range (Martin 1972a; Bluntschli 1933 and unpublished diary). Such synchronisation also increases the likelihood that individual females may be able to have two litters per season (Kaudern 1914; Martin 1972b), since a very large proportion of females in a population would produce and rear infants in the first half of the rainy season, following fertilization at the first oestrus, thus permitting many females to undergo gestation and rearing of a second litter before the end of the rains.

The fact that virtually all females in communal nests seem to come into oestrus and commence gestation at about the same time suggests that female Grey Mouse Lemurs reach sexual maturity in less than one year (7-10 months) in the wild. If any females from the previous breeding season had survived and remained in the area, perhaps remaining with their maternal female groups, they were not readily distinguishable from adult females of previous years. Neither in the data on body-weights nor in the records of oestrous activity is there any indication

Fig. 16.   Histograms showing the incidence of various stages of oestrus
and anoestrus in female Grey Mouse Lemurs collected at the
peak of the mating activity (6th-18th September) and soon
afterwards (24th-29th September). Note the clear signs of
synchronisation in the two samples.

A = anoestrus (pre- or post-mating)   F = open, large pink swelling
B = red colour of vulval area; no   G = swelling temporarily closed
    swelling   H = swelling collapsing (usually
C, D, E - Various stages of pro-   open)
    oestrous swelling   J = vulva fusing, white and flat

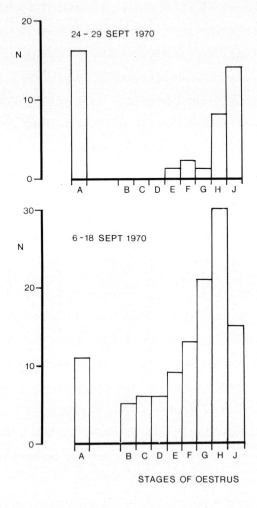

STAGES OF OESTRUS

of a distinction between adult females from previous years and younger females born only 7-10 months previously. If young females do not remain with their maternal female groups, but emigrate to form or join other females groups, it is surprising that the groups sampled in 1970 (and in 1968) did not show any sign of such immigrants. Overall, it seems highly likely that the female Grey Mouse Lemurs achieve sexual maturity within one year, and that they are indistinguishable from other adult females by the time that the next breeding season commences.

One final observation concerning stages of vulval activity in female Mouse Lemurs taken from tree-hollow nests provides indirect evidence of some degree of stability in female nesting groups. Within the individual nesting groups, synchronisation of oestrus stages seemed to be even more marked than in the overall sample collected at any one time. For example, a sample taken on 11.9.70 contained one nest in which 6 of 7 females all showed pro-oestrous red vulval swellings, whilst two other nests contained 3 and 4 females, respectively, all of which exhibited temporary post-oestrous closure of the swollen vulval area. Most of the nests collected indicated that the occupants of each nest were synchronised within a span of about 7 days, whereas the sample as a whole exhibited synchronisation over a wider range of 3-4 weeks. Similarly, in a sample taken on 18.9.70 most of the females showed recent fusion of the flattened vulval area, but three nests (containing 2, 5 and 2 females, respectively) contained females all of which showed temporary post-oestrous closure of the still swollen vulva. Finally, in a sample taken on 28.9.70 virtually all of the females exhibited no signs of vulval activity other than traces of scar tissue indicating recent vulval fusion. However, one nest containing four females included one which had a pro-oestrus vulval swelling and three others which exhibited incomplete post-oestrous vulval closure.

The fact that female Mouse Lemurs occupying communal nests exhibit greater synchronisation of oestrus than the population in general could indicate that the females in each nest associate with one another on a regular basis. It is possible that there are behavioural mechanisms operating to ensure tighter synchronisation than is achieved by simple reliance on the annual variation in daylength as a triggering device (Petter-Rousseaux 1970). In view of the fact that females rear their infants together in communal nests, refinement of synchronisation could have a number of advantages (see Martin 1972a). Behavioural synchronisation between females of nest-groups could be achieved in a relatively short space of time, but it seems more likely that the members of female groups are well acquainted with one another and that the relative stability of female groups is advantageous in the synchronisation of birth, and subsequent rearing, of their offspring.

2. Male Cycles:

Male Mouse Lemurs also exhibit an annual cycle of sexual activity in that there is a marked variation in testis-size (Spühler 1935; Martin 1972a). The testes remain scrotal throughout life, but during the greater part of the dry season (approximately May-August) they are reduced in size and retracted to the lower apertures of the inguinal canals. About one month before mating begins (i.e. in August), the testes increase in size such that the overall scrotal area measures a maximum of 30 mm in length and 25 mm in width by the beginning of September. Thereafter, the testes remain more or less stable in size until about one month after the end of mating activity, when they begin to regress again.

With all males examined in Mandena in 1970, the maximum
length and the maximum width of the scrotal area were measured with
calipers. Because of the copious growth of hair on the scrotum, these
measurements can only be approximate; but they do give some idea of
overall testis development. Nineteen males were measured in the period 6th-18th September, and a further 18 were measured between 24th
and 29th September. There was no difference in the average width
(20.7 vs 20.4 mm) or the average length (26.5 vs 26.8 mm) between
these two groups of males, indicating that the increase in testis size
had reached a plateau by the beginning of September. All males measured had at least the minimum scrotal area dimensions of 18 x 24 mm,
so it seems that all 37 were superficially sexually mature. Thus, one
can conclude that all of the males found in tree-hollow nests - usually
with females - had reached maturity. However, it cannot be concluded
that the males attain sexual maturity in one year, since it has already
been observed (Martin 1972a) that a large proportion of males seem to
occupy peripheral areas. It is quite possible that the young males from
any breeding season move to peripheral areas and that they may not have
access to females until two or more years after birth. Nonetheless, no
male Grey Mouse Lemur - peripheral or otherwise - was ever found to
have a small scrotal area during the breeding season in the 1968 and
1970 studies. Thus, it would seem that young male Mouse Lemurs may
attain overall physical maturity after 7-10 months, but that reproduction
at that age could well be ruled out by lack of breeding access to females.

3. Mating

Actual mating was observed in the Mandena study area on two
occasions in 1970. The fact that two such observations were made,

despite the limited occurrence of mating activities in Mouse Lemurs,
is a good indication of the relative ease with which these animals can be
observed at night. Once the mating sequence had started, the animals
seemed to be relatively insensitive to disturbance, and they could be
approached quite closely without interruption.

Both observations were made on the 14th September. At about
20.00 hours, high-pitched squeals were heard from one corner of the
study area (along the blind alley indicated near the top left of Fig. 12b).
It was already known that such squeals were uttered by Mouse Lemurs
either when fighting or when a female was unwilling to mate with a male.
The observer approached to within 10 m of a pair of Grey Mouse Lemurs
mating on a vertical branch about 3 m up in a shrub. The female was
clinging to the vertical support with all 4 extremities, and the male was
holding on to the female with the forelimbs whilst maintaining a grasp on
the support with the hindlimbs. The remainder of the mating bout lasted
about 3 minutes with intermittent sequences of pelvic thrusting, and the
two animals then separated and exhibited genital self-grooming. However, more squeals were heard from the same area 5 minutes later,
indicating a further interaction (e.g. chasing).

At 20.10 hours, further down the blind alley, a different male
Mouse Lemur was seen circling around a split, hollow tree-trunk at a
height of 1 m. Whenever he approached the entrance to the hollow, an
aggressive "snorting" vocalisation (see Martin 1972a) was heard from
within the trunk. The male continued to circle around the hollow for
about 15 minutes. On a number of occasions, the male attempted to
enter the tree-hollow; but each time there was a rapid burst of snorting
vocalisations, and the male re-emerged rapidly. In the course of circling around the tree-trunk, the male was repeatedly seen to wave his

tail from side to side (a characteristic sign of great excitation), and rhythmic, high-pitched squeaks were uttered intermittently. These rhythmic squeaks have been interpreted as a male mating call (Martin 1972a) and they indicated that the animal inside the trunk was a female. The animals were then left until two hours later (22.15 hours), at which time the presumed female was still in the tree-hollow, this time with the head emerging. The male was 3 m away from the hollow tree. The animal in the hollow then left (permitting the observer to establish definitively that it was a female), and the male followed fairly closely behind. Every time the male came within 1 m of the female, she uttered squeaks, which subsided once the gap between them was increased. The two animals continued this irregular pursuit within a fairly circumscribed area, until (after about 15 minutes) the female eventually permitted the male to approach. The mating posture was then adopted, once again on a vertical support with the same body postures and behaviour patterns as were seen with the previous mating pair.

It should be emphasised that the hollow tree in which the female was concealed did not seem to be a genuine nest. It was later found that the actual hollow was only about 30 cm in length, since the trunk had been split open with an axe lower down, making a second entrance. There was no sign of nest-material or debris of any kind, and no animals were ever found resting in that hollow again. This suggests that the hollow simply functioned as a temporary retreat whilst the female was resisting the approach of the male, and that the main nest(s) was elsewhere.

Apart from these direct observations of mating activity in mid-September, there were also a number of observations of females with

stages of vulval activity within the Mandena study area during September.
All of the females trapped and marked exhibited some sign of vulval activity, and a number of females identified with binoculars in torchlight at
night were clearly seen to have swollen vulval areas. This shows that
the overall synchronisation of oestrus and mating activity was widespread
in the Fort Dauphin region, since the females taken from nests came
from a forest area several miles away.

DISCUSSION

The value of short-term studies of primate behaviour and
ecology is necessarily limited. A detailed understanding of the relationships between ecology and behaviour can only be reached through careful
observations conducted over long periods of time. In addition, the factor of seasonal variation must be taken into account, particularly in an
area like Madagascar where seasonal changes are very marked. It is
quite possible that behaviour which is typical in the wet season may differ significantly from behaviour typical of the dry season, especially in
areas where there is pronounced annual variation in rainfall, and hence
in vegetation. Neither of the field-studies of the Mouse Lemur conducted
by the author has covered the latter part of the rainy season (mid-December
to April), and the early part of the dry season (May to July) remains to
be covered. For the Mandena study area, data are only available from
1968 and 1970 for the period from early September to mid-December.
Therefore any tentative conclusions reached in this paper apply only to
part of the annual cycle, and quite different conclusions may be reached
if Mouse Lemurs are studied at other times of the year. One particular
drawback has been the restriction of observations to the first half of the

breeding season. Until the entire breeding season has been studied, a number of important questions (e.g. estimation of overall reproductive capacity in Mouse Lemur populations) must remain unanswered.

Nevertheless, the two brief field-studies of the Grey Mouse Lemur conducted in 1968 and 1970 have provided a basic pool of data about the behaviour and ecology of this species, permitting a number of tentative conclusions about social organisation, mating and general habits. It seems to be fairly characteristic that Mouse Lemurs occur in localised population nuclei, especially since P. Charles-Dominique and C. M. Hladik (pers. comm.) observed the same pattern of distribution in semi-arid bush of the Berenty area. Within these nuclei, it is fairly obvious from data collected in 1968 and 1970 that there is a core with a high proportion of females to males (approx. 4:1). The sex-ratio at birth is virtually 1:1 (Martin, 1972a), so there must be a much higher death rate among the males, or exclusion of males to the peripheries of population nuclei, or a combination of both factors. Various observations made in 1968 and 1970 indicate that there is indeed a fringe of peripheral males around each core containing females and a few males. Thus it is probably justifiable to distinguish between peripheral males and central males. Independent confirmation of areas exhibiting a high proportion of female Grey Mouse Lemurs to males has been provided by observations conducted by Bluntschli in the Amboasary area in 1931, at a time when the semi-arid bush was still relatively untouched (Bluntschli 1933 and unpublished diary). Thanks to the kind assistance of Prof. F. Strauss of Bern, the author has been able to inspect Bluntschli's original diary of the 1931 expedition, and it is quite clear that Grey Mouse Lemurs collected from nests by villagers in the Amboasary area were mainly females. On the one hand this may be due to the fact that female

nests may have been easier to spot than male nests, and on the other
hand there is a strong possibility that Bluntschli's helpers were operating in the cores of population nuclei, where Mouse Lemurs were abundant
and there was a high ratio of females to males.

Within the cores of such population nuclei, it is apparent that
female Grey Mouse Lemurs tend to nest in groups, which may exceptionally have up to 15 members (Martin, 1972a). Males, on the other hand,
usually occur singly or in pairs, though 3 may be found together in nests
on rare occasions. As a rule, males and females do not tend to share
nests. However, during the period when many females have just completed oestrus - and perhaps during the time when females are actually
in oestrus - the incidence of nesting groups containing both males and
females seems to rise quite markedly. The fact that the highest incidence of male/female nest sharing seemed to occur after oestrus in this
study may indicate that there are non-sexual social contacts of some
kind between males and females in adjacent or overlapping home ranges.
However, most of the evidence indicates that male and female Grey Mouse
Lemurs do not show extensive overlap of their main areas of activity.
Outside the breeding season, contacts between males and females are
probably limited, though detailed study is necessary to establish this.

In the Mandena area, mating activity seems to begin in September.
There is clear synchronisation of the females, such that most or all of
them enter into oestrus within a period of 3-4 weeks. Various observations indicate that a high percentage of the females are fertilized, and
that most of them carry gestation through to term (Martin 1972a). Each
female typically gives birth to 2-3 infants in November. After these infants have been reared and weaned (i.e. after about $1\frac{1}{2}$ months), there
would be time for each female to have a second litter, and circumstan-

tial evidence indicates that this does actually occur (Martin, 1972a).

Within the female groups, synchronisation of oestrus is even more marked than in the local population generally, and this provides some evidence for a certain degree of stability of the female nesting groups.

Observations of Mouse Lemurs (mainly unmarked) whilst active at night has provided some indication of the areas of activity of male and female groups, as evident during the first part of the night during the latter part of the dry season and the early part of the wet season. Various lines of circumstantial evidence (e.g the observation that no known individual has been seen to range over any area greater than 50 m in diameter during the period of study) suggest that these inferred areas of activity do in fact - at least partially- correspond to "home ranges". It is therefore interesting that the observed areas of occurrence of females generally seemed to coincide with the areas richest in the two main inferred food-plants in the Mandena study area.

All the observations indicate that Mouse Lemurs born in one season are morphologically adult by the following season, and that the young females are then often fertilised along with their older nest-companions. Males are also physically mature after one year; but it is possible that confinement to peripheral home ranges excludes young males from breeding with the females in the population core. Accordingly, a young peripheral male could eventually achieve breeding access by usurping or replacing a central male in his own population nucleus, or in some other population nucleus. This kind of system would have many advantages. Mobility of peripheral males would ensure exogamy, whilst competition between males for central home ranges with breeding

access would ensure differential reproductive success. Meanwhile, the
females and a small proportion of adult males in the centre of each population nucleus would have access to local concentrations of suitable plant
foods, thus ensuring the survival of their offspring.

These general observations of Grey Mouse Lemurs are of
particular interest because of the overall similarities between this prosimian and Galago demidovii in Africa (Charles-Dominique and Martin
1970). The Cheirogaleinae are morphologically the lease specialised of
the lemurs, and the Galaginae are similarly less specialised than the
Lorisinae. This strengthens the assumption that Microcebus murinus
and Galago demidovii resemble one another because of the retention of
characters similar or identical to those present in the ancestral lemur/
loris (Strepsirhine) stock. The lemurs as a group are distinguished by
a number of morphological features quite clearly from the loris/bush-
baby group, and it is therefore extremely unlikely that the Cheirogaleinae and the Galaginae are derived from an ancestral stock distinct
from, and later than, the basic common stock which gave rise to all the
lemurs, bush-babies and lorises. It could, of course, be argued that
the Cheirogaleinae and the Galaginae have come to resemble one another
as a result of extensive convergent evolution; but this is relatively unlikely since both subfamilies contain the least specialised members of
their respective groups. It can, for example, be argued on quite independent grounds that the Cheirogaleinae have retained more primitive
characters than other lemurs, and the same can be inferred about behavioural characters (Martin, 1972c). Hence, it seems probably that
the Cheirogaleinae and the Galaginae have remained relatively close to
the ancestral primate condition in both morphology and behaviour, and
detailed study of these two subfamilies should yield valuable information

about the early radiation of the Primates. The fact that Galago demidovii
and Microcebus murinus live under similar ecological conditions - and
may have done so for some time - does mean that separate evolution of
similar characters may have occurred, and a certain amount of paral-
lelism must be expected. For this reason, a careful analysis of the
characters involved is obligatory.

A final note must be added about conservation of the lemurs.
As the smallest and most widespread of the lemurs, the Lesser Mouse
Lemur is of course the least threatened of all the Malagasy lemurs.
However, there were certain indications in 1970 that there may have
been changes due to human activity in the Mandena area since the 1968
study. Although these apparent changes are relatively slight, they do
highlight the inherent fragility of lemur populations faced with human interference. The need for effective conservation measures should be
obvious. In the Mandena area, heavy tree-felling is doubtless affecting
the resident lemurs. The maximum observed size of female nesting-
groups in 1970 was 7, as compared to 15 in 1968, and there were noticeable differences in tree-hollow nest dimensions. The nests examined in
1970 were generally in smaller trunks than those examined in 1968; but
the entrances to the hollows were generally larger. Finally, the average
weights of males and females measured in 1970 were somewhat lower
than those measured in 1968. Some or all of these differences could be
traced to a degradation of the habitat between 1968 and 1970. This would
seem to be a distinct possibility, since Avahi laniger - which was frequently observed in the Mandena area in 1968 - was not sighted at all in
the area in 1970. It is therefore a matter for urgent concern that the
International Conference on the Conservation of Natural Resources held
in Tananarive in 1970 should lead to increased international interest

and assistance, so that the Malagasy government will be enabled to restrict or arrest the destruction of the remaining forest areas and their lemur populations.

ACKNOWLEDGEMENTS

My thanks go to Dr. J. -J. Petter for his frequent advice and assistance, which was invaluable for both field-visits to Madagascar. The staff of the Malagasy Embassy in London - particularly the Ambassador, His Excellency Caesare Rabenoro, and the Cultural Attache, Mr. H. Razafindratovo - were extremely helpful. Valuable assistance was also provided by the Director of the Eaux et Forêts in Tananarive, Mr. Jules Ramanantsoavina, and by his assistant concerned with the Nature Reserves, Mr. J. M. Andriamampianina. The British Embassy in Tananarive provided frequent hospitality and assistance, and special thanks go to Mr. S. J. Warder and his wife for their friendship and help. The French Overseas Scientific Research Institute (O.R.S.T.O. M.) in Tsimbazaza also provided hospitality and valuable assistance, and thanks go to the Director, Mr. P. Roederer.

In the field, the support and assistance of my wife, Anne-Elise, was invaluable. Her assistance with preparation of the text-figures is also gratefully acknowledged. The hospitality provided by the de Heaulme family in Fort Dauphin and Berenty was once again magnificent. Thanks also go to Mr. Bidel and his son for arranging accommodation and transport in the Fort Dauphin area. Hospitality and assistance with transport was also provided by Mr. G. Mitshun, and his help is gratefully acknowledged. Finally, a word of thanks is due to Drs. P. Charles-Dominique and C. M. Hladik for their companionship, advice and encouragement in the field.

Thanks go to Dr. Gilbert Manley for his valuable assistance in revising the final manuscript.

The 1970 field-study was supported by a grant-in-aid from the Royal Society, which is gratefully acknowledged. This grant also permitted the purchase of a copy of Bluntschli's field diary, which was kindly provided by Prof. F. Strauss of Bern.

REFERENCES

Bluntschli, H. (1933). In den Urwäldern auf Madagaskar. Umschau i.d. Naturwiss.u.Techn. 36, 769-1019.

Charles-Dominique, P. (1971). Eco-éthologie des Prosimians du Gabon. Biol. Gabon. 7, 121-228.

Charles-Dominique, P. (1972). Ecologie et vie sociale de Galago demidovii (Fischer 1808; Prosimii). Z. Tierpsychol. Beiheft 9, 7-41.

Charles-Dominique, P. and Hladik, C. M. (1971). Le Lepilemur du Sud de Madagascar: Ecologie, alimentation et vie sociale. Terre et Vie 25, 3-66.

Charles-Dominique, P. and Martin, R. D. (1970). Evolution of lorises and lemurs. Nature, Lond. 225, 139-144.

Hill, W. C. O. (1953). Primates. Vol. 1 (Strepsirhini). Edinburgh University Press, pp. 798.

Kaudern, W. (1914). Einige Beobachtungen uber die Zeit der Fortpflanzung der madagassischen Saugetiere. Ark. Zool.,(Stockholm) 9, 1-22.

Martin, R.D. (1972a). A preliminary field-study of the Lesser Mouse Lemur (Microcebus murinus, J.F. Miller 1777). Z. Tierpsychol. Beiheft 9, 43-89.

Martin, R. D. (1972b). Breeding Lesser Mouse Lemurs (Microcebus
    murinus) for laboratory research: Paper submitted to the
    International Symposium on Breeding non-human Primates for
    Laboratory research, Bern June 1971 (S. Karger A.G., in
    press).

Martin, R. D. (1972c). Adaptive Radiation and Behaviour of the
    Malagasy Lemurs. Phil. Trans. Roy. Soc. Lond. ser.B. 264,
    295-352.

Petter, J. -J. (1962). Recherches sur l'écologie et l'éthologie des
    lémuriens malgaches. Mem. Mus. natn. Hist. nat. Paris,
    (nouv. ser.) Ser.A., Zoologie, 27, 1-146.

Petter. J. -J. and Hladik, C. M. (1970). Observations sur la domaine
    vital et la densité de population de Loris tardigradus dans les
    forêts de Ceylan. Mammalia, 34, 394-409.

Petter, J. -J., Schilling, A. and Pariente, G. (1971). Observations
    éco-éthologiques sur deux lémuriens malgaches nocturnes:
    Phaner furcifer et Microcebus coquereli. Terre et Vie, 25,
    287-327.

Petter-Rousseaux, A. (1962). Recherches sur la biologie de la
    reproduction des primates inferieurs. Mammalia 26, Suppl. 1,
    1-88

Petter-Rousseaux, A. (1970). Observations sur l'influence de la
    photoperiodicite sur l'activite sexuelle chez Microcebus murinus
    (Miller 1777) en captivite. Am. Biol. anim. 10, 203-208.

Spühler, O. (1935). Genitalzyklus und Spermiogenese des Mausmaki,
    Microcebus murinus. Z. Zellforsch, 23, 442-463.

DIFFERENCES IN BEHAVIOUR BETWEEN SOME

ARBOREAL AND TERRESTRIAL SPECIES

OF AFRICAN MONKEYS

N. R. Chalmers

National Primate Research Centre
Nairobi, Kenya *

*Author's present address:

Department of Biology,
The Open University,
Walton Hall, Bletchley,
Buckinghamshire,
England.

I. INTRODUCTION

Research into the social behaviour of free-living primates has three main preoccupations. First, it tries to describe the organization and behaviour of primate societies and to analyse the contribution which individuals within a particular society make to the organisation and behaviour of the society as a whole. Second, by relating inter-specific differences in social organisation and behaviour to inter-specific differences in habitat, it tries to assess the selection pressures to which primate societies are exposed and their responses to these pressures. Third, by comparing the social organisation and behaviour of primate species which vary in their degree of taxonomic affinity and in the adaptive pressures to which they are subjected, it tries to build up a picture of the evolution of primate social behaviour. Despite advances in all three aspects of primate research in recent years, the situation is still unsatisfactory. The diversity of interests, field techniques and methods of data analysis of different observers, not to mention the difficulties of observation, particularly on forest-living species makes meaningful inter-specific comparison difficult.

This paper indulges in all three of the preoccupations mentioned in the first paragraph, but rather than surveying a wide variety of primates it limits itself to five African cercopithecines in the hope that, by so limiting itself, something of the causal factors behind, and the adaptive features and evolutionary history of, these five types of primate society might be clarified.

The five primates in question are the redtail monkey Cercopithecus ascanius, de Brazzas monkey Cercopithecus neglectus, the patas monkey Erythrocebus patas, the white-cheeked mangabey Cercocebus

albigena and the baboons Papio cynocephalus and P. anubis (here treated as one species). Behavioural and ecological information in the
literature on these five types is briefly surveyed and compared. Following this, new information about the social behaviour in captivity of
redtails, patas and de Brazzas is presented and compared with similar
information on captive baboons (Rowell 1966a) and mangabeys
(Chalmers and Rowell 1971).

These five species can be divided taxonomically into two sub-
groups, one containing the two Cercopithecus species and the closely
related Erythrocebus and the other, Papio and Cercocebus, (Jolly,
1966). The habitats of species in both sub-groups are diverse. The
patas monkey is a ground living form typically living in open savanna
with few trees. The redtail, by contrast lives in semi-deciduous tropical rain forest, and typically occurs at forest fringes rather than in
the centre, (Haddow 1952, and personal observation). There is little
information in the literature on de Brazzas monkey but work on this
species in western Kenya by K. Simpson (personal communication) indicates that these monkeys live in tropical rain forest, particularly in
regions adjacent to swamps, into which the monkeys descend in situations of potential danger. In the other sub-group, the white-cheeked
mangabey is almost totally arboreal, living in similar forests to the
redtail monkey, but penetrating into the middle of the forest as well as
being at the edges (Chalmers 1968a). Cynocephalus baboons are primarily terrestrial, living in regions of savanna (Altmann and Altmann
1970, DeVore and Hall 1965), although anubis baboons, typically
savanna-living are also found in forests (Rowell 1966b).

The taxonomic affinities of these five species, and their habitats
are important because it makes it possible to compare the social

behaviour and organisation of closely related species living in dissimi-
lar habitats, and distantly related species in similar habitats. From the
literature on the five species it is possible to obtain a certain amount of
comparative information about group organisation and behaviour. Features which can be compared include group size, group composition,
home range size, dominance structure or lack of it, intra-group aggression, sexual behaviour and maternal behaviour. These are summarised
in Table 1 and commented on in more detail below.

(a)   Group size. DeVore's suggestion (1963) that terrestrial primates
tend to live in larger groups than arboreal species has not been supported by recent field data (Struhsaker 1969; Crook 1970). Even in the five
species listed in Table 1 there is no obvious relationship between group
size and habitat. It would seem therefore that adaptive pressures from
the environment are not sufficient to impose a general pattern upon
group size.

(b) Group composition. Again, there is little uniformity associated
with a particular habitat, but there are certain features of group composition common to some closely related species. Thus the majority
of Cercopithecus species, and all forest-living ones have one male
groups, but such a social structure is by no means unique to them
(Struhsaker 1969).

(c) Home range size.   Differences in home range size correlate well
with differences in habitat, and, as many authors have suggested, such
differences are likely to relate to the availability and particularly the
density of food resources within the home range. The data for the
species in Table 1 show this correlation, even though the figure for the
redtails may well be rather larger than is normal for this species.

(d) Dominance hierarchies and aggression. Again, there were early suggestions that terrestrial species possess aggressive societies with well-defined dominance hierarchies, whereas arboreal species do not (DeVore 1963). This suggestion, based as it was on comparisons between distantly related and, often poorly studied species (Chalmers 1968a) has proved in the light of more recent work to be a considerable over-simplification. As Table I shows, if one is comparing multi-male groups with single male groups, one cannot hope to have similar dominance-hierarchy-based societies, and hence statements about aggressiveness, hierarchies, etc. which are divorced from considerations of group composition are of little value. Inter-specific comparisons of behaviour frequencies are discussed further in the next section.

(e) Sexual behaviour. Of the species in Table 1, little is known about the sexual behaviour of the wild redtail and de Brazza monkeys. Hall (1965) reports that sexual behaviour in wild patas is rare. Mangabeys and baboons both show perineal swelling at and around the time of ovulation, whereas the other three species do not. Moreover, mangabeys and baboons have several other features of sexual behaviour in common (Chalmers and Rowell 1971), and this may well be an indication of taxonomic affinity.

(f) Maternal behaviour and infant development. Detailed data are available in the literature on infant development in baboons (Rowell, Din and Omar 1968), mangabeys and de Brazzas (Chalmers 1972) as well as two other African cercopithecines, the Sykes monkey Cercopithecus albogularis and the vervet, C. aethiops (Chalmers, op. cit. Struhsaker 1971). Comparisons by Chalmers show that in captive animals, infants of arboreal species become independent of their mothers at a later age than do those of terrestrial species such as vervets and

TABLE I. Comparisons of social organisation and behaviour of five African cercopithecines

Feature	Redtail	De Brazza	Patas	Mangabey	Baboon
1. Group size	Apparently flexible ranging from 3-5 while resting, 10-40 while travelling (Buxton 1952) – but see Struhsaker's criticism of these estimates (1969)	5-10 (K. Simpson pers. comm.)	5-31 (Hall 1965)	7-25 (Chalmers 1968a)	(a) 32, 58 (Rowell 1966b) (b) Mean of 51 groups, 51.4, mode 20-30 (Altmann and Altmann, 1970) (c) 12-87 (DeVore and Hall, 1965)
2. Group Composition	Possibly 1 male group	1 male group	1 male group	Multi-male group	Multi-male group
3. Home range size	130 hectares (Haddow, 1952)	Unknown	5200 hectares	13 hectares	(a) 380 and 500 hectares (b) 2330 hectares (c) 500+ – 3900 hectares
4. Dominance structure	Unknown	Unknown	Adult females aggression towards male. Females with rank order.	Not clear in wild animals. Some indication of rank order in captive animals. (Chalmers and Rowell 1971)	(a) absence of clear dominance structure. (b) – (c) Complicated dominance hierarchies in both males and females.

(Continuation of Table I)

5. Inter-group aggression	Unknown	Unknown	Rare – 0.073 aggressions per hour over 627 hours	1.26 per hour and 1.07 per hour (Chalmers 1968b)	0.88 per hour for P. ursinus (Hall 1962)
6. Sexual behaviour	No oestrous swelling	No oestrous swelling	No oestrous swelling	Oestrous swelling. Cyclicity of behaviour (Chalmers and Rowell 1971)	Oestrous swelling Cyclicity of behaviour (Rowell 1966c)
7. Intra-Specific communication	Staring open face (2) with face relatively immobile. Lip-smack rare. Infrequent grunts (van Hooff 1962)	As redtail Lip-smacks Infrequent grunts	As redtail. Lip-smacks Infrequent grunts	Staring open face (1) with eyebrows raised (van Hooff 1962) Lip-smacks Frequent grunts	As mangabey Lip-smacks (van Hooff 1962) Frequent grunts (Andrew 1963)

References for Items 2–7 as for Item 1 except where otherwise stated.

baboons. This is not due to a slower maturation on the part of the arboreal infants, nor to greater restrictiveness of their mothers. The arboreal infants do not leave their mothers as frequently as those of terrestrial species. Inter-specific differences here clearly relate to differences in habitat and are clearly adaptive. Other data on these species (Chalmers, in prep.) suggest that further aspects of socialisation, particularly the attitude of other adult group members, do not correlate with habitat, but with the taxonomic position of the species.

(g) Communication. Analysis of intra-specific communication by van Hooff (1962) Struhsaker (1970) and Chalmers (1968c) has shown that communicative gestures and vocalisations frequently betray evidence of taxonomic affinity, rather than of similarity of habitat, Andrew (1963).

In summary, this brief survey shows that two features of cercopithecine social behaviour and organisation are known which are unequivocally common to species living in similar habitats, and these are home range size and infant development. Certain aspects of behaviour are common to species which are taxonomically close. These include sexual behaviour and communication. In still other aspects, the interaction of ecological pressures and phylogenetic factors is complex and no clear pattern is visible. It is because of this and because of the many gaps in Table I that the present study, involving a detailed comparison of the social behaviour of several cercopithecines in captivity, was undertaken.

II. MATERIALS AND METHODS

1. Animals and their conditions of captivity

Small groups of redtails, de Brazzas and patas were kept each in an outdoor cage, measuring 8. 5 m x 3. 5 m x 4. 5 m high (de Brazzas and patas) and 11. 3 m x 4. 5 m x 2. 5 m high (redtails). The patas and de Brazzas in addition had a heated indoor section of the cage to which they had access at night. Each group consisted of one adult male (more than 5 years old) two or three adult females (more than 3 years old) and their young; (under 3 years old). The precise group composition is indicated in Fig. 2. Animals were watched for a total of 100 hours per species, one hour per day, 3 or 4 times per week over a period of 7 months. Observations were made at the National Primate Research Centre, Limuru, Kenya, at an altitude of 8000 ft. and a mean temperature of 18°C. Interactions were recorded in the same way as is described by Chalmers and Rowell (1971) for mangabeys. That is, all interactions were recorded, the majority being between pairs of animals, but where more animals were involved the interaction was split into its constituent diads. Which animal initiated each interaction, and the details of each interaction, such as grooming, aggression, etc. were recorded. The categories which are discussed in this paper are listed below with additional comments where necessary.

approaches	Who initiates the interaction, not the manner of approach
avoids	Either moves away from an approaching animal, or, if moving itself and the other animal stationary, makes a detour around it.
aggresses	Includes chasing, facial threats such as staring, biting, mouthing, pulling roughly to-

	wards or pushing away
	from aggressor.
grooms	
lip-smacks	As described by van
	Hooff (1962)
embraces	putting one or both arms
	round other monkey
genital contact	Touches genitals of other
	monkey either with hand,
	nose or mouth.
mounts	Does not necessarily
	include intromission,
	pelvic thrusts or ejaculation
tail-twining	two animals sitting side
	by side with tails hanging down,
	twined round each other.

The observations were carried out by the author, and by assistants. The categories of behaviour recorded were sufficiently distinct for there to be no ambiguity in their recording. (One pattern which proved to be ambiguous, and which therefore is not discussed here, is that of presenting and/or soliciting grooming.)

2. Analysis of data

All interactions except those involving infants were analysed. (There was one infant de Brazza born into the group 5 months before the end of the study, one redtail born 2 months before the end and one patas infant throughout.) This procedure is similar to that for the data presented by Rowell for baboons (1966): the mangabey group described by Chalmers and Rowell (1971) had no infants. The number of interactions and specific activities performed by each member of each group was totalled over the 100 hours of observation.

An important point in comparing behaviour frequencies between species is that an appropriate method of quantifying one's data must be chosen to make such comparisons meaningful. One of the most frequently used methods of quantifying observations is to express them as number of activities per unit time (see, for example, many of the field studies reported in DeVore 1965, also Hall 1964). If such a measure is expressed as a function of the number of members in the group, then such an index may have its uses for inter-specific comparisons. However, to any animal within a group, the significant feature of any encounter must be the probability of a given outcome following that encounter. It may be more meaningful therefore, to express events as percentages of a suitable total measure of activity, such as number of encounters in the whole group, or between given individuals. In the results section therefore, data on the total number of interactions per diad per 100 hours are presented for each group to give a comparative measure of group activity. A more detailed comparison follows by expressing the number of specific activities observed as a percentage of total interactions within the group. Following this, the contribution of each group member to the overall group is analysed by presenting the number of times each group member performed a specific activity as a percentage of the number of times that activity was performed in the group. Finally, the data are analysed to show the proportion of times each member of the group spends performing different activities.

For each of these methods of analysis, inter-specific comparisons are made, and adaptive interpretations sought. The data for

mangabeys and baboons are re-worked from the papers mentioned
above. Where appropriate, differences between individuals and between species were tested by X^2, with a 1% level of significance.

III. RESULTS

Fig. 2 summarises the interactions between group members in
the 5 species. (Original figures of which Fig. 1 gives percentages,
together with significance levels given in Table II). Fig. 1 (a) shows
how many interactions occurred per diad for each species, and (b) -
(j) show what proportion of these interactions involved specific activities such as grooming, aggression, etc. Fig. 1 (a) shows that the patas
and baboons had fewer interactions per diad than did the other species.
Chalmers and Rowell (1971) previously suggested that the difference in
number of interactions between baboons and mangabeys may not be a
real one, for the figures exclude any interactions with infants. While
Rowell's baboon group contained infants, the mangabey group did not,
and so the figure for baboons was lower than the total number of interactions, including those involving infants, in the group. Such an argument is valid provided that interactions of infants reduce the availability of adults to interact with each other. Such is not necessarily the
case; indeed, adults interacting with an infant might well be brought
into proximity with one another and so might interact more frequently
than they would have otherwise. Moreover, for redtails, de Brazzas
and patas, each group had at least one infant, and interactions between
adults and infants are likewise excluded from Fig. 1. Comparisons
can safely be made, therefore, between all except the mangabeys, and
even here a comparison may not be invalid. Such a comparison suggests

that the terrestrial forms interact less frequently than do arboreal.

Fig. 1(b) - (j) shows the frequency of various activities in the different species, each expressed as a percentage of the total number of approaches per species. Fig. 1(b) shows that the percentage of approaches involving aggression is higher for patas and baboons than for the other species. (It is interesting that, if the number of aggressive incidents per diad per 100 hours is used as an index of aggression, the following figures are obtained: baboons 6.6, mangabeys 4.8, redtails 28.9, de Brazzas 2.8, patas 9.3. This shows the rate to be similar for mangabeys and baboons, a fact which compares well with the figures for wild animals (Chalmers 1968b), which were, of necessity, obtained by the same method of quantification. Redtails, on this measure are by far the most aggressive of the groups studied.)

Fig. 1(b) shows that baboons had the highest percentage of encounters involving aggression, followed by patas, then by the three arboreal species. These figures must be treated with some caution. Chalmers and Rowell (1971) stated that the aggression rate in the mangabey group was markedly influenced by the composition of the group. An incompatible member can cause continuous fighting. However, each of the groups appeared to be relatively settled, and lacking in prolonged fights and chases directed against any one particular member.

This does not mean, however, that the aggression rates given in Fig. 1(b) can be taken as representative of aggression rates in the wild. In free-living mangabeys, for example, (Chalmers 1968) 37% of all encounters involved aggression. Nor does it mean that captivity alters each species' aggression rate to a similar extent. In the mangabeys studied so far the rate is lower in captivity than in the wild.

Fig. 1. Interactions within captive groups of five species of African
         cercopithecines.

         a number of interactions per diad per 100 hours
       b-j percentage of interactions involving specific activities

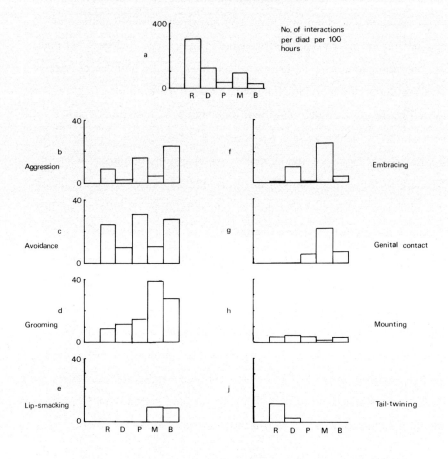

b-j % of interactions involving specific activities

R = redtail, D = de Brazza, P = patas, M = mangabey, B = baboon

Fig. 2.   Contribution of individuals to overall group behaviour within captive groups of five species of
African cercopithecines.
a   Percentage of interactions   b–f   Percentage of specific activities performed by each
group member

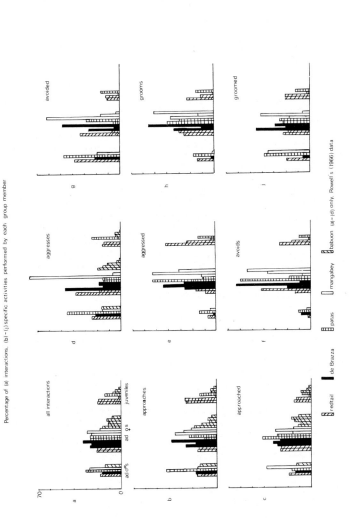

Percentage of (a) interactions, (b)–(j) specific activities performed by each group member

In the baboons studied by Kummer (1970) and by Rowell (1967) it
is higher. We can only say, therefore, that in these caged groups, living under their specific conditions, that the two predominantly terrestrial species showed a higher rate of aggression than the others.

As might be expected those species which showed a high aggression rate, also showed a high amount of avoidance. The cautionary
remarks made about the aggression figures must also be made about
these. However, the figures for avoidance are for each species higher
than those for aggression. This shows that on many occasions one animal avoids another, without the latter showing any aggressive behaviour.
The two species which showed the highest excess of avoidance over aggression were the redtails and patas, this excess being significantly
higher than that for the other species.

Fig. 1(d) shows that the mangabeys and baboons groomed more
frequently than the other species, the differences being quite substantial. They also lip-smacked more frequently than did the other species
(Fig. 1e), lip-smacking in the latter being almost non-existent. Conversely, tail-twining occurred exclusively in the redtails and de
Brazzas. These features, then, are common to animals with closer
taxonomic affinities. Genital contact (Fig. 1g) was most frequent in
mangabeys, followed by baboons. It was virtually non-existent in redtails and de Brazzas. The patas figures were unusual in that virtually
all the contacts (94%) were made by the adult male, whereas the figures
were fairly evenly distributed between all members of the group in
mangabeys and baboons. The figures for embracing are ambiguous for
it is not certain that the behaviour termed 'embracing' for each species
is necessarily homologous. In de Brazzas, for example, the embracing
animals frequently sat facing each other with their arms around each

other. In mangabeys, by contrast, one of the participants at least would stand, and back on to the other so that the two animals were head to tail when they put their arms around each other. Mangabeys and de Brazzas embraced more frequently than the other species. There was no obvious division of this behaviour pattern along either taxonomic or along ecological lines.

Finally, the frequency of mounting was similar for all species except the mangabeys, in which it was lower (Fig. 1h).

To summarise, the captive mangabeys and baboons groomed and lip-smacked more frequently than the other species. Excepting the adult male patas, this was also true of contacting genitals. De Brazzas and redtails alone showed tail-twining. In these captive groups, baboons and patas interacted less frequently than the other species; they also had a higher aggression rate. Baboons, patas and redtails avoided each other more frequently than other species, both after aggression and during non-aggressive encounters.

The data so far presented have given a picture of overall activity within each captive group. The following section presents data relevant to the contribution of individuals within the group toward the group's organisation and behaviour. These data are presented species by species and are summarised in Fig. 2. The totals of which Fig. 2 gives the percentages are shown in Table II.

Redtails

The adult male was involved in the same percentage of total interactions as the other members of the group. The percentage of approaches in the group made by the adult male was similar to that made by

each adult female, but the percentage of being approached was lower.
The male's contribution to group aggression was lower than that of one
of the females and higher than that of the other, while the percentage of
the group's aggression which was directed against the adult male was
slightly less than that against either female. The male's contribution
to avoidance within the group was lower than that of the females, and
the percentage of being avoided was higher for the male than for the
females. The male contributed to the grooming within the group less
than the females, but the percentage of grooming of the male was of the
same order as that directed to each female. In short, the male's contribution to the total activity of the group was in most respects not
markedly different from that of the females. The major difference was
the extent to which he avoided and was avoided.

De Brazzas

The adult male was involved in fewer interactions than the adult
females. He performed the same percentage of approaches as one
adult female, and less than the other two, while a lower percentage of
approaches were directed towards the adult male than to each adult
female. The figures for aggression are not particularly meaningful
because there were only 34 aggressive incidents overall but it is worth
noting that virtually none of them was directed at the adult male. The
figures for avoiding and being avoided are very variable for the females,
and so no comparison between the sexes is possible, beyond saying that
the figure for the male lies within the range of those of the females for
both categories of behaviour. A smaller proportion of grooming encounters involved the adult male than the adult females both in the role
as groomer and groomee. In summary, the contribution of the male's

TABLE II. Numbers of total interactions and numbers of specific activities recorded in 5 species of cercopithecine monkey

Species

Activity	Redtail	De Brazza	Patas	Mangabey	Baboon	Comments
Total interactions	6364	1568	1149	1237	7926	Baboons' figure for 300 hours' observation, others for 100 hours.
Aggression	577	34	185	58	1825	
Avoidance	1575	158*	354	130*	2210	
Grooming	547	186	174	481	2190	
Lip-smacking	1*	10*	3*	123†	714†	
Embracing	51*	158	16*	316	376	
Genital contact	18*	7*	66	273	621	
Mounting	211*	69*	43*	19	284*	
Tail-twining	714	42	0*	0*	0*	

Differences between species for the various activities are significant at the 1% level except where marked with identical symbols (* or †). (For example, redtails, de Brazzas and patas do not differ significantly from each other in the amount of lip-smacking they give, but they do lip-smack significantly less than mangabeys and baboons. Similarly, mangabeys and baboons do not differ from each other in the amount of lip-smacking.)

behaviour to the group's behaviour was not markedly different from that of the females, with the exception that the male appeared to be slightly detached from the group, being involved in fewer encounters than the females, and being involved in fewer grooming incidents.

Patas

The adult male was involved in more interactions than other members of the group. He approached more often than any adult female and was approached less often. The male aggressed much more than the females, but the amount of aggression directed against the females was very different. The amount of aggression directed against the adult male was similar to that of one of the females and lower than that of the other. The male avoided less than either adult female, and was avoided a great deal more. He also groomed less and was groomed more. The adult male's contribution to the group's behaviour is thus considerably different from that of the adult females.

Mangabeys

The male was involved in the same number of interactions as two of the adult females, rather more than the third. He approached less and was approached more than them, and thus formed the focus of the group's activities. There were only 58 aggressive incidents within the group, which makes intra-group comparisons meaningless. The adult male avoided less than the females, but the figures for being avoided are so disparate for the females, that no male:female comparison is possible, beyond saying that the figure for the male falls within the range of those for the females. The male groomed less than any of the females and was groomed more than two of them.

Baboons

Rowell's figures for baboons are rather difficult to compare with those for the previously mentioned species. With ten animals in the baboon group, not all animals could interact simultaneously with the male, and hence the chances of interactions not involving the male were larger than in the other groups. With this in mind, the figures show that the male was involved in more interactions than all but one of the adult females. He approached and aggressed more than all but one of the females and was approached to the same extent as the females. Rowell's paper does not give frequencies for individuals for other categories of behaviour; however, it is possible to extract from the paper figures for all males and all females, i.e. including sub-adults and juveniles. These figures are not shown in Fig. 2. They show that males avoided less and were avoided more than the females. Also, the males groomed less and were groomed more than the females. Figures for being aggressed are not available.

The contribution of any member to a group's behaviour depends upon how many interactions it is involved in, and what it does during an interaction. Thus differences between the contribution of two individuals within a group may stem from a different rate of approaching or being approached, and/or probability of a particular behaviour pattern occurring during an interaction. The previous method of analysis does not allow us to distinguish between these possibilities very clearly, although if the contribution of a male and female to a group's behaviour are different, but the number of interactions they are involved in is the same, then such a difference must stem from qualitative differences in behaviour during an interaction. Individual differences in behaviour can be analysed more rigidly by expressing the number of times an

individual performs a specific activity as a percentage of his total
interactions. Table 3 presents such an analysis and levels of significance. The Table shows that in redtails and de Brazzas, such differences between individuals that occur result primarily from differences
in how the different group members behave during encounters rather
than differences in the number of interactions in which they take part.
In the patas however, the male differs from the females both in the
number of interactions involving him and in the sorts of behaviour he
shows during an interaction. Thus the high frequency with which the
male aggresses, is avoided and is groomed is a result both of his high
number of interactions and his greater tendency to be involved in these
activities. Other categories of behaviour which occur less often in the
adult male than in the females (e.g. avoiding, grooming, being aggressed) do so in spite of the high number of interactions involving the male.

In mangabeys, differences in the individual's contributions to the
group's behaviour are a result of differences in the individual's behaviour during interactions rather than differences in number of interactions in which they take part. Finally, in baboons, inter-individual
differences in aggression rate stem primarily from inter-individual
differences in numbers of interactions, while other differences reflect
differences in qualitative behaviour.

The main feature of these results is the marked difference of the
adult male patas compared with the patas females, in contrast to the
less spectacular differences between the sexes in the other species.

IV. DISCUSSION

Any attempt to account for differences in social behaviour between primate species must take into account both their taxonomic position and their ecology (Chalmers 1968b, Struhsaker 1969). (Cultural
differences may also arise between groups (e.g. Crook 1970), but these
will not be considered further here.) Animals distantly related to one
another are likely to be more diverse in their behaviour than are closely related animals, just as they are in their morphology. However,
animals living in a similar habitat are likely to be subjected to similar
adaptive pressures, and hence they may evolve parallel features of
behaviour regardless of their degree of taxonomic affinity. Behavioural features which are common to a taxonomic group, regardless of
habitat must have been evolved early in the evolutionary history of the
group, before it diverged along different evolutionary pathways. Such
behavioural features are therefore likely to be older than are features
which are found to be common to animals of varied taxonomic affinity
in a given habitat. The problem is to tease out from the behavioural
repertoire of different species, those features which correlate with the
taxonomic position and those which correlate with the ecology of the
species.

In a discussion on behaviour characters in primate taxonomy,
Kummer (1970) suggests that primate behaviour traits which are
direct functional adaptations to the extra-specific environment are less
likely to reflect the taxonomic position of a species than the ecological
conditions in which they live. On the other hand, features of behaviour
which are adapted to the intra-specific environment, such as intra-
specific communication signals, are less likely to be influenced by the

TABLE III.   Number of times specific activities performed as percentage of total number of interactions for individuals in each group

Activity	Species	Ad ♂	Ad ♀					Juveniles			Significance
			1	2	3	4	5	1	2	3	
Approaches	Redtail	46.7	36.8	37.0				63.2	67.2		♂: each ♀ p<.01
	De Brazza	56.9	47.6	35.4	60.1			38.9	71.4		♂: ♀'s 1 & 2 p<.01 ♂: ♀3 p>.01
	Patas	71.7	19.5	43.8	59.0						♂: each ♀ p<.01
	Mangabey	29.2	68.8	47.4							♂: each ♀ p<.01
	Baboon	51.7	63.1	60.7	29.3	31.4	28.2	41.8	60.4	41.8	♂: each ♀ p<.01
Aggresses	Redtail	6.1	5.9	3.8				3.6	3.3		♂: ♀1 p>.01, ♂: ♀2 p<.01
	De Brazza	1.4	1.9	0.6	0.6						♂: each ♀ p>.01
	Patas	12.0	4.4	4.5	0			0	14.0		♂: each ♀ p<.01
	Mangabey	1.3	7.1	0.6	0						♂: ♀1 p<.01, ♂: ♀'s 2 & 3 p>.01
	Baboon	13.7	14.6	15.8	12.7	2.8	1.8	6.7	10.5	0.9	♂: ♀'s 1,2,3, p>.01, ♂: ♀'s 4,5 p <.01
Aggressed	Redtail	1.8	2.1	3.8				9.3	7.2		♂: ♀1 p>.01, ♂: ♀2 p<.01
	De Brazza	0.2	1.1	1.9	0.9						♂: each ♀ p>.01
	Patas	3.7	16.8	3.7				13.9	9.0		♂: ♀1 p<.01, ♂: ♀2 p>.01
	Mangabey	0.4	1.1	4.3	3.8						♂: ♀1 p>.01, ♂: ♀'s 2, 3 p<.01
	Baboon	No data									
Avoids	Redtail	1.7	7.6	25.6				16.3	9.8		♂: each ♀ p<.01
	De Brazza	2.6	3.8	12.4	1.5						♂: ♀'s 1, 3 p>.01, ♂: ♀2 p<.01
	Patas	5.1	35.6	10.7				19.4	11.2		♂: each ♀ p<.01
	Mangabey	0.6	1.4	6.5							♂: ♀1 p>.01, ♂: ♀'s 2, 3 p<.01
	Baboon	All ♂'s 6.7	All ♀'s 15.7					15.7			♂'s: ♀'s p <.01

TABLE III. (Continued)

								Statistics
Avoided	Redtail	25.8	19.4	3.9			6.3	7.2	♂: each ♀ p<.01
	De Brazza	6.8	4.9	0.9	7.6		8.3	17.4	♂: ♀'s 1, 3, p>.01, ♂: ♀2 p<.01
	Patas	23.8	2.9	17.1					♂: each ♀ p<.01
	Mangabey	3.7	12.7	2.9	0.9				♂: ♀'s 1, 3 p<.01, ♂: ♀2 p>.01
	Baboon	No data							
Grooms	Redtail	3.3	5.0	6.0			4.8	2.3	♂: each ♀ p<.01
	De Brazza	0.8	7.4	2.4	10.1				♂: ♀'s 1, 3 p<.01, ♂: ♀2 p>.01
	Patas	4.3	11.5	8.4			2.8	7.8	♂: each ♀ p<.01
	Mangabey	1.0	27.3	8.6	53.8				♂: each o p<.01
	Baboon	All ♂'s 9.2			All ♀'s 17.0				♂: ♀s p<.01
Groomed	Redtail	4.4	4.5	3.7			4.4	4.5	♂: each ♀ p>.01
	De Brazza	2.2	10.0	4.7	5.4		13.8	6.2	♂: ♀2 p>.01, ♂: ♀'s 1, 3 p<.01
	Patas	9.5	6.6	7.2					♂: each ♀ p>.01
	Mangabey	25.2	12.7	27.8	6.7				♂: ♀2 p>.01, ♂: ♀'s 1, 3, p<.01
	Baboon	All ♂'s 14.3			All ♀'s 15.9				♂: ♀'s p<.01

ecology of the animals, and more to reflect their taxonomic affinities.
Struhsaker (1970) supports this with evidence from Cercopithecus
vocalisations. Kummer cites feeding and digging movements as examples of behaviour likely to be influenced by ecological factors. It is
possible that this idea can be expanded further. Accumulating evidence
(summarised in Crook 1970, Kummer 1971) suggests that the distribution and nature of food supplies profoundly influences the spatial organisation of primate groups. Terrestrial forms tend to have larger home
ranges over which they forage, and spread out as a group more widely
than do arboreal forms. This suggests that any behaviour which affects
the spatial distribution of animals within a group is likely to have considerable adaptive consequences, and it is therefore probable that primates living in a similar environment will have similar spacing behaviour. This will essentially be behaviour which occurs between individuals at a distance, or as they are approaching each other. Once animals are in close proximity, however, it is less likely that behaviour
will depend on the nature of the environment for its functional consequences. Such behaviour might well, therefore, reflect taxonomic
affinities.

The data from the caged animals to some extent support this
hypothesis. Taking into account all the reservations mentioned earlier
about the reliability of measures of interaction frequency, group aggression and avoidance, these data are consistent with what one would expect from primate field studies. The baboon and patas groups both
showed fewer interactions than did the arboreal forms. This is consistent with the fact that in the wild, individuals of terrestrial, savanna
species are more widely dispersed than are individuals of arboreal
species. The fact that the baboons and patas groups both showed a high

aggression rate suggests that this may have been a mechanism by which this dispersion was maintained. An additional mechanism in the patas group may have been a tendency for members of the group to avoid each other, for the excess of avoidance reactions over aggressions was high. Conversely, in mangabeys and de Brazzas, the high interaction rate may be explained by the low amount of aggression and avoidance. The redtails were anomolous in this respect, having a high interaction rate, yet a high rate of avoidance.

By contrast, grooming, lip-smacking, and genital contact (all of which occurred to a greater extent in the baboon and mangabey groups than in the others - with the exception of the patas adult male's behaviour in genital contact) and tail-twining (found in redtails and de Brazzas, and also incidentally, in Cercopithecus campbelli lowei; Bourlière, Hunkeler and Bertrand, 1970) are confined to closely related species. In addition, they are all close contact encounters. (The fact that patas do not show tail-twining may be a consequence of the species' habitat. It is difficult for monkeys to tail-twine while sitting on the ground.)

It is hardly surprising that some categories of behaviour do not conform with this hypothesis; with small groups of animals living under conditions of captivity one could not expect otherwise. The figures for embracing and for mounting do not seem to fall into any pattern. Whether or not embracing is truly homologous in the species has first to be established, before a clearer picture can be obtained. The data of Fig. 2 help to clarify the role of each member of the group, and the contribution of each member's behaviour to the total behaviour of the group. In particular, they throw light on the role of the adult male. Some features are common to all five species. Thus the amount of being aggressed, avoiding and grooming was in all cases lower for the adult male than for the adult females. For other features there are inter-specific differences. Fig. 2 gives some indication that in the arboreal species, the adult male approaches less than the adult females, while in the terrestrial species, the male approaches more than adult females, or at least at the high end of the female range. Also, Fig. 2 suggests that arboreal males are no more aggressive than arboreal females (although the female figures admittedly fluctuate wildly), but that terrestrial males are either more aggressive than terrestrial females, or are at the high end of the latter's range. This again supports the idea that behaviour which maintains the dispersion of the group members is likely to reflect ecological affinities.

The other features of male and female behaviour summarised in Fig. 2 show no clear patterns.

V. SUMMARY

Data are presented comparing several features of social behaviour and organisation of five African cercopithecine monkeys. These are *Cercopithecus ascanius*, the redtail; *C. neglectus*, de Brazzas monkey; *Erythrocebus patas*, the patas monkey, *Cercocebus albigena*, the white-cheeked mangabey, and *Papio cynocephalus* and *anubis*. A survey of the literature suggests that only two features of their social life, home range size and infant development, show clear adaptations to the habitat which the different species occupy. For other aspects of behaviour, such as sexual behaviour and intra-specific communication, there is greater similarity between closely related species, regardless of their habitat, than between distantly related ones. Other aspects of behaviour, such as intra-group aggression and hierarchies fall into no simple pattern.

Data from captive animals support Kummer's suggestion (1970) that behaviour traits which arose as direct functional adaptations to the extra-specific environment are less likely to reflect the taxonomic position of a species than are features which are adapted to the intra-specific environment, such as communication signals. It is suggested that behaviour which affects the spatial distribution of group members is more likely to be subjected to adaptive pressures from theeenvironment than is behaviour which occurs when animals are in close proximity to one another. To a limited extent the present data support this idea.

VI. ACKNOWLEDGMENTS

This work was financed by the L.S.B. Leakey Foundation. I am grateful to Frances Wooldridge and Penny Magugu for carrying out the majority of the observations on which this study is based.

VII. REFERENCES

Altmann, S.A. and Altmann, J. (1970). Baboon ecology: African field research, 1-220. University of Chicago Press, Chicago and London.

Andrew, R.J. (1963). Trends apparent in the evolution of vocalisation in the old world monkeys and apes. Symp. zool. Soc. Lond. 10, 89-101.

Bourliere, F., Hunkeler, C. and Bertrand, A. (1970). Ecology and behavior of Lowe's Guenon (Cercopithecus campbelli lowei) in the Ivory Coast. In "Old world monkeys: evolution, systematics and behavior". (J.R. Napier and P.H. Napier eds.). Academic Press, New York.

Buxton, A.P. (1952). Observations on the diurnal behaviour of the redtail monkey (Cercopithecus ascanius schmidti Matschie) in a small forest in Uganda. J. An. Ecol. 21, 25-58.

Chalmers, N. R. (1968a). Group composition, ecology and daily activities of free living mangabeys in Uganda. Folia primat. 8,
247-262.

Chalmers, N. R. (1968b). The social behaviour of free living mangabeys in Uganda. Folia primat. 8, 263-281

Chalmers, N. R. (1968c). The visual and vocal communication of free
living mangabeys in Uganda. Folia primat. 9, 258-280.

Chalmers, N. R. (1972). Comparative aspects of early infant development in some captive cercopithecines. In Primate Socialisation
(ed. by F.E. Poirier). New York: Random House Inc.

Chalmers, N. R. and Rowell, T. E. (1971). Behaviour and female
reproductive cycles in a captive group of mangabeys. Folia
primat. 14, 1-14

Crook, J. H. (1970). The socio-ecology of primates. In "Social
behaviour in birds and mammals" (J. H. Crook ed.). Academic
Press, New York and London.

DeVore, I. (1963). Comparative ecology and behavior of monkeys and
apes. In "Classification and human evolution" (S. L. Washburn
ed.). Viking Fund publications in anthropology, No. 37. New
York: Wenner - Gren Foundation

DeVore, I. (Editor) (1965). "Primate behavior: Field studies of monkeys and apes." Holt, Rinehart and Winston, New York.

DeVore, I. and Hall, K. R. L. (1965). Baboon ecology. In: "Primate
behavior: Field studies of monkeys and apes" (I . DeVore ed.)
Holt, Rinehart and Winston, New York.

Haddow, A. J. (1952). Field and laboratory studies on an African
monkey, Cercopithecus ascanius schmidti Matschie. Proc.

zool. Soc. Lond. 122 (II), 297-394.

Hall, K. R. L. (1962). The sexual, agonistic and derived social behaviour patterns of the wild Chacma baboon, Papio ursinus.
Proc. zool. Soc. Lond. 139 (II), 283-327.

Hall, K. R. L. (1964). Aggression in monkey and ape societies. In
"The natural history of aggression" (J. D. Carthy and J. F.
Ebling eds.). Academic Press, New York.

Hall. K. R. L. (1965). Behaviour and ecology of the wild patas monkey, Erythrocebus patas, in Uganda. J. Zool. Lond. 148, 15-87.

Hooff, J. A. R. A. M. van. (1962). Facial expressions in higher primates. Symp. zool. Soc. Lond. 8, 97-125

Jolly, C. J. (1966). Introduction to the Cercopithecoidea with notes on
their use as laboratory animals. Symp. zool. Soc. Lond. 17,
427-457.

Kummer, H. (1970). Behavioral characters in primate taxonomy. In
"Old world monkeys: evolution, systematics and behavior" (J.
R. Napier and P. H. Napier eds.) Academic Press, New York.

Kummer, H. (1971). Primate societies: group techniques of ecological adaptation. Aldine Atherton, Chicago.

Rowell, T. E. (1966a). Hierarchy in the organisation of a captive
baboon group. Anim. Behav. 14, 430-443.

Rowell, T. E. (1966b). Forest living baboons in Uganda. J. zool.
Lond. 149, 344-364.

Rowell, T. E. (1966c). Female reproductive cycles and the behavior
of baboons and rhesus macaques. In "Social communication
among primates" (S. A. Altmann ed.) University of Chicago
Press, Chicago.

Rowell, T. E. (1967). A quantitative comparison of the behaviour of a wild and a caged baboon group. Anim. Behav. 15, 499-509.

Rowell, T. E., Din, N. A. and Omar, A. (1968). The social develop-
    ment of baboons in their first three months. J. Zool. Lond. 155,
    461-483.

Struhsaker, T. T. (1969). Correlates of ecology and social organisa-
    tion among African cercopithecines. Folia primat. 11, 80-118.

Struhsaker, T. T. (1970). Phylogenetic implications of some vocalisa-
    tions of Cercopithecus monkeys. In "Old world monkeys: evolu-
    tion, systematics and behavior" (J. R. Napier and P. H.
    Napier eds.) Academic Press, New York.

Struhsaker, T. T. (1971). Social behaviour of mother and infant ver-
    vet monkeys (Cercopithecus aethiops). Anim. Behav. 19, 233-
    250.

AN INTRODUCTION TO THE SOCIO-ECOLOGY OF

MALAYAN FOREST PRIMATES

David J. Chivers

Sub-Dept. of Veterinary Anatomy
Cambridge

I. INTRODUCTION

1. <u>General</u>.   Although the first systematic primate field studies were undertaken within the last 40 years (Carpenter, 1934), substantial progress was delayed until the last decade (De Vore, 1965; Altmann, 1967; Jay, 1968).   Carpenter himself studied gibbons in Thailand in 1938 (Carpenter, 1940), but research activity has centred since then primarily on the more accessible animals of Africa and India.   The dense tropical rain forests of South America and South-East Asia pose problems of observation that have, until very recently, deterred students of primate behaviour.   This can also be explained in part by an intense anthropological interest in the behaviour of the more terrestrial primates in a search for feasible models for hominid evolution.

It was not until different populations of the same species had been studied, that it was realised that primate behaviour patterns were not species-specific.   It was discovered that behaviour varied according to the habitat in which the population had been existing, and that while each species had its own diagnostic characters and fixed range of behavioural patterns, these would be strongly modified by environmental forces, e.g. Kummer (1971).

As interest has shifted towards these problems, so it has become necessary to penetrate the more inhospitable regions to elucidate the habitat and behaviour patterns of arboreal primates.   The problems in such studies are numerous, and have been described elsewhere (e.g. Aldrich-Blake, 1970).   Crook (1970) has reviewed in detail our present understanding of intra-specific variation in primate ecology and behaviour, and called for a more unified approach in observation and analysis so that generalizations beyond the tentative may be possible.

This can only be achieved by a detailed quantitative approach, e.g. Altmann and Altmann (1970); Gautier and Gautier (1969). The aim of this paper is to outline our approach in Malaya with reference to one species in particular, indicating some of the practical problems. We are attempting to coordinate studies over a long period on all the primate species inhabiting a tract of lowland dipterocarp forest in central Malaya. Following my two year study from 1968 of the siamang Hylobates syndactylus, Sheila Hunt of the University of California, Berkeley has just completed a 12-month study of the dusky and banded leaf monkeys, Presbytis obscura and melalophos. A follow-up study of the siamang was carried out over 3 months by Dr. Aldrich-Blake of Bristol University in 1971, and a similar study will be supervised by the author in 1972. It is hoped that by 1973 a second long term study of the siamang, and also the white-handed gibbon (Hylobates lar), will be under way, and that the two species of macaque, Macaca fascicularis and M. nemestrina, will also be under observation by this time.

In a 1-2 year study it is possible to produce a short-term description of the ecology and behaviour of a small conspecific primate population, but it will usually be impossible to fully interpret the significance of the observed behaviour, because the variables involved are so numerous and complex even for one species. Because one person rarely dedicates his working life to one species or habitat, it is necessary for several to persevere at one or more related problems. To facilitate their solution and comparison between species and habitats it is essential that methods of observation and analysis be standardised along the lines indicated by Crook (1970).

An attempt has been made here to produce a quantitative description of the environment of the siamang in Malaya in terms of climate, flora, and fauna, and of behaviour in terms of grouping, ranging, feeding patterns, and social interactions within and between groups. This paper will illustrate how this socio-ecogram is being constructed for a 'type' social grouping of siamang, with reference where possible to the other primate species. When completed it is hoped that similar information will be available for other species to allow the construction of an explanation of the differences that occur in feeding ecology and social organisation within species in different habitats, and between species in the same and different habitats.

2. Malay Peninsula   Although colonial adventurers and naturalists have been exploring South-East Asia for the last 200 years and describing the wild life they encountered in vivid detail, it is only in the last 10 years that systematic studies of free-ranging primates in Malaya have been made. Despite the interest shown in these man-like animals, activity previously centred on collecting and morphological description (Martin, 1841; Wallace, 1867; Beccari, 1904). It is surprising that in extensive explorations the Peninsula itself appears to have received scant attention, although travellers usually based their exploits on the west coast of Malaya. The mountain range running nearly the full length of the country behind the coast may have helped to deflect interest to the nearby islands of Sumatra, Java, and Borneo. Thus, the siamang was first described from Sumatra in 1778 by C. Miller, and then by Sir Stamford Raffles in 1821 (see Groves, 1972), but a distinct Malayan sub-species was not described until 1908 by Oldfield Thomas. Even in recent years primate studies have taken place at the forest edge. On the west coast are mangrove swamps inhabited by the silver

leaf monkey (Presbytis cristata); these have been studied by several observers in the parkland around Kuala Selangor (e.g. Bernstein, 1968). The long-tailed macaque, Macaca fascicularis occurs in the ornamental and botanic gardens and in patches of forest around major towns, such as Singapore, Kuala Lumpur, Taiping, and Penang, and these have been studied by Chiang (1968), and Judy Ellefson (1967) among others. But no one has yet studied these species in the forest; nor have they studied the pig-tailed macaque which usually inhabits those regions less disturbed by man. Bernstein (1967a and b) has made interspecific observations in a west lowland isolated forest, concentrating on Macaca nemestrina.

Also inhabiting the forest and exclusively arboreal are the other two leaf monkey species, the slow loris, Nycticebus coucang, and the gibbons and siamang. In the north between the Mudah and Perak rivers on the west, and north of the Kelantan river on the east, are the black-handed gibbons, Hylobates agilis. Elsewhere, the gibbons are white-handed, H. lar (Chivers, 1971);it has still to be decided whether these are two species or only subspecies. The siamang are restricted to the west and the more mountainous fifth of the remaining forested area.

Ellefson (1967) concentrated his detailed study of the white-handed gibbon on an isolated strip of coastal forest in east Johore. He was unable to penetrate deep into the forest range of this species. He claimed that the distinctive behaviour patterns of gibbons are so rigidly fixed phylogenetically as to be little different at the periphery of the population range. There may well be much truth in this, but I was determined to collect data on the siamang from more than one area, and to penetrate into the main siamang habitat - the hill dipterocarp forest.

It was therefore essential to work in the main mountain range.
Ulu Gombak, 15 miles north-west of Kuala Lumpur, contained many
siamang and gibbons, but, as Ellefson found, it was too steep for detailed study, although excellent discontinuous observations could be
made from the road. The Japanese have experienced similar problems at Fraser's Hill (Kawabe, 1970), and few results have yet emerged from their siamang studies. McClure (1964) made some very useful observations on primates over several years in Ulu Gombak, while
studying birds from a tree-platform.

During our population survey in 1968 we selected two main study
areas for detailed observations of siamang during 1969 and the first
half of 1970 - one on the remoter northern slopes of Fraser's Hill, and
the other at the foot of the central massif of Gunong Benom, at the east
end of the Krau Game Reserve. Because of difficulties in working in
the highland study area, Ulu Sempam, about 80% of observation time
was in the lowland study area, Kuala Lompat (Fig. 1). This paper con-
centrates on the primates of Kuala Lompat.

There is an important altitudinal zonation of the various primate
species concerned. During the 5-month survey the altitude was recorded for each primate sighting. Although there was extensive overlap of
samples, the means indicate the following separation: (1) Siamang 1836',
(2) gibbon 938', (3) dusky leaf monkey 1087', (4) banded leaf monkey
1441', (5) long-tailed macaque 665', and (6) pig-tailed macaque 1200'
above sea level. Medway (1972) obtained similar results on Gunong
Benom with gibbons up to 4700 and siamang near the summit at 6000';
dusky leaf monkeys were common between 700-2800' with bandeds
extending up to the final slopes of the summit (6,500'); and macaques
were seen at 700' (long-tailed), and 2400 and 3600 feet above sea

level (pig-tailed).

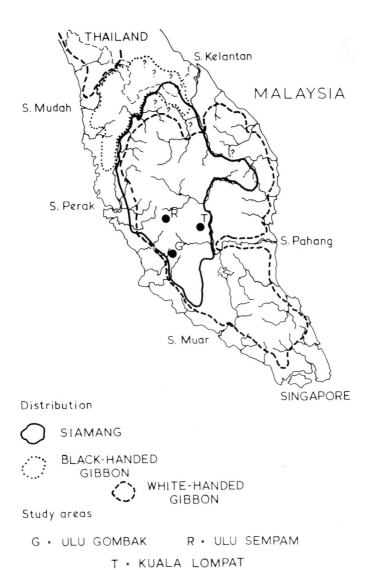

Fig. 1. Location of study areas and distribution of gibbons and
siamang in the Malay Peninsula.

II. ENVIRONMENT

1. <u>Climate</u>   From November to January the Malay Peninsula comes
under the influence of the north-east monsoon. This is the rainy season, which is most marked on the east coast where more than 150
inches per annum may be recorded in the Trengganu Highlands (Dale,
1959). This is followed by a dry season from late January until April.
During the rest of the year the weather is less predictable, although
the south-west monsoon usually brings rain to the west coast around
May; there may be a second dry period in September or October.

Kuala Lompat, nearly 4 degrees north of the equator, is located
in the rain shadow of both east and west mountain ranges, and is,
therefore, in one of the drier parts of the country with as little as 80
inches per annum. Prolonged cloud cover and periods of drizzle were
the main features of the rainy season, rather than prolonged heavy rain.
It was cooler with as little as 2 hours of sunshine/day, whereas in the
dry season there would be as many as 9 hours/day.

There are two main reasons for keeping a detailed record of
weather - because of the effect on primate behaviour during daily
activities, and indirectly through its effect on forest flora. This assumes greater importance when changes in annual pattern or intensity
result in differences in the variety, dispersion, and abundance of food.
Those species with the most varied diets, in terms of plant parts and
plant species, will be the least affected. The parameters measured
daily were maximum and minimum temperature (a continuous record
by thermo-hygrograph being preferable), daily rainfall at 0700 hours
and some measure of the daily pattern of sunshine, cloud cover and

rain. It was found useful to record which phenomenon occurred at 15 minute intervals during daylight hours. (Fig. 2).

2. Flora   The tropical rain forest flora of the Malay Peninsula is moist evergreen in the central part of the Indo-Malaysian flora (Corner, 1952). The altitudinal effects of temperature and humidity result in five climatic climax forest formations. We are concerned here with lowland (to 1,000 feet), hill (to 2,500 feet), and upper (to 4,000 feet above sea level) dipterocarp forest, which is characterised by the abundance and variety of tree species of family Dipterocarpaceae (Wyatt-Smith, 1953).

Ulu Sempam is an example of hill dipterocarp forest, whereas Kuala Lompat in the lowlands has a greater richness in species and in the numbers of each species. Apart from species of Dipterocarpus and Shorea, the canopy is dominated by species of Dyera, Parkia, Dillenia, Sindora, Intsia, Alstonia and the emergent giants Koompassia excelsa (Tualang) and K. malaccensis (Kempas). It is interesting that these trees give little nourishment for siamang (more for monkeys), providing arboreal pathways and resting positions.

The Kuala Lompat study area is nearly one mile from the Game Ranger Post at the confluence of Sungei Krau and S. Lompat, and is, therefore, sufficiently removed from the riverine flora characterised by a lower canopy with more smaller trees. (Fig. 3). There is evidence of human disturbance near the rivers in the past, although in the Game Reserve today orang asli (aborigines) from the nearby village harvest fruit, rattan and fish the rivers with a minimum disturbance to the wild life. It is in fact this peaceful exposure to man which has greatly helped primate studies at Kuala Lompat. East of S. Krau the

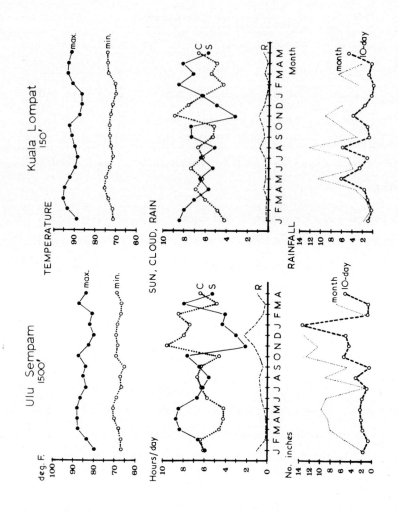

Fig. 2. Monthly pattern of (a) temperature, (b) sun, cloud, rain, (c) rainfall in two siamang study areas.

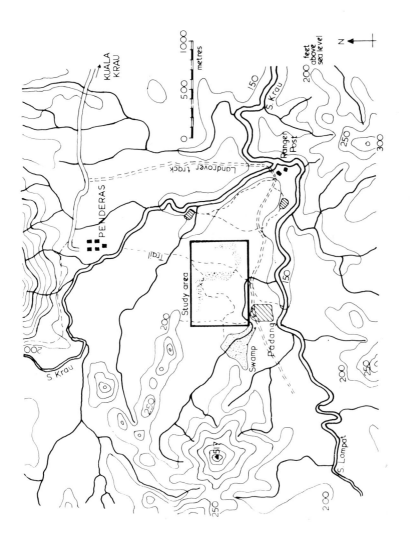

Fig. 3.   Study area at the east end of the Krau Game Reserve, Pahang – Kuala Lompat.

forest is disturbed and the land is being developed for cultivation; westwards is a vast expanse of undisturbed forest rising up to Gunong Benom.

Another factor facilitating field-work in the study area was that at the end of 1968 a government department surveyed the east end of the reserve, cutting the transects running north-south at 150 metre intervals from the Ranger Post, with one base line going due west. As can be seen from the map (Fig. 4, straight dashed lines) inaccuracies occurred as they proceeded west. These transects and a network of trails (many dating from the time when Jelutong trees, <u>Dyera costulata,</u> were tapped for latex used in the manufacture of chewing gum) provide sufficient reference points to readily plot the position and movements of any primate groups within the area. The transects also facilitate a vegetational analysis of ranging behaviour, and so forth, a grid of side 100 metres per unit, i.e. each square was 1 hectare in area, was over-laid onto all plots (Fig. 4, straight continuous lines).

This map also shows the location in the siamang territory of each specimen of each major tree species, indicating which were uti-lised by the siamang as sleeping trees; it shows the main landrover track going a further 12 miles along the S. Lompat to a Game Depart-ment grassland scheme for the conservation of large mammals, and the swampy areas or stream beds liable to flood after prolonged rain.

A count of trees within 10 metres of each transect in the siamang study area resulted in an estimate of 290 trees/hectare, i.e. those of 30' or more in height and 5" or more trunk diameter which could be used by siamang. (Fig. 5). Each tree was classified as high, medium or low according to its contribution to the forest tree cover. The main

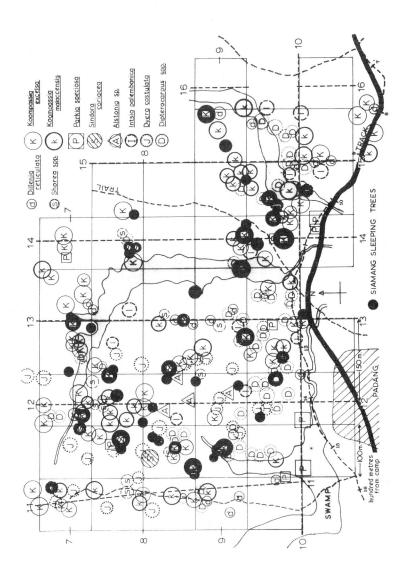

Fig. 4. Distribution of dominant tree species in siamang study area at Kuala Lompat. Siamang sleeping trees, both identified and unidentified, are indicated.

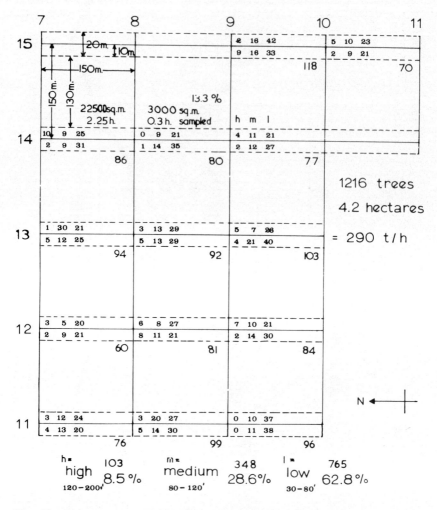

Fig. 5. Tree count and classification along sample transects at Kuala
         Lompat, e.g. going south for 150 m. along transect 13,
         1 high, 30 medium and 21 low trees were counted within
         10 metres to the east and a further 42 trees to the west -
         94 trees in all.

canopy, containing nearly 30% trees, usually extended between 80-120'; beneath were the low trees, nearly two-thirds of trees, through which the siamang could not travel continuously. Nearly 10% trees penetrated the canopy (emergents) to have their main foliage over 120' (some over 200' above ground). This does not indicate the proportion of foliage in each level, which has still to be measured. But it is clear that the main canopy, or middle layer provides the bulk. In the siamang study area it is estimated that there are 290 trees per hectare, but Sheila Hunt reports (pers. comm.) that in her leaf monkey study area immediately to the east near S. Krau, the canopy was lower with a density of 490 trees/hectare over 4" diameter.

3. <u>Fauna</u> In a primate field study the most important information to be acquired concerning other animals in the vicinity is about the closely related species, which are most likely to compete for the available resources. The other species of primate present in the siamang study area have already been indicated, and information on their distribution and behaviour will be summarised in later sections where available.

Apart from the occasional signs of elephant, tiger and seladang, the commonest terrestrial mammals observed were wild pig, deer and mouse deer. In the trees two species of giant squirrel, Prevost's squirrel were frequently seen with occasional sightings of colugo, flying squirrel, and civets. Also attracted to fruiting trees, especially figs, was a great wealth of bird life of which helmeted, rhinoceros, and black hornbills, and green pigeons were the most conspicuous. Owls, raptors and woodpeckers were not infrequently seen. A brief but intensive survey of birds and mammals at Kuala Lompat was organised by Lord Medway (Medway & Wells, 1971).

III. BEHAVIOUR

1. <u>Calling</u>   With elusive forest primates, loud calls can provide
important information, especially during the early stages of a study
when visual contact is low. Not only do they provide data on the group
on consecutive days, but in species where a small social group calls
together, groups may be identified and group size estimated. This is
possible for gibbons and siamang where sexually dimorphic calls and
individual peculiarities also denote the presence or absence of sub-
adult males or females in addition to the adult pair.

Macaques have loud contact calls, apparently used to keep contact throughout the group during group progression and foraging when
the group can be widely dispersed. The long-tailed macaque has a
sharp clipped 'kera' call, the pig-tailed macaque a gruff bark and roar
- 'broh'. (In most cases the Malay name for each primate is onoma-
topoeic). Leaf monkeys have louder calls used in alarm and location
situations, but probably with secondary spacing functions. The dusky
leaf monkey has a nasal 'cheng-kong' call; the banded leaf monkey a
trill and chatter (not unlike some calls of the giant squirrel). While
calls may be given frequently they are not as loud or sustained as the
family group calls of gibbons and siamang. The 'hoos' of a male
gibbon may be heard soon after dawn, followed within an hour or two
by group calls during which the female gives long, clear 'great calls'
(Ellefson, 1967). Within a tract of forest, gibbon calls tend to be synchronised, whereas siamang group calls pass sequentially around the
forest at a slightly later hour. Upon 'booms' resonating in inflated
throat sac are imposed regular 'bark series' by the female, culminat-
ing in male screams and 'bark-chatters'.

It appeared that each species had a daily pattern of calling which distinguished it from the others and implied differences in the nature and timing of group behaviours. Thus for 50 days in 1970 (10 consecutive days in each of the first five months) in addition to recording gibbon and siamang group calls in each hour of the day, the calls of the leaf monkey species were also noted. Plotting the number of days on which the calls of each species were heard calling in each hour (Fig. 6) also indicates the relative amount of calling by each species as well as its daily pattern. This was a time in the long-term forest cycle when the leaf monkeys were unusually noisy (compared with 1969) and only under these circumstances did patterns become apparent, with dusky leaf monkeys calling most often soon after dawn, and bandeds calling most often before dawn and after dusk.

Sheila Hunt (pers. comm.) points out that banded leaf monkeys (one adult male in each group) call at about 2-hour intervals throughout the night; groups chorus in a similar manner during the day, but dusky leaf monkeys do not call regularly.

Calling behaviour was recorded at three levels for the siamang · individual, group, and population. This has involved detailed analysis of the daily timing and frequency of group calls and their structural pattern (Chivers, in prep.). The same applies to the other aspects of siamang ecology and behaviour studied, and includes an investigation of changes in behaviour patterns from month-to-month, and at different seasons of the year.

2. Grouping pattern and territory   Siamang and gibbons were observed in monogamous family groups of one adult pair and 1-3 young in small territories of about 25 and 40 hectares respectively (based on

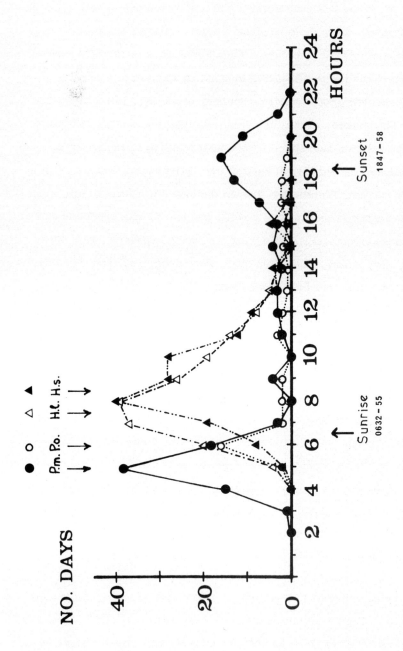

Fig. 6.   Daily pattern of calling over 50 days in 1970 at Kuala Lompat for siamang (H.s.), gibbon (H.l.), dusky leaf monkey (P.o.), and banded leaf monkey (P.m.).

estimates and measurements from Ulu Gombak, Ulu Sempam, Kuala Lompat; and from Ellefson, 1967). There was initially one group of siamang, but in mid-1970 the sub-adult male left the group (which ranged over 35 hectares), having attracted towards him a young female from across S. Lompat to the south. They were establishing a territory to the east of the parental group in Sheila Hunt's study area, when they were joined by an older female (Hunt, pers. comm.). It remains to be seen how this grouping will be resolved, but it seems likely that once one female gives birth, the other will be ejected from the group.

In the 46 hectares (grid) utilised by the original siamang group (Fig. 7) a group of 5 white-handed gibbons also ranged with almost complete overlap. There were two more groups with adjacent territories to the north and west (Fig. 8). A small group of pig-tailed macaques occasionally came into the area from the west, and a larger group of at least 20 long tailed macaques were seen more often - apparently the same one that ranged up to the Ranger Post and across the river. (Fig. 9). There were four groups of dusky leaf monkeys with 12, 18, 15+, and 5 monkeys living in territories of at least 10, 9, 12 and 5 hectares respectively. (Fig. 10). Also using the study area at least in part were three groups of banded leaf monkeys of about 20 individuals living in larger overlapping ranges of at least 13, 17, and 22 hectares. (Fig. 11).

In her adjacent study area Hunt (pers. comm.) observed 3 groups of dusky and 5 groups of banded leaf monkeys. Both species lives in groups of about 15 monkeys in territories of about 13 hectares. There was no overlap between dusky groups which rarely met, but banded groups had zones of overlap and the 'control' male called before entering a disputed zone; each group had 2-3 adult males.

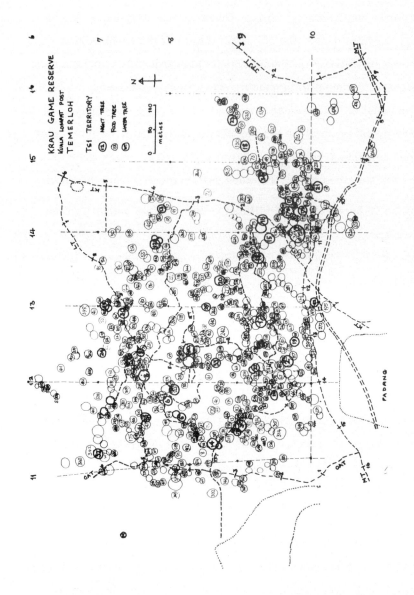

Fig. 7. Siamang group (TS1) territory showing location of all food trees used on 148 days over 14 months (numbered). Other trees regularly used in travel or for resting are also marked.

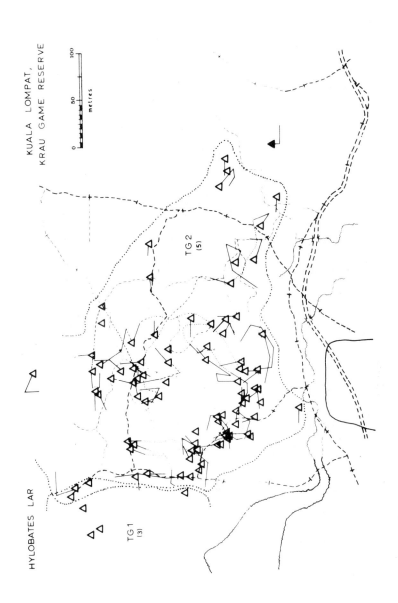

Fig. 8. Plot of gibbon sightings with direction of movement where observed and probably territorial boundaries.

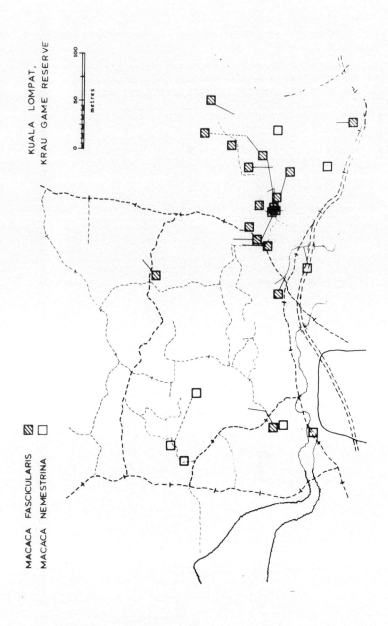

Fig. 9. Plot of sightings of long- and pig-tailed macaques, with direction of movement where observed and probable territorial boundaries.

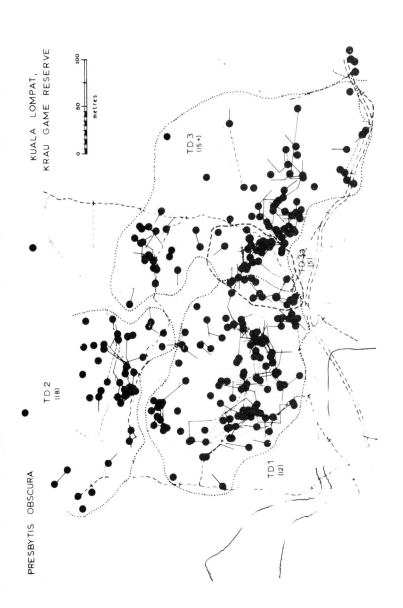

Fig. 10. Plots of sightings of dusky leaf monkeys, with direction of movement where observed, and probable territorial boundaries.

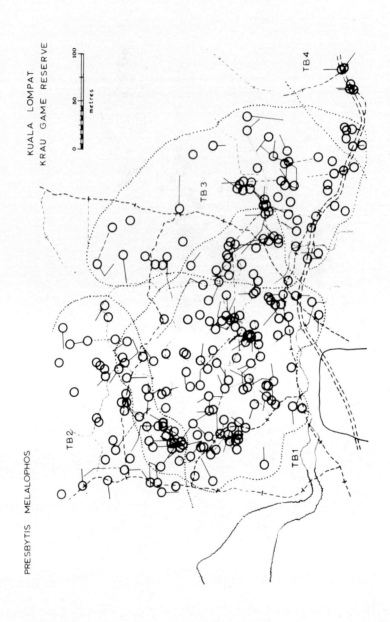

Fig. 11. Sightings of banded leaf monkeys, with direction of movement where observed, and probable territorial boundaries.

Whereas there were numerous leaf monkey births at the beginning of the study, no young infants of either species were seen after April at Kuala Lompat, and after August 1969 in Ulu Sempam. (1968 was the heaviest fruiting year since 1963.) Following this period of increase in group size, there were signs of new groups budding off by early 1970. In 1971 Sheila Hunt recorded a low level of steady recruitment. If group size does fluctuate in any regular or synchronous (inter- as well as intra-specific) pattern, this could be obscured at various phases in the cycle.

Territory has been used here in the traditional sense of an area defended for the exclusive use of the resident group. There has been some difficulty and confusion in applying this concept to primates. Although gibbons and siamang come closest among primates to fulfilling the definition laid down originally for other animals, the ranging behaviour of the siamang study group, in the absence of immediate neighbours (compared with those in Ulu Sempam), leads one to re-examine the traditional approach and explore alternatives. What is most significant for most primate populations studied so far is the strong affinity each social group shows for a particular tract of forest. They differ in the pattern of use of, and the intensity with which conspecifics are excluded from, this domicile.

3. Ranging Patterns   Siamang day ranges were measured in metres in terms of distance travelled by the group in its usual single-file manner of progression from one sleeping tree to the next. Also measured was the distance between these trees (night position shift), and the number of hectares (grid) traversed each day. These data were collected on 10 consecutive days in each month, from April 1969 until

May 1970 inclusive. The siamang group consistently utilised most of
its territory, even in the absence of adjacent groups, although ranging
increased in the dry season and was less extensive in the rainy season.
Day ranges averaged about 950 metres, night position shift 300 metres,
and about 9 hectares of grid were utilised each day - (nearly 30 in a
10-day period) (Fig. 12).

But generally the group spent 60% of daily activity time in 20% of
the territory (Fig. 13). Analysis in terms of a hectare grid provides a
useful quantitative method for investigating the pattern of use of space
by primates (e.g. Altmann, 1970). The form of presentation of this
material is aimed to assist intra- and inter-specific comparisons, and
the analysis of feeding behaviour (see below). The day ranges of the
two leaf monkey species tend to cluster around 305 metres (Hunt, pers.
comm.).

The siamang spent more than 60% time each day in the main canopy layer. The peak of activity in the lower layer of small or young
trees was before or after mid-day, whereas most activity in the high
level of the emergents was at dawn and dusk where they slept over-
night. (Fig. 14). For the other species data were used from first
sightings of each during the siamang study. The gibbon appeared to
concentrate its activity even more in the main canopy layer, but more
time was spent in the emergents. There seemed to be little distinct
separation of the leaf monkeys although the dusky were in the high and
middle layers mostly, and the banded in the middle and lower layers
(including the ground). Sheila Hunt (pers. comm.) confirms the
affinity of the duskies for the emergents. The terrestrial activities of
the macaques, especially the pig-tailed, are demonstrated by the high
proportion of time spent in the low levels of the forest (Table 1).

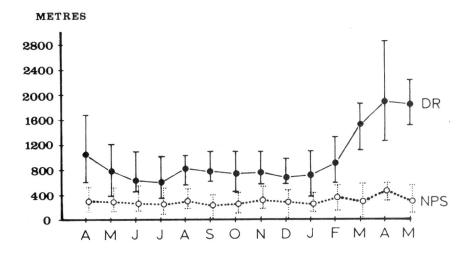

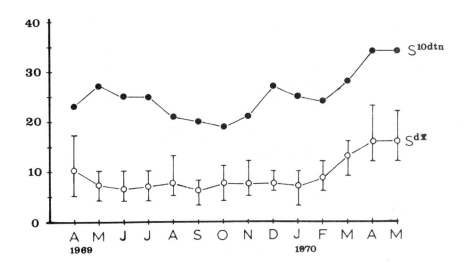

Fig. 12. Mean day range and night position shift, and mean no.
hectares (grid) utilised per 10 days, and per day, for each
month at Kuala Lompat (148 days).

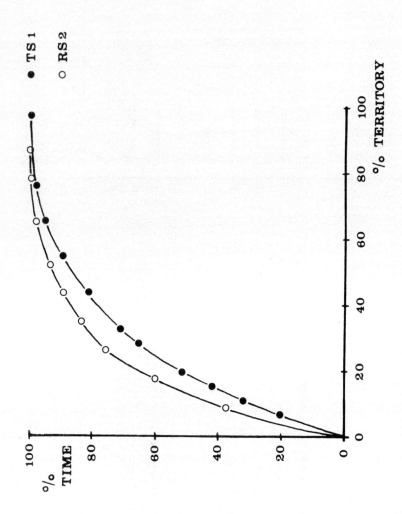

Fig. 13. Cumulative proportion of time in each hectare (grid) plotted against cumulative ranked hectares of territory for siamang groups at Kuala Lompat (TS1) and in Ulu Sempam (RS2).

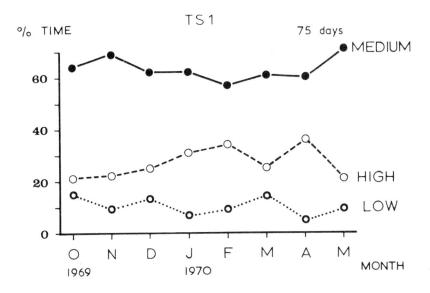

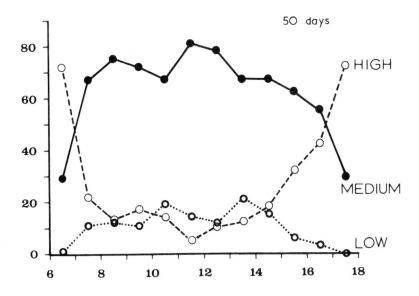

Fig. 14.   Monthly and daily pattern of the use of forest levels by
          siamang.

TABLE I. Inter-specific variations in use of different layers of forest high, medium, low – in Ulu Sempam and at Kuala Lompat.

	KUALA LOMPAT				ULU SEMPAM			
	n	H	M	L	n	H	M	L
		%				%		
Siamang		27	63	10		36	57	7
					295	17	64	20
					76	25	57	18
Gibbon	62	14	73	13	29	38	59	3
Dusky leaf-monkey	170	24	64	13	91	14	71	14
Banded leaf-monkey	104	13	62	25	40	17	67	15
Long-tailed macaque	27	15	48	37				
Pig-tailed macaque					23	0	39	61

Comparative analysis on the siamang in Ulu Sempam according to different intensities of observation, suggests that in these single sightings there is tendency to over-estimate time in both emergents and low levels.

4. Diet and food tree dispersion   Ellefson (1967), in agreement with Carpenter (1940), described the white-handed gibbon as mainly frugivorous. It obtained fruit from more than two-thirds of food trees. The siamang, however, has less than 30% fruit in its diet, whether measured in this way, or by the number of visits to, or the number of minutes feeding in, trees of each type (Chivers, 1972). This fact helps to explain the small territory size of the siamang (twice the weight of a gibbon) when compared to the gibbon, because the young leaves of many species on which siamang mainly feed are more plentiful per unit area. Ellefson relates territorial behaviour in the gibbon to the wide dispersion of preferred foods, and the need to preserve these sources from conspecifics; this also helps to explain the lower level of territorial behaviour in siamang (Chivers, 1972).

At Kuala Lompat food trees of siamang were tagged and identified where possible. The number of visits, feeding time, time of day and type of food consumed by the siamang group were recorded. This allows an analysis of the main food tree species, and the dispersion of food trees throughout the territory (Chivers, in prep.). 12% food trees belonged to the genus Ficus, 20% feed visits were to these fig trees, and 24% feeding time was on figs, young leaves, and new leaf shoots. 34 tree species (including 13 species of fig) accounted for 49% food tree sample and 56% of food visits. There were fig trees in 63% hectare squares; they were mainly absent from the periphery of the

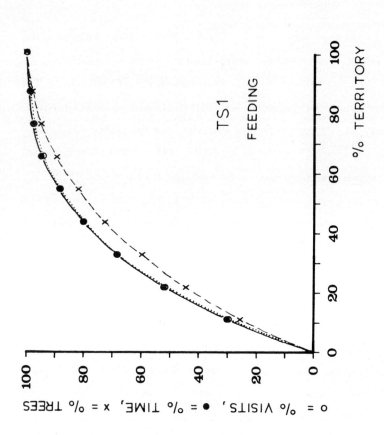

Fig. 15.   Cumulative proportion of (a) food trees, (b) feed visits, (c) feeding time in each hectare (grid) plotted against cumulative ranked hectares of territory for the siamang study group at Kuala Lompat.

territory. That this is a real pattern still has to be confirmed; it is
likely to be so in terms of floral activity at least.

In the siamang territory there were 15 food trees per hectare,
i.e. only 5% total estimated number of trees. 40% food trees were in
20% territory. The preference for these trees is illustrated by nearly
50% feeding visits and time being in this area (Fig. 15). The steeper
the slope, the more activity is confined to a small part of the territory.
55% feed visits and 65% feeding time were to 20% food trees. (Fig. 16).

It seems that the trees which are the major food sources of one
primate species are unlikely to be so important for the others. Where
overlap occurs it is likely that different parts of the tree are being consumed, possibly at different times of year. There appears to be more
overlap between tree species of only moderate importance, but these
patterns have still to be verified. Certainly fig trees are not of such
importance to the other primate species as they are to siamang. It
may be that the classification of food sources as primary and secondary for one species may have comparative significance. The smaller
size of the dusky leaf monkey territories detected in the siamang study
area possibly suggests that the dusky monkeys have a more varied diet
than the banded leaf monkeys, so that the former differs from the latter
as the siamang differs from the gibbon. It is, however, unlikely that
the banded leaf monkey is as frugivorous as the gibbon - or that the
differences between dusky and banded are so great.

5. Daily activity patterns. The siamang and gibbon commence daily
activities soon after dawn. Feeding and travel soon reach a maximum -
more than 75% of each hour - and then decline slowly as the day passes,
settling for the night about 2 hours before dusk. (Fig. 17). The diffe-

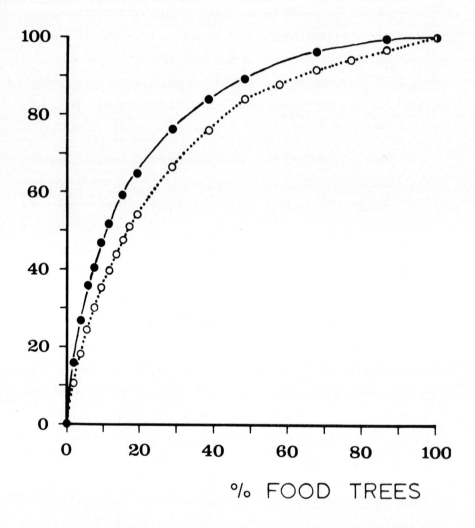

Fig. 16. Cumulative proportion of (a) feed visits, (b) feeding time in each food tree plotted against cumulative proportion of ranked food trees for siamang at Kuala Lompat.

rence in calling pattern has already been referred to; gibbons also differ from the siamang in their tendency to rest and groom at mid-day, rather than in the mid-afternoon (Ellefson). Three major day time activities can be recognised - rest, feed, travel - during which other activities take place. The gibbon is reported by Ellefson to feed from a greater variety of trees as the group travels scattered; he, therefore, uses a fourth category of foraging.

The leaf monkeys leave their sleeping trees at, or even before, dawn (0530-0600 hours, Hunt, pers. comm.). The author observed them moving before the siamang on nights when they slept close together, often not having seen them move to sleeping positions the night before. Hunt confirms that they do not settle for the night until dusk, (about 1900 hours) and that the late afternoon feeding bout while siamang and gibbon are in their night trees follows a long mid-day rest bout of $1\frac{1}{2}$-2 hours.

The determination of daily activity patterns from single sightings is less reliable because of the increasing bias in observations from the most conspicuous activity travel, through feeding, to rest. They might be very misleading, in fact, and contribute little to a quantitative description of the differences between species in activity patterns. This can only be satisfactorily achieved by a continuous sampling at 1, 5, or 10 minute intervals from dawn until dusk of the behaviour of primates of each sex and age class.

The daily pattern of association of each species with the siamang appears to support the different patterns that have been described. (Fig. 18). The two leaf monkey species are most often seen with the siamang at dawn and dusk. (The discrepancy between dawn and dusk

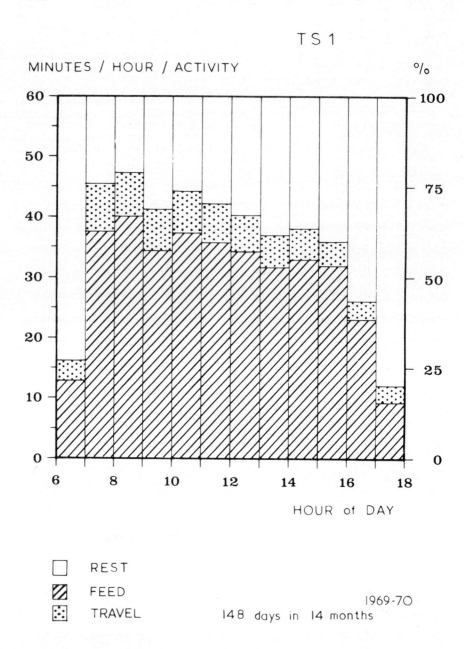

Fig. 17. Siamang daily activity pattern.

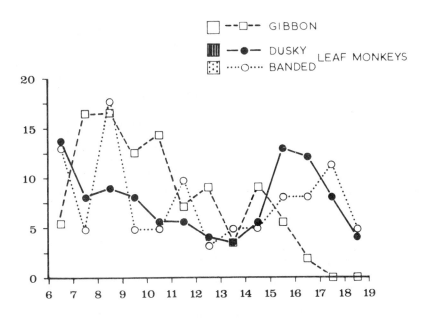

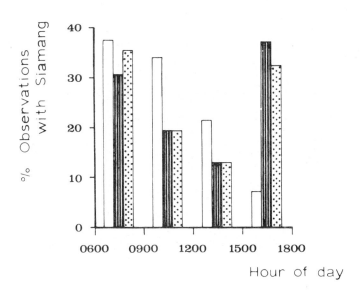

Fig. 18. Daily pattern of association of gibbon and leaf monkeys with siamang.

scores can be explained by the monkeys moving out of view, or further
away, during the final feed, to be found sleeping near the siamang the
next morning). Thus the time of greatest association was at night.
Because of the considerable numbers and wide dispersion of apparently
suitable night sleeping trees (Fig. 4) it seems that this has some behavioural significance. The low level of association after mid-day probably reflects the decreased activity of the monkeys as well as a greater
spatial separation. By contrast the gibbon is seen most with the siamang whilst foraging in the morning, decreasing as the day passes so that
they are rarely associated at night. Thus it may be possible to equate
these curves with daily activity patterns.

6. <u>Social organisation</u>   The social behaviour of the gibbon has been
described in full by Ellefson, that of the siamang has been outlined
(Chivers, 1971) and analysed in detail (Chivers, in prep.). The social
groups of the two leaf monkey species have still to be described, but
they differ from gibbons and siamang in size and complexity of interactions.

Social interactions can be classified as intra-group, inter-group,
and sometimes as a mixture of the two. Intra-group social activities
include sexual behaviour, grooming, communication by calls and gestures, agonistic behaviour and play. A quantitative measure of spatial
relations gives an indication of the form and frequency of interactions
between individuals (Chivers, 1971a). Social interactions may be quantified for each sex and age class over a specified period (such as one
year), so that inter-seasonal and interspecific comparisons may also
be made. If diurnal patterns exist for any activities they may be defined.

Fig. 19b. White-handed Gibbon (Hylobates lar) in typical feeding posture.

Fig. 19a. Siamang (Hylobates syndactylus). Sub-adult male climbing up vine.

Fig. 20a. Dusky leaf monkeys (Presbytis obscura) feeding on new leaf shoots of Intsia palem banica.

Fig. 20b. Banded leaf monkey (Presbytis melalophos) resting in small tree.

Fig. 20c. Pig-tailed macaque (Macaca nemestrina) adult male feeds in bamboo.

Fig. 20d. Long-tailed macaque (Macaca fascicularis) adult male.

There was little overt communication between individual siamang, activities being coordinated through visual signals. Sexual behaviour and play were limited to parts of a 2-3 year cycle. Agonistic behaviour was displayed mostly by the adult male towards the older immature animals. Social grooming mainly involved adult and sub-adult siamang, especially males; in the lowland study area the peak was mid-afternoon, but mid-morning in the highland area.

Inter-group interactions are based on the pattern of group dispersion; they either involve close visual, and possibly, physical, contact, or vocal communication at a distance initiated by visual or vocal cues. These interactions help to maintain the species-specific, or population-specific, pattern of dispersion. They may involve signals that increase, maintain, or decrease distance between groups, in contrast with signals that maintain the proximity of group members (Marler, 1968). Thus gibbons reinforce distance vocal interactions with calling and chasing displays across the territorial boundary, whereas siamang usually maintain distance by calls alone (less frequent). The latter appears to be true for dusky leaf monkeys, but the overlapping ranges of bandeds, and their frequent calling, indicate more contact in disputed areas.

IV. CONCLUDING DISCUSSION

As yet it is too early in this research programme to provide a satisfactory discussion of comparative results, or to come to any definite conclusions. Discussion of the results for each species (mainly the siamang) has taken place elsewhere, or where relevant above. None the less it is already becoming apparent that there are numerous mechanisms - some conspicuous, others subtle - enabling the

coexistence of six diurnal primate species at considerable densities in
the Malayan tropical rain forest to occur.

In the three siamang study areas there were nearly two primates/
hectare, at an estimated biomass of about 8 Kg./h. This may be almost
doubled in disturbed areas where populations are isolated (Bernstein,
1967). Elsewhere on the Sunda Shelf the figures tend to be lower than
in Malaya (Borneo, Rodman, pers. comm.; Sumatra, MacKinnon, pers.
comm.). It seems likely that the density of primates is as high in central Malaya as anywhere else in the world's tropical rain forests. In
South America densities are lower, and biomass greatly decreased per
unit area (Baldwin, Durham, Klein, pers. comms.). This further jus-
tifies the full investigation into inter-specific relations at a location
such as the Krau Game Reserve's Kuala Lompat.

Once the ecology and behaviour of each species has been described
over a long period, detailed comparisons may be made and observations
on each species more closely integrated. The seasonal variations that
occur in behaviour, and, more important, variations in the annual cycle
from year to year, pose problems as to the identity of environmental
pressures influencing these responses. What effects does the climate
exert on the forest to vary the diversity and abundance of food? What
is the effect on each primate species of the high density of birds and
mammals in the forest? And to what extent are reproductive cycles
synchronised within and between species, and correlated with years of
great food abundance?

V. SUMMARY

This paper aims at developing a quantitative comparative approach to the study of the six diurnal species of Malayan primates. Special reference is made to the siamang with analysis of ecology and behaviour in terms of environment (climate, flora, and fauna), and behaviour (grouping, ranging, feeding, intra- and inter-group social relations). Comparative data are presented where possible for the white-handed gibbon, dusky and banded leaf monkeys, and long- and pig-tailed macaque in the lowland study area in the Krau Game Reserve, Pahang.

VI. ACKNOWLEDGMENTS

The two-year field study in Malaysia was financed by a Malaysian Commonwealth Scholarship, a Science Research Council Overseas Studentship, and a Goldsmiths' Company Travelling Studentship, with additional grants from the Boise Fund, Oxford, the Royal Anthropological Institute, and the New York Zoological Society. This support is gratefully acknowledged.

The study would not have been successful without the help given by the State Game Wardens and their staff, particularly those in Pahang under Enche Abdul Jalil bin Ahmad. I am very grateful to Dr. T. C. Whitmore and Dr. E. Soepadmo for identifying leaves and fruit eaten by the siamang and other primates, and to Lord Medway, who advised me during the study and read critically the draft of this manuscript. I am also grateful to Sheila Hunt for her comments and for making available some of her unpublished data and to Dr. M. J. Simpson for his comments on the manuscript. My wife's continuing assistance in this work has been invaluable.

VII. REFERENCES

Aldrich-Blake, F. P. G. (1971). Problems of social structure in forest monkeys. In "Social Behaviour in Birds and Mammals" (J. Crook, ed.). Academic Press, London.

Altmann, S. A. (ed.) (1967). "Social Communication among Primates". University of Chicago Press.

Altmann, S. A. and J. (1970). "Baboon Ecology." University of Chicago Press.

Beccari, O. (1904) "Wanderings in the Great Forests of Borneo." Constable, London.

Bernstein, I. S. (1967a). Inter-taxa interactions in a Malayan primate community. Folia primat. 7, 198-207.

Bernstein, I.S. (1967b). A field study of the pig-tail monkey, Macaca nemestrina. Primates 8, 217-228.

Bernstein, I. A. (1968). The lutong of Kuala Selangor. Behaviour 32, 1-16.

Carpenter, C. R. (1934). A field study of the behavior and social relations of howler monkeys. Comp. Psychol. Monogr. 10, 1-168.

Carpenter, C. R. (1940). A field study in Siam of the behaviour and social relations of the gibbon, Hylobates lar, Comp. Psychol. Monogr. 16, 5, 1-212.

Chiang, M. (1968). The annual reproductive cycles of a free-living population of long-tailed macaques (M. fascicularis) in Singapore. Unpublished M.Sc. dissertation, U. of Singapore.

Chivers, D. J. (1971). The Malayan siamang. Malay. Nat. J. 24, 78-86.

Chivers, D. J. (1971a). Spatial relations within the siamang group. Proc. 3rd int. Congr. Primat., Zurich, 3, 14-21.

Chivers, D. J. (1972). The siamang and the gibbon in the Malay Peninsula. In "The Gibbon and the Siamang". (D. Rumbaugh ed.) Vol. 1. S. Karger, Basel.

Chivers, D. J. (in prep.) "The Siamang in Malaya: a field study of a primate in the tropical rain forest." Ph.D. dissertation, University of Cambridge.

Corner, E. J. H. (1952). "Wayside Trees of Malaya." Singapore.

Crook, J. H. (1970). The socio-ecology of primates. In "Social Behaviour in Birds and Mammals" (J. Crook, ed.) Academic Press, London.

Dale, W. L. (1959). Rainfall of Malaya. J. trop. Geogr. 13, 23-37.

DeVore, I. (ed.) (1965). "Primate Behavior: field studies of monkeys and apes," Holt, Rinehart, and Winston, New York.

Ellefson, J. O. (1967). "A natural history of gibbons in the Malay Peninsula." Unpublished Ph.D. dissertation, U. of California.

Ellefson, J. (1967). "Social communication in long-tailed macaques in Singapore." Unpublished Ph.D. dissertation, U. of California.

Gautier, J.-P. and Gautier, A. (1969). Les associations polospeci-fiques ches les cercopithecidae du Gabon. La Terre et la Vie, 2, 164-201.

Groves, C. P. (1972). Systematics and phylogeny of gibbons. In "The Gibbon and the Siamang" (D. Rumbaugh, ed.), vol. 1, S. Karger, Basel.

Jay, P. C. (ed.) (1968). "Primates: studies in adaptation and variability." Holt, Rinehart, and Winston, New York.

Kawabe, M. (1970). A preliminary study of the wild siamang gibbon, Hylobates syndactylus, at Fraser's Hill, Malaysia. Primates, 11, 285-291.

Kummer, H. (1971). "Primate Societies. Group techniques of ecological adaptation." Worlds of Man series, ed. W. Goldschmidt. Chicago. Aldine.

Marler, P. (1968). Aggregation and dispersal: two functions in primate communications. In "Primates: studies in adaptation and variability" (P. Jay, ed.) Holt, Rinehart, and Winston, New York.

Martin, W. C. L. (1841). "Natural History of Man and Monkeys - general introduction to the natural history of mammiferous mammals with a particular view of the physical history of man and the more closely allied genera of the Order Quadrumana or Monkeys." Wright and Co., London.

McClure, H. E. (1964). Primates in the dipterocarp forest of the Gombak valley. Primates 5, 39-58.

Medway, Lord (1972). The Gunong Benom Expedition 1967. 6. The distribution and attitudinal zonations of birds and mammals on Gunong Benom. Bull. Brit. Mus. nat. Hist. (Zool.) 22, 103-151.

Medway, Lord and D. R. Wells (1971). Diversity and density of birds and mammals at Kuala Lompat, Pahang. Malay. Nat. J. 24, 238-247.

Wallace, A. R. (1867). "The Malay Archipelago: the land of the orang-utan and the bird of paradise, a narrative of travel with studies of man and nature." MacMillan, London.

Wyatt-Smith, J. (1953). Malayan forest types. Malay. Nat. J. 7, 45-55.

SOCIAL AND ECOLOGICAL FEATURES OF TALAPOIN

MONKEY -

COMPARISONS WITH SYMPATRIC CERCOPITHECINES

A. Gautier-Hion

Station biologique de Paimpont
35380 PLELAN le Grand
University of Rennes

INTRODUCTION

The Talapoin is a small sized forest monkey, the average weight
of an adult male being 1380 g. Coat colour is relatively dull, varying
from pale yellow to green and facial hair is reduced. Slight sexual dimorphism makes identification in the field difficult unless the canines
or the testicles of the male can be seen and recognition of females is
easy only when they are pregnant or lactating. Indeed, the full-term
foetus may exceed 16% of the maternal weight, thus markedly distending
the abdomen of the mother. Gestation, lasting $5\frac{1}{2}$ months, can therefore be suspected from the second month. The newborn, already with
adult colouration, weighs about 175 g: the head is almost as big as the
body (fig. 1).

Such morphological, anatomical and physiological traits characterise the Talapoin, which, while classified within the sub-family Cerco-
pithecinae is clearly distinguished from related species. The males
are five to eight times lighter than those of sympatric forest species
(Genus Cercopithecus) among whom sexual dimorphism is greater.
Moreover, compared with the Talapoin, the majority of forest Cercopithecines have a brightly coloured pelage.

Although the Talapoin moves, in general, like arboreal monkeys,
it is also capable of a specialised locomotion allowing it to jump between
vertical supports much in the manner of the primitive Primates (Napier
and Walker, 1968). In addition, the Talapoin is an excellent swimmer.
Finally, adult females, unlike those of the genus Cercopithecus, possess a sex skin whose size varies with the course of the oestrus cycle.

Such specialisations, which have been used to classify the Talapoin

Fig. 1. Pair of Talapoin monkeys with their young.

Adult ♂ = 1200g
Adult ♀ = 1120g
Infant ♂, ten days old = 180g

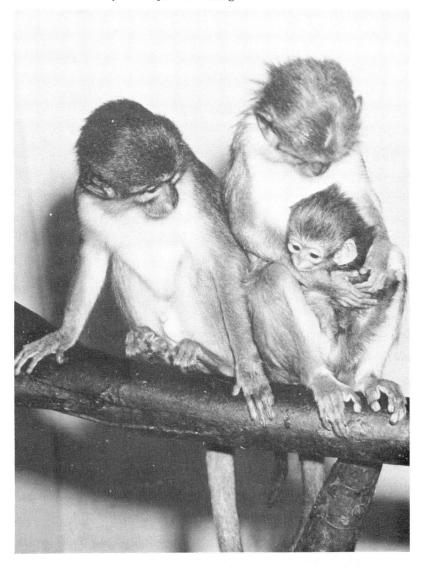

either as a separate genus, <u>Miopithecus</u>, or as a sub-genus or species
of the genus <u>Cercopithecus</u>, have ecological and ethological implications.
Following a summary of the results of 21 months of fieldwork in North-
East Gaboon, already published (Gautier-Hion, 1968, 1970, 1971a,
1971b), I shall attempt to discuss the specific adaptations of the Talapoin in parallel with what is known about sympatric forest-living Cercopithecines.

ECOLOGICAL RESULTS

<u>Population studied</u>:   24 troops; 17 of which, living in an environ-
ment inhabited by man, are "parasitic", utilising his resources.

<u>Habitat</u> (Figs. 2 and 3): essentially inundated rain forest. Such
forest is situated along the rivers, its undergrowth is dense and composed of lianas, palms and ripicole trees. For parasitic troops, living
in a degraded environment, the habitat is at least 50% of inundated
forest, the remainder being secondary forest and plantations.

<u>Distribution</u>: heterogeneous; a function of the hydrographic net-
work (see fig. 3).

<u>Troop density</u>: one troop on average every 4835m along large
rivers.

<u>Troop size</u>: non-parasitic troops - average: 66.5 individuals
(n = 6). Parasitic troops - average: 112 individuals (n = 4).

<u>Dimensions of the home ranges</u>:   mean, 1,216 km^2 (n = 3, para-
sitic troops). For these troops, the density of population is 92 individuals per km^2. It is lower for the non-parasitic troops (approximately
30 ind/km^2).

Sleeping sites: always situated along the water edge. The percent of stability is 78.7 for 343 controls made by night upon 8 troops.

Mean distance covered daily: 2323m (variation from 1500 to 2950m): results for a parasitic troop followed intensively.

Diet: frugivorous and insectivorous; animal food consumed may reach 50% of stomach contents.

Breeding season: November to April for 4 consecutive years upon 7 troops.

Intertroop interactions: never observed; territoriality unlikely - absence of visual and vocal spacing displays.

Social characteristics

Adult sex-ratio: 1:2 on average.

Mature reproductive animals in troops: 46% (n = 6 troops).

Solitary individuals: no permanently solitary individuals were observed but temporary ones were seen during the day (n = 10, of which 9 adult males and a pair of adults) and during the night (n = 3, all adult males).

Splitting up of the troops: rare; 7 observations of which 5 for the same troop followed intensively.

Sleeping sub-groups: 36 types for 523 sub-groups identified; mean size = 2.7 (range from 1 to 7).

Principal types: ♀ adult + infant + juvenile or sub-adult (n = 268)

2 to 4 juveniles or sub-adults (n = 157)

♂ adult isolated (n = 50)

♂ adult + ♀ adult (n = 10)

A. Gautier-Hion

Fig. 2. Aerial view of Ivindo river in the study area (N-E Gaboon, upstream from Makokou).

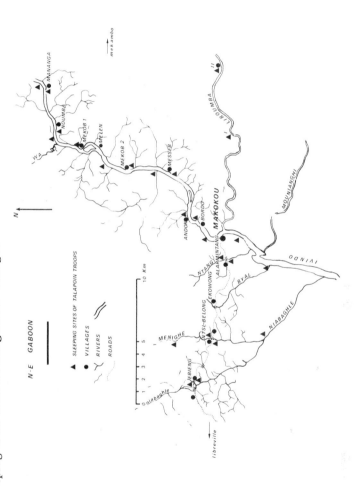

<u>Fig. 3.</u>   Map representing the different study areas, along the principal routes of the forest penetration, and the localisation of the sleeping sites of the 24 Talapoin troops observed. One can see that their distribution is correlated with the hydrographic network and that 17 troops possess their sleeping sites near an indigenous village.

Spatial organisation: varies according to activity but no splitting
of the troop occurs. The position of the adult males ensures defence of
the troop and its regrouping after alarm situations. When food items
are concentrated in a same place, the majority of adult males and the
females with their infants feed at the head of the troop.

Patterns of cohesion: essentially linked to vocal exchanges: (1)
presence of a cohesion call, associated with troop movements and inter-
individual distances; (2) call of adult male occurring in situations of
disturbance assures directional rallying of troop members; (3) numerous
emissions in chorus.

Social interactions: greater aggressivity of adult males; special
links between certain pairs of adult males (probably the dominant ones)
and females, between adult females and between young.

Numerous socio-ecological details tend to distinguish Talapoin monkeys from those of the tropical rain forest. Aldrich-Blake (1970) has
shown that there exists in the latter a "considerable degree of uniformity" with respect to troop membership, home ranges and population
densities. In the majority of tropical rain forest, this author notes:

- a high population density (up to 182 individuals/km^2 for C. mitis;

- troops of medium size from 12 to 20 individuals;

- home ranges of small size;

- frequent contacts between troops, often implying territorial and
vocal spacing behaviour.

In contrast to these data the Talapoin

- has a low population density (30 to 90 ind/km^2);

- lives in large troops (as numerous as some savanna troops);

- has large home ranges (15 times larger than those of C. mitis

for example), with important troop movements;

- does not possess spacing displays and does not seem territorial.

Discussing the argument developed by Crook (1970), that the size of the troop and the pattern of dispersion of savanna monkeys are dependent on three ecological factors (food, sleeping sites, predation), Aldrich-Blake (op. cit.) concludes that, as far as the tropical forest species are concerned, these factors may have only limited effects because:

- sleeping sites are widely available;

- predation seems feeble;

- food appears to be better sustained by a relatively constant production throughout the year.

What therefore is the impact of these factors on the Talapoin populations? Why does this typically arboreal monkey differ so much from the related species of the genus Cercopithecus; species with which it is sympatric and with which it may live in association (Gautier, Gautier-Hion, 1969).

The specialisation of the Talapoin is extensive; it lives in inundated rain forest (fig. 4), a particularly dense environment to which it is adapted by its small size and its method of movement from one vertical support to another. This specialisation tends to limit inter-specific competition: sympatric arboreal species such as C. nictitans or C. pogonias are too heavy to inhabit the lowest areas of inundated forest. It may be supposed that the Talapoin has been pushed into this type of habitat by heavier species of Cercopithecus.

This link with the water seems to be determined even more by the

choice of sleeping sites which are always situated near the water.
Their establishment requires:

    - a sufficiently wide and/or deep river

    - particularly dense vegetation along the banks, with numerous
lianas, branches or palm trees hanging over the water.

Detailed study of these sleeping sites shows that they are not available everywhere along the same river, certain portions of the banks,
thinly covered or devoid of vegetation reaching the water's edge, cannot
be used for sleeping sites. In the same way, certain zones of inundated
forest which border narrow rivers are devoid of Talapoins if there is no
water course sufficiently wide for the establishment of a dormitory.

Thus the Talapoin has a relative limitation of available sleeping
sites which seems primarily to influence troop distribution and may influence troop size secondarily.

The role of predation and the adaptative function of the sleeping sites

As with many other forest species and despite the large number of
observations made both night and day, the impact of predation on the
Talapoin population could not be estimated. Nonetheless certain ecological factors and types of behaviour observed do not seem explicable
except as a response to predation. This is particularly the case for
sleeping sites. We note that:

    - there was a vertical stratification of the different subgroups:
females and their young tend to sleep at the lower levels, on the supports overhanging the water. The adult males dominate the members
of the troop as a whole, in a way cutting off the paths of access from
the main trunks to the ends of the branches. Moreover one or two

adult males may occupy the lateral extremities of the dormitory, upstream and downstream.

- that the sites chosen by the different subgroups are always difficult of access, either because the animals sleep embedded in the very
dense foliage or because they are to be found suspended "in the air", on
thin lianas which transmit the slightest vibration (fig. 5).

- that when some danger presents itself during the night, the
animals which sleep lowest down (that is to say essentially females and
their young) plunge into the water and disappear by swimming under the
water.

It thus seems that the individuals of most importance for species
survival are protected both by the males who give the alarm and by
their proximity to water which allows them to dive, breaking olfactory
and visual contact with the predator. It is clear that even if a predator
has not alerted the males, it must descend on thin lianas to gain its
prey and will have little chance of reaching its goal without the monkey
being alerted by the vibrations and either mounting another liana or
diving.

The nocturnal predators seem to be mainly arboreal Carnivores
(golden cats, panthers) and the arboreal and aquatic reptiles such as
pythons and cobras. A Talapoin was found in a stomach tract of a
python and the aquatic cobras were frequently seen both day and night
in the sleeping sites of Talapoins (either in the water or looped around
the branches). Hunting essentially by smell, capable of stationing
themselves in the water and of sliding quietly along the branches, these
reptiles are, à priori, dangerous for Talapoins.

Fig. 4. General view of inundated rain forest

Fig. 5. Sleeping subgroup resting in a network of lianas above the water. It is composed of a female with her infant and a juvenile; this last one is hidden by the female but one can clearly see the three twining tails.

The choice of sleeping sites, the positionin g and spatial structure of different subgroups, the behaviour of fleeing into the water, are all suggestive of anti-predation devices.

The problem of feeding

The importance of food as a factor for socio-ecology has been examined for savanna monkeys (e.g. Kummer, 1968, Crook, 1966) but less often for the forest primates. In equatorial forest however, it has generally been assumed that food production is relatively constant throughout the year, and this has been used to explain for example the non-existence of a reproductive season   (Crook and Gartlan, 1966). However it is now established that several forest living Cercopithecines do have a reproductive season: this is particularly true for the Talapoin and for all the Forest Cercopithecines in N.E. Gaboon (Gautier-Hion, 1968).

As Aldrich-Blake (1970a, b) pointed out, the constancy of production of the tropical forest environment is perhaps only apparent: it may not be true at the level of the troop home ranges.

The home range of a "parasitic" troop, 115 individuals strong, was studied intensively. All the movements observed for the animals for a period of 21 months were plotted on a scale map. The Talapoins occupied an area of 1,400 km^2. The routes followed from January to July 1968 were subsequently analysed in two parts.

Fig. 6 shows that from January to April, the surface used by the monkeys reached 1 km^2, made up essentially of inundated and secondary forest and concentrated along the left bank of the Menighe river.

From May to July (fig. 6) the surface area used did not exceed

0.6 km^2. The movements of the animals were very different, distributed along one part and another of the river and frequently directed toward the manioc soaking sites (located along the two small rivers) and
towards plantations.

If we considered the number of fruit species collected monthly as
making up the diet of the animals for this period, it can be seen (fig. 7)
that the number is maximal in February and March, while it decreases
noticeably afterwards, reaching a minimum value in the month of July,
in the main dry season. Comparable observations upon fluctuations of
forest fruiting are also shown on the figure: they represent the number
of fruits collected on a fixed route in primary forest in the same region
(Charles-Dominique, 1971).

It seems, therefore, that during the main dry season, there is a
critical period in forest production. Now it can be seen that the change
in the home range of the troop of Ntsi-Belong (fig. 6) corresponds to a
decrease in fruiting in the forest. The animals then tend to approach
the villages and approach the manioc soaking sites and the different
plantations regularly. Manioc constitutes an important concentrated
source of food, which seems to compensate for the "deficit" in forest
fruiting. The Talapoin troop is, in fact, increasingly "parasitic" as
the fruit production of the neighbouring forest decreases.

The observed increase in size of "parasitic" troops is at least
partially the result of this supplementary source of food near the villages. (Thus some of the stomach contents studied consist entirely of
manioc). This constitutes a retrospective proof of the rapid influence
of the food factor on the socio-ecology of a species living in the tropical environment. Although manioc was relatively recently introduced

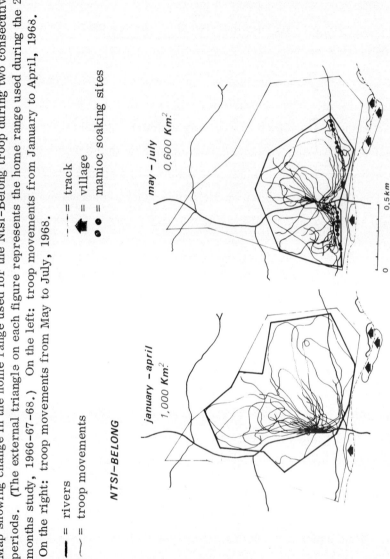

Fig. 6. Map showing change in the home range used for the Ntsi-Belong troop during two consecutive periods. (The external triangle on each figure represents the home range used during the 21 months study, 1966-67-68.) On the left: troop movements from January to April, 1968. On the right: troop movements from May to July, 1968.

— = rivers
~ = troop movements

---- = track
◄ = village
●● = manioc soaking sites

NTSI-BELONG

january – april
1,000 Km²

may – july
0,600 Km²

0   0.5 km

Fig. 7. Number of fruit species eaten by Talapoin monkeys, according to the season (December to July), in inundated rain forest and secondary forest --- Quantity of fruits collected on a fixed path, according to the season (March to August) in primary forest (Charles-Dominique, 1971).

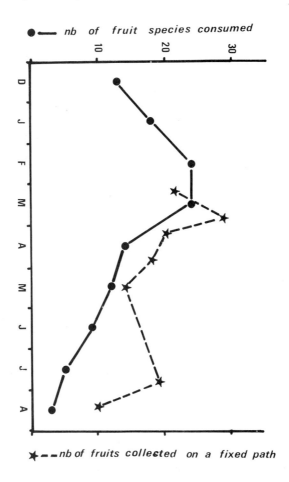

in Gaboon, more than 70% of the troops observed are parasitic. This shows that the social organisation of a Talapoin troop is sufficiently flexible to allow considerable augmentation in the number of individuals. In spite of this, the troops observed in N-E Gaboon remained coherent all the year, even out of the copulatory season, owing to a highly elaborate system of vocal communication. Splitting of the troops is very rare, contrary to what we have observed in sympatric arboreal Cercopithecines where there is great individual mobility.

Present studies in progress on the African forest monkeys, although still lacking in length, tend to show that the equatorial forest environment cannot be considered as a uniform milieu but that numerous ecological niches exist, of which the majority remain to be described. Such work would produce evidence of the role of environmental factors on the various systems of social organisation as clearly as some conclusions drawn from savannah monkeys (see Crook, 1970).

It is evident at the moment, that for the unique region of N-E Gaboon where I have worked, all the principal forms of social structures described for the Primates are found ranging from family groups in C. neglectus (Gautier, Gautier-Hion, under study) to troops of arboreal Cercopithecines (C. cephus, C. pogonias, C. nictitans) with a single male leader (Gautier, 1969) or socially mature male (Gautier, 1970, Eisenbergh et al. 1972) to troops with several adult males as found in Cercocebus albigena and Miopithecus talapoin. Finally in Cercocebus galeritus, a semi-terrestrial species, there is a variable structure, small groups of 7 to 10 individuals, including one adult male, occupy the same home range and may gather together occasionally to form larger troops. (Quris, pers. comm. work under progress). In the latter species, one cannot fail to make the parallel with phylogenetically close savannah species.

Cercocebus galeritus, Cercopithecus neglectus, M. talapoin, all inhabit inundated forest and their home ranges may overlap each other. However while the first two species are partially terrestrial, M. talapoin is typically arboreal. In addition, their diets show a large divergence: the Talapoin has a strong insectivorous tendency, while the Brazza monkey is only slightly or not at all, but has a high leaf intake. The diet of C. galeritus is still not known but this species feeds frequently at ground level on grasses and young shoots and explores the bog, probably for small organisms.

In the case of the Talapoin, one can, as Crook (1970) for Saimiri did, correlate the strong insectivorous tendency of species with large troop size. The movement of a large number of individuals probably reveals hidden insects. In addition, such prey being widely dispersed, the foraging troop can be very large without high competition appearing. In parallel, the mean troop movements are highly important (greater than 2 km by day while those of C. neglectus may be less than 200 m pers. obs.).

Furthermore, large troop size is possibly a response to predation. Within the troops, Talapoins possess an extremely complex system of choral vocalisations. Such mobbing choruses, composed essentially of calls intermediate between those of aggression and alarm (Gautier, in press), constitute a system of alert and rapid collective defence which is not only efficacious but doubtless contributes to the maintenance of social bonds.

However a system of defence may be assured by a totally different means. Thus, in relation to life in small groups, C. neglectus has no

social alarm call but reacts to danger either by fleeing at the ground
level, or by total immobilisation remaining completely silent. Such
"freezing" observed only in females and young, may continue for more
than ten minutes and is followed by a slow discreet departure, the animal moving much like a Potto. On the other hand, I have observed on
two occasions that the adult male, at ground level,may face the observer uttering violent barks during several minutes.

It is therefore clear that under similar ecological pressures (i.e.
predation in inundated forest) the responses developed by the two species are quite different from each other and cannot be resolved by simple
ecological facts.

We find in these two forest species that the two "major techniques
which have evolved for dealing with predators" (Kummer, 1971) in
savannah monkeys are developed in forest ones: the "baboon way" in
Talapoin (which consists more in discovering the danger and includes
attack and noisy mobbing) and the "patas way" in C. neglectus. In this
last species, as in E. patas, sexual differentiation is very high (adult
male Brazza is two times heavier than the adult female) and, during
alarm situation, the males play a defensive role while the females and
young stay motionless. It is perhaps also significant that the white
thighs of the Patas are replaced in the Brazza monkey by a superb and
very conspicuous white rump, which probably plays a role in the social
life of the group.

The primary and secondary forest of N-E Gaboon are inhabited by
three species of the genus Cercopithecus (C. nictitans, C. pogonias,
C. cephus). All these species have similar troop sizes, reaching the
modal size of 12 to 20 individuals discussed by Aldrich-Blake (op. cit.)

and possess in each troop, a fully adult male playing the role of leader by its vocal displays; in addition, their diet is essentially frugivorous. The influence of ecological factors on their social structures is far from clear. All these species live in polyspecific associations; this means that the total number of the foraging polyspecific troop is double or treble that of a single species (Gautier and Gautier-Hion, 1969). C. cephus shows a tendency to inhabit lower stratas in the primary forest and degraded forest; it is likely that a detailed study of its diet would exhibit some peculiarities related to this vertical stratification.

For C. nictitans and C. pogonias, the situation is less clear. In recent study in N- E Gaboon, I followed for 250 hours a troop of C. pogonias (13 individuals) associated with a troop of C. nictitans (13 individuals) and established that less than 5 hours of separation occurred during daily observations and that all the animals were regularly found in a same sleeping site. In spite of this, no obvious differences of vertical stratification implicating a differential exploitation of the environment occurred in the quantitative data, nor were any qualitative differences in feeding ascertained. Perhaps, however, a difference exists in the quantity of animal prey consumed. C. pogonias, the lighter species, is possibly more insectivorous. This hypothesis may be supported by the fact that C. pogonias tends to associate with the Talapoins, the troop changing its itinerary occasionally to meet with them, while C. nictitans does not exhibit this tendency. By this association (always temporary) C. pogonias could profit by the insects activated by the Talapoins.

Nevertheless, it is still difficult to understand from an ecological viewpoint, the function for which selection has favoured the formation of small sized troops since, by association, polyspecific troops increase the number of individuals. These polyspecific troops are durable and are far more numerous than monospecific ones for the three arboreal species of <u>Cercopithecus</u> described here.

Concerning the maintenance of the species itself, one must resort to behavioural barriers, possibly linked to phenomena of visual imprinting in which the facial markings play a part. Nevertheless, hybridisations between Cercopithecines have been reported in the wild (Aldrich-Blake e.g,, 1968) and in captivity (Gitzen, e.g., 1963).

Long term studies covering several annual cycles and including studies on environmental productivity and quantitative work on diets, are essential in order to elucidate the socio-ecology of African forest Primates. Difficulties of observation in forest conditions constitute as always the prime obstacle. But we should also, as Struhsaker (1969) and Eisenberg et al. (1972) have already noted, focus attention on phylogenetic affinity between species, on the history of their populations and on the study of specific ethological characteristics. It seems that at the present stage of our knowledge,the tropical forest milieu is a highly complex one in which have developed a wide range of monkeys differing in size and behaviourally adapted to multiple ecological niches. When we think of the multitude of African forest species about which we know nothing, it is apparent that theories on the evolution of Primate societies in forest conditions are currently of only heuristic value.

REFERENCES

Aldrich-Blake, F. P. G. (1968). A fertile hybrid between two <u>Cerco-pithecus sp</u>. in the Budongo forest, Uganda. <u>Folia primat</u>. 9: 15-21.

Aldrich-Blake, F. P. G. (1970). The ecology and behaviour of the blue monkey, Cercopithecus mitis. Ph.D. Thesis. Univ. of Bristol.

Aldrich-Blake, F. P. G. (1970). Problems of social structure in forest monkeys. In "Social Behaviour in Birds and Mammals" (J. H. Crook ed.). Academic Press, pp 79-99.

Charles-Dominique, P. (1971). Eco-ethologie des Prosimiens du Gabon. Biol. gabon 7. 2. 124-225.

Crook, J. H. (1966). Gelada baboon herd structure and movement: a comparative report. Symp. zool. Soc. Lond. 18. 237-258.

Crook, J. H. (1970). The socio-ecology of Primates. In:"Social Organisation of birds and mammals" (J. H. Crook ed.). Academic Press. pp 103-159.

Crook, J. H. and J. S. Gartlan (1966). Evolution of Primate Societies. Nature, 210: 5042. 1200-1203.

Eisenberg, J. F., Muckenhirm N. A., Rudran, R. (1972). The relation between ecology and social structure in Primates. Science 176: 863-874.

Gautier, J. P. (1969). Emissions sonores d'espacement et de ralliement par deux Cercopithèque arboricoles du Gabon. Biol. gabon. 5. 117-145.

Gautier, J. P. (1971). Etude morphologique et fonctionnelle des annexes extralaryngées des Cercopithèques; liaison avec les cris d'espacement. Biol. gabon. 7. 2.

Gautier, J. P., Gautier-Hion A. (1969). Les associations polyspécifiques chez les Cercopithecidae du Gabon. La Terre et la Vie. 23: 164-201.

Gautier-Hion, A. (1968). Etude du cycle annuel du Talapoin vivant dans son milieu naturel. Biol. gabon. 4: 163-173.

Gautier-Hion, A. (1970). L'organisation sociale d'une bande de Tala-poins dans le N-E du Gabon. Folia primat: 12. 116-141.

Gautier-Hion, A. (1971a). Répertoire comportemental du Talapoin (M. talapoin). Biol. gabon. 7: 3. 296-389.

Gautier-Hion, A. (1971b). L'écologie du Talapoin du Gabon. La Terre et la Vie. 25: 427-490.

Gitzen, A. (1963). Croisement accidentel entre deux espèces de Cerco-pithèques, C. mona m. et C. mitis dogetti. Zool. Hedelingen. 39: 522-525.

Kummer, H. (1968). Social organisation of Hamadryas Baboons. Bibl. primat. 6: 1-189.

Kummer, H. (1971). "Primate societies; group techniques of ecologi-cal adaptation" (Goldschmidt ed.) Aldine, Chicago.

Napier, J. R. and Walker, A. C. (1967). Vertical clinging and leaping; a newly recognised category of locomotor behaviour of Primates. Folia primat. 6: 204-219.

Struhsaker, T. T. (1969). Correlates of ecology and social organisa-tion among African Cercopithecines. Folia primat. 11: 80-118.

POPULATION COMPOSITION AND ADAPTIVE

ORGANISATION AMONG ORANG-UTANS

OF THE KUTAI RESERVE

Peter S. Rodman
Department of Anthropology,
Harvard University,
Cambridge, Massachusetts.

INTRODUCTION

The widespread occurrence among the Anthropoidea of stable social groups containing at least one adult male and one adult female has led some primatologists to assume that parallel evolution has occurred and to expect such groups in all anthropoid species. Early field studies showed the orang-utan to be unusually solitary and therefore anomalous with respect to social organisation (Davenport, 1967; Harrison, 1962; Schaller, 1961). Over the last ten years, however, it has been assumed that this anomaly was owing primarily to human disturbance and that when sufficient evidence was available from studies in undisturbed areas, a complex social organisation would be found.

George Schaller (1965) suggested that the social organisation of orang-utans was similar to the pattern of temporary, open groups formed by chimpanzees. Other scholars (e.g. Reynolds, 1966) have concurred. Schaller (1961) had observed orang-utans in Sarawak for $5\frac{3}{4}$ hours and Davenport (1967) had observed orang-utans in Sabah for 192 hours. These studies yielded ambiguous evidence: males and females were seen together, but the total observation time was low, and it was impossible to determine the normal frequency of such groups. Recent studies of undisturbed populations in three locations have demonstrated that orang-utans have a dispersed population structure similar to that of many other vertebrates but unlike that of other anthropoid species studied so far.

John MacKinnon (1971) studied orang-utans in Sabah for seventeen months in 1968, 1969 and 1970, and the results of his research will be

discussed below (see Secondary Groupings of Population Units). Dr.
David Horr initiated a long-term study of the orang-utan in Sabah in
1967, and he has kindly acquainted me with the results which are now
in preparation for publication and to which I refer frequently below.
Horr surveyed an area of 24 km^2 and began intensive observations of
orang-utans in a 4 km^2 area 70 miles north of MacKinnon's study area.
My wife and I joined Dr. Horr in August, 1969 with the intention both of
continuing the research on orang-utans and of broadening the base of
the study to include systematic observation of all primate species in
the 4 km^2 area. The government of Sabah would not allow us to continue the research because of internal political disturbance, but the
Department of Nature Conservation and Wildlife Management of Indonesia
invited us to begin research on the orang-utan in East Kalimantan.

Kalimantan stretches from approximately 4° south latitude to 4°
north, and from 109° to 119° east longitude; the province of East
Kalimantan comprises the eastern third of this area. In 1970 only one
million people lived in Kalimantan, concentrated in a few major population centres, so that until this year the major part of East Kalimantan
remained barely touched by man. While the practice of slash-and-burn
agriculture has destroyed large areas of forest between the west coast
of Kalimantan and the central highlands, there is practically no such
disturbance from the mountains to the east coast. Even in the relatively
accessible areas along the east coast the human population density is
low, and since the people are predominantly Moslem they do not hunt
primates for food. The people do not capture orang-utans for export
since there is little communication with the outside world where the
animals could be sold. Only within the last two years have mechanised
logging companies begun to work their way into the primary rain forest

of East Kalimantan, and, although they are working quickly, they have
not yet destroyed large areas of the forest. For these reasons, the
orang-utan population of East Kalimantan remains undisturbed in most
areas. We established a study area in the north-eastern corner of a
200 km^2 nature reserve called the Kutai Reserve, $0^{\circ}24'$ north and
$117^{\circ}16'$ east (Fig. 1). The study area supported a dense population of
orang-utans, and our observations of that population from May 1, 1970
to July 31, 1971 allow us to draw conclusions regarding the nature of
social organisation and dispersal in an undisturbed population.

BACKGROUND: VEGETATION AND CLIMATE

Within the study area genera of the family Dipterocarpaceae dominate the vegetation, and primary stands of dipterocarp forest grow on a
few long, gentle slopes. Certain species preferred as food sources by
the orang-utan, such as Dracontomelon mangiferum, Dillenia borneensis, Koordersiodendron pinnatum and Ficus spp., occur in clumps.
When these species are in fruit the resulting non-random distribution
of preferred food greatly influences the daily ranges of the orang-utans.
The most interesting effect is the increase in probability of encounters
between foraging units, and this effect is discussed briefly below.

Two natural processes disturb the vegetation and interrupt development of primary stands of forest. Frequent flooding of the river, and
fluctuations of its bed resulting from constant erosion, leave a strip of
secondary growth near the bank that is not to be confused with the after-
effects of human cultivation. Away from the river, along the ridges
where shifting, shallow soil lies over sedimentary rock, many trees
fall during wind-storms; in these areas the constant disturbance arrests

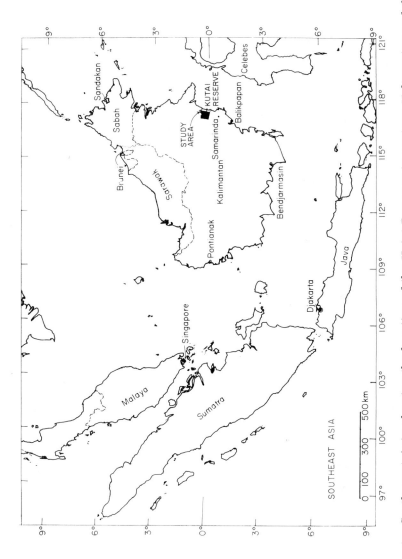

Fig. 1. South-east Asia showing the location of the Kutai Reserve in eastern Kalimantan and the principal cities of Kalimantan

development of true climax vegetation. In addition to these natural
disturbances, hand-loggers have recently cut about forty large diptero-
carps in two small sections of the study area (see Fig. 2) and young
secondary growth has replaced the forest there. A detailed report on
vegetation and the distribution of key plant species is now in preparation.

We kept daily records of rainfall and continuous records of temperature and humidity both at ground level and in the forest canopy from
August 1, 1970 to July 31, 1971. The minimum monthly rainfall came
in December, 1970 when 5.1 inches fell, and the maximum monthly
rainfall came the next month in January when 12.8 inches fell. The total rainfall for the year was 93.1 inches. Since most rain fell during
the night, there was only one day in the year when we were prevented
from working in the forest by heavy rain all day. Flooding of the river
was not directly correlated with the rainfall we measured; the heaviest
floods occurred in December, the month of minimum rainfall at the base
camp.

The maximum temperature recorded 1.5 metres from the ground
was $87^{\circ}F$, and the minimum temperature recorded was $66^{\circ}F$. The
relative humidity rose to nearly 100% during the night, but dropped to
80% on clear days between 1200 and 1500 hours. On cloudy days the
humidity remained above 90% for twenty-four hours. In the canopy
twenty metres above the ground temperatures were similar to those on
the ground, but the relative humidity was more labile. On clear days
the relative humidity dropped rapidly to 60% in the canopy from a night-
time figure of near 100%.

There are no distinct wet and dry seasons in the region probably
because of proximity to the equator and the orientation of the coast

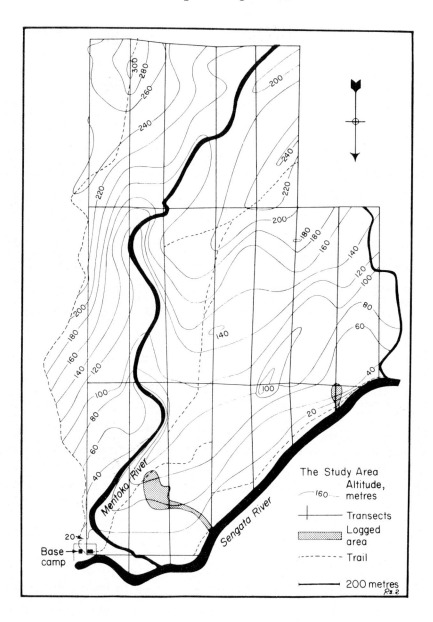

Fig. 2. The study area in the northeast corner of the Kutai Reserve showing topography of the area, principal landmarks and the grid of transects subdividing the area.

parallel to the prevailing winds. A few degrees north or south where the coast is more perpendicular to prevailing winds (e.g. Balikpapan or Sandakan; see Fig. 1), the climate is subject to seasonal variation caused by monsoons. The lack of seasonality in the region of our study area must influence the fruiting cycles of plants in the area since exogenous changes which may stimulate fruiting are at best extremely subtle and irregular. Marked seasons should cause synchronisation of fruiting in many plant species, and the resulting temporal clumping of food resources should affect the habits of fruit-eating animal species. One might expect, for example, that ranges of animals in areas where seasons are not marked will be different from ranges of the same species in areas with marked seasonality since food distribution in time and probably in space will be different. It is interesting that flooding of the river may be seasonal since the floods depend on rainfall far inland where monsoon winds coming from the south may bring rain. At least one plant species preferred as a food source by the orang-utan, Dracontomelon mangiferum, grows near the Sengata river and it fruited after the December and January floods. Remote seasonal changes in rainfall may therefore influence the distribution of food resources in the study area.

METHODS

The aim of this study was to describe the dynamics of distribution of primate groups in a small section of forest and to analyse direct and indirect interactions between groups of the same and of different species. The species of primary interest was the orang-utan, but systematic observations were made of all primate species present. In order to

carry out the study effectively it was necessary to work in a study area
large enough to include several groups of each of several species but
small enough to be surveyed thoroughly and regularly. We defined a
study area of 3 km^2 on the south side of the Sengata River by cutting
boundaries along compass lines; subsequent study was limited to the
area within the boundaries (see Fig. 2).

Grid system.

The study area was subdivided by six parallel transects running
from north to south 200 metres apart and two east-west transects 800
metres apart. These transects, marked every 50 metres, provided an
accurate basis for mapping locations of primate sightings and other
information such as movements of animals and the locations of food
trees. Profiles of elevation along the transects were translated into a
large-scale topographic map of the study area in a degree of detail un-
available in published maps of the region. Systematic use of the transects to search through the study area reduced a natural bias toward
walking and searching through areas where it was easiest to walk. The
set of baselines eliminated distortion in perception and mapping of distances within the study area. These may occur in an area where dense
vegetation limits the range of vision and obscures landmarks.

Multiple observers.

My wife and I carried out all observations with the aid of four
Indonesian assistants from the village down-river. Our four assistants
kept detailed notebooks recording all of their activities and observations,
and after an initial period of training they became reliable and accurate
observers. All their notes were translated and these notes are a sub-

stantial and valuable addition to the record of our research. We employed our assistants in two different ways: first, in taking a census of anthropoid primates present; and second, in searching for and tracking orang-utans.

Primate census.

Four observers walked in parallel along the north-south transects on pre-arranged itineraries. Each observer carried a schedule card specifying his route from intersection to intersection on the grid. We synchronised our watches each day and recorded the time of arrival at each intersection along the route. In this manner four observers, always including me either alone or with an assistant, could cover all transects in six hours. We equalised coverage of sections of the transects in each quarter of the day from 0600 to 1800 hours by varying the starting time and the daily itineraries. Each observer carried a notebook and recorded sightings of primate groups along the transects as follows:

1. Time of contact in hours and minutes.
2. Species sighted.
3. Number of animals counted and some indication of whether there were others who moved but were not actually seen.
4. Activity when sighted.
5. Location (e.g.: 225 m south of Transect A, 15 m west of Transect 3).
6. Height of animals in the canopy.
7. Direction of movement or flight.

Except in the case of orang-utans, we were never able to identify individual groups, but we have estimated the number of groups and individuals by inference from the data of many sightings. Details of the method of inference will be described in a subsequent report (Rodman, in prep.).

Searching for orang-utans.

The same method of systematic search was used to make contact with orang-utans, but with the following variations: 1) we often concentrated on subsections of the grid in order to contact particular individuals; 2) in the first half of the study, our assistants walked in pairs so that when one pair contacted an orang-utan, one man could stay with the animals while the other carried a message to my wife or to me giving the location of the animal contacted; 3) the pairs worked in two six hour shifts, from 0600 to 1200 and 1200 to 1800 hours so that once contact with an orang-utan was made, it could be maintained for days by rotating shifts; 4) when we obtained walkie-talkies, we all searched for orang-utans individually and made radio contact each hour. Radios doubled the area that could be searched effectively in a day.

Tracking orang-utans.

Once contact was made, we stayed with the animal for as long as possible or until we voluntarily broke contact. Our assistants kept notes on the activity of the orang-utan so that we had a constant record of behaviour even in our absence. The movements of the animals were recorded in relation to the grid of transects as the orang-utans travelled over the study area. We maintained contact with an orang-utan until it made a sleeping nest for the night, usually between 1800 and 1900 hours, and activity ceased within the nest. The observer then returned to camp,

and the same observer returned to the sleeping site of the orang-utan
the following morning before dawn. The animals normally did not move
before 0545 hours. We were able to maintain contact with two independent individuals or groups at a time; the longest period of continuous
contact with a single independent individual was eleven days at the end
of which we voluantarily terminated observation in order to search for
another orang-utan.

Individual recognition of orang-utans.

Some orang-utans have unnatural distinguishing marks. One adult
female, Afa, had a white mark on her facial skin over her right upper
canine; one adult male, BC, had a cut in his left cheek pad. Orang-
utans can be identified easily by many facial features which are not so
distinct as these two, however. The shape of the head, the height of
the hairline, and the direction of growth of hair on the head all vary
greatly. A few hours of observation of an individual were sufficient to
become familiar with the appearance of an orang-utan, and given a
small number of individuals, it was not difficult to distinguish between
them. Consistency in identification of an individual orang-utan by
several observers confirmed the identity in difficult cases.

RESULTS: CENSUS OF PRIMATES

In addition to the orang-utan, four other species of Anthropoidea
were always present in the study area. These were the Bornean gibbon,
Hylobates moloch, the Sunda Island leaf monkey, Presbytis aygula, the
crab-eating, or "kra", macaque, Macaca fascicularis and the pig-tailed
macaque, M. nemestrina. Three other species, the proboscis mon-

key, Nasalis larvatus, the maroon leaf monkey, P. rubicundis and the white-fronted leaf monkey, P. frontatus, entered the area infrequently. From July 16 to September 16, 1970 we walked the transects daily to make a census of the primate populations. We made 386 observations, including 26 observations of orang-utans, on 55 days in that period. The results of the first census are presented in Table 1. We repeated the census over a shorter time in May and June, 1971, but the results of that census have not yet been analysed. While we followed orang-utans, we made frequent observations of other primate groups so that the total observations of all other species during the study period including both censuses is more than 800.

TABLE 1. Results of a census of primates taken from 16 July to 16 September, 1970 within a 3 km^2 study area

Species	Estimated number of groups	Estimated total number of individuals
Macaca nemestrina	2	30
M. fascicularis	3	28
Presbytis aygula	8	45
Hylobates moloch	10	40
Nasalis larvatus	Spent 37 days in the study area during the period covered	
P. rubicundis	Sighted twice	
P. frontatus	Sighted occasionally; highly nomadic.	

THE ORANG-UTAN POPULATION

Primary units of the population

Between July 16, 1970 and July 31, 1971 the total observation time of orang-utans by all observers was 1639 hours and 4 minutes. The observation time was distributed between 281 independent observations; an independent observation is considered to be an observation of one independent orang-utan "unit" on one day. Thus the longest period of observation of a single independent animal -- eleven days -- counted as eleven independent observations. There were eleven different orang-utans who resided in or near the study area for the entire period of research, and they moved in six "primary units". Table 2 lists the membership of each of the primary units. The term "unit" is used here to avoid the confusion of calling single individuals a "group"; it includes both solitary orang-utans and combinations of individuals that travelled together constantly.

The membership of the six primary units was stable with one exception: Unit 1 often split when the juvenile female, Jfa, would leave the unit for several days and nights. We observed both subunits of Unit 1 during the time of separation as well as the complete unit when all three members were together.

Other orang-utan units were observed near the southern boundary of the study area (see Fig. 2). The difficulty of maintaining contact with orang-utans increased with distance from the base camp; there is consequently a bias in our observations toward units who ranged nearer to the base camp. We observed at least two adult females near the southern boundary. One of these females carried an infant, and the other was

TABLE 2. Primary units of orang-utans resident within the study area

Unit number	Membership	
	Name	Age/sex
1 a	Afa Ima	Adult female Infant male
b	Jfa	Juvenile female
2	Afd Imd	Adult female Infant male
3	BC	Adult male
4	Afb Jmb	Adult female Juvenile male
5	Afc Iuc	Adult female Infant, sex unknown
6	RT	Adult male

followed by a juvenile about the size of Jfa. Our original census and
continuous searching along the transects revealed that these orang-
utans were seldom within the study area, and I have ignored their contribution to the population density of the study area (see below). In
addition two young adult males passed through the study area; these two
males are discussed below (see Male Life Histories).

Ranges of population units.

The observed ranges of the six primary units are shown in Fig.
3. The ranges of Units 1, 2 and 3 are known from a total of 1517 hours
and 14 minutes of tracking; the ranges of units 4, 5 and 6 are estimated
from only 121 hours and 12 minutes of tracking and 22 brief sightings of
the members. The ranges are estimated by drawing boundaries around

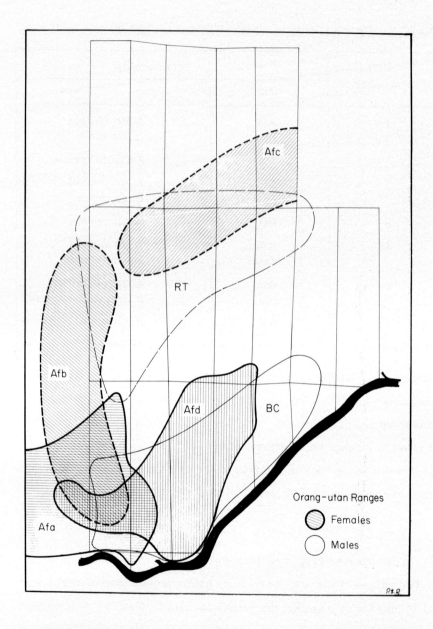

Fig. 3. Orang-utan Ranges: Ranges of the primary units of orang-utans resident in the study area; only the name of the adult member is given (see Table 2).

the smallest area that will include all observations of each unit. In Fig. 3 only the identification of the principal adult member of the unit is given. The juvenile female, Jfa, moved entirely within Afa's range when she left the primary unit.

Male ranges and spacing behaviour.

The two adult males, BC and RT, were never observed in the same locations and we conclude that they had discrete ranges. Any conclusion based on a sample of only two males must be tentative, but the generalisations suggested here are compatible with most observations made by Horr and some observations made by MacKinnon (1971). The similarities and discrepancies in the three studies will be discussed further (see below, Discussion).

One piece of evidence that suggests that adult males do establish discrete ranges at some point in their lives is the loud, throaty scream uttered by fully mature adult males. We heard the adult male RT give this call, which MacKinnon (1971) described as the adult male's "long call", about twice a month during the study. Depending on the intervening terrain, we could hear the call for up to a kilometre. MacKinnon was probably correct in arguing that the call functioned as a spacing signal between males since this interpretation fits the following evidence closely.

On December 17, 1970 one of our assistants encountered RT and Afc (units 5 and 6) together. We followed the pair and observed a single copulation between RT and Afc. That night RT and Afc slept 250 metres apart, and they rejoined in the morning. We lost track of them on December 18, but re-contacted them on the morning of December 19 before they left their nests. They had slept only five metres apart in the

same tree. Over the forty hour period between the time RT and Afc
were first contacted and the morning of December 19, RT called eleven
times. He called twice during the night of the 17th when he was separated from Afc, and he called five times during the night of the 18th when
he slept five metres from Afc. The calls on both nights were identical.
There is evidence that the long call attracts females (see below Male-
female communication), but the behaviour of RT on the night of December
18th strongly suggests that the call is used to repel other males and
that the increased frequency of his calls while in consort with a receptive female was a manifestation of strong competition between males
for fertile females. It would be reproductively advantageous for a male
to keep other males at a distance while he was in contact with a fertile
female, and repel other males at that crucial time. Similarly, natural
selection would favour structures which increase the effectiveness of
such behaviour, assuming, of course, that other males do respond to
the behaviour by staying away. Adult male orang-utans have an enlarged
laryngeal pouch which they inflate when they give the long call, and this
pouch presumably serves as a resonator and amplifier of the call, thereby increasing its range.

Female ranges and kin relations.

Female ranges were not discrete; they overlapped extensively
with each other and with male ranges (see Fig. 3). This pattern of
distribution -- discrete male ranges each overlapping several female
ranges which in turn overlap each other -- is unique among the
Anthropoidea, but occurs among other primates such as some nocturnal
prosimians (e.g. Galago demidovii, Charles-Dominique, 1972; and
probably Microcebus murinus, Martin, 1972). Female orang-utans

remained silent except during agonistic vocal displays. These agonistic
displays are not a frequent component of natural behaviour; in only two
instances were such displays observed to be directed at an object other
than the observer. In the first of these instances, the object was not
observed, and in the second instance, Afa drove BC from a fruit tree
with an agonistic display. Together these two instances accounted for
eleven minutes of observation time out of 20 hours and 8 minutes of
observed agonistic display by adult females. It is surely significant that
females, who occupy overlapping ranges, very seldom use loud vocalisations, whereas males commonly employ loud calls in the absence of any
direct visual stimulation by another animal. The comparison tends to
support the tentative conclusion that males occupy discrete ranges and
that long calls function to maintain spacing.

The juvenile female remained within Afa's range at all times.
When travelling alone she used the same paths through the range and fed
in many of the same fruit trees as she did when she followed Afa, or as
Afa did when they were separated. As the study progressed we learned
that Afd also used the same paths and fruit trees as Afa when in that
part of her range which overlapped Afa's range. Two other orang-utans,
BC and Afb, used completely different paths and food sources in their
areas of overlap with Afa and Afd. This evidence and the fact that Afa
and Afd met and moved together briefly while under observation suggest
to us that Afd may be a mature offspring of Afa. Their relationship is
discussed further below.

Male-female communication.

The consort pair, RT and Afc, has been described above, and RT's
calls have been interpreted as male-male spacing calls. It is likely that

RT's calls on the night of December 17th, when he was separated from
Afc, attracted Afc since on the morning of the 18th Afc woke and moved
directly toward the place where RT had been calling. On another occasion a male across the river from our camp called repeatedly from a
position near the river. Within an hour, Afa, Ima and Jfa (Unit 1)
appeared and moved directly over our house to a position on our side of
the river that placed them nearest to the male. One hour later Jfa
moved away, but Afa and Ima slept above our house and the male continued calling through the night. During the remainder of the study Unit
1 never came near our house except to feed. On that first occasion they
did not feed, and we conclude that the unit was attracted by the male's
long calls -- suggesting that the long call of the adult male orang-utans
may function not only to maintain spacing of males, but also to attract
females.

Population density

If population density is taken to be the number of individuals per
unit of area, it is necessary to distinguish between the maximum number of animals who never leave an area and the average number of
animals found within an area over a long period of time. If the estimated time each unit spent entirely within the study area is taken into
account, the average population density of orang-utans within the study
area was $3/km^2$ (see Table 3). The actual population density on any
given day must have varied from $2/km^2$ if all those who sometimes left
the study area left at the same time, to $3.67/km^2$ if all units were present within the study area. Schaller (1961) estimated 0.2 orang-utans
per km^2 in Sarawak; MacKinnon (1971) estimated $1+/km^2$ in the Segama
region of Sabah; and Horr estimates $2.1/km^2$ in his study area in Sabah.

TABLE 3. Population density of orang-utans within the study area

Unit number	Total members	Estimated time within the study area[1]	Time-corrected contribution to the population[2]
1	3	67%	2
2	2	100%	2
3	1	100%	2
4	2	50%	1
5	2	100%	2
6	1	100%	1
			Total 9

Total area = 3 km^2

Population density = approximately 3/km^2

[1]A convenient rough approximation to the fraction of observations of the unit made inside the boundaries of the study area.

[2]Time corrected contribution = total members x per cent time in the study area.

The probable reasons for a high population density in our area and in the larger Kutai region have been discussed above (see Introduction). The variation in population density between the four areas where Bornean orang-utans have been observed may be due to differences in average food densities of the areas as well as to differences in unnatural disturbance by man. If the Kutai region supports a richer edible flora, this could be due to the lack of seasonal variation described above (see Background: Vegetation and Climate).

There are obvious differences between the orang-utan populations

in our study area and in MacKinnon's study area in Sabah. MacKinnon
(1971) reported 160 different individuals in his 5 km^2 study area and
estimated that they spent an average of eleven days each within the
study area. It is therefore not surprising that he asserts that orang-
utans are, "... nomadic, wandering over enormous areas, ..." but
this is clearly not the case for the population in the Kutai area.
Detailed similarities between the populations in Horr's study area and
in our study area - particularly precise similarity between female
ranges in the two areas - suggest strongly that MacKinnon may have
been observing an atypical population of orang-utans. The differences
may have been the result of unnatural disturbance, but it will be much
more interesting if the dispersal and ranging patterns observed by
MacKinnon prove to be responses to unusual natural conditions.

Secondary groupings of primary units

Since they are organised in such small primary units it is clear
that orang-utans are highly solitary animals. The average size of our
six primary units is 1.83. We observed larger, secondary groupings
of the primary units on 13 occasions. The membership of the resulting
groups is listed in Table 4. A description of each of the observations
of larger groups follows.

Group 1. Units 5 and 6 combined to form Group 1; the behaviour of the group has been described above (see Male ranges and spacing behaviour and Male-female communication). This was the only
combination of units containing an adult male and an adult female (RT
and Afc) in which sexual behaviour was observed. Observations of the
two units in this group accounted for 2 of 281, or 0.7% of all independent observations of primary units.

TABLE 4.   Secondary groupings of primary units

	Membership	Number of sightings
1	RT Afc Iuc	1
2	RT Afb Jmb	1
3	BC Afd Imd	4
4	BC Afa Ima Jfa Afb Jmb	1
5	BC Afa Ima Jfa Afd Imd	1
6	Afa Ima Jfa Afd Imd	5

Group 2.   Units 4 and 6 combined to form Group 2 when the two
units fed in adjacent fruit trees of the species Koordersiodendron pinnatum. There was no co-ordination of movements between the units and no

observable reaction of one unit to the other. They arrived in the trees at different times and departed at different times.

Group 3.   Units 2 and 3 combined on four occasions to form Group 3. On three of these occasions the units met in the same fruiting tree of the species Dracontomelon mangiferum, and on one occasion they met in a fruiting tree of the genus Talauma. There was no coordination of their activities or reaction of one to the other on any of these occasions.

Group 4.   On May 25, 1971, Units 1, 3 and 4 converged on a single fruiting tree of the species D. mangiferum. Again, there was no co-ordination of movements of the units. We observed some reaction of Afb (Unit 4) to BC (Unit 3) since Afb urinated each time BC moved or shook the tree.

Group 5.   Units 1, 2 and 3 fed briefly together in another tree of the species D. mangiferum on March 2, 1970. During this observation Afa drove BC from the tree with agonistic display as described above (see Female ranges and kin relations). Shortly thereafter Afa left the fruit tree and joined Afd in the resting tree briefly before the two units separated.

Group 6.   Group 6 was first encountered when Units 1 and 2 were feeding together in a fruiting tree of the species Koordersiodendron pinnatum. Neither unit was habituated to observation at that time and both moved away upon discovery of the observers. Significantly, they moved in the same direction, at the same time, and they remained close together as they settled in a tree nearby. On the next occasion Unit 1 was feeding in a fruit tree of the species Dillenia borneensis when discovered. The three members of Unit 1 left the fruit tree and moved to a fruitless tree nearby where they encountered Unit 2. The members of the two units sat quietly in this tree for several minutes and then left together. Later in the study we found them sitting together in the same tree, and when Unit 1 moved, Unit 2 followed for several hundred metres before turning from the path. In each of the other two encounters we observed similar co-ordination of movements between the two units.

Secondary groupings and social behaviour

Each observation of a secondary group was at least part of one independent observation of each unit included in the group. There were eleven observations of two primary units in combination and two observations of three primary units in combination. This is a total of 28 out of 281 independent observations of primary units. The total observation time of secondary groups was 23 hours, or 1.65% of the total observation time of all orang-utans in this study.

Not only are both the frequency and duration of social interactions between primary units low but also only some of the secondary groups can properly be called social. According to the classical distinction of Allee (1931; also Tinbergen, 1953), there are two major categories of aggregations of individuals: in the first the aggregation remains together because of some external factor that influences each individual; in the second the aggregation remains together because the individuals react to each other. Only the latter aggregation is really a social group, and by this definition, only secondary groups 1 and 6 can be called social groups of primary units in this study. Groups 2, 3, 4 and 5, which resemble family groups or one male units, were combinations of units brought together by the common attraction of a fruiting tree; they are

classic cases of non-social aggregations. True social groups of more
than one primary unit therefore occurred in only 4.3% of all independent observations of primary units.

The frequency of combinations of primary units determined in this
study is consistent with observations reported by MacKinnon (1971).
MacKinnon observed 146 "sub-groups" of orang-utans formed by 160
different animals who were apparently individually recognised. Sub-
groups containing more than one adult orang-utan comprised 11% of the
total; this figure is close to the 10% frequency of observations of secondary groups in our study. It is difficult to compare the two studies
further because of differences in the two populations (see above,
Population density), but results of both studies show that a population
of orang-utans in distributed normally in small units of solitary animals
and females with young.

MacKinnon (1971) reports an interesting cross-section of frequencies of combinations of individuals; but because he observed each individual for an average of only 7.5 hours, it is impossible to assess the
frequency with which each individual joined in larger groups. The
results leave open the question of whether the few combinations of
adult animals found in orang-utan populations constitute some sort of
social organisation comparable to the social organisation found in local
populations of chimpanzees. My wife and I were able to follow a few
individually recognised individuals in well-known primary units for a
long period of time so that we could observe the details of interactions
between units. It is obvious from the results described above that
there are few social relationships between orang-utans outside of the
primary unit of mother and offspring. The only definite relationship
between primary units is the consort relationship of male and recep-

tive female, and it is brief. There is some indication that the tie between a mother and her female offspring persists into later life as in other anthropoid primates, but such rudimentary ties hardly constitute a social system comparable to that of the gregarious chimpanzees.

DISCUSSION

The dispersion of orang-utan populations and the simplicity of social relations within them are both striking and disappointing when compared with the complexity of social structures found among other primates. The data presented here raise, however, several interesting problems both within the context of the study of orang-utan behaviour and within the general field of primatology. In the following discussion I will treat only one of the questions that arise: given the observed differences observed between male and female ranges, what differential patterns of behavioural development lead to those ranges? In the absence of longitudinal observations of orang-utans it is intriguing to attempt to predict what the different life histories of the two sexes are and what sorts of observations will confirm or disprove the predictions. In an attempt to give some structure to our new knowledge of the behaviour of orang-utans, I will attempt such a prediction and discuss some of the data which are relevant.

Female Life History

Infant females have a range identical to their mother's range because they are totally dependent on their mothers. In adulthood females move in individual ranges that overlap with each other (see above, Female ranges and kinship relations). This pattern of adult female ranges has been confirmed by Horr's observations. I assume that the pattern observed in this study and in Horr's study is at least more common than the nomadic pattern reported by MacKinnon because it has been observed in two widely separated areas.

Table 5 lists the behavioural stages in the life history of females that have been observed both in this study and in Horr's. The stages are arbitrary sections of a continuum which could be subdivided further; the only possible abrupt change in the process of gradual separation from the mother is at weaning, and weaning probably marks the transition from stage 2 to stage 3 when the next infant is born. If my assumption that Afd is a mature offspring of Afa (see above, Female ranges and kin relations and Secondary groupings and social behaviour) and if their relationship is typical of females in the larger orang-utan population, distribution of females through the habitat is effected by conservative radiation of daughters from their mothers' ranges. An important implication of this mode of distribution is that neighbouring females must be closely related; the onus of genetic dispersal will be borne by male offspring.

Male Life Histories

I have concluded that adult males have discrete ranges (see Male ranges and spacing behaviour), but Horr's observations contradict this conclusion. Horr reports that there were more adult males than females in his study area and that males range over larger areas than females. He also reports that adult males move in overlapping ranges and that he frequently encountered new males. Adult females outnumbered adult males in the resident population of our study area, but over the entire study period we observed equal numbers of adult males and

TABLE 5. Stages in the life histories of female and male orang-utans

Female	Male
1. Constantly attached to mother, feeding only within her reach.[1]	1. (Same as female).............[1]
2. Forages independently of mother but carried by mother over long distances. Sleeps with mother.[2]	2. (Same as female).............[3]
3. Forages and travels independently but always follows mother. Sleeps near, but not with mother.[1]	3. (Same as female).............[1]
4. Spends several days and nights away from mother, but remains entirely within mother's range and frequently reunites with her.[1]	4. (Same as female).............[3]
5. Age of first reproduction. Daily travel completely independent of mother, range overlaps with mother's range, occasional encounters with mother.	5. Period of initial sexual maturity. Leaves mother's range and the ranges of any known resident males. Travels widely making random contact with females.[1]
	6. Competition for females with settled males and age-mates. Age of first reproduction.[3]
	7. Maintains contact with a few females and ranges over a fixed area which overlaps the ranges of those females.

[1] observed this study [2] observed by Horr [3] hypothetical

adult females within the study area: on two separate occasions, transient males passed rapidly through the study area. Strictly speaking,
this data indicates that male ranges overlap since the two transient
males crossed the ranges of the resident males. Judging by the size
of the two transient males and by the development of their secondary
sexual characteristics, these two males were distinctly younger than
the two resident adult males, BC and RT. The difference in age between resident and transient males suggests a stage of dispersal in the
life history of males not experienced by females.

Stages 1-4.   Stages 1 through 4 in the life of a male should be the
same as the first four periods in behavioural development of a female
(see Table 5). Males at each of the first and third stages of development have been observed in this study. Although a male has not been
observed during Stage 2, this stage is merely a logical transition from
Stage 1 to Stage 3, and the absence of observations is not significant.
Unfortunately, no male orang-utan has been observed during Stage 4.
Stage 4 is the theoretical period of developing independence of the
young male prior to sexual maturity. In the absence of evidence, it is
of course possible that males of this age have already begun to disperse.
It would be most interesting to know whether pre-pubertal Stage 4 males
travel together in pairs. Brief observations by Schaller (1961) of "two
subadults" and one observation of a subgroup containing two "adolescents" by MacKinnon (1971) suggest that this is a possibility. Unfortunately sex of the young animals was not identified by either observer.

Male dispersal: Stage 5.   One of the transient males was only
slightly larger than the resident Stage 4 female, Jfa. He had developing cheek pads which are a post-pubertal sexual characteristic. I
conclude that at physiological sexual maturity young males leave their

mothers' ranges and begin to travel widely. Initial dispersal could be
a response to the presence of resident Stage 7 males (see Table 5) or
to endogenous metabolic changes. In either case, dispersal of young
males is probably analogous to peripheralisation of subadult males in
multimale groups of baboons (Hall and DeVore, 1965), macaques,
(Kaufmann, 1967), and possibly mountain gorillas (Schaller, 1965).

A consequence of dispersal of males at an early stage of adult
life is that an observer working in a defined study area should see
more young adult males than either adult females or fully mature adult
males. The number of adult females and Stage 7 males who can possibly be observed depends on the size of the study area since both age/
sex classes have constant ranges. The number of young adult males
who can possibly be observed depends on the average distance travelled by a dispersing male and his average rate of travel; the longer the
average distance travelled by young males and the higher their rate of
travel, the more of them one should see in any fixed area of forest
over any fixed length of time. Even if relative age of males is not
determined, this system of wide-ranging dispersal will be manifest
in larger numbers of observations of males than of females and in
larger numbers of new males than of new females. This prediction
fits Horr's data, but the precise prediction can not be tested unless
relative ages of all males are known and at least some of the animals
are individually recognised so that appropriate distinctions may be
made between them.

Male reproductive strategy: Stage 6.   Gadgil and Bossert (1970)
have utilised a method of cost/benefit analysis - in which the "currency"
of cost and benefit is offspring - to predict the consequences of different life historical strategies for different sorts of breeders. Trivers

(1972) has applied the same method to interpretation of differential reproductive strategies by the sexes. The principles of these theoretical papers can be used to predict a major decision point in the life history of an orang-utan.

Trivers (1972) has argued convincingly that, "...the sex whose typical parental investment is greater than that of the opposite sex will become a limiting resource for that sex." Male orang-utans manifestly invest nothing in their offspring but the energy of sperm production; females must carry and nurture the offspring during an extended period of infant dependency. Even when the offspring are physically independent at Stage 3, the female must share the resources of her range with the offspring, and this sharing continues into the adult life of female offspring. We will therefore assume that females are a limiting resource for male orang-utans.

During Stage 6 males become interested in sexual access to females. The pattern of random wandering over a wide area adopted during Stage 5 will provide only random contacts with females. Comparative evidence from one captive lowland gorilla who is raising her infant in the Basel zoo (Jorge Hess, pers. com.) and from natural populations of chimpanzees (Van Lawick-Goodall, 1971; Reynolds, 1965) indicates that the birth interval among great apes is at least three and a half years. If we assume that a female orang-utan is fertile no more often than once every three and a half years and that she is sexually receptive for five or six days during oestrus, it can be shown that the probability of contacting a fertile female in random contacts with females is very low at each contact. A strategy of very rapid travel should increase the total contacts with females and thereby enhance the probability of contacting a fertile female in any unit of time,

but energy requirements would quickly limit the rate of travel. It is
interesting that MacKinnon (1971) reports observations of 15 consort
pairs of adult males and adult females; he also states that consort
pairs usually involved "younger or subadult' males and that no matings
occurred in the consort relationships. These observations are consistent with the predicted consequences of the dispersal pattern of males
described here.

Alternatively, the sexually mature male might choose to maintain
contact with a single female in a monogamous bond. In this way he
would be assured of access to her during all her fertile periods and
his energy expenditure in search for fertile females would be minimised. Given the long periods of sexual inactivity of a female and the
potential of a male to inseminate many females with no need for investment in the offspring, this strategy appears to be inefficient; it limits
the male to the reproductive capacity of a single female.

Somewhere between the extremes of random   contact with many
females and constant contact with a single female there must be a
strategy that will maximise the reproductive success of a male so that
his behaviour will be favoured by natural selection. Frequent communication with a few familiar females so that the male is continually
aware of the reproductive state of each female should maximise the
male's chances of successful mating. The energy budget of the male
and the population density of females will limit the number of females
who can be "monitored" since the amount of time necessary for feeding
and resting limits the time a male can spend moving between females.
The long call of the male (see above, Male ranges and spacing behaviour
and Male-female communication) probably increases the efficiency with
which a male can monitor several females since females are attracted

to the call.

Male-male competition: Stage 7.   Sometime during Stage 6 a
male will attempt to establish a permanent range. The exact point at
which he will do so probably depends on a chance encounter with a receptive female. The attempt to mate with an oestrus female must
carry some risk of direct conflict with a resident male, but delay in
establishing a range will also have a cost because the longer a male
waits to reproduce after sexual maturity, the fewer his maximum possible offspring. At an abstract level, the point in life at which a male
will attempt to displace a resident adult male will be the point at which
the difference is maximised between risk of conflict and benefit of
beginning to reproduce when both are measured in the currency of
offspring. A male's chance of success in his attempt will depend on
his condition and on the vigour of older adult males who reside in the
area.

Trivers (1972) reviews evidence that size is positively correlated
with reproductive success among males of several species: high dominance is rewarded with reproductive success, dominance is frequently
established by aggression and large size is advantageous in aggressive
encounters; therefore strong size dimorphism in the two sexes may
indicate aggressive competition between members of the larger sex.
Trivers also reviews evidence that among birds and mammals the
larger sex is normally the more aggressive sex. Adult male orang-
utans are approximately twice the size of adult females (Schultz, 1969).
In the absence of any other differential behaviour between sexes - such
as differential feeding and foraging - it is likely that larger size of
males is a manifestation of aggressive competition between males.
The size dimorphism of male and female orang-utans is therefore

consistent with the prediction of direct male-male conflict among orang-utans.

SUMMARY AND CONCLUSIONS

This paper presents some results from a fifteen month field study of orang-utans in the Kutai Reserve of East Kalimantan. Eleven orang-utans resided in the 3 km^2 study area; these orang-utans were individually recognised. The eleven individuals were normally organised in six primary population units: four adult females with offspring and two solitary adult males. Adult females were found in overlapping ranges while the two adult males maintained discrete ranges, each of which overlapped several female ranges. The primary units combined into larger secondary groups in only 10% of 281 independent observations of orang-utans during the period of research; observations of secondary groups accounted for only 1.65% of 1639 hours of observation. Seven of thirteen secondary groupings were aggregations rather than truly social groups. A mated pair was observed in consort once, and observations of a recurring secondary group containing two adult females suggest that the relationship between mother and female offspring persists tenuously into adult life of the daughter. I infer from the data that female orang-utans are dispersed by conservative radiation from their mother's ranges and that male orang-utans pass through a period of wide-ranging dispersal prior to the age of first reproduction. It is also predicted that a male orang-utan must compete for receptive females at some point in his life and that continued long-term study of an orang-utan population will yield observations of direct male-male conflict.

MacKinnon (1971) has suggested that the solitary nature of orang-utans in his study is a response to heavy human predation. In this study observations of orang-utans in an undisturbed habitat strongly suggest that the solitary nature of orang-utans is a normal condition and not a response to unusual pressures. In the preceding discussions I have attempted to show that the solitary nature of _male_ orang-utans can be explained as an adaptation to the distribution of females. If it is necessary to explain why orang-utans are not social, it is now necessary to explain the habits of females.

The behaviour of females must be an adaptation that maximises their foraging efficiency and their success at raising offspring. We will therefore arrive at a satisfactory explanation of the solitary nature of orang-utans by applying the models of socio-ecology formulated by Crook (1970) to the behaviour of _females_ and by analysis of: the feeding habits of females and offspring; the constraints of energy budgets on range size; and the distribution of resources in the habitat. At the very least this approach provides us with an interesting problem for analysis rather than a simplistic hypothesis linking the entire social pattern of orang-utans to the single influence of human predation. The work presented suggests furthermore that within the broader field of primatology understanding of social behaviour may be enhanced by reference to recent theoretical advances in the fields of evolutionary and behavioural biology.

ACKNOWLEDGMENTS

I am grateful to the Department of Nature Conservation and Wildlife Management of Indonesia for their initial invitation to study orang-utans in the Kutai Reserve. The enthusiasm of officers of the Provincial Forest Department of East Kalimantan encouraged my wife and me in the face of great logistic problems when we first arrived in East Kalimantan. The personnel of P. N. Pertamina and the Compagnie Generale de Geophysique in Kampung Sengata gave us constant practical assistance in the field. I am grateful to I. DeVore for introducing me to the study of primates and to Dr. David Horr and his family for introducing us to the pleasures of field research in the rain forest. My wife graciously accepted a two year intermission in her own career to accompany me, and she has contributed to every aspect of the research. R. L. Trivers introduced me to the theoretical work which I have treated briefly in this paper. I thank I. DeVore, R. L. Trivers and J. A. Kurland for reading and commenting upon drafts of this paper and for many hours of discussion. The research was supported by Grant 13156 from the U.S. National Institute of Mental Health to I. DeVore. The author is currently the recipient of a National Defense Education Act Title IV Graduate Fellowship.

REFERENCES

Charles-Dominique, P. (1972). Ecologie et vie sociale de Galago demidovii (Fischer 1808; Prosimii). Z. Tierpsychol. 9: 7-42.

Crook, J. H. (1970). The socio-ecology of primates. In: "Social Behaviour in Birds and Mammals" (J. H. Crook, ed.), 103-166. Academic Press, London.

Davenport, Richard K., Jr. (1967). The orang utan in Sabah. Folia Primat. 5: 247-263.

Hall, K. R. L. and I. DeVore (1965). Baboon social behavior. In:

"Primate Behavior" (I. DeVore, ed.), 53-110. Holt, Rinehart
and Winston, New York.

Harrison, B. (1962). "Orang-utan." Collins, London.

Gadgil, Madhav and William H. Bossert (1970). Life historical
consequences of natural selection. American Naturalist 104:
1-24.

Kaufmann, J. H. (1967). Social relations of adult males in a free-
ranging band of rhesus monkeys. In: "Social Communication
among Primates" (S. A. Altmann, ed.), 73-98. Univ. of Chicago
Press, Chicago.

MacKinnon, John (1971). The orang-utan in Sabah today. Oryx 10:
141-191.

Martin , R. L. (1972). A preliminary field study of the lesser mouse
lemur (Microcebus murinus J. F. Miller 1777). Z. Tierpsychol.
9: 43-89.

Reynolds, V. (1966). Open groups in hominid evolution. Man 1:
441-452.

Reynolds, V. and F. Reynolds (1965). Chimpanzees of the Budongo
Forest. In: "Primate Behavior" (I. DeVore, ed.), 368-424.
Holt, Rinehart and Winston, New York.

Rodman, Peter S. (in prep.). Doctoral dissertation, Department of
Anthropology, Harvard University.

Schaller, G. (1965). The behavior of the mountain gorilla. In:
"Primate Behavior" (I. DeVore, ed.), 324-367. Holt, Rinehart
and Winston, New York.

Schaller, G. (1961). The orang-utan in Sarawak. Zoologica 46: 73-82.

Schultz, Adolph (1969). "The Life of Primates." Universe, New York.

Trivers, R. L. (1972). Parental investment and sexual selection. In:

"Sexual Selection and the Descent of Man" (B. Campbell, ed.). Aldine, Chicago.

Van Lawick-Goodall, Jane (1971). "In the Shadow of Man." Houghton Mifflin, Boston.

SOCIAL COMMUNICATION AMONG SQUIRREL MONKEYS:

ANALYSIS BY SOCIOMETRY, BIOACOUSTICS AND

CEREBRAL RADIO-STIMULATION

Detlev Ploog and Manfred Maurus

Max-Planck-Institute for Psychiatry,
Munich
F. R. Germany

INTRODUCTION

The first phase of research in most, if not all fields of science and the humanities involves a thorough description of phenomena. In primate communication research this first phase has not yet been completed. Here one of the serious problems is how to sort out the communicative aspects of behaviour from the rest of the behaviour patterns. One may assume that only a certain percentage of the total behaviour pattern serves as an information carrier, and then one has to find out which specific behavioural units do or do not have communicative functions.

In the case of the squirrel monkey, observations in the laboratory under a variety of conditions have enabled us to describe this species' repertoire of motor and vocal behaviour during infancy, growth and maturation (Winter, Ploog and Latta, 1966; Ploog, 1967, 1969; Ploog, Hopf and Winter, 1967). Time and again the question arises of when to split and when to lump the behaviour patterns, that is, how to decide which elements of behaviour can be considered as a behavioural unit. However, within the behavioural repertoire of the squirrel monkey we can usually agree on what is definitely a unit serving communication, or, in other words, a unit that serves as a social signal. The difficulty is rather to determine what is not a signal, that is, which behaviour definitely has no communicative function. According to present findings, there is a certain set of signals that is built-in and species-specific. However, though the built-in or gene-determined signals appear to be the matrix for the communication system, they may not constitute the whole set of signals. The possibility that each observable unit of behaviour may take on communicative meaning has to be included in all functional analyses. Therefore, a substantial part of our research on social communication is devoted to the question of what signal carries which message in which social context, and we will deal with this question below.

Because of the high degree of complexity of the primates' communication system and because of our interest in the mediating brain mechanisms, it became apparent during earlier phases of our research that certain methods which are conventionally used for the analysis of signal function, such as dummy experiments, playbacks of vocalizations, and isolation from conspecifics, are insufficient if not supplemented by others. Therefore, we have additionally employed socio-metric methods and electrical brain stimulation, and examples of these will be given.

VISUAL MODE OF SOCIAL COMMUNICATION

I shall first describe the visual mode of social communication. Our paradigm in this paper is the phenomenon of genital display, which has been studied in detail and under various experimental conditions. This signal is used in various types of agonistic, dominance, and courtship behaviours. It is always directed towards a partner and has several components: laterally positioned leg with hip and knee bent and marked supination of the foot, abduction of the big toe and, according to the sex of the animal, an erection of the penis or enlargement of the clitoris. The display is frequently accompanied by specific calls (Ploog, Blitz and Ploog, 1963; Ploog and MacLean, 1963).

Fig. 1 shows genital display under four different conditions: on top, displaying of adults at a distance from each other and counter-

Fig. 1.   Genital display of the squirrel monkey (Saimiri sciureus)
          under four different conditions. (Drawing by H. Kacher
          after photographs and motion picture frames.)   (Ploog,
          D., S. Hopf and P. Winter, 1967).

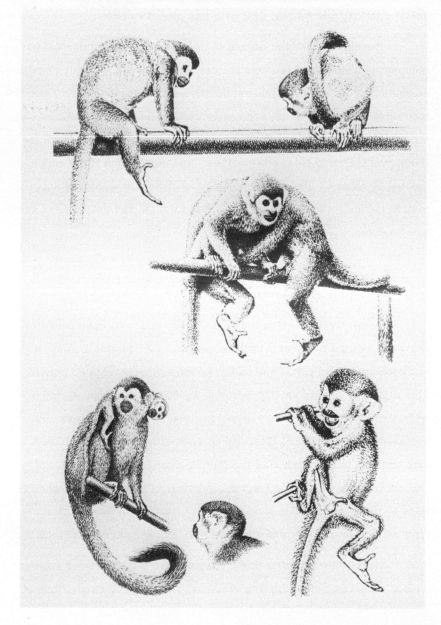

displaying in close proximity; on the lower right, a 7-week old infant displaying with vocalization to a human observer after having left its mother's back and, on the lower left, a $1\frac{1}{2}$-day old female infant positioned at its mother's neck displaying to a cage-mate; its mouth is slightly open for vocalization (as revealed by the original motion picture frames). The signal seems to be a highly integrated pattern that includes visual orientation and recognition, partner-directed relations, and coordination of motor and automatic functions. This indicates that the brain structures involved in this response are functionally mature at birth. The innate nature of genital display is also suggested by observations of a hand-reared male squirrel monkey, that directed this signal against its substitute mother, a stuffed woollen sock (Hopf, 1970; Ploog, 1969).

With increasing age there is a change in the functional significance of genital display, and this can be demonstrated by a quantification of interaction patterns between animals in a group. Such quantification is based on the question: "Who does what to whom, and how often?" This method, a form of sociometry, has been employed in our investigations of social behaviour for many years (Ploog, 1963; Ploog, Blitz and Ploog, 1963; Castell and Ploog, 1967; Hopf, 1971).

Fig. 2 shows an example of a young male, the dominant male, the mother and the "aunt" with regard to some age-specific interaction patterns and genital display. The distributions at the top of the figure shows mother and male infant in the process of intense weaning where the mother tries to avoid the child whenever contacted and where the child displays to the mother over and over again. Quite a different relationship is seen between infant and "aunt". Here there is almost no genital display, but much contact, and, for the first time, juvenile

Fig. 2.   Typical developmental phases of social interactions from the
5th to the 14th month. (Ploog, D., S. Hopf and P. Winter,
1967).

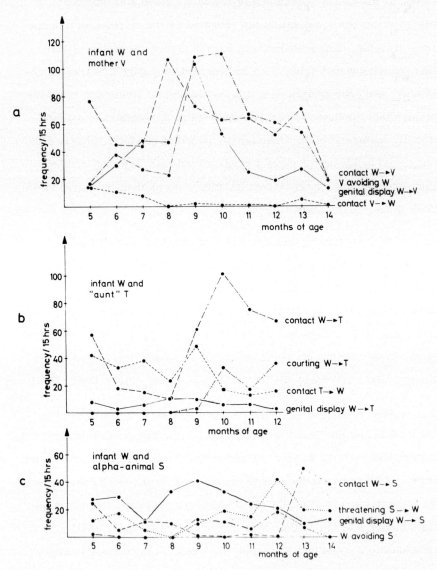

SOCIAL RELATIONS OF AN INFANT

features of courting. The relationship to the alpha male is different
again. Until the infant is about nine months old, the "boss" of the
group threatens only mildly and infrequently, even if the young male
displays towards him time and again. When the young animal grows
older, however, relations with the alpha male change radically. The
latter threatens severely and may attack the young male when it displays towards him. There is an amusing transitional phase during
which the young male does not want to give up its behaviour and so
turns its back to the boss while displaying but then glances over its
shoulder at him. At the beginning of the second year, the display behaviour decreases markedly, and the young male establishes a new
relationship with the dominant male. Contacts are more frequent and
consist mainly of huddling and playing. The play includes a characteristic pattern that is, no doubt, schooling in fighting - a playful but
well-controlled training by the alpha male (Ploog, Hopf and Winter,
1967; Ploog, 1969; Hopf, 1971). This phase comes to an end when
the adolescent approaches sexual maturity during his third year of
life.

The example of genital display as a social signal shows some
features that may be important for all primates. On the one hand, it
is a built-in, species-specific behaviour pattern. On the other hand,
as the infant matures, both the infant and the group change their interaction patterns with regard to a given signal. First, the infant
uses the signal over and over again with little or no consequence for
either sender or recipient. Despite this lack of reinforcement, the
signal persists up to a predetermined age. It is then followed by
severe consequences, and the young monkey learns, within a short
period of time, the context in which it may or may not use the signal.

This protracted maturation, which coincides with other biological
phenomena such as second dentition and final weaning, is characteristic of the social development of primates. This process of socializa-
tion is genetically determined by maturational processes in which innate
and learned components are interlocked.

RADIO-STIMULATION OF THE BRAIN

If one investigates developmental behaviour and social dynamics
under semi-natural conditions by collecting data on a day by day basis,
certain difficulties for the functional analysis of social signals are encountered. We feel that these difficulties can be overcome, by using
radio-stimulation of the brain (Maurus, 1967). One or more members
of a monkey colony of 4 to 5 members is implanted with indwelling
electrodes (Fig. 3). The remote-controlled brain stimulation is employed to generate certain social signals at any given time, as often
as desired, at the will of the experimenter. The function of the signal
and hence its information content or signal value is largely disclosed
by the response of the recipient to the signal. Therefore, there are
always two chains of events which are equally important, that is, the
sender's sequential behaviour triggered by the radio-stimulation, on
the one hand, and the recipient's sequential behaviour as the response,
on the other. Our earlier question: "Who does what to whom, and how
often?" can be advanced to the question: "Who does what to whom, and
in what order?" In such an experiment only one animal is stimulated
at a time. Whenever the stimulus leads to social interactions, the
scene is filmed and the film is evaluated later on frame by frame.

So far we have studied the reactions of group members to

Fig. 3.   View of a monkey's head with telereceiver. The total
           weight of the receiver including the box and batteries
           is 7-8 g. The diameter of the box is 25 mm and its
           height 12 mm. The wearing of the device does not
           alter the natural social behaviour of the monkey
           colony. Multi-lead electrodes are implanted in each
           monkey; there are 46 bare tips available for stimu-
           lation in each brain. Monkeys prepared in this way
           have lived quite normally for several years (drawing
           by H. Kacher).

various behaviours of the stimulated animal such as attack behaviour, dominance gestures, and reactions to specific signals from different distances. Our results have shown that the effects of social signals on the modification of social behaviour depend upon a whole range of variables, among them the intensity of a signal, the group context in which it occurs, and the space between sender and recipient (Maurus and Ploog, 1969, 1971). Because of the great variability of responses to signals, it became apparent that studies of signal functions should be done on a probabilistic basis. How we tried to proceed to this end will be shown in the next example.

In this experiment one particular animal, a subordinate male in one of the groups, was repeatedly stimulated over many weeks at only one brain site (the stimulus parameters being kept constant). The total number of stimulations was over 1200. These stimulations caused over 6700 actions in the group. (Maurus and Pruscha, 1972).

Fig. 4 shows a schematic presentation of an arbitrary experiment consisting of 12 stimulus repetitions. In the upper graph the ordinate shows the successive stimulus repetitions and the abscissa the number of seconds which elapsed after the film camera was turned on. The sequence of actions elicited by each stimulus repetition is shown as a chain in which each circle represents one action and is plotted at the time of its occurrence.

Within each sequence of actions there are three outstanding events, i.e., the beginning of the sequence, the end of the brain stimulation, and the end of the sequence. For each stimulus repetition, the latter two events - the end of stimulation and the end of the sequence - can have varying positions in the sequence. If one employs

Fig. 4.   Schematic presentation of an arbitrary experiment con-
          sisting of 12 stimulus repetitions. Upper graph: The
          sequence of actions elicited by each stimulus repetition
          is shown as a chain in which each circle represents one
          action and is plotted at the time of its occurrence.
          Lower graph: Illustration of rearranging the chains of
          actions for mathematical analysis. In section I the first
          actions of each of the 12 sequences are in one column;
          in section II the last actions before the end of stimulation
          are in one column; in section III the last actions of each
          sequence are in one column. Time between actions is
          neglected. (Maurus, M. and H. Pruscha, 1972)

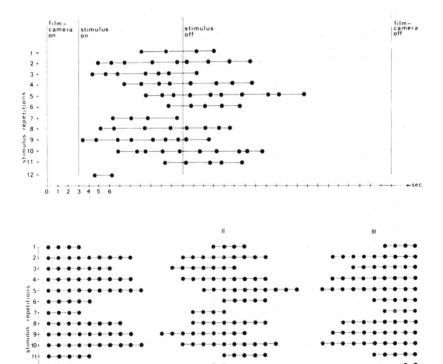

the obvious analysis proceeding from the beginning of each sequence,
no definite statements about the end of the stimulation and the end of
the sequence would be possible when employing the evaluation method
which is schematically shown in this figure. Thus, the sequences have
been evaluated in two other possible ways: starting with the end of the
stimulation and going backward and forward from here, and starting
with the end of a sequence and going backward. This procedure of re-
arranging the chains of actions in three different ways is shown in the
lower part of this figure. In section I the circles representing the first
action of each sequence are in one column, in section II those representing the last action before the end of stimulation are in one column
and in section III those representing the last action of each sequence
are in one column. Only the last possibility will be considered in the
following. Time between actions is neglected in this analysis. The
abscissa designates the occurrence of an action at a certain position
in the chain of events.

After this explanation of procedures, the results presented in
Fig. 5 will be understandable. It shows the relative frequency p_r of
the occurrence of certain actions at various positions in the chain of
events. These actions were performed by the dominant male (No. 1
in the first position of the four-digit numbers) or by the subordinate
male (No. 2). No. 3 stands for all females together. Our "Who does
what to whom" is reflected in the digits of the four-digit numbers:
the first digit is the "who", the sender animal, the second is the
"whom", the receiving animal, and the last two digits the "what",
that is, the behavioural unit whose function is analysed.

The left side of the figure shows actions which occurred more
often toward the end of a sequence, and the right side actions which

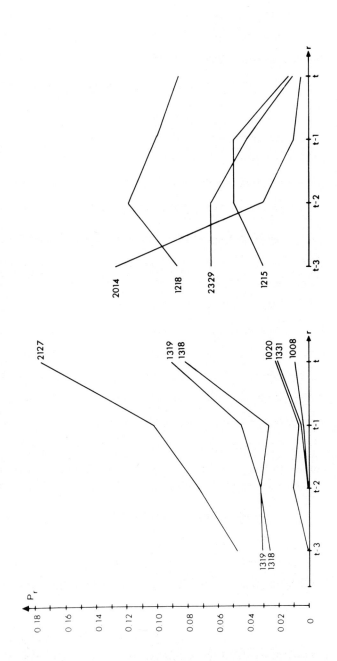

Fig. 5. Statistical analysis of all actions following more than 1200 stimulations to one animal. Relative frequency p_r of the occurrence of certain specific actions at various places in in the chain of events. The first two digits in the four-digit number refer to animals (No. 1 – dominant male; No. 2 subordinate male; No. 3 – all females), the last two digits refer to the behavioural units whose function is analysed. (Further explanation in the test.) (After Maurus and Pruscha, 1972.)

were less frequent toward the end.   The actions on the left occur
more frequently at the end of a sequence than at any other position in
the sequence. These are actions which terminate a sequence very frequently either by a submissive gesture if a lower-ranking animal is
the sender or by a dominance gesture if the top animal is the sender.

Actions on the right were less frequent at the end of a sequence
than at other positions and thus were frequently followed by other actions. We can conclude that actions which terminate a sequence and
actions which do not are functionally different.

We now look at those situations where behavioural unit No. 18
is involved. This is genital display as described before. On the left,
we see action 1318: the dominant monkey displayed towards the females. The frequency of this behaviour increased sharply, that is to
say, genital display frequently terminated a sequence when this signal
was directed from the dominant animal towards females. On the right
we see action 1218, which was less frequent at the end. In this case
of genital display from the dominant towards the submissive animal
the action usually did not terminate the sequence and was thus followed
by other actions. Here we can conclude that the signal function of
genital display differs, depending upon the sex of the recipient.

AUDITORY MODE OF COMMUNICATION

Among the many social signals of squirrel monkeys, we have
considered only one so far, namely genital display that is visually
perceived. However, an equally important aspect of the total communication system, at least in the squirrel monkey and possibly in most
primates, is auditory communication. In 1962, Rowell and Hinde were

the first to demonstrate the significance of vocal communication by the
rhesus monkey. They distinguish two major groups of calls, noise-
like calls and clear, vowel-like calls. Eight calls of the first group
are heard in various forms of agonistic behaviour and four calls in a
"friendly" context of cohesive behaviour. Some of the noise-like calls
express differential degrees of threatening and are partly dependent
upon the rank of the sender. In contrast to the high variability in specific calls of rhesus monkeys and most Old World monkey, the vocal
repertoire of the squirrel monkey consists of 26 to 30 rather discrete
calls which can be arranged systematically in groups of calls based
upon their physical characteristics. In an earlier study we made a
first attempt to show that calls of similar shape appear to have similar functions. We used four methods to investigate the functions of
the signal values of the calls. First, whenever possible, the calls
were elicited repeatedly by well-defined visual stimuli. Second, vocal
and motor behaviour patterns were elicited by playbacks of tape recordings of calls. Third, an animal's motivational state was varied,
and the accompanying vocal behaviour was recorded. Fourth, types
of calls were correlated with the social role and status of the emitters
and receivers of calls within the group (Winter, Ploog and Latta, 1966).

More recently we have been studying the functions of calls
through the use of electrical brain stimulation. In an elaborate study
the whole brain (including the cortex and excluding the cerebellum)
was explored. The majority of naturally occurring calls could be
elicited reliably and repeatedly in specific brain sites using implanted
electrodes and with the monkey sitting comfortably in a chair (Jürgens
and Ploog, 1970). The electrically evoked calls were classified into
eight fundamental types, which are schematically represented in the

following figure.

Figure 6: cackling calls are frequently heard and make up a
substantial proportion of the total vocal output of a group. This type
of call has been found in situations characterised by general aggressiveness and excitement; it is usually uttered by several animals simultaneously. Growling has been interpreted as an expression of directed
aggressiveness, for it often occurs in connection with specific dominance gestures of the vocalising animal. Chirping calls, which are the
most frequently heard calls under natural conditions, probably aid contact and group cohesion; furthermore, they seem to be performed particularly when the attention of the animals has been attracted by new
events. Trilling has been interpreted as a call whose function is to
maintain minimum distances between individuals; it probably also
serves to focus the attention of other group members on the emitter.
Moreover, trilling is strongly associated with all situations concerning feeding. Quacking is a typical call of irritation and expresses a
state ranging between uneasiness and threatening behaviour. Shrieking, finally, represents the highest degree of excitement.

NEUROANATOMICAL SUBSTRATES OF BEHAVIOUR

Without going into anatomical details and considerations, the
cerebral substrates for cackling and growling can be shown to give
a general impression of the specificity of the vocal system and its
correlation with limbic structures and their thalamic, hypothalamic
and midbrain connections. Furthermore, it is noteworthy that the
brain structures that mediate these calls, especially the amygdala,
the stria terminalis, the hypothalamus, and the midbrain periventri-

Fig. 6. Schematic presentation of eight fundamental vocalization types according to which all electrically elicited vocalizations were classified. (Jürgens, U. and D. Ploog, 1970)

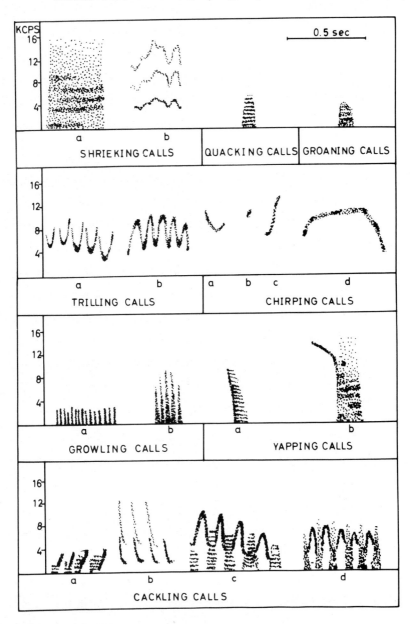

cular gray, are also associated with attack and defence behaviour.
Moreover, most structures that are shown to mediate vocalizations are
known to yield other behavioural or autonomic responses, including
genital responses (MacLean and Ploog, 1962; Jürgens, Maurus, Ploog
and Winter, 1967). The latter are of special interest in the context of
this contribution. For genital display, as mentioned before, is frequently accompanied by two types of vocalization - growling in an aggressive
context and chirping (especially in the form of peeping) in a cohesive
context.

Fig. 7 (1) shows schematically the anatomical substrate from
which cackling is elicitable. It leads from the caudal end of the periaqueductal gray through the periventricular gray of the diencephalon.
At the level of the inferior thalamic peduncle the system branches off
in three components: the first follows the inferior peduncle dorsally
toward the anteromedial thalamic nucleus; the second follows the inferior peduncle ventrolaterally into the amygdala and from there through
the external capsule and uncinate fasciculus to the rostroventral temporal cortex; the third follows the anterior thalamic radiation along
the ventromedial border of the internal capsule into the ventromedial
orbital cortex and the precallosal cingulate gyrus.

Fig. 7 (2) shows the system for growling calls that partly over-
laps the cackling system but also has its own extensions, e.g. into the
area ventralis tegmenti of Tsai and via the medial forebrain bundle into
the lateral hypothalamus. At the level of the inferior thalamic peduncle,
another important branch from the cackling system leads into the pre-
optic region just anterior to the anterior commissure, turns to the
stria terminalis, and follows these fibres into the amygdala. The distribution of the growling calls is essentially identical with that of the

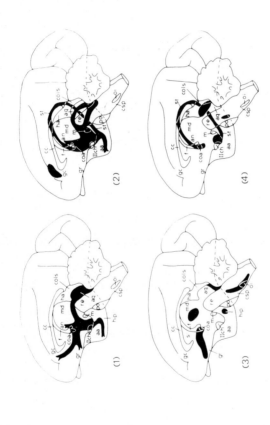

Fig. 7. General (sagittal) view of the cerebral system (in black) yielding vocalizations: (1) cackling calls, (2) growling calls, (3) chirping and trilling calls, (4) quacking and shrieking calls. (Jürgens, U. and D. Ploog, 1970; Jürgens, U., 1970.)

Abbreviations: aa, area anterior amygdalae; an, nucleus anterior; aq, substantia grisea centralis; cc, corpus callosum; coa, commissura anterior; cols, colliculus superior; csp, tractus corticospinalis; f, fornix; gc, gyrus cinguli; gr, gyrus rectus; ha, nucleus habenularis; hip, hippocampus; m, corpus mamillare; md, nucleus medialis dorsalis thalami; oi, nucleus olivaris inferior; po, griseum pontis; re, formatio reticularis tegmenti; st, stria terminalis, II ch, chiasma nervi optici.

hissing and growling of cats, with the amygdala, stria terminalis, per-
fornical hypothalamus, periaqueductal gray, and tegmentum as mediating structures.

Other groups of calls, such as chirping, trilling, quacking and
shrieking, are represented not in continuous systems but in circumscribed areas only. For example, the chirping calls, which aid contact and group cohesion, are elicitable in the subcallosal gyrus and
medioventral caudatum region, the midline thalamus, the rostral hippocampus, the caudal periaqueductal gray, and along the caudal spino-
thalamic tract (Fig. 7 (3)). Shrieking calls, which express a high degree
of excitement, are elicitable in the stria terminalis and its bed nucleus,
in the ventral hypothalamus and in a small section of the medial lem-
niscus (Fig. 7 (4)).

Knowledge about the cerebral substrates from which specific
calls can be elicited will help us further with the functional analysis of
vocal signals since it will now be possible in principle, though not quite
yet technically, to study vocal behaviour in the communal situation
under experimental conditions (Maurus and Szabolcs, 1971). What was
mentioned about the dominance gestures and other visually perceived
motor signals also holds for the vocal gestures perceived by hearing.
They also can be elicited at any time at the will of the experimenter.
At present it is quite true, of course, that the elicited social signal -
be it visual or auditory - occurs at the "wrong moment" most of the
time, if not always; that is, it occurs out of the monkeys' context of
communication. However, the experiments have shown that the monkeys' reaction to the evoked signals appeared as if the "out of context"
interference was originated from inside the group, that is from the
stimulated animal. In many ways one may compare this type of

experiment with dummy experiments on animals other than primates.
As in dummy experiments, with our method one can upset the continuous
flow of behavioural events and then provoke a reaction which restores a
balanced state of the group by means of natural communication processes.

Future research is aimed at the possibility of triggering social
signals in an appropriate context and thus establishing a feedback system between the ongoing natural communication processes and the
elicited test signals fed in by radio-stimulation (Maurus et al. 1970,
1972). From the technical point of view, however, we have a long way
to go.

REFERENCES

Castell, R. and D. Ploog (1967). Zum Sozialverhalten der Totenkopfaffen (Saimiri sciureus): Auseinandersetzung zwischen zwei
Kolonien. Z. Tierpsychol. 24, 625-641.

Hopf, S. (1970). Report on a hand-reared squirrel monkey (Saimiri
sciureus). Z. Tierpsychol. 27, 610-621.

Hopf, S. (1971). New Findings on the ontogeny of social behaviour in
the squirrel monkey. Psychiatrica, Neurologica, Neurochirur-
gica (Amsterdam) 74, 21-34.

Jürgens, U. (1970). Cerebral stimulation by remote control - a new
method in experimental behavioural research. Image 38, 2-8.

Jürgens, U., M. Maurus, D. Ploog and P. Winter (1967). Vocalization in the squirrel monkey (Saimiri sciureus) elicited by brain
stimulation. Exp. Brain Res. 4, 114-117.

Jürgens, U. and D. Ploog (1970). Cerebral representation of vocalization in the squirrel monkey. Exp. Brain Res. 10, 532-554.

MacLean, P.D. and Ploog, D.W. (1962). Cerebral representation of
penile erection. J. Neurophysiol. 25, 29-55.

Maurus, M. (1967). A new telestimulation technique for the study of social behavior of the squirrel monkey. In: Progress in Primatology. First Congr. of the Intern. Primatological Society, Frankfurt 1966. Stuttgart: G. Fischer.

Maurus, M. (1967). Neue Fernreizapparatur für kleine Primaten. Naturwissenschaften 54, 593.

Maurus, M. and D. Ploog (1969). Motor and vocal interactions in groups of squirrel monkeys, elicited by remote-controlled electrical brain stimulation. Recent Advances in Primatology 3, 59-63. Proc. 2nd Congr. Primatol. Atlanta 1968, Karger, Basel and New York.

Maurus, M. and D. Ploog (1971). Social signals in squirrel monkeys: analysis by cerebral radio stimulation. Exp. Brain Res. 12, 171-183.

Maurus, M. and H. Pruscha (1972). Quantitative analyses of behavioural sequences elicited by automated telestimulation in squirrel monkeys. Exp. Brain Res. 14, 372-394.

Maurus, M. and J. Szabolcs (1971). Kleinstsender für die Übertragung von Affenlauten. Naturwissenschaften 58, 273-274.

Maurus, M., H. -G. Peetz and U. Jürgens (1970). Elektronische Lauterkennungsschaltung zur automatischen Steuerung von Fernreizversuchen an Totenkopfaffen (Saimiri sciureus), Naturwissenschaften 57, 141.

Maurus, M., A. Höhne, H. -G. Peetz, and J. Wanke (1972). Technical requirements for the recording of significant social signals in squirrel monkey groups. Physiology and Behaviour, 8, 969-971.

Ploog, D. (1963). Vergleichende quantitative Verhaltens studien an zwei Totenkopfaffen-Kolonien. Z. Morph. Anthrop. 53, 92-108.

Ploog, D. (1967). The behavior of squirrel monkeys (Saimiri sciureus) as revealed by sociometry, bioacoustics, and brain stimulation. In: S. A. Altmann (ed.), Social Communication among Primates. The University of Chicago Press, Chicago, Illinois. pp. 149-184.

Ploog, D. (1969). Early communication processes in squirrel monkeys. In: R. J. Robinson (ed.), Brain and Early Behaviour. Development in the Fetus and Infant. Academic Press, London, pp 269-298.

Ploog, D. W., J. Blitz and F. Ploog (1963). Studies on social and sexual behavior of the squirrel monkey (Saimiri sciureus). Folia primatol. 1, 29-66.

Ploog, D., S. Hopf and P. Winter (1967). Ontogenese des Verhaltens von Totenkopfaffen (Saimiri sciureus). Psychol, Forsch. 31, 1-41.

Ploog, D. W. and P. D. MacLean (1963). Display of penile erection in squirrel monkey (Saimiri sciureus). Anim. Behav. 11, 32-39.

Rowell, T. E. S. and R. A. Hinde (1962). Vocal communication by the rhesus monkey. Proc. Zool. Soc. London 2, 279-294.

Winter, P., D. Ploog and J. Latta (1966). Vocal repertoire of the squirrel monkey (Saimiri sciureus), its analysis and significance. Exp. Brain Res. 1, 359-384.

SEXUAL BEHAVIOUR OF MALE PRIMATES AND

THE ROLE OF TESTOSTERONE

Richard P. Michael, Margo Wilson* and T. M. Plant

Department of Psychiatry, **
Emory University
Atlanta
Georgia 30322

** The original research described here was conducted at The Primate Behaviour Research Laboratories, Bethlem Royal Hospital, Beckenham, Kent.

* Present address: Department of Psychology, University of Toronto.

I INTRODUCTION

The majority of studies on the neuroendocrine bases of behaviour have been in rodents or other sub-primate mammals and, until
quite recently, investigations in primates have languished. This situation is now being corrected but, except in the rhesus monkey, data are
extremely fragmentary and there is a real need to widen the base of our
investigations by acquiring quantitative information on the behaviour of
a range of related primate species. This need for comparative studies
is particularly pressing in regard to the male where data are almost
completely lacking. Little is known, in fact, about the causation of sexual behaviour in male primates including man, although it is generally
thought that the secretory activity of the testis plays a significant role,
as it is also thought to do in the causation of male aggression. It seems
extraordinary, therefore, that there are no systematic studies in the
literature on the behavioural effects of castration and hormone replacement treatment in anthropoid primates. The view has been put forward,
especially for the male, that increasing encephalization during phylo-
genesis is associated with a corresponding decrease in the role of hormonal factors on behaviour, but until the hiatus in our knowledge is
made good, the argument can have little scientific basis. Similarly,
the behavioural events associated with puberty in male primates have
been little studied. In female mammals, puberty is signalled by the
occurrence of vaginal opening, the first ovulation or the menarche, but
the situation is less clear in males, particularly in primates, where
penile erections and intromissions are observed in juveniles. In our
studies, we have therefore used the first occasion of intromission and
ejaculation, with recovery of motile sperm by vaginal lavage, as the

criterion of behavioural puberty in the male rhesus monkey. Now that sensitive and specific competitive protein binding methods and radio-immunoassay methods are available for measuring steroid and protein hormones in plasma, rapid advances may be anticipated in our under-standing of the physiology of male puberty and also of the endocrine de-terminants of behaviour in the adult.

II PATTERNS OF SEXUAL BEHAVIOUR OF
ADULT MALE PRIMATES

The Primate Order provides an extremely diverse group of animals including, for example, the very small lesser mouse lemur of Madagascar which is nocturnal and has a loose social organisation of a few individuals and the large savanna baboon of Africa, which occurs in highly organised groups of up to as many as 200 individuals. For the purpose of this review, the phylogenetic approach has been adopted and the Prosimians, including the tree shrews whose classification as a primate is in some doubt, have been discussed first. The anthropoid primates have been grouped, in the usual manner, into New World monkeys, Old World monkeys and the Apes. Generally, in discussing male copulatory behaviour in a particular genus or species an attempt has been made to give a brief description of distribution, social organi-sation, the female reproductive cycle and seasonal changes in sexual activity in order to add perspective.

1. Prosimians

Tupaiidae

While these species are distributed throughout South East Asia,

most information on their behaviour and social organisation has been
obtained in the laboratory (Conaway and Sorenson, 1966; Sorenson &
Conaway, 1968; Martin 1968). With the possible exception of the
mountain tree shrew, Tupaia montana, the basic social unit appears to
consist of an adult male and female together with their young. In captivity, the social unit of the common tree shrew, T. glis, is the family,
but it is short-lived because of rapid maturation of the young and aggression between animals of the same sex. In free-ranging T. montana in
Borneo, however, social units of 8 - 12 animals were found. There is
no evidence for menstruation, an oestrous cycle or spontaneous ovulation; however, a post-partum oestrus lasting from 3 - 24 hours has
frequently been observed (Martin, 1968). A receptive female makes
short, darting runs which maintain her at a distance of a few feet from
the pursuing male. During mating the male licks the female's vulva,
which is exposed by tail deflection, mounts and takes a grip on the
female's neck with his jaws. The forelimbs are placed round the female's haunches and, during the female's lordosis response, intromission occurs with a series of pelvic thrusts terminating in ejaculation.
After dismounting each animal grooms its genitalia, and up to a dozen
intromissions with ejaculation may occur during the period of oestrus.
Another reproductive behaviour is the stereotyped courtship "dance" of
the predominantly terrestrial T. tana during which the male circles
about the female while vocalising. In a group of mixed species (T.
gracilis, T. tana, T. chinensis and T. longipes) studied in captivity,
males of the latter two species restricted their mounting attempts to
females of their own species. Although females appeared to tolerate
mounting attempts by alien males, intromission did not occur because
of differences in size and in mounting posture. A linear dominance

hierarchy among males was established in captive mountain tree shrews and the majority of copulations were made by the dominant male. There is evidence for seasonal breeding by captive T. glis and T. longipes with a birth peak in the summer in the United States, but no seasonal breeding was observed in T. belangeri in Germany. In Malaya, mean testicular weights of T. glis and T. minor were highest in spring and early summer; 1.60g and 0.54g for April–June compared with 0.81g and 0.20g for October–December in these two species (Harrison, 1955).

Lemuridae

The lemurs are confined to Madagascar and field studies have shown that their social organisation differs considerably in different genera (Petter, 1965; Jolly, 1966). In Phaner, Microcebus and Cheirogaleus there is a loose social organisation, while the black lemur, Lemur macaco, the ring-tailed lemur, L. catta, the mongoose lemur, L. mongoz and the red-bellied lemur, L. rubriventer, occur in small troops and the ruffed lemur, L. variegatus, and the grey gentle lemur, Hapalemur griseus, are found in family groups. . In the greater dwarf lemur, C. major, there is a 1 - 3 day period of oestrus with vaginal opening and 30-day polyoestrous cycles occur during the breeding season (Petter-Rousseaux, 1964). During oestrus, the male mounts the female, which usually lies with her belly close to a branch, by holding her with his forelimbs and grasping her ankles with his feet. Mounts last 2-3 minutes and are repeated several times at approximately 10-minute intervals but the numbers of ejaculations have not been documented. The mating pattern of the lesser mouse lemur , M. murinus, is closely similar to that described for Cheirogaleus and the 2 - 5 day oestrous period can be recognised by vaginal opening and swelling of the genitalia. Free-living troops of L. catta consist of 12-24 members in which females predominate (Jolly, 1966). Oestrous females are readily identified by pink and swollen genitalia but are sexually receptive for only a few hours when the vaginal epithelium is maximally cornified (Evans & Goy, 1968). Both free-living and individually caged laboratory females show oestrous synchrony and there is a clearly defined breeding season. As this approaches, a marked increase in aggression between males occurs, they emit high squeaking "spat" calls, and vigorous chasing and fighting develops with the males slashing each other with their canines. Increased male aggression is associated with increased marking behaviour: the palms of the hands are rubbed on branches and the tail is pulled between and arm and chest so that it picks up secretions from the brachial and antebrachial glands. Males face each other and wave their scented tails over their heads in the so-called "stink-fights". Females become attractive to males before they become receptive and males follow females, investigate their genitalia, and attempt to mount before females are fully receptive. When in oestrus, females either expose their anogenital region by standing with hind legs fully extended and tail fully forward, or crouch and show a lordosis posture. As with rodents, lordosis can be elicited during oestrous by manual stimulation of the lumbar region and perineum. The male mounts by wrapping his arms round the female's waist and gripping the female's hind legs with his feet. In the wild, copulation begins with the approach of two males towards a female, the eventual mate chasing and stink-fighting with his rival throughout the copulatory sequence; this consists of 3-12 mounts with or without intromission and thrusting. In captive pairs, however, copulation is quite brief, consisting of a mount with 2-7 episodes of pelvic thrusting, each episode consisting of 3-5 pelvic thrusts. Several ejaculations occur during the 4-10 hours the female is receptive and during this period a brief consort relation may be established. In the Lemuridae, breeding is seasonal. Mating in M. murinus occurs from September to January with spermatogenesis and an increase in testicular size beginning in July. Breeding occurs from April to June in L. m. macaco, L. m. fulvus, L. mongoz, L. rubriventer, L. catta, and from May to July in the sportive lemur. Lepilemur mustelinus, (Petter-Rousseaux, 1964; Petter, 1965; Jolly, 1966). Penile erections have been observed from one week prior to the onset of mating until the end of the short mating season, and seasonal fluctuations in androgen production have been reported in captive male L. catta as indicated by changes in plasma testosterone levels (Evans & Goy, 1968).

Indriidae and Daubentoniidae

Like the Lemuridae, the Indriidae and Daubentoniidae are found only in Madagascar and very few data are available on their reproductive biology. Verreaux's sifaka, Propithecus verreauxi, appears to be seasonally polyoestrous with four 6-week cycles between January and March (Petter 1965; Jolly, 1966), but patterns of copulatory behaviour have not been described.

Lorisidae

In contrast to the latter two families, the Lorisidae are widely distributed throughout Africa, India and South East Asia. All lorisoid primates are nocturnal, but captivity studies have provided useful information on their reproductive behaviour (Buettner-Janusch, 1964; Manley, 1966; Ioannou, 1966; Butler, 1964, 1967; Doyle, Pelletier &

Bekker, 1967; Doyle, Andersson & Bearder, 1971; Roberts, 1971). In
the bushbaby, Galago senegalensis, the oestrous cycle is 29-39 days,
and oestrus is characterised by vaginal opening, swelling and reddening of the external genitalia: vaginal smears are fully cornified for
periods of 7-10 days. Under reversed light cycle conditions, sexual
receptivity in G. s. moholi is maintained for about 2 days but male
interest in females appears to continue throughout the year. In the
thick-tailed galago, G. crassicaudatus, there are no marked seasonal
changes in the external appearance of males, and in feral male G. s.
senegalensis in the Sudan there was no histological evidence of seasonal
changes in the testes. In a captive colony of G. s. moholi in South
Africa, one of three males established dominance and monopolised
oestrous females (Doyle & Bekker, 1967). At the onset of oestrus,
females permit genital examination by males, the vulva opens and
there is a conspicuous white secretion. Olfactory and marking behaviour increases, males urinate into their cupped hands and thereafter
rub their feet on their hands. The male makes low clucking calls and
mounts by wrapping his forelimbs round the female's waist while pressing his chin firmly against the back of her neck, and makes a loud
vocalisation terminating in a whistle. Periods of intense sexual activity with chasing and frequent mounts of short duration (10-50 sec.)
alternate with periods of less intense activity with up to 30 min. between mounts: intromission and ejaculation probably occurs in these
latter periods during mounts of longer duration (6-8 min.) (Doyle et
al., 1967). Females become receptive from March onwards, giving
birth between July and September, when there is a post-partum oestrus
with a second birth peak between November and January which is not
followed by oestrus. In the Sudan, feral G. s. senegalensis showed

mating peaks between November and January and again in August but, as mentioned, seasonal changes in testicular activity are not marked.

There are few data available on the reproductive behaviour of the remaining lorisoid primates, potto, Perodicticus, slow loris Nycticebus, angwantibo, Arctocebus and slender loris, Loris, because breeding in captivity is difficult. All four genera are polyoestrous and the females' external genitalia redden and swell at intervals of 34-47 days. The receptive female of the slow-moving lorisoids (potto, slow loris, angwantibo, slender loris) suspends herself upside-down on a branch in a way that appears to be a sexual invitation. The male then investigates the genitalia and climbs on the back of the female so that intromission occurs with both partners upside-down (Manley - personal communication). Oestrus is brief, lasting only a few hours in some species. There is a single ejaculation and a large, visible copulatory plug is deposited which hardens rapidly into the consistency of firm wax and possibly prevents subsequent intromissions. Seasonal breeding has not been established in Perodicticus, Nycticebus and Arctocebus, however, the female L. tardigradus lydekkerianus comes into oestrus in winter and late summer in India, and increased seminal vesicle weights have been reported in May and December (Ramakrishna & Prasad, 1967). These weight increases did not coincide very precisely with periods of oestrus as determined by vaginal smearing.

Tarsiidae

Tarsiers are generally found in pairs on islands of the Malay Archipelago but are difficult to breed in captivity. Maximum vaginal cornification lasts for about 24 hr and recurs at approximately 24-day intervals (Catchpole & Fulton, 1943). Sexual activity in a pair of captive animals was associated with vocalisation and self-grooming by both members of the pair, and with increased urine marking by the male which persistently attempted to lick the female's genitalia (Harrison, 1963): however, copulation was only observed once.

2. New World Monkeys (Platyrrhina)

Callithricidae

This small family of South American platyrrhines consists of five genera of marmosets and tamarins: they live in small, territorial family troops in which the male and the female establish their dominance over the other young adults. As a result the latter are driven away as they attain sexual maturity (Epple, 1967; Christen, 1968). In the wild, the red-handed tamarin, Saguinus midas, is found in groups of 2-7 individuals that defend their territory (Thorington, 1968a). Marmosets breed quite well in captivity but there are few data on the oestrous cycle because, apart from the occurrence of copulation, there are few visible signs of oestrus (Epple, 1970). In captivity, male common marmosets, Callithrix jacchus, show sexual interest in the female 3 days after parturition and mating occurs 4-7 days later when the female has become fully receptive. Mounting and intromission is preceded by a courtship display in which the male and female follow one another about with their backs arched and limbs fully extended, activity that is associated with marked piloerection. This display is interrupted by scent marking when both partners drag their anogenital regions along a branch and also deposit drops of urine. The males make a characteristic lip-smacking approach to receptive females in which the tongue is moved rapidly in and out of the mouth, and females respond by crouching and making similar lingual gestures. Their tongues make contact and there is much facial and genital licking. The male then mounts the crouching female, clasps her waist and makes about 10 rapid intromitted pelvic thrusts before ejaculating; the lingual movements continue throughout the mount. The courtship display of Geoffroy's tamarin, S. geoffroyi, differs from that of the common marmoset in that the arched back display and licking is not observed. Instead, the female repeatedly wipes her tail across her genitalia, the male then takes hold of it and sniffs it intensively. Captive male pinchés, S. oedipus, mount by clasping the female's flanks and occasionally the female's hind legs with their feet. Intromission is prompt and copulation may be as brief as a few seconds (Hampton, Hampton & Landwehr, 1966). In this species, birth peaks have been noted in captivity from January to March but there are no good data to indicate seasonal breeding in other tamarins and marmosets.

Cebidae

The squirrel monkey, Saimiri sciureus, has been studied extensively in the laboratory (Rosenblum, Nathan, Nelson & Kaufman, 1967; Latta, Hopf & Ploog, 1967; Castellanos & McCombs, 1968; Clewe, 1969; Hutchinson, 1970; Srivastava, Cavazos & Lucas, 1970) and in the wild (DuMond & Hutchinson, 1967; Baldwin, 1968, 1971; Thorington, 1968b). The oestrous cycle is variously reported as having a mean of between 7 and 13 days, but the data are highly variable. Receptivity varies from a few hours to a few days and is associated with vaginal cornification and sometimes with a visible swelling of the external genitalia. Under free and semi-free conditions, males gain weight during the breeding season and the pelage becomes thicker when they are said to be "fatted". In this condition, males are aggressive, highly vocal and participate in mating activity, and there is an increase in testicular size with active spermatogenesis. Among adult males a linear dominance hierarchy is established during the mating season which can be determined by the frequency of highly ritualised penile displays (Ploog, Blitz & Ploog, 1963; Ploog & MacLean, 1963). Males that exhibit these displays more frequently are victorious in fights but not necessarily the most frequent copulators. Sub-dominant males also gain access to receptive females but have a less excitable and aggressive approach to them. Pre-copulatory activity by males includes leaping backwards and forwards between branches near the females and "silent vocalisation". The outcome of the male's approach is determined primarily by the female's behaviour: a non-receptive female reacts aggressively while a receptive one lags behind the troop and initiates mounting by presenting its anogenital region towards the male. Under free-ranging conditions, successful copulation involves temporary separation of the consort pair from the group. The male mounts the female by grasping her waist with his hands and the backs of her legs with his feet. Intromission occurs after a few rapid thrusting movements and from 1-15 slower pelvic thrusts ensue. The mating sequence, which comprises 10-25 mounts, may last from 6-20 minutes and terminates in a final ejaculatory mount. During the mounting series the partners frequently look at each other, display their genitals and vocalise. The frequency of urine washing, a behavioural pattern quite similar to that described for the galago, increases conspicuously. Ejaculation can be identified by a pause in the thrusting and maintenance of a tense copulatory posture: it is followed by mutual and self-licking and removal of ejaculate from the genital area. Captive and free-living squirrel monkeys both show a 3-month mating season but its timing depends on geographical location: in Peru mating occurs from July to September; in Florida from December to March; in Tennessee from February to March; and in New York and Munich from March to July.

The copulatory behaviour of the squirrel monkey is not typical for the Cebidae in general. In the night monkey, Aotus trivirgatus, and in the dusky titi, Callicebus moloch, copulation is not preceded by a display but there is increased inspection of the female's genitalia (Moynihan, 1964; 1966; Mason, 1966). In Aotus, ejaculation typically occurs during the first mount after some 3-4 thrusts. There have been several studies of free-ranging captive spider monkeys but copulation in Ateles has been described only recently (Klein, 1971). In the long-haired spider monkey, A. belzebuth, and the black-handed spider monkey, A. geoffroyi, the male "mounts" by sitting behind the female, placing his legs over her thighs, and grasping the branch upon which the female is sitting with his feet. By this means the female is "locked" in a dorso-ventral posture which may be peculiar to Ateles since it has not been described for any other species. A few rapid thrusts precede intromission, the intromitted ones being deeper and slower (1 per min.). As a consequence, intromission is maintained for a prolonged period before ejaculation. Changes in the females' external genitalia are not sufficiently prominent to provide an indication of oestrus, nor were specific female invitations observed. However, olfactory cues may be important in this species because males frequently manipulated the genitalia of females, both manually and orally, and sniffed or licked their hands thereafter. Reproductive activity and births in both wild and captive spider monkeys do not appear to show any seasonal fluctuations (Carpenter, 1935). The mantled howler monkey, Alouatta villosa, is

found in groups of up to 45 animals and they appear unsuited to captivity.
In field studies, both males and females initiate sexual interaction by
rapidly moving the tongue in and out of the mouth (Carpenter, 1934;
Altmann, 1959; Bernstein, 1964). The female crouches and the male
mounts by grasping the female's waist with his hands and, quite frequently, a branch with his tail. There is a series of mounts, each with
from 8-28 pelvic thrusts, but the number of ejaculations is not known.
Sexual receptivity lasts 3-4 days without any obvious changes in the
external genitalia. There is no good evidence for a mating season but
some indication of a winter peak in the frequency of births. In the remaining Cebidae, descriptions of copulatory behaviour appear to be
lacking.

3. Old World Monkeys (Catarrhina)

Macaques

Macaques are the only genus of catarrhine monkey common to
both Africa and Asia, and a great deal of information on their reproductive biology is available, particularly for the rhesus monkey, Macaca
mulatta. Field studies in India (Southwick, Beg & Siddiqi, 1965;
Prakash, 1962; Lindburg, 1967), and on the Caribbean Islands of Cayo
Santiago, La Cuera and Guayacan (Carpenter, 1942a & b; Altmann,
1962; Conaway & Koford, 1964; Sade, 1964; Kaufmann, 1965; Koford,
1965; Conaway & Sade, 1965; Vandenbergh and Vessey, 1968; Loy,
1970, 1971), have been complemented by systematic studies under
laboratory conditions, (Michael, 1965, 1968, 1971; Michael, Herbert
& Welegalla, 1967; Michael & Saayman, 1967; Michael & Zumpe, 1970):
these have provided a detailed account of sexual activity in the rhesus
monkey. Mating is seasonal and in India and the Caribbean most copu-

lations are observed during autumn and early winter. An annual variation in male sexual performance has been described in our colony in London with a winter peak in the frequency of ejaculations (Michael & Keverne, 1971). Under free-ranging conditions, there are seasonal changes in testicular size, in spermatogenesis and in the colouration of the sexual skin. Although associated with annual variations in mating activity, these changes have not been correlated, to date, with changes in plasma testosterone levels, nor were the latter related to the season at which plasma was collected from laboratory males (Resko, 1967). In contrast to prosimians and platyrrhines, several Old World species have an external menstruation, and in the rhesus monkey the cycle is about 28 days. Unless interrupted by pregnancy, menstrual cycles continue regularly for some eight months of the year, but from June to September there is a period of summer amenorrhoea (Corner, 1945; van Wagenen, 1945; Keverne & Michael, 1970). Sexual activity is not restricted to any one part of the menstrual cycle but, despite this, there are marked fluctuations in the amount of sexual behaviour, the highest levels being encountered near mid-cycle. In many pairs, the frequency of mounting and ejaculation by the male rhesus under laboratory conditions shows rhythmic variations from cycle to cycle, and these depend upon the phase of the partner's menstrual cycle: however, this aspect of their behaviour will not be discussed further here. The male mounts the female by grasping her waist with his hands and the backs of her legs immediately above the ankle with his feet. Copulation consists of 1-20 mounts, initiated by either sex, each mount usually being associated with intromission and from 1-15 rapid pelvic thrusts. The series of mounts terminates in a mount in which ejaculation occurs: this is characterised by deeper, faster thrusting and there is a pause at the moment of ejaculation associated with contractions of the thigh muscles and sometimes a characteristic facial expression and vocalisation. There are marked quantitative differences in the frequency of ejaculation by different males, in the rate of mounting, and in the rate and numbers of thrusts needed for ejaculation. From 1-7 ejaculations may occur in different males paired with the same females during a standard mating test of 1 hr. In the free-range situation, unlike the limited, dyadic situation in the laboratory, the position of an individual male in the dominance hierarchy of the group is a major factor in determining the formation of consort bonds and the frequency of copulation. In the rhesus colony on Cayo Santiago, four or fewer males, the highest ranking ones in the central hierarchy, had possession of 83-90% of receptive females. The alpha male was responsible for 35% of observed matings whereas when he was second in dominance, in a previous season, he was responsible for 7% of observed matings (Kaufmann, 1965). Social dominance has now been related to plasma testosterone levels (Rose, Holaday and Bernstein, 1971).

The sexual behaviour of the Japanese macaque, M. fuscata, has also been studied extensively under free-ranging conditions (Imanishi, 1957; Tokuda, 1961-62; Nishida, 1966; Hanby, Robertson & Phoenix, 1971). As in the rhesus monkey, there is a distinct mating season from December to March in Japan, and from October to January in the western United States. Although the colour of the males' sexual skin intensifies during the breeding season, there is no evidence for seasonal changes in spermatogenesis. Adult males mount females in a closely similar manner to that described for the rhesus monkey. Copulation consists of a series of 2-30 mounts each with from 1 to 8 pelvic thrusts (rather fewer than the rhesus), the series of mounts terminating in ejaculation. The duration of the mounting series is variable from a few minutes to an hour, with a mean of 6 min. being reported. The social organisation of large troops in Koshima, that were artificially provisioned, consisted of a central core of one dominant and several subdominant adult males, associated with adult females and their young under two years of age. More peripherally was a group of sub-adult and adult males and older juveniles. The central males were responsible for the majority of matings and, in the Oregon colony, the five highest ranking males of a total of twenty-six were responsible for 72% of the observed matings.

Copulation in the pig-tailed monkey, M. nemestrina, is also very similar to that described for the rhesus (Bernstein, 1967; Tokuda, Simons & Jensen, 1968). There is a series of 8-23 (mean about 9) mounts, which may be initiated by either partner, with some 12 intromitted thrusts per mount, terminating in an ejaculatory mount. Numbers of thrusts and also the intermount intervals tend to be greater than in M. fuscata. Ejaculation times are rather longer than in the rhesus monkey, and ejaculation is frequently associated with a facial grimace and a high-pitched vocalisation. Males initiate mounting attempts by a courtship approach with the ears retracted and the lips pushed forward and everted (van Hooff, 1962). The menstrual cycle is 32 days and, in marked contrast to the rhesus monkey, there is a conspicuous swelling of the sexual skin for about 21 days of the cycle: this reaches a maximum during the 10-12 days near mid-cycle. The menses may be slight and vaginal lavage or swabbing is required to determine menstruation accurately in some females. Mating occurs most frequently during the period of sexual skin tumescence and declines sharply with detumescence. There is no evidence for seasonal breeding in this species.

The bonnet monkey, M. radiata, is found in southern India and has been studied both in captivity and in the wild (Simonds, 1965; Kaufman & Rosenblum, 1966; Rahaman & Parthasarathy, 1969; Nadler & Rosenblum, 1969). During the mating season, which extends from October to November in the wild, males examine the females' genitalia frequently, insert their fingers in the vagina, and sniff them before mounting: a similar pattern of behaviour has been described in toque macaques, M. sinica, in Ceylon (Jay, 1965a). In both species, a copious, strong-smelling vaginal discharge occurs during certain days of the menstrual cycle. Mounts are usually initiated by the male as in M. nemestrina; he approaches the female, flips aside her tail, whereupon the latter assumes a presentation posture if receptive. In contrast to most macaques, copulation in the bonnet monkey is generally completed in a single mount with from 5-30 pelvic thrusts (cf. M. arctoides). Although certain high-ranking males assert their dominance over other males in respect of food, this is not observed in respect of mating frequency. In captive bonnet monkey, sperm were found in vaginal lavages almost exclusively near mid-cycle, and males only copulated with ovariectomised females when they received treatment with oestrogen (Hartman, 1938).

In the stump-tailed macaque, M. arctoides, the genitalia of both sexes possess some unusual anatomical features that appear to affect the behaviour patterns. The vaginal orifice is partly obstructed by a mid-dorsal ellipsoid structure, the vestibular colliculus, which protrudes from the roof of the vaginal introitus. The male's penis has an exceptionally long, slender glans (5-7 cm) that is ventrally flattened and tapers towards the tip giving a lanceolate shape that undoubtedly facilitates intromission: the glans in other macaques is dome shaped and about 2.5 cm long. It has been hypothesized that the specialisation of

these structures in M. arctoides prevents hybridization with sympatric
species (Fooden, 1967). Mounts are usually initiated by the male who
flips aside the female's tail and sometimes inserts a finger in the
vagina; the male sniffs his fingers before mounting. Females occasionally initiate mounts by adopting the presentation posture typical of
macaques (Blurton-Jones & Trollope, 1968). As in the bonnet macaque,
copulation consists of a single mount (occasionally two), with many
intromitted thrusts, up to 170 have been reported, terminating in ejaculation (Chevalier-Skolnikoff, 1971). During intromission, the male
lip-smacks with exposed teeth, and this is accompanied by a chattering
and finally a barking vocalisation. At ejaculation, the male bites the
female's back, sometimes causing superficial injury to the skin, and
thereafter the penis characteristically remains intromitted for a few
minutes. A comparison of some indices of sexual activity for macaques
is given in Table I.

Papio

The taxonomy of the baboons is still unsettled (Roth, 1965;
Napier & Napier, 1967; Jolly, 1967; Hill, 1967), and for present purposes the following five species are considered: the chacma baboon,
Papio ursinus, the olive baboon, P. anubis, the yellow baboon, P. cynocephalus, the sacred baboon, P. hamadryas, and the Guinea baboon,
P. papio. Baboons are found in troops of as many as 200 individuals
throughout much of Africa south of the Sahara except for coastal regions
of Nigeria, Ghana, Ivory Coast, and the Congo basin. Data on the copulatory activity of this genus are provided by both field studies and studies on captive colonies: in the chacma baboon (Bolwig, 1959; Hall,
1962; Hall & DeVore, 1965; Saayman, 1970), in the olive baboon

Table I.   Comparison of data on male sexual activity in several related anthropoid

Species	No. of males	No. of ejaculations observed	Condition of female partner	Ejaculations per unit time (mean or range)	No. of mounts to ejaculation (mean or range)	Total no. of intromitted thrusts to ejaculation
M. mulatta	3	60	Oestrogen treated	–	7-9	–
M. mulatta	8	207	Intact	1-4/hr	10.7	–
M. mulatta	6	84	Oestrogen treated	1.9/hr	8.4	32.7
M. mulatta	4	142	Oestrogen treated	2.1/hr	10.9	34.6
M. mulatta	12	272	Intact	2.2/2hr	7.4	61.7
M. fuscata	6	13	Intact	–	17	63.0
M. fuscata	19	648	Intact	–	7.4	–
M. nemestrina	4	–	Intact	–	8.8	–
M. radiata	–	28	Intact	–	1	5-30
M. radiata	5	20	Oestrogen treated	1.5/hr) 1.8/hr)	2.9) 1.4)	14.5) 20.7)
M. arctoides	2	63	Intact	–	1	60-70
P. ursinus	18	–	Intact	–	–	–
P. anubis	3	50	Intact	1.2/hr	2.0	10.9

[1]Ejaculation time = time from 1st mount to 1st ejaculation

[2]Total number of mounts to ejaculation divided by ejaculation time x 60

[3]Total number of thrusts to ejaculation divided by ejaculation time x 60

[4]Refractory period = time from 1st ejaculation to 1st mount of next mounting series

primate species

No. of intromitted thrusts per mount (mean or range)	Ejaculation time (min,[1] mean)	Mounting rate to ejaculation[2] (mean)	Thrusting rate to ejaculation[3] (mean)	Refractory period (min,[4] mean)	Type of study	Authors
-	-	-	-	-	Laboratory	Freedman & Rosvold, 1962
7.8	13.7	96.1	885.8	11.2	Laboratory	Michael & Saayman, 1967
4.7	10.0	67.1	367.2	22.5	Laboratory	Present Study
6.0	8.0	88.3	624.9	19.3	Laboratory	Present Study
8.8	6.3	-	-	-	Laboratory	Missakian et al, 1969
3.7	6.3	-	-	-	Field	Tokuda, 1961-62
1-8	10.0	-	-	-	Captive Colony	Hanby et al, 1971
13.0	-	-	-	-	Captive Colony	Tokuda et al, 1968
5-30	-	-	-	-	Field	Simonds, 1965
19.6	0.1) 4.1) (median)	-	-	24.2) 32.8)	Laboratory	Nadler & Rosenblum, 1969
60-70	2.5	-	-	-	Captive Colony	Chevalier-Skolnikoff, 1971
11.1	-	2.8) 16.3)	-	56	Field	Saayman, 1970
5.8	5.7	111	743	16	Captive Colony	Evans & Michael, unpublished

(Washburn & DeVore, 1961; DeVore, 1965; Hall & DeVore, 1965;
Rowell, 1967), and in the sacred baboon (Kummer, 1968). The menstrual
cycle is generally between 31-35 days with a menstrual flow of about 3
days. Female baboons exhibit well-marked changes in the sexual skin
and tumescence starts a few days after menstruation, reaches a maximum during the middle part of the cycle, and detumescence occurs
more abruptly in the luteal phase (Zuckerman, 1937, 1953; Gillman &
Gilbert, 1946; Hendrickx & Kraemer, 1969). In chacma baboons, consort pairs form when an adult male follows a swollen female to the periphery of the troop. Mounting is initiated by both sexes, the female presents her anogential region to the male, and the male grasps the female's
haunches with both hands. In the mount that follows, the male grasps
the backs of the female's legs with his feet. Copulation consists of a
series of mounts each with 1-20 intromitted thrusts, and the intermount interval varies widely (4-21 min). During intromission, the
female makes a series of short barking calls and, when the male stops
thrusting, she rapidly bounds away from him. Females are mounted
most frequently during the tumescent phase when mating is performed
almost exclusively by dominant males. Juvenile and sub-adult males,
however, mount females most frequently during the early part of the
cycle when the sexual skin begins to inflate. Mating behaviour in the
olive baboon differs conspicuously from that described in the chacma
baboon because ejaculation typically occurs in one to three mounts,
sometimes in a single mount of 6-30 sec, and there is an average of
6 thrusts per mount. Males rarely grimace while copulating, but
females may withdraw vigorously from males and bound away from
them at the termination of thrusting (Michael & Evans - unpublished
observations). Sacred baboons, unlike yellow and olive baboons, live

in one-male groups with from 1-10 females, some 80% of adult males are harem leaders. The male exercises exclusive control over his harem and herds the females by threat behaviour. Mating occurs most frequently in the morning and evening when groups are near their sleeping sites, and males copulate only with females showing maximal sexual skin swelling. There is a variable number of mounts at 3-8 min intervals terminating in ejaculation; they are initiated by both sexes and are similar to those in other papio species. In the olive baboon, a birth peak has been described from October to December in Kenya and, in the sacred baboon, there is a birth peak between May and July in Ethiopia.

Mangabeys

The mangabeys are arboreal, living in dense, high, wet forest in Africa in groups of 9-23 individuals. The grey-cheeked mangabey, Cercocebus albigena, has been studied in the wild (Chalmers, 1968; Jones & Sabater Pi, 1968) and in captivity (Rowell & Chalmers, 1970; Chalmers & Rowell, 1971). The modal menstrual cycle length is 30 days and, as in the baboon, the sexual skin swells near mid-cycle. Ejaculation is generally restricted to the period of maximal swelling which lasts about 5 days. The male mounts the female by putting his hands on the small of her back and grasping her ankles with his feet. Before intromission, pelvic thrusting is gentle but becomes more vigorous thereafter. Ejaculation is completed after a series of mounts and is signalled by rapid vibration of the male's legs, the entire copulatory sequence being conducted in silence and without any facial gestures. There are insufficient data to draw conclusions about seasonal influences on behaviour in this genus.

Guenons

The guenons are a diverse genus of some 23 species distributed widely throughout Africa south of the Sahara. In the vervet monkey, Cercopithecus aethiops, mounts may be initiated by either sex, but only the most dominant males are observed to copulate (Struhsaker, 1967; Gartlan, 1969). The female initiates a mount by crouching, deflecting the tail and looking back over her shoulder at the male. The male mounts by grasping the female's waist with his hands and the backs of her legs with his feet. After a few rapid, shallow thrusts, intromission occurs and ejaculation takes place in a single mount after some 25 deeper, slower thrusts. There is a breeding season determined by local geography and climatic factors; in Amboseli, mating occurs from May to October, while on Lolui Island in Lake Victoria, it occurs from October to May. The diameter of the seminiferous tubules of males introduced to the West Indian Island of St. Kitts is greatest during the winter mating season, but annual fluctuations in the testes of vervets are less marked than in the rhesus (Conaway & Sade, 1969). In the Sykes' monkey, C. albogularis, in the blue monkey, C. mitis, and in De Brazza's monkey, C. neglectus, ejaculation is also completed in a single mount (Booth, 1962). The talapoin monkey , Miopithecus talapoin, one of the smallest Old World monkeys, is potentially useful for laboratory studies because the female shows well-marked changes in the sexual skin during the menstrual cycle (Scruton & Herbert, 1970). Sexual activity is initated by both sexes, is maximal near mid-cycle, and noticeably reduced during the luteal phase. Males initiate mounting by following the female, sniffing her anogenital region, and by flicking aside her tail. Ejaculation is generally completed in a single mount. Free-ranging talapoin monkeys in the Gabon show a mating season between May and August during which time the males are "fatted" (Gautier-Hion, 1968 and personal communication).

Patas monkeys

The patas monkey, Erythrocebus patas, of Uganda occurs in groups containing one adult male and as many as 12 adult females together with their young. Mating has been observed infrequently in the wild, and in a total of 638 hr of observation, only 7 series of mounts with pelvic thrusting were observed in the period between July and September, (Hall, 1965). In captivity, mounts are initiated by both sexes, the male places his hands on either side of the female's abdomen and lifts her into a quadripedal posture, the female initiates by making a cringing, half-run towards the male with her tail drooping. This is accompanied by a toneless vocalisation ("blowing") produced by inflating and deflating the cheek pouches (Hall, Boelkins & Goswell, 1965). The male usually examines the female's anogenital region both maually and olfactorily before mounting. During the mount the male's feet remain on the ground or branch and slow pelvic thrusting continues (1-2 per sec) until ejaculation occurs.

Langurs

The Hanuman langur, Presbytis entellus, of northern India is found in large, multimale troops of up to 120 individuals. Troops in southern India tend to be much smaller and may contain one adult male together with females and their young (Jay, 1965b). Mating behaviour in the Hanuman langur and in the silvered leaf-monkey, P. cristatus, is generally confined to a 5-day period about mid-cycle when the female is receptive, and it consists of a series of mounts terminating in ejacu-

lation (Jay, 1965 b; Sugiyama, Yoshiba & Parthasarathy, 1965;
Bernstein , 1968). During a mount, which is always initiated by the
female presenting her anogenital region to the male, dropping her tail
to the ground and shaking her head, the male grasps the female's
waist with his hands but his feet remain on the ground or branch. Sexually excited males sometimes chase receptive females while making
repeated low-pitched vocalisations. Females do not have any cyclic
sexual skin swelling. Increased sexual activity appears to occur within a troop at times when its social organisation is changing, particularly
when this involves changes in group leadership. Additionally, there is
evidence for a seasonal peak in births, but this is not conspicuous and
appears to vary with geographic locale.

4. Apes

Lesser apes

Under free-ranging conditions in South East Asia, the white-
handed gibbon, Hylobates lar, occurs in small family groups consisting
of an adult male and female together with from 1-4 young (Carpenter,
1940; Ellefson, 1968). The adult pair appears to be monogamous and
stable and, as young males approach maturity, the adult pair becomes
aggressive towards them so that they are forced to the periphery of the
group. Carpenter observed two copulations in the wild and on both
occasions these were initiated by the female who presented her anogenital region to the male which examined the vulva before copulating. More
detailed descriptions of copulation in this lesser ape have been obtained
from studies on captive gibbons (Carpenter, 1940; Ibscher, 1967). The
female usually hangs by her hand from a branch directing her anogenital

region towards the male which swings beneath the female pushing his pelvic region under hers. Because the erect penis of the male gibbon is rather small (about 4 cm), a close juxtaposition of the pelvic regions of the pair is necessary for successful intromission, and the female will reach back with her arm to hold the male close to her body. Pelvic thrusting occurs at a frequency of about 1 per sec, ejaculation occurs in 30 sec. and the pair then separate.   The social organisation of the siamang, Symphalangus syndactylus, is similar to that of the gibbon (Kawabe, 1970), but copulation in this species has not been described in detail and has only been observed infrequently (Koyama, 1971).

Orang-utans

The arboreal orang-utan, Pongo pygmaeus, of Borneo is primarily a solitary animal, and the majority of sub-groups observed consisted of an adult, usually a female, accompanied by dependent young (Davenport, 1967; MacKinnon, 1971; Rodman, 1973). Copulation in the orang-utan has only been observed infrequently in the wild. Seven of the eight matings reported by MacKinnon in the Ulu Segama Reserve in Sabah appeared to involve the "rape" of relatively unreceptive females by aggressive males. The male usually clasped the female by her thighs or round the waist with his prehensile feet but because the female continually appeared to try to escape, intromission was seldom described. A typical sequence of "rape" lasted for about ten minutes and differed from the behaviour observed in captivity where females adapt to their mates and become less timid. For pregnancy to occur, mating must take place in the context of pair-bonding but data from the wild are very sparse.

Chimpanzees

The chimpanzee, Pan troglodytes, has been widely studied both in captivity and in the wild in different habitats throughout its range in West and Central Africa (Kortlandt, 1962; Goodall, 1965; Reynolds & Reynolds, 1965; Itani & Suzuki, 1967; Nishida, 1968; Sugiyama 1968, 1969). Observations on their sexual behaviour have been obtained under both captive and free-living conditions (Yerkes & Elder, 1936; Yerkes, 1939; Young & Yerkes, 1943; Young & Orbison, 1944; van Lawick Goodall, 1968; Albrecht & Dunnett, 1971). The menstrual cycle is about 30 days in length with a menstrual flow of 3 days. Sexual skin swelling is extreme, reaching its maximum during the middle 10 days of the cycle. During the period of sexual skin swelling, the female's social status increases and she is most attractive and receptive to the male. Females may initiate copulation by crouching low in front of the male and presenting their anogential region towards him. The male initiates copulation by means of a courtship display which includes bipedal loco-motion with a swaggering gait, beckoning arm movements, tree leaping and associated gestures - all directed towards the female. The male approaches the female from the rear with an erect penis and "mounts", usually by placing one hand on her back and adopting a squatting posture behind the female with his buttocks almost in contact with the ground. Ejaculation is typically achieved during a single intromission lasting 5-10 sec with up to 20 pelvic thrusts. When ejaculation does not occur during the first intromission it may be repeated. Ejaculation is asso-ciated with a rapid panting vocalisation, resembling a grunt, and lip-smacking by the male, and higher pitched squealing or a scream by the female who frequently looks back at her partner. In captive pygmy

chimpanzees, P. paniscus Schwarz, a ventro-ventral copulatory posture
has also been described (Kirchshofer, 1962). Sexually active males do
not appear to form extended consort bonds with receptive females, the
latter are promiscuous, copulating with several males in the group.
Such activity in anubis baboons, for example, would result in increased
inter-male aggression. During the period of maximum sexual skin
swelling, a female may be accompanied by six or more males, and has
been observed to mate with three different males in a period of 15 minutes. Sexual activity increases during periods of heightened social activity, for example at the time of inter-group encounters when males
make charging displays. At the Gombe Stream Reserve, 70% of the
copulations observed at the feeding site took place when the group first
arrived there. There are no data to indicate seasonal breeding in this
species.

Gorillas

Although the lowland gorilla has now been successfully bred in
several zoos, adequately detailed descriptions of copulatory behaviour
have only recently become available (Hess, 1973 and personal communication). The western lowland gorilla, Gorilla gorilla gorilla, studied
in the Basel Zoo has a menstrual cycle of about 31 days, but data on
menstrual flow are few. There is a well-circumscribed period of sexual receptivity in this species which is of 2-3 days' duration, presumably
near mid-cycle. There is no obvious sexual skin swelling but turgidity
of the external genitalia has been mentioned (Noback, 1939; Eckstein &
Zuckerman, 1956). Before the stage of full receptivity there is a period of about 3 days when there are marked behavioural changes and
also a change in the body odour of the female. During this time the

female displays and orients her posture towards the dominant male.
During periods of receptivity almost all copulations are initiated by the
female and at its height mating occurs at intervals of 30-60 min. Hess
has described several invitational behaviours, including a gesture with
the outstretched, supine hand, and a crouch with the anogenital region
directed towards the male. There is also a supine posture associated
with rhythmic pelvic movements. The mating position is very variable
in this species: ventro-dorsal with the male squatting behind the female,
ventro-ventral with the male squatting in front of the supine female, and
the male may also take the female on his lap with her facing either towards or away from him. Intromission usually lasts 1-2 min and consists of 30-40 pelvic thrusts at a rate of about 2 per sec. During copulation, the female's lips are pressed together, the cheeks are slightly
puffed out and the eyes are closed intermittently; she also utters a
long, vibrating vocalisation. The male's facial expression is similar
but he only vocalises near or at ejaculation. It is unusual to see visible
ejaculate. Data on the sexual behaviour of gorillas in their natural
habitat are extremely few: in more than 450 hr observation on 10
groups of mountain gorilla, Gorilla gorilla beringei, in the Virunga
volcano region of the Congo, only two copulations were observed
(Schaller, 1963). During one, a silver-backed, sub-dominant male
clasped a prone female by the hips at the beginning of copulation and
subsequently by the armpits, nearly covering her back. The couple
remained juxtaposed for a period of about 15 min during which there
were episodes of pelvic thrusting and male vocalisation which became
a roar towards the end of the mating sequence. The other copulation
was initiated by the female which mounted the male. This sequence
lasted for about an hour and consisted of three separate "mounts" with

the female sitting on the male's lap and on each occasion there were over 70 thrusts. There are no adequate data on seasonal breeding.

5. Summary

In attempting to bring together the available data on the sexual behaviour of male primates, the paucity of detailed information and the lack of quantitative, comparative results becomes apparent. There is, nevertheless, an obvious progression from the more stereotyped rodent-like reactions of the lower prosimians to the greater variety of soliciting gestures and postures shown by the Old World monkeys and the Great Apes. Interestingly, for quite closely related species within the macaque and baboon genera, ejaculation may be achieved either in a single mount, sometimes with many intromitted pelvic thrusts, or by means of a series of mounts each with fewer thrusts. The particular form of social organisation of a species may influence the type of consort bonding and also the extent of sexual promiscuity, but it seems to have little direct bearing on the pattern of copulatory activity itself. Where adequate data are available it is clear that the majority of primate species show evidence of seasonal changes in reproductive activity; this should not in itself be taken to imply an exteroceptive causation.

III DEVELOPMENT OF SEXUAL BEHAVIOUR IN MALE PRIMATES

The males of many mammalian species show some components of the fully adult pattern of sexual behaviour well before puberty and, in monkeys and apes where puberty is long delayed, mounting activity between members of the peer age group is commonly observed. Mounting attempts, pelvic thrusting and erections have all been described from

infancy (in C. aethiops, Struhsaker, 1967; in M. radiata, Rahaman &
Parthasarathy, 1969; in P. troglodytes, van Lawick-Goodall, 1968,
1969). When the juvenile stage is reached these behaviours occur more
frequently and more completely (S. sciureus, Ploog, Hopf & Winter,
1967; Baldwin, 1969; C. aethiops, Struhsaker, 1967; P. entellus, Jay,
1965b; M. radiata, Rahaman & Parthasarathy, 1969; Rosenblum &
Nadler, 1971; E. patas, Hall, 1965; P. anubis, Hall and DeVore, 1965;
P. hamadryas, Kummer, 1968; P. ursinus, Saayman, 1970). Juvenile
chimpanzees have been reported occasionally to achieve intromission
during a mount (Goodall, 1968; Albrecht & Dunnett, 1971) as have
baboons. During the sub-adult stage, attempts by male chacma baboons
to form consort relations begin to appear along with the development of
mature copulatory behaviour which includes intromission and ejaculation
(Saayman, 1970).

In the male rhesus monkey a similar pattern of development has
been observed with mounting attempts occurring from as young as 6
weeks of age but more usually appearing between 12–46 weeks (Hinde &
Spencer-Booth, 1967). Adult-like mounting and pelvic thrusting, but
not ejaculation, have been observed in juvenile males (Mason, 1960;
Southwick, Beg & Siddiqi, 1965); erections have been described even
during the third post-natal week (Hines, 1942). The importance of early
social interactions for the development of adequate behaviour patterns
in adulthood has been clearly demonstrated in the well-known studies of
Mason and Harlow (Mason, 1960; Harlow, 1962, 1965; Harlow and
Harlow, 1965). Socially restricted male rhesus monkeys show less
mounting and thrusting activity and less adequate body orientation for
copulation than a control group, and the fertility of socially isolated
males is extremely low. The role of social factors in the ontogeny of

adult behaviour patterns has also received attention from other workers
(Meier, 1965; Missakian, 1969; Rogers and Davenport, 1969). The
available evidence indicates that puberty in the male rhesus monkey
occurs between 3.5 and 4.5 years of age (van Wagenen & Simpson,
1954; Kaufmann, 1965; Meier, 1965; Conaway & Sade, 1965; Sade 1968).
The behavioural changes associated with puberty have been little studied
but, as in the human, puberty is not an abrupt phenomenon but results
from a prolonged period of growth and maturation. There are few systematic data on the development and maturation of patterns of sexual
behaviour in the period immediately following puberty. A description
of the behaviour of male rhesus monkeys in the pre- and post-pubertal
periods is needed to permit comparisons to be made with the behaviour
of adults.

1. Comparison of Sexual Behaviour Before and After Puberty with
That of Adult Males

To study the maturation of behavioural patterns during puberty
in a primate species, a choice must be made between using feral males
of uncertain age and unknown past history and animals whose dates of
birth and histories are known but which have been, as a consequence,
born and reared under artificial conditions in the laboratory. We have
chosen to use animals born and reared in the wild in North India because
they were most likely to provide us with normal behavioural data.
Special care was therefore taken to make an assessment of the age of
the subadults using several somatic measures. We recognised that the
age of an adult male may be important in determining its behaviour, but
here we were primarily interested in the maturation of behaviour patterns during the peri-pubertal period and in a comparison of these with the
behaviour of fully adult males. For this purpose we selected adult males

that were fully mature on the basis of their general appearance, body
weight and dentition.

(i)   Determination of age

Data for the estimation of the ages of sub-adult males and a
comparison with data for the fully adult group are given in Table II.
All sub-adult males were paired on each weekday with an ovariectomised,
oestrogen-treated female until ejaculations were established. On the
day of the first ejaculation the following data were obtained:

1. Body weight - these were also obtained for all animals
   at regular intervals.

2. Testicular size - the length and breadth of each testis
   was measured within the scrotal sac using calipers and
   the sum of these two dimensions was used for comparison with other published data (Sade, 1964; van Wagenen
   & Simpson, 1965) for males of known age.

3. Scrotal skin colouration - this was assessed in a manner
   similar to that described by Vandenbergh (1965) by the
   Munsell Colour Notation system (Munsell, 1929) which
   identifies colour in terms of hue, value and chroma.
   Fifteen Munsell colour cards with hues ranging from 10
   RP to 5R were ranked independently by ten people according to chroma. The card considered by each individual to
   have the weakest colour was assigned the rank of 1 and
   that with the strongest the rank of 15. The rank assigned
   to each card by the ten individuals was averaged to
   provide a mean rank value for that colour card. The
   mean rank value of the Munsell colour card judged to be
   the best match with the colour of the male's scrotal sac

Table II. Criteria for the determination of age in the group of sub-adult male rhesus monkeys

Male number	97	95	102	96	Adult male (range)
Date of 1st test with female	22.4.69	22.4.69	17.11.69	22.4.69	–
Date of 1st ejaculation with female	24.9.69	3.9.69	24.11.69	4.7.69	–
Data at 1st ejaculation:					
1) Body weight (kg)	7.25	7.25	7.00	7.50	8.0 – 12.5*
2) Testis dimensions (mm)	62	63	61	61	79 – 90 *
3) Scrotal skin colour index	1.5	1.5	1.5	2.3	7 – 11 *
4) Canine:incisor ratio	0.75	1.50	1.87	2.83	2.4 – 3.2 *
5) Presence of sperm	+	+	+	+	+ *
Duration between 1st ejaculation and castration (days)	392	163	81	145	–
Data at castration:					
6) Testis weight (g)	10.7	10.6	12.1	23.5	19.3 – 28.2
7) Tubule diameter (μ)	115.9 ± 0.03	99.8 ± 0.03	108.8 ± 0.03	133.4 ± 0.05	120 – 140
Estimated age at first ejaculation (yr)	3 – 4	3 – 4	3 – 4	4 – 5	–

*Data obtained at the start of the study.

skin by two observers under standard conditions of illu-
mination provided the scrotal skin colour index (Table II).

4. Dentition - the lengths of the canine teeth and of the
    incisors were measured and the ratio of these two dimen-
    sions was calculated and compared with other published
    data (Hurme & van Wagenen, 1961) for animals of known
    age.
5. Spermatozoa - immediately following the first ejaculation
    during coitus by sub-adult males, the vaginal contents of
    their partners were collected by lavage and examined
    microscopically for motile sperm.

At the time of castration 81 to 392 days after the establishment
of ejaculation (see Table II), testicular weights and seminiferous tubule
diameters were obtained. The mean diameter of the seminiferous
tubules for the left and right testis of each male was obtained by measuring the diamater of 20 tubules in cross section from 6 representative histological sections (120 tubules for each male). These data were
then compared with those from animals of known age (Conaway & Sade,
1965; van Wagenen & Simpson, 1965).

(ii)   Behavioural observations

All four sub-adult males were held in the colony without being
given access to females for 6 months, and were then paired with three
ovariectomised females receiving 5 μg oestradiol monobenzoate s.c.
per day for periods of between 83-474 days (total 616 tests); their behaviour was followed until ejaculation became established. To provide
the sub-adults with known but different amounts of sexual experience,
testing was stopped after 14 ejaculations (male 102), 39 ejaculations

(male 95), 55 ejaculations (male 96) and 111 ejaculations (male 97) respectively. Six fully adult males were paired with five ovariectomised females also receiving 5 μg oestradiol monobenzoate s.c. per day for periods of between 14-41 days (total 84 tests). Two of these males and two additional males were also paired with two ovariectomised females receiving 10 μg oestradiol monobenzoate s.c. per day for periods of between 24-70 days (total 142 tests). As in the previously reported studies all mating tests were of one hour duration, conducted under standardised conditions, and animals were trained to enter and leave transfer boxes of their own volition so that they could be introduced into and removed from observation cages without being handled (Michael, Herbert & Welegalla, 1966; Michael & Saayman, 1967; Michael, 1968).

(iii)   "Unestablished" copulatory behaviour.

        In these studies we have used the first occurrence of intromission and ejaculation with the recovery of motile sperm from vaginal lavages as the criterion of behavioural puberty. By "unestablished" copulatory behaviour we mean the patterns of sexual activity occurring in tests up to, but not including that in which the first ever ejaculation during coitus took place. Behaviour in tests in which the first ejaculation occurred has been dealt with separately. Behaviour in tests subsequent to that in which the first ejaculation occurred is referred to as "established" copulatory behaviour (see below): it is, however, very different from that of fully mature males.

        When sub-adult males first made mounting attempts, only some features of the typical copulatory posture of adults were observed. Although the male's thrusting movements were oriented towards the hind quarters of the female, the erect penis was not directed accurately

R.P. Michael et al.

Table III. Comparison of the sexual behaviour of sub-adult, male
the first ejaculation occurred.

Male No.	No. of tests	No. of Hand Clasps			No. of Mounts		
		1 hand	2 hands	2 hands + thrusts	1 foot	2 feet

Behaviour in Tests Before First Ejaculation (Unestablished Behaviour)

Male No.	No. of tests	1 hand	2 hands	2 hands + thrusts	1 foot	2 feet
97	101	16	62	6	61	114
95	86	4	14	0	2	13
102	5	0	9	0	1	1
96	43	11	6	0	2	40
Totals	235	31	91	6	66	168

Behaviour in Tests with First Ejaculation

Male No.	No. of tests	1 hand	2 hands	2 hands + thrusts	1 foot	2 feet
97	1	2	1	1	0	45
95	1	0	0	0	0	10
102	1	0	0	8	1	0
96	1	0	2	0	1	5
Totals	4	2	3	9	2	60

Behaviour in Tests After First Ejaculation (Established Behaviour)

Male No.	No. of tests	1 hand	2 hands	2 hands + thrusts	1 foot	2 feet
97	278	35	258	2	56	2,656
95	114	28	57	0	11	843
102	56	5	47	10	10	89
96	58	80	68	0	14	694
Totals	506	148	430	12	91	4,282

rhesus monkeys in tests before, during and after the test in which

No. of Un-intro thrusts	No. of intro thrusts	Latent Period to 1st Mount (mins)	Ejaculation Time (mins)
2,333	30	21.8 ± 7.7	-
61	0	19.7 ± 6.9	-
3	0	38.5 ± 13.5	-
426	8	24.2 ± 6.4	-
2,823	38	23.3 ± 3.8 (mean)	-
723	55	7.5	50.5
84	15	10.5	12.5
6	57	6.0	18.0
48	18	26.0	5.0
861	145	12.5 (mean)	21.5 (mean)
7,448	10,166	16.5 ± 1.4	14.5 ± 1.0
2,083	1,617	14.6 ± 1.9	19.3 ± 1.6
169	355	19.6 ± 4.3	13.0 ± 3.7
3,109	1,571	7.7 ± 1.5	8.5 ± 0.7
12,809	13,709	14.9 ± 1.0 (mean)	14.0 ± 0.7 (mean)

towards the vaginal orifice. After several such mounts during a 2-3 week period, the males' movements and orientation improved. Two of the four sub-adults ejaculated during the test in which intromission first occurred, and the remaining two animals did so in the second test in which intromission occurred. Differences in the "unestablished" behaviour of individual sub-adult males during 235 hr observation are shown in Table III. The "unestablished" copulatory behaviour of the sub-adult group consisted of (i) hand clasps (one or both hands), and (ii) mounts that involved clasping the female's waist with both hands and her legs with both feet, or with one foot only, or with both feet on the ground while thrusting. Most noteworthy was the very large number of pelvic thrusts without achieving intromission, and usually the long latent period from the start of the test to the occurrence of the first mount. For example, the youngest male (97), on the basis of canine-incisor ratio, made a total of 2,333 unintromitted thrusts and 30 intromitted thrusts during the 181 mounts in tests that preceded the first ejaculation: one or both of the male's feet remained on the cage floor in 37% of these mounts.

(iv)   Behaviour in tests in which the first ejaculation occurred

These were somewhat unusual tests because of the high numbers of unintromitted and intromitted thrusts that occurred, and it seemed preferable to deal with them separately (Table III).

(v)   "Established" copulatory behaviour

By "established" we mean the patterns of sexual behaviour in tests following that in which the first ejaculation occurred. Data for the behaviour of sub-adult males during 506 hr observation are shown in Table III. These are indices that can be compared with those

obtained from the same animals in the period before the first ejaculation: the latent period to the first mount of the test decreased, the
number of mounts per test increased, and the number of intromitted
and unintromitted thrusts per test increased. After the first ejaculation, incomplete mounting postures with one or both feet on the floor
while thrusting were still observed but less frequently, and the
majority of these incomplete mounts occurred during the period of the
first ten ejaculations. Males gripped the female's legs with both feet
in 70% of the mounts before achieving their first ejaculation, in 90%
of the mounts during their first ten ejaculations, and in 99% of the
mounts thereafter. An interesting comparison can be made between the
"established" copulatory behaviour of sub-adults, i.e. their activity
in the period immediately following behavioural puberty, and that of a
group of fully mature males. Comparisons were made during tests
conducted over approximately the same periods of time when sub-adults
were paired with ovariectomised females receiving 5μg oestradiol
daily (506 tests), and when the adults were paired with ovariectomised
females receiving either 5μg (84 tests) or 10 μg (142 tests) oestradiol
daily. The results in Figure 1 are for the following behavioural
indices: mean number of ejaculations per test; mean latent period to
the first mount in a test (mins); mean ejaculation time (time in mins
from the first mount of the test to the occurrence of ejaculation).
Fully adult males achieved four times as many ejaculations per test as
sub-adults (X^2 test, p < 0.001), and did so in significantly shorter
ejaculation times (t test, p < 0.001). There was a conspicuous difference in the rapidity with which sub-adults and adults approached
the females, and the latent period to the first mount in a test was
three times longer for sub-adults (t test, p < 0.001). It is clear
from these data alone that the sexual performance of the sub-adult group,
even after they had attained the capacity to ejaculate, was still greatly

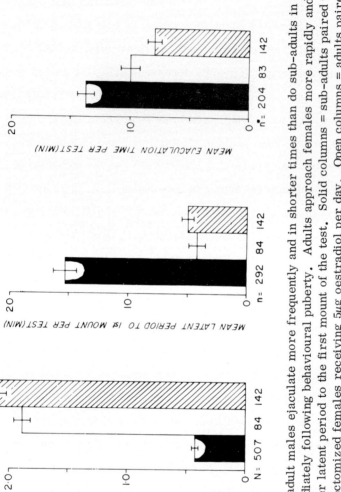

Fig. 1.   Fully adult males ejaculate more frequently and in shorter times than do sub-adults in the period immediately following behavioural puberty.   Adults approach females more rapidly and there is a shorter latent period to the first mount of the test.   Solid columns = sub-adults paired with ovariectomized females receiving 5μg oestradiol per day.   Open columns = adults paired with ovariectomized females receiving 5μg oestradiol per day.   Hatched columns = adults paired with those receiving 10μg oestradiol per day.   N = total number of tests.   n = number of tests in which mounting occurred.   n* = number of tests with ejaculation.   Vertical bars give standard errors of means.

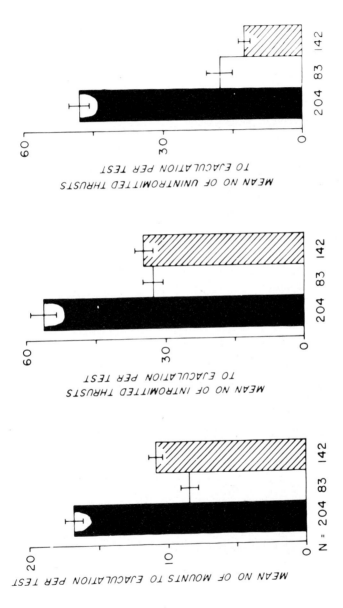

Fig. 2.   Sub-adult males in the period immediately following behavioural puberty required markedly more mounts and pelvic thrusts, both unintromitted and intromitted, in order to achieve ejaculation than did fully adult males.   N = number of tests in which ejaculation occurred. Column code as in Fig. 1.

below that of fully mature males. There were marked differences
also in mounting and thrusting activity (Fig. 2). The sub-adults
required a significantly greater number of mounts to achieve ejaculation than did the adults (t test, p < 0.001, data for first ejaculation of
test), and the numbers of both unintromitted and intromitted thrusts
were very greatly increased (t test, p < 0.001 in each case). Thus, the
sub-adults appeared to work harder and exhibit more behavioural
activity in order to attain ejaculation. Clearly, there are continuing
behavioural processes in the period following puberty in these male
primates but, at this stage in the investigation, it is not really possible
to ascribe the differences in the behaviour of the two groups to hormonal,
experiential or simply maturational factors.

IV EFFECTS OF CASTRATION AND ANDROGEN REPLACEMENT ON THE BEHAVIOUR OF SUB-ADULT AND ADULT MALE RHESUS MONKEYS

1. Castration

The effects of castration on the behaviour of male mammals
have been known for centuries. Systematic laboratory studies have
been carried out in many infra-primate species: in rat (Stone, 1939;
Beach, 1944; Beach & Holz, 1946; Beach & Holz-Tucker, 1949; Larsson,
1966; Davidson, 1966); in hamster (Beach & Pauker, 1949; Warren &
Aronson, 1956, 1957); in guinea pig (Grunt & Young, 1952, 1953); in
rabbit (Stone, 1932; Macmillan, Des jardins, Kirton & Hafs, 1969); in
cat (Rosenblatt & Aronson, 1958); in dog (Hart, 1968; Beach, 1970;
Schwartz & Beach, 1954); in sheep (Banks, 1964; Clegg, Beamer &
Bermant, 1969). Despite the attention given to this matter in laboratory and farm animals, there is a marked lack of systematic data on
the role of the testes in the control of primate behaviour. In some
early studies (Thorek, 1924; Antonius, 1930; Zuckerman & Parkes,

Fig. 3. Silicone rubber testicular prostheses made to match the sizes of the testes to be removed. These were inserted into the scrotal sacs of males at the time of castration. (cm scale)

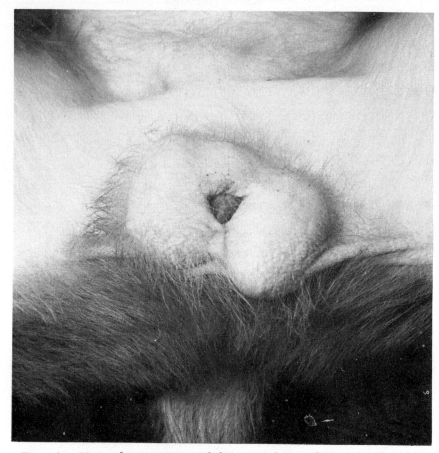

Fig. 4. Normal appearance of the scrotal sac after castration and insertion of testicular prostheses. Animal's abdomen is above and the tail is below.

1939), castration was reported to decrease the frequency of penile erections in several Old World species whereas testicular transplants or testosterone treatment reversed this effect and enhanced male dominance. Under free-ranging conditions on Cayo Santiago and at La Parguera, four males that had been castrated between 4-6 years of age were never seen to mount females and were also low in the dominance hierarchy (Wilson & Vessey, 1968).

Four sub-adult males used in the study already described and four fully mature males were castrated, and the behaviour of the two groups was compared by Dr. M. Wilson during a period of $4\frac{1}{2}$ years involving some 4,000 hr observation. In order to minimise changes in the external appearance of males which might in itself have an effect on behaviour, silicone prostheses were inserted into the scrotal sacs at the time of castration. These were made from non-toxic silicone rubber using a plaster of paris mould shaped to match the sizes of the testes to be removed (Fig. 3). Except for pallor of the sexual skin, the appearance of the scrotal sac was indistinguishable from normal when incisions had healed (Fig. 4). Following castration, there was a marked decline in the number of ejaculations and intromissions per test for both groups: this was more conspicuous for adults which had a higher level of performance when intact (Fig. 5). Whereas ejaculations ceased entirely in the sub-adult group about 12 weeks after castration, they persisted in some adults males, as did intromissions, throughout the 32 week period to which these observations refer. In contrast, a marked decline in mounting activity was only observed during this time in sub-adults, and mounting continued more or less unchanged in the adult group. There was no explanation for the transient increase in mounting by some sub-adults 18 weeks after castration

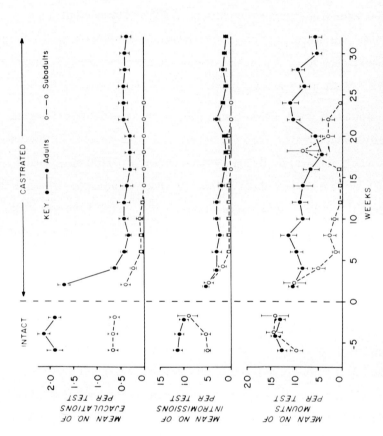

Fig. 5.   Castration resulted in a marked depression in ejaculations and intromissions in both sub-adults and adult males whereas mounting behaviour was much less affected in the adult group (1006 tests).   Vertical bars give standard errors of means.

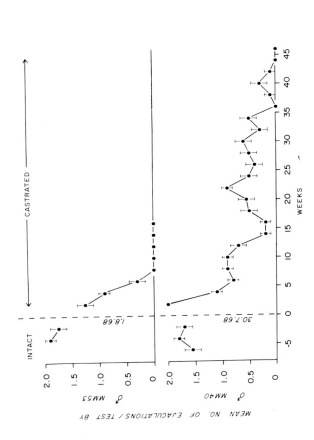

Fig. 6.   Illustrating individual differences in the effects of castration on the ejaculatory behaviour of two adult male rhesus monkeys when tested with the same ovariectomized, oestrogen-treated partners throughout.   One male (MM 53) stopped ejaculating 37 days after castration while the other male (MM 40) continued doing so for 762 days.   The gradual decline in activity over the first 45 weeks is shown.

Dates give days of gonadectomy.   Vertical bars give standard errors of means.

(Fig. 5). These data refer to the initial 32 weeks after castration, but the behaviour of the castrated adults was followed for an additional 6-90 weeks. During this extended period of observation, sexual activity declined further, and all four males ceased ejaculating by 109 weeks. Mounting also declined to very low levels (Fig. 8) but, unlike ejaculation and intromission, mounting continued to occur in occasional tests throughout the entire period of study.

Marked individual differences in the effects of castration on adult males were observed. This is illustrated in Fig. 6 which shows two adult males with approximately the same levels of ejaculatory behaviour when intact, castrated within 24 hr of each other, and tested with the same ovariectomised, oestrogen-treated partners throughout. In one case, ejaculations ceased entirely 6-8 weeks after gonadectomy, and in the other, they gradually declined to zero over a 45-week period.

Testosterone has been shown to be the principal androgen secreted by the testis of adult dogs, bulls, rams, boars and men (Lucas, Whitmore & West, 1957; West, Hollander, Kritchevsky & Dobriner, 1952; Lindner, 1961a, b). In the present study, plasma testosterone was estimated using a competitive protein binding technique (Plant & Michael, 1971) involving the extraction of plasma samples with methylene dichloride, purification by thin layer chromatography on silica gel and competition of testosterone with tritiated testosterone for the binding sites on protein obtained from human pregnancy serum. This method has been shown to be sufficiently precise, sensitive and specific for the estimation of testosterone in 0.5 ml plasma from intact adult male rhesus monkeys and in 3.0 ml plasma from castrates. The coefficient of variation was 10.5% and the value for a 0.5 ml water blank taken through the entire procedure was 0.33 ± 0.28 ng (mean $\pm$ S.D.) with a mean recovery of 65%. Animals were adapted to the bleeding procedure, and concentrations of plasma testosterone in saphenous vein blood from intact adult males collected at 08.00 hr ranged between 323-1,254 ng per 100 ml (849 ± 287 ng per 100 ml, mean ± S.D.), which compared with a range of 30-135 ng per 100 ml (84 ± 31 ng per 100 ml, mean ± S.D.) for castrates. The changes in plasma testosterone after castration were extremely rapid, and Fig. 7 shows that levels had fallen by 50% within 30 min of gonadectomy. This was also the case when LH treatment (HCG) prior to castration produced exceptionally high intact plasma levels, and within 24 hr plasma testosterone values were in the range of those of long-term castrates. Clearly, levels of circulating testosterone fall much more abruptly than the decline in behaviour which takes weeks rather than hours to become apparent. It was of interest, therefore, to ascertain if the dissociation in time between changes in the level of circulating steroid and changes in the behavioural parameters would show the same kind of relation during replacement treatment with testosterone propionate.

2. Androgen Replacement

Both the sub-adult and adult groups of males studied after castration received 2 mg testosterone propionate i.m. per day for periods exceeding 20 weeks (the experiment is continuing), and behavioural testing was maintained with the same partners as previously. Restoration of ejaculatory performance occurred rather gradually in both groups and, at the end of the period of observation described here (Fig. 8), it had not returned to intact levels in either group. However, in the adults, both intromissions and mounts were fully restored after 14 weeks of treatment whereas, in sub-adults, intromissions and, to a lesser ex-

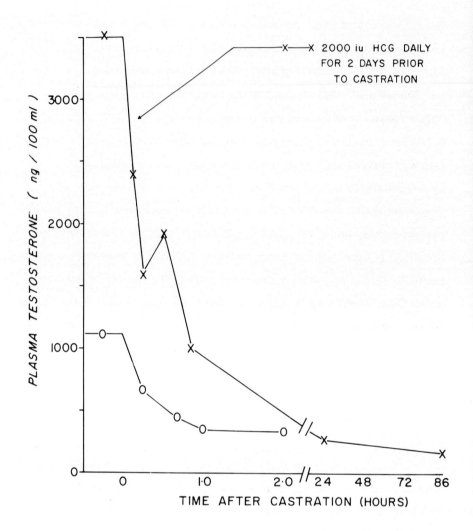

Fig. 7. Decline of plasma testosterone values after castration in two adult male rhesus monkeys. Within 30 min., plasma levels were reduced by 50%. One male (X—X) was treated with LH (HCG) prior to castration to stimulate androgen production by the testis. Each point is the mean of duplicate determinations.

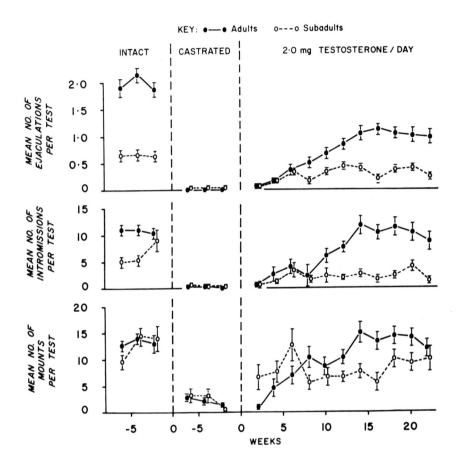

Fig. 8. Testosterone replacement treatment resulted in a gradual
increase in the sexual activity of both sub-adult and adult
male castrates. Ejaculations were not restored to intact
levels in either group, whereas intromissions were fully
restored in adults but not in sub-adults. Mounting was
fully restored in adults and nearly so in sub-adults.
Vertical bars give standard errors of means (1001 tests).

tent, mounts remained below intact values. Thus, some 22 weeks of
daily treatment with testosterone, although producing a marked im-
provement, did not fully restore the behavioural patterns to those observed before castration in either group. This is perhaps more clearly shown in the group data (Fig. 9) where for both the sub-adults and
adults, ejaculatory performance during testosterone replacement treatment reached only some 50% that of intact levels. However, individual
differences in the effects of replacement treatment on behaviour were
as marked as were the effects of castration. In one male, ejaculation
was fully restored in about 16 weeks of treatment whereas, in another
male paired with the same females, although ejaculation reappeared
earlier, it failed to reach pre-castration levels during the following
6 months of treatment (Fig. 10).

    Replacement treatment in these primates presents certain diffi-
culties; prolonged periods of treatment are required, and intact males
exhibit fluctuations in plasma testosterone during a 24 hr period. While
it would be premature to describe a nycterohemeral rhythm in plasma
testosterone in the rhesus monkey on the basis of samples collected at
only four times throughout the 24 hours, our data nevertheless indicate
clearly that plasma levels are usually higher at 22.00 hr than at 08.00
hr (Plant & Michael, 1971). Fig. 11 shows that means for samples
collected between 08.00 hr and 16.00 hr were about 800 ng per 100 ml,
whereas the mean for samples collected at 22.00 hr was about 1,600
ng per 100 ml (analysis of variance $F = 10.9$, df 3, 52, $P < 0.001$); a
substantial difference, and one not observed after castration. By administering 2 mg testosterone propionate as a single intramuscular
injection in the afternoon at 16.00 hr, the changes in plasma levels of
testosterone during the next 24 hr were quite similar to those seen in

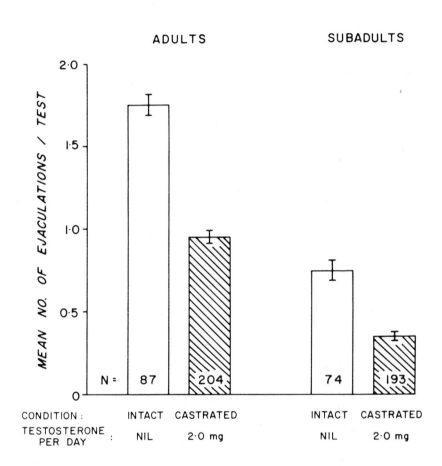

ADULTS   SUBADULTS

Fig. 9. Testosterone replacement treatment failed fully to restore
        the ejaculatory behaviour of both sub-adult and adult male
        castrates to pre-castration levels. N = number of tests.
        Vertical bars give standard errors of means. (10 pairs)

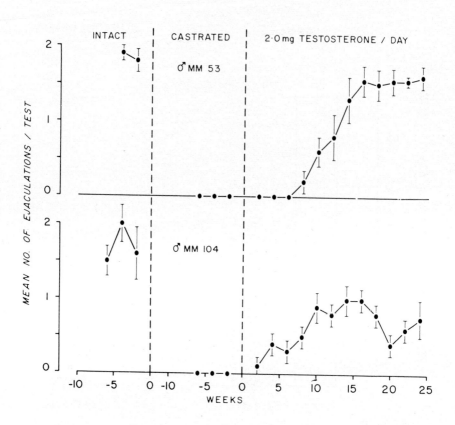

Fig. 10. Marked individual differences in the behavioural responses of
male castrates to testosterone replacement treatment were
observed. In one adult male (MM 53), ejaculatory behaviour
was fully restored within 16 weeks of starting treatment,
while in the other adult male (MM 104), tested with the same
females, it failed to reach intact levels after 25 weeks.
Vertical bars give standard errors of means.

intact animals (Fig. 11). The mean plasma levels that resulted were
above those for intact adult males but not outside their ranges. It seems
clear from these data that the failure of this dosage of testosterone completely to restore the sexual behaviour of both groups of males to intact
levels was unlikely to be due simply to inadequate replacement therapy.
The lack of correlation between plasma testosterone and behaviour observed after castration was seen again during the period of replacement
treatment. Plasma testosterone was fully restored within 24 hr of
starting intramuscular injections, but the restoration of behaviour did
not begin to occur until between 2 and 4 weeks later (Michael, 1972;
Wilson, Plant & Michael, 1972). The behavioural decrement after
castration and its restoration after instituting androgen treatment clearly indicated that the behavioural changes were, at least in part, dependent upon the secretion of androgens by the testis, but the dissociations
in time between changes in plasma levels and the behavioural events
implied that the causal relations were indirect: other factors, perhaps
growth-dependent ones, would seem to intervene. An interesting contrast occurs between the rapid and abrupt behavioural effects of oestrogen treatment in ovariectomised female rhesus monkeys (Michael,
Zumpe, Keverne & Bonsall, 1972), and the slow, progressive changes
produced by androgen treatment in castrated males. Furthermore, the
behavioural changes consequent upon castration in this highly evolved
primate species, with well-marked neocortical development, occurred
as rapidly as in a lissencephalic species such as the laboratory rat.
Thus, hormonal factors have not lost their role in mediating sexual
behaviour in male rhesus monkeys.

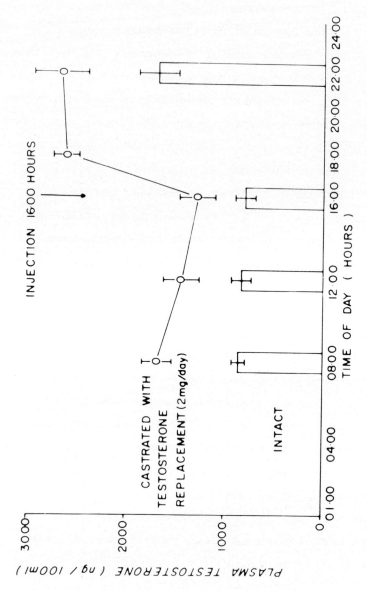

Fig. 11. In intact males, mean plasma testosterone levels were significantly higher at 22.00 hr than at the other three times of day. By injecting testosterone daily i.m. to castrates at 16.00 hr., the variations in plasma testosterone during the next 24 hr. were similar to those of intact males (62 samples, 9 males). Vertical bars give standard errors of means.

V   SUMMARY AND CONCLUSIONS

The development of sexual behaviour in male primates gradually unfolds from infancy through the time of puberty and, as we have described here, continues through the post-pubertal period. The attainment of the capacity to ejaculate in coitus was closely related in time to the occurrence of the first intromission. The sexual behaviour of sub-adult males in the period immediately following behavioural puberty differed quantitatively from that of fully mature males, particularly in the frequency with which ejaculation occurred, and in the number of mounts and thrusts required to achieve it.

Castrating adult male rhesus monkeys resulted, contrary to expectations, in a relatively rapid decline in the incidence of ejaculation and intromission during the ensuing 6-week period: however, individual males continued to ejaculate, although less frequently, for periods of up to 2 years after removing the testes. In contrast, mounting activity was not immediately affected in the fully mature group. Castrating sub-adult males, whose sexual experience had been limited, resulted in the abolition of ejaculation within 19 weeks of gonadectomy, and in greatly decreased mounting activity.

Administering testosterone daily to sub-adult and adult castrates resulted in a progressive increase in the level of sexual activity over a 5-10 week period. However, at the end of five months' replacement treatment, ejaculatory performance was not fully restored in either group. This was not due to inadequate testosterone replacement since plasma levels were fully and rapidly restored to pre-castration values. It might be speculated that the absence of an androgen-dependent maturational change, in addition to the experiential factor, was responsible for the persisting deficit in the behaviour of the sub-adult group. Nevertheless, the possibility should be held in mind that the testis elaborates other hormones in addition to testosterone that are important for the development and expression of sexual behaviour in the male primate. It may safely be concluded at this time that the sexual behaviour of male rhesus monkeys possesses a large component that is androgen-dependent.

VI ACKNOWLEDGEMENTS

The original work described here was supported by grants from the Foundations' Fund for Research in Psychiatry, the Population Council and the Medical Research Council, which are gratefully acknowledged. Miss Margo Wilson was supported by a Commonwealth Scholarship awarded by the Association of Commonwealth Universities.

VII BIBLIOGRAPHY

Albrecht, H. & Dunnett, S. C. (1971). Chimpanzees in the West of their range. Ethologische Studien 11. Piper, Munich.

Altmann, S. A. (1959). Field observations on a howling monkey society. J. Mammal, 40, 317-330.

Altmann, S. A. (1962). A field study of the sociobiology of rhesus monkeys (Macaca mulatta). Ann. N.Y. Acad. Sci., 102, 338-435.

Antonius, O. (1930). Eine Beobachtung an Affenkastraten in Schonbrunn. In Der Zoologische Garten (Zweiter Band). Akademische Verlagsgesellschaft M.H.H., Leipzig, pp. 134-135.

Baldwin, J. D. (1968). The social behaviour of adult male squirrel monkeys (Saimiri sciureus) in a seminatural environment. Folia primat., 9, 281-314.

Baldwin, J. D. (1969). The ontogeny of social behavior of squirrel monkeys (Saimiri sciureus) in a seminatural environment. Folia primat., 11, 35-79.

Baldwin, J. D. (1971). The social organisation of a semi free-ranging troop of squirrel monkeys (Saimiri sciureus). Folia primat., 14, 23-50.

Banks, E. M. (1964). Some aspects of sexual behavior in domestic sheep, Ovis aries. Behaviour, 23, 249-279.

Beach, F. A. (1944). Relative effects of androgen upon the mating behavior of male rats subjected to forebrain injury or castration. J. exp. Zool., 97, 249-285.

Beach, F. A. (1970). Coital behavior in dogs: VI. Long-term effects of castration upon mating in the male. J. comp. physiol. Psychol., 70, 1-32.

Beach, F. A. and Holz, A. M. (1946). Mating behavior in male rats castrated at various ages and injected with androgen. J. exp. Zool., 101, 91-142.

Beach, F. A. and Holz-Tucker, A. M. (1949). Effects of different concentrations of androgen upon sexual behavior in castrated male rats. J. comp. physiol. Psychol., 42, 433-543.

Beach, F. A. & Pauker, R. S. (1949). Effects of castration and subsequent androgen administration upon mating behavior in the male hamster (Cricetus auratus). Endocrinology, 45, 211-221.

Bernstein, I. S. (1964). A field study of the activities of howler monkeys. Anim. Behav., 12, 92-97.

Bernstein, I. S. (1967). A field study of the pigtail monkey (Macaca nemestrina). Primates, 8, 217-228.

Bernstein, I.S. (1968). The Lutong of Kuala Selangor. Behaviour, 32, 1-16.

Blurton-Jones, N. G. and Trollope, J. (1968). Social behaviour of stump-tailed macaques in captivity. Primates, 9, 365-394.

Bolwig, N. (1959). A study of the behaviour of the chacma baboon Papio ursinus. Behaviour, 14, 136-163.

Booth, C. (1962). Some observations on behaviour of cercopithecus monkeys. Ann. N.Y. Acad. Sci., 102, 477-487.

Buettner-Janusch, J. (1964). The breeding of Galagos in captivity and some notes on their behaviour. Folia Primat., 2, 93-110.

Butler, H. (1964). The reproductive biology of a strepsirhine (Galago senegalensis senegalensis). Int. Rev. gen. exp. Zool., 1, 241-296.

Butler, H. (1967). Season breeding of the senegal galago (Galago senegalensis senegalensis) in the Nuba mountains, Republic of the Sudan. Folia primat., 5, 165-175.

Carpenter, C. R. (1934). A field study in Siam of the behavior and social relations of howling monkeys (Alouatta palliata). Comp. Psychol. Monogr., 10, 1-168.

Carpenter, C. R. (1935). Behavior of red spider monkeys in Panama. J. Mammal., 16, 171-180.

Carpenter, C. R. (1940). A field study in Siam of the behavior and social relations of the gibbon (Hylobates lar). Comp. Psychol. Monogr., 16, 1-212.

Carpenter, C. R. (1942a). Sexual behavior of free ranging rhesus monkeys (Macaca mulatta). Specimens, procedures and behavioral characteristics of estrus. J. Comp. Psychol., 33, 113-142.

Carpenter, C. R. (1942b). Sexual behavior of free ranging rhesus monkeys (Macaca mulatta). II. Periodicity of estrus, homosexual, autoerotic and non-conformist behavior. J. Comp.

Psychol., 33, 143-162.

Castellanos, H. and McCombs, H. L. (1968). The reproductive cycle of the New World Monkey. Fertil. Steril., 19, 213-227.

Catchpole, H. R. and Fulton, J. F. (1943). The oestrus cycle in Tarsius: Observations on a captive pair. J. Mammal., 24, 90-93.

Chalmers, N. R. (1968). The social behaviour of free-living mangabeys in Uganda. Folia primat., 8, 263-281.

Chalmers, N. R. and Rowell, T. E. (1971). Behaviour and female reproductive cycles in a captive group of mangabeys. Folia primat., 14, 1-14.

Chevalier-Skolnikoff, S. (1971). The female sexual response in stumptail monkeys (Macaca speciosa), and its broad implications for female mammalian sexuality. Annual Meeting of the American Anthropological Association, New York.

Christen, A. (1968). Haltung und Brutbiologie von Cebuella. Folia primat., 8, 41-49.

Clegg, M. T., Beamer, W. and Bermant, G. (1969). Copulatory behaviour of the ram, Ovis aries. III: Effects of pre- and postpubertal castration and androgen replacement therapy. Anim. Behav., 17, 712-717.

Clewe, T. H. (1969). Observations on reproduction of squirrel monkeys in captivity. J. Reprod. Fertil. (Suppl.), 6, 151-156.

Conaway, C. H. and Koford, C. B. (1964). Estrous cycles and mating behaviour in a free-ranging band of rhesus monkeys. J. Mammal., 45, 577-588

Conaway, C. H. & Sade, D. S. (1965). The seasonal spermatogenic cycle in free ranging rhesus monkeys. Folia primat., 3, 1-12.

Conaway, C. H. & Sade, D. S. (1969). Annual testis cycle of the green monkey (Cercopithecus aethiops) on St. Kitts, West Indies. J. Mammal., 50, 833-835.

Conaway, C. H. & Sorenson, M. W. (1966). Reproduction in tree shrews. Symp. Zool. Soc. London, 15, 471-492.

Corner, G. W. (1945). Development, organization and breakdown of the corpus luteum in the rhesus monkey. Contr. Embryol. (Washington, D.C.)., 31, 117-146.

Davenport, R. K. (1967). The orang-utan in Sabah. Folia primat., 5, 247-263.

Davidson, J. M. (1966). Characteristics of sex behaviour in male rats following castration. Anim. Behav., 14, 266-272.

DeVore, I. (1965). Male dominance and mating behavior in baboons. In Sex and Behavior (F. A. Beach ed.) pp. 266-289. John Wiley & Sons, New York.

Doyle, G. A. & Bekker, T. (1967). A facility for naturalistic studies of the lesser bushbaby (Galago senegalensis mohili). Folia primat., 7, 161-168.

Doyle, G. A., Andersson, A. & Bearder, S. K. (1971). Reproduction in the lesser bushbaby (Galago senegalensis mohili) under semi-natural conditions. Folia primat., 14, 15-22.

Doyle, G. A., Pelletier, A. & Bekker, T. (1967). Courtship, mating and parturition in the lesser bushbaby (Galago senegalensis mohili) under semi-natural conditions. Folia primat., 7, 169-197.

DuMond, F. V. and Hutchinson, T. C. (1967). Squirrel monkey reproduction: The "fatted" male phenomenon and seasonal spermatogenesis. Science, 58, 1467-1470.

Eckstein, P. & Zuckerman, S. (1956). The oestrus cycle in the mammalia. In A. S. Parkes (Ed.), Marshall's Physiology of Reproduction, Vol. 1, Part 1, Longmans, London. pp. 226-396.

Ellefson, J. O. (1968). Territorial behavior in the common white-handed gibbon, Hylobates lar, Linn. In P. C. Jay (Ed.), Primates. Holt, Rinehart & Winston, New York. pp. 180-199.

Epple, G. (1967). Vergleichende Untersuchungen über Sexual- und Sozialverhalten der Krallenaffen (Hapalidae). Folia Primat., 7, 36-65.

Epple, G. (1970). Maintenance, breeding and development of marmoset monkeys (Callithricidae) in captivity. Folia primat., 12, 56-76.

Evans, C. S. and Goy, R. W. (1968). Social behaviour and reproductive cycles in captive ring-tailed lemurs (Lemur catta). J. Zool. London, 156, 181-197.

Fooden, J. (1967). Complementary specialisation of male and female reproductive structures in the bear macaque, Macaca arctoides. Nature, 214, 939-941.

Freedman, L. Z. and Rosvold, H. E. (1962). Sexual, aggressive and anxious behavior in the laboratory macaque. J. Nerv. Ment. Dis. 134, 18-27.

Gartlan, J. S. (1969). Sexual and maternal behavior of the vervet monkey, Cercopithecus aethiops. J. Reprod. Fert. (Suppl.), 6, 137-150.

Gautier-Hion, A. (1968). Etude du cycle annuel de reproduction du talapoin (Miopithecus talapoin), vivant dans son milieu naturel. Biologie gabonica, 4, 163-173.

Gillman, J. and Gilbert, J. (1946). The reproductive cycle of the chacma baboon (Papio ursinus) with special reference to the prob-

lems of menstrual irregularities as assessed by the behaviour of
the sex skin. S. Afr. J. Med. Sci., 11, 1-54.

Goodall, J. (1965). Chimpanzees of the Gombe Stream Reserve. In
I. DeVore (ed.), Primate Behavior. Holt, Rinehart & Winston,
New York. pp. 425-473.

Grunt, J. A. and Young, W. C. (1952). Differential reactivity of individuals and the response of the male guinea pig to testosterone
propionate. Endocrinology, 51, 237-248.

Grunt, J. A. and Young, W. C. Consistency of sexual behavior patterns in individual male guinea pigs following castration and androgen therapy. J. Comp. Physiol. Psychol., 46, 138-144. (1953).

Hall, K. R. L. (1962). The sexual, agonistic and derived social behaviour patterns of the wild chacma baboon, Papio ursinus.
Proc. Zool. Soc. London, 139, 283-327.

Hall, K. R. L. (1965).   Behaviour and ecology of the wild patas
monkey, Erythrocebus patas, in Uganda. J. Zool. Lond., 148,
15-87.

Hall, K. R. L. and DeVore, I. (1965). Baboon social behavior. In
I. DeVore (ed.), Primate Behavior. Holt, Rinehart & Winston,
New York. pp. 53-110.

Hall, K. R. L., Boelkins, R. C. and Goswell, M. J. (1965). Behaviour of patas monkey, Erythrocebus patas, in captivity with notes
on the natural habitat. Folia primat., 3, 22-49.

Hampton, J. K., Hampton, S. H. and Landwehr, B. T. (1966). Observations on a successful breeding colony of the marmoset, Oedipo-
midas oedipus. Folia primat., 4, 265-287.

Hanby, J. P., Robertson, L. T. and Phoenix, C. H. (1971). The sexual
behavior of a confined troop of Japanese macaques. Folia primat.

16, 123-143.

Harlow, H. F. (1962). The heterosexual affectional system in monkeys. Am. Psychol., 17, 1-9.

Harlow, H. F. (1965). Sexual behavior in the rhesus monkey. In F. A. Beach (ed.), Sex and Behavior, John Wiley & Sons, New York. pp. 234-265.

Harlow, H. F. and Harlow, M. K. (1965). The affectional system. In A. M. Schrier, H. F. Harlow and F. Stollnitz (eds.) Behavior of Nonhuman Primates, Vol. II. Academic Press, New York. pp. 287-334.

Harrison, B. (1963). Trying to breed Tarsius. Malay Nat. J., 17, 218-231.

Harrison, J. L. (1955). Data on the reproduction of some Malayan mammals. Proc. Zool. Soc. London, 125, 445-460.

Hart, B. L. (1968). Role of prior experience in the effects of castration on sexual behavior of male dogs. J. comp. physiol. Psychol., 66, 719-725.

Hartman, C. G. (1938). Some observations on the bonnet macaque. J. Mammal., 19, 468-474.

Hendrickx, A. G. and Kraemer, D. C. (1969). Observations on the menstrual cycle, optimal mating time and pre-implantation embryos of the baboon, Papio anubis, and Papio cynocephalus. J. Reprod. Fert., Suppl., 6, 119-128.

Hess, J. P. (1973). Some observations on the sexual behaviour of captive lowland gorillas, Gorilla g. gorilla. (Savage & Wyman). In R. P. Michael and J. H. Crook (eds.), Comparative Ecology and Behaviour of Primates. Academic Press, London.

Hill, W. C. O. (1967). Taxonomy of the baooon. In H. Vagtborg (ed.)

The Baboon in Medical Research. Vol. II. University of Texas Press, Austin. pp. 3-11.

Hinde, R. A. and Spencer-Booth, Y. (1967). The behaviour of socially living rhesus monkeys in their first two and a half years. Anim. Behav., 15, 169-196.

Hines, M. (1942). The development and regression of reflexes, postures, and progression in the young macaque. Contr. Embryol., 196, 153-210.

Hooff, J. A. R. A. M. van. (1962). Facial expressions in higher primates. Symp. Zool. Soc. London, 8, 97-125.

Hurme, V. O. and Wagenen, C. van. (1961). Basic data on the emergence of permanent teeth in the rhesus monkey (Macaca mulatta). Proc. Am. Phil. Soc., 105, 105-140.

Hutchinson, T. C. (1970). Vaginal cytology and reproduction in the squirrel monkey (Saimiri sciureus). Folia primat., 12, 212-223.

Ibscher, L. von. (1967). Geburt und Frühe Entwicklung zweier Gibbons (Hylobates lar L.). Folia primat., 5, 43-69.

Imanishi, K. (1957). Social behaviour in Japanese monkeys (Macaca fuscata). Psychologia, 1, 47-54.

Ioannou, J. M. (1966). The oestrus cycle of the Potto. J. Reprod. Fert., 11, 455-457.

Itani, J. and Suzuki, A. (1967). The social unit of chimpanzees. Primates, 8, 355-381.

Jay, P. (1965a). Field Studies. In A. M. Schrier, H. F. Harlow and F. Stollnitz (eds.), Behavior of Nonhuman Primates, Vol II. Academic Press, New York.

Jay, P. (1965b). The common langur of North India. In D. DeVore (ed.) Primate Behavior. Holt, Rinehart & Winston, New York, pp. 197-249.

Jolly, A. (1966). Lemur Behavior: A Madagascar Field Study.
University of Chicago Press, Chicago.

Jolly, C. J. (1967). The evolution of the baboons. In H. Vagtborg
(ed.) The Baboon in Medical Research, Vol. II. University of
Texas Press, Austin. pp. 23-50.

Jones, C. and Sabater Pi, J. (1968). Comparative ecology of Cercocebus albigena (Gray) and Cercocebus torquatus (Kerr) in Rio Muni,
West Africa. Folia primat., 9, 99-113.

Kaufman, I. C. and Rosenblum, L. A. (1966). A behavioral taxonomy
for Macaca nemestrina and Macaca radiata: based on longitudinal
observation of family groups in the laboratory. Primates, 7,
205-258.

Kaufmann,J. H. (1965). A three-year study of mating behavior in a
free-ranging band of rhesus monkeys. Ecology, 46, 500-512.

Kawabe, M . (1970). A preliminary study of the wild siamang gibbon
(Hylobates syndactylus) at Fraser's Hill, Malaysia. Primates,
11, 285-291.

Keverne, E. B. and Michael, R. P. (1970). Annual changes in the
menstruation of rhesus monkeys. J. Endocr., 48, 669-670.

Kirchshofer, R. (1962). Beobachtungen bei der Geburt eines Zwergs-
chimpansen (Pan paniscus Schwarz 1929) und einige Bemerkungen
zum Paarungsverhalten. Z. Tierpsychol. 19, 597-606.

Klein, L. L. (1971). Observations on copulation and seasonal reproduction of two species of spider monkeys, Ateles belzebuth and
A. geoffroyi. Folia primat., 15, 233-248.

Koford, C. B. (1965). Population dynamics of rhesus monkeys on
Cayo Santiago. In I. DeVore (ed.) Primate Behavior. Holt,

Rinehart & Winston, New York. pp 160-174.

Kortlandt, A. (1962). Chimpanzees in the wild. Scientific American, 206, 128-138.

Koyama, N. (1971). Observations on mating behavior of wild siamang gibbons at Fraser's Hill, Malaysia. Primates, 12, 183-189.

Kummer, H. (1968). Social Organisation of Hamadryas Baboons. University of Chicago Press, Chicago.

Larsson, K. (1966). Individual differences in reactivity to androgen in male rats. Physiology and Behav., 1, 255-258.

Latta, J., Hopf, S. and Ploog, D. (1967). Observations on mating behaviour and sexual play in the squirrel monkey (Saimiri sciureus). Primates, 8, 229-246.

Lawick-Goodall, J. van. (1968). The behaviour of free-living chimpanzee in the Gombe Stream Reserve. Anim. Behav. Monog., 1, 161-311.

Lawick-Goodall, J. van. (1969). Some aspects of reproductive behaviour in a group of wild chimpanzees, Pan troglodytes schweinfurthi, at the Gombe Stream Reserve, Tanzania, East Africa. J. Reprod. Fert., Suppl., 6, 353-355.

Lindburg, D. G. (1967). A field study of the reproductive behavior of the rhesus monkey (Macaca mulatta). Ph.D. Thesis, University of California.

Lindner, H. R. (1961a). Androgens and related compounds in the spermatic vein blood of domestic animals. I. Neutral steroids secreted by the bull testis. J. Endocr., 23, 139-159.

Lindner, H. R. (1961b). Androgens and related compounds in the spermatic vein blood of domestic animals IV. Testicular androgens in the ram, boar and stallion. J. Endocr., 23, 171-178.

Loy, J. (1970). Peri-menstrual sexual behavior among rhesus monkeys. Folia primat., 13, 286-297.

Loy, J. (1971). Estrous behavior of free-ranging rhesus monkeys (Macaca mulatta). Primates, 12, 1-31.

Lucas, W. M., Whitmore, W. F. and West, C. D. (1957). Identification of testosterone in human spermatic vein blood. J. Clin. Endocr. Metab., 17, 465-472.

MacKinnon, J. (1971). The orang-utan in Sabah today. A study of a wild population in the Ulu Segama Reserve. J. Fauna Preser. Soc., 11, 141-191.

Macmillan, K. L., Desjardins, C., Kirton, K. T. and Hafs, H. D. (1969). Seminal composition and sexual activity after castration and testosterone replacement in rabbits. Proc. Soc. Exp. Biol. Med., 131, 673-677.

Manley, G. H. (1966). Reproduction in Lorisoid primates. Symp. Zool. Soc. London, 15, 493-509.

Martin, R. D. (1968). Reproduction and ontogeny in tree-shrews (Tupaia belangeri), with reference to their general behaviour and taxonomic relationships. Z. Tierpsychol., 25, 409-495 and 505-532.

Mason, W. A. (1960). The effects of social restriction on the behavior of rhesus monkeys. I. Free Social behavior. J. comp. physiol. Psychol., 53, 582-589.

Mason, W. A. (1966). Social organisation of the South American monkey, Callicebus moloch: A preliminary report. Tulane Studies in Zoology, 13, 23-28.

Meier, G. W. (1965). Other data on the effects of social isolation during rearing upon adult reproductive behaviour in the rhesus monkey (Macaca mulatta). Anim. Behav., 13, 228-231.

Michael, R. P. (1965). Some aspects of the endocrine control of sexual activity in primates. Proc. Roy. Soc. Med., 58, 595-598.

Michael, R. P. (1968). Gonadal hormones and the control of primate behaviour. In Endocrinology and Human Behaviour, (R. P. Michael ed.). Oxford University Press, London. pp. 69-93.

Michael, R. P. (1971). Neuroendocrine factors regulating primate behaviour. In Frontiers in Neuroendocrinology, (L. Martini and W. F. Ganong, eds.). Oxford University Press, New York, pp. 359-398.

Michael, R. P. (1972). Determinants of Primate Reproductive Behaviour. In The Use of Nonhuman Primates in Research on Human Reproduction, (E. Diczfalusy and C. C. Standley, eds.) pp. 322-363. Proc. WHO Symposium, Sukhumi, U.S.S.R.

Michael, R. P. and Keverne, E. B. (1970). Primate sex pheromones of vaginal origin. Nature, 225, 84-85.

Michael, R. P. and Keverne, E. B. (1971). An annual rhythm in the sexual activity of the male rhesus monkey (Macaca mulatta) in the laboratory. J. Reprod. Fert., 25, 95-98.

Michael, R. P. and Saayman, G. (1967). Individual differences in the sexual behaviour of male rhesus monkeys (Macaca mulatta) under laboratory conditions. Anim. Behav., 15, 460-466.

Michael, R. P. and Zumpe, D. (1970). Rhythmic changes in the copulatory frequency of rhesus monkeys (Macaca mulatta) in relation to the menstrual cycle and a comparison with the human cycle. J. Reprod. Fert. 21, 199-201.

Michael, R. P., Herbert, J. and Welegalla, J. (1966). Ovarian hormones and grooming behaviour in the rhesus monkey (Macaca mulatta) under laboratory conditions. J. Endocr. 36, 263-279.

Michael, R. P., Herbert, J. and Welegalla, J. (1967). Ovarian hormones and the sexual behaviour of the male rhesus monkey (Macaca mulatta) under laboratory conditions. J. Endocr., 39, 81-98.

Michael, R. P., Zumpe, D., Keverne, E. B. and Bonsall, R. W. (1972). Neuroendocrine factors in the control of primate behaviour. Recent Prog. Horm. Res., 28, 665-706.

Missakian, E. A. (1969). Reproductive behavior of socially deprived male rhesus monkeys (Macaca mulatta). J. comp. physiol. Psychol., 69, 403-407.

Missakian, E. A., Del Rio, L. R. and Myers, R. E. (1969). Reproductive behavior of captive male rhesus monkeys (Macaca mulatta) Comm. Behav. Biol., 4, 231-235.

Moynihan, M. (1964). Some behavior patterns of Platyrrhine monkeys. I. The night Monkey (Aotus trivirgatus). Smithson, Misc. Coll. (Washington, D.C.), 146, 1-84.

Moynihan, M. (1966). Communication in the Titi monkey, Callicebus. J. Zool. London, 150, 77-127.

Munsell, A. H. (1929). Munsell Color Company, Inc., Baltimore.

Nadler, R. D. and Rosenblum, L. A. (1969). Sexual behavior of male bonnet monkeys in the laboratory. Brain Behav. Evol., 2, 482-497.

Napier, J. R. and Napier, P. H. (1967). A Handbook of Living Primates. Academic Press, London.

Nishida, T. (1966). A sociological study of solitary male monkeys. Primates, 7, 141-204.

Nishida, T. (1968). The social group of wild chimpanzees in the Mahali Mountains. Primates, 9, 167-224.

Noback, C. R. (1939). The changes in the vaginal smears and associated cyclic phenomena in the lowland gorilla (Gorilla gorilla). Anat. Rec., 73, 209-221.

Petter, J. J. (1965). The lemurs of Madagascar. In I.DeVore (ed.) Primate Behavior. Holt, Rinehart & Winston, New York. pp. 292-319.

Petter-Rousseaux, A. (1964). Reproductive physiology and behavior of the Lemuroidea. In J. Buettner-Jaunsch (ed.) Evolutionary and Genetic Biology of Primates. Academic Press, New York. pp. 91-132.

Plant, T. M. and Michael, R. P. (1971). Diurnal variations in plasma testosterone levels of adult male rhesus monkeys. Acta endocr. (Kbh.) Suppl., 1971, 155, 69.

Ploog, D. W. and MacLean, P. D. (1963). Display of penile erection in squirrel monkey (Saimiri sciureus). Anim. Behav., 11, 32-39.

Ploog, D. W., Blitz, J. and Ploog, F. (1963). Studies on social and sexual behavior of the squirrel monkey (Saimiri sciureus). Folia primat., 1, 29-66.

Ploog, D., Hopf, S. and Winter, P. (1967). Ontogenese des Verhaltens von Totenkopfaffen (Saimiri sciureus). Psychologische Forschung, 31, 1-41.

Prakash, I. (1962). Group organisation, sexual behavior and breeding season of certain Indian monkeys. Jap. J. Ecol., 12, 83-86.

Rahaman, H. and Parthasarathy, M. D. (1969). Studies on the social behaviour of bonnet monkeys. Primates, 10, 149-162.

Ramarkrishna, P. A. and Prasad, M. R. N. (1967). Changes in the male reproductive organs of Loris tardigradus lydekkerianus. Folia Primat., 5, 176-189.

Resko, J. A. (1967). Plasma androgen levels of the rhesus monkey: effects of age and season. Endocrinology, 81, 1203-1212.

Reynolds, V. and Reynolds, F. (1965). Chimpanzees in the Budongo

Forest. In I. DeVore (ed.). Primate Behavior. Holt, Rinehart & Winston, New York. pp. 368-424.

Roberts, P. (1971). Social interactions of Galago crassicaudatus. Folia primat., 14, 171-181.

Rodman, P. S. (1973). Behavior and ecology of orang-utan: population density, population composition, and individual variation in diurnal patterns. In R. P. Michael and J. H. Crook (eds.) Comparative Ecology and Behaviour of Primates. Academic Press, London.

Rogers, C. M. and Davenport, R. K. (1969). Effects of restricted rearing on sexual behavior of chimpanzees. Developmental Psychology, 1, 200-204.

Rose, R. M., Holaday, J. W. and Bernstein, I. S. (1971). Plasma testosterone, dominance rank and aggressive behaviour in male rhesus monkeys. Nature, 231, 366-368.

Rosenblatt, J. S. and Aronson, L. R. (1958). The decline of sexual behavior in male cats after castration with special reference to the role of prior sexual experience. Behaviour, 12, 285-338.

Rosenblum, L. A. and Nadler, R. D. (1971). The ontogeny of sexual behavior in male bonnet macaques. In D. H. Ford (ed.) Influence of Hormones on the Nervous System. S. Karger, Basel. pp. 388-400.

Rosenblum, L. A., Nathan, T., Nelson, J. and Kaufman, I. C. (1967). Vaginal cornification cycles in the squirrel monkey (Saimiri sciureus). Folia primat., 6, 83-91.

Roth, W. T. (1965). The taxonomy of the baboon and its position in the order of Primates. In H. Vagtborg (ed.), The Baboon in Medical Research. University of Texas Press, Austin. pp. 3-16.

Rowell, T. E. (1967). Female reproductive cycles and the behavior of baboons and rhesus macaques. In S. A. Altmann (ed.), Social Communication Among Primates. University of Chicago Press, Chicago. pp. 15-32.

Rowell, T. E. and Chalmers, N. R. (1970). Reproductive cycles of the mangabey Cercocebus albigena. Folia primat., 12, 264-272.

Saayman, G. S. (1970). The menstrual cycle and sexual behaviour in a troop of free-ranging chacma baboons (Papio ursinus). Folia primat., 12, 81-110.

Sade, D. S. (1964). Seasonal cycle in size of testes of free-ranging Macaca mulatta. Folia primat., 2, 171-180.

Sade, D. S. (1968). Inhibition of son-mother mating among free-ranging rhesus monkeys. Science and Psychoanalysis, 12, 18-37.

Schaller, G. B. (1963). The mountain gorilla-ecology and behavior. The University of Chicago Press, Chicago.

Schwartz, M. and Beach, F. A. (1954). Effects of adrenalectomy upon mating behavior in castrated male dogs. Am. Psychol., 9, 467-468.

Scruton, D. M. and Herbert, J. (1970). The menstrual cycle and its effect on behaviour in the Talapoin monkey (Miopithecus talapoin). J. Zool. Lond., 162, 419-436.

Simonds, P. E. (1965). The bonnet macaque in South India. In I. DeVore (ed.), Primate Behavior. Holt, Rinehart & Winston, New York. pp. 175-196.

Sorenson, M. W. and Conaway, C. H. (1968). The social and reproductive behavior of Tupaia montana in captivity. J. Mammal., 49, 502-512.

Southwick, C. H., Beg, M. A. and Siddiqi, M. R. (1965). Rhesus monkeys in North India. In I. DeVore (ed.), Primate Behavior. Holt, Rinehart & Winston, New York. pp. 111-159.

Srivastava, P. K., Cavazos, F. and Lucas, F. V. (1970). Biology of reproduction in the squirrel monkey (Saimiri sciureus): I. The Estrus cycle. Primates, 11, 125-134.

Stone, C. P. (1932). The retention of copulatory activity in male rabbits following castration. J. Genet. Psychol., 40, 296-304.

Stone, C. P. (1939). Copulatory activity in adult male rats following castration and injections of testosterone propionate. Endocrinology, 24, 165-174.

Struhsaker, T. T. (1967). Behavior of vervet monkeys (Cercopithecus aethiops). Univ. Calif. Publ. Zool., 82, 1-74.

Sugiyama, Y. (1968). Social organisation of chimpanzees in the Budongo Forest, Uganda. Primates, 9, 225-258.

Sugiyama, Y. (1969). Social behavior of chimpanzees in the Budongo Forest, Uganda. Primates, 10, 197-225.

Sugiyama, Y., Yoshiba, K. and Parthasarathy, M. D., (1965). Home range, mating season, male group and inter-troop relations in Hanuman langurs. (Presbytis entellus). Primates, 6, 73-106.

Thorek, M. (1924). Experimental investigations of the role of the Leydig, seminiferous and Sertoli cells and effects of testicular transplantation. Endocrinology, 8, 61-90.

Thorington, R. W. (1968a). Observations on the tamarin Saguinus midas. Folia primat., 9, 95-98.

Thorington, R. W. (1968b). Observations of squirrel monkeys in a Colombian forest. In L. A. Rosenblum and R. W. Cooper (eds.) The Squirrel Monkey. Academic Press, New York. pp. 69-85.

Tokuda, K. (1961-62). A study on the sexual behavior in the Japanese

312   R. P. Michael et al.

monkey troop. Primates, 3, 1-40.

Tokuda, K., Simons, R. C. and Jensen, G. D. (1968). Sexual behavior in a captive group of pigtailed monkeys (Macaca nemestrina).
Primates, 9, 283-294.

Vandenbergh, J. G. (1965). Hormonal basis of sex skin in male
rhesus monkey. Gen. comp. Endocr., 5, 31-34.

Vandenbergh, J. G. and Vessey, S. (1968). Seasonal breeding of
free-ranging rhesus monkeys and related ecological factors. J.
Reprod. Fert., 15, 71-79.

Wagenen, G. van. (1945). Optimal mating time for pregnancy in the
monkey. Endocrinology, 37, 307-312.

Wagenen, G. van and Simpson, M. E. (1954). Testicular development
in the rhesus monkey. Anat. Rec., 118, 231-251.

Wagenen, G. van and Simpson, M. E. (1965). Embryology of the
Ovary and Testis, Homo sapiens and Macaca mulatta. Yale
University Press, New Haven.

Warren, R. P. and Aronson, L. R. (1956). Sexual behavior in castrated-adrenalectomized hamsters maintained on DCA. Endocrinology, 58, 293-304.

Warren, R. P. and Aronson, L. R. (1957). Sexual behavior in adult
male hamsters castrated-adrenalectomized prior to puberty.
J. comp. physiol. Psychol., 50, 475-480.

Washburn, S. L. and DeVore, I. (1961). The social life of baboons.
Scientific American, 204, 62-71.

West, C. D., Hollander, V. P., Kritchevsky, T. H. and Dobriner, K.
(1952). The isolation and identification of testosterone, Δ^4-andro-
stenedione-3, 17 and 7-ketocholesterol from spermatic vein blood.
J. clin. Endocr. Metab., 12, 915-916.

Wilson, A. P. and Vessey, S. H. (1968). Behavior of free-ranging castrated rhesus monkeys. Folia primat., 9, 1-14.

Wilson, M., Plant, T. M. and Michael, R. P. (1972). Androgens and the sexual behaviour of male rhesus monkeys. J. Endocr., 52, 11.

Yerkes, R. M. (1939). Sexual behavior in the chimpanzee. Human Biol., 11, 78-111.

Yerkes, R. M. and Elder, J. H. (1936). Oestrus, receptivity and mating in chimpanzee. Comp. Psychol. Monog., 13, 1-39.

Young, W. C. and Orbison, W. D. (1944). Changes in selected features of behavior in pairs of oppositely-sexed chimpanzees during the sexual cycle and after ovariectomy. J. Comp. Psychol., 37, 107-143.

Young, W. C. and Yerkes, R. M. (1943). Factors influencing the reproductive cycle in the chimpanzee; the period of adolescent sterility and related problems. Endocrinology, 33, 121-154.

Zuckerman, S. (1937). The duration and phases of the menstrual cycle in primates. Proc. Zool. Soc. London, 107 (A), 315-329.

Zuckerman, S. (1953). The breeding seasons of mammals in captivity. Proc. Zool. Soc. London, 122, 827-950.

Zuckerman, S. and Parkes, A. S. (1939). Observations on secondary sexual characters in monkeys. J. Endocr., 1, 430-439.

INTERGROUP ENCOUNTERS IN THE WILD

BARBARY MACAQUE <u>MACACA SYLVANUS L.</u>

John M. Deag

Department of Zoology
University of Edinburgh

INTRODUCTION

Although there are numerous reports of intergroup encounters in macaques, there is almost no information from natural, forest living populations. The present report is an attempt to provide such information and to show that the dynamics of individual involvement in intergroup encounters is an aspect of primate biology deserving close attention. The Barbary macaque Macaca sylvanus was studied during 1968-69 in the Moroccan Middle Atlas Mountains (Deag & Crook, 1971; Deag, in prep). At the Aïn Kahla study locality (altitude, 2,010M, Long 5°13' W; Lat. 33°15' N) the animals lived in a forested habitat of cedar with some holm oak and juniper trees. The forest is dissected by open grassland 'bleds', devoid of trees. The only permanent water supply in the study area is at two wells, also used by the semi-nomadic Berber people and their herds. With the exception of the Aïn Kahla forestry post (that lies outside the forest) the nearest village is 12 km away. The animals were entirely dependent upon natural food.

During the early weeks of this project apparent fluctuations in party size made it difficult to understand the grouping tendencies of the population. It was later shown, however, that the basic social unit of the population was the multimale group (12 to approximately 36 individuals) and that the previously observed fluctuations in party size were due to groups moving in close proximity or uniting. No solitary individuals were recorded (Deag and Crook, 1971).

An intergroup encounter was scored when the behaviour of animals in one group was modified as the result of the behaviour of animals in another. Apart from the first type of encounter to be described, where the changes in behaviour were subtle and usually the result of auditory and not visual contact between groups, intergroup encounters were accompanied by a reduction of the distance between groups. The actual distance between groups varied with the circumstances. With the exception of type A encounters (described below) the definition of encounter used here corresponds closely to the "group interactions" defined by Vessey (1968) and "intergroup relationships" or "intergroup social behaviour" defined by Southwick (1962).

Within this population several different types of encounter were seen. It appeared that the outcome of an encounter depended upon the identity of the groups involved and possibly upon the context of the encounter. During the population study it proved difficult to predict what would happen when two groups met. The study of a single group showed, however, that after a sufficient number of encounters it was possible to predict more accurately how the group studied in detail would behave.

METHODS

A two month survey of Macaque habitats in Morocco, including a preliminary study at Aïn Kahla (carried out jointly with J. H. Crook), was followed by a detailed two phase study in the Aïn Kahla forest. In a 7 month populations study I observed several groups. This was followed by a 6 month single group study during which one group (Group 6) was researched intensively. Results from both studies are presented here. The population study was valuable in revealing one encounter type that might have been overlooked if only the single group study had been made.

Monkey groups were followed as they moved through the forest.

As encounters occurred, I usually stopped other forms of data collection in order to record details of the encounter.

The positions of groups and parties were marked on day range maps and times recorded. Encounter details were recorded either by notes or on a tape recorder. Large scale diagrams were drawn in the field to record the movements of individuals as these occurred. These diagrams formed the basis of the figures used in this paper. Where examples of encounters have been given, the field protocols have been edited to avoid repetition and to illustrate most clearly the point under discussion. In the study area groups were unequally habituated to the observer. In order therefore not to influence the course of an encounter, the observer had to position himself with caution. It was impossible to record full details for all encounters. In some cases observations commenced after the start of the encounter: alternatively the animals were disturbed in some way or obscured by vegetation. Comparisons are therefore limited to encounters for which the relevant details were available, the incompletely observed encounters being excluded. The start and finish time of encounters were recorded and their duration measured to the nearest five minutes. Since the sample size for each encounter type is small, the variation in duration within each type cannot be meaningfully determined.

The term 'party' refers to associations of monkeys of unknown affinity, composition or size limit. Encounters involving one or more parties (either with or without known groups) are included as intergroup encounters only when they were known to be moving independently previous to the encounter. Definitions of the age-sex classes used are given by Deag and Crook (1971). Group 6 contained, 3 adult males, 2 subadult males, 3 juvenile males, 6 adult females, 3 subadult females,

3 juvenile females, 3 infants and 2 babies. Where numbers are used
to identify individuals these correspond to social ranks within age-sex
classes. When data has not been given this will be found in Deag (in
prep.). All times are G.M.T.

TYPES OF INTERGROUP ENCOUNTER

The encounters observed between groups were varied, but could
be arranged on a scale of increasing tendency for the groups to remain
in each other's proximity. The encounter types represent points on a
continuum of possibilities. The classification must be taken as flexible.
It is based on a variety of features that include: the distance between
groups, their behaviour at meeting and while together, the duration of
the encounter and their movements subsequent to the initial meeting.

1. Type A encounters. Noticing the presence of other groups.

As a group moved through the forest various noises and calls
were made. The response of animals in other groups to these sounds
represented the simplest form of encounter. Such simple encounters
were of considerable importance for they provided a group with information on the position of other groups. Noises produced by the animals
included the knocking of stones, as these were turned in search for
food, and the sound of moving branches. Often upon hearing such a
sound individuals stopped what they were doing and, after briefly looking towards the source of the sound, resumed their previous activity.
Loud calling, for instance during intragroup fighting and calling at
predators, lead to the same response. Groups were usually not in visual contact. They responded to calls given almost 1 km away. No calls
appeared to have the primary function of influencing inter-group spacing.
More complex encounters commenced with individual groups noticing

each other's presence, from sounds produced within each group. There was no noticeable change in the spatial arrangement of individuals following this behaviour, unless this was a prelude to another type of encounter.

2. <u>Type B encounters. Groups in close proximity with little or no interaction</u>

This type of encounter can be considered as an extension of Type A. It involved a closer proximity of groups (e.g. 40 - 120 m) and a greater response by each group to the other's presence. They had a mean duration of 15 minutes (range = 50, N=7). Groups were usually in visual contact. There was little if any change in the spatial distribution of individuals within the groups, a feature which contrasts markedly with subsequent encounter types. Upon noticing the presence of the other group, individuals would glance towards it briefly soon resuming their previous activity. Tree shaking occurred in some encounters. It was not always possible to observe under forest conditions the movements of groups both previous and subsequent to tree shaking displays. There was therefore a possibility that some type B encounters involving tree shaking might in reality by type C encounters. Tree shaking is discussed in more detail later.

Example 1. 22.12.68. Two parties.

As one party crossed a forest track moving north, the second party moved down from the north, sat by the track and crossed to the south. The parties were within 40 m of each other. No interaction was seen or heard.

Example 2. 4.10.69. Group 6 and a party

At 1127 Ad♂1 gave a tree shake. At 1128 Ad♂2 gave a tree shake and the observer detected a party ca 100 m from Group 6. There

was intra-group agonistic behaviour and calling in the party, and Group
6 monkeys looked towards this. There was no subsequent interaction.

3. Type C encounters. Approach - retreat encounters not followed by
    coordinated group movements.

During these encounters one group retreated upon the other's
approach. In contrast to some subsequent encounter types this was not
followed by prolonged contact between moving groups. They had a mean
duration of 50 minutes (range = 100, N=10). In this and several other
types of encounter, adult, subadult and older juvenile males, played a
major part in intergroup behaviour. One very characteristic type of
behaviour, called here 'intergroup monitoring behaviour', was observed only during intergroup encounters and then principally by these categories of animal. Intergroup monitoring involved a decisive move towards another group, followed by sitting (principally without feeding or
other activity) and looking towards the encountered group in an alert
fashion. The dynamics of this behaviour were studied in detail in Group
6 and are described later. The retreat of one group, followed either
monitoring behaviour (by individuals from one or both groups) or a more
rapid movement towards the other group by either part or the whole of
the displacing group. In both cases adult and subadult males were usually the leading animals of the approaching group.

These encounters were observed both near and away from the
wells. In both cases one group either displaced the other actively,
with agonistic interaction between individuals from different groups,
or one group simply moved away as the other approached. Usually the
group which retreated from a well was the one that had already drunk.
Away from the wells it was difficult to understand the reasons for
approach-retreat encounters. In two cases, during the course of an

encounter the role of displacing and displaced groups was reversed.
The encounters varied in the extent to which the approach of one group
was directed towards the other.

Example 3. 19.9.68. Group 2 and a party.

     The observer had been following Group 2. At 1350 members
of a party were seen drinking at a well and at that time Group 2 gradually advanced feeding towards them. The leading animals of Group 2
were two adult males and several infants. The adult males moved forwards approximately five paces at a time, sat and moved again. The
party at the well suddenly ran off into the trees behind the well. One
adult male returned to drink. At that moment one of the movements
forward by the Group 2 males suddenly turned into a run and they chased
the party through the trees behind the well. At 1405 the first animal
from Group 2 drank and a tree shake was heard from the party. At
1424 another loud tree shake was given by the party but Group 2 monkeys made no move. Under the trees there was an occasional chase but
it is unknown whether this involved only the party or both groups. By
1507 Group 2 were moving away from the well and at 1520 there were
only 9 monkeys left. At 1530, 11 of the party returned led by two adult
males and several juveniles and infants. The remaining animals of
Group 2 withdrew but there was no further intergroup agonistic behaviour.

Example 4. 2.1.69. Group 8 and a party. Fig. 1.

     At 0849 when some Group 8 monkeys were in their sleeping
trees and others feeding nearby, a party was heard approximately 65 m
away. Several of Group 8 looked in that direction. Those in the trees
descended and joined those feeding. An adult female moved towards
the east and away from the party. Group 8 followed her. The monkeys
on the edge of the party appeared, fed and then at 0920 moved west into
the forest. At 0923 the same female moved back towards the original
position and again Group 8 followed her. While the rest of Group 8 fed,
she moved further west and sat looking in the direction of the party.
She climbed a tree and continued looking, again without feeding. At
0950 she descended, moved to the east, as at 0849, and Group 8 followed behind her.

Fig. 1. Type C encounter. Group 8 avoided a party (Example 4)

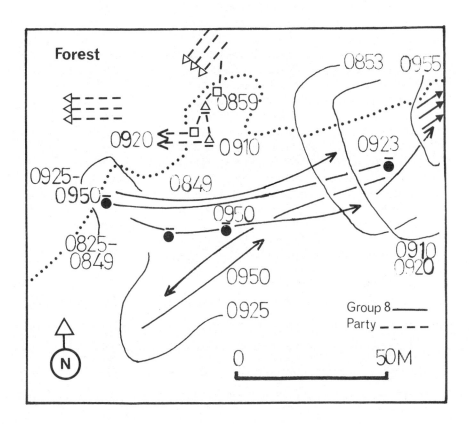

Convention:

Ad♂ ◉, O, Sa♂ ◼,☐, J♂ ▲, △, J (unsexed) <u>▲</u>, <u>△</u>, Ad♀ ◉̄, Ō, I ▼;
unspecified X.

················· edge of forest or clearing

lines enclosing majority of group

——————⟶ routes taken by individuals or groups

routes taken by groups before and after encounters

Numbers, (e.g. 1500) refer to times.

Example 5. 19.4.69. Group 11 and a party. Fig. 2.

At 1440 the party was heard moving ca 250 m from Group 11.
It was on a route which would take it ca 70 m east of Group 11. At 1515
the party had arrived in that position. Members of the party looked towards Group 11 after intragroup calling in the latter. At that time a
subadult male of Group 11 performed a vigorous tree shaking display.
The subadult male and an adult male in the same tree sat looking towards the party. At 1524 they both descended and walked towards the
party. At the same time a subadult male of the party ascended a tree
and shook it vigorously. Some of Group 11 looked in that direction.
Following the shake he sat, looked towards Group 11 and then descended.
While the subadult male of Group 11 sat watching the party the adult
male sat, watched, advanced and sat. The subadult male fed but the
adult male did so only occasionally. The party gradually moved away
to the north-east. At 1529 the adult male (Group 11) moved down to the
tree which the subadult male of the party had shaken, and at 1535 and
1536 shook the tree. Following each shake he sat and looked towards
the party. 1537 the adult male returned to Group 11 which had advanced eastwards. The party had moved completely out of sight.

Other cases involved a more complex series of movements. The
following example illustrates a case where a group which was first displaced, followed this by displacing the group which displaced it. The example also illustrates how, in some circumstances, a whole group moved directly towards another and settled down in its vicinity. In subsequent encounter types this was often the start of a prolonged contact between groups.

Example 6. 25.2.69. Party and Group 4. Fig. 3.

At 1116 an Ad♂ of the party performed a tree shake. Performed on a living tree this made little noise. He then sat, without feeding,
looking towards the north and occasionally autogroomed. At ca 1125
he descended and joined the rest of the party. From 1135 until 1207
this was stationary and feeding. At the latter time Group 4 was seen
moving swiftly towards the party from the north. Two Ad♂♂ and two
Sa♂♂ were at the front of Group 4, followed closely by other age-sex
classes. Their movement was completely orientated towards the party
and the speed was such that some of the last animals were running to
keep up with the group. The party took little notice of Group 4's approach

Fig. 2.   Type C encounter.   Males from Group 11 approached a party
which avoided them.   (Example 5).   Conventions as Fig. 1.

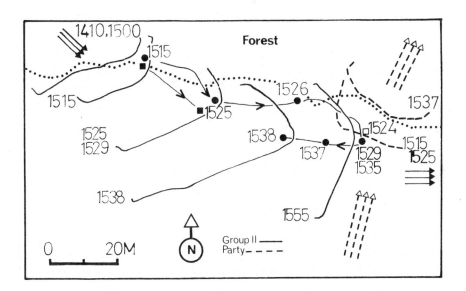

Fig. 3. Type C encounter. Retreat of a party was followed by retreat of Group 4. (Example 6.) Conventions as Fig. 1.

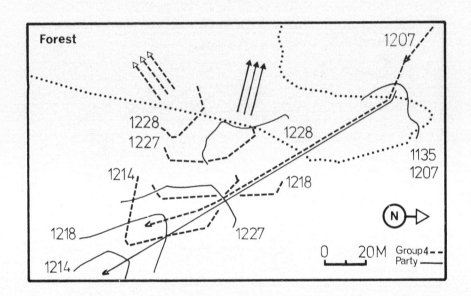

and most animals continued feeding and facing south. When Group 4 got to within 20 m of the party the advancing monkeys sat and immediately started to feed. At the same time monkeys from the party got up and moved decisively to the south. This was followed by a gradual advance of Group 4. The movement picked up momentum and the party moved as a tightly packed unit. There was no feeding. During the initial stages of this movement infants and juveniles from the two groups were involved in chasing but no agonistic calls were given. A single Ad♂ was at the front of the party; the other Ad♂♂ and Sa♂♂ were spread out throughout the party. In group 4 two Sa♂♂ were in the lead but two Ad♂♂ later moved so that they were closest to the party.

At 1214 the movement stopped and the groups were positioned as shown in Figure 3. The groups started to feed. While two Ad♂♂ and Group 4 were closest to the party the latter's Ad♂♂ and Sa♂♂ were spread out throughout the party. At 1218, following a movement of females, juveniles and infants towards Group 4, the Ad♂♂ of the party moved through and sat closest to Group 4. There followed a gradual retreat to the west by Group 4. At 1228 males from the party chased members of Group 4. After a further chase by the party at 1229, during which agonistic calls were given, Group 4 moved away from the party. The final details of separation were obscured by the vegetation.

4. Type D encounters. Approach followed by sitting together which was not followed by coordinated movements.

In this type of encounter either one group moved towards another, or they approached more or less simultaneously. In some cases the whole groups sat, rested and fed in close proximity. In other cases (as in Example 7) the approximation of groups was restricted to the males, the rest of the groups remaining spatially distinct and removed from the encounter zone. They had a mean duration of 57 minutes (range = 120, N=5). In contrast to the following types of encounter, the groups separated and were not seen to move in a coordinated fashion. The separation of groups was casual and did not involve displacement of one group by another. A variation of this encounter type was seen at the wells. There, one group sometimes approached a drinking group and before moving in to drink, waited until the latter had moved. Water was the only localised commodity in the forest and this waiting behaviour was not seen elsewhere. The following example illustrates further the intergroup monitoring behaviour.

Example 7. 4.9.69. Group 6 and a party. Figs. 4 and 5.

At 1619 the observer became aware of a party 40 - 50 m to the east of Group 6. Eight Group 6 monkeys sat looking towards the party. This was done in absolute silence. At 1626 some of the males of the two groups started to advance towards each other (fig. 4) and sat between the groups (fig. 5). At this time a Sao♂ from the party gave a tree shake but this produced little sound. From then until 1648 there was further movement of Group 6 males. These movements, plotted on Figs. 4 and 5, were restricted to the two Sao♂♂ and the oldest J♂. The two visible Ad♂♂ of Group 6 remained with the major part of that group. The major parts of both groups actively fed and only a total of three Sao♂♂, one Ad♂ and a J♂ were engaged in intergroup activities. At 1636 a Sao♂ and J♂ of Group 6 moved closer towards the Sao♂ of the party. This moved back a little. A further movement left the two Sao♂♂ sitting facing each other and 1 m apart. At 1648 the party Sao♂ moved back slightly and an Ad♂ from the party rushed in threatening the Group 6 Sao♂♂. An Ad♂ of Group 6, having moved into the area without the observer's knowledge, chased one of these. The other Sao♂ moved back towards Group 6. Both the first Sao♂ and the Ad♂ returned and sat again in front of the Ad♂ from the party. At 1652 Group 6 males withdrew as did the party Ad♂. By 1655 the groups were moving independently.

5. Type E encounters. Approach, with or without sitting together, followed by coordinated fast progressions

In this type of encounter one group approached another, or the two approached simultaneously. In some cases the two groups sat together as in type D encounters or, as in type C encounters, one group withdrew on the other's approach. In either case this preliminary phase of the encounter was followed by one group walking quickly in front of the other group. Such progressions were swift, the groups moving in narrow (not necessarily single) file with little feeding. These progressions were therefore very different from normal travel feeding progres-

Figs. 4 and 5. Type D encounter. Males from Group 6 and a party
                approached, sat looking at each other and interacted.
                (Example 7). On Fig. 5, numbers refer to minutes of
                1600 hrs. Conventions as Fig. 1.

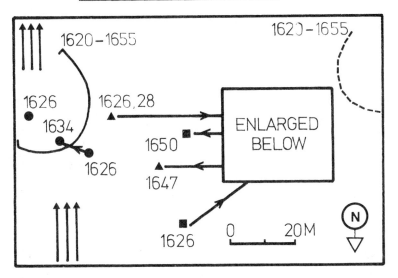

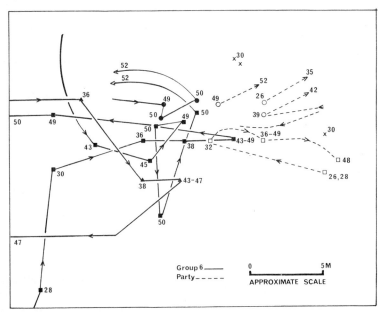

sions and were more like the swift progressions seen when a group
crossed an open area of 'bled' between two areas of forest. Such fast
progressions were almost never confirmed under other circumstances.
(Deag, in prep.) For two complete progressions the speed of movement
from the start of the progression until the groups were moving independently was 0.72 and 0.88 km/hr. The distances covered were 0.33 and
0.51 km respectively. The speed for one incompletely observed progression of 0.30 km (total length unknown) was 0.69 km/hr. The mean
speed for the two complete progressions, 0.80 km/hr is eight times
greater than the mean speed of the linked progressions seen in type F
encounters. Type E encounters had a mean duration of 112 minutes
(range = 5, N = 2).

Example 8. 3.6.69. Groups 6 and 13. Fig. 6.

At 1126 Group 13 was heard calling 180 m from Group 6 and
monkeys from the latter group looked towards Group 13. Group 13 gradually advanced towards Group 6 which had been stationary in its present position for one hour. A Group 6 subadult male was on the edge of
its group. It stopped feeding at 1209 and sat looking at Group 13 for
one minute before resuming feeding. An adult and subadult male were
the leading monkeys in Group 13. At 1211 and 1213 they advanced further towards Group 6 having both previously paused and looked towards
Group 6 without feeding. In response to their movement Group 6 animals made no move. The remainder of Group 13 moved close behind
the adult and subadult male. Monkeys in both groups glanced towards
each other. By 1217 Group 6 monkeys had started to move east with
Group 13 monkeys following close behind. By 1225 all monkeys were
in a progression moving east and away from the encounter site. By
observing various parts of the progression line it was seen that Group
6 continued to advance in front of Group 13. By 1320 the groups were
moving independently. They appeared to have separated by moving at
different speeds rather than by changing direction. (In the above example it appeared that the groups kept separate throughout the progression.
On another occasion close continuity was noted between the last monkeys
of the first group and the leading monkeys of the second group. Two
subadult males from one group and one from the other moved in close

Fig. 6. Type E encounter. An approach by Group 13 was followed by Group 6 retreating. Group 13 moved behind it for over 0.5 Km. (Example 8). Convention ●, O, positions of groups at times shown.◯ , positions of sleeping trees.

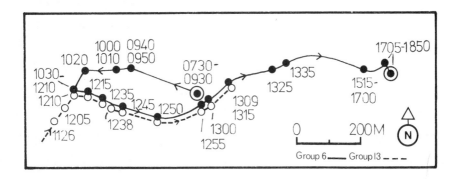

proximity. Group 6 moved in front of Group 13 in each of the three type E encounters between the two groups.)

6. Type F encounters. Approach, with or without sitting together, followed by coordinated linked progressions.

This type of encounter proceeded in its preliminary phases like type D encounters. The coordinated movements shown by the groups were however very different to that shown by type E encounters. Here groups moved in a linked manner, more or less side by side in contrast to moving one behind the other. Each group moved on a broad front. The speeds of four linked progressions, timed from the start of the progression until the groups were moving independently, were 0.07, 0.22, 0.07 and 0.05 km/hr. The distances covered were 0.34, 1.11, 0.49 and 0.27 km. The mean speed of 0.10 km/hr is much slower than that characteristic of Type E encounters. There is probably little difference between the speed of linked progressions and normal travel feeding movements through the home range. Both are slow and casual in contrast to the rapid, little feeding movement typical of fast progressions. Type F encounters had a mean duration of 340 minutes (range = 140, N = 4).

Throughout a linked progression the groups were not continually interacting. They drifted together and apart for a variable number of times. The groups appeared to be drawn together by the monitoring and agonistic behaviours. Groups drifted apart apparently by a reduction of monitoring behaviour as the males moved to catch up with their own groups. On occasions the groups were in close proximity during the period of reduced movement around midday and monitoring was reduced during resting and grooming. In some cases linked progressions were resumed as travel feeding recommenced. Separation finally occurred by the groups moving in different directions or speeds. In the early

phases of such encounters each time the groups came together inter-

group monitoring usually occurred. In some encounters (not for instance

in Example 9) monitoring was noticeably absent when the groups came to-

gether during the later stages. Example 9. 23.8.69. Groups 6 & 13. Fig.7.

Group 6 was followed from its sleeping trees and it moved independently until 1020 when Group 13 was heard nearby. Group 13 approached Group 6 and the two groups moved in a more or less coordinated
manner until 1730. The groups first interacted at 1044 but the details
were obscured by the vegetation. This was followed by Group 13 moving
behind Group 6 and at 1107 the groups interacted again, with the two
subadult and one adult males from Group 6 performing monitoring movements. By 1130 the groups were separate and although they stayed in
the vicinity while grooming and resting they did not meet again until
1512 (see Fig. 7). At that time Group 13 approached Group 6 and an
adult male and subadult male of the former group performed monitoring
movements. The groups moved approximately side by side and at 1525
there was some chasing, following monitoring behaviour. This was possibly intergroup antagonism. It was followed by further monitoring by
both groups. Males from both groups withdrew and the groups continued
independently until 1700 when Group 13 again moved close to Group 6.
Group 6 males advanced towards Group 13 in monitoring movements and
Group 13 withdrew slightly. Monitoring by Group 6 subadult males
continued until 1730 when they moved back to the main part of their group.
The two groups continued to move in the same vicinity but with no further
close interaction. The sleeping trees of the two groups were 100 m
apart. The following morning Group 6 moved away from the sleeping
trees independently of Group 13.

7.   Type G encounters. The unification of groups

Part of the operational definition of 'group' used in this project

was that the individuals comprising a group moved as a coordinated

unit for several days. If a party was located twice with recognisable

individuals and known to be approximately the same size, it was called

a group and given a number. The long term continuity of such groups

was shown during the single group study of Group 6 (Deag, in prep).

Fig. 7. Type F encounter. Group 6 was approached by Group 13 and
the two groups moved side by side for over 7 hours. *indicates
the points where the groups came close together. Other conventions as Fig. 6. (Example 9).

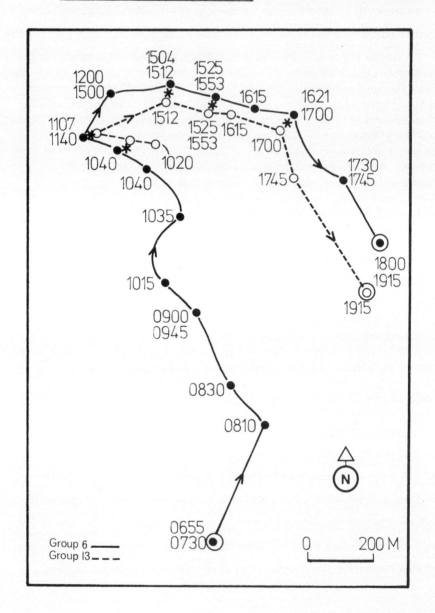

This definition of a group might, however, be compromised by the finding that two such groups could unite to form a larger unit or herd which moved as an apparently integrated unit for several days. Long term observations would be necessary to determine the proportion of time spent by the groups in the independent and herd states. As the group chosen for detailed study was not observed to unite with any other group such data was not obtained. While the details of this process (in particular the behaviour of known individuals while in a herd) remains to be elucidated, sufficient observations were obtained to describe its occurrence.

Example 10. Group 3 and a party.

When Group 3 was located at 1005 on 24.1.69 it was part of a larger unit the exact nature of which could not be determined. Between 1230 and 1300, following a fast progression, during which Group 3 maintained a rear position, the groups involved separated. This movement was not unlike the coordinated fast progressions seen in type (E) encounters. From 24.1.69 to 5.2.69 Group 3 was followed by the observer on six days. With the exception of an adult male which may have temporarily left the group its size (ca 26 individuals) was, as far as could be determined, constant. On 6.2.69 Group 3 met and united with a party but it is unknown whether this was the same party involved on the 24.1.69. Group 3 moved towards the party and until the groups were ca 20 m apart there was no noticeable change in the spatial distribution of individuals. After this, however, two adult males from Group 3 made the first direct approach to the other group, and the two united following some intergroup chasing.

The groups slept in the same stand of trees. On the second day the groups kept together and moved as one. The adult males from each group appeared to keep closer to the males of their own group, but the adult females appeared to maintain no particular positions. The next morning there were several tree shakes and the groups descended and moved off with considerable chasing. This may have been intergroup antagonism. The groups moved in a fast coordinated type progression until lost at 1040.

Example 11. Groups 4 and 9.

From 0930 to 1245 on 20.3.69 Group 4 was observed alone. By 1530 this group had united with Group 9 and the two groups moved as one unit integrated from that time until the 23.3.69. On that date between 1000 to 1235 (exact time unknown owing to observational conditions), the groups separated and moved independently. Group 9 was followed. While this was in the vicinity of a well Group 4 approached the well at 1435 and united with Group 9 at 1505. This took place with no intergroup monitoring behaviour. The animals were completely intermingled and moved again as a single unit. They continued to do so until observation ended at 1015 on 25.3.69.

Less definite examples of unification are as follows. On one occasion a party drinking at a well was disturbed by a herdsman. It ran by the shortest route to the forest some 50 m away and there united with another party which had previously drunk at the well. The arrival of the two parties at the well was separated by one hour. This and the parties' size and cohesion would indicate that they were separate groups. The herd moved and fed as one unit until lost from sight in the forest 10 minutes later.

On another occasion a large herd of monkeys was seen feeding on the slopes of the forest. This included Group 10 and a party. Shortly after observation commenced the herd was disturbed by a man and it separated into two groups, one running north and the other south. Before disturbance no evidence for separate groups was seen. Subsequent observation showed that separation had been complete, no strange individuals being identified in Group 10. It has been necessary to exclude from this analysis large parties (some of which contained over 70 animals) when these were not seen to join or divide, and incompletely observed encounters between known groups and parties. It is likely that some of these large parties involved type E, F or G encounters.

Not all encounters fitted into this frame-work. For example, on one occasion two groups met 'head on' and passed through each other with some intergroup agonistic behaviour.

The relative frequency of encounter types is shown in Table I. Type A encounters are omitted since these were not systematically

quantified. For each group they usually occurred at least several times a day. During the preliminary study a minimum of 11 encounters were recorded. 9 of these were seen during watches at the wells.
They included Type C(4), D(1), D or C(1); type B ending possibly in
type G upon disturbance (1) and two encounters of unknown type. The
two encounters away from the wells were also of unknown type.

It is likely that a localised commodity, such as water, affects
the relative frequency of encounter types. Unfortunately, a proposed
analysis on the influence of well visiting upon the rate and type of encounter was not possible during the single group study. During that
summer (1969) these animals were able to obtain sufficient water in the
forest and no visits to the wells were made. I believe that type C encounters may be relatively more common at the wells than elsewhere.

The data is inadequate to consider the relationship between a
group's size and its performance during encounters. In many cases
complete counts of group or party size could not be made and encounters between groups of known size were relatively rare. This is unfor-
tunate since in _Macaca mulatta_ performance in approach-retreat encounters is correlated with group size (Vessey, 1968). In the present
study, type C encounters included two in which the displacing group was
the larger and one in which displacement of a larger group (29 individuals,
minimum) by a smaller one (20) was followed by a reversal of this position. Other types of encounter involved groups of different size as follows. Type B (15 and 24 individuals), Type D (15 and 24; 23 and ca 47),
Type 'others' (24 and 35 minimum).

No encounters of types E and F were recorded in the population
study. Since it appears, (Table I) that the type of encounter varied with
the groups involved little can be gained from comparing the overall

Table I. Frequency of encounter types

Type*	Population study All groups and parties	Single group study			
		Group 6 with:			
		Group 12	Group 13	Parties	Totals
B	3	1	0	3	4
C	6	1	0	3	4
D	2	2	0	1	3
E	0	0	3	0	3
F	0	0	5	0	5
G	3	0	0	0	0
Other	1	0	0	0	0
Unknown	5	0	2	9	11
Totals	20	–	–	–	30
Number of contact hours	598.2				630.4
Encounters per hour*	0.033				0.047

*Type A encounters excluded.

frequency of encounters in the population study. In the single group study encounters can be divided according to the groups involved. With Groups 12 and 13 the encounters fell into restricted parts of the scale: with Group 12, Group 6 had encounters of types B to D, with Group 13 types E to F. It should be noted that some of the encounters with parties could have been with these groups. Group 6 had no type G encounters. Within the limits of the sample size it appears that the type of encounter seen when two groups met depended upon their identity. This is supported by the observation from the population study that Groups 4 and 9 had a type G encounter twice.

The evidence therefore suggests that pairs of groups may be characterised by the extent of their tendency to remain together during an encounter.

The mean duration for all encounters of known duration was 86 minutes (N=30). This does not include any type A or G encounters.

THE FREQUENCY AND DIURNAL DISTRIBUTION OF ENCOUNTERS

The frequency of encounters was calculated by dividing the number of encounters (excluding Type A) by the contact time (Table I). There were 0.033 encounters/hr in the population study and 0.047/hr in the single group study. (Contact time is defined as the total time during which the observer was with at least one group of monkeys. Only the hours of daylight are included.) The best estimate of encounter rate is that from the single group study. Group 6 was usually followed for several days at a time and this effectively eliminates error due to short periods of observation. The estimate from the population study, based on several groups followed for different lengths of time, may be subject to such errors. In the population study it was also necessary to elimi-

nate from the records some large parties that were probably engaged
in type E, F and G encounters. These were only included when they
were observed to split or join, or involved a known group.

During the preliminary study with J. H. Crook two watches at
the wells revealed 3 encounters between 3 parties in 185 minutes and a
mimimum of 5 encounters between 6 parties in 215 minutes. It is most
likely that the encounter rate was higher when visits to the wells were
necessary.

Encounters were unevenly distributed during the day. (Table
II p 0.<05, x^2 one sample test). Relatively few encounters started after
1500 hours. No attempt has been made to correct for this in the results
presented in other tables,

THE LOCATION OF ENCOUNTERS

For the purpose of studying home range phenomena, the study
area was divided into hecatre quadrats   and entry to these was used
to define a group's home range. 36% of group 6's home range included
80% of its sleeping sites and accounted for 75% of its entries to the
quadrats. This area was arbitrarily designated the 'core area'. Fig.
8 records the position of group 6 during encounters. The three type
E encounters were movements away from the periphery of the range
towards the core area. The five type F encounters involved movements
near, and parallel to, the edge of the core area. Of the remaining
eleven classifiable encounters, 9 occurred either at or near the edge
of the core area. The three type C encounters that involved retreat
of group 6 were on the edge of the core area; the fourth, involving

TABLE II.   The diurnal distribution of encounters (single group study)

Time of day	Number of observation hours	Number of encounters starting in time period	Expected number of encounters
1. Before 0900	94.6	7	4.3
2. 0900 - 1059	100.9	4	4.6
3. 1100 - 1259	112.3	9	5.2
4. 1300 - 1459	112.0	6	5.1
5. 1500 - 1659	108.9	3	5.0
6. 1700 - 1859	101.7	0	4.7
	630.4	29	28.9

When time periods 1 and 2; 5 and 6 are lumped $X^2 = 8.17$ df = 3 $p < 0.05$

Fig. 8.   The location of encounters within Group 6's home range
            (single group study).

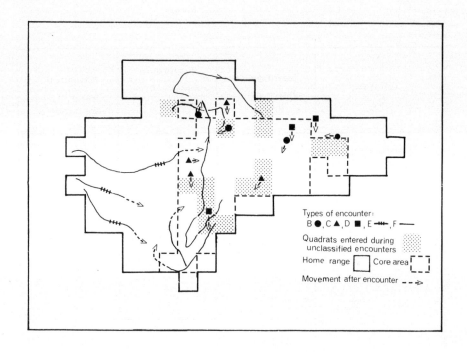

retreat of the other group, was in a more central position. After almost every encounter the group either kept within the core area or moved towards its centre. Was the core area a territory? To what extent can the different types of encounter be interpreted as defence of the area and did they result in group 6 having preferential access to the area? This is possible but until more information is available (including data on the relative positions of the core areas of adjacent groups) I believe that such speculation should be made with caution. At times when well visits were necessary, or when a group's home range included a well, encounters probably occurred more frequently around the wells and in the corridors of forest en route to them.

BEHAVIOUR DURING ENCOUNTERS

1. Tree shaking.

A monkey shook a tree by bouncing rapidly up the trunk, pulling itself up simultaneously with both hands and bouncing down onto the trunk with both hind feet together. When it reached the top these movements were repeated several times before stopping. They were also given during a descent. When performed on a dead trunk the vibrations produced a loud echoing sound clearly audible in the forest (Deag, 1970; Deag, in prep.). Tree shaking occurred during intergroup encounters and also at times when no other monkey groups were known to be near. In the latter situation, another group was sometimes seen near after the tree shake had occurred. It is not, of course, known how many times another group was close but obscured from sight by the vegetation.

Tree shakes were seven times more frequent during encounters than during non-encounter periods. (Table III). The data in this table is restricted to the single group study where the data for non-encounters and encounters is directly comparable. Before and after shaking the animal usually sat looking towards the other group. Sitting and looking around appeared to be less frequent during non-encounter situations.

Tree shakes were recorded in 46% of encounters (18 out of the 39 for which data was available) and during most encounter types. Owing to the small sample it is not possible to analyse the tendency for tree shaking to occur with different types of encounter. During encounters the context of tree shaking was variable. In some cases (particularly during type B encounters) the animal shook without first moving towards the other group. On other occasions it was given after the initial approach towards another group. In both displaced and displacing groups shakes were recorded both before and after the withdrawal of the displaced group. Examples 3, 4 and 5 (earlier) provide typical examples of tree shaking during encounters. Since other behaviour occurred during encounters, it is difficult to determine the effect of tree shaking per se upon another group's subsequent movement. The shaking generally had little effect upon the individuals of the shaker's group. The animals usually ignored the movements and sound, or simply looked towards the tree-shaking monkey. It produced no immediate change in the group's movement or spatial distribution. Tree shakes from other groups produced the same lack of reaction. This behaviour was never used as part of an intragroup threat sequence.

Table III records the age-sex class of the Group 6 individuals known to tree-shake during the single group study. It is based on the number of tree shaking bouts. Bouts were considered separate from

TABLE III.   Tree shaking by group 6 monkeys (single group study)

Age-sex class	Frequency of tree shaking	
	Not during encounters	During encounters
Ad♂	11	6
Sa♂	1	3
J♂	2	0
Ad♀	5	0
Sa♀	2	0
J♀	0	0
unsexed J< 2 years	7	0
I/B	2	0
unidentified*	8	11
Totals	38	20
Number of contact hours	585.1	45.3
Shakes/hour	0.06	0.44

*principally animals heard but not seen to shake.

previous and subsequent bouts if they were separated by other activities,
such as sitting and looking around. In non-encounter situations a variety of age-sex classes shook trees. Young juveniles (ca <2 years) and
infants performed these movements as part of play sequences, either
alone or with their peers. Such shakes rarely produced an appreciable
noise and were accompanied by either running and leaping through the
branches or social play. During encounters only adult and subadult
males were identified as tree shakers and this emphasises again the
importance of these age-sex classes during encounters. Table III is
based on visual and auditory information. In some cases the latter led
to the tree-shaking animal being seen. There might therefore be a
higher probability of including an animal in such a table if its shake produced noise. Combining tree-shaking in encounter and non-encounter
situations, the frequency with which individual Group 6 males shook was
as follows: Ad♂1 (10); Ad♂2 (4), Ad♂3 (2); Sa♂1 (4); Sa♂2 (0); J♂1 (1).
(Plus one by either Ad♂1 or 2 and one by an unidentified J♂. Based on
single group study). In this group there was therefore a positive correlation between the numbers of shaking bouts and rank within age
classes. While subadult males shook during encounters, this was relatively infrequent compared with their high level of intergroup monitoring behaviour (see below).

Occasionally it seemed that tree shaking during non-encounters
was stimulated by the observer's presence. In these cases the shake
sometimes followed a movement by the observer and the shaking animal
then sat and looked towards the observer. This was recorded in 7/54
tree shakes during non-encounter situations (population and single group
study data). The frequency with which this occurred appeared to decrease as the group became more habituated to the observer's presence.

Compared with the number of occasions on which it did not occur, tree shaking at the observer was a very rare event.

2. Intergroup monitoring behaviour.

This term refers to a behaviour seen only during intergroup encounters. Intergroup monitoring behaviour involved a decisive move towards another group (monitoring movements) followed by a prolonged period of sitting in the encounter zone, i.e. the area between the two groups. Such animals sat in a relaxed posture, alert and looking towards the other group. (Fig. 10). Monitoring animals only occasionally fed or engaged in other activities. A monkey from one group occasionally moved back in response to movements by an individual from another group. It is important to note, however, that for most of the time these animals did not show any overt threatening behaviour. For instance, during monitoring movements an animal would stride easily and was alert. It did not, however, push its head forward in a threatening posture or lunge towards the animals of the other group. While prolonged staring may be a form of threat, the seated animals did not raise their eyebrows or push their heads out towards the animals from the other groups. Occasionally, monitoring animals subsequently did threaten and chase individuals from other groups. Then the agonistic behaviour patterns seen during intragroup behaviour were used. Monitoring animals were silent. Individuals from each group took up positions facing each other. Movements across the encounter zone by members of one group were followed either by eye or with a corresponding movement in the other group. As explained earlier (type C encounters) monitoring behaviour was sometimes followed by one group retreating.

Monitoring movements showed that the spatial distribution of

individuals in one group was directly affected by the other group's presence. In most non-encounter situations there was no evidence to suggest that some individuals were spatially central or peripheral (Deag,
in prep.). In encounters where monitoring movements were seen this
position was clearly changed; the individuals engaged in monitoring behaviour took up positions in the encounter zone. Individuals nearest to
the other group did not simply turn around to face it. This occurred,
but they also moved from all parts of the group to take up positions
between the two groups. Although the distance between monitoring animals of opposite groups varied considerably, they were usually closer
to each other than they were to the majority of their own groups. On
occasions they were only one metre apart but a more frequent distance
could be 5-10 metres. While these individuals were in the encounter
zone, the majority of individuals from both groups were not involved
and intragroup activities would proceed as in the non-encounter state.
This does not mean that these individuals were not affected by monitoring behaviour. In several cases, particular type F encounters, the
whole direction of group movement was changed. Here the remainder
of the group eventually moved up behind the monitoring animals.

81% of Group 6's encounters were known to include monitoring
behaviour. (Table IV). Since, by definition, it was excluded from Type
B encounters, the proportion for other encounter types was effectively
higher. Intergroup monitoring behaviour was primarily an activity of
adult, subadult and juvenile (ca > 2 yr) males. (Table IV). The number
of encounters in which individual males (J. and older) were known to
monitor were compared (X^2 one-sample test) with the number expected
if all males monitored equally. The males differed significantly (p <
0.001), owing to subadult males monitoring more frequently than expected,

TABLE IV. Group 6 animals seen to perform intergroup monitoring behaviour (single group study)

Encounter type	Number of encounters known to include monitoring	Number of encounters for which data is available	Number of encounters in which individuals were observed to monitor								
			Ad♂$_1$	Ad♂$_2$	Ad♂$_3$	Sa♂$_1$	Sa♂$_2$	J♂$_1$	J♂$_2$	J♂$_3$	Others
B (4) *	0	3	0	0	0	0	0	0	0	0	0
C (4)	3	3	1	0	1	3	1	1	0	0	0
D (3)	3	3	1	0	0	3	3	2	0	0	0
E (3)	3	3	0	0	0	2	3	0	0	0	0
F (5)	4	5	3	2	1	3	4	1	1	0	0
G (0)	–	–	–	–	–	–	–	–	–	–	–
unknown (11)	4	4	2	0	0	3	4	2	1	0	J and Sa♀
Totals (30)	17	21	7	2	2	14	15	6	2	0	2
Number expected if all males monitored with equal frequency. $X^2 = 38.33$ 7df $p<0.001$			6	6	6	6	6	6	6	6	–

81% (17/21) of encounters were known to include monitoring.

* Total number of each encounter type.

and some individuals monitoring less often than expected. Juvenile and
adult males appeared to monitor in relatively short bouts. No quantitative data on time spent monitoring was however collected. The population study confirmed that this behaviour was characteristic of the population. The proportion of the male age-classes in each group, and individual differences in behaviour, may produce a small difference between
groups. An adult male in Group 13 appeared to monitor more frequently
and with greater persistence than any Group 6 adult male. Group 12
adult and subadult males seemed to monitor less than those of Group 6.

While females and other juveniles would look towards another group
and occasionally pause and watch it between bouts of feeding and other
activities, they rarely performed the full monitoring behaviour. An
interesting exception is provided by Example 4.

To illustrate the details of intergroup monitoring behaviour the following example is given. Example 6 illustrated the initial movements
of males towards another group and gave some details of monitoring behaviour. In the following example it was possible to plot the positions
of most of the group members.

Example 12. 2.9.69. Groups 6 and 13. Fig. 9.

This encounter (Type F) commenced at approximately 0955 with a
tree shake by a member of Group 6. Group 6 was stationary. Group 13
gradually moved south towards Group 6 and by 11.30, when Group 13
was first seen by the observer, the two groups were in close proximity.
Intergroup monitoring was in progress. Fig. 9 records diagrammati-
cally the positions of 21/25 Group 6 individuals.

While the diagram plots the movements of individual males, it is
perhaps more important to note the overall effect of a band of monitoring Group 6 males in the encounter zone. Only one female entered this
zone and this was I♀3. She was shown elsewhere (Deag, in prep.) to be
spatially close to the group's males. She did not engage in monitoring

Fig. 9.   The movements of individual males during intergroup moni-
           toring behaviour.   (Example 12.) Superscripts (e.g. ▲¹)
           give the rank within age-sex classes. Conventions as for
           Fig. 1.

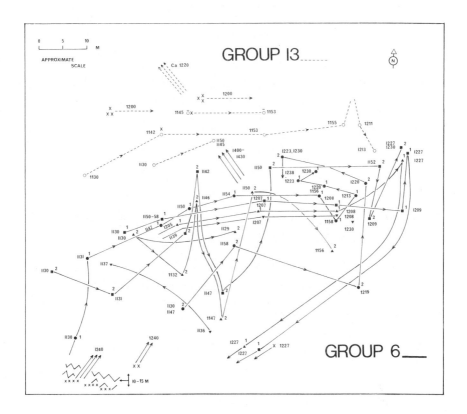

behaviour. The majority of the group, known to include adult and sub-adult females, babies, infants and one adult male, were located approximately 40-50 m from the encounter zone. These animals stayed there from the beginning of the encounter until they moved north at 1240. By that time the intergroup monitoring had more or less ceased and Group 13 was slowly moving away to the northwest. The monitoring individuals were Ad♂♂ 1 and 2; Sa♂♂ 1 and 2; and the oldest J♂♂, 1 and 2. In Group 13 the closest individuals were two adult males. The activities of the two groups' males were correlated. For instance, at 1130 Sa♂1 sat facing a Group 13 Ad♂. At 1139 Sa♂2 moved position and took up a new position at 1142. During this movement the Group 13 Ad♂ followed him with his eyes and then moved to a new position as shown. At 1147 Sa♂2 moved again and the Group 13 Ad♂ moved around and eventually took up his 1155 position. These movements were followed by further movements in the same direction by both groups. At 1223 Ad♂2 ran at an unidentified Group 13 monkey. By that time most of Group 13 had moved slightly north-west and continued to do so. With the exception of Ad♂♂ 1 and 2 the monitoring by Group 6 monkeys had ceased by 1220. The two Sa♂♂ and one J♂ fed, and at 1227, two of these moved back to the rest of the group (as shown) in response to a call given by a baby male. The major part of the group moved north-east at 1240. By then monitoring had been relaxed and Ad♂2 moved from his last monitoring position at 1238. While Group 13 remained near, the behaviour of Group 6 was then directed towards intragroup activities with only occasional glances towards Group 13. At 1400-1430 Group 6 moved after Group 13 and the two moved side by side in a coordinated, linked progression until separating at 1530. During these subsequent movements monitoring behaviour was reduced in frequency and at times absent.

The possible functions of monitoring behaviour are examined in the Discussion.

3. Agonistic behaviour

Encounters were analysed according to the presence or absence of overt agonistic behaviour and agonistic contact between monkeys of different groups. Overt agonistic behaviour refers to any aggressive behaviour pattern, in a series between either the tense mouthed or staring open mouthed pout faces (both with head pushed towards object) and actual attack. Agonistic contact refers to any attack which leads to any physical contact between the fighting animals. For those encounters which were seen clearly, 46% (6/13) of the population study encounters and 50% (10/20) of the single group study encounters involved overt agonistic behaviour. No cases of agonistic contact were recorded. This reflects the low level of agonistic contact seen during intragroup behaviour. It is important to note the low level of wounding in these animals. No wound involving broken skin was observed. Owing to the small sample it is not possible to discuss the relationship between encounter type and the occurrence of overt agonistic behaviour. It was recorded in all types of encounter with the exception of types A and B. This exception would be expected by definition.

Agonistic interactions between individuals of different groups usually started with one of the males engaged in monitoring behaviour, threatening or being threatened by another (see Fig. 10).

Females, younger juvenile males and infants became involved primarily when chasing brought monkeys from one group towards the major part of another. Table V lists for Group 6 the involvement of age-sex classes in intergroup agonistic behaviour. Only males were aggressors. The proportion of adult : subadult males involved was as expected from their relative proportion in the group. In contrast, while adult males were never victims, subadult males were victims frequently. This involvement of males (particularly subadult males) is related to their close proximity to other groups during encounters.

In some cases agonistic interactions commenced with an adult male running towards the monkeys at the edge of the other group, without previously performing monitoring behaviour. Threatened monkeys ran

Fig. 10. Agonistic behaviour during an encounter. Black arrow points
to members of one group (B), white arrows to members of
other (W). In the encounter zone a WSa♂ (almost adult) sat
facing a BSa♂ and a BSa♂ and BJ♂ were grooming (a). Approach of the WSa♂, followed by a threatening gesture (b) broke
up the grooming pair (d). Subsequently, this WSa♂ chased the
B group animals until he was himself chased by a BAd♂ (d).
The seated posture of the BSa♂ on the left in (c), was typical
of intergroup monitoring animals.

TABLE V. The frequency with which Group 6 monkeys were involved in overt agonistic behaviour with monkeys from other groups (single group study).

Number of interactions during which age-sex classes were:	Ad♂	Sa♂	J♂	Ad♀	Sa♀	J♀	I/B	Unidentified
Aggressors	7	4	1	0	0	0	0	0
Victims	0	10	4	3	3	0	4	5+?*

*Unknown number from two interactions

back towards their own group. This was followed, in some cases, by adult and subadult males from the victims' group running to the encounter zone. These animals either, threatened or chased the victim, took up monitoring positions, or threatened individuals from the other group. Fig. 10 gives an example of such an interaction. The squealing of females and young animals appeared to be particularly effective in bringing adult males running to the encounter zone. Once there, they often stayed in the zone only briefly. In contrast, subadult males often continued monitoring until the groups finally separated.

4. Non-agonistic behaviour

No intergroup non-agonistic behaviour (other than monitoring) was observed in encounter types A to F. Since the single group study included only a short part of the mating season, the absence of intergroup copulation needs to be confirmed. There is probably extensive contact between individuals of different groups during type G encounters but, as so few individuals could be recognised at that stage, only one was confirmed: a subadult female groomed an infant from another group.

INTERGROUP ENCOUNTERS IN OTHER MACAQUES

1. The frequency of encounters

Intergroup encounters have been observed in most of the studied macaque populations. Two exceptions are the studies of Nolte (1955, M. radiata) and MacRoberts (1970, M. sylvanus, on Gibraltar). Few studies give details of encounter rates. Vessey (1968), working with the La Cuevan rhesus, reported 0.36 encounters/hour. On Cayo Santiago Loy (1970) recorded 1.1 displacements/hour. Lindburg (1967 p. 99) reported that in India "rarely did a group pass through a day without coming into contact with at least one of the other four groups in the area". One can therefore infer that the encounter rate was lower than those quoted above. In a less densely occupied forest habitat he found that encounters were less frequent. In the present study the rate was 0.047/ hr. These differences reflect differences in population density and patterns of habitat use. The mean duration of 204 encounters on La Cueva was 7 minutes (Vessey, 1968); much shorter than the mean duration of 86 minutes recorded in the present study.

2. Types of encounter

Most encounters described for other populations fit into the classification used in this paper. Type A and B encounters probably occur in most populations but have almost never been reported. Type C encounters have been seen in M. mulatta, M. radiata, M. fascicularis, M. silenus, M. cyclopsis and M. fuscata. On Cayo Santiago island, La Cueva Island and in the Indian temple habitats (M. mulatta), type C encounters are exaggerated in frequency by high population density and localised sources of food. They are also more violent, involving extensive intergroup fighting. Of the 112 type C encounters observed by Wilson (personal communication) on Cayo Santiago, only 13 were away from the feeding stations. Sugiyama (1968) observed type C encounters between M. silenus groups when they came into contact at food trees.

Several studies have noted a positive correlation between a group's size and its ability to displace other groups (Altmann, 1962; Koford, 1963; Koyama, 1970; Neville, 1966; Nishida, 1963; Rahaman and Parthasarathy, 1969 a and b; Southwick, 1962; Southwick et al, 1965; Sugiyama 1968; Vessey, 1968, 1971; Wilson personal communication).

These and other studies (Vandenbergh, 1967; Imanishi, 1963; Loy 1970) indicate a definite group dominance hierarchy, revealed by approach-retreat encounters. A group's rank may also be based on the relative rank of the highest ranking males (Koyama, 1970; Koford, 1963; Vessey, 1968). One group may, however, recognise the other's status without seeing the highest ranking male (Koford, 1963).

According to Vandenbergh (1967) a group's rank may depend upon its 'central group of females' since group rank did not change when high ranking males changed groups. Vessey (1968 and 1971) speculated that 'peripheral males' may play an important role in determining group rank; when he removed alpha males this had no effect on group rank. Marsden (1971, abstract only) has shown in enclosed groups that "instability of intergroup dominance can be experimentally induced by the removal or introduction of young, 'peripheral' males". Several of these studies report reversals of the intergroup hierarchy. Such reversals may depend upon the locality of the encounter (Southwick, 1962; Furuya, 1965).

Encounters approximating to type D have been reported by several studies (Rahamen and Parthasarathy 1969 a and b; Sugiyama 1968, Wilson, personal communication). Vandenbergh (1967) found that in 6% of 92 encounters the bands "remained together for one to fifteen minutes duration without antagonism". This occurred between two groups in particular. Working on the same population Vessey (1968) noted that two groups remained close for up to three hours. He also reported encounters, lasting up to 45 minutes, which correspond to the type E encounters described here. On La Cueva type C encounters developed into type E encounters when the two groups were moving along a common pathway, one group being continually pushed in front of the other. This explanation does not, however, fit for the present study. In the more uniform habitat of the Aïn Kahla forest, special pathways were not defined.

It is speculated later that type G and F encounters may be more common among related groups. Evidence for or against this might be found in studies of group division. Unfortunately most of these studies give little detail of the ranging patterns of the groups prior to, during or after division. Southwick et al (1965) found that in M. mulatta the groups became increasingly independent and their relationship with each other increasingly antagonistic. In M. fuscata studies of group division have concentrated upon the social changes within the dividing group (Furuya 1960, 1968, 1969; Koyama, 1970). According to Furuya (1968) division occurs abruptly. Sugiyama (1960), however, found that the branch troop became gradually more and more independent until separate sleeping sites were used. From that point the groups were fully independent and encounters between them led to no unification, temporary or otherwise. Nothing is known of group division in M. sylvanus and so comparisons should be made with caution. If division occurred in a similar way then type G encounters would represent an early stage in division. My impression, admittedly based on little hard evidence, is that type G encounters represent either the late stages of division or a post division behaviour. Type F encounters have not been described in any other macaque.

3. Agonistic and non-agonistic behaviour

One important result of the high population density of the Temple habitat and Cayo Santiago rhesus populations may be that the animals have become, in one respect, habituated to the frequent close proximity of other groups. Sounds from one group do not seem to warn of another group's presence. Apparently, type A encounters carry no meaningful information. Southwick et al (1965) and Southwick (1962) reported rhesus groups surprising each other, since they relied on visual and not auditory cues to detect another group's approach. On Cayo Santiago the banging of hopper lids may indicate that a feeder is occupied; calls apparently do not. The surprising of groups and the blocking of retreat in urban areas may be responsible for the almost extensive daily occurrence of intergroup fights (Southwick 1962). Southwick (1962) classified rhesus encounters as "usually antagonistic" with "direct overt fighting between groups". Lindburg (1967, p. 99) reported that in the Asarori forest, where encounters were "relatively rare", they were "invariably marked by a high degree of antagonism". This was in spite of population density in the forest area being lower than at his other study site. Encounters in the forest population studied by Neville (1966) appear to have been less violent. Probably only one out of ten encounters involved fighting between groups. In 219 encounters Vessey (1968) saw 3 cases of agonistic contact. Wilson (personal communication) saw 10 cases in 112 type C encounters. Vandenbergh (1967) recorded gestural and vocal threats in 12% of 92 encounters and fights in 22%. Wounds are common in some Cayo Santiago animals (Koford, 1965). In both the present study and Vessey's (1968) c.a. 50% of encounters included overt agonistic behaviour. Neither the frequency of agonistic contacts nor the proportion of encounters involving overt agonistic behaviour fully reveal the more violent nature of encounters in M. mulatta when compared with the study population of M. sylvanus. A more sensitive measure is required for adequate comparison. Encounters in M. radiata (Rahaman and Parthasarathy, 1969 b) and in M. fascicularis (Shirek-Ellefson, quoted by Marler 1968, Furuya, 1965) may also be violent.

Other studies have noted the involvement of adult and subadult males during encounters (Rahaman and Parthasarathy, 1969 b; Southwick, 1962; Koford, 1963; Marsden, 1968; Neville, 1966; Sugiyama 1960; Wilson, personal communication). Vessey found that 'peripheral males' were most often involved in the overt aggression between groups and this is upheld by the observations of Marsden (1968). Vessey concluded that involvement correlated with the spatial distribution of individuals within the group. This is supported by the observations of Neville (1966) in wild forest living animals. The present study, however, shows how the presence of another group produced a marked change in the spatial distribution of individuals. Involvement could therefore be explained primarily in terms of movement into the encounter zone rather than the relative positioning of individuals in the non-encounter state. This highlights the active participation of these age-sex classes.

Non-agonistic contact between individuals from different groups has been reported. Wilson (personal communication) observed intergroup copulation and grooming. Nishida (1963) only saw inter-group copulations when the groups were brought together by artificial feeding. Some 'intergroup copulations' involve males changing groups and not copulation during encounters (Lindburg 1967). Vessey (1968) saw intergroup play and copulation.

4. Tree shaking and intergroup monitoring

Tree, branch or timber, shaking during encounters by adult or subadult males has been reported from most studies. Altmann (1962) considered that timber shaking, in the Cayo Santiago rhesus, indicated an occupied region, but it was not given at any territorial boundary.

Marler (1968) classified it as a signal that increased

the distance between groups: if this were the case in the study popula-

tion one would expect tree shaking to be more frequent during the early

encounter types. In the two cases when tree shaking was recorded

during type G encounters, the unified groups appeared to be in the pre-

liminary stages of separation. Southwick (1962) considered tree shaking

to be a form of threat. While this may be so, it is not essential to the

interpretation of the behaviour as a signal that increases the distance

between groups. M. fuscata call while tree shaking and these calls are

related to calls given during agonistic situations. Tree shaking is giv-

en during intergroup encounters, following intra-group fighting and

leader males use tree shaking to indicate the departure of the troop

and its direction of movement (Itani, 1963, Yamada, 1966). Rahamen

and Parthasarathy (1969b) considered that branch shaking had two func-

tions; signalling the presence of one group to another and warning group

members of the other group's approach.

Branch shaking outside encounter situations has been recorded by

Altmann (1962), Itani (1963) and Simonds (quoted by Marler, 1968).

Marler (1968) suggested that this may function as a signal that main-

tains the distance between groups. In the present study it occurred too

infrequently to be ascribed this function. M. silenus has a loud whoop-

ing call, given by large males, with the apparent function of influencing

intergroup spacing. Given during encounters, one group moves away

after a short period of calling (Sugiyama, 1968). Adult male M. fasci-

cularis call before and during movements and this is thought to keep

groups spaced out (Shirek-Ellefson, quoted by Marler, 1968).

Intergroup monitoring behaviour has not been discussed in detail

for any other macaque. Simonds (1965 p 195), however, noted that

"When the two groups met the subadult and adult males would move towards the other group, and then sit and look at each other with approximately 20 ft. between them. Then the males in one of the groups would begin to drift back in the opposite direction and the groups would separate". This closely corresponds to the behaviour described in this paper.

DISCUSSION

The encounters described for this population cannot be explained simply in terms of a group dominance hierarchy. Some groups clearly displaced others (Type C encounters) and, with a larger sample, it might be possible to show that the approach-retreat relationship of groups was relatively constant. The remaining encounters do not fit into this limited theoretical framework. To call type D encounters 'stalemates', because they result in no displacement, has no explanatory value. A wide variety of factors most likely influence the nature and frequency of encounters. Table VI lists some of these. (See also Bates, 1970). Only long term studies of a population could fully determine the relative importance of these factors. The purpose of the following is therefore to speculate how some of them may have influenced the encounters recorded in this paper.

Ranging characteristics determined which groups could possibly meet. Group 6 met Group 12 less often than Group 13, most probably because it had greater home range overlap with the latter. The individuals within groups that met frequently may have been more familiar with each other's behaviour and encounters, and may therefore have proceeded differently to those between groups which met less often. This may be one reason for the different types of encounter between

TABLE VI.   Factors which may determine the frequency and nature of encounters between two groups of this population

(A) Possible determinants of the frequency of encounters

      Size of home range

      Length and pattern of day ranges

      Extent of home range overlap

      Density of habitat use (time and frequency in particular areas)

      Localised commodities - e.g. water

      Group size

(B) Possible determinants of the nature of encounters

      Whether or not the groups originated from a common group

      Manner of group division

      The extent of kinship between individuals in the different groups

      Time since division

      Proportion of different age-sex classes

      Group size

      The location of the encounter

      Time since previous encounter

      Major activity of individuals and the rate of group movement at the start of encounter

      Personality of males involved in monitoring and tree shaking

      Pugnaciousness of individuals, in particular adult and sub-adult males

      Personality traits of males and/or females which may partially determine group rank

      The personality of individuals which lead or influence group movements

      The outcome of previous encounters between the groups

Group 6 and these two groups. At some seasons one might expect a
higher encounter rate at wells and it is likely that at such times groups
would encounter groups from outside their own (wet season) home range.
Type C encounters (involving approach-retreat) may have been more
frequent at the wells than elsewhere. It is likely that if the animals
were dependent upon localised food sources the frequency of this encounter type would be higher. In this population there was no active
competition between groups for food trees or sleeping sites. The order
of progression in type E encounters (essentially Type C but with a long
retreat) was probably an expression of the approach-retreat relationship between the groups. There is other evidence to show that locality
influenced the encounter type. For instance, Groups 6 and 13 meeting
on the western edge of Group 6's home range had type E encounters.
Elsewhere their encounters were type F.

Groups recently formed by the division of another group may have
had a large home range overlap, a close knowledge of the individuals in
each group and kinship with some members in the other group. This
may explain the type G encounters and possibly, if division occurred
longer ago, the type F encounters.

As in other macaques, adult and subadult males played a major part
in encounters. They were involved in moving towards other groups,
monitoring, tree shaking and agonistic behaviour. The persistence
and frequency of involvement of individual males in these types of behaviour may have affected the type of encounter. The repeated monitoring by the Group 6 subadult males and one adult male from Group 13
may have been partially responsible for the long type F encounters.
Group 12 males seemed to monitor less than those of Group 6 and
there were no type F encounters between these groups. Since the rest

of the group sometimes moved after the monitoring individuals the extent to which these individuals were followed by others may have influenced the encounter and in particular, the speed with which separation occurred. An individual's experience in past encounters probably
influences its behaviour in subsequent encounters and consequently the
overall performance of the group.

What is the function of monitoring behaviour? The term monitoring
was used since males appeared to sit, observe and respond to movements by the other group's males. This knowledge of the other group's
position might be particularly important if a relatively strange group
was encountered. Presumably if groups met frequently, then individuals
could predict, on the basis of previous experience, the probable behaviour of the other group's individuals. With strange groups, the males
in the encounter zone may sense changes in the behaviour of the other
group and would be the first individuals to respond. It is interesting to
note in this context, the apparent reduction of monitoring during the
later phases of Type F encounters. Also, when two groups united for
the second time on one day (Example 11), they did so without monitoring behaviour. These cases suggest that familiarity of the groups may
be important in determining whether or not monitoring occurs.

There was little evidence for the exchange of males between groups
in this study. Nevertheless this is known to be common in some macaque populations (Lindburg, 1969). It should therefore not be excluded
as a possibility, especially when only a few days of detailed study were
possible during the mating season. Intergroup monitoring might facilitate the exchange of males between groups by familiarising the males
of one group with those of another and by conveying information about
the number and condition of males in other groups. A group with few

males might be quickly indicated by a low level of monitoring behaviour.
Marsden (1968) suggests that the frequent contact between peripheral
rhesus males may facilitate group exchange.

When groups live in overlapping home ranges then they can be expected to meet on the basis of chance alone. Vessey (1968) considered
that there was no evidence that groups actively sought each other out
for encounters. When groups were some distance apart this applied to
the study population. Once they were closer a definite attraction existed between some groups. Why did some groups meet and have lengthy
encounters when complete avoidance would be possible? We know little
of why home ranges have the shape and overlap pattern that they do.
Encounters may not only familarise individuals in one group with another (and so facilitate group exchange and permit group recognition),
but may also play a major role in the spacing out of groups over the
habitat. When home range overlap is imposed by ecological conditions
then the extent of overlap might be adjusted by keeping encounters with
identified neighbouring groups down to a minimum. When population
density is high, encounters become more frequent and violent (cf Cayo
Santiago studies). On Cayo Santiago this may be partially due to competition for food and Loy (1970) found a small, but non significant drop
in the encounter rate when food was short. On an island, dispersal is
impossible and the encounter rate is likely to be a function of group
size, density and ranging behaviour. In the study population, tolerance
between groups would be expected to some extent during dry seasons
when groups moved to wells to drink. In territorial species encounters
have a spacing function and contain stereotyped components. Here,
tree shaking (see Marler, 1968) and intergroup monitoring were the
most stereotyped components of encounter behaviour. These elements

may therefore be the most important in maintaining the separation of groups and in bringing about the ultimate dispersal of groups.

It must be emphasised that the classification used is a preliminary one. The headings given to each encounter type summarise the overall course of an encounter. In future studies it would be preferable to analyse a larger sample of encounters using numerical taxonomy techniques. This would test the overall validity of the present classification and place any new classification on a more empirical basis.

SUMMARY

Intergroup encounters within a population of wild Macaca sylvanus were varied in type but could be arranged on a scale of increasing tendency for the groups to remain in each other's proximity. The outcome of an encounter depended upon the identity of the groups and possibly upon the context of the encounter. One group had approximately 0.05 encounters/hr with a mean duration of 86 minutes. Many encounters occurred on the edge of the group's core area. Approximately 50% of encounters included overt agonistic behaviour between individuals from different groups. Adult and subadult males played a major part in encounters. They participated more frequently than other age-sex classes in the intergroup behaviour which included tree shaking, agonistic behaviour and intergroup monitoring. The latter involved a decisive move by an individual towards another group followed by a prolonged period of sitting and watching in the zone between the groups. In other macaques adult and subadult males also play a major part in encounters. Several of the encounter types have been observed in other macaque populations. In some provisioned populations the relative frequency and approach-retreat encounters may be exaggerated by the localised resources. The results are discussed in terms of the wide variety of factors likely to influence the nature and frequency of encounters in this and other species of macaques.

ACKNOWLEDGEMENTS

This project was undertaken while the author was a post-graduate student in the Department of Psychology, University of Bristol. Field research was financed by a Leverhulme Overseas Scholarship and a Wenner-Gren Foundation Pre-Doctoral Fellowship. Research in England was carried out during the tenure of a S.R.C. Research Studentship. A vehicle for the project was supplied by Leverhulme with assistance from the University of Bristol. I am grateful to these organisations for their support. In Morocco the 'Administration des Eaux et Forêts et de la Conservation des Sols', provided invaluable assistance. I thank M. Msougar, Director of the 'Institut Scientifique Cherifien', University Mohammed V, Professor J. B. Panouse, formerly of the 'Laboratoire de Zoologie', the staff of the British Embassy, Rabat, and the foresters of Aïn Kahla for their hospitality and assistance.

I am indebted to Dr. J. H. Crook for his help throughout the project and to Drs. W. C. McGrew, D. L. G. Noakes and T. Rowell for their helpful comments on an earlier draft of this paper. Dr. A. P. Wilson kindly permitted me to quote his unpublished observations. J. J. Holmes drew some of the figures. It is a pleasure to acknowledge the assistance given by my wife Rosemary, at all stages of this project.

REFERENCES

Altmann, S. A. (1962). A field study of the sociobiology of rhesus monkeys Macaca mulatta. Ann. New York Acad. Sci., 102, 338-435.

Bates, B. C. (1970). Territorial behaviour in primates: a review of recent field studies. Primates 11, 271-284.

Deag, J. M. (1970). The Apes of Barbary. 30 minute, 16 mm. colour film. Produced in association with J. H. Crook and with the University of Bristol, Audio-visual Aids Unit.

Deag, J. M. (In prep.) A study of the social behaviour and ecology of the wild Barbary macaque, Macaca sylvanus L. Ph. D. Thesis, University of Bristol.

Deag, J. M. and Crook, J. H. (1971). Social behaviour and 'agonistic buffering' in the wild Barbary macaque Macaca sylvana L. Folia Primat. 15, 183-200.

Furuya, Y. (1960). An example of fission of a natural troop of Japanese Monkeys at Gagyusan. Primates 2, 149-179.

Furuya, Y. (1965). Social organisation of the crab-eating monkey. Primates, 6, 285-336.

Furuya, Y, (1968). On the fission of troops of Japanese monkeys. I. Five fissions and social changes between 1955 and 1966 in the Gagyusan troop. Primates, 9, 323-350.

Furuya, Y. (1969). On the fission of troops of Japanese monkeys. II. General view of troop fission of Japanese monkeys. Primates, 10, 47-69.

Imanishi, K. (1963). Social behaviour in Japanese monkeys. Macaca fuscata, in C. H. Southwick (ed), 'Primate social behaviour', 68-81 (Van Nostrand, Princeton).

Itani, J. (1963). Vocal communication of the wild Japanese monkey.

Primates 4 (2), 11-66.

Koford, C. B. (1963). Group relations in an island colony of rhesus
    monkeys in C. H. Southwick (ed), 'Primate social behaviour',
    136-152 (Van Nostrand, Princeton).

Koyama, N. (1970). Changes in dominance rank and division of a wild
    Japanese monkey troop in Arashiyama. Primates 11, 335-390.

Lindburg, D. G. (1967). A field study of the reproductive behaviour of
    the rhesus monkey. (Macaca mulatta). Unpublished Ph.D. disser-
    tation. University of California, Berkeley.

Lindburg, D. G. (1969). Rhesus monkeys: mating season mobility of
    adult males. Science 166, 1176-1178.

Loy, J. (1970). Behavioural responses of free-ranging rhesus monkeys
    to food shortage. Am. J. Phys. Anthrop. n.s. 33, 263-272.

MacRoberts, M. H. (1970). The social organisation of Barbary Apes
    (Macaca sylvana) on Gibraltar. Am. J. Phy. Anthrop. n.s. 33,
    83-100.

Marler, P. (1968). Aggregation and dispersal: two functions of primate
    communication in P. C. Jay (ed), 'Primates. Studies in adapta-
    tion and variability', 420-438. (Holt, Rinehart & Winston, New
    York).

Marsden, H. M. (1968). Behaviour between two social groups of rhe-
    sus monkeys within two tunnel-connected enclosures. Folia Pri-
    mat. 8, 240-246.

Marsden, H. M. (1971). Intergroup relations in rhesus monkeys
    (Macaca mulatta). In A. H. Esser (ed), 'Behaviour and Environ-
    ment: the use of space by animals and men', 112-113. (Plenum
    Press, New York).

Neville, M. K. (1966). A study of the free ranging behaviour of rhesus monkeys. Unpublished Ph.D. thesis. Harvard University, Cambridge, Massachusetts.

Nishida, T. (1963). Intertroop relationship of the Formosan monkey (Macaca cyclopsis) relocated on the Nojima islet. Primates 4, 121-122.

Nolte, A. (1955). Field observations on the daily routine and social behaviour of common Indian monkeys, with special reference to the Bonnet monkey (Macaca radiata Geoffrey). J. Bombay Nat. Hist. Soc. 53, 177-184.

Rahaman, H. and Parthasarathy, M. D. (1969a). Studies on the social behaviour of Bonnet Monkeys. Primates 10, 149-162.

Rahaman, H. and Parthasarathy, M. D. (1969b). The home range, roosting places and the day ranges of the Bonnet macaque. J. Zool. 157, 267-276

Southwick, C. H. (1962). Patterns of intergroup social behaviour in primates, with special reference to rhesus and howling monkeys. Ann. N.Y. Acad. Sci. 102, 436-454

Southwick, C. H., M. A. Beg and M. R. Siddiqi, (1965). Rhesus monkeys in North India. In I. DeVore (ed), 'Primate Behaviour'. (Holt, Rinehart & Winston, New York). pp. 111-159.

Sugiyama, Y. (1960). On the division of a natural troop of Japanese monkeys at Takasakiyama. Primates 2, 109-148

Sugiyama, Y. (1968). The ecology of the lion-tailed macaque Macaca silenus (Linnaeus) - a pilot study. J. Bombay Nat. Hist. Soc. 65 283-293.

Vandenbergh, J. (1967). The development of social structure in free-ranging rhesus monkeys. Behaviour 29, 179-194

Vessey, S. H. (1968). Interactions between free-ranging groups of rhesus monkeys. Folia Primat. 8, 228-239.

Vessey, S. H. (1971). Free ranging rhesus monkeys: Behavioural effects of removal, separation and reintroduction of group members. Behaviour 40, 216-227.

Yamada, M. (1966). Five natural troops of Japanese monkeys in Shodoshima Island (I) - Distribution, and social organisation. Primates 7, 315-362.

Additional Reference

Lindburg, D. G. (1971). The rhesus monkey in North India: an ecological and behavioural study. In Rosenblum L. A. "Primate Behaviour" Vol. 2. Academic Press, New York and London. pp. 1-106

Addendum

Since this paper was completed, Lindburg (1971) has published a more comprehensive account of intergroup encounters in wild rhesus. His forest population showed some interesting similarities with the population discussed here. Encounters occurred at a rate of 0.03 per hour, several different types were seen (but not apparently types E and F) and the participation of sub-adult and juvenile males in an intergroup monitoring-like behaviour was noted.

THE SOCIAL STRUCTURE OF WILD CHIMPANZEES

A REVIEW OF FIELD STUDIES

Yukimaru Sugiyama

Kyoto University
Primate Research Institute
Inuyama, Aichi, Japan

I. INTRODUCTION, RECOGNITION OF SOCIAL UNIT

OF CHIMPANZEES

During the last decade or so studies of ecology and behaviour of wild chimpanzees have progressed rapidly. In particular the work of Kortlandt (1962, 1963, 1967, etc.), Goodall (1965, 1968, etc.) and Reynolds (1965, etc.) is well known. Here, I wish to present the chimpanzee study of the Kyoto University Research Party which is currently little known in Europe, and to focus particularly on the social structure and relationships of chimpanzees.

Ecological and sociological studies on chimpanzees by Kyoto University started in 1961 in the vast savanna area from Kabogo Head through Kasakati Basin on the east coast of Lake Tanganyika (Fig. 1). Although these studies encountered difficulties as the chimpanzees were so shy that they could neither be traced in movement nor be observed within a short distance for many hours successively, the continuous study piled up observations and extensive ecological data on the chimpanzee's daily life (Azuma and Toyoshima, 1961-2; Izawa and Itani, 1966; Suzuki, 1969; Izawa 1970; Kano, 1972).

In the early stages of this study the members of our Research Party found, as had Jane Goodall, that chimpanzees form a temporary group or party which lasts for a few hours or days. The animals freely unite or separate from time to time, as if they had no stable social unit except the mother-offspring social bond. We were impressed by the difference between the social structure of chimpanzees and that of other old world monkeys and apes studied so far, which always have a closed or semiclosed group with permanent membership of individuals.

Fig. 1. Study areas of wild chimpanzees by Kyoto University Research
Party (shaded area).

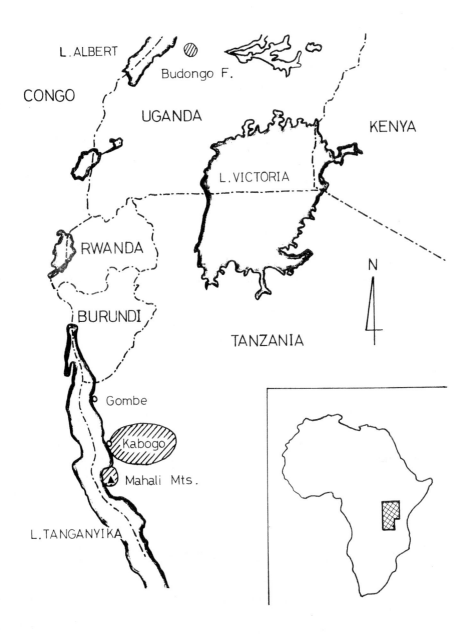

We found it difficult to believe in a group life without any permanent social unit.

During this time we sometimes met large chimpanzee parties of which the membership appeared rather stable. An observation of a large party travelling in savanna was especially significant (Itani and Suzuki, 1967). The procession order of the whole party, consisting of 43 head, was recorded.

Gradually we concentrated on studying the chimpanzee social unit, its structure and the relationships between social units. We worked in two main study areas (Fig. 1). The first was in the high forest of Budongo of north-east Uganda where we tried to observe chimpanzees intensively by habituation and without artificial feeding. The second was in a ecotone of lowland forest and savanna-woodland at the foot of the Mahali Mts. of east coast of Lake Tanganyika where we baited chimpanzees.

II.   OBSERVATIONS ON FOREST CHIMPANZEES
OF BUDONGO

The Budongo Forest covers an area of about 430 km^2 and the canopy reaches nearly 50 m in height (Photo 1). Few sunbeams reach the forest floor in the wet season but many of the trees shed their leaves in the dry season; between December and February the forest floor is exposed to the sun (Eggeling, 1947).

Reynolds and Reynolds (1965) studied the ecology and behaviour of chimpanzees in this forest in 1962 and I tried to examine chimpanzee social structure through the identification of individuals utilising the studies of the Reynolds as a basic reference. I traced the same chimpanzee population as the Reynolds studied, trying to habituate the animals to me and naming each individual whom I met. As in all other studies chimpanzees were observed in temporary parties though sometimes as singletons. Party membership changed frequently (Fig. 2). Sometimes two or more parties came together at a food tree and sometimes one party divided into two or more parties as if there was no integration between them.

1. Population

Recording as many chimpanzee names as possible I found that the splitting of a party and the gathering of individuals is not carried out at random but is done within the membership of a loosely resident population. That is, most of the party members of the main study area were chimpanzees recorded in my name list. In the study period of half a year I succeeded in identifying 41 chimpanzees in the regional population of the centre of my main study area by their face, features, behaviour and other individual characteristics, though chimpanzees were still shy and some could not be identified. 5 km^2 was confirmed as the ranging area of this group. I estimated that a group size of about 50-60 chimpanzees occupied a total range of about 7-8 km^2 (Fig. 3) (Sugiyama, 1968). Partly overlapping with the range of the central group, there were adjacent chimpanzee groups having their respective ranges and similar group sizes. Succeeding to my study, Suzuki followed the same population of chimpanzees continuously for 17 months and he found that this group actually consisted of more than 80 chimpanzees with a range of about 20 km^2 (Suzuki, 1971). Reynolds, when he studied here, estimated that about 13 km^2 of his main study area was distinct from the neighbouring area and contained the movement of about 70-80 chim-

Photo 1.　Interior of the Budongo Forest.

Fig. 2.   Continual division and conflux of chimpanzee parties observed
in October 2 and 3, 1966, at a <u>Ficus</u> <u>mucuso</u> tree.

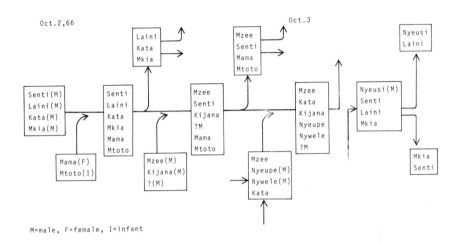

M=male, F=female, I=infant

Fig. 3. Moving ranges of chimpanzee groups of the study area,
         Budongo Forest, which were drawn by Reynolds and Reynolds
         (1965) (Break line), Sugiyama (1968) (solid line) and Suzuki
         (1969, 1971) (chain).

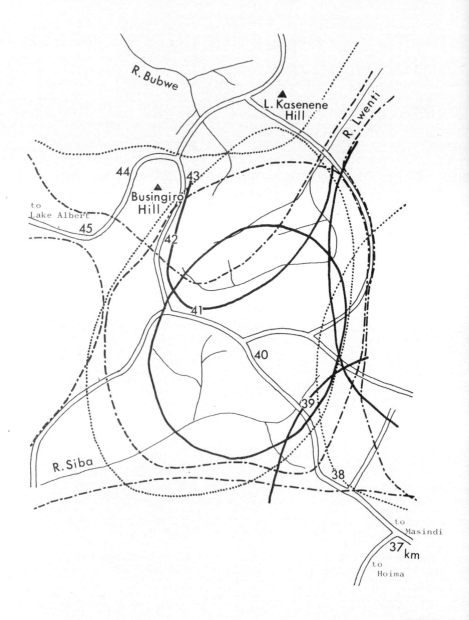

Table 1. Group composition of the main study area, Budongo Forest

Estimated by	Adult Male	Adult Female	Immature Male and Female	Total	Moving range (km^2)
Reynolds	20	23-30	27-32	70-80	13
Sugiyama	18	14	24	56	7-8
Suzuki	25	30	30	85	16-17

panzees and he named this area the Eastern Valleys Siba Region, though he could not identify each chimpanzee (Reynolds and Reynolds, 1965). Although Reynolds' way of estimating group size and range is different from ours, the results of these three successive studies give us a fairly clear picture of the chimpanzee population of our study area.

Although there might be some misidentification of chimpanzee individuals in my estimation, a group of about 70-80 chimpanzees maintained itself in the same area for more than 7 years (1962 to 1968) without much change (Table 1). It persisted in being separated from surrounding adjacent groups and the population density of the study area was estimated as about 4-5 head/km^2. Some of the characteristic chimpanzees lived in the study area as residents for more than 7 years and most of the adult male chimpanzees were seen for more than two years of our study period. For example, a male of ginger-coloured hair who had been recorded by Reynolds in 1962 as an infant of two years old or less was still alive in 1966 as an adolescent male and nearly matured in 1968. Mkono, who had no right hand, was found in 1966 and was accustomed to me (Photo 2). He was one of the dominant males of the main study area through 1968, but recently he was killed by a biologist for serological study (Suzuki and Suzuki, 1971). (So now our research material for naturalistic study is being destroyed not only by industrial needs but also by modern scientists.) Thus in natural forest, each chimpanzee persists in staying in a certain restricted area which he knows well for some years. Here he lives with some fellow animals whom he knows well. The group size, its membership, its range and, perhaps the social structure appear more stable than we suspected previously. This kind of regional population can be considered to be a loosely integrated group separated from neighbouring groups as a social unit.

2. Greeting

How are the social relations among individuals maintained?
Among chimpanzees, besides grooming, there are many kinds of
friendly and associative behaviour patterns used for appeasement or to
ease social tension. When excited party members produce a booming
noise (see page 391) and the social tension among individuals becomes
high. When two parties are confluent at a fruit-bearing tree, when
two individuals come too near on a narrow branch, or in other situations, one grooms the other, one stretches out its hand and touches
the other's hand or body, one grips or faces the genital area of the
other (Photo 3), one embraces the other, or some other behaviours
may occur. These greeting behaviours are not always forms of appeasement directed by a subordinate to a dominant individual. In many situations, when two or more individuals meet, tension-easing behaviours
occur on an equal base, independent of the actions of the dominant and
subordinate relationship (Sugiyama 1969).

When two parties join at fruit-bearing tree, some kind of greeting behaviour between members of both parties, especially between big
adult males, occurs. One observation follows (Fig. 4). After crying
vigorously and beating the buttress of a tree with both hands, a big
male climbed the tree composedly. Hearing the greeting cry and beating, a big male from the former occupying party approached the newly
arrived big male. The two males almost embraced and mutually
groomed for a long time. Then, they began to eat. No other chimpanzee performed any greeting ceremony.

Sometimes a newcomer approaches a former occupant, stretches

Photo 2. An old male chimpanzee, Mkono, had no right hand and was most accustomed to us.

its hand and both chimpanzees touch each other's hands. Big males may sometimes feel the necessity to solve the psychological friction which occurs with a male of another party. The greeting occurs between the leading animals of two parties, as other animals in the joining parties neither greet nor exhibit aggression. Young animals may not have such a psychological tension with others and they cannot carry out the complete greeting behaviour.

3. Leadership

The role of permanent leader is unlikely to exist in a flexible society in which members form only temporary parties in their daily life. Although it may not be essential for females and immature animals to follow a leader, big males were often observed leading their party to a safe place, informing other animals of the presence of a villager, or displaying against him in a critical situation.

Finding me in the forest, shy chimpanzees who were not accustomed to me usually went away by themselves leaving their fellows. This kind of reaction to me was typical in mother parties or in parties lacking big males. Males may learn how to cope with emergencies with an enemy, and with other critical situations while other animals understand the meaning of the warning behaviour of big males and react appropriately.

4. Sexual Relations

Coexistence of individuals of equal status in a group is also observed in the sexual behaviour of chimpanzees. A sexually excited male and an estrous female neither form an extended consort couple nor do they copulate exclusively. An oestrous female may mate with

Photo 3. A middle-sized adult male, Laini (lower), grasped and
          shook the scrotum of a big adult male, Simo (upper), and
          groomed his thigh for easing their tension.

Fig. 4. Conflux of two parties after greeting by big males of both
sides (December 17, 1966. 7:30)

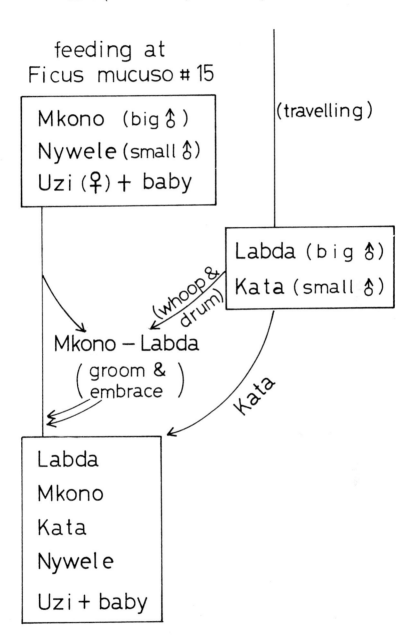

many males within a short time, even in sight of other dominant animals.
An œstrous female was observed to mate with three males within 15
minutes. Another observation revealed that an œstrous female stopped
grooming a big adult male, approached a young adult male on a nearby
branch and copulated with the latter before returning to the former for
further grooming with him.

These examples show that sexual relations, as well as other
social relationships among chimpanzees, are formed without a rigid
dominance hierarchy. However, according to a personal communication
of P. R. McGinnis, dominant males of Gombe Stream Reserve form
exclusive consort couples with particular females, though subordinate
or peripheral males mate promiscuously.

5. Dominance

Although I emphasize the uniqueness of the chimpanzee society in
the friendliness and associativeness among individuals, inter-individual
friction is not always solved by friendly and associative behaviour.
Sometimes a big male exaggeratedly attacks and chases a small male,
putting the whole party into excited confusion. This is especially common during the dry season during which chimpanzees form large parties and travel noisily covering a wide area. Even so the dominant
and subordinate relationship does not govern the whole of their daily
life. I recognised only 31 dominant and aggressive-submissive behaviours among chimpanzees of the study area during the 360 observation
hours. This is because each individual can move itself freely away
from a particular animal if it does not want to move with the latter
according to its own volition.

Along with differences in the individuality of each chimpanzee differences of intimacy among individuals and differences in associations between individuals when moving may occur. So, some individuals were frequently recorded in a same party but others were not. Many kinds of physical, behavioural and psychological differences between individual chimpanzees may contribute to their loose social integration. Correspondingly, the loose social organisation permits free movement of each individual in a population.

6. Booming Clamour

Excited chimpanzees frequently produce the booming noise, that is, they cry, whoop and bark desperately, drum by spanking tree trunks and buttresses, run and brachiate from branch to branch and vigorously shake branches. Although the booming noise may sometimes function to express antagonism against an adjacent group, chimpanzees within hearing range of the separate party which belong to the same group frequently respond by whooping and run in the direction of the sound. The two booming parties often meet and join at a fruit-bearing tree with or without greeting behaviours. Even though chimpanzees of a group cannot recognise each other visually in the thick forest, they may be able to communicate the existence of fruit-bearing trees, potential predators, or their own location and demeanor (Reynolds and Reynolds 1965, Sugiyama 1968).

The booming clamour of chimpanzees occurs when a party divides and half of it moves away, when two parties meet, when a party finds or reaches a fruit-bearing tree, and when a party begins to travel after feeding or resting as well as in many other situations. The booming clamour may function to maintain friendly communication with other group members and, as such, to strengthen their social bonds. I was impressed by the fact that chimpanzees often raise clamour without an apparent economic purpose in their daily life but simply when they want to behave in an excited fashion. The excitement of one chimpanzee may then release that of others and the whole party soon becomes frenzied by a feedback mechanism.

Having contacted with each other by means of these communicative behaviours group members gather and join at fruit-bearing trees. Yet they also split and move away at will. This kind of group or regional population consists in a group of chimpanzees having associative social bonds and living in a same range. The members are acquainted with each other and frequently move together, although they do not always move as a troop.

7. Wanderer and Inter-group Relations

I sometimes found strangers in the main study area. They were not positively identified because they went away within a few days or so. These strangers probably wandered into the main study area from neighbouring groups, and might be slightly acquainted with the study area and its resident chimpanzees. When a lone stranger joined a party of resident chimpanzees it was quite calm, the residents neither showed aggression nor attempted to exclude it. Most of the strangers which I recognised were adult males but there may have been females which I could not recognise because they were very shy.

In the overlapping part of their ranges mixed parties of members of two adjacent groups were sometimes observed together without the occurrence of any agonism. However, I twice observed that when many chimpanzees of neighbouring groups met, they mixed together excitedly, ate exaggeratedly leaves and fruits which they seldom eat, ran and leaped about the ground and branches, drummed and beat the buttresses of the huge trees and uttered their desperate cry and bark. After nearly one hour of noisy booming clamour, the chimpanzees of each group returned to their own proper ranges. During the time no direct aggression against the other group between animals of separate groups could be observed. Although chimpanzees of neighbouring groups are acquainted with each other and have neighbourhood relations, they usually avoid mixing as whole groups. Even when they do meet they maintain their neighbourhood relations by such 'ritual' or 'festivalised' behaviour without showing direct aggression.

I was convinced that each chimpanzee living in the continuous large forest recognises its own group fellows and that non-aggressive relationships with chimpanzees of neighbouring groups exist. Not only do smooth, friendly social relationships stem from this, but genetic exchange among groups is also quite likely.

8. Hunting and Food Sharing

Although Dr. Reynolds and I could find evidence neither for hunting nor for meat-eating, Suzuki (1971) observed three episodes of hunting or meat-eating at the Budongo Forest. In one case he observed a black-and-white colobus which was attacked by several chimpanzees and captured by a big male (Fig. 5). Chimpanzees came to gather round the captor to look at the prey and some eagerly groomed him and touched the prey as if begging for some meat. A few chimpanzees succeeded in sharing a piece of meat or a small bone with the captor. The begging, grooming and meat-sharing proceeded between the second meat-holder and other chimpanzees as in a chain reaction. In another case Suzuki found a big male holding a new-born baby chimpanzee

Fig. 5. The relations among individuals during the eating of a black-
and-white colobus monkey. (From Suzuki, 1971a)

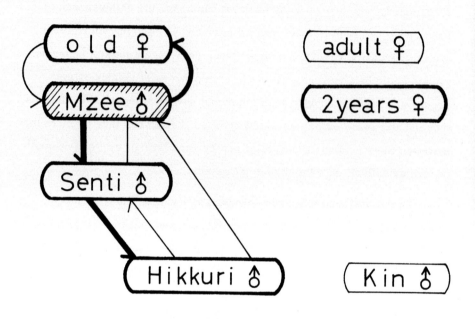

: possessor

: individuals who were shared

: direction of sharing

: direction of begging and grooming

without its right leg but still carrying the navel-cord. Some males and females gathered near the male, presented themselves to him, touched the baby and licked the root of the right leg of the victim, but he continued to hold and lick the blood of the root of the right leg of the baby which was still living and uttering a feeble scream. Although the above observation was a fragmental one, D. Bygott (personal communication) has now observed a complete episode of cannibalism among chimpanzees of the Gombe Stream Reserve, from the tragic meeting of the captor and the prey to the eating and throwing away of the carcass.

III. WOODLAND CHIMPANZEES OF MAHALI MTS.

1. Population

The Mahali Mts. lie at the Kungwe Head projecting into Lake Tanganyika from the east. They are covered by thick riverine forest and woodland (Photo 4). Following information from villagers that some years ago chimpanzees damaged cultivated fields, Nishida tried to bait chimpanzees by banana and sugar-cane. In February 1966 the first chimpanzee appeared in front of the observer and since then the number of chimpanzees who appear on the feeding ground has gradually increased (Photo 5). Although chimpanzees appeared in parties of several animals and showed both joining and splitting as in all other studies on chimpanzees, we confirmed that the whole population of this area consisted of only 29 permanent members (Table 2). This population was named Group-K. Since that time, 1966, the basic membership of this group has not changed although some died or deserted the group and some temporarily joined the group. It has a ranging area of about 10 km^2 which contains the feeding ground at its south end (Nishida 1968)

Photo 4.   View of the Mahali Mountains.   (Photographed by Dr. J. Itani)

Photo 5.   Chimpanzees feeding in the Mahali region.

Table 2.   Age/Sex composition of Group-K of Mahali mountains
            (July, 1967). (From Nishida 1968).

Age class	Male	Sex Unknown	Female	Total
Adult	6		9	15
Subadult-Adolescent	1		3	4
Juvenile			2	2
Infant	2	4	2	8
Total	9	4	16	29

(Fig. 6). The population density of the range is calculated at about 3
head/km^2 but that of Mahali Mts. area as a whole is estimated at about
one head/km^2.

2. Begging and Sharing Interaction

During the first stage of the baiting at Mahali, Nishida observed
that adventurous males came to the feeding ground, took bananas and
sugar-canes and carried them back to the jungle where the females and
juveniles were waiting, hesitating to move closer. A female stretched
her hand timidly to the male begging for food. He cut his food into two
and gave one part to her. Begging behaviour was performed almost
exclusively by adult or adolescent females, who begged food of adult or
adolescent males on 28 of the 32 total occasions of begging interaction
observed. On 16 occasions males who were begged at for their food
willingly gave part upon request (Nishida, 1970). All begging and food
sharing behaviours were carried out with food provided at or near the
artificial feeding ground.

Fig. 6.   Feeding ground near the Mahali Mountains.

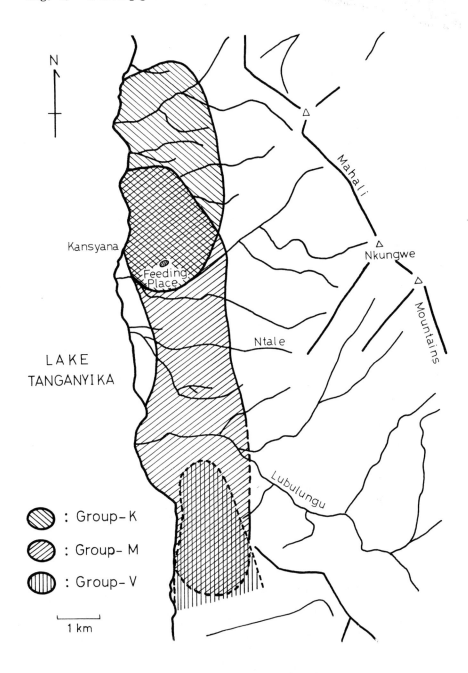

3. Intergroup Relationship

To the south of Group-K, a larger population of about 60-80 chimpanzees, Group-M, has a range of about 17 km^2. This group moves to the north in September seeking the juicy fruits of the particular species, Garcinia huillensis, and Saba florida. At this time chimpanzees of Group-M gradually increase at Kansyana valley area where the artificial feeding ground exists. Chimpanzees of Group-K then move to the north of their range grouping in parties. They decrease their appearances at the feeding ground, perhaps avoiding the dominant population, Group-M. No chimpanzee of Group-K can be seen near the feeding ground at the end of October. The feeding ground and its vicinity are occupied by Group-M until next January or February when the fruiting season of the particular food species finishes, and the Group goes back to the south of its range. Then, members of Group-K come back to the Kansyana Valley area once more grouped in small parties. During the succession of the chimpanzees of the two groups at the feeding ground chimpanzees of both groups sometimes coexist in the Kansyana valley area. Occasionally some females of Group-K remain there after their group has deserted the feeding ground and gone north. These females joined Group-M without being rejected. According to Nishida and Kawanaka (1972), altogether 5 adult and adolescent females changed their membership from Group-K to Group-M between 1966 and 1970. Afterwards, three of them returned to Group-K (Fig. 7).

Other than these 4 females, one mother with her baby and an extremely old male were missed from Group-K. The latter must be dead. During 4 years 4 mothers with their babies and 6 adult and adolescent females were found to join Group-K temporarily but they deserted it after some days (Table 3). Altogether 39 episodes of

Fig. 7. Individual transferring between Group-K and M. (From
         Nishida and Kawanaka,1972).

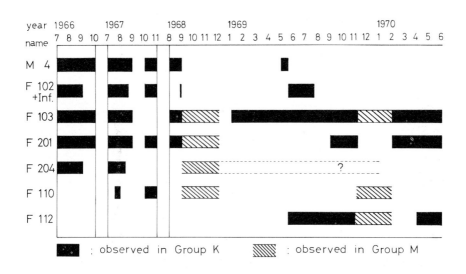

Table 3. Observations of Temporary Immigrations

			Observed Date
1.	Subadult female	1966	24.7
2.	Adolescent female		31.7 1.8
3.	Adult-I female		5.9
4.	Adult-I female Infant-II Juvenile-I		10.9 11.9
5.	Adult-I female		12.9
6.	Adult-I female Infant-II		1.10
7.	Adult-I female Infant-II		1.11
8	Adult-I female Infant-II	1967	9.8
9.	Adolescent female	1968	14.8 16.8
10.	Adolescent female		28.8

of emigration or immigration were observed in this small population containing only 12 adult females as permanent members. There must have been more episodes which observers could not count. An important point here is that most of the emigrants and wanderers were females and their children.

In all examples of immigration and emigration chimpanzees were received without any antagonism and no behaviour characterising the newcomer could be recognised. But females who deserted their group and joined to Group-M were sometimes observed together in the same party. These 4 females were in oestrus at least once during their stay in Group-M. Females who joined Group-K were also observed in oestrus during their stay in it. These observations show that sexual excitement may be one of the factors predisposing females to move from their maternal group and to join another group. Although almost all emigrants and immigrants which were confirmed at Mahali were females and their children, the social composition of Group-K suggests that males may leave their mother-group during their lifetime too.

IV. DISCUSSION: SOCIAL STRUCTURE OF CHIMPANZEES

The basic structure of chimpanzee society can be recognised in both the thick forest of Budongo as well as in the woodland of Mahali. The Budongo chimpanzees live in natural conditions while chimpanzees of Mahali are artificially baited. Chimpanzees usually spend their daily life grouped in a small party or moving alone. Frequently a party divides into two or more parties and parties merge into one. Even so, the gathering and splitting of the party and individuals are carried out mostly within a basic population of between 30-80 individuals or so which is loosely separated from neighbouring others. This account is also supported by the extensive observations in the savanna of Kasakati Basin, east coast of Lake Tanganyika (Izawa 1970). The population size of the chimpanzees' basic social unit at our research sites does not contradict other studies. Although   Kortlandt (1962, 1967) recognised 48 or 49 head as a maximum in his study area in high forest of East Congo, he estimated that a total population may be 70 or 80. Goodall (1965, 1968) estimated that the total population of Gombe chimpanzees is about 150 and that each individual in this community is an independent unit with the exception of infants and young juveniles; but only 38 chimpanzees frequently visited her research station throughout the year of 1964-5.

The social integration of the chimpanzee population of the Budongo Forest is characteristically loose and the chimpanzees seldom move all together as a group. The relationship between adjacent groups is also loose and their members sometimes mix in a party without any trouble. On the other hand the chimpanzee population of Mahali moves as a group at least twice a year over a long distance. As a social unit its membership is more stable and the outlines of the regional population are more clear in Mahali than those in Budongo. The relationship between adjacent groups is more antagonistic in Mahali. However, the semiclosed social unit could be found without any geographic barrier in both habitats. Whether there are two or three loosely separated groups in the Gombe chimpanzee community or not, it may be that the social integration of the Gombe chimpanzee population is more loose than others. I must emphasise that chimpanzee social structure has a wide variety from place to place. The variation of rigidity, compactness and closedness of the structure of a social unit may depend, firstly on the population density and the distribution pattern of food and shelters and, secondly, on the vegetation type, geographic conditions and some other factors. Although it is still to be fully described, Kano estimated that the population density of the widely scattered chimpanzees of the huge savanna of Western Tanzania is much like that of the dense Budongo Forest, where only the riverine forest part of the savanna is considered as the ecological base for the daily life of savanna dwelling chimpanzees (Kano, 1972).

So flexible and loosely united society is never found in old world monkeys and apes so far studied except in the chimpanzee. Members of the group always move together, though there are some temporary exceptions. In most of the old world monkeys and apes the social and psychological frictions between individual members of a group is solved mainly by aggression or avoidance. This kind of social relation is called the dominance relationship. In chimpanzees aggression between individuals is not frequently seen although many kinds of associative, appeasement and greeting behaviours are found more frequently than in other kinds of monkeys and apes. This difference between chimpanzee and other kinds of monkeys and apes may show that chimpanzees solve the social and psychological friction among individuals mainly by a highly developed tolerance of individuals which suppresses the appearance of the dominance. The flexible society of the open group (Reynolds, 1966) allows each member to move freely from others so that they can avoid particular individuals before aggressive behaviour takes place. These must be the principles for the peaceful coexistence of chimpanzees in a group. Although among Mahali chimpanzees a dominance hierarchy is seen, it is to be emphasised that the dominance relationship among individuals must become more rigid as a consequence of the artificial baiting and severe food competition.

All hunting episodes by chimpanzees against monkeys observed by Kawabe (1966) in the savanna of the east coast of Lake Tanganyika and by Suzuki (1971) in the Budongo Forest as well as by Goodall (1965) at the Gombe Stream Reserve, were carried out by two or more male chimpanzees. Some of them involved coordinated pincer attacks. These observations show that chimpanzee hunting behaviour requires cooperation among hunters, more or less with foresight as to the result. Although nimble monkeys are not always very afraid of chimpanzees, they are none the less a potential prey of cooperatively hunting chimpanzees.

In the Budongo Forest the begging and food sharing behaviours were seen in relation to meat and in Mahali they concerned the food thrown at the feeding place. Although the situations seem different to each other, the begging and food sharing were carried out when a particular animal obtained the exclusive possession of valuable foods.

Now, it can be said that the maintenance of the unique social structure of chimpanzees is deeply correlated not only with individual tolerance but also with the development of active cooperation and mutual assistance.

Considering the evolution of mammals, primitive species must have aggregated or dispersed very loosely. The discrimination of place and individual animals must have developed in relation to the evolution of the central nervous system. Then, territorially among dispersed animals and the dominance hierarchy among members of an aggregation must have developed gradually when the population density in a given area was high. All primate species, except some prosimian species, developed group life with stable membership, dominance hierarchy and the closedness of the group. The rigid dominance hierarchy in a social unit, typically seen in macaques, must be one of the peaks of the social evolution. On the other hand chimpanzees must have followed a contrasting path in which they evolved a flexibility of social structure and the development of behaviour patterns as a "buffer" or "lubricant" of the social and psychological friction among individuals which did not require the establishing of a rigid hierarchy (Sugiyama,1972a). Although chimpanzees of a group do not always stay together in one gathering, to maintain the loose but regulated social structure described above must require a highly developed ability of memory and identification. The importance of such a kind of loosely organised social structure must be related to the independence of individuals. That is, while it may have enhanced the development of individuality it also requires it as a basic factor. Besides, it suggests that such a flexible social structure might have had an important role during hominisation in the establishment of personality, family and flexible hunting society in man (Reynolds 1966).

V. ACKNOWLEDGEMENTS

I am most grateful to Prof. Junichiro Itani for his kind encouragement and suggestions throughout the period of my field work and in preparing the manuscript. Thanks are extended to Dr. K. Kawanaka for his valuable suggestions and discussions and to people in our research field for their associative friendship. Acknowledgement is also extended to Dr. R. Michael for his kind help in preparing the English manuscript.

VI. REFERENCES

Azuma, S. and Toyoshima, A. (1961-2). Progress report of the survey of chimpanzees in their natural habitat, Kabogo Point Area, Tanganyika. Primates 3 (2), 62-70.

Eggeling, W.J. (1947). Observations of the Ecology of the Budongo Rain-forest, Uganda. J. Ecol. 34, 20-87.

Goodall, J. (1965). Chimpanzees of the Gombe Stream Reserve. In: "Primate Behavior" (E. DeVore ed.) Holt, Rinehart & Winston, New York.

Itani, J. and Suzuki, A. (1967). The social unit of chimpanzees. Primates 8, 355-381.

Izawa, K. (1970). Unit groups of chimpanzees and their nomadism in a savanna woodland. Primates 11, 1-46.

Izawa, K and Itani, J. (1966). Chimpanzees in Kasakati Basin, Tanganyika (1) Ecological study in the rainy season 1963-1964. Kyoto Univ. Afr. Stud. 1, 73-156

Kano, T. (1972). Distribution and adaptation of the chimpanzee on the eastern shore of Lake Tanganyika. Kyoto Univ. Afr. Stud. 7, 37-129.

Kawabe, M. (1966). One observed case of hunting behavior among wild chimpanzees living in the savanna woodland of western Tanzania. Primates 7(3), 393-396.

Kortlandt, A. (1962). Chimpanzees in the wild. Sci. Amer. 206 (5), 128-138.

Kortlandt, A. and Kooij, M. (1963). Protohominid behavior in primates (preliminary communication). Symp. zool. Soc. Lond. 10. 61-88.

Kortlandt, A. (1967). Experimentation with chimpanzees in the wild.

In "Progress in Primatology", (Stark, D.R. Schneider and H.J.
Kihn eds.) Gustav-Fischer, Stuttgart. pp. 185-194.

Nishida, T. (1968). The social group of wild chimpanzees in the Mahali
Mountains. Primates 9, 167-224.

Nishida, T. (1970). Social behavior and relationship among wild chimpanzees of the Mahali mountains. Primates 11, 47-87.

Nishida,T. and Kawanaka, K. (1972). Inter unit-group relationship
among wild chimpanzees of the Mahali mountains. Kyoto Univ.
Afr. Stud. 7, 131-169.

Reynolds, V. (1966). Open groups in hominid evolution. Man 1 (4),
441-452.

Reynolds, V. and Reynolds, F. (1965). Chimpanzees of the Budongo
Forest. In: "Primate Behavior" (I. DeVore ed.), Holt, Rinehart
& Winston, New York. pp. 368-424.

Sugiyama, Y. (1968). Social organisation of chimpanzees in the Budongo
Forest, Uganda. Primates 9, 225-258.

Sugiyama, Y. (1969). Social behavior of chimpanzees in the Budongo
Forest, Uganda. Primates, 10, 197-225.

Sugiyama, Y. (1971). Evolution of primate society with special
reference to the individuality. Proc. Symp. Prim. Res. Inst.
"Primates with special reference to the evolution of mammals",
119-129. (in Japanese)

Sugiyama, Y. (1972a). Social characteristics and social organisation
among wild chimpanzees. In: "Primate socialisation" (F. E.
Poirier ed.) Random House, New York.

Sugiyama, Y. (1972b). Social organisation of a wild chimpanzee
colony. In: "Behavior regulators of behavior in primates",
(C. R. Carpenter ed.) Pennsylvania State Univ. Pr. (In press).

Suzuki, A. (1966). On the insect-eating habits among wild chimpanzees
living in the savanna woodland of western Tanzania. Primates 7,
481-487.

Suzuki, A. (1969). An ecological study of chimpanzees in a savanna
woodland. Primates 10, 103-148.

Suzuki, A. (1971). Carnivority and cannibalism observed among
forest-living chimpanzees. J. Anthrop. Soc. Nippon 79, 30-48.

Suzuki, A. and Suzuki, T. (1971). Requiem for a chimp. Africana
4 (7), 23.

Van Lawick-Goodall, J. (1968). A preliminary report on expressive
movements and communication in the Gombe Stream Chimpanzees. In: "Primates --- Studies in adaptation and variability"
(P. C. Jay ed.), Holt, Rinehart & Winston, New York. pp. 313-374.

(All first hand reports written in English by the members of our
research party until 1971 on the study of wild chimpanzees which
were carried out at East Africa are included in this reference list.)

THE SOCIAL GROOMING OF MALE CHIMPANZEES

A study of eleven free-living males in the
Gombe Stream National Park, Tanzania

M. J. A. Simpson

MRC Unit on the Development and Integration of Behaviour
University Sub-department of Animal Behaviour
High Street, Madingley
Nr. Cambridge, England

I. INTRODUCTION

Adult male chimpanzees who visit the provisioning area in the
Gombe Stream National Park do not groom all their fellows equally
(van Lawick-Goodall, 1968), nor do they all groom equally often, or
equally long. This study attempts to characterise 11 adult males in
terms of how much each groomed the other 10, and how he distributed
his grooming among them.

Previous studies on free-living chimpanzees (van Lawick-Goodall
1968, in the Gombe Stream in W. Tanzania, and Sugiyama, 1969, in
the Budongo Forest in Uganda); and on captive chimpanzees (Crawford,
1942, and Reynolds and Luscombe, 1969), suggest that an individual's
status, and other behaviour patterns possibly related to his status, such
as his displaying, are correlated with the amount of grooming he receives from the others. Crawford (1942) showed that, of two females
who had been allowed to compete for food in the test compartment, the
'dominant' individual, who had been the first to get the food, was more
groomed by her partner than vice versa, when the two were together at
times when the food was not available. Sugiyama (1969) found that, of
males of different sizes, the smaller was the one more likely to groom.
Reynolds and Luscombe (1969), working with a captive colony of chimpanzees, found that an individual who displayed frequently was much
groomed, while other individuals, who could be ranked high on how
soon they had access to food, were not necessarily much groomed.

This study also examines the relations between grooming, status
and display. The individual males are taken one by one, and the distribution of each male's grooming toward his fellows is related to those
others' statuses, and to aspects of their displaying behaviour. Such a

limited project is offered as a starting point for further work on how an individual distributes his social behaviour among his fellows. In its use of correlational methods to look for relations among the frequencies of different behaviour patterns by an individual towards his several partners, its methods resemble those of Bertrand (1969) and Bernstein (1971). These methods must be distinguished from those of van Hooff (1970 and 1971), which are also correlational. Van Hooff measured the proximity in time of different behaviour patterns in the same individual, and he found, for example, a cluster of behaviour patterns which he called 'aggressive' to occur closer to each other than to behaviour patterns constituting other clusters, including grooming behaviour. Thus he confirms that excited episodes of display and aggression occur at separate times from the peaceful and prolonged grooming sessions. But it is still possible that what an individual does to one partner as opposed to the others during the displaying episodes - perhaps directing his own displays away from that partner - can be correlated with what that individual does to that partner, as opposed to the others, during the grooming sessions - perhaps grooming him most. Findings by the two methods are not contradictory: van Hooff shows how an individual's behaviour is organised in time, while the present method could show how an individual organises his behaviour among his fellows, perhaps directing his displays least at those whom he grooms most.

It is now a commonplace in primate studies that individuals from the same age-sex class behave in their own characteristic ways (e.g. Gartlan, 1968; van Lawick-Goodall, 1968; Ransom and Ransom, 1971). While such differences raise further problems for the description of the social organisation of a group, some of them may explain how the group maintains its present form of organisation. For example, the

apparent ranking of individuals in a captive baboon group was most readily understood in terms of differences in its members' avoiding action
of others, rather than differences in their assertiveness towards others
(Rowell, 1966). When possible, the categories for describing the individuals should be applicable across species. Such categories include
the inter-individual distances of Kummer (1968), but many categories,
like 'displays', will not be so widely applicable. Of those applied, only
some will differentiate individuals consistently. For example, an individual chimpanzee might always be the one to groom longest in grooming sessions, but not always the one to groom others most frequently.

Once those social behaviour patterns by which individuals can be
consistently differentiated are known, it may be found that the differences
can be fitted into a common scheme, as when rhesus monkey females
have different favourite grooming partners, and for many of them, the
favourite partner is often the one ranking immediately above her in their
dominance hierarchy (Richards, in prep.). On the other hand, different
individuals in the group may distribute their behaviour among the others
consistently, but according to their own patterns: one according to the
statuses of his fellows, another according to the time he spent with them,
and so on, revealing new depths of complexity in social organisation.
The 'open' social group structure of chimpanzee regional populations
(Sugiyama, 1968, van Lawick-Goodall, 1968), which is such that one
individual will see others for different proportions of the time, and may
also do different things with different partners, suggests that the differences between individuals could be very complex (e.g. discussion in
Reynolds, 1968 and 1970).

The foregoing paragraphs raise two main classes of methodological question. First, should criteria of survival value be included

when one is describing a social group in terms of the ways in which its individuals behave consistently? Secondly, to what extent is it meaningful to ascribe behaviour in which as individual is involved to that individual, when he is interacting with a number of others in the social group?

In this study, descriptions of the ways in which individuals behave consistently avoid issues about how such differentiations between the individuals' activities are of survival value to them, or to the group. It is arguable that a study of primates in their natural habitat should concern itself with the survival values of the behaviour patterns being described. Gartlan (1968) has shown how different members of the same age-sex class can be described in terms of their 'role profiles', which are their contributions to different 'roles of adaptive significance', such as leading, looking out, territorial defence and social focus. However, to emphasise the few classes of consequences of individuals' behaviour which are believed, at this stage in primate studies, to have survival value, could lead to an incomplete description (see also Hinde 1971). For there are probably other consequences with positive survival value yet to be recognised; others with strong negative survival value; and yet others with relatively little survival value. Gartlan's system has the great advantage of suggesting ways in which different social groups, of the same and different species, can be compared, in terms of how characteristics common to all are distributed among their individuals. Bernstein (1971) and Reynolds (1970) have also developed such systems, without referring to survival value. Many of the categories of behaviour developed in this study, and those described by Kummer (1968) can also be used across species.

The second methodological difficulty raised above must be faced by all studies which attempt to describe how individuals in social groups distribute their behaviour among their fellows, and it is introduced with the following two examples. Does the frequency with which an individual chimpanzee grooms his fellows reflect 'his preferences among' those individuals, or is he often involved in grooming sessions because they 'chose' him, and perhaps even demanded grooming from him (e.g. van Lawick-Goodall, 1968)? A particular vervet monkey spends much time out on the limb of a tree, away from the centre of his group, and consequently in a place where he must spend much time looking out and it thus often the first to warn the group of impending danger. Is he there because the others have driven him there, or because he has chosen to fill the altruistic role of 'looking out'? To rephrase these questions in more general terms: to what extent is the individual's behaviour his own, and to what extent is the consequence of what the others do to him? In studies of human beings, concepts of role can help analysis of such problems, because we know who has what roles, because we can decide and agree about such matters. Brown (1965) defines roles, as applied to individuals in human groups, as norms applying to categories of persons, where 'norms' are prescriptions for behaviour. When describing species whose members probably cannot use normative and prescriptive procedures, role concepts are not applicable in the ways that they are to human groups (Reynolds, 1970).

In studies of free-ranging non-human primates, the problem of each individual's contribution to the activity in the social group can be avoided: we can say that a chimpanzee is more involved in grooming with partner A than he is with partner B, or that a particular young vervet male is less involved with the large males in the centre of the group. We can visualise human and animal-laboratory procedures which isolate an individual's contribution to his involvement in different activities.

Can we be more definite about the individual's contribution to the social behaviour in which he becomes involved? I maintain that we can, because a study of a free-running interaction (e.g. Simpson, 1968) usually reveals stages where there are several things an individual can do next, and what he does next depends partly on who the interactors are. For example, an individual chimpanzee arrives to find a group already engrossed in a grooming session, and none of those already in the group even looks up as he approaches. On such an occasion, the partner he grooms first will be his own choice. Those stages where an individual can show his choice must be distinguished from those stages in his interactions where what he does next depends only on what has been done to him. For example, the act of presenting by any male chimpanzee may always lead any recipient to groom the presenter. Had one of the group presented to the new arrival, we would have discovered nothing about the arrival's choice of grooming partners, but something about the presenter's eagerness to groom with the arrival, for chimpanzees do not invariably present to new arrivals, whomever they are. Note that to recognise a stage in an interaction where an individual's next action seems not to be influenced by the behaviour of those present, but by who those are, is to be confident that those present are all behaving in the same way at the moment when the individual makes his choice, or to be confident that observed differences in their behaviour are irrelevant to his choice. Such confidence presupposes extremely thorough studies of interaction, such as we do not yet have, and perhaps cannot have.

After the methods of this study have been described in Section

II, Section III shows how individuals can be characterised in terms of
how much they groom others as a group, and in terms of how they distribute their grooming among their partners in the group, grooming
some more than others. Section IV explores grooming as an interaction, and concludes that two of three measures of grooming can be used
only to describe an individual's involvement with others, while the third
reflects that individual to a greater degree than it reflects his partners.
Section V describes the measures of status used, and shows that they
correlate with each other well enough for it to be possible to describe
an individual in terms of his status. Section VI shows how each individual's grooming given to others and received from them reflects his
status, and how each individual distributes his grooming among his
fellows according to their statuses. Generalisations that can be made
about all the individuals are idealised in Figures 1 and 2. No less important than the generalisations arising out of this study are the rich
characterisations of the different individuals that emerged in the
attempts to make the generalisations.

II. METHODS

1. Subjects

The eleven adult males who visited the feeding area most often
were chosen as the subjects for this study. The youngest, Satan, only
just came within van Lawick-Goodall's (1968) class of "adult" (10 to 13
years). Then came Figan (13 to 14), Evered (14 to 15) and Faben (16
to 17). Figan and Faben were brothers (van Lawick-Goodall, 1968 and
1971). The relative ages of the remaining 7 males can only be guessed.
Humphrey, then Charlie, probably came next, followed by Mike and

Rudolph. Hugh, Leakey and Goliath seemed to be the oldest males. During my study period, Goliath looked oldest of them all, being thin and having a bald crown and a balding lumbar region, but subsequently he has gained weight and hair. Leakey has disappeared, and is presumed dead.

Mike was clearly the dominant male, and Goliath, from whom Mike took the top position (described in van Lawick-Goodall, 1968 and 1971) was clearly subordinate in some ways (see Section V).

2. Feeding policy

The object of feeding bananas at a particular place (called 'the feeding area' or 'in camp') was to ensure that chimpanzees would visit regularly, so that they could be contacted and then followed away into the park. The day on which an individual received bananas was recorded and so far as possible he was not fed again for seven to ten days. Nevertheless, individuals who had recently fed often reappeared while another was being fed, and then they were not prevented from taking more bananas. Subsequently, the banana feeding has been further reduced. Wrangham (in prep.) is reviewing the effects of the changes in banana feeding on this group.

3. Animals present during grooming sessions

When the males were present at the feeding area, as many females plus their infants and adolescents of both sexes were often present too. (See van Lawick-Goodall, 1968 and 1971, for a full description of the regional population.) Prolonged grooming sessions biased numbers of animals present in favour of the adult males, because these were the most persistent groomers (van Lawick-Goodall, 1968). More full

descriptions of the wider social context must await completion of
broader social studies on females (McGinnis, in prep., van Lawick-
Goodall and others, in prep.) and on the adult males (Bygott, in prep.).

4. Times spent by males in the feeding area (i.e. in camp)

For every individual, records are available (see acknowledgements) for the time he spent in the area during the daylight hours
(07.00 to 19.00). During the period of this study, Mike was the male
who spent most of the daylight time in the area (10.2%) and Hugh spent
least (2.6%).

5. Times spent by pairs of males together in camp

Mike and Rudolph was the pair seen most together in camp,
spending 5.5% of the daylight hours thus. Mike's time with Rudolph
constituted 53% of Mike's total time in camp, and Rudolph's with Mike,
59% of Rudolph's total time in camp. This value was the highest: even
in the feeding area, where there is presumably a common external factor (bananas) attracting individuals, no male spent more than 60% of
his time with any other male. In contrast, Evered and Goliath constituted the pair least together (0.4% of the time), and each was with the
other for 9% of his time in camp.

As would be expected from the fact that the chimpanzees were
provisioned, total time spent together by a pair of individuals always
exceeds total time they would be expected to spend together. The expected value can be calculated, for any one pair, from the total times the
two individuals are observed to spend in camp. (If one spends half the
daylight time in camp, and the other one sixth, then the time they would
be expected together is 1/2 x 1/6, or 1/12 of the total time.)

6. Sociabilities of pairs of males

The factor obtained for each pair, by dividing time the two individuals are observed together by time they are expected together, called the Sociability of that pair (work in prep.), is consistently greater in some pairs than it is in others. This finding suggests that, in addition to the common attraction of bananas, some individuals are more attractive to each other than are others. For example, the highest sociability, of the pair Hugh and Charlie, is more than 12, whilst the lowest, of the pair Goliath and Evered, is 2. Moreover, the pair Hugh and Charlie appears in the top quarter of the ranks for pairs' sociabilities in eight out of eight separate months.

In order of ranking for sociability are the pairs Hugh and Charlie, Humphrey and Leakey, Hugh and Mike, Faban and Figan, Rudolph and Mike, Charlie and Mike. In each of the eight months, when their sociabilities were calculated and ranked separately, these pairs were in the top 27 of the 55 ranks of the possible pairs of the 11 males. The younger males, especially Evered, Faben and Figan, were rather consistently involved in the pairs ranking lower for sociability, confirming the impression they gave of being "peripheral" males. Note that Mike, the dominant male, was in three of the high-sociability pairs.

7. 'Open grouping'

These details underline the 'openness' of the groupings of the males (see Sugiyama, 1968, and van Lawick-Goodall 1968). Thus no male-male pair was observed to exist for more than 60% of the time when one of the males involved was in sight, and in the median pair (Leakey and Hugh), neither individual spent more than 25% of his time in camp with the other. While 'open', the grouping did not seem to be random, for some individuals were consistently more strongly attracted to a particular male than were others, as measured by their sociabilities (above).

8. Recording methods

On every recording day I would centre my observations on one of the eleven males, but I would also record the grooming interactions of any of the other males while they were in sight. When there was a choice of males arriving at the feeding area, I would choose to centre my record for that day on the one on whom I had spent fewest hours so far. The observations would continue until a grooming session had ended (the individuals had dispersed), or, if there was no grooming, until midday. If, however, individuals left camp before midday, they would be followed out into the park.

My observations cover the 12 months starting in May 1969, and during 304 hours of recording, each male was watched fairly evenly through the year for totals varying from 83 hours (Rudolph) to 37 hours (Hugh).

The analyses described in this paper combine results from grooming sessions occuring out of camp, with the majority, which I recorded in camp. As did van Lawick-Goodall (1968), I found that grooming sessions could last as long outside the feeding area as in it.

Grooming sessions started soon after males had arrived and met, and many of the prolonged sessions occurred after feeding. The sessions lasted an hour on average, with three hours as a rare extreme. The median total number of chimpanzees present at the grooming sessions recorded in this study was nine, and the median total number of adult and adolescent males present was five. The individuals were recognisable, and so well habituated to human observers that there were few problems of visibility, for it was easy to walk around to find the best vantage point.

9. Data recorded

At every fifth minute, animals visible to the observer, and presumed to be in sight of the male on whom the record was centred, were listed, and those within arm's reach of the male were noted. Arrivals and departures were noted as they occurred. All approachings and leavings involving the eleven males were recorded. The approacher (or leaver) was that individual moving when the three-foot (one-arm's-length) distance between him and another was entered. If one male approached another, and the other left within a second, that was defined as a displacement, the first being said to displace the second.

While my chosen male of the day was not grooming, I recorded continuously his travel, feeding, resting, self-grooming and scratching. For all those in sight, I recorded displaying, pant-hooting, greetings and reassurances (van Lawick-Goodall, 1968).

Whenever any of the males started to groom, I noted who approached, who presented for grooming (van Lawick-Goodall, 1968) and who started grooming first. Then, on every half-minute, I recorded who was grooming whom, who was scratching himself, and who was grooming himself. Also recorded were the distances from the group and from each other of those who were more than three feet from the grooming group and from each other.

When the grooming groups comprised fewer than four individuals, in addition to sampling the state of affairs among the groomers on every half-minute, I would make a continuous record of the behaviour of the chosen male, and his partners. This could include changes in his orientation (facing, sideways-on, back-to), and the parts of himself and his partner groomed and scratched by himself and partner. The occurrence in sequence of other grooming activities, such as adjustments of groomer's and groomee's posture, use of lips, and tooth-clapping, were also noted.

Records were put onto check-sheets, the sequences of events within half-minutes being preserved by numbering. With a pair of males, there were usually about two such changes per half-minute, rarely six or eight. At first a portable tape-recorder was used, and the check-sheets were filled in from it later. With practice, the check-sheets could be filled in directly.

10. A comment on the accuracy of data obtained by this method of recording

This method limits the accuracy with which the timing of grooming and pausing bouts can be described. Information about every change in behaviour and its place in sequence relative to every other change is preserved. For example: "Mike grooms Rudolph, and continues thus over the minute; Mike then pauses, and the pause extends over the half-minute, Rudolph then scratches himself, and Mike resumes his grooming of Rudolph, and Mike is grooming Rudolph when the next minute comes up". But information about durations of activities, like grooming bouts and pausing bouts, is limited in accuracy: in the preceding example, Mike's pausing bout was long enough to cover the half-minute time-check (longer than a second or so) but the pausing bout is shorter than a minute. From such records, bout lengths can be classified accordingly as they cover no time check, one half-minute time-check, two time-checks, and so on. It is convenient to call such bout-lengths half-minute, one-minute, one and a half-minute bouts, but it must be borne in mind that there is a possible range of nearly a minute for each category of bout-length. Obviously the scope for error decreases as the bout-lengths become longer relative to the spacing of the time-checks.

III. MEASURES OF GROOMING

1. The grooming session

Grooming sessions usually had clear-cut beginnings and ends, although the grooming activity could be taken up by different males as they arrived at different times. For the purposes of the analyses in this study, each individual's grooming session was defined separately, because each individual could be present for a different part of the time when grooming was occurring. For a particular male, a session was that period of time when he was in sight of, or participating in, a grooming session involving other males. A male could be 'present' at a grooming session without participating in one. It follows that each male's record included all those with whom he was present, including those with whom he was not involved in grooming. It was rare for a male to leave and then return to the same grooming session. If an individual was present at more than one session in one day, the second session was usually somewhere else. Although some of the records involving some of the males were made in particularly great detail, this Section refers to measures of grooming available from all records.

Two of the three measures used in this section refer to the grooming a male gives to each of the ten other males, without regard to who else is present when he grooms those others. In any one session, a male may or may not groom a particular partner*. The proportion of different sessions involving a male and a particular partner in which the male grooms that partner once or more is called the Frequency Measure of his grooming towards that partner. Note that a male cannot groom a partner in more than 100% of their sessions together. The Duration Measure of a male's grooming toward a particular partner refers only to those sessions in which at least one of the particular male-partner pair groomed the other. For each pair, there were usually several sessions which provided measures of duration, and the measure for each male is his median, with that partner, from those sessions. This median value must be distinguished from his overall median duration, which is his median value with his median partner.

This Section starts with the third measure of a male's grooming, the Comparative Measure, which makes it possible to compare the degree to which a male is involved with each of two partners when they are present together with him in the same sessions. Although this last measure is more complicated to use, it provides the most direct picture of a male's grooming in situations where at least three groomers are present.

2. The Comparative Measure of Grooming

This study is particularly concerned with male grooming in social

---

*The terms 'partner' and 'male' are used in abstract discussions about pairs of interacting individuals, instead of proper names. So far as their relative roles in interactions go, no difference of the kind implied by such terms as 'actor' and 'reactor' is intended: a 'partner' can play as active a part in an interaction as a 'male'.

situations where there are sometimes several partners simultaneously available for him to groom. How does an individual distribute his grooming among them? When there are two others with him, does he groom longest that individual whom he grooms longest and most often when only one partner is available?

The Comparative Measure takes each male in turn, and focusses on his grooming behaviour toward every pair of other males that was simultaneously present in one or more grooming sessions with him. For example, Charlie groomed both Mike and Leakey in one of his sessions with them, and he groomed Mike for longer than he groomed Leakey. In the next session, during the time when both Mike and Leakey were available to Charlie, Charlie groomed Mike, but not Leakey. In both sessions, Charlie was regarded to have groomed Mike more than he groomed Leakey. In all, there were six sessions when this trio was together, and in five of them, Charlie groomed Mike more than he groomed Leakey. Table I summarises Charlie's grooming involvement with all the pairs of partners occurring together in grooming sessions at least once with him. Each cell refers to Charlie and the pair of individuals from the corresponding column and row of the table. The table is filled according to the convention that a plus be given to a row partner (e.g. Mike) whom Charlie grooms more than the corresponding column partner (Leakey, in this example) in the majority of their sessions together.

The empty cells refer to pairs of partners whom I never observed in the same grooming session as Charlie; (and see also the note at the foot of Table I). The ='s refer to pairs whose members tied. For example, there were four occasions when Charlie groomed Leakey more than Goliath, and four occasions when Charlie groomed Goliath more than Leakey.

Table I.　Charlie's grooming with the members of different pairs of partners: the Comparative Measure

	Hh	Ru	Mk	Ev	Gol	Ly	Hm	St	Fb	Fg	+s	rank
Hugh	.	+	+	+	+	=	+	+	+	+	8	1
Rudolph	−	.	+	+	=	+	+	+	+	+	7	2
Mike	−	−	.	+	+	+	+	+	+	+	7	3
Evered	−	−	−	.	+	=	=	+	+	+	4	4
Goliath	−	=	−	−	.	=	+	+	+	+	4	5.5
Leakey	=	−	−	=	=	.	+	+	+	+	4	5.5
Humphrey	−	−	−	=	−	−	.	+			1	7
Satan	−	−	−	−	−	−	−	.			0	9
Faben	−	−	−	−	−	−			.		0	9
Figan	−	−	−	−	−	−				.	0	9

　　　　Each cell in the table refers to a pair of partners, both of whom were simultaneously present at one, or more, of Charlie's grooming sessions. A + for a row partner means that Charlie groomed the row partner more on the majority of the occasions when that row partner was with the corresponding column partner. For example, partner Mike scores a + over Leakey, because Charlie groomed Mike more than he groomed Leakey, on 5 of the 6 occasions when Charlie, Mike and Leakey were present at the same grooming session.

The conventions by which partners are ranked are explained in the text.

Note that the +s and −s in some cells are based on only one session involving the relevant trio. In an ideal study, every cell would be based on at least six sessions.

Such a table is rather a cumbersome way to represent Charlie's comparative involvement with his different partners. If Charlie's grooming behaviour with the partners were 'transitive' (cf. Struhsaker, 1967) in the sense that when he groomed A more than B, and B more than C, he also groomed A more than C, then the information about Charlie's involvement with all pairs could be contained in a rank for each individual. In this hypothetical case, A would have rank 1, B rank 2, and C rank 3.

In order to rank Charlie's partners on their involvement with him, the pluses scored by each partner, over the other 9 with whom he is paired, can be counted, and rank 1 can go to the partner who scores most pluses. Thus Hugh, with whom Charlie is more involved in grooming than with 8 of the 9 others, can be given first rank. On pluses, Rudolph and Mike tie second. In the case where two of Charlie's partners tie, the individual of the two most groomed by Charlie is given top place. Charlie grooms Rudolph more than he grooms Mike on the occasions when they are together, so it is Rudolph, not Mike, who comes second to Hugh.

This procedure was repeated for each of the eleven males. In some cases, such as Mike's, triangular relationships were overridden by this ranking procedure, but these cases were considered to be few enough not to constitute too drastic a loss of information.

Table II summarises, for each male (row) the ranks he gave to his partners, on the Comparative Measure of grooming. Such a table raises the question of how consistent each male's distribution of grooming among his different partners was. The table also suggests that some individuals, like Charlie, Rudolph and Mike, were rather popular

Table II. Each male's partners ranked according to the Comparative Measure of his grooming with them

Male	Partners										
	Ch	Ev	Fb	Fg	Gol	Hh	Ru	Hm	Ly	Mk	St
Charlie	.	4	9	9	5.5	1	2	7	5.5	3	9
Evered	1	.	2	5	5	9.5	3	7	5	8	9.5
Faben	3.5	6	.	9.5	5	7	1	3.5	8	2	9.5
Figan	2.5	8.5	4	.	1	5.5	5.5	2.5	8.5	8.5	8.5
Goliath	5	9.5	7	8	.	4	1	6	3	2	9.5
Hugh	6	7	9	9	5	.	2	3	4	1	9
Rudolph	3	8	5	9	1	2	.	6.5	4	6.5	10
Humphrey	4	7.5	7.5	9.5	2.5	2.5	5	.	6	1	9.5
Leakey	4.5	7	9	9	3	4.5	2	6	.	1	9
Mike	1	9	7	9	2	6	5	4	3	.	9
Satan	1.5	6.5	9.5	4	6.5	9.5	6.5	1.5	6.5	3	.
Ranks of mean ranks of partners											
	1	9	8	10	4	6	2	5	7	3	11

partners, while others, like Figan and Satan who were never ranked above 4, were rather unpopular.

The question of how consistent or stable the males were in their grooming behaviour towards their partners, can be answered by repeating the analysis of their Comparative Grooming separately, over the first and second six months of this study. The Spearman Rank-order correlations between the ranks the males gave to their partners in the first and second six month periods ranged from -0.31 to +0.92, with the median rS at +0.72. Seven of the rSs were above +0.57, a value significant at the 5% level (1-tailed) for a N of 10. Ten of the eleven males had positive rSs. On a one-tailed binomial test, the probability of getting ten out of eleven results in the same direction is 0.006.

As a group, the males seem to be rather stable in their preferences, as judged by this measure of grooming. Note that the eleven constitute a group of interacting individuals. Each cell in each male's comparative grooming table, like Table I for Charlie, refers to three of the males, and each cell refers to a different trio. Thus it cannot be assumed that each male makes an equal contribution to this stability: some could have been making active choices among their partners, while others may have waited passively until they were groomed. From this it follows that statistically improbable results of the group's behaviour, such as ten out of eleven positive rSs, or seven statistically significant ones, should not be taken to reflect an equal degree of organisation in every individual, until the individuals' interactions with each other have been elucidated.

The observation that some individuals (like Charlie, Rudolph and Mike) seemed to be more popular as grooming partners than others

(like Figan and Satan), can be confirmed with a test of the degree to
which the males concur in ranking them high, or low. A modified test
of concordance (based on Kendall's, described by Siegel, 1956, and
further described in this Section, page 437) shows that this distribution
of ranks among partners has a probability of less than 0.001. Note that
to find that an individual is relatively highly ranked by many of the
males says nothing about how he achieves such a happy result. He may
indeed be a much sought-after grooming partner, or he may be an in-
trusive and demanding grooming acquaintance. Section IV considers
such questions of interaction further.

To summarise: the Comparative Measure shows that males are
consistent from one six-month period to the next in how much they
groom individuals from pairs of partners simultaneously present.
Partners which are ranked high by one male, in the sense that he
grooms them more than others in sessions when those others are present with the male and the partner, are likely to be ranked high by the
other males. Charlie, Rudolph and Mike rank highest, Faben, Evered,
Figan and Satan rank lowest as partners. (See Table II for 'ranks of
mean ranks as partners'.) It will be recalled (Section II) that the last
four are youngest, and that Mike was the clearly dominant male.

3. The Frequency Measure

While the Comparative Measure has the advantage of referring
directly to social situations involving trios of animals, it has the limitation of confounding how long a male groomed the partners being compared, and how frequently he groomed them. On the Comparative
Measure, one of a male's partners can score over the other by being
groomed when the other is not groomed, and he can also score by being

groomed long when the other is groomed briefly. Thus, to describe a
male's grooming behaviour more fully, both Frequency and Duration
Measures are required. Of course, it may be found that these two are
well correlated with each other, and with the Comparative Measure.
In such a case, an individual's grooming behaviour toward his partners
is adequately described by referring to one of the three. Meanwhile, it
is possible that the three measures are not well correlated, and that a
male does not necessarily groom long those partners whom he grooms
often.

The Frequency Measure, for each male, with each partner, is
derived by dividing the number of sessions in which the male was observed to groom his partner, by the number of sessions in which the
male occurred with that partner. Note that the Frequency Measure
refers to all the sessions when the two occurred together, not just
those when they were together with some third partner, as the Comparative Measure.

Table III shows the percentages of occasions in which the males
(rows) groomed their partners (columns). (To explain how the cells
were filled: Mike, for example, was with Leakey in 43 grooming sessions, and Mike groomed Leakey in 20 of them, or 48%, while Leakey
groomed Mike in 17 of them, or 40%.)

On the right-hand side of the table are the male's percentages
with their median partners. Values over 25%, which was near the
median of all the medians, are underlined, to emphasise that individuals who groomed particular partners more frequently than once on
four occasions were also usually groomed more frequently than that
by those partners.

Table III   The Frequency Measure of Grooming: for each male (row) the percent of grooming sessions with each of his partners (column) in which he grooms that partner is shown.

Males	Partners											Med-ian	Rank of Median
	Gol	Mk	Ru	Ch	Hm	Ly	Hh	Ev	St	Fb	Fg		
Goliath	.	100	90	57	56	85	75	0	42	50	21	57	1
Mike	83	.	53	48	38	48	56	4	0	19	0	43	2
Rudolph	80	45	.	75	32	48	64	22	3	24	13	35	3
Charlie	72	52	69	.	25	26	55	31	6	0	0	29	4
Humphrey	38	27	29	20	.	31	50	5	0	0	0	28	5.5
Leakey	85	40	39	32	42	.	25	12	3	19	0	28	5.5
Hugh	67	47	55	25	43	19	.	0	0	0	0	24	7
Evered	0	9	25	38	21	24	0	.	7	40	0	16	8
Satan	42	7	17	13	15	15	0	27	.	0	19	14	9
Faben	50	24	24	0	5	10	0	31	0	.	17	13.5	10
Figan	33	5	19	7	5	0	20	0	0	17	.	6	11
Medians	58	34	35	28	28	26	39	9	2	8	0		
Ranks of medians	1	4	3	5.5	5.5	7	2	8	10	9	11		

The figures at the foot of the table refer to the percentages partners receive from their median males. Thus Hugh, whose grooming
toward his partners is not very frequent (median 24%), is groomed
comparatively much (a median of 39%), which could be more than once
in every session that he shares with four of the males, a usual number.

The males were tested for their consistency from the first to the
second six-month periods of the study. For each male, in a table corresponding to Table 3, but based on the data for the first six months
only, partners were given ranks based on the frequencies with which
he groomed them, with rank 1 going to the partner most frequently
groomed. This was repeated for the second six-month period, and the
rankings were compared for the two periods. All eleven males had
positive rSs, which ranged from +0.08 to +0.91. The median rS was
+0.79, and nine males had values above +0.56, which is significant
(i.e. P < 0.05, 1-tailed). Thus the males were as consistent on this
measure as they had been on the Comparative Measure.

Did the males also concur in ranking their partners on the
Frequency Measure? The frequencies for the males with their partners in Table III were converted into ranks. Thus for the male Goliath,
partner Mike was ranked 1, Rudolph 2, Leakey 3, and so on. A modified Kendall test for the males' concordance was run, and they proved
to be significantly concordant (K = 0.62 and P < 0.001). Such a result
could be a consequence of the fact that the seven oldest males, called
the Senior Males, and excluding Evered, Figan, Faben and Satan,
groomed each other more than they groomed the other four, the Junior
Males. Do the Seniors also discriminate among their Senior partners?

Table IV suggests that the Seniors also concur in the ranks they

Table IV   Ranked Frequencies with which Senior Males Groom their
Partners: the frequencies with which each male (row)
grooms his partners (columns) are ranked.

Males	Partners						
	Ch	Gol	Hh	Ru	Hm	Ly	Mk
Charlie	.	1	3	2	6	5	4
Goliath	5	.	4	2	6	3	1
Hugh	5	1	.	2	4	6	3
Rudolph	2	1	3	.	6	4	5
Humphrey	6	2	1	4	.	3	5
Leakey	5	1	6	4	2	.	3
Mike	4.5	1	2	3	6	4.5	.
Ranks summed	27.5	7	19	17	30	25.5	21
Ranks of summed ranks	6	1	3	2	7	5	4

Analysis with 'dummy ranks' inserted:

	Partners						
	Ch	Gol	Hh	Ru	Hm	Ly	Mk
Charlie	4	1	3	2	7	6	5
Goliath	6	4	5	2	and so on		
Hugh	6	1	4	2	5	and so on	

give to their partners. As a partner, Goliath receives high ranks, and Humphrey low ranks, except from Leakey. Table IV, like Tables II and III, lends itself to tests of the probabilities of the observed distributions of ranks across the columns, though the gaps, where males are their own partners, constitute a problem. If the gaps can be filled, using some procedure which is the same for all males and partners, then such a table lends itself for such tests of distribution of ranks as Kendall's test for concordance, and Friedman's two-way analysis of variance. I chose to fill the blank cells with the same rank for all males, and the rank chosen was the median one: 4 when there were seven males (6 when all eleven males were included in the analysis). In the analysis of the seven Seniors, shown at the foot of Table IV, all ranks of partners of 4, or more, are increased by one. Thus, Charlie's partner Mike, originally with a rank of 4, now ranks 5th.

The effect of this procedure on the tests used is to make them more conservative, for the 'dummy' ranks add to N and K by 1, and they also homogenise the variance to some degree. In Table IV, Goliath as a partner now has a 4th rank, and so does Humphrey: the former is to some degree dragged down, and the latter raised up. This effect becomes relatively greater as N and K become smaller. Thus probabilities from tables of different sizes are not strictly comparable. For comparing different analyses involving the same number of individuals, the procedure seems useful. In this case, the seven Seniors are moderately and significantly concordant in ranking their Senior partners on the grooming they give to them (K = 0.41, P = 0.01 to 0.001).

4. Relationship between Frequency and Comparative Measures

If a male grooms one partner more often than a second, when
the Frequency Measures are derived from all his sessions with each,
will he also groom the first partner more on the majority of those
occasions when both first and second partner are together with him in
the same sessions? From the rankings a male gives to his partners
on the Frequency Measure, such as Charlie grooming Rudolph more
frequently than Mike (Table III), it can be predicted that Charlie should
also groom Rudolph more than Mike in those sessions where the three
are simultaneously present. Table I shows that this is the case. For
each male, there are 45 possible pairings to test, though results will
not be available for all of those pairings. Among the seven Senior males,
the wrong predictions about individuals' behaviour toward pairs of partners, based on the Frequency Measures, ranged from 3 of Hugh's pairs
of partners, to 5 of both Leakey and Goliath's pairs, and 8 of Mike's
pairs. Note that in this context 'a wrong prediction' means an incon-
sistency between the pairings described by the Comparative and Frequency Measures: no implication that one measure is 'better' than the
other is intended at this stage. The two do, however, refer to different
situations: the Comparative Measure restricts itself to situations where
three or more chimpanzees are present at a grooming situation, while
the Frequency Measure includes situations where there are only two
groomers. The Comparative Measure also restricts the comparisons
to a male's grooming towards members of pairs of partners present at
the same time.

Another, but less direct, way of testing how well males' rankings of their partners on the Frequency Measure reflect their rankings
on the Comparative Measure, is to run correlations for each male's

rankings of his partners on the two measures. For the eleven males, the rS's range from -0.03 to +0.97, and ten of these rS's are positive. All seven Seniors had rS's above +0.75, a value significant at better than the 1% level (1-tailed test). Thus the Frequency Measure adequately predicted the Seniors' grooming behaviour toward pairs of partners simultaneously present. Part of the reason for its failure to do so in the cases of the Juniors may have been that fewer data were available for them.

The practical implication of this success is that the more easily derived Frequency Measure reflects the Comparative Measure, so that not too much information about how males distribute their grooming among pairs of partners simultaneously present is lost. Nevertheless, one would expect to lose information by this procedure, for the Frequency Measure is derived from situations where the individuals groomed when there was only one partner available for grooming, which could not be said to provide a social choice in the way that two-partner situations did. Moreoover, the procedure of describing a male's grooming involvement with several partners in terms of a unidimensional ranking of those partners can obscure non-transitive grooming relationships. Information about such relationships can be recovered from the matrices (e.g. Table I) from which the Comparative Measures were derived. For example, the comparative study showed that Mike groomed Charlie more than he groomed Rudolph, when that pair was with him, and Mike groomed Rudolph more than Hugh, when those two were with him. While it might be expected that Mike groomed Charlie more than he groomed Hugh (Table II), the opposite was the case.

5. The Duration Measure

Every time a male was present in a grooming session with a partner, and grooming by the male and/or that partner occurred, the number of half-minutes on which he was seen to groom that partner was recorded. If that male did not groom a partner who groomed him, the male was given a score of 0 for that session. Each session could provide one score, and the median of all scores toward the partner, including the 0 s, is entered in each cell of Table V. If the partner never groomed the male in a particular session, and the male did not groom the partner, then he was given a blank in the table. Thus, in Goliath's row, Evered received a -, because neither groomed the other, while in Mike's row, Satan received a 0, because Mike did not groom Satan, although Satan groomed Mike. In Table V, the original half-minutes are converted into minutes.

At the extreme right-hand side of the table is the median of each male's medians for his different partners. Thus, for Goliath, Mike, whom Goliath groomed 10.0 minutes in his median session, is the median partner. At the foot of the table are the median values for grooming durations received from the partners. These medians for grooming given to and received from partners as a group are called 'Overall Medians'.

6. Relationship between the Duration and Comparative Measures

For each male, partners' median durations of grooming received were used to predict which of the two that male would groom most, on the comparative analysis. The Duration Measures predicted the males' behaviour toward their partners less well than the Frequency

Table V. The Duration Measure of Grooming: for each male (row) the median number of minutes spent grooming each of his partners. Read across for grooming given by each male.

Males	Partners											Overall Median
	Gol	Fb	Mk	Ru	Ev	St	Hh	Ly	Fg	Ch	Hm	
Goliath	•	15.5	10.0	5.5	—	13.6	18.0	10.8	0.3	3.0	4.3*	10.0
Faben	13.0	•	9.0	23.8	14.5	—	—	1.0	1.0	—	1.5	9.0
Mike	6.3	9.8	•	14.0	5.0	0	13.8	8.3	0	14.8	9.5	8.9
Rudolph	6.0	29.3	7.5	•	2.5	0	23.8	2.5	1.0	10.0	7.5	6.8
Evered	—	13.0	5.5	9.0	•	0	—	7.0	—	2.0	2.3	5.5
Satan	21.0	—	22.0	1.8	2.3	•	—	8.3	3.0	0	6.3	4.7
Hugh	7.0	—	8.0	6.5	—	—	•	4.5	0	0.3	3.0	4.5
Leakey	7.5	3.8	9.5	4.0	0	0	5.5	•	—	2.0	5.8	4.0
Figan	0.5	2.8	9.0	6.8	—	0	9.0	—	•	1.5	0.5	2.2
Charlie	1.0	—	11.3	7.5	2.0	0	3.3	2.0	0	•	2.3	2.0
Humphrey	3.8	1.5	4.3	3.5	0	0	10.5	1.5	0	2.3	•	1.9
Overall medians	6.5	9.8	9.0	6.6	2.3	0	10.5	4.5	0	2.0	3.6	
Ranks of medians	5	2	3	4	8	10.5	1	6	10.5	9	7	

*There were values from 8 sessions. The median value is that lying between the 4th, at 4.5 minutes, and the 5th, at 4.0 minutes.

Measures. The range of wrongly predicted pairs extended from 1,
through 9 (Mike and Rudolph's partners) to 18 (Goliath's partners).
Correlations were also run for each male's ranking of his partners on
the Duration and Comparative Measures. For the eleven males, the
rSs ranged from -0.80 (Figan) to +0.94. Two of them, (Figan and Satan)
had negative rSs. Of the seven Seniors, all had positive rSs, ranging
from +0.25 to +0.94, with a median of +0.61. Four of the rSs were
significant at the 5% level (1-tailed). For six of the seven Seniors, the
correlation between the Comparative and Duration Measure was lower
than that between the Comparative and Frequency Measure. Clearly,
the Duration Measure of a male's grooming behaviour toward his partners is less closely correlated with the Comparative Measure than is
the Frequency Measure.

7. Relationship between the Duration and Frequency Measures

The rSs for the seven Seniors' rankings of their partners on the
Frequency and Duration Measures were positive, ranging from +0.15
to +0.78, with a median of 0.56. Only one of the correlations was significant*. While a male who grooms a particular partner often is also
likely to do so for long, the correlation is not so high that one of the
measures can be discarded. In scanning through the raw records, it
was notable that the Junior males, although grooming Seniors rarely,
groomed them for long periods on the occasions when they could.

8. Discussion and conclusions

The main aim of this section was to discover how the males

*The Ns for the correlation tests involving Duration Measures were
not always 10 (Table V).

distributed their grooming among their partners, where grooming was measured in three ways. The results are contained in Tables II, III, IV and V. The range of grooming behaviour, from individual to individual, and with each individual, from partner to partner, is wide. For example, Goliath groomed Mike in every one of their sessions together, while there were other pairs in which the individuals never groomed in their sessions together. Goliath also has the longest overall median duration, of 10 minutes, though some individuals groomed their partners more than 25 minutes in some sessions.

From Table III, it can be seen that the median frequency that the median males Humphrey and Leakey groom their median partners is about once in four sessions. Table V shows that a median duration for all the male-partner pairs is about five minutes per session.

Senior males emerge as rather a distinct group, being groomed much more often than the Juniors (Evered, Faben, Figan and Satan), and grooming each other more often than they groomed the Juniors (Table III).

Some generalisations can be made about the results presented in this section.

(i)   The Comparative and Frequency Measures of grooming were well correlated with each other, and positively, but less well correlated with the Duration Measure. Thus, to describe an individual's grooming behaviour, measures of the durations with which he grooms are needed in addition to the Comparative or the Frequency Measure. Of the latter two, the Comparative Measure refers more directly to males' grooming in sessions with three or more individuals present at once, while the more easily derived Frequency Measure refers to

each male's grooming in all his sessions with each of his partners. For
detailed studies of how males distribute their grooming among partners
simultaneously present, ranking methods are not adequate when they obscure triangular relationships of the kind: M grooms A more than B, M
also grooms B more than C, and contrary to simple expectation, he
grooms C more than he grooms A.

(ii)   The different males tended to concur in the rankings of the Frequency and Comparative grooming measures they gave to their partners,
so that some partners, such as Charlie, were generally more popular
groomees than others, such as Satan. However, there were some differences between males in how they ranked their partners, but the data
were not sufficient to show whether such differences were statistically
significant. In some cases, the differences could have been explained
in terms of which partners were their closest associates (Section II).
Thus Table II shows that Hugh, Charlie's closest associate, ranked
Charlie less highly as a grooming partner than did the other Senior males,
although Charlie ranked Hugh highest of all. Both the members of the
two other strongly associated pairs, Mike and Rudolph, and Leakey and
Humphrey, groomed their closest associates less than might be expected
from those associates' mean ranks as partners.

(iii)   Table III, showing how often each male grooms each of his partners, suggests that most males groom their partners as often as the
partners groom them. Field impressions at the time confirmed this:
it was rare for a partner not to groom the male who groomed him during
a particular session, except when that male was very much his junior.
When the individuals in Table III are ranked as groomers and groomees
(i.e. according to the medians respectively at the right-hand side and
foot of the table), the Spearman rank-order correlation between the two
rankings is +0.84, which is significant at the 1% level (1-tailed). It is

also possible to take the males one by one, and rank the grooming each
gives to his partners (i.e. to rank the cells in his row) and to compare
this ranking of his grooming towards his partners with the ranking of
the grooming he received from his partners (i.e. to rank the cells in
the same individual's column). The Senior males all have rS's above
+0.90 (Table VIA). For these males, the Frequency Measure gives us
little idea as to whether one individual of a pair is more responsible
for their grooming sessions than is the other.

Figure 1 idealises the frequency with which four different
individuals groom each other. Male A's median frequency is the highest, and his partners B, C and D also groom him more frequently than
they groom their other partners. In this model, a male, e.g. A,
grooms his partner, e.g. D, as frequently as vice versa (10 units).
Such a symmetrical situation makes it impossible to infer anything
about the direction of cause and effect: male A may groom male D
only because male D approaches him and starts the sessions, or vice
versa, or both may contribute to the starts of their sessions.

(iv)   The Duration Measure (Table V) can also be used to rank individuals as groomers and groomees. The rS for the rankings of the
eleven males according to their overall median durations of grooming
given, and their overall median durations of grooming received, is
+0.47, which is not statistically significant. Table VIB shows the correlations between the durations with which individuals groom their different partners, and the durations with which the partners groom those
individuals. Six of the seven are lower than those using the Frequency
Measure. Three are significant at the 5% level (1-tailed test). Obviously, while a partner will usually groom when he is groomed, he will not
necessarily groom for as long as he is groomed, especially when he is

Table VI. Does a Male Groom More Often with those who Groom him More Often, and Longer with those who Groom him Longer? Correlations for each male; A between partners ranked according to the frequency with which the male grooms the partner, and the partner grooms male; and B: between partners ranked according to the median duration per session he grooms them, and the duration per session that they groom him.

Male	Ch	Gol	Hh	Ru	Hm	Ly	Mk	+s	Median
A: Frequency Measure	0.92	0.92	0.97	0.99	0.92	0.90	0.96	7/7	+0.92
B: Duration Measure	0.80	0.92	0.73	0.51	0.44	0.38	-0.14	6/7	+0.51

rSs above 0.60 are significant at better than the 5% level, 1-tailed test.

Figure 1. Model Idealising the Social Grooming of Four Males

Male	Status	Grooming with partner	Frequency measure of grooming
A	1st	B C D	******************** with B *************** with C ********* with D
B	2nd	A C D	************************ with A *********** with C ********* with D
C	3rd	A B D	***************** with A ************* with B ********* with D
D	4th	A B C	********* with A ********* with B ********* with C

with Mike or Leakey.

(v)   Finally, it must be emphasised that to describe a partner as ranking high on the Comparative Measure of a male's grooming towards him, or to characterise a male like Goliath as grooming his partners frequently, as compared with other males like Hugh, is to say nothing about the relative contributions of those males and their partners to the results. Field impressions suggested that some partners were demanding groomees, and some males were generous groomers. Section IV attempts to analyse individuals' contributions to the beginnings and maintenance of the grooming sessions in which they became involved.

IV. ASSESSING AN INDIVIDUAL'S CONTRIBUTIONS TO HIS GROOMING SESSIONS

1. Introduction

The preceding section showed how the males' involvement in grooming with their various partners differed, but it could not establish how far the males concerned were responsible for the differences, and how far their partners were. This section is concerned with events occurring at the starts of, and within, grooming sessions, and it attempts to discover those events in a male's grooming that are least affected by the partner's behaviour during and at the start of the grooming session. In a limiting case, a male's grooming may be entirely independent of what his partners do: in reality some aspects of it will to some degree be affected by some of his partner's activities during the session. The aim of the analyses described in this section is to discover how far the measures of grooming described in the previous section reflect the males', rather than their partners', behaviour during the sessions. If, for example, the duration with which an individual grooms his partner is unaffected by what his partner does, then the finding that a male grooms A more than he grooms B will suggest that the male, rather than differences between the behaviour of A and B, was responsible for the difference in his grooming behaviour towards them.

First, the relative contributions of pairs of individuals to the starts of grooming sessions are considered. Then I return to the question of the partner's influence on the duration of a male's grooming, once he has started.

One object of the following analysis of the starts of the grooming sessions was to discover whether the individuals made symmetrical contributions to the starts of the sessions. If they did, the frequency of grooming would show an individual's preferences among his partners. In the event, however, there were several pairs where one of the males was first to start in the majority of the sessions. In such cases, the question arises as to whether the asymmetries can be explained in terms of differences in the two members' presenting frequencies, and/or differences in their responsiveness to such presentings. Moreover, were the asymmetries also reflected in the contributions of the two individuals in the pairs to the approaches which brought them together?

2. Who starts first?

Table VIIA, row i, shows, for each male, with how many of his grooming partners he was usually the first to start the session, where 'usually' means 'in more than half their sessions together'. Mike, with one of his partners, Charlie, was involved in 16 grooming sessions

Table VII.   A i.   The number of his grooming partners whom each male usually starts grooming before they start on him, in the majorities of their sessions together. (see text.) A ii.   Treating the males' partners as equivalent, the number of sessions/total, in which each male starts grooming his partner before his partner starts grooming him.

B i.   The number of grooming partners whom each male approaches first (rather than them approaching him) in the majority of their grooming sessions together. B ii.   Treating all partners as equivalent, the number of sessions, out of the total sessions with all partners, in which the male, rather than the partner, made the approach.

Senior Males:	Mk	Gol	Hh	Ch	Ru	Hm	Ly
A i	5/10	3/9	0/7	4/10	6/10	4/10	5/9
A ii	59/114	35/72	5/34	27/66	52/86	36/78	48/87
Junior Males:	Fb	Fg	Ev	St			
A i	1/7	6/9	3/8	8/8			
A ii	14/40	15/24	23/46	23/26			
Senior Males:	Mk	Gol	Hh	Ch	Ru	Hm	Ly
B i	2/10	5/9	4/7	3/8*	5/10	4/10	4/9
B ii	45/113*	46/77	24/38	35/72	54/96	36/91	45/92
Junior Males:	Fb	Fg	Ev	St			
B i	4/7	5/10	1/8	6/8			
B ii	26/43	13/24	15/47	20/26			

*Total partners (rows i) and sessions x partners (rows ii) did not always match in parts A and B of the table, because it could not always be judged who approached first, and vice versa. (See text.)

in which it could be judged who was first to groom the other. In 10 of these, Mike made the first start, in the remaining 6, Charlie. Mike was thus 'usually' the first to start with Charlie. Where the figures for particular pairs were based on more than 6 sessions, in 19 pairs (out of the 55 pairs possible) no pair was found to be significantly asymmetrical by the binomial test. Mike was usually first to start with five of his ten partners. Hugh, for whom records of starts are available for only seven males, was not usually first to start with any of them, and Satan, in contrast, was usually first to start with all his partners.

Row ii in Table VIIA treats each male's sessions with all his partners as equivalent. For Mike, there were 114 sessions altogether, in which it could be judged whether Mike, or his partner, was first to start. Mike was first in just over half (59). It was rare for Hugh to start first, and usual for Satan to do so. The rule that Juniors generally start first when grooming with others was confirmed in five other males regarded as 'Junior' during the period of this study (Flint, Goblin, Jomeo, Sniff and Godi).

3. Who approaches first?

Table VIIB, row i, shows for each male, with how many of his grooming partners he usually made the approach. By my definition of approach (Section II), only one individual of a pair could be said to approach. Doubtful cases, where each approached the other, were excluded from the analysis. Such rare cases account for the discrepancies between the sessions available for analyses of starts and approaches in the respective parts A and B of Table VII. Table VIIB, row i, shows that Mike approached more often than he was approached with only two of his ten partners. For example, there were 13 sessions involving

Mike and Goliath, but in only 3 was Mike the approacher. Few pairs,
however, were as asymmetrical in this respect as Mike and Goliath.
Of 21 pairs for which there were more than 6 sessions where the approacher could be determined, three had a binomial probability of less
than 0.05: Goliath with Mike, Goliath with Humphrey, and Charlie with
Evered, where the first-named male in each pair made the majority of
the approaches.

As in Table VIIA, row ii combines each male's partners, to show
his relative contribution to the approaches at the beginnings of his sessions with all his partners combined. Mike approached in less than half
his sessions ($X^2 = 4.68$, P = 0.05 to 0.02). Humphrey, Evered and
Satan also had values sufficiently different from the 50% expected by
chance to reach statistical significance. The reservations about the
meanings of statistically improbably results achieved by individuals in
a group such as this one have been made above (Section III). The procedure is merely a way to locate divergent individuals in the group. It
is notable that Mike, who was usually approached more than he approached with eight of his partners, was the clearly dominant male (Section V).
In this respect he is similar to the dominant baboons described by
Rowell (1966). Satan, the most junior male, approached in the majority
of his sessions. Evered, Faben and Figan did not conform with Satan
in this respect, however.

Is an individual's starting behaviour consistent with his approaching behaviour? Observations in the field quickly showed that this was
not an invariable rule. Moreover, Table VIIA and B show that individuals who started first only occasionally, were not necessarily relatively reluctant to approach. Although Hugh rarely started first, it
was usually his approach that led to the sessions involving him and

another male. Satan was the only male whose approaches and starts were clearly consistent with each other: he was usually the one to approach, and the one to start first. Mike started first as often as his partners, although his partners approached him more than vice versa.

4. Presenting behaviour

Discrepancies between the results for approaching and those for starting could be accounted for by individuals' presenting behaviour, and their responsiveness to their partners' presents. For example, Table VIII shows that Mike is presented to more than any of the others, and that he starts grooming his partner first after 18 out of 19 presents. Table VIII also shows that presenting is too rare an event to explain discrepancies between approaching and starting behaviour in the other males. There are too few records of presents to distinguish males according to their responsiveness, though the results suggest that Goliath is less responsive than Mike, Leakey, Rudolph and Humphrey.

Table IX shows how often the different males were observed to present. Goliath and Hugh presented most often altogether, and inspection of Table VIIB, row ii, shows that they also presented most often per 100 grooming sessions involving them. With Goliath and Hugh, the other males almost invariably responded to these presents by starting to groom first. Unfortunately, the figures are too small to show differences in how readily presents by different males were responded to, though they suggest that they may have responded less readily to Leakey. If to present is to demand grooming from the partner, then it is apparently paradoxical that the dominant male should receive most of these demands. But presenting could also be regarded as a particularly clear statement, by the presenting individual, of the fact that his approach is

Table VIII. Males' Presenting and Starting Behaviour: All presents by all partners to the different males: for each male the number of 'starts first' by the male following the presents.

Males	Mk	Ly	Ru	Hm	Gol	Fg	Ev	Ch	Fb	Hh	St
Presents by partners	19	9	9	8	7	5	5	4	3	1	3
Male starts first	18	9	9	5	3	5	1	2	0	0	3
Male starts first per 100 occasions when partners presented	95	100	100	63	43	100	20	50	0	0	100
No presents by partners	95	78	77	70	65	19	41	62	37	33	23
Male starts first per 100 occasions when partners did not present	43	63	56	44	49	53	53	40	38	15	87

Table IX.   Males' Presenting and Starting Behaviour: All presents by each male to all his partners in relation to the number of occasions when for each male his partner starts first after his presents to the partners, and the percentage of occasions when his partners start first after no present by the male.

Males	Gol	Hh	Ru	Ly	Hm	Ev	Fb	Mk	Ch	St	Fg
He presents	18	10	9	9	8	5	5	4	4	1	0
Partners start first	15	9	6	5	5	4	5	4	4	1	0
Partners start first per 100 occasions when male presented	83	90	67	56	63	80	100	100	100	100	–
He does not present	54	24	77	78	70	41	35	110	62	25	24
Partners start first – per 100 occasions when male did not present	69	83	36	44	53	46	60	46	57	8	38

peaceful, i.e. with intent to groom. Rowell (1966) has argued how especially important it can be for subordinates to make their intentions
about their behaviour near dominants clear. It is also possible that
Mike is much presented to because it is worth being groomed by him:
he is a generous (see Section III) and perhaps also an accomplished
groomer.

5. Conclusion

    Table VII shows that not all pairs are asymmetrical in their in-
dividuals' contributions to the starts of the grooming sessions. In
pairs involving Mike and Hugh, it was usually the partners who made
the greater contributions: in Mike's case, being the ones who usually
approached; in Hugh's case, being the ones who usually started first.
In pairs involving Satan, in contrast, it was Satan who made the greatest contributions to the sessions, both by approaching and starting.

    It follows from this lack of symmetry in the pairs, that a male's
preference for his grooming partners cannot be inferred from his involvement in grooming with them, as measured by grooming frequency.
For the purposes of further analysis, the Frequency Measure, and also
the Comparative Measure, which is determined to some degree by the
relative frequencies with which males groom partners simultaneously
present (Table VI), can be used only as measures of males' involvement with their partners, and not as measures of the degrees to which
they select their partners.

    This analysis of the starts of grooming sessions suggests that
there is still much to discover about the individual males. For example, why does Goliath make so many of the approaches to Mike and
Humphrey, and why is Hugh so reluctant to start grooming first?

6. The Durations of Grooming Sessions involving pairs of males

To what extent is a male's grooming duration independent of his partners' behaviour during their grooming sessions? Section III showed that some males groomed for longer those partners who groomed long. The rank-order correlation coefficients are not high, and it seems unlikely that a male will groom exactly as long as his partner does. Thus the medians for Goliath and Hugh as groomers and as groomees (Table V) suggest that Goliath will usually go on grooming for longer than his partners, while Hugh will usually groom less than they do.

Nevertheless, when a series of sessions involving one pair is taken, the durations of the two individuals are usually rather well correlated. With Mike, there were data available for at least six separate sessions with each of seven different partners. The grooming durations of Mike and each partner, in the series of sessions involving those two, were ranked, and the ranks of the two were tested for rS. Seven values of rS were available for Mike and his partners, and Table X shows the median value for Mike, and also the medians for the other males. Out of 21 possible separate pairings of 7 Senior males, there were data for 16, and the median rS of the separate pairings was +0.78.

This finding, that the longer a male grooms, the longer a particular partner of his grooms, seems to contradict the finding that males who groom all partners long (e.g. Goliath, Table V) do not necessarily get groomed long. This contradiction is resolved easily. For example, when Goliath and Mike groomed together, Goliath always groomed longer than did Mike. Over a series of sessions involving those two, the longer Mike groomed, the longer Goliath groomed. In contrast, when Mike and Hugh groomed together, Mike always groomed for longer than

Table X. Do Males Groom Longer with Particular Partners in those
Sessions when the Partners Groom Longer? Grooming
times per session: correlations between the times of the
two members of particular pairs over successive sessions,
run for each pair for which there are data for more than
6 sessions.

Median of the 7 pairs involving	Mike	:	+ 0.84
" 4 "	Goliath	:	+ 0.83
" 4 "	Charlie	:	+ 0.87
" 4 "	Hugh	:	+ 0.70
" 7 "	Rudolph	:	+ 0.78
" 5 "	Humphrey	:	+ 0.76
" 5 "	Leakey	:	+ 0.80

For these 7 Senior males, there was a total of 16 pairs involving
them, for which this analysis could be carried out. The median
rS from the 16 different pairs is + 0.78

Hugh. The longer Mike groomed in a particular session, the longer Hugh groomed (usually), but Mike still groomed more than Hugh. In short, a partner who grooms very long will not shift a male's grooming duration very far outside the male's characteristic range of durations, although the longer the partner grooms, the longer that male will groom, within his range of durations.

The finding that, with some pairs, one of the individuals was consistent in grooming longer than his partner, suggested that for any particular pair of males, the one who groomed longer could be predicted from his overall median grooming duration, shown in the right-hand-column of Table V. That value is based on a male's grooming toward all 10 partners. If the male grooming longer in any particular pair can be so predicted, that is some evidence that differences in the individuals' durations reflect merely the characteristic durations with which the individuals concerned groom, and the durations need not be explained in terms of interactions peculiar to the particular pairs.

For every pairing, all the sessions were taken, and the individual who groomed the longest in the majority of the sessions was given a +. In Table XI, the convention used is that a + for a column individual over his row partner means that the former groomed longest in the majority of their sessions together. Thus, reading along Goliath's row reveals that only Satan groomed Goliath for longer than vice versa in the majority of their sessions together. In contrast, all Hugh's partners groomed Hugh more than he groomed them, in the majority of their sessions with him. In the 47 pairings for which such data are available, there were 14 where one member groomed longer often enough for the asymmetry to be significantly greater than that expected by chance (P < 0.05, 1-tailed sign test and marked * in the table). To discover

Table XI.   In Every Pair of Males, which Individual usually Grooms Longer? Observed and Predicted Results are Compared. The cells are filled with the results observed in pairs of individuals' sessions together. A + for a column individual over a row individual means that, of the pair comprising the two, the first grooms longer in most of their sessions together.

	Gol	Fb	Mk	Ru	Ev	St	Hh	Ly	Fg	Ch	Hm	Cells wrongly predicted
Gol	.	-	-	-*		+*	-	-	-	-	-	1
Fb	+	.	+	-	+			+	+		+	5
Mk	+	-	o	-	+	+	-*	-	+	-*	-*	4
Ru	+	+	+	.	+*	+*	-*	-*	-	-	-*	2
Ev		-	-	-	.	+	-			-	-	4
St	-		-	-	-	.	-*	-	-	-*		4
Hh	+		+	+	.		.	+	+	+*	+	4
Ly	+	-	+	+	+	+	-	.		-	-*	4
Fg	+	-	-	+		+	-		.	-	-	3
Ch	+		+	+	+	+	-	+	+	.	+	2
Hm	+	-	+	+	+	+	-	+	+	-	.	2

Note.   The order of the males is that of their median grooming durations, so that if the prediction is fulfilled perfectly, the space above the diagonal will be filled with -s, and the space below, which mirrors that above, with +s.

*One of the individuals in the pair represented by the particular cell grooms for longer in a statistically significant proportion of their sessions together (P < 0.05) whether such asymmetries were consistent over time, the analysis was repeated separately for the first and second six-month periods of the study. Pairs whose members tied in one half of the study were discarded, as were those for whom data were available only for one half of the study. Of the 26 pairs remaining, only 5 showed reversals, compared with the 13 expected by chance (P < 0.002, 1-tailed binomial test). The pairs' behaviour was therefore considered to be consistent.

In Table XI, the males are arranged along the top and side in order of their overall median grooming durations. If each male's grooming in every one of his pairings perfectly reflected his overall median duration, then all the cells above the diagonal would be filled with -'s. In the 47 spaces above the diagonal, there are 30 -'s. For the group of males taken as a whole, the individuals' overall median durations do not predict very well which one in every pairing will usually groom more.

The analysis was repeated with the 7 Seniors only.

In Table XII, the Seniors are ordered along the top and left-hand side according to their median grooming durations with their 6 Senior partners. On the 21 cells, only 4 are wrongly predicted. A Senior male's characteristic grooming duration predicts rather well whether he will groom more or less than a particular Senior partner. Who usually grooms longer, in a particular pair, can be predicted from the individual Seniors' characteristic grooming durations, without resource to special hypotheses about the interactions of particular pairs.

In Table XIII, the results shown in Table XI are shown again, but the ordering of males along the top and sides is different: Seniors are kept separate, and arranged so that no Senior is placed before

M. J. A. Simpson

Table XII. <u>In every pair of Senior Males, which Individual usually Grooms Longer?</u> See also Table XI. A + for a column individual over a row individual means that, of the pair comprising the two, the first grooms longer in most of their sessions together. The males are placed in order of the median durations for grooming Senior partners. (Note that this order is not the same as that for their median grooming duration with all partners, shown in Table XI.)

	Mk	Gol	Ru	Hh	Ly	Hm	Ch	Cells Wrongly Predicted
Mike	.	+	–	–	–	–	–	1
Goliath	–	.	–	–	–	–	–	1
Rudolph	+	+	.	–	–	–	–	0
Hugh	+	+	+	.	+	+	+	3
Leakey	+	+	+	–	.	–	–	1
Humphrey	+	+	+	–	+	.	–	1
Charlie	+	+	+	–	+	+	.	1

Table XIII. In every pair of Males, which Individual usually Grooms Longer? The Junior Males (Faben, Evered, Figan and Satan) are shown separately. The Seniors are arranged in terms of the numbers of Senior Partners who usually groom longer than they do. Thus all six of Hugh's Senior Partners usually groomed more than he did, while none of Goliath's did.

	Hh	Ch	Hm	Ly	Ru	Mk	Gol	Fb	Ev	Fg	St
Hh	•	−	−	−	−	−	−	−			
Ch	+	•	−	−	−	−	−		−	−	−
Hm	+	+	•	−	−	−	−	+	−	−	−
Ly	+	+	+	•	−	−	−	+	−	−	−
Ru	+	+	+	+	•	−	−	−	−	+	−
Mk	+	+	+	+	+	•	−	+	−	−	−
Gol	+	+	+	+	+	+	•	+		+	−
Fb			−	−	+	−	−	•	−	−	
Ev		+	+	+	+	+		+	•		−
Fg		+	+	+	−	+	−	+		•	−
St		+	+	+	+	+	+		+	+	•

another Senior who usually grooms more than he does. From the table, generalisations about the grooming relationships between and within the classes of Seniors and Juniors can be made. Among the Juniors, Satan grooms more than Evered and Figan, and both Evered and Figan groom more than Faben. Satan, who usually grooms more than all the partners with whom he grooms, was a more willing groomer in this respect, as well as in the way in which he started his grooming sessions.

In 16 out of the 22 Senior-Junior pairings, the Juniors groom more than their Senior partners. Faben (a Junior) accounts for four of the six pairs where Juniors groomed Seniors less than vice versa. This result may be explicable in terms of Faben's paralysed polio' arm (van Lawick-Goodall, 1968 and 1972).

7. Discussion and conclusions

In subsequent analyses, the Frequency and Comparative measures of grooming will be used to represent individuals' degrees of involvement in grooming with their partners, because the analyses of how grooming sessions started showed that such grooming measures could not in all cases be assumed to reflect an individual's selection among his partners.

To what extent can an individual's grooming duration be regarded as characteristic of him, rather than of his partners' behaviour towards him in their sessions with him? The analyses described above have shown that, for a Senior Male, his overall median Grooming Duration towards the others is so characteristic of him that, when particular individuals are paired, it is usually possible to predict who will groom longer from their overall median durations. This result can be explained most economically be concluding that overall median grooming duration reflects the male, rather than any special interaction with his partners. To product a result like that shown in Table XII, all each male has to do is to groom for a fixed amount of time, whoever he is with, the times decreasing for the males in the order Mike to Charlie.

In fact the variance of individual males' grooming durations across their different partners (Table V), and across different sessions with the same partner (this Section, and Table X) is considerable. Moreover, within his characteristic range of grooming duration, an individual tends to groom those others who usually groom him longer than those who do not (a correlation described on p. 445, which is not statistically significant). When an individual is with the same partner on separate occasions, he grooms longer when his partner grooms longer (p.459 above). It thus remains possible that, within his range of grooming durations around his characteristic median, differences in an individual's grooming durations reflect differences in his part- ners' behaviour during their grooming sessions together. Thus a male's grooming duration depends to some degree on whether his partner is grooming or not: when his partner is grooming, he grooms on twice as many half-minutes as he does when his partner is not grooming. This partly explains the result in Table 10, but does not explain the differ- ences between the grooming durations of members of grooming pairs. If the partner's grooming behaviour affects that of the male, then com- parisons between one male's grooming durations with different partners must take into account the grooming durations of those partners. For example, Mike usually grooms Hugh for longer than he grooms Goliath (Table V). But Goliath grooms Mike longer than Hugh does. Thus the difference in Mike's behaviour toward these two others does not reflect only their grooming durations; Mike may be discriminating between

between Hugh and Goliath according to some other properties than
their moment-by-moment behaviour during the grooming sessions.
Note that if Hugh groomed Mike for longer than Goliath did, then we
could not have come to this conclusion.

There are other ways in which partners' within-grooming-session
behaviour could be affecting males' grooming behaviour. Some partners
could be 'demanding' more grooming than do others, by scratching themselves (see van Lawick-Goodall, 1968). Thus, in the preceding example
Mike could be grooming Hugh for longer than he groomed Goliath, because Hugh was demanding more grooming, by scratching more frequently when Mike paused. In fact, Goliath scratched more frequently
than Hugh, when Mike paused in his grooming. Partner-scratching during the grooming sessions does not explain this difference.

Analyses of scratching and grooming half-minute by half-minute
(Simpson, in prep.) nevertheless confirmed an effect of scratching on
grooming: if a male had paused in grooming a partner, and the latter
scratched himself, the male was more likely to resume grooming than
he was during those pauses in which the partner had not scratched.
But the effect was small, and scratches did not occur during every
pause. While small, the effect shows up interesting male-male differences: Mike as a scratching partner caused others who had paused to
resume grooming him sooner than did the other males.

This discussion has revealed some of the difficulties of inter-
preting differences in duration measures of grooming: first, differences
between males' grooming towards the others considered as a group
(i.e. differences in overall medians of the males); and then difference
by the same male shown in his grooming toward different partners.

The differences between males' overall median duration measures of
grooming could be regarded as characteristic of those males, and did
not require more complicated explanations in terms of those males'
interactions with their partners. However, differences by the same
male toward different partners must be considered in more detail,
because a partner's behaviour during a grooming session can affect a
male's grooming duration. If a difference in a male's grooming towards
different partners cannot be explained in terms of differences in those
partners' behaviour, (their grooming durations and their scratching
frequencies), then it remains possible that the male is discriminating
between the partners according to properties they show at other times,
such as their aggressiveness, or whether they are his siblings (e.g.
Goodall, 1968). Section VI considers the relations between the duration
measures of a male's grooming towards his different partners, and
measures of those partners' aggression.

V. MEASURES OF STATUS AND AGGRESSION

1. Introduction

It was my field impression that individuals who supplanted many
others also displayed (van Lawick-Goodall, 1968) often and pant-grunted
(ibid.) to few of the others, while they received pant-grunts from many
of those others. It was tempting to describe such individuals as having
high status, and as being aggressive. The 11 males' ratings on these
four separate measures were examined to discover whether the measures were so well correlated that it would be useful to describe individuals in terms of a ranking of status or aggression. (See also
Simpson, 1968, for an exploration of an aggressive display for the

for the number of dimensions along which it varied.) If the four measures were very well correlated, then in the further analyses of their relations to the grooming measures, only one of the four would need to be used. If, however, the correlations were not high, so that (for example) the male who displayed most frequently only supplanted 5 of his 10 fellows, then it would be necessary to examine the relations of the 'status' measures to the grooming ones, separately. For it is possible, as the work of Reynolds and Luscombe (1969) suggests, that while those much involved in grooming display frequently, they are not the animals who supplant most others.

van Hooff's (1970 and 1971) work on how soon one behaviour pattern occurs in time relative to another behaviour, in the same individual chimpanzee, suggests that chimpanzee aggression is unitary. But he does not examine individuals separately, nor does he compare their interactions with others. Thus, in accordance with his results, displays could be followed by supplantings in all individuals, but one of those individuals might spend all his time displaying at and displacing only one other male, while another could distribute an equal number of displays and supplantings among all the other males. In such a hypothetical case, status, measured by the number of males supplanted, would not be correlated with status measured by frequencies of display. This study is concerned with the question of whether an individual who supplants more different males also displays more frequently.

2. Definitions

One male was said to supplant another if, after moving to within three feet of that other, the latter moved to beyond three feet, within a second. A supplanting thus always refers to two males. It does not distinguish cases where the first just happaned to be passing as the second was getting up to go elsewhere from the cases where the first charged the second, who then fled precipitately away. Further, it is obvious from the definition of supplanting that both individuals contribute to such an episode. Thus any ranking based on supplantings involving pairs says as much about the behaviour of the subordinates as it does about that of the dominants.

About a third of the supplantings observed in this study occurred during displays by the supplanting individual. 26 of the 76 displays by Mike caused at least one other individual to move away, and the proportion of displays with this effect was 0.30 in the median male (Humphrey). This study will reveal correlations between displays and supplantings only if the individuals who display more frequently also displace more of the 10 other individuals.

For the purposes of this study, displays comprised sustained brisk runs, with hair erect, and some slapping of own chest, and/or ground, and/or vegetation, and/or resonating objects. The directions of the displays relative to other chimpanzees, baboons or human beings were not criteria for this definition of display. This definition is wide and includes elements which van Hooff's (1970 and 1971) work shows are not perfectly correlated with each other. In other words, it lumps together more than one type of display, including the silent charging display of a relatively subordinate individual near a group of more senior males, but mainly out of their sight; and the case when an individual will display noisily in concert with, or soon after, another. The descriptions of van Lawick-Goodall (1968 and 1971) and van Hooff reveal the variety of displays, and Bygott (in prep.) is studying this variety, with special reference to the social contexts of the displays. Of the context of a display, my records noted only which others were present, and which of those were supplanted during the display.

I also recorded pant-grunts by each male (see van Lawick-Goodall 1968, and van Hooff, 1971, for descriptions of this vocalisation: van Hooff called pant-grunts 'oh-oh'). A male who had been supplanted was especially likely to pant-grunt to the one who displaced him, and males are also likely to pant-grunt to individuals returning after displaying. In such a case, and also when high-status males arrive, the pant-grunting males might approach before pant-grunting to the arrival.

3. Absolute measures of rates of supplanting and display

The object of my study, which was restricted mainly to a limited social situation (male grooming) and a limited time (morning) in a special part of the chimpanzees' range (the provisioning area) was to discover differences between the individuals. The figures in this paragraph must therefore be treated with caution; current and subsequent work in the Gombe National Park, by McGinnis (in prep.), Bygott (in prep.) and others will produce more complete data. In the 300 hours I spent recording, I saw 87 supplantings, 40 of which were by Mike. Mike's rate of supplanting was one in just over two hours, and that of the male with the median rate (Leakey), one in 25 hours. Mike's rate of display was about once per hour, and that of the median male (Hugh) about once per 5 hours. These rates are greater than those observed in the Budongo forest by Reynolds (1970) and Sugiyama (1969). The latter observed about one display per 10 hours of his observation time, which is presumably equivalent to more than 10 chimpanzee-hours-in-sight.

Results: Comparison of the males' supplanting behaviour.

Supplanting results are available for 30 different pairs of the

Table XIV. Individual Supplanted by the Males in this Study

Male	Supplants									Supplanting rank of male
Mike	Ch	Hh	Hm	Fg	Ru	Fb	Ly	Ev	St	1
Charlie			Hm	Fg	Ru	Fb		Ev	St	2
Hugh			Hm	Fg						3
Humphrey				Fg			Ly	Ev	St	4
Figan					Ru			Ev	St	5
Rudolph						Fb			St	6
Faben								Ev	St	7
Leakey									St	8.5
Goliath									St	8.5
Evered										10.5
Satan										10.5

11 males, and these are shown in Table XIV. Mike's row shows that he supplanted every male except Goliath at least once. Satan and Evered, in contrast, were never observed to supplant any of the others. Satan was supplanted by every male except Evered and Hugh (read down Satan's row).

From the fact that a total of 87 observed supplantings were distributed among 30 pairs, it follows that there was more than one for many of the pairs. In the 23 pairs, for which there was more than one record of a supplanting episode, I never saw a reversal. This suggests that, in the situation where I was observing the males, their supplanting behaviour was stable, in spite of the fact that the compositions of the groups varied from occasion to occasion. Such stability may, of course, reflect the crudeness of my criterion for a supplanting episode: more subtle measures would almost certainly reveal reversals, especially among those pairs where I never observed any supplanting behaviour (represented by gaps in Table XIV). van Lawick-Goodall (1968) has described how an individual's rank can depend on the situation, and on who else is nearby.

For further analysis, it would be convenient if each male's supplanting behaviour could be represented by a rank. This has been done in Table XIV by arranging the males so that if each of them had been observed to supplant every male ranking below him there would be no gaps, and the position of each male on the left-hand side of the table would provide all the information about who he displaced. In fact, the data are not so complete: the gaps remain. The procedure of assigning ranks to the males thus involves the following assumptions: first that a male is not, within the year's time-scale of this study, supplanted by any whom he has supplanted; and second, that the ranking is always transitive (Struhsaker, 1967), so that if one male, say Figan, supplants a second, such as Rudolph, and if that second male supplants a third, Faben; then the first, Figan, will also supplant the third, Faben. Both assumptions are supported by such data as I have: first, in the 23 pairs where there was more than one supplanting episode, there was no reversal; second, the 30 pairs for whom data are available provide 13 trios in which transitiveness can be looked for, and in none of these is there a triangle.

To summarise the procedure by which the males were ordered in the table: first, no male was put above one who supplanted him. This rule leaves the relative positions of Charlie and Hugh open, and it also leaves Leakey in any position below Humphrey, and above Satan, and Goliath in any position above Satan. A second rule was used to place these last males: when two males are not themselves involved in any supplanting episodes, the male who supplants most others is given the higher position. Then Hugh, who supplants two others, comes below Charlie who supplants 6 others, and Goliath and Leakey tie, below those males who supplant more others than they do. This second rule is arbitrary, although its assumption that, of two males who do not supplant each other, the one most likely to supplant the other is the one who supplants most other males, is reasonable. It must be emphasised that, to squeeze different individuals into any one-dimensional system of ranking is almost always a process of simplification. Table XIV reveals Leakey, Goliath and Hugh as interesting in so far as they are among the four oldest males, and involved in fewer supplanting episodes than might be expected. Thus Hugh did not supplant many others, and Goliath and Leakey were not supplanted by many others. Perhaps the latter two were treated with special respect, as was an old baboon described by Rowell (1966). They may also have been adept at avoiding situations where they might get supplanted. Thus Hugh and Goliath sometimes withdrew into nearby undergrowth when there was much displaying. Hugh and Leakey may have avoided situations where they were supplanted, through staying close to Charlie and Humphrey, respectively.

Pant-grunting

If pant-grunting is regarded as a submissive action, then the pant-grunting data confirm the Supplanting Ranking, including the positions of Leakey and Goliath. Thus Leakey pant-grunted to Rudolph, as well as to Mike, Charlie, Humphrey and Goliath. Goliath pant-grunted to all the males except Evered and Figan. If the males are ranked according to how many of the others they pant-grunt to, with Mike, who pant-grunted only to one other (Humphrey) ranking lowest, and Satan who pant-grunted to every one of the others at some time, ranking highest, then the Spearman rank-order correlation between the males' Supplanting and Pant-grunting rankings was -0.87 (Table XVII, below).

The males were also ranked according to the numbers of partners they received pant-grunts from, and the correlation between this ranking and their Supplanting Ranking was +0.79. Both this and the preceding rS is significant at the 1% level (1-tailed).

5. Displaying: Measures of Display Frequency

Whenever a male displayed, there was a record of which other males were present with him. Also available from the records is the total time I observed each male in the presence of every other male. For each of them, in the presence of each of his partners, it was possible to calculate how frequently per hour he displayed. Such frequencies were called Display Rates. Thus, for every male, data are available for the rate with which every partner displayed in his presence, and for the rates with which he displayed in the presence of every partner.

In Table XV, each male's Display Rates in the presences of his ten partners are ranked, and at the right-hand end of the row is shown the male's rate with his median partner. Thus, Mike displayed most frequently in Goliath's presence, and least frequently in Rudolph's. His median rate was between that in Charlie's presence, and that in Humphrey's. This was also the highest median rate of the males.

At the foot of Table XV appear the median rates which the column individuals experience* from the row males. Thus Mike, who displays most frequently, experiences one of the lower median display rates.

This study can say little about the causation of the situation as represented by the different display rates of the males in the presences of their partners. Thus Leakey may experience low rates because he avoids social situations where there is much display, Mike because he inhibits display in situations where the other males might otherwise display often.

Table XV does, however, suggest that different partners may have different effects on males' display rates. For example, four males have their peak display rates in Evered's presence. Thus a

*In this context, to say that a particular male experiences 0.13 displays per hour from his median male partner is merely to say that his median partner displays with this frequency in the male's presence.

Table XV. Display Rates of the 11 Males. In each row, a male's rate of display per hour spent in the presence of each partner (column) has been ranked, with rank 1 for the partner in whose presence the male displayed most frequently. To the right of the row is the male's rate in the presence of his median partner.

Male	Partners											Median rates of Males	Rank
	Mk	Ch	Hm	Ev	Hh	Ru	Fb	Fg	Ly	St	Gol		
Mike	–	5	6	4	9	10	3	2	8	7	1	1.09	1
Charlie	7	–	5	1	10	8	2	4	6	3	9	0.64	2
Humphrey	5	3	–	1	10	8	2	9	7	4	6	0.38	3
Evered	7	5	10	–	2	8	3	4	9	1	6	0.34	4
Hugh	8	2.5	1	6	–	2.5	5	7	9	4	10	0.23	5
Rudolph	8	4	9	2	1	–	5	6	10	3	7	0.16	6
Faben	8	10	5	1	4	6	–	3	9	2	7	0.16*	7
Figan	8	7	9	2	10	4	5	–	6	1	3	0.15	8
Leakey	6	9	5	3	8	7	4	10	–	1	2	0.15*	9
Satan	4	2	9.5	1	5	8	3	9.5	6	–	7	0.09	10
Goliath	†	.	.	.	.	.	.	.	.	.	–	0.00	11
Median rates of partners in males' presences	.13	.16	.13	.31	.19	.22	.23	.16	.09	.43	.30		
	*	*	*					*					
Rank	9	7	10	2	6	5	4	8	11	1	3		

*These results differed at 3 places of decimals, so were given different ranks

†Goliath displayed once while I was recording, in Mike's presence.

male may have a high Display Rate not only because he displays often whatever the social situation, but also because males in general cause him to display often, or because some particular males are specially provoking. The disadvantage of measuring an individual's display behaviour by his Display Rate in the presences of different partners is that there is no indication of his Display Rate in the absences of the same partners, for the males are usually present in groups of three or more, so that one particular partner may still be present for some of the time when the male's rate in the presence of a second is being measured.

However, the effect of a particular partner can be isolated more effectively by comparing the male's rate in the presence of that partner, with his rate in the absence of the same partner. The result

of $\dfrac{\text{Rate of display in the presence of a particular partner}}{\text{Rate of display in the absence of the same partner}}$ was called

the Display Ratio. If groups formed and reformed at random, such a ratio could reflect the effects of a particular partner on the male's display rate. In fact the groups do not thus form and reform, because certain combinations of individuals associate more strongly than others (Section II), so that the effects of particular partners will be contaminated if they have relatively persistent associates.

Table XVI shows the males' display ratios with their median partners. It also shows how many of each male's partners increased his display rate (i.e. gave him a Display Ratio of more than 1.0). Note that Mike, who had the highest Display Rate, did not have the highest Ratio. However, the three males ranking highest on Displacement have positive ratios with at least five of the partners.

Table XVI.   Display Ratios: The Median Value for Each Male

Males	Ru	Hm	Ch	Mk	Hh	Ev	Fb	Fg	Ly	St	Gol
Median display ratio	1.67	1.23	1.15	1.02	0.94	0.78	0.48	0.57	0.48	0.20	–

The number of each male's partners, in whose presence his display ration exceeded 1.0 is given below, under each male:

Males	Ru	Hm	Ch	Mk	Hh	Ev	Fb	Fg	Ly	St	Gol
Number	9	7	6	6	5	4	3	2	2	0	–

For each male, with each of his partners, the ratio $\dfrac{\text{male's display rate when that partner was present}}{\text{his display rate when that partner was absent}}$ was calculated, and the median of the values for each male's ten partners is given under each male in the table.

6. Conclusions: The relations among the measures of status and
aggression.

Table XVII shows the rSs for all the correlations run between
the rankings of the males on the measures discussed in this Chapter.
The only non-significant correlations involve the male's rankings on the
rates with which others display in their presences, although these correlations are in the expected direction. (Thus the more partners a
male supplants, or the higher his Display Rate, the less frequently do
others display in his presence; the more of the others the male pant-
grunts to, the more frequently do they display in his presence, and
fewer of them pant-grunt to him.)

At a level of description that accepts all rSs greater than +0.60
or -0.60 as showing correlations, it is possible to subsume Supplanting Ranks, pant-grunting behaviour, Display Frequencies by males, and
their Display Ratios, under one heading, which could be called "status"
or "aggression". A more detailed description of the individuals, however, must refer to them separately, for the correlations are not near
1.0. In other words, although Evered displayed very frequently he had
a low Supplanting Rank, while Hugh, who displayed infrequently, had a
high Supplanting Rank. Rudolph, who displayed rather infrequently, had
the highest median Display Ratio. Although Goliath hardly displayed at
all, and supplanted only Satan, I never saw any of the others supplant
him.

Finally, it must be emphasised again that there are probably
many types of display, only some of which are simply occasions when
a male asserts his own status. Many displays do not supplant other
individuals, and many of those displays are not even directed at others.
Some are performed in concert with others (e.g. the 'rain dances' of

M. J. A. Simpson

Table XVII. Correlations between rankings of males' statuses, as measured by 1-6 below.

		1	2	3	4	5	6
1	Number of others chimp. supplants	x	0.72 **	-0.47	0.62 *	-0.87 **	0.79 **
2	Display rate by chimp.	0.72 **	x	-0.37	0.73 **	-0.93 **	0.89 **
3	Rate others display in presence of chimp.	-0.47	-0.37	x	-0.29	0.52	-0.76 **
4	Display ratio by chimp.	0.62 *	0.73 **	-0.29	x	-0.72 **	0.70 *
5	Number of others chimp. pant-grunts to	-0.87 **	-0.93 **	0.52	-0.72 **	x	-0.75 **
6	Number of others who pant-grunt to the chimp.	0.79 **	0.89 **	-0.76 **	0.70 *	-0.75 **	x

$*$ = $P < 0.05$ (1-tailed test)

$**$ = $P < 0.01$ (1-tailed test)

Note that positive Spearman rank-order correlation coefficients are not given signs in this table.

van Lawick-Goodall, 1972), and may even strengthen social bonds between those individuals, rather than assert one individual's status as against that of another.

VI. THE RELATIONS BETWEEN MEASURES OF AGGRESSION AND GROOMING

1. Introduction

The males have been characterised in terms of three measures of grooming given to and received from their partners as a group, and they have also been characterised in terms of four measures of status. This section first uses the whole group of the males to discover how these characteristics are related in individuals. For example, does an individual with high status groom his fellows for longer or shorter times than one with low status? This section then takes the individual males singly, to discover:

a. whether each grooms his partners of status greater than his more than they groom him;

b. how each individual distributes his grooming among pairs of partners with different statuses, who are simultaneously present; and

c. how each distributes his grooming among all ten partners with different statuses, when those partners are not necessarily all present at once.

Similarly, the way in which each male distributed his grooming with partners defined according to other properties, like hairiness, relative age, Sociability (Section II) etc. were explored. This is a method for discovering what aspects of their common social environment make differences to the individuals' behaviour, and thus of discovering how each individual classifies his own social environment. It is quite possible that different individuals within the same social group could classify their social environments differently. For example, very high-status males, and pre-adolescent males, might not groom individuals of different statuses differently, and the remaining males might discriminate only among pairs of individuals who had statuses higher than their own. An account of the ways in which an individual distributes his behaviour among fellows with different properties, which include different ways of behaviour towards him, does not alone suggest how far the individual's social environment is of his own making, and how far it is forced upon him by the others. Nevertheless, it will be argued that there are occasions when an individual's behaviour in his social environment can be seen to reflect that individual, more than his fellows.

2. The relations between grooming and status characteristics in individuals

Table XVIII shows that the frequency with which a male grooms his median partner is positively correlated with his own Supplanting Rank, Display Rate and Display Ratio. While high-status males groom more often, they do not, however, groom for longer when they do so. The correlations between the Durations with which males groom their median partners, and their own status measures, are negative. In Table XVIII, tests of correlation involving the Duration and Frequency measures were also run without Goliath. The justification for excluding Goliath is that he was more obviously anomalous than any of the other males (Section V); not only in being nearly the lowest-ranking male with the highest Frequency and Comparative measures of grooming,

Table XVIII.   How Grooming and Status Measures Correlate.
Spearman rank-order correlation coefficients for correlations between the males' rankings on measures of grooming given to their median partners (from Section III) and measures of the males' status, in Table XVIIIA. Table XVIIIB shows rSs for correlations between the measures of grooming received by them from their median partners (from Section III) and measures of the males' status.

Table XVIIIA

Status Measures	Measures of their own grooming	
	D	F
Supplanting rank	-0.26	+0.31
	-0.22	+0.58
Display rate	-0.29	+0.22
	-0.06	+0.63*
Display ratio	-0.08	+0.69*

Table XVIIIB

Measures of their partners' grooming		
D	F	C
-0.32	+0.38	–
+0.32	+0.59	+0.62*
-0.18	+0.19	–
+0.26	+0.58	+0.72*
+0.32	+0.73*	+0.84*

* = P < 0.05   (1-tailed test)

D = rankings according to the Duration Measure of grooming

F = rankings according to the Frequency Measure of grooming

C = rankings according to the Comparative Measure of grooming

Note that males cannot be compared on the Comparative Measure for grooming given to the group as a whole but they can be compared as partners, on mean ranks received (foot of Table II).

The lower lines of rSs are from analyses run without Goliath.

Goliath was also excluded from analyses involving Display Ratio, as explained in the text.

but also as the one male who once had a clearly dominant position (van Lawick-Goodall, 1968 and 1972); a low-status male in many ways whom I never saw supplanted; and one whom I saw display only once. During my study period, he may also have been sick and/or depressed (Section II). Without Goliath, the correlations between the Frequencies with which individuals groom, and their statuses, become stronger.

If higher-ranking individuals groom more frequently, but perhaps for less long, do they also receive grooming more frequently from their median partners, and are they groomed for shorter or longer periods of time when they are groomed? Table XVIII shows that, as would be expected from the fact that males usually groom when they are groomed by their partners, the higher-status individuals are also groomed more frequently, whether Goliath is included in, or excluded from the analysis. Higher-status males are also more involved in grooming, as measured by the Frequency and Comparative Measures. Fig. 1 (Section III) idealises the result for the Frequencies with which four different individuals groom their partners, where those individuals are arranged in order of their statuses. Thus the top individual A has the highest median frequency.

The Duration of grooming received by an individual seemed to be negatively correlated with that individual's status if Goliath was included in the analysis, and slightly positively correlated if Goliath was excluded. But all correlations between median duration received and the status measures were non-significant. The slightly positive correlations, when Goliath was excluded from the analysis, could be taken to suggest that higher-status individuals received more grooming from their partners, in spite of the fact that those higher-status individuals did not themselves groom for longer. If their partners do groom higher-status individuals for longer, it is probably not because those individuals groom longer. (See also the discussion, below, p. 493.) If it is true that the higher an individual's status, the less long he grooms, and the longer his partners groom him, then, when two individuals of differing status groom together, the lower-status one should groom longer. Examination of paired individuals' grooming durations confirms this.

3. Grooming by individuals towards partners with different statuses

(a)   When two of different statuses groom together, does the lower-status individual groom his higher-status partner longer than vice versa?

Table XIV (Section V) shows the 30 pairs of individuals, for which observations of who supplanted whom are available. Table XI (Section III) shows, for 28 of these pairs, which individual groomed longer in the majority of their sessions together. Two pairs are excluded, because the individuals concerned tied on who groomed more. Of these 28 pairs, 19 have the subordinate member grooming the dominant more than vice versa, a result in the direction predicted (subordinates grooming more) but not statistically significant. Six of the 9 wrong predictions involved Mike, who was an exceptionally generous groomer. With Mike removed from the analysis, 16/19 pairs were correctly predicted (P = 0.002, 1-tailed binomial test). I have argued that Goliath is also an exceptional male, and when he is also excluded from this analysis, 15/18 of the pairs are correctly predicted (P = 0.04, 1-tailed test).

So far, only those pairs who were actually involved in observed supplanting episodes have been considered. But every male was given a Supplanting Rank (p. 472) so that it is possible to make predictions for every pair of the males. In Table XIX, the males are arranged

Table XIX.   Can Males' Grooming Behaviour Toward Each Other be Predicted from the Supplanting Ranks of the Individuals Involved?   The males are considered pair by pair, and a + means that the column male usually grooms more than his row partner.   The males are arranged along the top and left-hand side of the table, so that if the predictions from individuals' Supplanting Ranks were perfectly fulfilled, all the cells above the diagonal would be filled with +s.   The cells are filled with the observed results, from Table XII.

	Mk	Ch	Hh	Hm	Fg	Ru	Fb	Ly	Gol	Ev	St	Cells wrongly predicted
Mike	•	−	−	−	+	−	−	−	+	+	+	6
Charlie	+	•	−	+	+	+	−	+	+	+	+	2
Hugh	+	+	•	+	+	+		+	+			2
Humphrey	+	−	−	•	+	+	−	+	+	+	+	2
Figan	−	−	−	−	•	+	−	−	+		+	1
Rudolph	+	−	−	−	−	•	+	+	+	+	+	2
Faben	+	−	−	+	+	−	•	+	+	+	+	3
Leakey	+	−	−	−	−	+	−	•	(+)	+	+	2
Goliath	−	−	−	−	−	−	−	(−)	•	.	(+)	0
Evered	−	−	−	−	.	−	−	−	−	•	+	0
Satan	−	−	−	−	−	−	−	−	−	(−)	•	0

( ) refer to comparisons between males who tied on their Supplanting Ranks.

along the top and left-hand sides in order of their Supplanting Ranks.
If a column male usually grooms more than his corresponding partner,
the cell for that pair is given a +. (Two of the pairs could not be used
in this analysis because the individuals concerned tied on their Supplanting Ranks.) A perfect prediction would have filled every cell above the
diagonal with a +. In fact there were 35/45 +s above the diagonal in
Table XIX. The probability of getting this value is less than 0.001, by
a X^2 test. Although the form of such a table lends itself to such statistical treatment, it is difficult to interpret a particular level of statistical significance applied to the data in the table, because the grooming
behaviour of the pairs represented by the different cells was not always
observed when the members comprising the pairs were isolated from
members comprising other pairs. For example, it is possible that Hugh
was almost always groomed more than he groomed back, because
Charlie - the male most often with Hugh - somehow inhibited Hugh's
grooming. In fact there is no evidence that this occurred.

Males' rankings on other measures of their status, their Display
Rates and their Display Ratios, can also be used in the same way, to
predict which individual in every pair should usually groom the most.
From Display Rates, it was possible to make predictions for 47 pairs,
of which 32 were correct; and from rankings on Display Ratios, predictions for 38 pairs, of which 24 were correct. Clearly, Supplanting
Ranks of the individuals in the pairs provided the best predictions of
who should groom more. An alternative way to describe the results
in Table XIX is to say that, for each of 10 of the 11 males, the majority
of the predictions involving him is correct (cells wrongly predicted for
each male and his partners are shown in Table XIX). The exceptional
male is Mike, for whom 6/10 predictions are wrong.

(b)   In a male's grooming sessions with <u>pairs</u> of partners,
         simultaneously present with that male, does he groom the
         higher-status partner more?

Table XVIIIB showed that higher-status individuals tended to
rank higher on grooming received from their median partners, measured
by the Comparative Measure. This result could be a consequence of
some or all of the males grooming higher-status individuals more than
they groom lower-status ones. The analysis that follows (and that under
(c) below) examines, one by one, the males' distributions of grooming
among individuals of different statuses. Under (b), each male's grooming toward pairs of partners simultaneously present in grooming sessions
with him, is considered.

For Charlie (Table I, section III) there were 35 pairs of partners
about which predictions about his grooming towards them could be made.
First, the Supplanting Ranks of those males were used to make predictions about the pairs. In 23 of the 34 pairs available for the present
analysis*, or 68% of them, Charlie usually groomed the higher ranking
of his two partners more. Charlie's result is shown in the top row of
Table XX. The results from the other males are also shown.

In Table XXB, the results of the analyses without Goliath are
shown. Predictions were also made from each individual's pairs of
partners' Display Rates, and their Display Ratios. For these predictions, the Display Rates and Display Ratios by the partners in the particular individual's presence were used, not the median Display Rates
and Display Ratios of the partners. (The analysis of Display Ratios
could not include Goliath, because I only had one display from Goliath.)

*Why only 34 of the 45 possible pairs of partners were used is
 is explained in Section III, and at the foot of Table XIX.

Table XX. Distribution of Individual Males' Grooming among Pairs of Partners Predicted from the Partners' Rankings on their Supplanting Behaviour, Display Rates, and Display Ratios.

A. Goliath included in the analysis

Male		Ch	Gol	Hh	Ru	Hm	Ly	Mk	Ev	Fb	Fg	St
Supplant-ing	%	68	71	68	63	76	81	66	48	61	40	55
	N	†34 *	38 **	34 *	38	37 **	31 **	38	23	23	15	22
D. Rate	%	63	63	67 *	54	66	74 **	61	37	65	25 *	55

B. Goliath excluded from the analysis

Male		Ch	Hh	Ru	Hm	Ly	Mk	Ev	Fb	Fg	St
Supplant-ing	%	70	75	69	83	88	70	55	60	43	61
	N	27 *	28 **	29 *	30 **	25 **	30 *	20	20	7	18
D. Rate	%	61	76 **	65	80 **	80 **	63	40	70	43	56
D. Ratio	%	79 **	68 *	86 **	73 *	80 **	70 *	60	75 *	57	39

% = percent correctly predicted; N = number of pairs available for testing the prediction, for each male.

*   P < 0.05, X^2 Test

** P < 0.01, X^2 Test

† Ch's N = 34, not 35 as in Table I, because pair Evered/Satan, who tied on Supplanting Ranks, is excluded.

For each male's number of partner-pair grooming predictions correct, a X^2 was calculated. The values of X^2 facilitate comparison of males for whom there were different numbers of pairs of partners available, but the interpretations of particular levels of statistical significance meet the difficulties mentioned above.

From Table XX, it can be seen that, for all seven Senior males, more than half the predictions about their grooming from their partners' Displacement and Display Rate, were correct, and for all six of the Seniors excluding Goliath; the majorities of the predictions from their partners' Display Ratios were correct.

(c) How much does each individual groom his ten partners with different statuses?

This analysis was restricted to the Seniors. As would be expected from the mainly successful predictions from partners' status to the grooming of the males towards members of pairs of those partners, (Table XX), there were positive correlations between the Comparative Measure of grooming with partners, and the rankings of those partners on the Supplanting and Display Rate scales. The median males' rSs for the two correlations are respectively +0.49 and +0.35 when Goliath was included in the analysis, and +0.59 and +0.55 when he was excluded. When the Frequency Measure was used instead of the Comparative Measure, to rank the males' partners, the respective median males' rSs were +0.41 and +0.22 with Goliath included in the analysis, and +0.63 and +0.53 when he was excluded. All rSs were positive. This finding, that the higher a partner's status (measured by his Supplanting Rank and his Display Rate) the more often he is groomed, does not add much to the results in Table XX.

4. Summary of the relations between grooming frequencies and status

Figure 1 (Section III) provides a convenient framework for sum-
marising the generalisations about grooming frequencies made so far.
The figure idealises the result, as applied to four males, whose statuses
decrease in the order A, B, C and D. In accordance with Table XVIII
above, the highest-ranking male A also has the highest median grooming
frequency. Figure 1 also shows how each individual distributed his
grooming among his three partners. In accordance with the high correlations between the frequencies with which individuals groom their partners, and get groomed by them (Table VI, Section IV), each male grooms
his partner as often as his partner grooms him. Thus, the frequency
with which A grooms D = the frequency with which D grooms A = 10
asterisks. In accordance with the positive correlations between the
status rankings of each male's partners, and the frequencies with which
he grooms them, higher-status partners are groomed more frequently.
Because a male grooms a particular partner as often as vice versa (because one chimpanzee almost always grooms one who grooms him at
some stage in the session), it is impossible to say whether the lower
status, or higher status individuals are responsible for these results.
The analysis of how grooming sessions start suggests that, when a very
low-status individual is involved with high-status partners, it is usually
the low-status one who has approached and started the session (Section
III). When very high-status individuals are involved, however, they do
not necessarily wait to be approached by others; and once another has
approached, they do not necessarily wait for the other to start first.

5. Summary of the relations between grooming durations and status

Figure 2 represents schematically the grooming durations of

Fig. 2.   Schematic Representation of the Grooming Durations of
Four Males of Different Statuses

Male	Status	With partner	Median grooming duration
A	1st	B	******
		C	*****
		D	****
B	2nd	A	********
		C	*******
		D	******
C	3rd	A	**********
		B	**********
		D	********
D	4th	A	****************
		B	***************
		C	**************

four individuals with different statuses, with three partners of different statuses. The evidence that higher-status individuals have lower over-all median durations is contained in Table XVIIIA.

Table XXIA shows the correlations between the duration with which each male grooms his different partners, and the statuses of those partners, as measured by their Supplanting Ranks. With every male except Goliath, the higher the rank of his partner, the longer he groomed that partner. This effect was as marked in the highest rank-ing males, like Mike and Charlie, who also groomed their higher rank-ing partners longer, as it was in the others. In the idealised Figure 2, Mike is represented by Male A.

It can be seen that Figure 2 also fits the finding that a male usu-ally grooms a partner with higher status more than that partner usually grooms him.

From Figure 2, it would be expected that a male (say B) would receive more grooming from low-status partners than from high-status ones (in the model in Figure 2, more from C - 9 units - than from A - 6 units). For Mike and Goliath, Table XXIB confirms this expecta-tion, but not for the other Senior males. It is possible that any tendency of higher-status partners to groom the males less (Table XVIIIB) was counteracted by the tendency of those high-status partners to groom longer when they were groomed longer (Table VI).

The finding that a male grooms his higher-status partners for longer could reflect the male's behaviour, discriminating among his partners, or it could be a consequence of greater demands for grooming by the higher-status partners. Section III showed that differences in males' grooming times with different partners were not accounted for

Table XXI.   Correlations Between Each Senior Male and his Partners Ranked According to their Supplanting Ranks, and A his Grooming Behaviour towards each Partner; and B each Partner's Grooming Behaviour toward him.

Male	Ch	Gol	Hh	Ru	Hm	Ly	Mk	+s	Median
A: with Gol	+0.60*	-0.06	+0.42	+0.62*	+0.75*	+0.52	+0.68*	6/7	+0.60*
no Gol	+0.64*	—	+0.65*	+0.56*	+0.73*	+0.70*	+0.65*	6/6	+0.65*
B: with Gol	+0.09	-0.60*	-0.29	+0.35	+0.04	+0.09	-0.13	4/7	+0.04
no Gol	+0.21	—	+0.03	+0.38	+0.12	-0.02	-0.10	4/6	+0.08

Grooming behaviour is ranked according to

A   median duration given by the male to his different partners; and

B   median duration received by the male from each of the partners.

*rSs significant at the 5% level (1-tailed test)

by differences in the scratching behaviour of those partners. It can be concluded that, apart from their grooming behaviour, partners' behaviour during the grooming sessions probably have rather small effects on the males' grooming durations. And higher-status partners' grooming behaviour could not have had much effect on the males' durations, because higher-status partners did not usually groom longer than lower-status ones (Table XVIII).

VII. GENERAL DISCUSSION

This description of male chimpanzee grooming and aggressive behaviour, based on a group of eleven males and on the behaviour of each of the eleven to their ten partners, is very incomplete. First, because only some of the ways in which the individuals' behaviour can differ are examined; second because those dimensions and categories of behaviour applied could conceal further important individual differences.

Some of the dimensions of individual behaviour touched upon in this study have been tested for their relations to the measures of grooming. Partners' times spent with males were slightly positively, but not significantly, correlated with the males' grooming toward them, in the cases of the majority of the Senior males. The median rS for the seven Senior males was +0.34 when the Frequency Measure of grooming was used, and +0.14 when the Duration Measure was used. The respective numbers of Seniors with positive correlations were 6 and 4 for the two grooming measures. When the correlations between the degrees to which partners were associated with the males (their Sociabilities, Section II) and the Frequency and Duration Measures of grooming were run, the respective median rSs were +0.35 and +0.42, with five of the seven Seniors having positive rSs in both cases. Thus there was a slight (non-significant) tendency for males to groom those with whom they were more strongly associated more frequently per opportunity, and longer. In Mike's case, the rS for partners' Sociabilities and the Frequencies with which Mike groomed them was +0.64, which is significant at the 5% level. In spite of this trend, some males groomed their very closest associate rather less than would be expected (Section III). There are many more ways in which partners could be characterised, and not all these ways would provide dimensions by which the partners could be ranked: some would be dichotomous classifications, such as 'of higher-status' or 'not of higher-status'. Obviously any description of the patterns of an individual's involvement in social behaviour with his fellows should include a list of those relations among the social behaviour which were tested for, and found not to be statistically significant. For the failures of relations to hold, such as the failure of the Gombe Stream males' grooming distribution to correlate strongly with time spent with fellows, become interesting when such relations do hold in other social groups. Thus a chimpanzee from Kasakati basin, who ranges over wider areas than do the Gombe chimpanzees, (Izawa, 1970), might show a closer relation between grooming involvement with fellows, and time spent with those fellows.

The pitfalls of applying tests of correlation to large numbers of measures have been mentioned by Spencer-Booth and Hinde (1969), and debated by Meehl (1967). Organisms and social groups are to some degree integrated systems, so that correlations between rankings according to any two aspects of them will almost always reveal some relationship, whether positive or negative, and if the Ns used are sufficient, the correlation will be statistically significant. Moreover, if many correlations are run, statistically significant differences arising by chance will arise: about one per twenty tests when a 5% level of probability is chosen. These two observations suggest that the statistical level of significance of a result is no guarantee of any other significance: judgement of the meaning of a result in the pattern of results already obtained should be made independently of its statistical level of significance. Those correlations that arose by chance in one study can be eliminated only by repeating the study with another group, and/or when the present group's members' properties have changed substantially. Thus the present study could be profitably repeated now (1972) that Humphrey is top male, and Satan's status is higher than Mike''s (Bygott, pers. comm.).

The second way in which a description using such dimensions of behaviour as were used in this study could be inadequate, follows from the fact that categories and dimensions applied to the group as a whole can miss some of the most striking characteristics of the individuals in it. Thus, if there is more than one sort of display, this study could never show differences between the males, such that (for example) Mike used mainly the first sort, and Humphrey used mainly the second. Another example is the way in which the Duration Measure of grooming gives no indication about the parts groomed: some males may groom mainly the backs of their partners, others mainly the chests.

The dimensions and categories used in this study also lend themselves to generalisations, which could override possible important individual characteristics. Thus the generalisation that it is the higher-status males who groom for less long conceals the fact that the top male, Mike, usually groomed for very long (ranking second in Table III). Other special characteristics which could be concealed include

Hugh's reluctance to start grooming first, and to continue for any length of time, in spite of his relative readiness to join in a session; Goliath's eagerness to approach Mike and Humphrey; the high frequency with which Goliath presents to be groomed; and the rarity of occasions when Goliath was supplanted.

To what extent can the grooming and aggression results be interpreted functionally and casually? The prolonged grooming by Mike, as top male, suggests that functional interpretations will not be simple. It is obviously in the interests of relatively low-status individuals to keep others calm, by grooming them, but what advantages does Mike's generous grooming provide? His grooming may counteract the exciting effects of his displays on the others and it may increase their attachments to him. (Displaying, too, could have a social cohesive, as well as assertive, function.)

Comments about causation must be made separately from those about function, for the causes leading to behaviour with adaptive consequences can be many and devious (Section I). It is tempting to apply a simple 'arousal' explanation to male grooming (prompted by Fentress, pers. comm.). When males are in a situation where they could rest and do nothing, the more aroused individuals groom themselves, and also those others who are in reach, rather than do nothing. Mike was especially aroused because he was anxious about his social position; and Goliath, because he was a relatively frail subordinate. In accordance with this hypothesis, both these males not only groomed others longest, but they also self-groomed longer than Charlie and Hugh, in spite of the fact that their diligent allo-grooming left less time for self-grooming. Of course, this simple explanation leaves open the question of why some males are more 'aroused' than others in the grooming sessions, and why some partners have a more arousing effect than do others. The obvious social consequence of this arousal effect is a socially homeostatic one: excitement in the group promotes arousal in some of its individuals which causes them to groom, which calms both groomers and groomees (Mason, 1965).

VIII. CONCLUSION

This study developed methods for characterising different individuals in terms of their involvement in social activities with others. Each male was characterised in terms of measures of his grooming toward his 10 partners considered as a group, and by the way in which he distributed his grooming among his partners. In the same ways, the males' displaying, and other status-related behaviours, were used to characterise them. They were then fitted into schemes, whereby their grooming and status were related to each other. Such schemes are shown in Figures 1 and 2. A male would groom his partner for longer, the higher that partner's status, although higher-status partners did not themselves groom in return much longer than the lower-status ones. A male was also more often involved in grooming sessions with higher-status partners, and such individuals were generally more frequently involved in grooming. The lower-status individuals contributed most to the durations of the sessions, usually grooming longer; but higher-status individuals contributed nearly as much to the starts of their sessions as did their partners.

These generalisations provide a common, status-related, scheme in which to place individuals who groom others for different amounts of time, with different frequencies. It remains possible, however, that other schemes, as yet untried, will also fit, and that some of them will fit better. In the attempt to relate each individual's grooming and status it has become clear that generalisations applicable to the group as a whole do not fit all the information about the individuals in it, which this study has made available.

IX. SUMMARY

The subjects of this study were 11 adult male chimpanzees who commonly visited the provisioning area of the Gombe Stream National Park, in Tanzania. Methods were developed for characterising individual chimpanzees in terms of their involvement in social activities with others. Their grooming and aggressive behaviour toward their fellow males were examined. Each male was characterised in terms of:

(i)   his behaviour toward the group as a whole, and the behaviour of the group towards him; and

(ii)   the distribution of his behaviour among his fellows, and how they differed in their behaviour towards him.

The 7 oldest males were more involved in grooming with each other than the 4 younger ones. There were many ways in which each individual was unique, but the following generalisations could be made:

1.   It was meaningful to order the males in a status hierarchy, with the top male (Mike) supplanting most others, displaying most frequently, pant-grunting to fewest others, and being pant-grunted to by most others.

2.   Some individuals (including Mike) were more frequently involved in grooming with the majority of their fellows than were certain

other individuals.

3.   The males most frequently involved in grooming usually had the higher statuses.

4.   The higher an individual's status, the less long he usually groomed his fellows, on those occasions when he groomed them, except for the top male, who groomed others long.

5.   Whatever his status, a male tended to groom others for longer, the higher their statuses.

Methodological problems faced by this study included:

(i)   The fact that an individual's involvement in a social activity does not necessarily reflect only his contribution to that activity. For example, he may be much involved in grooming because he is much chosen as a grooming partner. A detailed knowledge of the usual sequences in the interactions in which the individuals are involved can provide a starting point for assessing each one's contribution to his interactions.

(ii) To describe the distribution of an individual's behaviour among his fellows by ranking those others according to how much of the particular social activity he does with them is made difficult when the groupings of the chimpanzees are 'open' so that one individual is seldom present with all 10 possible partners together, and when such small groups as he does join differ from time to time. To rank an individual's partners on a single scale is to assume that his behaviour toward different individuals is consistent in all groupings of those individuals. Such assumptions were examined in this study.

X. ACKNOWLEDGEMENTS

The observations on which this study is based were made in the Gombe Stream National Park in Kigoma, Tanzania, while I was a Research Fellow of St. John's College, Cambridge. I was also supported by the Science Research Council. I wish to thank Dr. Jane van Lawick-Goodall and Baron Hugo van Lawick for giving me the air fare to Tanzania, and for their help during my time at the Gombe Stream. The data about the males' attendance at the feeding area (Section II) were collected by Lori Baldwin, Janet Brooks, David Bygott, June Cree, Cathleen Clarke, Ruth Davis, Carole Gale, Pat McGinnis, Anne Shouldice-Simpson, Dawn Starin, Geza Teleki and Neville Washington. I wish to thank these people, and those many others at the Gombe Stream National Park, and at the Sub-department of Animal Behaviour, Cambridge, without whose support and encouragement I could not have completed this study.

XI. REFERENCES

Altmann, S. A. (1965). Sociobiology of rhesus monkeys. II. Stochastics of Social Communication. J. Theoret. Biol. 8, 490-522.

Bernstein, I. S. (1971). Primate status hierarchies. In "Primate Behaviour. Developments in Field and Laboratory Research." Vol. 1. (L. A. Rosenblum, ed.) Academic Press, New York and London.

Bernstein, I. S. (1971). Activity profiles of primate groups. In "Behavior of Non-human Primates." Vol. 3. (A. M. Schrier and F. Stollnitz, eds.) Academic Press, New York and London.

Bertrand, M. (1969). The Behavioral Repertoire of the Stumptail
Macaque. Bibliotheca Primatologica, 11.

Brown, R. (1965). Social Psychology. The Free Press, Macmillan
Company, New York.

Crawford, M. P. (1942). Dominance and the behavior of pairs of female chimpanzees when they meet after varying intervals of separation. J. Comp. Psychol. 33, 259-265.

Gartlan, J. S. (1968). Structure and Function in Primate Society.
Folia. Primat. 8, 89-120.

Hinde, R. A. (1971). Development of Social Behavior. In "Behavior
of Non-human Primates," Vol. 3. (A. M. Schrier and F. Stollnitz
eds.) Academic Press, New York and London.

Izawa, K. (1970). Unit groups of chimpanzees and their nomadism in
the savanna woodland. Primates 11, 1-46.

Kummer, H. (1968). "Social Organisation of Hamadryas Baboons."
Univ. Chicago Press, Chicago and London.

Mason, W. A. (1965). Determinants of social behavior in young
chimpanzees. In "Behavior of Non-human Primates." (A. M.
Schrier and F. Stollnitz, eds.) Academic Press, New York and
London.

Meehl, P. E. (1967). Theory-testing in psychology and physics: a
methodological paradox. Philosophy of Science 34, 103-115.

Premack, D. (1971). Language in chimpanzee? Science 172, 808-822.

Ransom, T. W. and Ransom, B.S. (1971). Adult male-infant relations
among baboons. (Papio anubis). Folia. Primat. 16, 179-195.

Reynolds, V. (1968). Kinship and the family in Monkeys, apes and
man. Man 3, 209-223.

Reynolds, V. (1970). Roles and role change in monkey society: the consort relationship of rhesus monkeys. Man 5, 449-465,

Reynolds, V. and Luscombe, G. (1969). Chimpanzee rank order and the function of displays. Sec. Conference of the International Primatological Society, Behaviour, Vol. 1, (C. R. Carpenter ed.) S. Karger, Basel and New York.

Rowell, T. E. (1966). Hierarchy in the organisation of a captive baboon group. Anim. Behav. 14, 430-443.

Spencer-Booth, Y and Hinde, R. A. (1969). Tests of behavioural characteristics for rhesus monkeys. Behaviour 33, 179-211.

Siegel, S. (1956). Nonparametric Statistics for the Behavioral Sciences. McGraw-Hill, New York, Toronto and London.

Simpson, M. J. A. (1968). The display of the Siamese Fighting Fish (Betta splendens). Anim. Behav. Monogs. 1, No. 1.

Sugiyama, Y. (1968). Social organisation of chimpanzees in the Budongo Forest, Uganda. Primates 9, 225-258.

Sugiyama, Y. (1969). Social behavior of chimpanzees in the Budongo Forest, Uganda. Primates 10, 197-225

Struhsaker, T. T. (1967). Social structure among vervet monkeys (Cercopithecus aethiops). Behaviour 29, 83-121.

Struhsaker, T. T. (1969). Correlates of ecology and social organisation among African Cercopithecines. Folia. Primat. 11, 80-118.

van Hooff, J. A. R. A. M. (1970). A component analysis of the structure of the social behavior of a semi-captive chimpanzee group. Experientia 26, 549-550.

van Hooff, J. A. R. A. M. (1971). "Aspecten van het sociale gedragende communicatie bij humane en hogere niet-human primaten." (A structural analysis of the social behavior of a semi-captive group of chimpanzees.) Bronder-offset, Rotterdam.

van Lawick-Goodall, J. (1968). The behaviour of free-living chimpan-

zees in the Gombe Stream Reserve. Anim. Behav. Monogs. 1,
No. 3.

van Lawick-Goodall, J. (1971). In the Shadow of Man. Collins, London.

Additional References.

Sade, D.S. (1972). In Sociometrics of Macaca mulatta I. Linkages
and Cliques in Grooming Matrices. Folia Primat. 18, 196-223,
presents elegant methods for preparing matrices of social data
for statistical analysis, and he refers to relevant sociological
literature.

Richards, S.M. (1972). Tests for Behavioural Characteristics in
Rhesus Monkeys. Ph.D. Thesis, Cambridge.

SOME OBSERVATIONS ON THE SEXUAL BEHAVIOUR OF

CAPTIVE LOWLAND GORILLAS, GORILLA G. GORILLA

(SAVAGE AND WYMAN)

Jorg P. Hess

University of Basel
Zoological Department

supervised by Professor Dr. Rudolf Schenkel

I INTRODUCTION

In the spring of 1968 I began a comparative study of the mother-
infant behaviour of the lowland gorillas living in the Basle Zoological
Gardens (Dir. Prof. Dr. E. M. Lang).

During the course of my work opportunities arose every now and
then to observe the sexual behaviour of all the individuals in the population. These observations comprise the behaviour of individual animals
as well as scenes in which two, or, more rarely, several partners participated and which refer to oestrus and inter-oestrus periods in adult
females. As more and more interesting information accumulated, my
attention was drawn to the individual oestrus phases of Goma and Kati
in particular.

Up to the present time (November 1971), literature on the sexual
behaviour of the gorilla has been meagre. Schaller compiled the data
existing before 1963 on captive and free-living mountain and lowland
gorillas and published them together with his own observations in his
monograph "The Mountain Gorilla". From Schaller's monograph,
three passages concerning sexual behaviour of free living gorillas will
be cited here: "page 275 ... My work on free-living gorillas yielded
remarkably few observations on sexual behaviour. In 466 hours of
observation I witnessed only two copulations and one invitation to do
so." - "page 278 ... In the wild, not a single observation on play
mounting, homosexual behaviour, or any other type of sexual behaviour
was noted, except two copulations and one invitation to do so." - "page
278 .... Free-living gorillas showed no sexual activity while young,
and even blackbacked males were never seen to indulge in any beha-

viour during my presence which could be construed as erotic." Later publications amount, on the whole, to hardly more than brief notes on copulatory behaviour and on oestrus in females in connection with reports on gorilla births in zoological gardens.

In this study the term "sexual behaviour" includes

- the behaviour of one or more animals which involves direct contact with its or their own genitals or genital region or those of a partner.
- behavioural sequences that correspond largely to the phases of copulatory behaviour during an inter-oestrus phase.
- behaviour which is clearly connected with the oestrus in females.

This study contains qualitative rather than quantitative data. The observations and their interpretation form the basis for further quantitative studies of the group in Basle.

The sexual behaviour observed during the inter-oestrus phases of the females takes many different forms. As it is described at length the impression might be given that the gorillas in Basle constitute a hypersexualized society. This is not the case. The above-mentioned behaviour occurs comparatively rarely.

II MATERIAL AND METHOD

(a) Material

The Basle Zoological Gardens at present (1971) owns a group of nine lowland gorillas (Gorilla g. gorilla, Savage and Wyman). The group is composed of three adult females (Achilla, Goma and Kati),

two silverbacked males (Stefi and Pepe), one blackbacked male (Jambo),
one subadult male (Migger), one infant female (Quarta) and one baby
male (Tamtam). During one of her oestrus periods which are considered in this study, Kati conceived and gave birth to another baby female (Uzima) in spring 1972. Data on the individuals such as age,
name, sex and origin can be found in Table I.

Until the spring of 1969 the group, with the exception of Tamtam
and Uzima, lived in the old bird house. The animals had three, occasionally four, exhibition cages (two indoors and two, screened with
glass, out of doors) as well as seven small sleeping-boxes at their
disposal.

Stefi and Achilla were kept together from 1954 until Achilla's
first pregnancy which ended in March 1958 with an abortion. Afterwards
Stefi and Achilla were together only to allow copulation and were separated as soon as pregnancy was ascertained. During the pregnancies
and the time when Achilla was rearing her infants (Jambo, Migger and
Quarta) she was given one of the indoor cages to herself. At three
years of age the infants were normally separated from their mothers
and were incorporated into the juvenile group. The members of this
group (Pepe, Goma, Jambo, Kati and Migger) always stayed together.
While Achilla was rearing her third infant, Migger, the juveniles
(Pepe, Goma, Jambo and Kati) were allowed to visit the mother and infant for an hour from time to time. As Stefi occupied one of the outdoor cages and the juvenile group the other, they enjoyed acoustic, optic and olfactory contact with each other. Within the juvenile group,
the particularly close relationship between Pepe and Goma, who were
both handreared and had been together since 1960, should be especially
mentioned.

In the new ape-house, into which the gorillas were moved in April 1969, they have at their disposal three large inside cages which can be connected by hydraulically operated sliding doors. Even when these are closed, the iron barred doors and windows between the cages allow all the animals a limited contact with each other. The enclosure also comprises two outdoor cages and a number of sleeping-boxes which are usually left open during the day for resting and retiring. The size and structure of the enclosure on the one hand, and the ideal age and sex composition of the group on the other made a gradual integration of all the individuals into one unit seem feasible.

At first Stefi, Achilla and Quarta were put together for a few hours during the day. The young animals remained in the right-hand cage until they, in their turn, were gradually introduced to Stefi, Achilla and Quarta. During this phase which lasted for a fortnight, frequent rank contests took place between Stefi and Pepe who had meanwhile become adolescent. Later on Stefi usually refrained from entering the right-hand cage, limiting himself to the middle and the left-hand one. Pepe took defensive action only when Stefi intruded upon his quarters; he generally avoided those occupied by Stefi. Since 2nd May 1971, the birth-date of Goma's first infant, Tamtam, mother and child together with Pepe have shared the right-hand cage. To avoid disturbing the mother with her infant, she was given the company only of the partner most familiar to her; direct contact with the other animals was interrupted. Optic, acoustic, olfactory contact and limited possibilities of touching continued to exist. Keeping all the individuals in one large community has proved to be a valuable measure and has, moreover, rendered possible the study of sexual behaviour in a group.

Table I.   The gorillas living in Basle Zoo.

name/sex		age	born	in Basle Zoo since	further notes
Stefi (S)	♂	22 silverbacked	ca. 1949 in the wild The Cameroons	1954/from Columbus Zoo, Ohio	Father of G, J, M, Q and probably So.
Achilla (A)	♀	24 adult	ca. 1947 in the wild The Cameroons	1948/from Vincennes	Mother of G, J, M and Q. J, M, Q raised by A herself.
Pepe (P)	♂	12 silverbacked	ca. 1959 in the wild	1960	
Goma (G)	♀	12 adult	23. 9. 59 Basle Zoo	birth	First infant of A + S. Hand-raised by E. M. Lang. Mother of T.
Jambo (J)	♂	10 blackbacked	17. 4. 61 Basle Zoo	birth	Second infant of A + S. Mother-raised. Father of T and probably So
Kati (K)	♀	10 adult	ca. 1961 in the wild The Cameroons	1962	Mother of So, the infant died 6 days after birth
Migger (M)	♂	7½ subadult	1. 6. 64 Basle Zoo	birth	Third infant of A + S. Mother-raised.
Quarta (Q)	♀	3½ infant	17. 7. 68 Basle Zoo	birth	Fourth infant of A + S. Mother-raised, at present still in close contact with A
Souanke (So)	♀	-	23. 11. 70 Basle Zoo	died 6 days after birth	First infant of K. Father S or J.
Tamtam (T)	♂	½ baby	2. 5. 71 Basle Zoo	birth	First infant of G + J. Mother-raised, is still completely dependent on his mother.

(b) Method

Observations were made with the naked eye and from time to time with binoculars. They were recorded simultaneously on tape. In addition the study was documented with photographs as far as exposure conditions allowed. Scenes during two consecutive oestrus periods were recorded with 16mm black and white film. This film supplied further data which have been considered in the study.

III SEXUAL BEHAVIOUR OF ALL THE MEMBERS OF THE GROUP EXCEPT DURING OESTRUS IN FEMALES

1. Mother and infant

(a)   Genital inspections

From the very day of birth, the mother carries out minute inspections of the infant's body. She examines each part, treating various places carefully with her fingers, lips, teeth and tongue. These activities can roughly be described as picking, scratching, rubbing, plucking, poking, licking, sucking, biting and nibbling. They occur several times every hour and serve many functions, which shall not be discussed in this paper. The regions which particularly interest the mother are the ears, face, shoulders, hands and feet, navel, anus and genitals. The frequency of application to a particular part during an inspection phase and the duration of absorption in this part show its degree of attraction. The genitals are stroked, plucked at and poked or held and moved to and fro, mostly with the fingers (chiefly the thumb or index finger - Fig. 1 - the little finger being employed for more delicate manipulations). Touching with the lips, teeth and tongue, combined with sucking, do occur but are less frequent. The mother performs

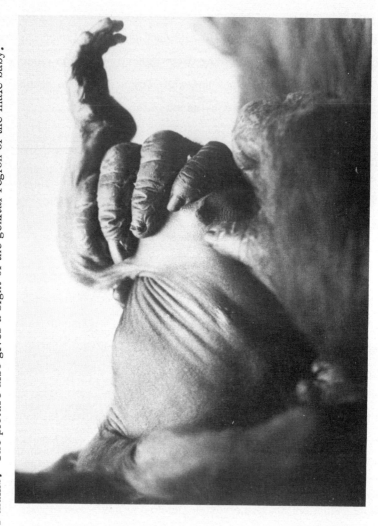

Fig. 1. Genital inspection / mother G and male baby T. The mother manipulates the infant's penis with her thumb. The picture also gives a sight of the genital region of the male baby.

Fig. 2. Genital inspection / mother G and male baby T. From the
         first day of life the mother is occupied with the genital region
         of the infant in the context of general body inspections. The
         picture shows the mother's interest and concentration.

this treatment either sitting (Fig. 2) in various positions or lying on
her back (Schaller gives in free-living gorillas only one observation of
a mother manipulating the infant's penis with subsequent sucking). Already during the first days after birth the mother's occupation with the
infant's genital region does not only occur in the context of general body
inspections but also independently. After having touched the genitals,
the mother smells her finger (Fig. 3) then places it in her mouth, or
touches it with her tongue. Her occupation with the infant's genitals is
clearly influenced by the child's reactions; scenes occur with differentiated participation by both partners.

- If the touching behaviour is of brief duration, gentle and tender,
  the infant hardly reacts at the beginning; later it makes the
  same face as when being tickled by its mother.

- If the touching lasts a long time or is rough, the newborn utters
  faint grunts and squeaks whereupon the mother's activity is dis-
  continued.

- Towards the end of the first month, the faint vocalisations become screams and are accompanied by increasingly violent arm
  and leg movements. As the locomotory faculties develop, sliding and crawling away, sitting up, turning, walking and finally
  running away can be observed. The mother may respond to
  these evasive movements by gripping the infant firmly when she
  wishes to touch its genitals, moreover she no longer necessarily
  reacts to its expressions of discomfort and resentment.

- Towards the middle of the first year the mother sometimes uses
  genital touching as a training method; she thereby urges the
  infant to crawl, climb, walk and run; in certain cases it is used

Fig. 3. Genital inspection / mother G and male baby T. After genital touching the mother smells at her finger or touches it with her tongue.

as a means of "getting rid of" the infant for a short time.
Pulling at the genitals can also serve as a punishment.

Already during the first few days after birth, genital touching causes urination and defecation provided that the infant is ready for excretion. (Similar observations on A and J in earlier studies of the gorilla group in Basle are reported by Schenkel and by Lang. The baby J reacted to touching of the genital region also with excretion. A similar report by Fisher on Kumba the son of Mumbi at Lincoln Park Zoo shows the same reaction of the infant. Lang used the genital-touching-method to provoke excretions with G, while she was raised in his home).

Possibly the expectation of such reactions is one factor motivating the mother to occupy herself directly with the infant's genitals. From the second or third day onwards infants of both sexes react to genital touching by erection of their genitals. G, the mother of the male baby T, handled her infant's genitals in a far more differentiated manner than A, the mother of the female baby Q. The difference is astonishing. It seems unlikely that the difference in maternal experience is responsible. The explanation may rather be found in the different sex of the infants. The erection of the penis and the wide arc described by the squirting urine (Fig. 4) in the male baby are reactions which are highly rewarding for G and which induce more intensive exploration.

The frequency of the genital touching decreases as the infant grows older but can be regularly observed almost until the end of the third year, later on only sporadically.

(b)   Other sexual activity

Apart from genital touching A shows a further type of sexual

Fig. 4.   Urination / mother G and male baby T. A typical situation of
           urination after the touching of the genitals in a male baby.
           The urine squirts in a wide arc and the mother seems im-
           pressed.

occupation with her infant. During Q's first three years, A repeatedly laid the infant on its back on the floor in front of her, placed her own genital region on that of the infant, then crouching down, either slid around with the child beneath her or performed rhythmic pelvic movements. In the earliest stage A used to put a protective hand between the floor and the infant's back. This behaviour was often elicited by the appearance of familiar persons but was also observed without their being present. (A had acted similarly with her two earlier infants M and J as reported by Lang and by Schenkel.)

Up to the time of writing (November 1971) G has only shown tendencies to such behaviour with T, and only rarely.

On the other hand a corresponding scene involving the gorilla mother Delilah and her six month-old son, Daniel, was observed in the Bristol Zoo (three personal observations and personal communications with G. R. Greed and M. Colbourne). The mother holds the infant to her face and touches the penis orally thus causing an erection; then she lays the child down in front of her, spreads its thighs apart and fixes them with her hands, supporting herself with her arms, she then places her genital region on that of the infant and moves her pelvi rhythmically. (A comparable situation, but not so closely related to the genital region is reported by Rumbaugh, involving the mother Vila and her infant Alvila of San Diego Zoo.)

All the described performances did not take place at the same ages of the different infants under observation. The time of the occurrence of a special pattern is certainly determined by the individuality of the mother and by her experience.

As yet there is not sufficient material to be able to state what may be considered as a norm for the mother-son or mother-daughter behaviour.

2. The infant (until 3rd year)

During the first few weeks the infant explores its own body with its hand either in scratching or palpating excursions. Thereby the hand comes into contact with the genital region. The manner of touching does not differ from the manner of manual exploration of other parts of the body. The different frequency with which the infant turns to various regions of its body corresponds to their degree of attraction. For the infant, too, its own genitals belong to the attractive parts for this kind of exploration. Touching of its own genitals may cause an erection. With increasing age the touching of the genital region with the hand becomes more direct and often occurs immediately before or during urination and defecation. At no moment during the first two years of life may the touching of the genital region, in the cases I observed, be called "masturbation". Continuous touching and manipulation can easily be observed, but such prolonged periods of exploration of their own or their mother's body are typical for infants of this age. "Masturbation-like" behaviour has been observed in Bristol Zoo with the $3\frac{1}{2}$ month old Daniel, son of Delilah (personal communication G. R. Greed and M. Colbourne).

In a social group, infants of more than one year of life are sometimes involved in more complex sequences of sexual behaviour while playing with other young individuals. By the age of $1\frac{1}{2}$ years Q was for the first time indulging in a play copulation with M. At the age of 2 years and 2 months Q has for the first time been seen to assume a copulatory position on her own; sitting ventrally against the back of her mother, embracing her she imitated copulatory movements. Later on, she also showed forms of offering behaviour towards her father, S, while playing.

Schaller's wife observed a two year old male infant, belonging to Cordier, which was sitting in a copulatory position behind a seven-month old female and making several thrusting movements.

3. Other members of the group

The following behaviour patterns, or very similar ones, can be observed in different individuals. The activities have been divided into those without and those with a partner. Table III indicates which particular performance occurred in which individual or between which partners and characterises the frequency in occurrence.

(a) Sexual activities without a partner

On the one hand we find patterns belonging to the field of comfort or explorative behaviour (sgt), on the other hand patterns with a definite sexual motivation (rgt, rpm, sco and rgr).

Simple genital touching - sgt - (observed in all animals).

The genital region or the genitals are touched once or several times with the whole hand, or with one finger. As a rule, after each contact, the hand or finger is held to the nose and/or licked.

Rhythmic genital touching- rgt - (observed in males, P and M). The genital region or the genitals are touched rhythmically for a comparatively long time (up to 30" or more) with the hand, a single finger or, more rarely, the foot. The animals have an erection, sometimes even before the contact. Many individual variations of this behaviour occur. P, for instance, uses his index finger, or else he presses his feet rhythmically against his erect penis. On five observed occasions, P finally reached ejaculation as a result of this stimulation.

Schaller compiles different cases of masturbation-like behaviour in captive gorillas, but he never saw this occupation or similar forms in free living animals. In captive gorillas however, masturbation seems to be common, (personal observations Zurich Zoo, Frankfurt Zoo, Bristol Zoo, personal communication G. R. Greed and M. Colbourne, Bristol Zoo).

Rhythmic pelvic movements - rpm - (observed in K, J and M). The animal performs rhythmic upward and downward movements with the abdomen in a supine (female K only) or sitting (males M and J only) position. In the supine position K's legs are flexed and the feet hold onto the bars of the door, or the wire netting, or are pressed against a firm object (Fig. 5). In the sitting position, M and J hold onto the bars or an iron door with hands and feet; the knees are bent to an extent that the genital region is rubbing against the bars or the door while the whole body is continuously lifted and lowered. The direct rubbing-contact of the genitals is only observed in males. The frequency of movement in the female is higher (average 31.8 down movements/10″) than in males (average 18-20 down movements/10″, Table II).

Substitute copulation with an object - sco - (observed in males only).
One possible form, out of a great number of varieties, is the

Fig. 5. Female K performing rhythmic pelvic movements.

following:

An object (rubber block or tyre) is pushed under the body,
the rump is, in a quadrupedal posture, lowered until the genitals
touch the object and normally a brief series of copulatory
thrusts follows. Another form is in a sitting position to press
an object against the genital region and to perform thrusting
movements against it.

Rhythmic genital rubbing - rgr - (observed only in females)
While sitting or in supine position the genital region is
pressed against the wall or the bars or another firm object and
rubbed sideways, or up and down; always of brief duration
(5 to 10"). This activity may be repeated for a few times.

Table II. Data on the rhythmic pelvic movements

	Kati ♀	Jambo ♂	Migger ♂
number of phases measured	7	1	5
number of measurements during the above phases	28	3	8
frequency of pelvic movements			
maximum mov. / 10"	41.1	20.2	23.6
minimum mov. / 10"	25.0	20.0	16.0
average mov. / 10"	31.8	20.0	18.1

(b) Sexual activities with a partner

All partner-related behaviour can be observed between partners of the same or opposite sex. On the one hand it involves explorative touching of the partner's genitals (sgt, lgmp), as a rule with one partner taking the initiative and the other being tolerant, on the other hand, scenes with typical sexual motivation (gocp, cpcp, ocpp) frequently develop out of play context. Also in the latter case one partner is generally the initiator while the other accepts the corresponding role. Table III gives information about the partners in the various scenes.

Simple genital touching - sgtp - (Figs. 6 and 7) and
Long lasting genital manipulation - lgmp -

The genitals (or the genital region) of the partner are, with a single finger or the hand, either quickly touched (sgtp), or manipulated for a longer period (lgmp). These activities may be repeated. In both cases finger or hand are then smelled at, and/or licked. The partner remains motionless and tolerates being touched.

Genital-oral contact - gocp -

Several variations occur. In the scene most frequently observed, one partner lies on its back, the other stands over it, facing in the opposite direction, and lowers its rump to the former's face. Except during oestrus one partner only was oral-genitally active in this position and never both simultaneously. M, for instance, often exposes his erect penis in a standing position in front of the sitting A. He then may with the penis even touch his mother's lips to provoke her being orally active.

Fig. 6. Simple genital touching - sgt - /female A and female infant Q. Q touches the genital region of her mother, A.

Table III. Frequency of sexual patterns in inter-oestrus periods and notes on partners.

indi-vidual	sexual activities without a partner					sexual activities with a partner					
	sgt	rgt	rpm	sco	rgr	part-ner	sgtp	lgmp	gocp	cpcp	ocpp
S ♂	◑										
P ♂	●	●		◑		G ♀ M ♂			O	O 	O ◑	
A ♀	O				O	S ♂ M ♂ Q ♀	◑		 O	 O O	
G ♀	O				O	P ♂	●	◑	◑		●
J ♂	O		◑			S ♂ G ♀ K ♀ M ♂	● O O ●	 ◑		 O ●	
K ♀	●		O		O	S ♂ J ♂ M ♂	 O 		◑ ◑		O
M ♂	●	O	●	◑		S ♂ G ♀ J ♂ K ♀	● O ● ●	● 	 ◑	 ● ●	
Q ♀	O					S ♂ A ♀ J ♂ K ♀ M ♂	◑ O O O ◑			 ●	◑ O

● more than 10 observations / ◑ 3-9 observations / O 1-2 observations

sgt: simple genital touching / rgt: rhythmic genital touching / rpm: rhythmic pelvic movements /sco: substitute copulation with an object / rgr: rhythmic genital rubbing / sgtp: simple genital touching of partner/ lgmp: long lasting genital manipulation of partner /gocp: genital-oral contact with partner /cpcp: copulation developing out of play context / ocpp: offering for copulation out of play context.

The table contains observations from 1968-1971.

Copulations developing out of play context - cpcp - (Figs. 8 and 9)

Often the older partner plays the masculine role, females have also been observed to assume this role. The positions and the activity during such copulations correspond to the oestrus behaviour (see Section IV).

Offering for copulation out of play context by females - ocpp

The behaviour corresponds to the form of offering preceding copulations in oestrus periods and has only been shown by females. It need not result in copulation, the invited partner may react by renewing the scuffle or "chase". Q showed these forms while playing with her silverbacked father S by the age of two and a half years.

IV SEXUAL BEHAVIOUR OF ALL THE MEMBERS OF THE GROUP DURING OESTRUS IN FEMALES

In the adult female gorillas of the Basle Zoological Gardens the menstrual cycle comes to approximately 30 days (for detailed data see Table IV, these data largely correspond to similar ones given in literature for gorilla females in other zoos, Schaller 1963, Tijskens 1971). During the major part of this period the females are in non-oestrus condition. The comparatively short oestrus period is in this paper divided into "the pre-oestrus period" (1) and "the oestrus period" (2). This classification is chiefly methodological, in reality the two phases overlap, precluding a clear definition of their boundaries.

The pre-oestrus period begins 1 to 3 days before the oestrus period. The latter lasts from 2 to 4 days (for detailed data see

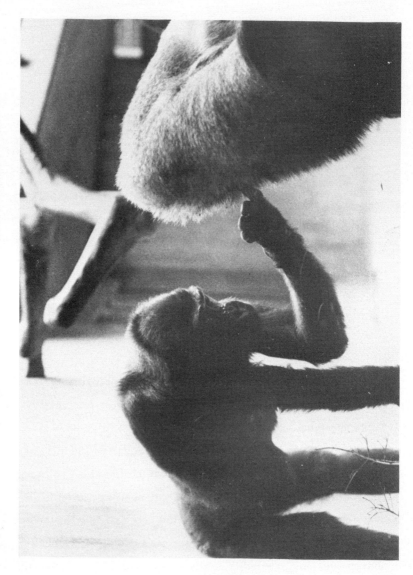

Fig. 7.   Simple genital touching – sgt – /female K touches the genital region of male S.

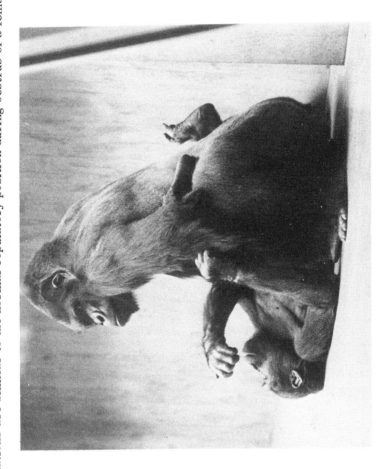

Fig. 8.   Play copulation – ventro/ventral / male P and subadult male M.   The adult male P in a sitting position, the subadult male M in supine position.   The positions adopted in such copulations are similar to the normal copulatory position during oestrus of a female.

Fig. 9. Play copulation – dorso/ventral / young adult male J and subadult male M. The older male is sitting behind and thrusting, and as a rule the younger one assuming the female role.

Table IV). During the pre-oestrus period there is evidence of a change
in the behaviour of most individuals as compared with inter-oestrus
periods, particularly of the female directly concerned. Only during
the oestrus period the female shows "inviting" and "offering" behaviours
which may lead to copulations.

Apart from this difference many behaviour patterns occur in
both periods, especially those compiled in Table III.

The above classification might be extended to include a third
period, the "post oestrus". Certain after effects of oestrus periods
were observed, mainly in the young males J and M, resulting in increased but otherwise normal sexual activities with a partner as described in III. b), but sufficient quantitative data to justify the term are
not yet available.

The observations on pre-oestrus and oestrus described subsequently were collected mainly during these periods in K. Observations
on A and G are included occasionally.

1. The pre-oestrus period

During this period there is a noticeable change in the female's
body odour. Anyone familiar with gorillas will register a more potent
smell. I shall now describe the principal changes in the behaviour of
all the animals in the group during the pre-oestrus period. Many
changes occur less distinctly or less frequently in social situations
other than pre-oestrus period.

(a) Female K during pre-oestrus.

K's displays are aimed exclusively at S. She often maintains

Table IV.   Data on oestrus periods and menstruation cycles (based on keeper's reports)

	Achilla	Goma	Kati
first oestrus (age in years)	$6\frac{1}{2}$ ($\pm\frac{1}{2}$)	$6\frac{1}{2}$	$6\frac{1}{2}$ ($\pm\frac{1}{2}$)
duration of menstrual cycles			
(a) total number of cycles	63	30	29
(b) duration of one cycle			
maximum (days)	52	44	48
minimum (days)	8	21	22
average	29.7	31.4	32
duration of oestrus periods			
(a) total number of periods	74	28	31
(b) duration of one period in days			
(estimation)	3-4	3	2
oestrus periods after conception			
during the following number of months after conception, oestrus was observed: (neither oestrus periods nor menstrual cycles show the normal duration, the motivation of the ♀ decreases)	G: 2 J: no data M: $5\frac{1}{2}$	$6\frac{1}{2}$	5
oestrus periods after birth of an infant, separation of the mother from the infant or abortion			
first oestrus (months after)	G: $1\frac{1}{2}$ J: $1\frac{1}{3}$ M: 1 abort: $1\frac{1}{2}$		2

a display posture, standing stiffly on all fours, with neck and head raised, staring unwaveringly at S. At other times, she poses with her stiff arms erected on a platform (rubber block, tyre or the threshold of the sliding door), so that the front part of her body is raised even more (Fig. 10). Her lips are pressed together, the corners slightly drawn in.

On S's shifting his position, K immediately adjusts her stand to face him and continues to fix him with her gaze. When S turns his head towards her, K almost immediately turns hers away for a short moment. Even in the old birdhouse she was similarly fascinated by S, although she never had direct contact with him.

(Recently, September 1972, the gorilla female Copina from Zurich Zoo has been introduced in Basle to M and S for purpose of mating. During her first pre-oestrus period at Basle, she behaved in the same way and was similarly concentrating on S only, even when she was in a cage together with M and having no direct, but only visual, contact with S. She had been introduced to S about one month before, but until that time of pre-oestrus no sexual interactions between S and Copina ever took place.)

K tolerates J and M but seems uninterested, that is to say, neither her look, posture nor movement are directed at the young males. Any invitation to play, on their part, is ignored. She is more reserved than usual towards her keeper.

(b) Typical scenes between K and S

- S maintains a similar stiff display posture between frontal and lateral, with face and eyes turned away, frequently changing from one side to the other. From time to time brief turns of his head

<u>Fig. 10.</u> Pre-oestrus / female K. Typical display posture of female
K during pre-oestrus. She is facing the dominant male S and
staring at him.

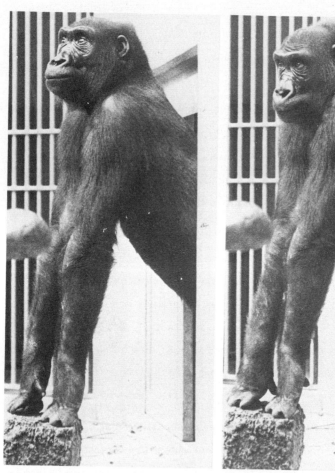

towards her and glances out of the corner of his eyes occur upon which K turns her head away.

- When S attempts to approach K, she evades him. Either she turns round and walks off stiffly or she backs away from him, always intent on keeping the greatest possible distance between them. In this situation S's display may be intensified in the following manner:
    - Maintaining a rigid posture he advances with a strutting run and if he succeeds in reaching her, rushes past her. At the same moment he strikes out sideways either with an arm or with a shambling movement of the leg. More rarely, as he runs past, he throws an object he happens to be carrying in her direction.
    - In a state of intense excitement S stands up bipedally, beats his chest increasingly rapidly with the palms of his hands and then starts a rush bipedally which ends in the described stiff quadrupedal posture. Sometimes the rising- and chest-beating-display is initiated and accompanied by a sequence of dull roaring UUUU-sounds. The frequency and volume of the vibrating sounds increase and, towards the end, the pitch rises. The vocal climax coincides with that of the chest-beats.

(c) Other members of the group.

G and A (females) : During K's pre-oestrus period, A and G seem but little influenced by the special atmosphere and show approximately their normal behaviour.

M and J (subadult and young adult males) : The two males, on the other hand, who are particularly familiar with K, show some

very interesting traits. They persistently follow K. If K sits
down, they hang around her or sit down near her. They often
try to come into copulatory contact with her from behind. Again
and again they can be observed trying to touch her genitals or
armpits either with the index finger or the hand. If successful
they either smell at the hand or finger, touch it with the tongue
or put their fingers into their mouths. This behaviour indicates
that mainly the genitals and the armpits secrete the smelling
substances characteristic of the oestrus by which chiefly the males
are aroused. More rarely J and M try to touch S's genitals or
armpits. S tolerates M fully but may chase J away. J is permitted to touch S only after a pacifying ceremony. He stands
facing S and stretches out his arm, with the hand hanging down
in front of S's face; S then takes J's wrist into his mouth, bites
it gently and releases it again. Even while acquiescing, S maintains a stiff display posture. J and M have an erect penis and
from time to time proceed to rpm as described above (Section
III). Both occasionally perform a strutting walk in front of K,
J showing a more pronounced form, very similar to that of S.
J utters the same sounds as S but not quite so loud and not so
clearly coordinated with the other acts of the chest-beating sequence.

J often lies prone facing K for 10 to 15 minutes; he rests on his
elbows with the upper part of his body slightly raised, staring at
her steadily. J disobeys the keeper's command to come to the
place where he is normally fed and often even refuses to eat at
all.

Q (female infant): The infant Q is extremely interested in what is going on and often watches absorbedly. She is interested in J and M as well as in A, S and K. When J and M try to touch S or K, Q immediately imitates them. Isolated "copulations" occur out of play context.

P (adult male): The behaviour of the handreared male P is not at all influenced by the pre-oestrus period. The impression that his auto-sexual behaviour during the pre-oestrus period of females is enhanced, needs corroboration with quantitative methods.

(d) Comments on the pre-oestrus of G.

During the pre-oestrus period the handreared G shows no interest in S. The keeper and other familiar persons seem of primary importance to her, J and M come second. Only J's and M's reactions are clearly directed at her.

2. The oestrus period

During the oestrus period (duration on an average of 3 days) the female's sexual motivation increases towards a central phase which lasts $\frac{1}{2}$ to 1 day. During this phase offering scenes with subsequent copulations follow at intervals of 15 to 45 minutes. Before and after this central phase these intervals come to 1 to 2 hours and more peripherally they are even larger. During one observation period (6 hours), including the central phase, in a maximum 16 copulations between S and K have been counted; on the other hand in an observation period of the same duration, but including the peripheral phase, a minimum of two copulations occurred.

A low sexual motivation of the female with a corresponding decline in the number of copulations can also be found in oestrus periods which do not show the normal duration. Such periods can be observed after conception as pregnancy progresses, after the loss or the separation of a newborn infant and after weaning of an infant. For further information on irregular periods see Table IV.

In all cases copulation of S and K was preceded by inviting and offering. The copulatory behaviour will be described in the following four paragraphs: (a) inviting and offering, (b) copulatory behaviour, (c) phases between copulations, (d) difference in behaviour of K and S when not in the group environment. Finally, in a fifth paragraph, (e) the behaviour of the other members of the group will be sketched.

(a) Inviting and offering

In inviting which occurs either before or during offering, K clearly makes a gesture to S with her hand (Fig. 11). Her arm is stretched out, suspended in the air or lying on the floor, and is directed at S, the palm facing upwards. K's eyes always rest upon S. If S alters his position, K changes the direction of her eyes and arm accordingly. In some cases K touches S's forearm with her extended hand or even takes hold of him and pulls him slightly towards her. This gesture of invitation, with variations, has only been observed in Kati. It occurs in all forms of her offering behaviour.

A similar gesture with the extended arm and the open hand, palm facing upwards, I observed as an invitation to play among young and subadult animals. Schaller, 1963, and Fossey (1971) refer to a similar gesture as a means of getting in contact with another individual.

Offering chiefly develops from two main forms of the foregoing scene. I specify them, according to their characteristic form of offering, as "offering in cowering, crouching or prone position", and

Fig. 11. Inviting / female K and male S. K's inviting gesture is aimed exclusively to the dominant male S.

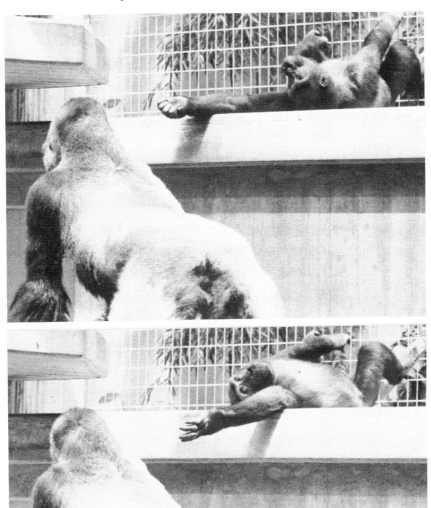

"offering in supine position" respectively. These forms are decisive for the ensuing mode of copulation.

(i) Offering in cowering, crouching or prone position.

This form often develops from a scene characterised by K's walking or running away and S's following or pursuing her (Fig. 12). A second possibility consists of S's standing quietly on all fours, sitting or lying, while K approaches him from the side or the front. Should S follow her, as in the first case, K suddenly stops, crouches and looks back at S over her shoulder or between her upper body and arm. She either waits quietly until S joins her or turns her abdomen more pronouncedly towards him and backs a few steps towards him. With her inviting hand she often reaches back to S. If S is standing during K's approach from the front or the side, she usually halts at a distance of some two metres and extends her hand as described above. If S remains relaxed, she turns her back towards him in the cowering or crouching position and either waits or pushes her way backwards between his arms and underneath his body. If S sits or lies, K follows the same patterns of approaching and offering (Fig. 13).

(ii) Offering in supine position

In the group environment S frequently ignores the initial signs indicating K's readiness for copulation. She thereupon lies down on her back and begins to perform the rpm described above, meanwhile extending her hand invitingly towards S and staring at him. Should S move, K changes her position accordingly. Should he approach, she either just waits or slides along on her back directing her abdomen at him.

Twice during the course of such offering S was observed to stand over K, facing the opposite direction, and to lower his rump until his genital region rested on her face; he then lowered his head, until his face touched K's genital region. A clear oral occupation with S's genital region was observed in this situation in K. During the whole scene head movements were performed by both animals and S jerked his abdomen slightly sideways. Following this prelude S turned round, slid between K's legs, which were held slightly apart, and copulated. K continued her rpm until S started copulation. K's predominant motivation while performing rpm seems to be the urge to copulate. The activity may function as a stimulating signal for the males and probably as a surrogate for copulation. If S fails to join K, she continues these movements for quite a long time and then stops abruptly. Subsequently she reacts in the same way as after copulation. Once the rpm set in and no other animals is disturbing her, they invariably work up to a climax; a change in events depends solely on whether S actually copulates.

K reacts to S's manner of approach, to his posture and his intention movements, even to minute changes in his bearing. If he turns his head away, and appears relaxed K tends towards him and shows inviting and offering. As soon as he looks at her, assuming a stiffer posture, she stops inviting and either tends to walk away or to place her hand on her head. When he starts a strutting run she either walks away in time or holds her forearm over her head to ward off a possible blow. Sometimes, in moments of obvious indecision, she rubs her head with the palm of her hand.

Fig. 12. Offering/ female K and male S. Offering sequence, developing from a scene characterised by K's walking away and S's
following or pursuing her. (Sequence out of a 16mm film
documentation)

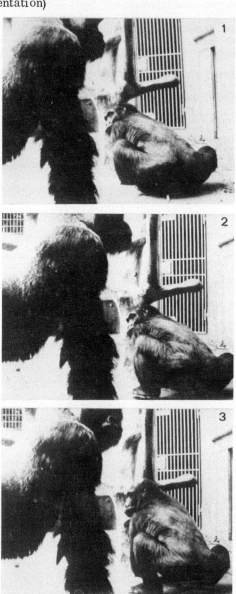

Fig. 12 (continued)

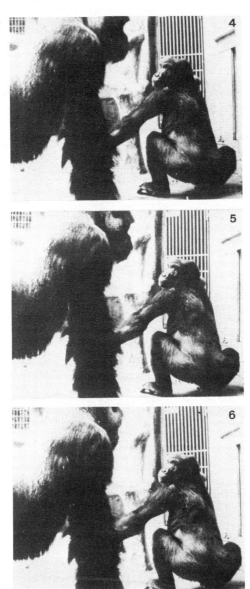

Fig. 12 (continued)

Fig. 12 (continued)

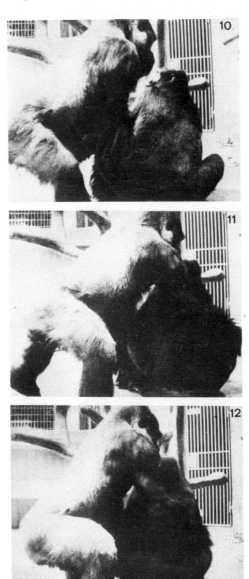

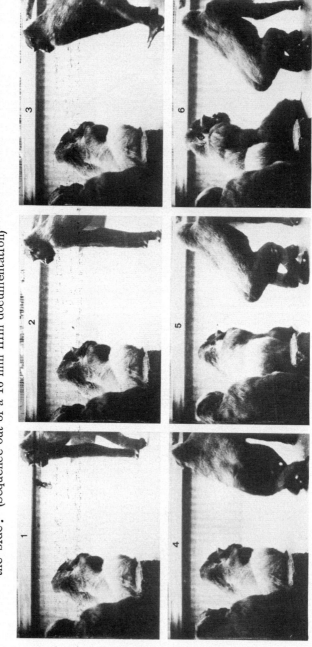

Fig. 13. Offering / female K and male S. K offers herself to the lying S, after approaching him from the side. (Sequence out of a 16 mm film documentation)

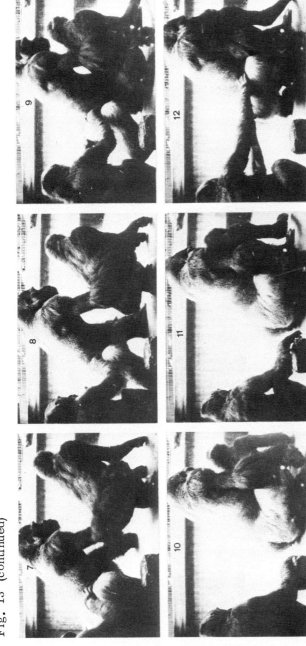

Fig. 13 (continued)

Fig. 14. Genital-oral contact /female K and male S. This form of
contact between the couple has been observed twice as a
prelude to copulation.

Fig. 14 (continued)

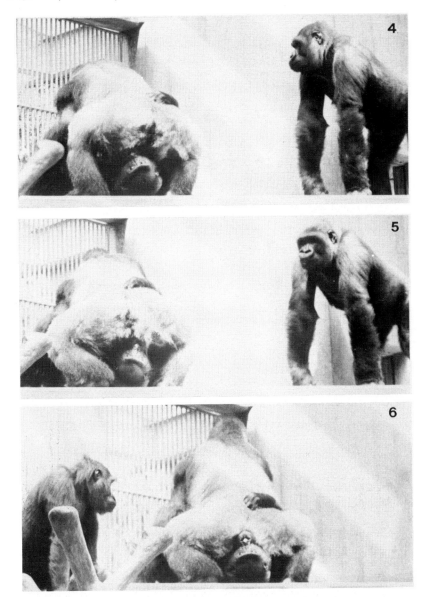

Inviting and offering behaviour varies considerably depending on the individuals involved. Obviously there is a rather pronounced tension in the relation between S and K, whereas familiarity and confidence prevail between the females K and G in interactions with the younger males M and J. In the latter cases inviting and offering behaviour in the above shown form may even lack at all. Confidence itself might depend on

- phase of life of males and females when they joined into one social group,
- age difference between males and females
- social status of both partners and
- personalities of the different individuals.

Different reports from other Zoos show that couples had been brought together with no tension between the partners during oestrus periods of the female (Bristol Zoo, personal communication G. R. Greed and M. Colburn).

(b) The copulatory behaviour

The two main forms of offering result in copulation, either in a dorso-ventral or ventro-ventral position.

(i) The dorso-ventral copulatory position - dv - (Fig. 15).

According to the motivation K either stands still in an offering position or backs, in this position, towards S. In the first case S quietly approaches, repeatedly averting his head and eyes; he then crouches down just behind K with his knees turned outwards, supporting himself on his hands.

In the second case K pushes her rump between S's arms and under his body. S crouches. In both cases S holds K by the hips and pulls her closer towards him. K cooperates by making a hollow back, thus clearly exposing her genital region.

In the course of copulation in the dv position the following variations can be observed between S and K:

- S either remains holding the hip region of K or places his arms on the floor in front of K's legs. The female's legs are bent and held slightly sideways.

- S puts his arms at his sides or slightly behind him, thus adopting a position with the genital region exposed ahead (this was even more frequently observed in J - Fig. 16).

- K either remains in the above position, or following intromission, lowers herself until lying prone; the upper part of her body is still slightly raised and she rests on her elbows (Fig. 17).

- Sometimes K lies flat on her belly with her arms sideways practically outstretched.

(ii) The ventro-ventral copulatory position - vv - (Fig. 18).

Also when offering in a supine position, K can either help to accomplish the copulatory position or leave it, more or less, to S. The possible differences are the following:

- When S approaches, K, sliding on her back, turns to direct her abdomen at him. Her legs are slightly bent and held apart. S, crouching, with his knees turned outwards, advances in between her legs and towards her abdomen. K lifts her legs a little and puts them between S's thighs and hips. S leans on his arms which are placed on the floor on either side of K.

- If K does not react when S approaches, he advances in between

Fig. 15. The dorso-ventral copulatory position. Male S and female K. (Photograph by W. Angst)

Fig. 16. Dorso–ventral copulatory position of the young adult male J with female G.

Fig. 17. Dorso-ventral copulatory position. Male S and female K. Variation with the female lying on her belly.

Fig. 18. The ventro-ventral copulatory position. Male S and female K. (Photograph by W. Angst)

her legs, crouches, takes hold of her thighs and, sometimes
also her hips and puts her into the above position. He subsequently supports himself with his arms on the floor on either
side of K's hips, as before.

- In this position S can either lean forward or backwards, or take
a vertical position, depending on whether his arms are in front
of him, behind him or at his sides. K retains her position,
modified only by the copulatory activities yet to be described.

In the dv as well as in the vv positions S makes adjusting movements sideways and forwards which most probably lead to intromission.

On the whole, copulations with J and M follow similar patterns
except that K hardly assists in any way when the partner advances in a
copulatory position. In the dv position males may also stand behind
the female during copulation or even lean in a standing position ventrally on the female's back. These forms are often seen in copulatory attempts and in copulations of subadult and young adult males (Fig. 19).
Table V gives information on copulatory positions observed in animals
of the group in Basle. Table VI compiles data on copulatory positions
and copulatory behaviour given in literature, mostly in Schaller's book.

(iii) The course of copulation

The duration of copulation (S) comes on average to 52, 5 seconds.
Copulation comprises, as a rule, 3 to 6 sequences of 30 to 60 copulatory thrusts with an average frequency of 24, 2 per 10". The frequency
varies from sequence to sequence and often a slight increase in frequency in a particular sequence can be observed. Intervals between
sequences are characterised by adjusting movements similar to those
preceding the first copulatory sequence. Further information can be

Fig. 19. Standing copulatory position. Young adult male J and female K. This position is often seen in copulatory attempts and in copulations of younger males. (Photograph by W. Angst)

Table V: Copulatory positions

couple ♀ ♂		modus	further notes
A	S	dv and vv	inadequate personal observations (see additional notes Lang)
K	S	dv and vv	couple separated : normally dv, rarely vv. couple in the group : normally dv and vv
K	J	dv and vv	normally dv, vv very seldom. K does not offer herself to J in a variety of forms; J often takes the initiative by sitting behind her.
K	M	dv and vv	normally dv, M initially sits behind her or mounts her in a standing position; not all copulations seem to be accomplished; vv has only been observed in play context and K was the initiator in regard to the position.
G	J	dv	G normally offers herself by lying on her belly, therefore only dv positions occur.
G	M	dv	idem G/J

found in Table VII.

Table VII.   Duration of copulation and frequency of copulatory thrusts.

Duration of copulations (S + K)	
11 copulations were measured	
maximum in seconds	110
minimum in seconds	20
average	52.5
Frequency of copulation thrusts (S)	
23 measurements during 11 copulations	
maximum number of thrusts in 10"	30
minimum number of thrusts in 10"	14
average	24.2

During copulation characteristic facial and vocal expressions can be registered in both partners. K's lips are slightly pressed together with the edges drawn in forming a bulge. They remain, however, a trace apart. Her cheeks seem slightly puffed up and her eyes are closed at times. During copulation she utters a long sequence of vibrating sounds, very similar to the male's strutting vocalisation except for being much quieter, hoarser and rather more voiceless.

Two to three times during copulation S screws up his eyes for a short while. His lips are pursed. The corners are pulled backwards and slightly downwards. S utters copulatory sounds only in the final phase and, even then, not always. They are very similar to the strutting vocalisation.

In so far as K's eyes are open they are always directed to

Table VI.   Data on copulatory behaviour given in literature.

Institutions	Positions adopted and behaviour displays		Duration	Further remarks
	female	male		
Bronx Zoo, New York (Quinn, 1959, cited by Schaller)	quadrupedally	covers her from behind, thrusts several times and they part	10–15"	Apparently first copulatory attempts of the male. After copulation the male lay on his back and the female fondled his testes and licked them.
National Zool. Park Washington (Reed and Gallagher, cited by Schaller)	straddled male, crouched down, copulated, most of the thrusts done were supplied by the female	lying supine		first coitus observed
" subsequently observed during the first period	standing position and abdominal juxtaposition, male dorsal			
" in later cases normally observed	crouching down, knees drawn up under her abdomen, arms folded under her chest, chest lowered.	squatting position behind, hand either on her hips, or on the floor, or just hanging at his sides		
" notes of Emlen, 1960, cited by Schaller	backs up to the male crouching down, after 30–40": fast high hooting	pushes her head down with his wrist, throws his leg over her rump, starts thrusting harder and more rhythmically and gets directly behind her, after 30–40": soft rhythmical hooting	1–1½′	

Location	Position	Duration	Remarks
Columbus Zoo, Ohio (Schaller 1963, Thomas, and Ambrose, cited by Schaller)	dorso-ventral On all fours. Squatting. Standing bipedally. / Standing upright. Squatting behind female. Standing bipedally. latero-ventral Lying on the side, arms and legs tucked in front of her. / Kneeling behind her. ventro-ventral Lying on her back, legs spread. / Squatting between her legs. Lying on her back, clasping male's back. / Standing on all fours over her. Entirely lifted from the ground and supported by his arms, her legs clasping him. / Male standing upright.	90 " total time spent in mounting position.	Strutting walk, wrestling and running preceded copulation. During three consecutive days, 8 mounts have been observed, with a total of 109 thrusts, varying from 1 to 40. Copulation was initiated by the male or the female.
I.R.S.A.C. Station, Congo (Van den Berghe, cited by Schaller)	dorso-ventral		
Zoological Gardens, Basle (Lang, 1959).	dorso-ventral and ventro-ventral		The female usually plays the active part, by embracing the male or drawing him to her.
(Hess, this paper)	dorso-ventral and ventro-ventral (For detailed information see Section IV, 2, b, and figures 15, 16, 17, 18, 19.)	average 52.5 "	
Free living mountain gorillas (observations by Schaller, 1963)	dorso-ventral Sitting or resting on her knees, belly and elbows. / Sitting behind, holding on to the hips. Lying prone, moving in this position downhill. / Covers the back of the female.		Schaller gives a detailed description of all activities displayed by both partners, during the two copulations he witnessed.

meet S's. In the dv-position she often turns her head round towards
him whereas, in the sitting position, she bends it as far back as possible. S often turns his head away and does not return K's gaze.

K also seems to caress S with her hands. She places them on
his knees or hips and gently scratches him. This form of contact is very
noticeable in the vv-position. She often stretches up both her arms and
with her palms resting on either side of S's head, or more seldom on
his shoulders, continuously scratches him gently.

The final copulatory phase is indicated by a rising intensity,
in S as well as in K. S increases the frequency of copulatory thrusts and
the characteristic facial expressions and vocalisations are intensified;
he sometimes utters the sounds described above or screws up his eyes.
Finally the copulation ends with several spasmodic movements in the
hip and thigh region and S's look becomes glazed. At this moment K
immediately breaks off the copulatory contact. S remains, on an average, for another ten seconds in this final state before relaxing.

K's facial expressions also become more intense in the final
phase and her copulatory vocalisation increases rhythmically; moreover the individual sounds become somewhat more voiced.

(c) The phases between two copulations.

After the couple has separated both animals remain clearly
inactive for a while. They sit or lie at a distance from each other, displaying mutual interest only by their head movements. They glance at
each other from time to time.

During this period K is frequently occupied with her genitals.
She inserts her finger into her vagina, then smells at and licks it,

often repeating the process many times. No extrusion of the ejaculation fluid from the vagina has been seen after the partners have separated.

On occasions K is observed to raise herself out of a sitting to a crouching position and drop her rump with a jerk. After this the finger is invariably inserted again into the vagina and smelled and/or licked. A possible interpretation of this behaviour may lie in the fact that by this jerking movement downwards the ejaculation fluid in the vagina is brought to a region which can be reached with the finger.

The vaginal inspections seem to be of particular interest to J, M and Q, as the three often come either alone or together and try to touch K's genital region or at least her finger.

S touches his genitals less frequently than K but the younger animals repeatedly try to do so immediately after copulation (Fig. 20).

After the first phase of complete inactivity S and K's mutual interest increases. In either animal this is indicated by the stiff display posture, more intense head turning towards and away from each other and fairly composed walking and climbing after each other. During this time K also starts to stare again in S's face. Occasionally very short "chasing" scenes occur. At first K avoids letting S get too close to her. Then the outward signs become gradually more intense and result in the inviting and offering scenes described above which are preliminary to the next copulation.

(d) Contact between S and K outside the group environment.

K and S were sometimes separated from the other animals for a few hours or half a day during K's oestrus period. Under these conditions copulations, although they were not disturbed by other animals, did not last longer than those taking place in the presence of the whole group, disregarding the rare cases in which copulation had to be interrupted or broken off owing to extreme pressure.

The behaviour of S and K differed from that in the group environment as follows:

- When alone with K, S seemed less affected, in the phases between copulations, by scenes irrelevant to his direct sexual interest in K. He accepted K's invitations more quickly and with less preamble. Under these conditions the rhythmic pelvic movements in K could not, or only very rarely, be observed.

- The main difference emerged in the phases between copulations. After the period of inactivity described above, S and K pursue each other for 5 to 10 minutes at a stretch, resuming the "chase" after a short rest. The sequence is brought to an abrupt end by K's offering herself with subsequent copulation. The actual "chasing" is occasionally interrupted by brief "roughing" lasting 5 to 10 seconds.

(i) The "chase" (Fig. 21)

One of the partners advances, striding or running, upon the other. The pursued remains facing his pursuer and retreats, at a walking or running pace. As a rule S finds himself in the defensive role, but nevertheless shows a strutting attitude. The distance between the two animals is rarely greater than $1\frac{1}{2}$ to $2\frac{1}{2}$ metres. K shows, when following S, an expression which changes between complaint and reactive aggression.

From time to time S responds to K's pursuit with intense strutting scenes and utters the characteristic sounds described above.

K is temporarily deterred but continues to pursue him as soon as he ceases strutting. If the distance between the animals is reduced to less than $1\frac{1}{2}$ metres, they stand up bipedally facing each other, raise their arms in inhibited aggression over their heads directed towards their partner and try to seize each other by the arms, shoulders or head. While in the upright position facing each other, their mouths are open, baring the upper and lower teeth, rarely the upper lip covers the upper teeth, revealing only the points of the canines. Renewed "chasing" or "roughing" scenes follow.

(ii) The roughing scenes.

S usually tries to force K to the ground beneath him and bites her in the upper part of her arm, shoulder region or back, while K shrieks incessantly. More seldom S lifts K up a little then lets her fall onto the floor; before turning away from her, he may drag her after him a step. K retaliates by pulling S's hair or biting, but her main aim is to free herself from S and run away. On three occasions during "roughing" bouts I observed that K lay down on her side, drew her legs close to her body, covered her head with her arms, tucking it between her shoulders with her face close to her breast, and stayed in this position. In each case S immediately left her alone. (For this submissive posture further examples in other contexts are given by Schaller, 1963). Roughing seems to involve considerable violence of which the tufts of hair left lying around bear evidence.

Similar roughing scenes with preliminary bipedal standing were observed during serious rank contests between S and P. They also occur in play behaviour among younger animals accompanied

Fig. 20. Chasing is often seen in the phases between two copulations but only when the couple has been separated from the group. (Sequence out of a 16 mm film documentation)

Fig. 21.   Genital touching / young adult male J and dominant male S.   J often touches G's genitals
immediately before or after a copulation of S.

by the typical play-face.

In chasing and roughing scenes the motivation seems to be aggressive, of which the aggressive coughing sounds and facial expressions bear evidence. Despite this specific character of the scene, K never quite evades S in order to prevent his reaching her as she does during the pre-oestrus period. S and G behaved similarly under the same circumstances, but without subsequent copulation as G never offered herself to S. A similar situation between S and A has been observed and noted by W. Angst at Basle Zoo. (In literature reports with equal descriptions of aggressive interactions in isolated kept pairs during oestrus of the female are given by Schaller, by C. J. Hardin et al., and W. D. Thomas). (Fig. 20).

(e) The behaviour of non-participants during copulation and the phase between

The following section is based on observations on K's actual oestrus period. It will be confined to the behaviour and scenes which have not yet been described in section III or IV in connection with the interoestrus and pre-oestrus.

The interest taken by non-participants in the copulation is evident. Their particular activities differ according to age and sex. The individual animals will be mentioned separately:

A (female) : A's participation is purely hostile. As a rule she tries to intervene, coughing aggressively (Fig. 22), as soon as S copulates with K. She usually either advances on them with a strutting run and endeavours to tear K away or, if the pair is copulating on a platform, she tries to grap K's arms, jumping from below, and

Fig. 22.　Aggressive interference / male S copulates with female K and female A intervenes aggressively coughing and grabbing at K.

pull her down. But often she simply waits until another animal in the strutting posture disturbs the couple whereupon she runs shrieking and coughing towards them abetting the aggression. If J or M are sitting near S and K, they try in a similar aggressive manner, to drive their mother away. A's role is not clear. It is obvious that the cause of her aggression, which is usually directed at K, and more seldom, at S, lies in S's intimacy with K. A might be regarded as S's most intimate partner, ranking at times second to S in the social hierarchy. During immaturity she clearly dominated S until he was practically sexually mature and became her physical superior. These circumstances partly explain her behaviour. Curiously enough in the central phase of the oestrus she neglects the supervision of her infant Q. This may further indicate her preoccupation with the copulating pair. When copulation is not taking place, she shows interest in the group as a whole, but is not active in any particular way.

Q (infant female) : The three and a quarter year old Q makes use of her freedom to gain contact with the copulating pair. She runs up to them, stands beside them, watches them and touches S or K timidly on the head, shoulders or arms. Again and again she bends down to see or touch the genital regions. Her attention is obviously drawn to these regions. Q is also to be observed standing upright with her arms hanging down, staring absorbedly at S's face. Moreover Q is the only individual during this phase to indulge in play, mostly with an object or by herself, rarely with a partner. If play with a partner occurs, it usually ends, amid brief chasing and roughing, in a playful copulation scene. Q responds to K's inviting gesture directed at S as though it

were an invitation to play. In the phases between copulations Q
is clearly more interested in S than in K.

J and M (young adult and subadult males) : The two males are the most
active members of the group, apart from S and K. They are considered together as their behaviour is distinctly related. J frequently attempts to copulate with K, mainly in the phases between
copulations of S and K, when K is beginning to concentrate on S.
But there the matter usually rests because K, who is virtually
only interested in S, breaks off the contact as soon as S comes
near her. This is a frequent situation; it seems as though S's
sexual motivation is increased by J's activity. On S's approach
K walks away, leaving J sitting or standing. If S is tolerant, K
returns and offers herself. J withdraws but, if S and K copulate,
comes back immediately and sits down nearby. Moreover, I have
observed K inviting S with a gesture of her hand, while copulating
with J. M is also eager to copulate with K but is rarely a main
actor as he always gives J the priority; his attempts to mount
K comprise either standing or sitting behind her. M performs
rpm more frequently than J, most likely to compensate for K's
refusing him on J's account. Copulations between S and K are
closely followed by both J and M. At first they beset the couple,
trying to touch them on the head, shoulders, arms and face or to
slip their hands between the two and touch the genital regions.
Exceptionally they succeed whereupon they immediately smell
at their hands. Towards the middle and the end of a copulation
phase the touching becomes more obtrusive and often causes
great disturbance. Frequently they try to tear K and S apart;
they pass the pair with a strutting run and hit them or hurl them-

selves at K at full speed. S and K are remarkably tolerant. At
the most S tries either to push J and M away, to break the force
of their onslaughts with his outstretched arm or to parry a blow
with his forearm. His attitude is all the more remarkable as J
distinctly opposes his father at this time. Aggressive coughing
by S or K is very rare. It would appear as though this supreme
tolerance is, at least, partly a reaction to the oestrus of the female. In the phases between copulations J is only interested in
touching S's genitals directly, particularly immediately before
or afterwards; the same applies to his interest in K. When S
copulates with K, M often sits behind his father in a copulatory
position, embracing S from behind, and imitates his father's
movements. Beside touching S and K's genitals after copulation,
M often tries to sit behind his father when the latter is lying down
and to perform copulatory thrusts.

G (female) : G reacts very similarly to A but only when the aggressive
scenes create a generally hostile atmosphere. During a considerable time while these observations were being made, she was
pregnant which presumably explains her much quieter behaviour.
She was interested in what was going on around her but avoided
any direct contact.

P (adult male) : The comments given on P in connection with the pre-
oestrus period can also be applied to his behaviour in the
oestrus period.

V   SUMMARY

The Zoological Gardens in Basle own at present a group of nine lowland gorillas, <u>Gorilla g. gorilla,</u> living at times all together in one social unit. All observations presented here originate from that group.

In the study the term "sexual behaviour" includes

- the behaviour of one or more animals which involves direct contact with its or their genitals or genital region or those of a partner.
- behavioural sequences shown during inter-oestrus periods that correspond largely to sequences of copulatory behaviour.
- behaviour which is clearly connected with the oestrus in females.

1.   From the first day of life the mother is occupied with the genital region of the infant in the context of general body inspections. She soon develops several types of touching and manipulation which are often carried out directly and on their own. Such treatment often stimulates urination and/or defecation in the infant and these reactions seem to act as a positive feedback on the mother. Later the touching of the child's genitals is sometimes aimed at stimulating infantile sexual reactions, mainly erection; sometimes it serves as a punishment or rejection, or as a training method. During the first years of the infant's life the mother carries out "pseudo-copulations" in which she adopts the male role.

2.   During oestrus periods of females sexually motivated behaviour

is emphasised in almost all members of the gorilla group. But
also outside these periods more or less sexually motivated behaviour, either with or without a partner, occurs occasionally
in all the animals. Such behaviour without a partner is more
frequently observed in handreared animals and the one with a
partner is more often in individuals brought up by their mother.
Manipulation of the animal's own genital region may occur as
comfort behaviour, exploration, or "masturbation"; stimulation of the genital region is also observed as "surrogate copulation" with objects, and as rubbing of the genitals against objects, and as rubbing of the genitals against objects (tyres,
iron bars, e.g.). Touching of a partner's genitals is always
combined with chemoreceptory testing, thus showing an aspect
of exploration. Pseudo-copulations can occur in the context
of play; sometimes out of playing sexual motivation can develop.
Generally such activity with a partner is rarely observed in
fully adult males and females, whereas young adult, subadult
and juvenile individuals indulge more often in activities of this
type.

3. When a female comes into pre-oestrus, its smell appears al-
   tered, its behaviour changed, and also the other members of
   the group reflect the change in the social situation and contribute
   to it. The males and juvenile individuals generally are interested in the female while a special relationship develops between the latter and the dominant male. In both reciprocal
   imposing display is conspicuous.

4. During the oestrus period the female is, at intervals, ready to
   mate. This is expressed by the gesture of "inviting" and

"offering" which are addressed to the dominant male.
Between these two partners tensions of varying degree are
observed in the intervals between copulations, evidenced by
the special type of looking at each other, a stiff posture,
strutting and maintenance of distance between them.
Inferior males are tolerated by the female when hanging
around or following her, their attempts to copulate are
sometimes tolerated, sometimes eluded, but throughout, her
interest as well as her gestures of inviting and offering are
aimed at the dominant male.

5. During the whole oestrus period, all animals of the group
appear specially stimulated. Their interest is focused on the
female in oestrus, the dominant male, and above all theipair
in copulation. In addition sexual behaviour as mentioned in
3. occurs frequently, especially scenes of sex-play between
subadult and juvenile partners.

6. Copulation takes place when the male reacts positively upon
inviting and offering by the female. If the female is offering
in a quadrupedal more or less crouched position, copulation
is effected in dorso-ventral fashion; offering in supine position leads to ventro-ventral copulation. Occasionally reciprocal oro-genital contact can precede ventro-ventral copulation.
During copulation - especially in vv-fashion - forms of tender
touching of the male by the female are conspicuous.
Copulation comprises 3 to 6 sequences of up to 30 to 60
thrusts. A climax is reached in the last sequence, characterised by more intense facial and vocal expressions and

higher frequency of the male's copulatory thrusts.

7. Aggressive display of the dominant male against the female in oestrus can stimulate all members of the group to become involved in aggressive activities. Such aggressive scenes normally only last for a few seconds. Copulation between the dominant male and the female provokes different kinds of participation, interference and investigation depending on age, sex, and social relation between the actor and the copulating partners. During copulation the couple is extremely tolerant of all sorts of interference.

8. If the male addressed to does not positively respond to the female's inviting and offering, she will, in supine position, perform rhythmic pelvic movements while still inviting. This seems to function as a surrogate for copulation and a stimulus for the male as well.

9. If the couple is kept isolated from the other members of the group, in the phase between copulations, scenes revealing initiative and reactive aggression occur, with "chasing", roughing and on the part of the female, screaming. It seems that such scenes cannot develop in the social environment, interference by other members of the group then being imminent.

VI ACKNOWLEDGEMENTS

My heartfelt and deep gratitude goes to my wife, whose attitude to my work has at all times been selfless and devoted. I thank Professor Dr. Rudolf Schenkel and Professor Dr. E. M. Lang for their advice, guidance and active support without which these studies would not have been possible. Included in my thanks are also his collaborators, Dr. Hans Wackernagel, Dr. Peter Studer, Dr. D. W. Fölsch and Paul Steinemann. I am grateful to my friend, Dr. Walter Angst for his constant advice and help. Professor Dr. Rudolf Geigy and Fred Hufschmid of the Swiss Scientific Film Association gave much help and generously supported the cost of filming. I have received much practical help from the keepers in the ape house, Walter Bayer, Markus Ruf and Helmuth Müller. My thanks also go to Susan Shaw and to Cathleen Tobler for helping to translate and revise the manuscript. I would also like to thank G. R. Greed and M. Colburn of the Bristol Zoo for information and permission to make observations there.

VII REFERENCES

Angst, W. (1966). Begegnung Achilla-Stefi, observation protocol, Zoological Gardens Basle, unpublished.

Colbourne, M. (1971). Information on the gorillas at Bristol Zoo, pers. communication.

Fisher, L. E. (1970). Kumba, Lincoln Park Zoo, privately printed, A 18806.

Fossey, D. (1971). More years with mountain gorillas, National Geographic, Vol. 140, No. 4.

Greed, G. R. (1971). Information on the gorillas at Bristol Zoo, pers. communication.

Hardin, C. J., Danford, D., Skeldon, P. C. (1969). Notes on the successful breeding by incompatible gorillas at Toledo Zoo, Int. Zoo Yearbook, Vol. 9; 84-88.

Lang, E. M. (1959). The birth of a gorilla at Basle Zoo. Int. Zoo Yearbook, Vol. 1; 3-7.

Lang, E. M. (1961). Goma, das Gorillakind, Albert Müller Verlag, Rüschlikon.

Lang, E. M., Schenkel, R. and Siegrist, E. (1965). Gorilla Mutter und Kind, Basilius Presse AG, Basel.

Rumbaugh, D. M. (1965). The birth of a lowland gorilla at San Diego Zoo. Zoonooz, Gorilla issue, September 1965.

Schaller, G. B. (1963). The Mountain Gorilla, Ecology and Behavior, University of Chicago Press, Chicago and London.

Schenkel, R. (1964). Zur Ontogenese des Verhaltens bei Gorilla und Mensch. Z. Morph. Anthrop., 54; 3, 233-259, Stuttgart.

Thomas, W. D. (1958). Observations on the Breeding in Captivity of a Pair of Lowland Gorillas. Zoologica, Vol. 43, Part 3.

Tijskens, J. (1971). The oestrus cycle and gestation period of the Mountain gorilla. Int. Zoo Yearbook, Vol. 11.

Film Reference

Hess, J. P. On sexual behaviour of captive lowland gorillas, Gorilla g. gorilla. 16 mm black and white film, light sound, duration 30 min., available through Swiss Scientific Film Association, Kapellenstrasse 33, 4000 Basel, Switzerland.

PRIMATES AND HUMAN ETHOLOGY: INTRODUCTION

Detlev Ploog

Max-Planck-Institute for Psychiatry, Munich, F.R. Germany

Whatever I can say in introducing briefly such a complex and far-reaching subject as "Primates and Human Ethology" has been said before, and probably much of it in the Meeting Rooms of the Zoological Society of London. Whether I took the position of those who have stressed the similarities between man and the rest of the primates or the position of those who have put the emphasis on the differences, I would be on the wrong side of the fence. It is not only the gap between man and ape that always was and still is under discussion, it is also the dispute about nature and nurture, about natural and cultural evolution which, in my opinion, raises questions that cannot be resolved completely on a scientific basis (Morris, 1967). Although it became rather evident during the past decade that questions related to this issue cannot be asked in a dichotomic manner, it still seems to be difficult to avoid this sort of conceptual thinking. For the sake of briefness, I will call this thinking the layer cake concept. It has a neurological and a behavioural aspect. It conveys the idea that the phylogenetically old heritage - be it brain structures or behaviours - is on the bottom of the cake and the most recent products of evolution - human language, arithmetic and reasoning - are on the top. Consequently, reflexes, fixed action patterns, drive states, conditioned responses, learned behaviour, etc. and their neuronal correlates are on top of each other. And on top of this the cultural development of man takes place. However, a more detailed analysis of the brain structures as well as of the inferred functions of these structures shows that new developments in evolution are not brought about by adding new elements to old ones but by structural changes of the whole, with the new elements intimately embedded. Hence the evolution of the brain and of behaviour cannot be understood as an additive process of increasing faculties. This may sound rather trivial, but the consequences of this are four-fold:

1.   New faculties in man have their special biology which is characteristic of homo sapiens; for instance, the biology of language and speech with its special brain mechanisms and the appropriate vocal apparatus.

2.   The new faculties are functioning in a structural framework of older functions whose biology has been adapted to the new situation.

3.   Wherever we encounter behaviours in man which share common features with the behaviour of other primates we have to take into account that the observed behaviour is part of the total structure of human behaviour.

4.   The result of this is that there is no pure "animal" behaviour in man which can be dissected from human behaviour, and, vice versa, there is no pure "human" behaviour which can be separated from animal behaviour or for that matter, even from subhuman primate behaviour.

In this context I should like to quote a statement from Professor Thorpe's book of Science, Man and Morals: "..... that man is a social animal gives a glimpse of the obvious; but it is a truism that cannot be too often repeated and no inquiry into human nature can be any use at all unless it is founded on the study of social behaviour. So we need to consider all the evidence we can get as to the origin of man as a social animal; we need to probe into the dark and misty areas where zoology, anthropology and pre-history meet" (p. 66). This volume is, indeed, devoted entirely to central aspects of human social behaviour, namely to sexual behaviour, motivation, social interactions and nonverbal communication. It takes a primate - man, ape or monkey - many years to attain not only physical maturity but also the social maturity typical of adult social behaviour. The struggle to obtain food and to meet certain other needs seems, under normal conditions at least, less frequent and less intense than the struggle for partner relations and social status. Social interactions seem to be a basic need of all primates, including man. Nonhuman primates handle their affairs by means of visual, vocal and other nonverbal communication. In man, a similar communication system, with representation in limbic and other subcortical structures, still plays a role and is seen clearly in all facial, vocal, postural, and other motor expressions of emotions, in songs without words, and in the cooing and babbling of small infants. In fact, this system is involved in every human conversation and in every direct partner interaction, but it is dominated by spoken language, the most effective and unique communication system that Nature has produced.

Because of the importance of speech, interest in human communication was, for many years, focused on language problems. During the last decade, probably under the influence of ethological concepts, nonverbal human communication has become a new research area. For example, smiling as a visual social signal, and crying as an auditory one have been investigated (Koehler, 1954; Ambrose, 1961; Wolff, 1963, 1969; Ploog, 1964; and others). The role of gaze direction, of body movements and of postures in human partner interaction has been studied under a great variety of experimental conditions (Argyle, 1967; Ekman et al., 1969; Cranach, 1971; and others). Nonverbal communication has also become of interest to psychiatry since this part of behav-

iour undergoes dramatic changes in the so-called endogenous psychoses.
It appears to me that ethological concepts can contribute a great deal to
the explanation of these profound changes in behaviour. In child psychiatry the breakdown of nonverbal communication is most obvious in the
syndrome of infantile autism (Ploog, 1964, 1969, 1971). Corinne Hutt
and Ounsted have pointed out the biological significance of the gaze,
with particular reference to this syndrome. It seems to me that this
is a most challenging clinical paradigm for abnormal human ethology.

Comparative studies in different cultures on facial expressions,
gestures and postures have indicated the innate nature of nonverbal
communication (Ekman et al., 1969; Eibl-Eibesfeldt, 1968, 1970). As
the linguists speak of the universals of language in the Chomsky sense,
one may also speak of the universals in nonverbal communication which
would be those basic traits of communication which all humans share
(Ploog and Melnechuk, 1969, 1971). Eibl-Eibesfeldt did a transcultural
study on what he calls the "Augengruß" (greeting with the eyes) which
is a synergism of a quick smile, gaze direction towards the partner
and a rapid lifting of the eyebrows which lasts for only about a sixth of
a second. This signal, which invites a flirt and can be considered as
a low intensity courtship signal, has been filmed in Samoa, Kenya,
Japan, France and elsewhere. It has been studied together with other
signals from the eye region and various complex signals used in greeting situations, praying, begging, mother-child interactions, etc. (l.c).

In animal experiments, particularly those involving monkeys
and apes, it is always difficult to find out what response is equivalent to
a stimulus and what detail of a known signal is really perceived (Kluver,
1933, 1936, 1937, 1965; Ploog, 1971). In a social setting, it often becomes impossible to discover which signal properties produce a certain

behavioural response. In man, the situation is different. He can report what he perceives. Since the human gaze is considered an important social signal, we wanted to know more about how the recipient perceives it. Von Cranach and his coworkers from our institute approached this problem by conducting a series of experiments of the following type:

The sender of the gaze looked in random order at target points on lines that crossed the receiver's eye region horizontally and vertically; some of these points were within and some were outside the receiver's face area. The receiver of the gaze announced his opinion as to whether the sender was looking at his face, and an impartial observer was asked to do the same. In these experiments, gaze direction, gaze movement, head position, and head movement were investigated as cues for the perception of gaze direction. The receiver responded differently to the different stimulus configurations. Unnoticed by the receiver, head position, gaze movement and head movement influenced his perception of gaze direction. In general, the recipient's judgment proved wrong a significant number of times: the sender's gaze actually was directed to target points outside the face. The errors increased significantly with increasing distance between the partners, the best distance being 80 cm. This is an interesting result because it tells us that a normal person tends to feel his face is being looked at more often than is actually the case. So it seems that each person has a slight predisposition to a paranoid response. Whether this tendency has a built-in component is an open question. For an explanation of the genesis of the receiver's reaction, we must consider that, in early childhood, eyes and ocula (the area around the eyes) have the function of releasers. In further development this results in very marked attention to the ocular component of orientation towards a partner.

The disproportionately high subjective certainty in the judgment of
gaze direction might originate from the innate basis of this reaction.
On the other hand, early learning may also play an important role,
since eye contact between mother and child serves an important function in the early interaction patterns. Therefore, the gazing of the
baby at the mother is probably positively reinforced by the mother
(Cranach, 1971; Ploog, 1970).

REFERENCES

Ambrose, A. (1961). The development of the smiling response in
early infancy. In: Determinants of Infant Behaviour (B. M.
Foss, ed.). John Wiley & Sons, New York, vol. 1, 179-201.

Argyle, M. (1967). The Psychology of Interpersonal Behaviour.
Penguin Books Ltd., Harmondsworth, Middlesex.

Cranach, M. v. (1971). The role of orienting behavior in human interaction. In: Behaviour and Environment (A. H. Esser, ed.).
217-237. Plenum Press, New York.

Eibl-Eibesfeldt, I. (1968). Zur Ethologie des menschlichen Gruβver-
haltens. I. Beobachtungen an Balinesen, Papuas und Samoanern
nebst vergleichenden Bemerkungen. Zeitschr. Tierpsychologie
25, 727, 744.

Eibl-Eibesfeldt, I. (1971). Zur Ethologie menschlichen Gruβverhal-
tens. II. Das Gruβverhalten und einige andere Muster freund-
licher Kontaktaufnahme der Waika (Yanoama). Zeitschr. Tierpsychologie 29, 196-213.

Eibl-Eibesfeldt, I. (1970). Ethology: Biology of Behavior. Holt,
Rinehart and Winston, Inc., (German edition: Piper Verlag,
Munich 1967).

Ekman, P., E. R. Sorenson and W. V. Friesen (1969). Pan-cultural
elements in facial displays of emotion. Science 164, 86-88.

Hutt, C. and C. Ounstedt (1966). The biological significance of the
gaze with particular reference to the syndrome of infantile autism. Behavior. Science 11, 346-356.

Kluver, H. (1933). Behavior Mechanisms in Monkeys. University of
Chicago Press, Chicago. (Reissued 1957, Phoenix Science
Series, New York.)

Kluver, H. (1936). The study of personality and the method of equivalent and non-equivalent stimuli. Character and Personality 5,
91-112.

Kluver, H. (1937). Re-examination of implement-using behavior in a
cebus monkey after an interval of three years. Acta Psychol. 2,
347-397.

Kluver, H. (1965). Neurobiology of normal and abnormal perception.
In: Psychopathology of Perception (P. M. Hoch and J. Zubin
eds.). Grune and Stratton, New York. pp 1-40.

Koehler, O. (1954). Das Lächeln als angeborene Ausdrucksbewegung.
Zeitschr. für menschliche Vererbungs-und Konstitutionslehre
32, 390-398.

Morris, D. (Editor) (1967). Primate Ethology. Weidenfeld and
Nicolson, London.

Ploog, D. (1964). Verhaltensforschung und Psychiatrie. In: Psychiatrie der Gegenwart (H.W. Gruhle et al., eds.) 1; 291-443.
Springer Verlag, Berlin, Heidelberg, New York.

Ploog, D. (1969). Verhaltensbiologische Hypothesen zur Entstehung
endogener Psychosen. In: G. Huber (Hrsgb.), Schizophrenie
und Zyklothymie. Ergebnisse und Probleme. Thieme

Verlag, Stuttgart. 19-28.

Ploog, D. (1971) Neurological aspects of social behavior. In: J. Eisenberg and W.S. Dillon (eds.), Man and Beast. Comparative Social Behavior. Smithsonian Institution Press, Washington, D.C. and In: Social Science Information 9 (3), 71-97 (1970).

Ploog, D. (1970). Social communication among animals. In: The Neurosciences (F.O. Schmitt, ed.), 349-361. The Rockefeller University Press, New York.

Ploog, D. (1971). The relevance of natural stimulus patterns for sensory information processes. Brain Research 31, 353-359.

Ploog, D. (1972). Kommunikation in Affengesellschaften und deren Bedeutung fur die Verstandigungsweisen des Menschen. In: Neue Anthropologie (H. G. Gadamer and P. Vogler, eds.) Thieme Verlag, Stuttgart, 2, 98-178, and In: dtv (Deutscher Taschenbuch Verlag, Munich), 98-178, 1972.

Ploog, D. and T. Melnechuk (1969). Primate Communication. Neurosciences Research Program Bulletin 7, 419-510.

Ploog, D. and T. Melnechuk (1971). Are apes capable of language? Neurosciences Research Program Bulletin 9, 599-700.

Thorpe, W. H. (1965). Science, Man and Morals. Methuen and Co. Ltd., London.

Wolff, P. H. (1963). Observations on the early development of smiling. In: Determinants of Infant Behaviour (B. M. Foss, ed.). John Wiley and Sons, New York, 2, 113-138.

Wolff, P. H. (1969). The natural history of crying and other vocalizations in early infancy. In: Determinants of Infant Behaviour (B. M. Foss, ed.). 4, 81-109. John Wiley and Sons, New York, and Methuen and Co. Ltd., London.

A DESCRIPTION OF SOME HUMAN GREETINGS

Adam Kendon[1]

Project on Human Communication
Bronx State Hospital
Bronx, N.Y.

and

Andrew Ferber
Family Studies
Bronx State Hospital

INTRODUCTION

In this paper we describe certain instances of human greetings.
The examples are all taken from films or video-tapes prepared for research on communicative behaviour. They were all recorded in the
Eastern United States, among members of the professional middle
class. Most of them were taken from a film made at an outdoor party
held at a private house in a suburb of New York City. They include both
greetings accorded to guests as they arrived at the party and also those
that took place among the guests during the party.

The term "greeting" will be used to refer to that unit of social
interaction often observed when people come into one another's presence,
which includes a distinctive exchange of gestures or utterances in which
each person appears to signal to the other, directly and explicitly, that
he has been seen. Such an exchange may be as fleeting as an exchange
of glances between strangers as they pass on the street, or it may be
as prolonged and elaborate as the salutations that may sometimes be
observed at airports or docksides, when loved ones are reunited after
a prolonged absence.

There are a number of reasons for choosing to study greetings.
First of all, they have an important function in the management of relations between people. It is by way of the greeting that a guest is made
to feel properly part of a party. It is by way of a greeting that friends
acknowledge, and so confirm and continue their friendship. In the manner in which the greeting ritual is performed, the greeters signal to
each other their respective social status, their degree of familiarity,
their degree of liking for one another, and also, very often, what roles

they will play in the encounter that is about to begin.

Secondly, since greeting occurs among people all over the world, it would appear to be an excellent unit of social behaviour to study if one is to begin to examine systematically what is universal and what is traditional in human communicative behaviour. The value of the greeting for this kind of study has already been recognised by Eibl-Eibesfeldt (1968, 1970, 1972). Although no cultural comparisons are attempted in this paper it is hoped that the detail we provide and the format we have developed will prove useful in comparative studies[2].

Finally, greetings occur in animal species other than Man. If an effective comparative ethology for human behaviour is ever to be developed, we need to be able to make detailed comparisons between human behaviour and behaviour of other animals. This, however, cannot be useful unless we are comparing behaviour that occurs in contexts that can be compared. It would seem that the greeting, as an interactional event, provides us with a unit of behaviour which occurs in closely similar contexts and thus makes comparisons between human and animal behaviour meaningful.

There are few students of greeting. Early writers such as Roth (1889) provided accounts of the great variety of greeting behaviour that may be found throughout the world, but it is only within the last five years that anyone has again taken a systematic interest in it. Eibl-Eibesfeldt (1968, 1970), and Blurton-Jones and Leach (1972) have devoted papers to it. Callan (1970) and Goffman (1971) have devoted chapters to it. Work pertinent to the greeting has also been done or is now being done by Harvey Sacks (unpublished), Schegloff (1968), and Sherzer (in preparation). This work will not be reviewed here. We shall confine

ourselves to description in an effort to show that a common structure
appears to characterise at least those greeting transactions we have
looked at, and also to show what the repertoire of behaviours that occurs
within such transactions includes.

MATERIALS AND METHODS OF STUDY

The specimens of greetings examined for this paper were taken
from films and video-tapes made for the purpose of studying communication conduct. These included two films and a video-tape made specially for this study. The films will be known herein as the Birthday
Party Film and Wedding.[3] The video-tape will be referred to as the
Thanksgiving Tape. Use was also made of three other films made at
other times for other purposes. These are known as TRD Band, TRD
Picnic and An Observation. Details of all these films will now be given.

1. Birthday Party Film. As this was our principal document it
will be described fully. The film consists of 4,800 feet of 16mm colour
film, much of it with synchronised sound, taken on an afternoon in early
July 1969 at an outdoor birthday party held for the five-year-old son of
one of the authors (AF). The party took place in the back garden and
adjoining private beach of the boy's home in Westchester County, N.Y.
Forty-five people were present, though not all of them at the same time.
There were twenty-three adults and twenty-two children, aged between
23 and 65 years, and 2 and 11 years respectively. These included the
parents of the five-year-old, his little sister, the parents, father-in-
law, sister and her husband, of the boy's father, seven adults who were
close friends of the boy's parents and their children, and several children who were schoolmates of the boy, together with their parents. The

great majority of these people were of Jewish background and members
of the professional middle class.

A sketch-map of the site of the party is given in Fig. 1. The
guests arrived by way of the Brick Walkway. In the early part of the
party many of them were greeted on this walkway or on the Lawn where,
for a while, they remained. Eventually, however, all of the guests
gathered on the beach. Latecomers or parents coming to fetch their
children, thus had to walk all the way to the beach before being greeted.
When all the guests were gathered on the beach, the birthday cake was
brought out and cut and served from the Beach Deck. Before and after
serving the cake, many of the children, and some adults, clustered at
the water's edge, while some of the children were taken for rides in a
small sailing boat. The others mostly remained near the Beach Deck,
the source of food and drink. After about two hours had passed, the
guests again gathered on the Lawn where the children played, or watched as the five-year-old opened his presents. The adults sat on the grass
or in deck chairs, chatting. Then gradually, they began to leave.

In filming this event, three cameras were used. All filming was
done with 16mm Commercial Ektachrome. Two cameras were fixed,
one on the beach to command a view of the Walkway and the Lawn.
These cameras were fitted with 1200 ft. magazines, to allow for up
to half an hour of continuous filming, if necessary. The third camera
was hand-held, and it was used to acquire a second angle on much that
was filmed by the two fixed cameras. A shot-gun microphone and synchronised portable tape-recorder was used with the hand-held camera.
A wireless microphone worn by the hostess was tuned to the recorder
synchronised with the Lawn camera, while the microphone for the
Beach Camera was placed on the Beach Deck. The sound recording

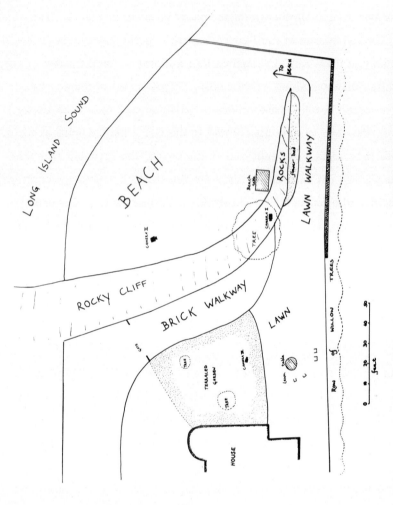

Fig. 1.   Sketch map of the site of the Birthday Party to show its main areas and the
approximate locations of the cameras.

was not as successful as had been hoped, but some use of it has been possible.

The cameras were kept to the edges of the site, well away from people. Zoom lenses were used to compensate for this distance, but in filming, complete groupings of people were always kept in frame. No attempt was made to film in close-up. This meant, of course, that we lost details of the face. However, for the analysis of interactional events it is necessary to have all participants in the frame simultaneously as much as possible. Additional cameras would have to be used to get close-ups of faces, but these were not available to us.

At the beginning of the party the cameras were turned on as soon as a guest could be seen approaching down the walkway and were kept running until the guest finally parted from the host or hostess. Since a number of guests arrived in fairly quick succession, the first twenty minutes of the party were recorded by nearly continuous filming. The camera on the beach was allowed to run continuously for approximately forty minutes, from the time that the first guests were received there. Filming was resumed towards the end of the party, and an additional fifteen minutes of continuous filming was done.

No attempt was made to conceal the cameras, but since they were on the edges of the site at all times, they intruded very little. All of the guests knew that some filming was to take place. They knew that this was for research purposes, but they did not know that the main interest was in greetings. Nineteen of the adults and one of the children were interviewed afterwards in an attempt to find out, among other things, how they had reacted to the filming. Of these, three appeared to be totally unaware of the cameras, while the seventeen who reported they were aware of them, only four described their feelings as negative, ten said that the cameras made no difference at all, and three of them, including the child who was interviewed, felt excited and interested in the filming. These responses seem to confirm our observations of the guests. They appear in the film to be almost completely unaffected by the cameras, and there are very few instances in which someone is seen to look at the camera. This lack of camera effect is not really surprising. As we have said, the cameras were kept away from the people, Furthermore, the party was a real event. It had not been staged in any way for the purposes of the film. Furthermore, to most of those present the people and the site were all highly familiar. The event gathered its own momentum and proved to be absorbing enough for both adults and children for them not to care very much about the filming.

2. The Wedding. This film was made at a wedding in Manhattan in March 1970. Footage was taken as the guests approached the chapel, and afterwards in the foyer of the chapel as they emerged from the ceremony. Filming was also done at the reception. This footage proved much more difficult to work with, mainly because we could not get far enough away from the people, and because it was so crowded. However, it has been possible to include some examples from this film in our corpus.

3. Thanksgiving Tape. This consists of one hour of video-tape made in a Manhattan apartment during a party held at Thanksgiving. It contains a sequence in which the successive arrival of the guests was recorded.

4. <u>TRD Band.</u> Half-an-hour of high school adolescents in a parking lot waiting for a band practice. Filmed in a small town in Connecticut in 1964. It was made by Van Vlack at Eastern Pennsylvania Psychiatric Institute, as part of a project in the study of adolescent behaviour.

5. <u>TRD Picnic.</u> Footage shot in a picnic ground in a park near Philadelphia, when a local organisation were having a picnic as part of Fourth of July celebrations. Two or three useful instances of greeting have been used from this film.

6. <u>An Observation.</u> This consists of four hours of unstaged activity at a Nursery School. It was made by the Child Development Center of the University of West Virginia, for the purposes of training students in child observation. Three examples have been used from this material.

The aim of this work was to develop a description of how people greet one another. We began by carefully watching and re-watching the examples available to us. The films were prepared for research by having a number printed on each frame which can be seen when the film is projected. We used an Athena L-W and a Bell & Howell 385 projector, converted to be operated by a hand-crank. In this way very small stretches of film could be examined at a time, and the events recorded could be analysed in great detail. As a result of this process of intensive watching, we were able to formulate a list of behavioural units that appeared over and over again in the examples, and this formed the basis of a check-list which was used to record the presence or absence of these elements in the greeting studied. Additional specific procedures, such as how we analysed behaviours such as gaze direction, will be given in the account of our findings.

The total number of greeting incidents that we have made use of in this study is ninety-two. However, it should be made clear that by no means all of these could be used for all parts of the analysis. In some of the examples only one participant in the greeting could be seen. In others we could see only a fragment of what was obviously a much longer event. Thus the size of the sample upon which our general statements are based may vary according to the statement being made. Where we have presented quantitative statements to show the distribution of a given feature of greeting within our corpus, no attempt has been made to evaluate these statistically. What we offer here is a synthetic picture of what we believe to be the main features of the organisation of greeting interaction. It should not be taken as more than a guide for the more refined and systematic studies that undoubtedly should follow.

The greetings may be classified in various ways, according to the context of the greeting, its apparent function, and who was involved in it. Tables 1a and 1b, present some of this data, so that a more complete picture of the sample we have worked with may be available.

THE STRUCTURE OF GREETING INTERACTIONS

The distinctive gestures and utterances that occur in a greeting interaction will be referred to as salutations. In some greeting interactions the participants exchange salutations while there is considerable distance between them. Such a distance salutation exchange may be all that there is to the interaction, and afterwards the participants go their separate ways. At other times it is a prelude to further interaction which occurs at close range. In these cases, which include most of the cases we are to consider in this paper, such interaction at close range is opened with another salutation exchange, here to be referred to as the close salutation.

As we shall come to see again later, it is characteristic of the close salutation that the participants enact it in a distinct location, and that they orient to one another in a way that is distinctive. Once the gestures of salutation have been completed, the participants then move away from the location taken for the exchange. If they continue in one another's presence as for instance when they remain together for conversation, they will adopt a different orientation to one another.

The close salutation may thus be said to occur within a distinct spatial and orientational frame. Obviously, the establishment of this frame is done jointly by the participants. The greeting interaction will be said to have begun once either of the participants has begun to move toward the other, whether or not any explicit interaction has taken place. The greeting interaction will be said to be over, for present purposes, as soon as the spatial and orientational frame of the close salutation is dissolved.

The diagram in Fig. 2 displays the structure of a typical greeting. This was a greeting, taken from the Birthday Party Film, between two men, who were a considerable distance from one another at the outset. The converging lines in the centre of the diagram represent the movement of the two men towards one another. Where the line is broken, the individual represented is in motion. Where the line is solid he is standing still. The arrows above and below these lines represent the orientation of the bodies of the participants in relation to one another.

Table Ia.   Types of Greetings in the Birthday Party Film

Total number of greetings	63
Number of greetings between	
Host/Hostess and Guest	31
Guest and Guest	32
Number of greetings between	
Adults	56
Adult–Child	7
Males	18
Male-Female	26
Females	19
Members of same Family	20
Close Friends	15
Acquaintances	28

Table Ib.   Number of Individuals Observed in the Greeting Examples
and the Number of Times Each was Observed, for the
Birthday Party Film

Number of observations per individual	Number of individuals
22	1
13	1
11	1
8	1
7	3
6	2
5	1
4	5
3	2
2	4
1	11
0	6
82	38

The outer oblongs, above and below the converging lines and arrows represent the segments of p's[4] during which a given bodily orientation is sustained. Broken lines again represent movement through space, continuous lines represent standing still. The short blocks inside the outer oblongs represent short elements of behaviour such as gestures of the arm or head, the occurrence of utterances, and so forth. These actions, as they may be called, are conceived of as occurring within the frame provided by the orientation of the whole body.

It will be seen from the diagram how, after an initial turn of the body in which each faces toward the other, the two men approach one another, and sustain a frontal orientation to one another. It will be noted that they both come to a halt (WF a little before JH) and while they are thus halted, facing one another, they engage in a handshake. The location each occupies and his orientation to the other at this point, constitutes the spatial-orientational frame of the close salutation that we spoke of above. Thereafter JH moves further towards WF, but as he does so he steps round him. WF takes a few steps backwards, also altering his orientation. As they move into this side-by-side arrangement, they begin their conversation.

In this paper, the greeting interaction in this example would be regarded as having begun at the point where WF turns towards JH. It would be regarded as over at the point where WF finally turns from the position he had adopted for the duration of the handshake. It will be seen that JH is engaged in the greeting interaction slightly later than WF, and that he begins to move into the phase of the interaction that follows the greeting slightly sooner than WF.

The frontal orientation of each greeter to the other, sustained

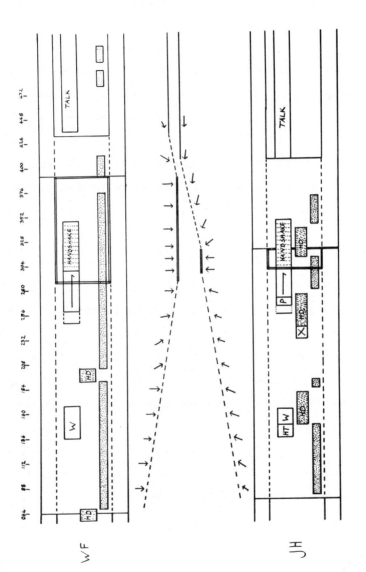

Fig. 2   Diagram of a greeting.   For explanation see text.

through the approach and until the end of the close salutation, provides
a frame within which a number of actions may be observed. In the present example we may note how, shortly after each has oriented to the
other and begun his approach, they engage in a distance salutation exchange. This is the typical pattern. It will be noted, however, that
there are certain conditions that must be established before the distance
salutation can occur and these conditions are sometimes brought about
by observable actions. Thus before any greeting can begin the participants must sight each other, and in so doing they must identify the other
as someone they wish to greet. Sighting may sometimes be observed
as a distinct action, though this is not usual in our sample. What we
observe first, as a rule, is the orientation and the beginning of the
approach of one participant to the other.

It will be noted that p will not begin an approach to q unless he has
some indication that he is aware of him and of his intention to greet. In
some circumstances, for example where q is preoccupied and p is in a
hurry to greet him, p may announce his presence to q explicitly. He
may do this by calling his name, by coughing discreetly, or by knocking
on the door. In the present example, as in most of those in our corpus,
q responds to p's orientation to him, by himself orienting to p so no distinct announcement is apparent. We mention it here, however, for it
may sometimes occur as a distinct step, and when it occurs it always
precedes the distance salutation.

As the greeters continue to approach one another following the
distance salutation, a number of different behaviours may be observed,
some of which are illustrated in the example. Thus we note that people
do not usually look at one another continuously as they approach one
another, and they may often look sharply away just prior to the close

salutation. We may also observe how they may touch their hair or adjust their clothing. Sometimes they may be seen to draw one or both arms across their own body in an action we refer to as the 'body cross'. This is seen in JH in the present example. These behaviours, which tend to occur toward the end of a long approach, are quite unformalised.[5] In their 'withdrawing' character they contrast sharply with the behaviour that occurs in the final stage of the approach, when the greeters are close enough to begin interaction with one another by means of speech.[6] Here, they characteristically look at one another, they usually smile, and they get ready for whatever gestures are to be involved in the close salutation. Whether the unformalised 'withdrawal' behaviours appear will depend in part upon how long the approach is. It will also depend upon the kind of relationship that exists between the greeters. Likewise, the behaviour characteristic of the final phase of the approach may appear immediately after the distance salutation and be sustained thereafter. This also seems to depend upon the kind of relationship that obtains between the greeters.

Following the close salutation the greeters move out of the distinct spatial and orientational frame they established for it and the greeting is now said to be over. However, though what follows the close salutation is quite variable, there is one phase that is quite often observed, and in some circumstances has become quite formalised and should be described in any full treatment of greetings. We call this phase the "How Are You." Here people engage in an exchange of information about one another. This commonly concerns their state of health, and is frequently highly formalised and quite brief. In some circumstances the exchange of information may be prolonged, however. People may relate news of one another and of mutual acquaintances, they may explain the purpose of their visit, or they may provide information about their identity. In our investigations to date we have done little more than merely note the existence of this phase. However, since it plays an important part in the process by which relationships and maintained and and developed in any further study of greeting this phase will merit much more consideration.

In the rest of this paper we shall describe in more detail the behaviour we have observed in each of the phases of the greeting as they have been sketched above, up to and including the close salutation. It should be noted that we are concerned with greetings between two people at a time. Sometimes such dyadic greetings occur within the context of a larger unit of interaction, as when several people are being greeted together. However, in this paper we shall not be concerned with the ways in which successive greeting exchanges may be related together, though there is much of interest here that could be described. It should also be noted that our descriptions are confined to greetings between adults, except in a few cases.

THE ELEMENTS OF GREETING INTERACTIONS
AND THEIR INTERRELATIONS

We now turn to an account of the behavioural elements that occur at the various stages of the greeting we have described above. To do this we shall describe examples which illustrate, for each phase, the behaviours we have observed in our corpus of filmed greetings.

1. How Greeting Interactions Begin: Sighting, Orientation and the Initiation of the Approach

p must first sight q if he is to greet him. He must perceive him

and identify him as the particular individual he may wish to greet.
Sighting is a pre-interactional step. It need not be marked in any overt
behaviour. For example, p may become aware of q's presence in a
passing glance, or by overhearing his voice. Once he has sighted him
he must decide whether or not to initiate a greeting interaction. Whether he does so or not immediately upon sighting will depend upon (a)
the urgency of p's intention to greet q, (b) what p is doing at the time of
sighting (c) what q is doing at the time of sighting.

If p is already engaged in a conversation with someone when he
sights q, he may have to postpone an initiation of a greeting with him
until that conversation is ended. Similarly if, when he sights him, q
is busy, p may have to wait until q has completed what he is doing before initiating a greeting. How ready p is to interrupt himself, and how
ready he will be to interrupt q will, of course, depend upon the importance of initiating a greeting with q, relative to the importance of other
things. Sometimes p's role in the situation may be that of a greeter, in
which case his other involvements may all be interrupted the moment
anyone who must be greeted appears. This was the case for the hostess
at the birthday party, for example. At other times, p may be prepared
to interrupt himself to greet q because it is the only opportunity he may
have of doing so, or because he has not seen q for a long time, or because q is a valuable friend or a person of importance to p. How ready
p will be to interrupt q will likewise depend upon a variety of factors.
If p is high in status in the gathering, he may be more likely to interrupt
q no matter what q may be doing, than if he is low in status. p may also
have special rights in relation to q. For example, spouses or very
close friends can interrupt one another for a greeting, whereas p is
less likely to interrupt q if he does not know him well. In general, p

will only initiate a greeting if he is confident that the greeting will be
returned. To be rebuffed or unrecognised is gravely embarrassing,
and people rarely risk this.

The ways in which p begins a greeting with q in our corpus are
quite various. Here we will cite a series of examples which illustrate
how, at one extreme, p may begin upon a greeting with another as soon
as he has sighted him and how, at the other extreme, p may not begin
upon a greeting until he has received some explicit signal from q.

Where p begins upon a greeting with q without any prior interaction with him, we find that p either has a special obligation to greet him
or he has a special right to a greeting from him. First greetings between host and hostess and guests were initiated in this way. We also
have instances of greetings between spouses that are begun by one of
the pair without any prior interaction. Many of the greetings between
guests, on the other hand, have a more tentative beginning. In these
cases we see p hinting to q that he wants to approach him, for example
by subtly synchronising his movements with him, but not approaching
him until this hint has been acknowledged with an explicit signal.

In the first few greetings recorded in the birthday party film,
the hostess crossed the lawn and walked part of the way up the brick
walkway where she would then stand and wait as the guests approached
her. In these instances (G1, G2, G4, G5, G10), sighting could be observed as a distinct action. JF turns her face in the direction of the
approaching guests, tilts back her head slightly and maintains this
orientation for a perceptible length of time. Immediately following
sighting she would begin her approach, usually combined with a distance salutation display. In these instances the hostess, upon sighting,

would interrupt whatever else she might have been doing to embark upon the greeting. Greeting new guests was given priority over other involvements at this stage of the occasion, as befitted her role at the party as hostess. It may be noted here, however, that though the hostess did not depend upon any explicit signal from the approaching guests before she initiated an approach to them, she nonetheless would not begin her approach until they were close enough so that, upon walking towards them she would meet them at the edge of the site of the party. In the early stages of the party, where the guests could be seen from the lawn entering the gateway to the drive, JF would begin her approach upon sighting. In this way she had time to walk part of the way up the drive and stand and wait for them, when they were between fifteen and twenty feet away from her. Much later in the party, when the guests had all moved down to the beach, though a new arrival could be seen clearly from the beach as he walked down the grassy walkway, the hostess neither explicitly acknowledged him nor began her approach until the guest had turned on to the beach itself (G59, G57). The point at which she began her approach allowed her so to time her movement across the beach, that she could meet the guest at the edge of the gathering on the beach.

These examples reflect a general point that has to do with the location on the site of the occasion of the close salutation between host and newly arrived guest. In most of the examples this would take place at some point well removed from the centre of the site of the occasion. In the above example the hostess took an active part in determining the location of the close salutation by timing the moment she began her approach. In other instances the arriving guests would not be seen by the hostess and they thus had an opportunity to fully penetrate the party's arena. In most of these cases they did not do so, however, remaining on the edge of the main area until they had been greeted by the hostess.

How freely a newly arrived guest will penetrate the site of an occasion and how far away from the centre of it the host or hostess will move towards them, depends in a complex way upon the nature of the relationship between the guest and the host or hostess. In general, it would appear that the further the host moves from the centre of the occasion's action, the greater the show of respect for the guest he creates.[7] The more fully the guest penetrates the arena of the occasion before being greeted, the greater is his familiarity with the host. Thus, at the birthday party, the guest who penetrated the site most fully before being greeted was the host's mother who, upon her arrival on the lawn, immediately set about some rearrangement of the furniture on the lawn, and gave some instructions to the host's maid, before being greeted either by the host or the hostess. On the other hand, guests who did not know the hostess or host well and who were not immediately greeted waited on the lawn until they were greeted. Only then did they move down on to the beach, nearer the centre of the occasion. However, it should also be noted that how far the host will move to the edge of the arena and how far the guest may penetrate the arena may also depend upon the stage the party has reached when the guest arrives. Later arriving guests typically get a less elaborate welcome than guests arriving early and, correlatively, guests arriving late may often enter more fully into the activities of the occasion before being greeted.

It will be noted that these expectations make it possible for hosts and guests to give expression to their attitudes toward one another. At the birthday party the host, piqued because his mother, father, and sister and her husband arrived much later than he expected, remained down on the beach and waited for them to come to him. He did not go to greet them, upon learning of their arrival. This little violation of etiquette was noticed by his wife who, as she left the beach to go up the lawn to greet them, called to her husband: "Aren't you going to come up and meet them?" with a sharp contrast in pitch over the last two syllables evidently expressive here of her pained surprise at his insistence on remaining on the beach.

In a number of the greetings between host or hostess and guest, the guest could be said to take the initiative. This occurred, for example, in G23a, G23b and G62, where a guest was awaiting his turn for a close salutation from the host or hostess, while he or she was engaged with someone else. Here, what is observed is that the guest would begin his approach to the hostess or host, fully oriented to him and ready to engage in a close salutation, the moment the host or hostess began a behavioural element that would count as marking the beginning of the end of his involvement with the other. Here, thus, p begins upon a greeting with q, not upon receipt of any signal addressed to him, but upon a change in q's activity that is indicative of his relinquishment of his current involvement. He makes bold to approach here, either because he is clearly next in line (as was the case in G23a and G23b) or because, since he has a right to receive a greeting from the other, he can count on him to turn to him next, should the other be made aware of his desire for a greeting (G62).

> For example, in G62 a recently arrived guest, MG, is chatting to the hostess while, about ten feet away, his host is engaged with another recent arrival, GG. MG, who has been standing with arms akimbo, his hands splayed on his hips, takes a step towards the host, extending his right hand first upwards in a little gesture by which he apparently indicates to her that he wishes to greet the host, and then forwards to the host in an offer of a handshake. By the time MG is near enough to the

host to grasp his hand, the host has already turned to him, also with hand extended. Though the host has not looked at MG before this, he is nonetheless able to turn to him for a handshake coordinately with MG's approach. This was brought about, apparently, by the guest picking his moment to begin his approach to the host to coincide with a juncture in the host's conversation with the other guest. The first movement MG makes as he begins his approach is to lift his right hand away from his hip. He initiates this at frame number 72554. One frame before this the host had begun to lower his head, looking away from GG to attend to the plate of cake he is holding. MG, thus, though engaged in conversation with JF, was nonetheless sufficiently attuned to his host's behaviour to identify the moment at which he began a pause in his conversation with GG, a moment at which he became more accessible to interruption than he would were he fully oriented to GG. Similarly, in G23a JF, the hostess, is engaged in a greeting with WF. BA, who she next greets, is standing with her back turned about ten feet away from JF. As JF begins to step sideways, the first of the steps she takes to move out of the spatial and orientational frame she had been in for the close salutation with WF, BA turns and begins her approach to her. In this case, BA had presumably overheard the concluding utterance of the greeting exchange between JF and WF. And again, in G23b, BA's husband HA, begins his approach to JF as she steps away from BA, though before she had begun to orient to him.

In contrast to these examples in which p coordinates the beginning of his approach to q with a movement, or a change in speech pattern that indicates that q is going to relinquish a current involvement, there are a number of examples in which p does not begin his approach to q until he received an explicit signal from him, a signal which may nonetheless be distinct from a salutation display. Whereas in the examples we have described so far, p begins to approach q as if on the assumption that q will engage in a greeting with him, in the examples we shall now describe p defers his approach until q has directly signalled his readiness for an approach. The greetings in our corpus in which the approach was preceded by this "catching the eye" of the other are all between guests, between people, that is, who do not know each other very intimately and who do not have any special reason for greeting one another, as hosts and guests do.

Some examples of greetings initiated by an exchange of signals will now be described.

In G44 (see Fig. 5) CB is standing alone with his five-year-old son, looking out to sea. Twenty feet away to his left DW is standing in conversation with HS and, like CB, he is facing the sea. DW's conversation with HS lapses and DW turns his head to direct his face to CB, though he does not turn his trunk or lower body towards him. Shortly thereafter CB turns his face in the direction of DW and then away again. He then looks at DW again, but this time smiling slightly, whereupon DW immediately throws back his head in a distance salutation. After CB has replied to this with a brief utterance and a much increased smile, DW then begins to turn his lower body and trunk to face CB, and then approach him. In G40 SW approaches the beach deck in front of which WF is standing, fully oriented to CB and BA who are talking together. SW stops about eight feet from this group, but stands so that she is fully facing at right angles to the axis between CB and BA, smiling, but looking down slightly. WF, who turned his head to her as she approached, but then resumes his orientation to CB and BA, now turns his head to her again, this time smiling. As she raises her head, apparently looking at him, he initiates his approach to her and directly thereafter they engage in a close salutation. In G41 SW, her encounter with WF over, turns to fully face the interactional axis between CB and BA. She remains in this position for two seconds and then begins to approach CB. Her approach here, however, begins only after CB has turned his face to her, away from BA. SW begins her approach one second after CB has looked at her, and as she begins her approach CB looks back at BA.

In these examples, we see p orienting to q, but not approaching him until q has oriented his eyes to p. p by his orientation to q may be said to announce his intention to approach, but he does not do so until q has given his "clearance". It is to be noted that in two of these exam-

ples the initial orientation of p̱ is by a turn of the head only, the rest
of the body being retained in p̱'s current orientation. This perhaps
serves to give the initial move a certain tentativeness. If the other
does not offer a clearance signal p̱ can easily turn his head in another
direction and his look at q̱ can pass as a mere glance. To turn his
whole body to q̱ is to commit himself much more fully to an approach to
him, and this is less easily discounted if he is rebuffed. Correlatively,
it is easier to ignore someone who merely turns his head in one's direction, than if he turns his whole body towards one.

Sometimes one may see what would appear to be an even more
tentative form of beginning a greeting. Here p̱ avoids catching the eye
of the other, but at the same time he synchronises his movements with
those of the other and he may also glance at the other fleetingly, looking
away each time the other looks towards him, until the other actually
directs a salutation display to him. An example of this kind of greeting
is provided by G60:

> Here MG is standing talking to JF while about eight feet away
> from him at JF's right GG is standing, arms folded, not engaged
> in any focused interaction. At frame 71340 GG turns his head
> left slightly, focusing on MG while, at the same time, MG turns
> his head, focusing his eyes on JF. GG thus looks at MG as MG
> looks away from GG. Then, MG rotates his head away from
> JF into an orientation in which he would catch GG's eyes. Simul-
> taneously, GG looks away from MG. MG then directs a distance
> salutation to GG, who looks back at him and replies with a salu-
> tation. Here, thus, GG, by synchronising his head turns with
> movements of MG may be said to have signalled his wish for
> contact. However, he consistently avoided catching MG's eye
> until MG offered him an explicit salutation. (See Fig. 7.)

Synchronising one's movements with another but yet not meeting
the other's eyes or in some other way signalling a request for contact

in an explicit fashion is commonly followed by explicit contact between p and the person whose movements p "picks up". An example within an established focused gathering has been described in detail by Kendon (in press). Initiating an explicit interaction with another person is always a somewhat risky business, since there is always the possibility that the other party does not wish to reciprocate. By simply picking up the rhythm of another person's movements one can establish a connection with him which, at the same time, does not commit one to a positive initiation. If, after having joined the rhythm of another, the other makes no move toward establishing explicit contact with one, one can continue to go about one's business as if one had not made the initiation attempt.

Another way in which a greeting interaction may begin should now be mentioned. This is where p makes an explicit announcement of his presence. In the Birthday Party film all the greetings recorded took place in the open air, with relatively few barriers screening people from one another. Where p is to enter someone's house or office, however, he must almost always announce his presence explicitly - as with the knock on the door or the bell-ring or, perhaps, the secretary who informs her superior of his visitor's presence. A few greetings in our corpus, however, were initiated by explicit announcements. For example, in G46, KH standing by the beach deck saw BA approaching the table, put down her cup and then immediately called out: "Why if it isn't BA." This was followed by BA orienting to her and a distance salutation was then exchanged. In G52 BA follows HR as he moves across the beach, runs around and confronts him, announcing her presence to him. In G4, G10 and G14 JF, upon sighting the approach of children who she is going to greet, calls out, as if to announce to anyone in earshot, who is coming. Following this she proceeds to approach and engage in a distance and close salutation.

Finally, there is the introduced greeting. In the examples in our corpus (G3, G 18, G19 and G42) one member of the pair is accompanied by the hostess or host who then calls to the other announcing to him who she is with. In these instances a close salutation immediately follows the introduction. The introduction stands in for sighting, orientation, announcement and distance greeting, since it serves to create the context in which a close salutation is possible.

2. The Distance Salutation

At some point following p's orientation to q, he is likely to address an explicit display to him, such as a call or a wave. This is generally reciprocated in kind by q. We refer to this as the distance salutation since it always occurs at such a distance that the greeters if they continue to interact, move closer to one another afterwards. The absolute distance at which distance salutation occurs is not fixed, of course. In some cases in the birthday party film it occurred at a distance of more than thirty feet. In some cases it occurred between greeters who were only a few feet apart. How far away the participants are when they engage in the distance salutation depends upon such factors as (a) how far p is from q when p initiates his approach to him; (b) how eager p is to greet q; (c) how crowded the setting is. In crowded settings, for example, p may move closer to q before he initiates a salutation with him than he does in less crowded settings.

In the distance greeting the greeters may be said to recongise one another explicitly and they thereby establish, both for each other and for anyone else within range, that they are now engaged to greet

one another. We may expect, perhaps, that distance greetings are
more likely to occur in settings such as the one at the birthday party,
where there might be some ambiguity for q as to whether p was approaching him or someone else. However, as we shall see, two exchanges of
salutation displays appears to be extremely common, even where the
greeters are, from the outset, but a few feet from one another. We may
expect, however, that the amount of time that separated the first salutation from the second will be greater, and that the first or distance
salutation will be more vigorous in its enactment, in circumstances
where there is more than one possible partner for a greeting exchange.

In the material we have examined we have observed several different kinds of distance salutation displays. These will now be described,
and we shall also indicate the characteristic contexts for the different
forms we have observed, insofar as we know what these are.

(a)   The Head Toss

The distance display most commonly observed in the birthday
party film may be called the head toss display. Its most characteristic
feature is that the head is tilted back rapidly and then brought forward
again. It is usually combined with a call - such as 'hi' or 'hi' followed
by a name. Typically, the head is first raised and then, as it is lowered again, the call is uttered. As the head is raised, the mouth is
opened and generally the lips are drawn back in a smile which tends to
expose the upper teeth. In a few instances in our material we have been
able to see enough facial detail to see that the eyebrows are raised
sharply as the head is raised or tilted back, and they are then lowered
again as the head begins to be lowered. [8] Commonly, only the head and
face and voice are involved in this display, though in some instances the

trunk and arms are involved as well. Here, as the head is thrown back there is an associated marked straightening of the trunk, it is often bent back at the hips, or the hips themselves may be thrust forward. At the same time, the elbows are extended, so that the arms are held straight at the sides of the body and drawn back at the shoulders so that they extend dorsally. There may also be some adduction at the shoulder so that the arms are spread somewhat to either side. The forearms may be rotated to a prone position, with the fingers of one or both hands extended, so that the palms of the hands are oriented so that they face towards the person to whom the display is addressed.

The occasions when the body and arms are involved in the display, as well as the head, face and voice, are rare in our corpus. When they are, the enacter seems to be somewhat excited. The head toss display may thus be said to be enacted to varying degrees of intensity. At the very least we may have a slight raising of the head, coupled with an almost imperceptible eyebrow raise. More usually, a definite toss of the head is observable. At the higher intensities the body and arms are also involved in the way we have described. An example of the head toss display is seen in Fig. 4b.

The head toss display does not appear to be reciprocated with a headtoss. In none of the eleven examples in the birthday party material in which a head-toss display occurred and in which both parties to a distance greeting could be clearly observed, was the headtoss display seen in both partners. In all but one of these instances, furthermore, the headtoss display was the first explicit greeting display to be observed - in other words, it was performed by the individual taking the initiative in the sequence of greeting displays.

Other forms of the distance salutation display include the head
lower, the nod, and the wave, which can itself take various forms.
These are generally, though not always, associated with a smile and a
call.

(b)   The Head Lower

In the head lower, as the name we have given it implies, the head
is lowered, or tilted forward, and it is distinguished from the nod only
in its duration. In the head lower the head is tilted forward, held in that
position, and then raised, whereas in the nod the head is lowered and
then raised without a hold intervening. The head lower may be combined
with a smile, but if it is, the smile is different from the open mouth
upper-tooth smile observed in the head-toss greeting. In the head lower
smile the mouth is not opened, or at least it is not opened widely, the
lips are drawn back, sometimes so that both rows of teeth are exposed
and the circum-orbital muscles of the eyes are much more likely to be
involved, producing "crinkled eyes." The head lower may also be combined with a wave. In the instances in which we have observed this, the
arm is not fully raised, the hand being lifted not much above the top of
the head. An example of the head lower is to be seen in Fig. 8c.

The head lower is commonly seen in response to the headtoss.
However, we have also observed it in an initiator of a greeting exchange,
but in these cases the initiator is either an adult greeting a child or, in
a few cases, we have seen an older man greeting a much younger woman
with this head-action.

(c)   The Nod

The head nod display, in which the head is lowered and then at

once raised, is characteristic of greetings-in-passing. Here both parties to the greeting enact a nod. It is possible that the nod is closely
related to the head-lower. Whereas when p head-tosses, he initiates
contact with q and perhaps thereby invites further interaction, when p
head-nods he is not initiating but responding to the other. Where each
responds to the other, but neither initiates, we have a greeting in passing. The head-nod display is not often accompanied by facial involvement, or if it is this is relatively slight. Non uncommonly, a quiet
vocalisation occurs, such as 'hi' or 'good-day.'

(d)   The Wave

Waving is a common element in distance salutations, though the
birthday party material provided us with only five examples. There are
a number of different forms of waving. Here we shall describe the
forms we have been able to observe from a variety of sources. No
claims to exhaustiveness are made, however.

In waving, the hand and usually the forearm and upper arm as
well are raised up. This may or may not be combined with flapping or
wagging of the hand or limb. In all the waves we have observed, the
fingers of the hand are extended at least partly. They may be either
drawn together or spread, but the palm of the hand is always oriented
toward the person being waved at.

Waves vary in the extent to which the limb is extended. Sometimes it is only the hand that is raised, sometimes it is only the forearm. At other times, of course, the whole arm is lifted, usually to a
steep angle in relation to the vertical of the body, though occasionally
the arm is held straight up above the head.

The wave may consist of a simple up-down movement of the hand or hand and arm. The hand, once raised, may be 'flapped' - or it is moved from side to side or 'wagged'. When it is 'flapped', the wrist is alternately flexed and extended rapidly two or more times. In 'flapped' waves, the hand is held high and flapped. Successive up-down movements of the whole arm are not observed. In 'lateral' waves, the movements may be confined to a back-and-forth rotation of the forearm, with the wrist held somewhat extended, or the forearm, or sometimes the whole arm may be moved laterally back and forth.

The degree of limb extension in a wave is probably related in part to the distance over which signals are exchanged. Thus when people wave to one another at distances of fifteen feet or less they are not likely to do more than raise their hand by flexing their elbow, thus raising the hand to the level of the shoulder. At distances greater than this, how-ever, the hand may be raised to the level of the eyes or above. At very great distances the arm is fully extended above the head. The degree of limb extension is also related to the vigour of the wave. The more vigorously the hand is 'flapped' or 'wagged' the more the rest of the limb is involved in the movement and the more it will be extended.

The simple wave, in which the hand is merely raised and lowered, seems to occur as a reply to a more elaborate wave, or as an acknow-ledgement of another's greeting. We also see the simple wave when the wave is part of a distance salutation that is performed while the indivi-dual is already approaching the person he will greet. 'Flap' waves and 'lateral' waves are characteristic of waves where the waver is trying to catch another's attention. They also seem to occur where the waver is making contact with another, but will not or cannot thereupon proceed to have further close interaction with him. Whether there are any con-

sistent differences in the contexts in which 'flapped' waves as opposed
to 'lateral' waves occur, we do not yet know.

(e)   Discussion

The distance salutation occurs in all of the greeting interactions
we have examined in which close interaction also occurs, with the exception of greetings preceded by an introduction. How far away the individuals are when they exchange a distance greeting is a matter of considerable variation, however. In some circumstances the distance greeting
will occur as soon as the greeters come into one another's presence, in
which case it will be followed by the close salutation almost directly.
Thus, in the series of greetings recorded on the Thanksgiving Tape,
guests were entering the hallway of an apartment. As soon as they could
be seen through the door they would greet the host or hostess who was
already waiting for them. This greeting, which would include an utterance such as "Hullo, nice to see you" would then be followed by another
greeting ritual such as a handshake, or an embrace. Similarly, in G60,
in the birthday party film, where before the transaction occurs MG and
GG are already within ten feet of one another, when GG catches MG's
eye, MG initiates a headtoss greeting and GG responds with a head-lower
and a small wave. Then they lean forward to one another and shake
hands (see Fig. 7). The distance salutation also occurs just prior to the
close salutation where p and q are approaching one another in circumstances where they are bound to pass close to one another. For example
if p sets off down a corridor at the other end of which he sights q, no
distance greeting is likely until they are already close enough to begin
close interaction. It occurs when the greeters are much more widely
separated where, as frequently in the birthday party film, the greeters

had sighted one another a considerable distance away, but where there were several different directions in which either of them could move, and often several other people about whom they might greet. Here the distance greeting serves, perhaps, as an official ratification of the partners into a greeting relationship, a move that is not necessary in the corridor situation and not possible in the hallway referred to above.

3. The Head Dip

In many instances, one of the participants in the greeting transaction (though usually not both) will follow his distance salutation display with a head dip. Here the head is lowered by means of a forward bend of the neck. An example may be seen in Figs. 4 and 5. In the birthday party film, of the fifty separate distance salutations observed, twenty-five were followed by a clear head dip.

It may be noted that the head-dip is not only observed in association with greetings. A number of observations of it have been recorded which have suggested to us the hypothesis that the head-dip is associated with those points in an individual's flow of behaviour where he is changing his attention, where he is changing from one major unit of involvement to another. This hypothesis led us to compare all the instances of distance salutations that are followed by head-dips with those that are not, from the point of view of the location of the distance greeting in relation to changes in the greeter's direction of movement or orientation, and to changes in his activity or involvement.

As we have seen, some distance greetings occur just after p has oriented to the other. At other times, the distance greeting occurs just before p and q begin to move close enough to one another for the close salutation. Distance greetings were classified according to whether

they followed shortly upon p changing his orientation to begin his approach
to q or whether they immediately preceded the close salutation phase.
Whether a head-dip followed the distance greeting or not was in each
case noted. It was found that whereas no distance salutation that occurred during the final stages of the approach to the other were followed by
head-dips, sixteen of the distance salutations associated with head-dips
did occur just after p had begun his new orientation and approach to the
other. This would seem to support the hypothesis that the head-dips
here, as elsewhere, occurred in association with a change in p's principal involvement. We suggest that it may mark a shifting of "atten-
tional gears".[9]

Whether the head-dip has any regular signal function in greeting
interaction or not we cannot, from our present corpus of material,
determine. It is a conspicuous action, however, and insofar as it is
regularly associated with the onset of new phases of activity in the individual, it could serve to forewarn others of this change. In the context
of greetings it may perhaps serve to forewarn the recipient of a distance
salutation of the greeter's firm intention to relinquish whatever he was
doing before, and give his whole attention to the person he has just
saluted. It is significant in this connection that a head dip does not follow a distance salutation which is not followed by further interaction.
It is also significant that head-dips do not follow distance salutations
that immediately precede close salutations. In these cases, the individuals are already fully oriented to one another, and by this orientation,
and by the other's previous approach, there is no ambiguity about who
is attending to whom.

4. Approach

When people engage in a close salutation they always move to a distinct location to do so. Thus in any greeting which includes a close salutation we shall observe an approach, that is, a period during which the participants move toward one another to meet at a spot that is distinct from the one that either was occupying at the beginning of the transaction. How much each moves is, of course, a matter of considerable variation, depending upon the circumstances at the beginning of the transaction, such as how great a distance separates the interactants at the outset, and what each of them happens to be doing when sighting occurs. It is also to be noted, however, that the pattern of approach that is observed - whether one walks over to the other person, waits until they have approached instead, or whether each times his walk in the direction of the other so that each covers about the same amount of ground by the time they reach each other - is also dependent upon tendencies of the individuals in their behaviour toward one another which are not dependent upon the immediate situation. In other words, how far one "goes out of one's way" to meet another, appears to have a communicational significance. As we noted in an earlier section, for instance, how far from the central area of the party the host moves to greet a new arrival at a party, can be taken as an indication of how important the new arrival is for the host.

The communicational significance of mode of approach would appear to derive from the fact that, in moving from one location to another, an individual must perforce change the segment of the environment with which he can involve his attention. In moving away from one's current location, that is to say, one must necessarily give up whatever involvements were associated with it. In a greeting thus, the further p̱ moves from his location at sighting, in his approach to the other, the more fully will he be putting aside whatever his previous involvements were. He thus provides information about the relative importance he gives to his various involvements.

The precise significance of the mode of approach in a particular greeting, of course, will depend upon the combination of circumstances in which it occurs. In the birthday party material approach patterns are quite various and few general statements appear to be possible. A more detailed attempt at working out the rules which govern approaches in greetings will be reserved for another report. Here we shall examine some of the behaviour that may be observed during the approach.

(a)   Behaviour during approach: facial orientation

Earlier, in discussing how greeting transactions begin, we described examples in which p̱ did not begin his approach to q̱ until q̱ apparently looked at him. These examples support the observations of Goffman (1963) that an exchange of glances is one of the ways individuals give one another "clearance" for further interaction. In all of the instances of greetings in which we were able to observe both individuals from the outset of the transaction, there is a moment, early on, when each do appear to exchange glances with one another. This glance exchange is generally associated with the distance greeting by which the partners to the greeting may be said to give explicit acknowledgement to one another that they are such. After this moment of looking, however, one or other of the greeting pair, or sometimes both, look away, and they may continue to avoid looking at the other until they are almost close enough for the close salutation. [10]

We have investigated "looking" during the approach by recording changes in the orientation of the face. This can be seen readily in the films available to us, although in most cases we cannot arrive at a reliable estimate of the point of convergence of the eyes. Where an individual orients his face nevertheless indicates where he is most likely to be looking. Furthermore, in natural social interaction, it appears that a change in the direction of the glance from "looking at" one's partner to "looking away" from him, and vice versa, is almost always associated with a change in the orientation of the face (Vine, 1971). In the present study, we shall confine ourselves to observations on whether the face is oriented in the direction of the other member of the transaction - in which case p will be said to be "looking at" the other; or whether his face is oriented in some other direction - in which case p will be said to be "looking away" from the other.

In examining face orientation or "gaze" during approach, all those greetings in the birthday party film were selected in which (a) at least ten feet separated the individuals at the start of the transaction and (b) at least one member of the transaction could be observed from the beginning. The period of time during which observations could be made was then divided into twelve frame segments (half-second segments) and the number of frames in each segment in which the individual had his face oriented to the other was counted. The combined results of this analysis are presented in Fig. 3. This gives an overall picture of "gaze" during approach for a maximum of forty-seven individuals drawn from twenty-five greetings. These individuals could be observed for between two and fourteen seconds. All forty-seven of them could be observed for the last two seconds of the greetings studied, twenty of them could be observed for the last eight seconds, while seven could

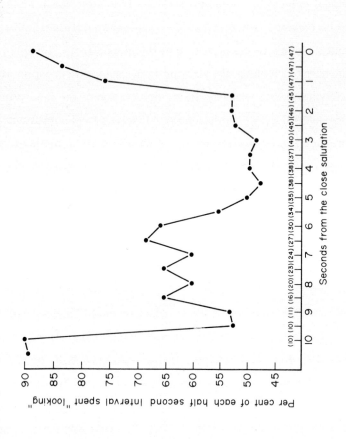

Fig. 3.   Variation in the proportion of time spent in face orientation to other during approach. Abscissa: time intervals in seconds from the close salutation. Figures in parentheses are the number of individuals observed at each interval. Ordinate: proportion of each half second interval (in percent) spent in face orientation at other combined for all individuals observed at each half second interval.

be observed from the point at which the greeting transaction began. The later parts of the curve are thus more reliable as an indicator of overall "looking" trends than are the earlier parts.

The composite curve shows the proportion of time spent "looking at" the other during approach at each of the twenty-eight twelve frame segments. The most outstanding feature of this curve is that although within the half second immediately preceding the start of the close salutation almost all the greeters are "looking at" one another, during the previous three seconds the proportion of time spent "looking" is sharply lower. Thereafter the curve tends to rise, though irregularly, until ten seconds before the close salutation the greeters are much more likely to be "looking at" one another. In general, it would seem, we can say that as the approach begins the greeters tend to look at each other. It is here, at the beginning of the approach, that the distance salutation tends to occur, and during the distance salutation the greeters look directly at one another. This is often followed, as we have seen, by a head-dip, and it is this that no doubt accounts for the irregularities observed in the early parts of the curve. Thereafter, some looking is likely to occur, but less and less as the approach continues until, when the individuals are within but a few feet of one another, as the curve shows, they look comparatively little. This dip in the curve just before the close salutation reflects a definite dip or turn of the head by which gaze to the other person is sharply "cut off". This "cut off" tends to occur when the individuals are just a little more than ten feet from one another, a distance just a little greater than the one at which interaction by means of utterance exchange can become possible (see Fig. 8).

This aversion of gaze just before the close salutation is observed in 72% of the individual approaches examined. It may perhaps be interpreted in terms of a theory of the role of the look in the regulation of "intimacy" or degree of interpersonal involvement in social encounters (Argyle & Dean 1965, Kendon 1967).

First of all it may be noted that when p looks at q he may thereby be said to reduce his behavioural distance from him. Conversely, to look away is an act of withdrawal. In the situation studied here, in which two individuals are physically approaching one another, we may expect that, the closer they get to one another the stronger will be any tendencies either may have to withdraw from the other. We may expect, thus, that behaviours associated with withdrawal will be more likely to appear the closer the individuals get to one another.

This expectation seems to be fulfilled by the face-orientation data, if we accept that to look away from someone is to partly withdraw from him. Not only do we find that p is more likely to look away from q the closer he gets to him, we also find that the partner who looks the least in a given transaction is also the one who we would expect to have stronger withdrawal tendencies. The relevant data are given in Table II. Here we present the mean number of frames per twelve frame block in which p's face was oriented to q, for the fifteen greetings in which this could be observed simultaneously in both partners for three or more seconds. It will be seen that in all but one of the seven greetings in which the hostess was involved, the hostess spent substantially more time looking at her approaching guests than the guest did looking at her. It will also be seen that in the eight other greetings included here, in six of these cases it is the individual who covers the least amount of ground in his approach who looks the most. It seems that the partner to a greeting who looks the least, is the one who must enter a space that is already occupied by the other.

Table II. Average "Looking" Time Per Twelve Frame Block During the Approach

	Hostess–Guest Greetings				Guest–Guest Greetings		
Greeting	Participants	Mean "looking"	No. of seconds observed	Greeting	Participants	Mean "looking"	No. of seconds observed
G1	Hostess (JF) Guest (RG)	12.0 3.7	7	G16	Waits (MR) Approaches (DG)	7.5 5.9	14
G2	Hostess (JF) Guest (RC)	11.1 6.2	18	G48	Waits (WF) Approaches (JH)	11.9 6.0	18
G5a	Hostess (JF) Guest (CB)	8.9 8.9	16	G26	Waits (DG) Approaches (RG)	8.0 6.2	12
G6	Hostess (JF) Guest (SK)	11.2 3.9	13	G28	Waits (MR) Approaches (AF)	6.0 3.0	16
G10	Hostess (JF) Guest (DG)	9.0 5.4	14	G39	Waits (CB) Approaches (HR)	10.8 5.0	10
G17	Hostess (JF) Guest (JR)	12.0 0	6	G41	Waits (CB) Approaches (SW)	6.7 7.3	29
G24	Hostess (JF) Guest (DF)	8.0 6.1	17	G40	Waits (SW) Approaches (WF)	10.5 7.5	6
				G44	Waits (CB) Approaches (DW)	7.1 10.5	21

However, as we see from Fig. 3, though looking away increases sharply in most cases just before the close salutation, thereafter looking at increases even more sharply. Almost everyone is looking directly at the other as he begins the close salutation. There is thus a reduction in withdrawal tendencies in the final phase of the greeting. This reduction, it is now suggested, may be brought about by the gaze aversion we have described. The very performance of an act of withdrawal may serve to decrease the tendency to withdraw.

Aversion of gaze may have the effect of facilitating further approach for two reasons, neither of which excludes the other. On the one hand, by looking away from q, p sharply reduces stimulus input from him, and this may reduce his tendency to withdraw because it reduces the very input that is inducing that tendency. The aversion of gaze just prior to the close salutation thus could function as a "cut off" in the sense intended by Chance (1962). At the same time, of course, for p to avert his gaze from q as he gets closer to him, may make it easier for q to remain where he is. This could come about because q's tendency to remain is likely to increase with any manifestation by p of his tendency to withdraw. A look directed at another is also, in many circumstances, a threat, and this, in another who is physically approaching q, might either frighten q away or provoke him to attack. If, as he approaches him, p averts his gaze, either of these agonistic tendencies in q will be reduced.

(b)   Behaviour during approach: the "Body Cross"

In several of our examples, at about that point in the approach where we see the sharp aversion of gaze, one of the members of the greeting transaction may be observed to bring one or both of his arms in front of him, "crossing" the upper part of the body. This may be done momentarily, or this arm position may be sustained, persisting either until the close salutation or, in some instances, persisting right through it. It may take a variety of forms. Either one arm may be moved across the mid-line of the body, or in some examples, both arms are brought into play, the hands being clasped together in front. In other instances an object the individual is carrying may be raised up in front. In still other instances, which we have counted as examples, the hand is raised to the mouth or it is raised to grasp the neck. The body cross may be seen in Figs. 4 and 6.

In all of our examples, the body cross occurs in only one of the greeting partners. The one who does it is either the younger of the pair or he is entering a territory from the outside - as in the case of a guest entering the site of a party - or he is the one who covers the most distance in his approach. Of the three instances in which a body cross occurs when the greeting is between a male and a female, it is the female who body crosses in each case. Only two of our eighteen instances of body crosses occur in greetings between people of apparently the same age on what may be regarded as "neutral" territory.

This survey of the circumstances in which the body-cross occurs in our sample of greetings, suggests that it is likely to occur in the partner to the greeting transaction who may be expected to have the stronger tendency to withdraw. It seems to occur, in a word, in the more vulnerable of the two participants. It is tempting to describe it as a protective movement, and indeed a body cross may be observed as part of a pattern of rapid withdrawal, when an individual is confronted with a sudden and apparently dangerous situation.[11]

In all the instances of the body cross in our examples, the body cross is a very casual, unformalised movement. Nevertheless, we can still ask if it has any communicative function. From the data available to us, we cannot decide this question. We may suppose, however, that like the aversion of gaze we have already discussed, it may betoken non-aggressive intent, and so it may facilitate further approach. From the point of view of p, we may suppose that a protective move on his part may enhance his ability to approach more closely, for he is safer from an aggression that might occur. On the other hand, a protective display by p may be reassuring to q. For p to protect himself mildly as he approaches q may signal to q that p perceives him as powerful. Thus the body cross could be a signal of subordination to q and, like withdrawal of gaze, reduce the degree to which p may appear threatening. p's own tendencies to withdraw could thus thereby be reduced.

(c) Behaviour during the approach: Grooming

Another action that may be observed during the approach is the "groom". We counted as a groom any instances where p adjusts his clothing - straightening a sweater or a tie, for example; where he strokes or smooths his hair; scratches his head; pats himself or appears to brush something off himself; or rubs any part of his face. Such actions are typically unformalised, brief, and they are performed quite incidentally to the main flow of behaviour.

In greeting sequences a groom is observed most commonly either just before or just after the distance salutation, or just before the close salutation. It may also be observed just before an individual is to leave a gathering, or just after he has left and after the parting

ceremony is over. There are other circumstances in which grooming
is observed besides these, of course, but these are the ones most
pertinent to this paper.

In the birthday party material relatively little grooming was observed. It seems to be characteristic of only a few individuals and
each of them has a characteristic style of grooming. Thus CB usually
strokes his beard, drawing the palm of the hand downwards towards the
tip. He may be observed doing this repeatedly just prior to an engage-
ment in interaction at close range. RC was observed either to touch
the right side of her glasses or she would place the tips of the fingers
of her right hand on the left side of her head, and draw the hand over
her hair, in an apparent hair adjustment movement. HA would either
pull down the sweater he was wearing, or he would run the fingers of
his right hand through the long lock of hair than hangs over his forehead. DF's groom consisted in a brief patting of the buttocks.

In other material much more grooming has been observed. Thus,
a study of grroming was made using the TRD Band film. This is a film
of a gathering of about seventy adolescents who are milling around in a
parking lot prior to a practice of their high school band. Conversational knots constantly form and break apart. During the first twenty minutes of the film over one hundred separate instances of grooming were
recorded, and their occurrence was classified according to whether the
groom occurred during interaction, just before it or as it was beginning,
just after it or as it was ending, or when the individual was alone. It
was found that seventy percent of the grooms observed occurred with
the onset or offset of interaction, while only ten percent were observed
in individuals who were alone. A fuller account of grooming will be
published elsewhere. Preliminary findings suggest, however, that it

will be commonly observed where an individual is changing his involvement with others, as he is moving into interaction with another, or as he is moving out of interaction with him.

Whereas most of the examples of grooming we have observed are unformalised in character, formalised grooming does exist. One relatively well known form may be seen in females, where it seems to be part of the system of flirting gestures. Here, the head is tilted to one side and, at the same time, the hand moves down the side of hair and it is so turned that the palm of the hand is oriented toward the person being addressed. In its full fledged form it is accompanied by the eyebrow-flash and smile display, and also, if the individual is standing, by a sway of the hips. Fragments of this display are not uncommon. It has been described by Scheflen (1964) as part of what he calls "quasi-courtship", where he indicates that it has the function of heightening the attention of individuals to one another. Self-grooming has also been incorporated into the close salutational ritual in a few cultures. Among the Ainu of Northern Japan, the traditional formal close salutation is reported to include stroking the beard and arms or, with women, smoothing locks of hair away from the forehead. (Hitchcock 1889-1890; Batchelor 1927.) In Tibet, the salutation by which an individual of low station addresses someone of high station is reported to include opening the mouth and protruding the tongue, bowing forward slightly and scratching the back of the head (Tsybikov 1919, Bell 1946).

5.   The Final Approach

We noted, in the discussion of gaze during approach, that as the partners got closer to one another, they were increasingly likely to look away but that this aversion of gaze was highly likely to be followed by a

phase in which each looked at the other. This phase immediately precedes the start of the close salutation. It generally begins when the
greeters are within ten feet of one another, or less. It also appears to
have certain distinctive behaviours associated with it, which are less
likely to occur at earlier stages of the transaction. Thus vocalisation
is most likely to occur here. A distinctive facial display appears - almost always a smile in our data - and the greeters assume a set of the
head that is distinct from the headsets they have adopted during earlier
phases of the transaction. Finally, we have sometimes observed a distinct gesture in one of the hands, in which the palm of the hand is oriented toward the other. This gesture may precede or it may be combined
with the movements associated with getting ready for the close ritual.
These phenomena will now be discussed in more detail.

(a)   Smiling.   The quality of the films available to us did not permit
a fine-grained analysis of facial displays. However, it did prove possible to distinguish "smiling face" from "non-smiling face". Within the
category of "smiling face", furthermore, we could distinguish "broad
smiles" from other smiles on the basis of whether or not the teeth were
could be seen.

Smiling, as we have seen, is commonly associated with the distance salutation. Thereafter, however, the smile either rapidly fades
in intensity, or even disappears altogether, until the participants are
close to one another and once again are looking at one another. In
some cases, to be sure, a smile could be clearly seen throughout the
approach. This was the pattern observed in the hostess when she was
greeting guests as they entered the site of the party. Very often, however, a definite smile could not be distinguishable again until the final
approach phase. In this phase, however, a smile was very common.

Of the seventy separate observations of faces that were possible in this phase of the greeting transaction, only eight showed no smiling.

The distribution of smiles with teeth as compared to smiles without teeth is presented in Table III. It will be seen that smiles with teeth ("broad smiles") were overall more frequent than smiles without teeth; males were somewhat less likely to show a smile with teeth than were females; smiling with teeth appears less often in greetings between family members than in greetings between friends and acquaintances. Thus, in the forty-three greetings in which the record was such that some smiling could be observed, twelve of these were between members of the same (extended) family, thirty-one between friends and acquaintances. In only one of the twelve family greetings was smiling with teeth observed in any party to the greeting, in contrast to twenty instances out of the thirty-one non-family greetings observed.

The only definite conclusion that seems to be warranted by these data is that smiling is a common feature of the greeting ritual. The distribution of the different types of smiling we have reported, however, do suggest that there will be much more to be said about smiling in greeting if a special effort is being made to study it.

(b) Headset. In the final approach phase, the greeters not only look at one another and smile, but as they do so they are likely to hold their head in a way that is distinct from the way they have been holding it at earlier phases of the approach.

The head positions of greeters in the final approach were classified into five categories: erect head, head tilted forward, head tilted back, head cocked to one side, and head held erect or forward, but with neck extended forward. Out of a total of eighty-three observations in the birthday party film, the forward position was observed

Table III.   Observed Smiling in the Final Phase of the Approach for
Forty-three Greetings in Birthday Party Film

	p's members of same family	p's not members of same family
No. showing tooth smiles	1	20
No. showing no-tooth smiles	11	11

thirty-five times while the cocked to one side position was observed twenty times. It was further noted that eighteen of those cocked to one side positions were performed by females, whereas twenty-seven of the forward positions were performed by males. Of the twenty-four females observed, nine adopted headcock at least once, in contrast to the nineteen males observed, of whom only two adopted headcock in the final approach. It is our impression that this apparent tendency for females to adopt headcock in the final approach, in contrast to the male's erect or forward head position appears to be more obvious in male-female greetings. Perhaps head erect or forward and headcock are kinesic gender markers of males and females, respectively. Head forward may be seen in Fig. 9a. Headcock may be seen in Figs. 4 and 6.

(c)   The "palm presentation". A gesture in which the palm of the hand is oriented toward the other, often with the arm extended forward or laterally, may sometimes be observed, either in association with a distance salutation or, more often, just before p prepares for the close salutation. This gesture will be referred to as the "palm presentation".

Seventeen instances of it have been seen in our present material. It may appear in a conspicuous and well developed form, though in most of the examples in our corpus it has a more fleeting character. It is also of interest to note that it may occur in quite small children. Two of our examples, one of them a very clear one, were enacted by five-year olds.

The palm presentation as a gesture of greeting has been recognised by Eibl-Eibesfeldt (1970) who reports that it occurs in greetings in many different parts of the world. The orientation of the palm to another has also been described by Scheflen (1964) in so-called "quasi-courtship" displays which, according to him, function to heighten the attention of one individual upon another. When the gesture is performed, p is at the same time face oriented to (or "looking at") the other. It is thus addressed to another. It is also associated with an increase in the closeness of interaction. It may thus be reasonably supposed that the palm presentation is a signal of openness to social contact - it may be seen perhaps both as a signal of p's intentions and also, at the same time, as a signal to q serving to invite further approach from him. Palm presentation is illustrated in Fig. 9.

6.   The Close Salutation

The close salutation may be regarded as the culmination of the greeting transaction. Up till now, the participants have been reducing the distance between them. Eventually they stop doing this. They stand, often face to face, generally at a distance of five feet or less, [12] and engage in a highly formalised unit of interaction, usually recognisable as a handshake, an embrace, or some other well known category of greeting ritual. It is this ritual which is usually thought of as the

greeting ceremony. Insofar as greetings have been described by other
writers, it is generally this part of the transaction that has been described. Most of what we have considered in this paper so far can be
regarded as having the function of preparing a context in which this close
ritual may be performed.

Regardless of the actual form of the ritual, there are certain
characteristics that are associated with all the close salutations we have
observed. First, both partners to the greeting come to a halt as they
perform the salutation. Sometimes this halt is very brief, and key elements of the close salutation may be begun before it starts, or continued
after one or both of the participants have begun to move again. But coming to a halt is always observed. Secondly, the participants, in coming
to a halt, tend to face the ventral surfaces of their bodies toward one
another, and each typically orients his face directly at the face of the
other. Close salutations are not, as a rule, performed when the individuals are standing side-by-side, both facing the same way, nor are
they performed when the individuals are standing so that the angle of
their bodies to one another in the horizontal plane is a right angle (such
right angle arrangements are commonly adopted in conversations).
Thirdly, the position and orientation associated with the close salutation is not maintained after it is over. Both participants move away
from the spot at which they came to a halt during the salutation, and
both participants alter their orientation to one another. In many cases
this is a large and obvious change - having shaken hands, the guest and
hostess walk together to the centre of the party, or the two greeters
move into the room and sit down. In other cases the change may be
slight as when, following the close salutation, the two stand and talk,
close to the location of their greeting. But even here the participants

change their orientation and location in relation to one another, even if
they do this by merely moving the position of a foot, or by shifting the
distribution of weight in the body.

Since such a postural and positional change can always be observed
in association with the end of the gestures of salutation, and since following upon it some distinct kind of interaction is to be observed, we
have taken this change as the point at which the close salutation may be
said to be over. This is also the point at which, in the present paper,
we bring our analysis of the greeting transaction to a close.

There are many variations to be observed in the form of the close
salutation. Here we shall describe what has been observed in our birthday party corpus under three main headings: close salutation which involves no body contact; handshakes; and kisses and embraces.

(a)   Close Salutation Without Body Contact.   In some examples, the
participants approach one another and stop, facing one another but,
apart from speaking, do not appear to engage in any behaviour distinctive of salutation.

> Thus in G10, JF waits at the bottom of the brick walkway as
> DG, bringing up the rear of a group of four children, approaches
> down the walkway. When this group of guests is about twelve
> feet away, JF calls a greeting to each of them, (a "hi" followed
> by the name) and then takes two steps backwards. The children
> come to a halt in front of her, as does DG. JF's face is
> oriented down and forward - she is apparently looking at the
> children. The children are looking either to their left or to
> their right. DG also looks down, apparently at the children,
> talking meanwhile. JF then turns and begins to tell them
> where to go as they go into the party, and they walk forward
> onto the lawn. Though both JF and DG stop in a face-to-face
> orientation, an orientation distinctive of greeting, no clearly
> distinguishable gestures of salutation can be observed. All

the gestures of salutation -greeting calls by JF, and a smiling response from DG - were completed before the greeting parties stopped, facing one another.

More usually, in the non-contact close salutations we have observed, the greeters come to a halt in front of one another and simply sustain the head-eye orientation, the headset and the facial display they had already assumed when they were a few feet away from one another.

> This is seen in GW1, for example, where a girl crosses from some distance away to greet someone who is standing still. Here, as the girl approaches, she cocks her head on one side. She then stops within two feet of the person she is greeting, who holds her head erect. As the approaching girl comes to a halt, the other turns, so that she is now oriented at approximately right angles to the other (Fig. 4).

In this instance, stopping in the "salutational frame" (which here was only momentary) was not itself marked by any distinctive gestures. Sometimes, however, the participants do not assume the head orientations, head sets and facial display characteristic of the close phase of a greeting, until they enter the salutational frame.

> This is exemplified in G44, where CB is approached by DW from a distance of about twenty feet after an initial distance salutation. During most of the approach DW looks at CB, while CB looks down and to the side. However, when DW is within five feet of CB, CB orients his face to him. As he does so, DW stops moving and cocks his head to one side. At the same time CB steps sideways in such a way as to bring his body more fully into a frontal orientation to DW. As he does so, his smile broadens, and he pronates his right forearm in what appears to be the beginnings of a palm presentation. (Fig. 5).

These examples are, perhaps, the most typical of the non-contact close salutations we have observed. Sometimes, however, gestures distinctive of the close salutational frame itself occur.

(a) p̲ sights q̲

<u>Fig. 4.</u>   <u>Tracings from stills from</u>
<u>film of GW1</u>

(b) p̲ showing head toss display in distance salutation. Note the raised eyebrows and the open mouth smile.

(c) Head-dip following distance salutation.
Note the eyes are now shut.

(d) p̲ is now closer to q̲ and is looking
at her. Note that p̲ has her head tilted
to one side, an example of one of the
"head-sets" characteristic of the final
phase of a greeting encounter.

(e) Following the salutation p̲ and q̲ move
out of their vis-a-vis orientation into one
in which their bodies are set more nearly
at 90°. Note that p̲ has her arm across
the front of her body, illustrating "body-
cross".

Thus in G18, MR headtosses three times to HS as HS bends forward at the trunk in a slight bow and then raises the cup he is
holding as if to offer a toast to MR. He then nods three times.
During this gestural exchange, MR is saying "Hi, I remember
I met you at Jane's party" - HS probably makes some verbal
reply here, but this cannot be heard. Likewise, in G6 SK
head tosses twice to AF while AF stands before her with a
slight headcock.

In these two examples, it will be noted, one member of the
pair engages in repeated headtosses, while the other engages with nods
or bows or with a headcock. Observations made outside the present
corpus, without the aid of films suggest that this is the typical pattern.
We saw earlier, in the account of the distance salutations, that the
headtoss is characteristically reciprocated with a head lower or head
nod. The same seems to be true of the non-contact close salutations
we have observed in which a gesture distinctive of the salutational
frame occurs.

b)   Handshakes.   In the handshake each extends, typically, his
right hand to grasp that of the other and the joined hands are then
squeezed or moved up and down one or more times. A common form
in our corpus was for the hands to be raised and lowered three times,
the first stroke of the handshake having much greater amplitude than
those that follow. Just before the head disengages there is a brief
pause in the movement. In some instances, however, much more prolonged shaking occurred. As is well known, handshakes also vary in
the strength of the grip. The handshake may also vary in that additional gestures may be associated with it. In our corpus we have observed
it associated with head nodding (G3), with a marked forward tilt of the
head combined with a head-cock, or with a kiss. The handshake combined with a kiss is quite common, but occurs only between males and

Fig. 5　Tracings from a sequence of stills from film of G44.
(Figure on left is CB, figure on right is DW.)

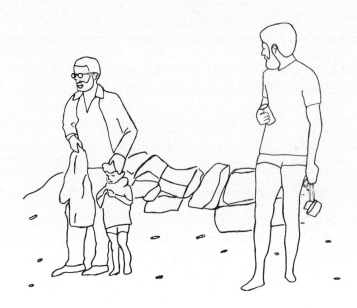

(a)　DW orients face to CB

(b)　CB looks back at DW　　　　(c)　DW lifts head in "headtoss"
　　　　　　　　　　　　　　　　　for a distance salutation

(d) DW begins his approach. Note his dipped head. CB has also turned his face away from DW.

(e) CB and DW look at each other. DW stops approaching and sets head on one side.

(f) CB walks forward and turns to face DW.

(g) After the close salutation CB stepped back to his previous location and DW has come closer to him. They now stand with their bodies at approximately 90° to one another, a common arrangement for pairs of individuals as they stand and talk.

and females, and generally speaking it is the female who offers her cheek which the male then touches with his lips. Where the handshake is combined with a head nod or forward cock lower (as in G62), it seems to be performed by only one of the pair, not both. Another form of the handshake is when it is combined with a partial embrace. Here one member of the (usually male) pair, places his hand upon the shoulder of the other. Finally, another form may be mentioned, in which one of the greeters takes the other's hand with both hands grasping with his right hand in the usual way, bringing his other hand to cover the back of the other's hand that he is grasping.

(c) Embraces. In our present corpus, seven instances of cheek kissing occurred, all except one of them in association with an embrace. In six instances this form of close salutation occurred between males and females, in one instance it occurred within an all female greeting.

The performance of the embrace is subject to some variation. We may note here what we have observed. In all the embraces between males and females, with one exception, the male's arms are lifted outwards, and placed around the female. The female lifts her arms and places her hands against the male's chest or waist, or she may slide her forearms under the male's arms to place her hands on his back. In the exceptional case (G22, JF/WF), JF placed her hands on WF's shoulders, but WF, instead of encircling JF with his arms, placed the palms of his hands under JF's chin. This gesture, it may be noted, is the close salutational gesture used by JF in greeting children. In this instance in some respects JF stands in relation to WF as a child, since she is his daughter-in-law.

In two instances of male/female embraces, the embrace had a two-phasic form. In the first phase, associated with a kiss by the male on the female's proffered cheek, the female placed her hands against the sides of the male's thorax. In the second phase, the hands of both greeters were placed on the other's back - each thus encircles the other with their arms, and they pulled each to the other in a hug, cheeks in contact.

(d)   Distribution of the Main Close Salutational Forms in the Corpus. The fifty-six instances of close salutation examined were divided into non-contact forms, handshakes and embraces. The distribution of the forms so classified in relation to the sexes of the participants is given in Table IV. The figures suggest the following:

The most frequent forms of close salutation between males is the hand-shake, whereas between females the no-contact forms prevail. With cross-sex pairs, however, the frequencies of handshakes vs. no-contact forms is about equal. Though the figures of the present sample are small, this distribution is of interest because it exactly follows what would be expected on the basis of what is recommended as correct practice in leading North American etiquette manuals. Thus Emily Post (Post 1965), McCall's (Bevans 1960) and Vogue's (Fenwick 1948) eti-

Table IV.   Occurrence of Close Salutations of Different Types According to the Sex of the Participants

Type of CS	Male-Male	Male-Female	Female-Female
No contact	1	9	11
Handshake	10	7	2
Embrace	3	10	3

quette manuals are all agreed that men shake hands with men, but that women do not do so as a rule though "there is no reason why they shouldn't." Between men and women it is, according to these works, up to the woman to decide whether to shake hands or not, and thus the man should not offer his hand unless she offers hers first. In our corpus this is found to be the case. It seems unlikely that this distribution of close salutational forms has come about because the people observed in the corpus have studied etiquette manuals. Rather, it suggests that these manuals are accurate guides to what is, in fact, common practice.

As for the embraces and kisses, nine of the fifteen embraces occurred in male-female greetings, three occurred between females, and three between males. In these instances, one was between father and son (G 33, AF/WF) and one between brothers-in-law (G30, HA/HF). It should be noted that HA is Mexican, and Mexicans are said to follow the common Latin practice of mutual embrace combined with back patting. This is exactly the form the close salutation in G30 takes. AF here, probably, is accommodating to HA's style.

The data we have discussed in this section are too scant for any firm conclusions, yet they are suggestive. In a later paper a much more detailed study of the close salutation will be reported, where we shall attend not only to the distribution of the various forms, but in particular, to details as to how they are performed. In this way we hope to gain insight into how personal relationships are stated in the enactment of the form of the greeting itself.

Fig. 6. Tracings from a sequence of stills from film of G2.

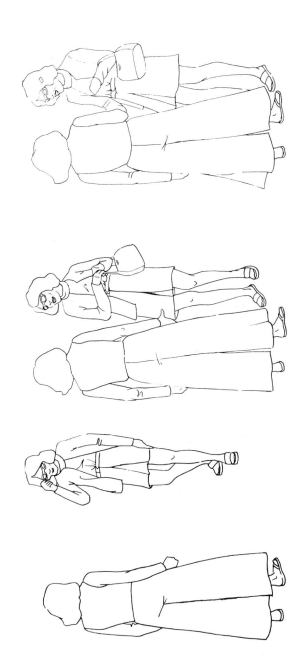

(a) guest is approaching hostess. Hostess stands and faces guest as she approaches. Note guest is touching her hair ("groom") and has her head tilted forward.

(b) just before guest offers her hand for the handshake. Note that her head is on one side and her right arm is held across her body in a "body cross".

(c) hostess and guest shake hands

Fig. 7.   Tracings from a sequence of stills from film of G60.
(a) MG (on left) in conversation with hostess. DG (on right)
looks at him. (b) MG offers a head-toss salutation to DG.
(c) DG responds to MG's head-toss with a head-lower and
a raised hand with an open palm. (d) MG and DG shake
hands (e). (e) MG and DG step back. Note their symmetry
in the handshake and in the postures they assume afterward.

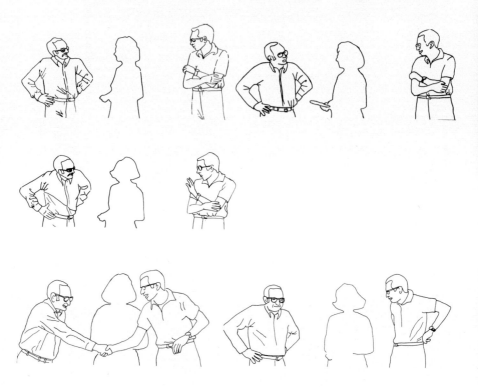

Fig. 8.　Tracing to show the horizontal rotation of the head characteristic of the exaggerated turning away of the face that often occurs just before the greeters are close enough to begin the close salutation. From the Wedding film.

Fig. 9   Examples of palm presentation.

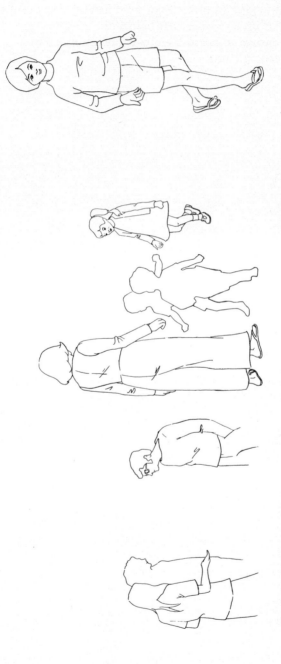

(a) JS (left) turns to AF (right as AF approaches. Note JS's hand extended toward AF with palm uppermost. AF shows head forward on neck, one of the headsets observed in the final phase of greeting interaction.

(b) A six year old girl approaching the hostess. Note how her right hand is open with palm oriented toward hostess.

(c) A well developed example of palm presentation in a five year old boy. Reconstructed from two views of KC in G2, from the Birthday Party film.

CONCLUSION: THE STUDY OF GREETINGS AND
THE DEVELOPMENT OF HUMAN ETHOLOGY

Human ethology may be understood as a study of human behaviour in which an attempt is made to throw light upon its evolutionary
history. Such a study has to begin with a close analysis of what human
behaviour presently consists in. This means that the first task of a
human ethologist, like that of an ethologist who sets out to study a bird
or a fish or a monkey, must be systematic description. He must set
out to see what behavioural structures the human being has, and how
these structures are related to his mode of life. In doing this with
people it would seem best to begin with those aspects of behaviour which
are most likely to be shared with other animals, for a comparison of
human behaviour with the behaviour of related species will be an essential step in this enquiry. Thus while detailed analyses of language, or
of perceptual and conceptual processes must eventually find a place in
a human ethology, these do not seem to be the best aspects of human
behaviour with which to start. Likewise, the more complex aspects of
human social behaviour, such as the development of a self-image,
mechanisms of leadership, the formation of attitudes, and all the other
common topics of social psychology, are not appropriate aspects of
behaviour for a human ethologist to study. He must look for something
more elementary. This is why the close analysis of communication
conduct seems to offer so rich a vein. Since it is in his behaviour in
his immediate relationship to others that we most easily recognise
similarities between human and animal behaviour, it is here that an
effective start on a human ethology may be possible.

The foregoing descriptive analysis of some human greetings

may be understood as a contribution to this initial phase of human ethology. It is limited in many ways. There are many aspects of the behaviour we have had to leave undescribed. We have been severely
limited by the sample we have had available so that we have not been
able to explore properly the contextual distributions of the various elements we have described. This has meant we have had to be extremely
cautious in making statements about the signal function of these elements.
Nevertheless it is hoped that the detail we have provided, and the format within which this detail has been set, will offer a guide to those who
would follow with more rigorous observational and experimental studies.

In the analysis presented in this paper, we have drawn a distinction between the structure of the greeting as an interpersonal transaction, and the specific gestures and other actions that comprise its
various stages. We suggest that the greeting transaction could be seen
as a unit having certain general features, even though the salutational
gestures might be different from greeting to greeting. Thus we suggested that greetings would have a pre-phase of sighting and announcement,
a distance salutation, an approach phase and a close salutation; that the
close salutation has a distinct location, and the participants as they engage in it orient themselves to each other in a way that is distinctive.
Each of these components of the greeting transaction can be thought of
as a spot in a programme where one of a number of different actions
can be performed. We expect that for each of these spots there will be
a restricted class of actions that will be "selected" from. Thus the
kinds of actions that will be observed in the distance salutation will
comprise a rather different set from those that will be observed during
the approach phase, and different again from those that will be observed
in the close salutation.

From the point of view of an ethological study of greetings, the question of the diversity of salutational forms is one that must soon be faced. One may gather from reading such writers as Roth (1889) or LaBarre (1964) that the forms of salutation are very diverse indeed. Yet, as Eibl-Eibesfeldt has shown, the display that we have here described as the head-toss display, appears to be universal to man. If the programmatic structure of greeting transactions is borne in mind, however, this seeming conflict is clarified, for it will be seen that whereas Eibl-Eibesfeldt has confined his observations to what we would call the distance salutation, such writers as Roth and LaBarre have collected together descriptions of close salutational rituals.

It would seem from what we have just said, that the range of gestures or other actions that occur in the greeting transaction is greater at some spots in the programme than it is in others. Thus it appears that the range of variation in close salutational rituals may often be greater than is the range for distance salutations. This could well be due to the difference in function that these two steps in the greeting programme have. Thus whereas the distance salutation often seems to function merely to establish that the two greeters have seen one another and that they are now ratified in a greeting relationship, the close salutation would seem to have several additional functions. These have to do with establishing or reaffirming the kind of relationship that the two greeters have to one another, both in reference to all the different situations in which they may meet, and in reference to the specific situation in which the greeting is taking place. Thus in the close salutation, we may expect that such aspects as relative dominance, friendliness, familiarity, and identity will be signalled. It would seem reasonable, therefore, that there should be greater variation in close salutational gestures than those of the distance salutation.

Even within a single culture, or indeed within a small sample from a single culture such as the one we have examined in this paper, we will encounter a good deal of variation in the kinds of greeting transactions performed. In understanding this variation we shall have to consider not only whether the greeters are friends, relatives or strangers; whether they are males or females; whether they differ greatly in social status; but also with in what occasion the greeting occurs, and how long ago it was that the participants last met, if they have met before.

It is further to be noted that not only may the greeting transactions vary in what salutation or other actions are performed at any given spot in the programme, but they will also vary in how much of the programme is performed. Some transactions will include only a distance salutation. Others may include only a distance salutation and an approach. A few instances of this occurred in the Birthday Party where individuals were greeting one another for a second time. Mutual sighting would occur, followed by a distance exchange, followed by an approach in which the individuals moved directly into a formation in which conversation can take place. It will also be seen that for a given situation, how many of the stages of the greeting programme are enacted will depend upon the kind of relationship that exists between the greeters. There are some with whom a mere distance exchange is all that is needed. There are others with whom one must engage in close salutation in addition. But again, this is related to the situation. For a given kind of relationship, there are situations in which all of the steps of the programme will be appropriate, but others in which only some of them will be necessary. In situations where close interaction is to follow, for example, it appears that upon an initial encounter (i.e., the first time the two individuals encounter one another within the context of a given occasion) both a distance and a close exchange of salutation will occur. Upon subsequent encounters only a distance salutation is necessary. In some contexts where repeated encounters between the individuals are likely, all that is left of the greeting is the approach, and salutations appear to be omitted altogether.

Thus we see that which parts of the programme are enacted is a function both of the situation that is prevailing, and also of the relationship that prevails between the greeters. It will be seen that insofar as p can decide how much of the programme to enact, he can take an initiative in defining the situation or the relationship between the participants.

Another question is: how can we account for the forms of action that do occur in the greeting? We might ask, for instance, why do we see the eyebrow flash and head-toss display in the distance salutation? Or we could ask about the origin of the palm presentation, the handshake, or any of the other forms.

To deal with this sort of question, three kinds of inquiry seem to be necessary. First, we must have a thorough understanding of the contextual distributions of the various forms. We need to know (a) at what stage in the greeting programme the form is observed, (b) in what greeting situations the given form is observed, and (c) between what categories of person the given form is observed. Answers to these questions would enable us to infer much about the function of the given form in the greeting transaction. Second, we need to know, for a given form whether it can be observed in other contexts besides that of greeting. If it can be observed in other contexts, is it different in any way, or is it clearly the same element in every respect? Third, we need to know its developmental history.

In this way, we may be able to see how a formalised action in the greeting has arisen from some unformalised form, such as an intention movement of contact, or of withdrawal, or of attack. With some elements, such as the smile, it will be found that it appears in the human being as a formalised display from the very first. In this case we would have to resort to comparisons between the various species of primates to understand its derivation (Van Hooff 1972). Some of the other elements of greeting, however, appear to be only partly formalised in some cultures but not in others. Thus in the Ainu salutation, in which the participants stroke their own beards, we can entertain the hypothesis that the Ainu salutation is a formalised version of this action since we have noted that self-grooming in an unformalised form occurs in many greetings in so divergent culture as our own. Why this element should have become formalised among the Ainu, and not among other peoples, is yet another kind of question. An answer to it will be suggested from an understanding of the place of this form of salutation in Ainu life, and also from an understanding of the nature of Ainu life as compared with life in other cultures. Needless to say, we are very far from such understandings.

These then, represent some of the further ways in which the human greeting may be investigated. A further step in the development of an ethology of greetings will be the comparison of the behaviour of greetings in man with those observed in closely related species. As Jane Van Lawick-Goodall (1968) has shown, there are patterns of behaviour in the chimpanzee that may reasonably be described as greetings, and there appears to be considerable overlap in the forms assumed by

the actions that comprise these greetings. Until we know far more
about the nature of human greetings and of those of the chimpanzee and
other primates, little can be concluded beyond the rather general point
that much in human greeting behaviour appears to be phylogenetically
quite ancient.

NOTES

[1]Adam Kendon is a Research Scientist associated with the Project on
Human Communication and Andrew Ferber is Director of the Family
Studies Section at Bronx State Hospital. Much of the detailed analysis
and all of the writing was done by Kendon, but the collection of the
material and essential formative discussion and analysis was done
collaboratively. We are both very grateful to the Director of Bronx
State Hospital, Dr. Israel Zwerling, for granting facilities for this
research. Kendon is deeply grateful to Dr. A. E. Scheflen, Director
of the Project on Human Communication, for giving him the freedom
necessary for doing this research. Both of us are also indebted to Dr.
Schefl n for his constant encouragement and for many stimulating discussions. For financial support we would like to thank Ralph Freedman,
Emory Kleiman and Mike Chernow for much needed grants-in-aid. We
are also both indebted to the State of New York Department of Mental
Hygiene and to the National Institutes Health Grant No. 15977-03. Some
of the film analysis equipment was bought with funds from the Van
Amerigen Foundation grant to the Project on Human Communication,
and we are much indebted for this. Mrs. Adele Herman and Mr. John
Schoonbeck have been invaluable as research assistants. We would
like to express our deep appreciation to all those who appear in the
films we have studied, and who gave their permission for this. We are
particularly grateful to Jane Ferber who made possible the filming of
the Birthday Party.

[2]One of us (A. K.) has begun a study of the forms of salutation used in
different parts of the world in collaboration with J. M. Roberts of
Pittsburgh.

[3]These films were made under the technical supervision of Jacques
Van Vlack of Eastern Pennsylvania Psychiatric Institute. We are

very much indebted to him, both for his supervision of the productions, and also for making available some of the facilities and equipment of the Studies in Human Communication Division of Eastern Pennsylvania Psychiatric Institute. We would also like to thank Paul Byers and Joseph Schaeffer of Columbia University, and Sander Kirsch, for acting as cameramen. We are also indebted to Ronald Goodrich and John Frikor for their assistance with filming for the Wedding Film.

[4]Throughout this paper p will be used to designate the individual whose behaviour is being discussed, and q will be used to designate the person he is in interaction with.

[5]Behaviour may be said to be "formalised" when it becomes stereotyped in form, conspicuous, sharply differentiated from other actions, and when it is explicitly addressed to another. Where it is known that the action in question has become formalised through natural selection, the term "ritualised" may be used. Where it is known that the action in question has become formalised through tradition or habit, the term "conventionalised" may be used. We have used the term "formalised" throughout this paper since we do not commit ourselves as to which processes have been involved in the evolution of the behavioural forms we discuss. We are indebted to W. John Smith (unpublished material) for these terms.

[6]The distance within which individuals can sustain interaction by means of utterances which use interpersonal levels of voice projection (in contrast to public voice projection levels, or private levels - as in talking to oneself) will be referred to as the close interaction distance. It varies according to the situation and the kind of interaction taking place, but is probably rarely greater than ten feet; c.f. Hall's (1966) treatment of interpersonal distance and its relationship to interaction.

[7]The host may also move to the edge of his territory to deal with intruders, of course, and how far he moves will be related to how threatening he perceives the intruders to be.

[8]The display we have described here appears to be identical with that described by Eibl-Eibesfeldt (1968, 1970) in which the eyebrows are raised and lowered rapidly, together with a smile, commonly enough, and also a little toss of the head. According to Eibl-Eibesfeldt this display can be found to occur among people from very diverse parts of the world.

[9]To dip the head is effectively to cut visual input from the surrounding environment, except for the terrain immediately in front of one's feet. It is possible that this momentary cut-off of environment input is associated with those internal processes by which an individual re-programmes himself for the next unit of action, whatever this may be. In studies of changes in gaze direction in conversation, it was found that a conversationalist would look away from his partner, usually down, either just before beginning a long utterance or during hesitations in speech which, on other grounds, are supposed to reflect periods of planning in speech (Kendon 1967).

[10]For both individuals to approach one another from a distance and sustain mutual gaze throughout is rare. When it happens we would probably say the relationship is very intense. The one instance in which we do see mutual face orientation over the whole length of the approach is in a greeting between JF and her two year old daughter.

[11]For example, in a film in our collection, a couple may be seen seating themselves on a grassy hillock in Central Park in New York City. Just as the girl was settling, a pack of large dogs charged by, very close. As they did so, she drew up her legs, bent her body forward, and crossed her body with her arms. In the same film, a girl is seen walking down some steps. As she does so she stumbles and, as she stumbles (but does not fall), she crosses her body. In the birthday party film, a small boy charges up to a nine year old girl, his fists raised as if to box with her. As he approaches, she lifts her shoulders and bends them forward, at the same time crossing her arms in front of her.

[12]The distance between people in greeting referred to here is the distance as estimated from pelvis to pelvis.

REFERENCES

Argyle, M. and Dean, Janet (1965). Eye contact, distance and affilia-
    tion, Sociometry, 28, 289-304.

Batchelor, John. Ainu life and lore: echoes of a departing race.
    Kyobunkwan 1927 Tokyo.

Bevans, Margaret (1960). McCall's Book of Everyday Etiquette. Golden Press, New York.

Bell, C. A. (1946). Portrait of the Dalai Lama. Collins, London.

Blurton-Jones, N. G. and Leach, G.M. (1972). Behaviour of children and their mothers at separation and greeting. In Ethological studies of child behaviour (Blurton Jones, N.G. ed.). Cambridge University Press, Cambridge.

Callan, Hilary. (1970) Ethology and Society. Clarendon Press, Oxford.

Chance, M. R. A. (1962). An interpretation of some agonistic postures; the role of 'cut-off' acts and postures. Evolutionary Aspects of Animal Communication, Symp. Zool. Soc. Lond. 8, 71-89.

Eibl-Eibesfeldt, I. (1968). Zur Ethologie des menschlichen Grussverhaltens. I Beobachtungen an Balinesen, Papuas und Samoanern nebst Vergleichenden Bemerkungen. Z. Tierpsychol. 25, 727-744.

Eibl-Eibesfeldt, I. (1970). Ethology: The Biology of Behavior. Holt, Rinehart & Winston, New York.

Eibl-Eibesfeldt, I. (1972). Love and Hate: The Natural History of Behaviour Patterns. Methuen, London.

Fenwick, Millicent (1948). Vogue's Book of Etiquette. Simon & Schuster, New York.

Goffman, E. (1963). Behaviour in Public Places. The Free Press of Glencoe, New York.

Goffman, E. (1971). Relations in Public. Basic Books, New York.

Hitchcock, Romyn. (1890). The Ainos of Yezo, Japan. U.S. National Museum, Report 1889-90: 429-502.

Kendon, A. (1967). Some Functions of Gaze Direction in Social Interaction. Acta Psychologica, 26, 22-63.

Kendon, A. The role of visible behaviour in the organisation of social interaction. In "Social Communication and Movement" (M. Von Cranach & Ian Vine eds.). Academic Press, in press.

LaBarre, Weston, (1964). Paralinguistics, kinesics and cultural anthropology. In "Approaches to Semiotics" (T. Sebeok, A. S. Hayes and Mary C. Bateson eds.). Mouton & Co., The Hague.

Post, Elizabeth L. (1965). Emily Post's Etiquette: The Blue Book of Social Usage, 11th edition, Funk & Wagnalls Co. Inc., N.Y.

Roth, H. Ling (1889). On Salutations. J. Royal Anthropological Institute, Vol. 19, 164-181.

Sacks, Harvey. Unpublished lectures 1970. University of California at Irvine.

Schegloff, E. A. (1968). Sequencing in conversational openings. American Anthropologist, Vol. 70 (New Series) 1075-1095.

Sherzer, J. Greetings among the Cuna. Unpublished. University of Texas, Department of Anthropology.

Tsybikov, G. T. (1919). Buddist palomnik u sviatyn' tibeta. po dnevnikam, redennym v 1899-1902 gg. (A Buddist pilgrim to the holy places of Tibet; from diaries kept from 1899 to 1902). Petrograd, Russkoe Geograficheskoe Obschestvo 10. [Translation in Human Relations Area Files, Yale University, New Haven, Conn.]

Van Hooff, J. A. R. A. M. (1972). A comparative approach to the phylogeny of laughter and smiling. In "Non-verbal communication." (R. A. Hinde ed.). Cambridge University Press, Cambridge.

Van Lawick-Goodall, Jane (1968). A preliminary report on expressive movements and communication in the Gombe Stream chimpan-

zees. In "Primates: Studies in adaptation and variability"
(Phyllis Jay ed.). Holt, Rinehart & Winston, New York.

Vine, Ian, (1971). Judgement of Direction of Gaze: an interpretation
of discrepant results. Brit. J. Soc. Clin. psychol. 10, 320-331.

PRIMATE ETHOLOGY AND HUMAN SOCIAL BEHAVIOUR

M. J. Waterhouse and H. B. Waterhouse

Department of Sociology
University of Reading

The authors may be contacted at Newport College of Art and Design, Monmouthshire.

I. INTRODUCTION

The recent developments in primate fieldwork have led to speculation about the origins of human social groups and to attempts at the explanation of human behaviour. Although the research on monkeys and apes has been objective and of a high standard, the human comparisons have been largely based on personal experience and not on factual information. This type of work, however, is not new.

In the late nineteenth and early twentieth century, after the publication of Darwin's "The Origin of Species", a number of anthropologists, influenced by Darwin, used what little information there was available about the primates, based mainly on travellers' tales, to support their evolutionary models of human development. (Hayes, 1958). For example, Westermarck suggested that the origin of human society was to be found in the monogamous group. He backed up his supposition with evidence from various species, more specifically the gorilla, which was thought to live as pairs with their offspring. Later, Briffault (in Hayes, 1958) used the same species to prove the opposite, that the mother/offspring relationship was the basis of group life. His information was that the gorilla was polygamous, the male jealously guarding his females.

The gorilla was used yet again by Sigmund Freud to support his hypothesis about the origin of the incest taboo. Taking Darwin's idea of the "primal horde", dominated by a "violent and jealous father who keeps all the females for himself and drives away his sons as they grow up" (1950, 141), Freud suggests that one day the brothers, who had been driven out, banded together and killed their father. This type of thinking failed for two reasons: their work was not based on adequate field data and was purely speculative, and they are responsible for much of the scepticism found today amongst sociologists for evolutionary thought in the social sciences.

This is not the place to attempt a review of the many ethological studies of monkeys and apes which have been made since the 1950's. Recently stress has been laid on the variability of social behaviour between and within species. A number of field workers have used their data to make generalisations about man and the other primates. Washburn and De Vore (1961) compared and contrasted their study of baboons with the behaviour of man in "pre-agricultural society". They state that unlike the baboon man is territorial, defending boundaries against strangers. Reynolds (1966), on the other hand, argues that "the typical hunter-gatherer society evolved naturally out of an ape-like system of nomadism, open groups, wide recognition of relationships, sexual differences in temperament and exploratoriness, lack of territoriality....." (441). Inter group aggression and territoriality, he suggests, are the result of permanent settlement. Whereas such authors have made first-rate studies of their respective animals, they have not been able to use equivalent data about man.

A third group of writers has extrapolated from the primate field research to make models of "typical" monkey groups, "protohuman" and human groups. These range from speculations about the social relations of "proto-" man to explanations of human behaviour (Watson and Watson, 1969; Morris 1969). The data from field studies is so varied as to make it difficult to generalise about primate social organisation, and there is again little comparative data for Homo sapiens. Finally, models of "protohuman" life are untestable and therefore seem unfruitful except as pure speculation.

II. ETHOLOGY OF SMALL HUMAN GROUPS

Ethology has potential for the study of small human groups. In its painstaking observation, it allows for the objective description of recurring units of behaviour, and the analysis of the function and causation of these behaviours. As a comparative method it should lead to more valid cross-specific comparisons and contrasts, which may shed light on the evolution of human behaviour.

The observer of any species must have become completely familiarised with his subjects. Many primate field workers have suggested that their first contact with the group under observation caused temporary alteration to the behaviour of the animals. The subjects must therefore be given time to become acclimatized to the presence of the observer (Schaller, 1963). If this is so of non-human primates it is even more true of man. Fortunately children below the age of five quickly become used to the presence of an observer and if he does not encourage contacts they appear to forget him. It is therefore possible to sit in the same room as the subjects, or even to follow them while recording behaviour. It is for this reason that pre-school children are often used as subjects in Human Ethology. A useful method of recording behaviour has been found to be the handwritten commentary. This was used by Leach, who preferred it to "check-lists" because of flexibility, and also by Krebs and ourselves. Disadvantages of this method are that recording is slow, one is continually looking away from the subjects in order to write and analysis is more difficult. More sophisticated methods have been used by other workers. Reynolds and Guest (Pers. Comm.) tried time lapse cinematography but for their purposes preferred a running commentary. McGrew and McGrew (1970) have used check-lists of behavioural items and have recorded the location of subjects on floor plan sheets at regular intervals. McGrew (1969) used film, which allows more detailed analysis. (Unless stated, the above references are to unpublished material).

It is much more difficult to study adult humans for they are more conscious of their behaviour. Grant (1965) used a one way glass screen in order to observe without being seen by his adult subjects, who had however been told of his presence. Eibl-Eibesfeldt (1968), used mirror lenses in a cross-cultural study of human expressions to film people without their knowledge.

An extensive taxonomy of facial expressions has been published by Grant (1969). For example, the commonest expression in an aggressive situation is "aggressive frown", whereby the eyebrows are drawn together, and drawn down in the centre. "Upper smile", a smile showing top teeth, is the most common social smile and is used in greeting situations. A flight element is "mouth corners back", the corners of the mouth being drawn well back, but not lifted, with the lips together. Human greetings are being fully studied by Kendon (this volume). No analysis has been made of verbalisations, although Grant (1965) correlates commands with other non-verbal scores of dominance. Evidence has been put forward by Brannigan (this volume) and Eibl-Eibesfeldt (1968) which suggests that certain motor units may be innate. For instance, Eibl-Eibesfeldt (1968, p. 483) in a cross-cultural study, has stated that, "..... complex flirting behaviour can be reduced to a few variables that occur in human females of very different cultural backgrounds."

Another aspect of ethology is the description and analysis of social interactions. In our own research on pre-school age children (see appendix), we were not primarily interested in the motor units ex hibited _per se_ but rather in the distribution of these units. We were interested in the occurrences of a specific unit between individuals or between sex categories. From these a picture of the social organisati of the group could be drawn. For example, Grant, (1969) analyses "beat", a blow from open or closed hand, as an aggressive element. We wished to quantify the distribution of such a unit amongst the indi- viduals and to derive a pattern of dominance from it. Similarly, an element such as "upper smile" was used in scoring associative interac tions.

An early attempt to use ethology in the description of human social interaction was made by Grant (1965) on adult schizophrenic pa- tients in a Birmingham hospital. He was able to rank his subjects into a dominance hierarchy; this correlated with the giving of commands. The spatial arrangement of the individuals reflected their rank, the dominant three remaining close together and those less dominant stay- ing on the periphery. Evidence for dominance ranking was not as clea cut in other groups he studied at the hospital.

III. STUDIES OF NURSERY SCHOOL CHILDREN

Blurton Jones (Morris ed., 1967) studied London nursery scho children between 1963 and 1964 and found that, "........'dominance' s nothing useful or instructive about the social organisation of the class three- to five-year-olds I observed or of the groups within it". (351). By this he means that although some children regularly won fights, the were not leaders, and were not given priority access to objects. McGrew's (1969) results from another nursery school differ from those above in that dominance ranking was related to the number of interactions initiated, "a possible measure of leadership." (155).

Our own results on a study of Reading nursery school children are interesting in this context. We used three categories of agonistic interaction:

1. Approach-withdrawal. By this we mean that at the approach of one individual, another "gives place" or "flees". No threats are given by the approaching child. This was of rare occurrence, comprising only 5% of the total number of agonistic interactions.

2. Threat. By this we refer to such units as "aggressive frown" and "intention beat" in one child. This category comprised 17% of the total of agonistic interactions.

3. Take from/beat. This involves a struggle over objects and/ or the hitting of one child by another. 76% of all agonistic interactions were of this type.

The total number of agonistic interactions observed was 157 and the distribution was such that a hierarchy was obtainable for the boys, i.e. agonistic behaviour was uni-directional. We have obtained similar results from other groups studied. However, unlike the other groups, it was not possible to obtain a hierarchy for the Reading girls. The child at the top of the hierarchy, in all cases, received the highest score for being watched or followed by other children. Chance (1967) has suggested that a hierarchy is maintained by those less dominant directing their attention to the most dominant individuals.

Among nursery school children, then, it seems that most agon-istic behaviour involves struggles over objects, or the beating, kicking or punching of one child by another. McGrew (1969) stated that 30% of agonistic and quasiagonistic interactions involved a struggle over objects. Blurton Jones has stated that, ".....fights occur over pro-perty and little else". (1967, 354). This is in striking contrast with findings from our research on adult rhesus monkeys in Bristol Zoo (1969, 1971). There, over a period of one year, 70% of all dominance interactions were of the approach-withdrawal type; that is one monkey avoided another more dominant, without the latter threatening. Only 5% of the Reading children's agonistic behaviour was of this type. In other words children were not spatially orienting themselves in rela-tion to those more dominant. Young monkeys at Bristol, up to $2\frac{1}{2}$ years old, acted in a similar way to the children, in that the only way to as-sess their relative dominance was to observe them fighting over objects. Grant's study of adult schizophrenic patients suggests an increase in the approach/withdrawal and threat categories, and a lower take from/beat score. Observations by Brindley (unpublished), of interactions in the street, have illustrated spatial orientation in human adults. Apparently approach/withdrawal interactions, leading to spatial orientation in a group, develop sometime after the age of five.

A number of workers have noted sex differences in the amount of agonistic behaviour exhibited. McGrew (1969) studied a group of children in which males constituted 70% of the group, but were involved in 99% of agonistic and quasiagonistic interactions. (See also Hutt, this volume). We have results from a study of children in two Bristol play-groups which support the contention that females are less aggres-sive than males; the boys, who constituted about half of each group,

were responsible between themselves for 66% and 80% of all agonistic
behaviour. In Reading however the 9 girls were involved in more
agonistic interactions between themselves than the 11 boys. As we
have said, it was not possible to obtain a hierarchy for these girls.
They spent much time quarrelling between themselves, first one winn-
ing then another.

So far we have discussed intra-group agonistic behaviour.
A recurring problem for human groups is the introduction of a new
member. Evidence from other primates suggests that species can be
arranged along a continuum from those who tolerate strangers to those
who do not. Recent research has modified the opinion that bands of
ground-living species, such as rhesus and baboon, are completely
'closed' to outsiders. Lindburg (1969), for instance, has observed
some rhesus males changing groups during the breeding season. Acceptance is gradual, and occurs after threats have been exchanged at the
periphery of the group. Our own observations on captive rhesus monkeys showed that the introduction of a new male led to increased
fighting, but that the dominant male intervened to curtail each quarrel.
Reynolds (1966) has suggested that chimpanzee bands are "open". It is
doubtful, however, whether the animals involved are, in fact, strangers
(see Sugiyama, this volume). Chimpanzees in captivity are much less
likely to tolerate the introduction of a new animal (Reynolds, pers.
comm.).

In observing young children in her own nursery school during
the 1920's and 1930's Susan Isaacs (1933) found extreme hostility towards newcomers. Similar data has recently been collected by Krebs
(pers. comm.). Some interesting behavioural units were observed by
us when new children were introduced into two play groups. Mothers

usually left fairly quickly and the introduction for the new child was traumatic. Extreme flight behaviour was exhibited by the children; for example, they attempted to leave the room, kicked, screamed, and finally collapsed on the floor weeping. This would be followed in time by exploratory behaviour. However, out of nine children introduced to the groups, four left after a few weeks, two were still unsettled and only three were well-integrated by the end of the study. Of these three, one had a sister in the group, one a friend and the mother of the third helped. The reaction of group members to newcomers varied from indifference to mild hostility, frowning, eyes fixated on the stranger.

Small attempts at association would at last be made by the newcomer or a group member , and often a "gift" was exchanged. The "gift" was usually refused. Such positive responses to a newcomer were, in all but one case, made by a low ranking group member. An analysis was made of the objects passed between children in social interaction. During interaction objects such as toys, sweets and personal belongings pass between individuals. These may be differentiated between those which are solicited and/or part of a game, and those which do not appear to be solicited, nor part of an existing play sequence. It is the latter we refer to as "gifts". The behaviour involves stretching out the hand containing the object, at waist level with a serious face and the eyes fixed on the face of the recipient. Forty-five objects were observed to be passed from one individual to another. Twenty-seven of these were what we refer to as "gifts", and the other eighteen were passed in play or solicited. Of the twenty-seven "gifts", 78% involved a newcomer whereas only 11% of the objects passed in play or solicited involved a newcomer. Blurton Jones (1967) refers to gift-giving but only in relation to himself or other strange adults.

It is interesting to speculate on the role of gift-giving in the assimilation of a new child. Chimpanzees may pass food to other group members (Nishida, 1970) but the giving of a "gift" by or to a newcomer appears new in the repertoire of primate behaviour, and perhaps functions as a reassurance or appeasement gesture.

IV. ASSOCIATIVE BEHAVIOUR

By "association" is meant that two or more individuals are interacting freely, smiling, talking, sitting next to each other. It parallels huddling and grooming without the exhibition of any sign of flight or agonistic behaviour in non-human primates. Associative units of behaviour are not distributed equally over all possible pairs of individuals in a group. In other primates mother/offspring and sibling relationships score highly for association, as do sub groups of males. Southwick et al. (1965) have noted the peaceful, co-operative relationship between certain adult rhesus males. Young monkeys associate frequently together in play, groups of young males having particularly high association scores. Young females associate more frequently with their mothers.

Parallels are found in human children. Our data supports that of Hutt (this volume) and McGrew and McGrew (1970). The latters' study of group formation in nursery children found that females stayed nearer adults and that boys indulged more in rough-and-tumble play in peer groups. In the Reading nursery group, the average number of interactions per observed pair was 5.66, but whereas most male/male pairs had an above average number of interactions few female/female pairs did. The total number of male/male interactions (442) was almost double that of female/female interactions (250). Interactions between the sexes were lower still, only 145 having been observed.

Males then, had wider and more social contacts with each other, than females did with each other. The girls tended to interact in pairs or to play alone. They were rarely observed in large groups, whereas as many as eleven males frequently ran around the field together, chasing, play-fighting, and shouting. This helps account for the low number of interactions between males and females recorded. The males tended to move to the periphery of the space available, the girls remaining closer to the staff.

Seven hundred occurrences of voluntary play were recorded. Females were seen to play in groups of three or more only twenty-nine times, and males 178 times. The largest single category of play was male rough-and-tumble, which occurred between pairs of boys 40 times, and in groups 50 times. Females exhibited this behaviour 13 times in pairs, and only 3 times in groups. The main play category involving girls was solitary locomotor play with apparatus, for example swinging, rolling tyres, and climbing ladders, of which there were 32 occurrences. Only 87 play sequences involved both sexes simultaneously.

V. GROUP FORMATION

In modern Western society a child's first experience with a group of children of the same age is often in the nursery or play-group setting. At the beginning of a nursery year the introduction of a large number of new children allows for the observation of group formation and development, and changes in the behaviour of individuals over a short period of time. McGrew and McGrew (1970) observed group formation in an Edinburgh nursery over a seven day period. Five of the children had previous nursery experience, and they were joined by eight younger children who had no such experience. Unlike findings from rhesus monkeys (Bernstein and Mason 1963) there was a low initial level of aggressive behaviour; the newcomers were inhibited and subdued, whereas the experienced children were noisier and more active. Over the next seven days struggles over objects and pushing both increased and the experienced children won more often. Digit sucking and "automanipulation" decreased during this period. Sex-differences had become apparent, boys pushing and beating, laughing and chasing more often than girls. The girls sought out adult contact and sucked their fingers more often than the boys.

We had an opportunity to observe group formation at the start of a new play-group year. Two groups were studied for six meetings each. Each group met one morning a week. All dominance interactions were noted and they were at first rare:

Group C	week 1	8 occurrences
Group C	week 6	20 occurrences
Group D	week 2	2 occurrences
Group D	week 4	34 occurrences

At any one time there were approximately fifteen children in each group, eight with previous nursery experience and seven newcomers. The main distinction in dominance interactions was between those children with nursery experience and the newcomers:

GROUP C	Number of domi- nance interactions	%
nursery experienced/nursery experienced	32	42.7
nursery experienced/newcomer	30	40
newcomer/nursery experienced	9	12
newcomer/newcomer	4	5.3
GROUP D		
nursery experienced/nursery experienced	36	41
nursery experienced/newcomer	21	24
newcomer/nursery experienced	13	15
newcomer/newcomer	17	20

(In the above the first named category is the dominator.)

The cases where a newcomer dominated a child with nursery experience are interesting. In each case (22 examples) the newcomer had been put into such a position that he or she had to use force to retain or protect an object. For example, newcomer D has an engine. K tries to take it. D retains it. K beats D. D runs towards K, who flees with taut face.

Associative interactions between children were equally rare on their first visit, but rose steadily. Only a quarter of the possible number of relationships between children were observed, and by the end of the study, the sixth visit, only a few strong relationships had developed.

Our observations like those of McGrew and McGrew (1970) show that a child's initial response to a novel social environment is caution. Hutt (1966) has provided some experimental findings about a child's reaction to a novel object, which parallel the behaviour in the social situation. A child presented with a novel stimulus, explores it visually and manually, with intent facial expressions and postures. The presence of a known adult makes the child less apprehensive. Over time exploration decreases and play-behaviour characterised by a relaxed expression, lack of concentration, and the incorporation of the novel object in a game, increases. In the nursery school, social behaviour and play only occur when the environment has been carefully explored.

VI. TOWARDS THE FUTURE

Most research in Human Ethology has been carried out on small groups of children in Western Societies, usually under-fives in nursery schools. This is largely because the formal organisation is minimal and the activities of the children are relatively free from adult supervision. Secondly, the under-fives apparently pay little attention to an observer. Thirdly, children in nursery schools are usually freely available for study. Older children of five to seven years of age are being studied by Reynolds and Guest in Bristol schools. Other research has been carried out on adult schizophrenic patients in a hospital setting, and current research programmes include the study of some American prisoners. An attempt is being made in this study to correlate observable behaviour with psychiatric diagnoses, previous prison experience and other factors. (Pfeiffer, pers. comm.).

Comparative data is badly needed from non-Western societies. Blurton-Jones (this volume) has contributed in this field with a comparative study of London children, and Bushman children of the same age. This sort of comparison will give useful insight into constants in human behaviour and social organisation. From our knowledge of other primates we may expect a wide range of intra-specific variation. Ethology, as a method for the objective description of behaviour, should allow for more meaningful cross-specific comparisons and contrasts to be made.

Much more research is needed in the behaviour of normal human adults in small groups. This is obviously more difficult to arrange than studies of the behaviour of children. Within the area of nursery school research, a follow-up study would be useful, observing the introduction of individual new children to a group, noting the behaviour of children prior to introduction, the behaviour of the introduced child, the reaction of the group to the newcomer, and the subsequent assimilation process. Experimental manipulation of the environments in which groups interact may be fruitful. It should be noted that Iona and Peter Opie (1969) have criticised the observation of children in the school of playground situation, on the grounds that the children are "captive", and their behaviour may consequently be distorted. It is difficult to know how a systematic programme of research could be attempted on groups of children outside the formal setting, but such an attempt would be of obvious value.

From a practical point of view the study of behaviour could guide nursery school management in making a newcomer's entry into a school a smoother and less traumatic experience. The description and analysis of play, and the study of behaviour in various environments could help in the design of better facilities and buildings for both children and adults.

Much of the research we have discussed is as yet unpublished. The ethological study of man is a new development stemming from research into the non-human primates. Any review of the work is at present no more than a presentation of introductory themes. The number of new workers in the field suggests that within the next few years a large amount of material will become available for study.

VII. ACKNOWLEDGEMENTS

We should like to thank The Bristol, Clifton and West of England Zoological Society, Bristol W.R.V.S. Playgroups, and Norcot Nursery School, Reading for working facilities. For useful discussion we should like to thank Prof. S. Andreski, Dr. V. Reynolds, K. Krebs and T. Pfeiffer. We thank especially Dr. W. M. S. Russell for invaluable help. The research was financed by Reading University Research Board.

VIII. REFERENCES

Bernstein, I. S. and Mason, W. A. (1963). Activity patterns of rhesus monkeys in a social group. Anim. Behav. 11, 455-460

Blurton Jones, N. G. (1967). An ethological study of some aspects of social behaviour of children in nursery school. In "Primate Ethology" (D. Morris ed.) Weidenfeld and Nicolson, London.

Brindley, T. (1971). unpublished B.A. dissertation. Social Sciences Library, University of Reading.

Chance, M. R. A. (1967). Attention structure as the basis of primate rank orders. Man (N.S.) 2, 503-518.

Darwin, C. (1962). "The origin of species." Collier, New York.

Eibl-Eibesfeldt, I. 1968. Ethological perspectives on primate studies. In "Primates - studies in adaptation and variability" (P. Jay ed.) Holt, Rinehart and Winston, New York.

Freud, S. (1950). Totem and taboo. Routledge and Kegan Paul, London.

Grant, E. C. (1965). An ethological description of some schizophrenic patterns of behaviour. Proc. Leeds symp. on behaviour disorders. 13pp. mimeo.

Grant, E. C., (1969). Human facial expression. Man (N.S.) 4, 525-536.

Hayes, H. R. (1958). From ape to angel. Methuen, London.

Hutt, C. (1966). Exploration and play in children. In "Play, exploration and territory in mammals". (P. A. Jewell and C. Loizos eds.) Symp. Zool. Soc. Lond. No. 18. Academic Press, London.

Isaacs, S. (1933). "Social development in young children." Routledge, London.

Leach, G. M. (Undated). A comparison of the social behaviour of normal and problem children. 34pp. mimeo. Dept. of Growth and Development, Institute of Child Health, University of London.

Lindburg, D. G. (1969). Rhesus monkeys: mating season mobility of adult males. Science 166, 1176-1178.

McGrew, W. C. (1969). An ethological study of agonistic behaviour in pre-school children. Proc. sec. inter. congr. primat. (C. R. Carpenter ed.) Karger, Basel, New York.

McGrew, W. C. and McGrew, P. L. (1970). Aggression and group formation in nursery school children. Proc. 3rd inter. cong. primat. Karger, Basel, New York.

Morris, D. (1969). The human zoo. Cape, London.

Nishida, T. (1970). Social behaviour and relationship among wild chimpanzees of the Mahali Mountains. Primates 11, 47-87.

Opie, P. and Opie, I. (1969). Children's games in street and playground. Clarendon Press, Oxford.

Reynolds, V. (1966). Open Groups in Hominid Evolution. Man (N.S.) 1, 442–452.

Reynolds, V. and A. Guest. (1970). Nuffield pilot project on primary school children aged 5-7 years. Mimeo.

Schaller, G. B. (1963). "The mountain gorilla: ecology and behaviour" Univ. of Chicago Press, Chicago.

Southwick, C. H., M. A. Beg and M. R. Siddiqi (1965). Rhesus monkeys in North India. In "Primate behaviour: field studies of monkeys and apes" (I. DeVore ed.) Holt, Rinehart and Winston, New York.

Virgo, H. B. and Waterhouse, M. J. (1969). The emergence of attention structure amongst rhesus macaques. Man (N.S.) 4, 85–93.

Washburn, S. L. and De Vore, I. (1961). The social life of baboons. Sci. Am. 204(6), 62–71

Waterhouse, M. J. and Waterhouse, H. (1971). Population density and stress in zoo monkeys. The Ecologist Vol. 1 No. 10, 19-21.

Watson, R. and Watson, P. (1969). "Man and nature: an anthropological essay in human ecology." Harcourt, Brace and World Inc., New York.

IX. APPENDIX

The authors' research programme, from which results are quoted in the text, was carried out between 1967 and 1971. Observations were made on a colony of rhesus monkeys (Macaca mulatta) at Bristol Zoo, England. We have also studied three-five year old children attending play-groups in Bristol. Altogether four play-groups were observed; two of the groups had been formed for eight months when we began work, and the other two groups were being set up. There were approximately equal numbers of boys and girls in each group. The children attended once a week, for three hours and interacted in a room 14' x 40', which they were unable to leave without permission. There were two observers recording independently in written commentaries the behaviour of subjects. Each subject was studied for equal periods of time. The study totalled approximately 100 hours.

A further study was made of a Reading nursery school group comprising 20 children for six weeks in the summer of 1971. The children were observed each weekday for three hours, a total of 90 hours' observation. There was only one observer per day. Recording was done in same way as above. These children, 9 girls and 11 boys, had the free run of three rooms, and a large field with apparatus in it.

A distinction should be made between play-groups and nursery schools. The former were set up by voluntary organisations and usually involve attendance once or twice a week. The latter are usually run by Local Education Authorities and involve attendance each weekday. The ages of the children in both cases range from three to five years. Because of the lack of facilities for this age group, there is a tendency for deprived and "problem" children to be over represented. There is no formal teaching and the accent is on free-play.

SEX DIFFERENCES IN BEHAVIOUR OF LONDON

AND BUSHMAN CHILDREN

N. G. Blurton-Jones

Department of Growth and Development,
Institute of Child Health,
University of London.

and

M. J. Konner

Department of Anthropology,
Harvard University.

INTRODUCTION

Differences in the behaviour of boys and girls are of topical and controversial interest. They are also of social importance, in so far as they have to do with the reasons for differences between the current roles of men and women in adult society. Sex differences are also of interest as an area in which to study the development of individual differences. It therefore seems worthwhile to report some quite unlooked-for findings on sex-differences in behaviour of children in a pre-agricultural, hunter-gatherer culture, the Zhun/twa, or !kung bushmen; and to compare them with results of data gathered by the same observers in the same way in an industrial culture. The main aims of our study were:-

1. To look at the way different items of behaviour relate to each other in the two cultures, and particularly whether facial expressions accompany the same bodily actions in both cultures, and

2. To look for the differences in the frequencies of various features of social behaviour in the two cultures.

However, this inevitably meant we had data on behaviour of both sexes and it is a preliminary analysis of these aspects of the data that we wish to report and discuss here. We also indicate some of the ways in which we intend to analyse the data further to examine some of the many possible reasons for the differences discovered.

Sex differences (i.e. different scores of boys and girls) have been found repeatedly in a variety of studies of a wide range of psychological measures in Europe and North America . These have been reviewed by Garai and Scheinfeld (1968) and reviewed and discussed by

Hutt (1972)   and Gray (1971) among others. It is often forgotten that the explanation of these sex differences is another question from their measurement. This is a field in which, as much as in any other field of development, argument focuses about an exaggerated nature-nurture dichotomy. While there is much evidence from experiments on a variety of mammals, e.g. Phoenix, Goy and Resko (1968) that early exposure to androgens has a fundamental "sex-typing" effect on the brain, there is less evidence about how this is translated into differences in behaviour, (but see Valenstein 1968). Developmental psychologists such as Moss (1967), Kagan (1971) and Lewis (in press) have also made some progress in this direction, looking more closely at the interaction with the external environment. On other primates there is work such as that of Jensen,Bobbitt and Gordon (1967, 1968) on development of sex differences and their relationship to mother-infant interaction and environmental complexity in Pig-tailed Macaques. Gray (1971) reviews some of the evidence on endocrine and neurological bases of sex-differences in behaviour, and Gray and Buffery (1971) discuss adaptive causes of these differences, though using a rather limited sample of the comparative data.

There is a vast body of cross-cultural data on human adults that shows great variation in behaviour reported (either by informants or more directly by the anthropological fieldworker himself) as typical of adult males and females in different cultures. However, Murdock (1949) and Tiger (1969) have argued that it is universal to all cultures to have a sex role differentiation, a view that some things are women's work and other things are men's work. Nonetheless, much cross-cultural information is recorded by methods which are open to very damaging criticism if they are regarded as methods of gathering data on behaviour (rather than data on attitudes etc.) and which would certainly not be used by anyone investigating behaviour of animals. In addition, relatively little of the cross-cultural work on sex differences in children has been quantitative in approach (e.g.: Mead, 1967), noteworthy exceptions being the as yet only partially analysed "six cultures study" (Whiting 1963), and Caudill and Weinstein's (1969) elegant examination of mother-infant interactions in Japanese and American families.

The main traditional method of recording and analysing observed behaviour of children is to rate each child along a scale of the extent to which it shows some predetermined characteristics such as aggression, dependency, nurturance, sociability, to name the more comprehensible. Another method is to count instances of behaviour which the observer (or an assistant) codes as being an example of predetermined large categories of behaviour such as aggression, dependency, etc. Both of these techniques leave the question of the nature, in particular the unidimensionality, of the major categories untested, and untestable. This procedure is questionable even within the observer's own culture. Millet (1970) shows how dangerous it can be for comparisons of the sexes. Between cultures it may be even more unreliable (Smith and Connolly, 1972).

The data presented in this paper were gathered in a form based on studies of social behaviour in animals and applied successfully to children in the U.K. and U.S.A. by an increasing number of workers such as Grant (1965, 1969), McGrew (1972) and contributors to Blurton-Jones (1972). Basically our method differs from traditional interview and rating methods in that we record the occurrence of small, easy to describe items of behaviour. Since the items are described in almost anatomical terms they stand a good chance of being observable in any people. (Evidence is now accumulating that this is indeed the case, Eibl-Eibesfeldt 1972). If they are, and since they are small items, this allows very precise descriptions of the ways in which behaviour differs between cultures in terms equally applicable in either culture.

1. The significance of studies of non-agricultural people

Information on child development in hunter-gatherer peoples has an additional interest, particularly to biologists, in that such people are living in the ecological niche (though not necessarily with the climate, flora or fauna) in which man evolved, indeed in which over 90% of Homo sapiens generations have lived, and before them H. erectus and his predecessors. It thus represents in terms of durability the most successful phase of human evolution. Although it is wrong to assume that any one surviving foraging culture is typical of all evolving man it is possible to observe behaviour in its natural context, subject to the selection pressures that constructed Homo sapiens. Howell (1971) has shown that peak mortality in Bushmen occurs below the age of five, so that the adaptiveness of child behaviour for survival as a child is clearly as important as its function as a prelude to adulthood. Konner (1972) has also indicated the correctness of Bowlby's view on the adaptiveness of the child's attachment to its mother, and adds to this its significant effect on acquisition of adult subsistence technology.

It is worth pointing out that Lee (1968) has shown that the area where Zhun/twa live, while clearly marginal for agriculture is by no means marginal for hunting and gathering. Woodburn (1968) holds the same to be even more clearly true for the Hadza, whose life greatly resembles that of the Zhun/twa, (differing primarily in a preoccupation with gambling, rather than music and trances). Among these peoples plant foods form about 70% of their excellently balanced and adequately-sized diet. Yellen (in press) and Yellen and Harpending (in press) have shown that people, living much as the contemporary Zhun/twa do, inhabited the same area in both drier and wetter climates throughout the past 10,000 years. Quantitative observations of adult work patterns and other activities are fortunately replacing idle speculation on matters such as the role of the sexes in pre-agricultural society. Demographic studies such as those of N. Howell replace speculation on birth rates and spacing, longevity and the insignificance of predation. These studies are part of a long-term multi-disciplinary study of the Bushmen organised by I. DeVore at Harvard. (Readers of this symposium will of course know DeVore best for his work on non-human primates, and his example provides a good argument for the inclusion of a section on human behaviour in this symposium.) DeVore and Lee's project, as does their Man the Hunter symposium (Lee and DeVore 1968), illustrates the intimate relationship of the human sciences with biology, and of the branches of the human sciences with each other. It is possibly easier to see this unity when studying pre-agricultural man but it should be remembered that (a) even the most advancedly human features of man are present in such people, and (b) that even post-industrial man has a historical, evolutionary and ecological position with attendant problems of survival, which soon enough make the inter-relationships of the separate branches of the biological and human sciences evident even to the most sectarian.

Theoretically, the presence or absence of differences in behaviour of boys and girls in a forager society should be of special interest. Not because these differences directly imply any more about the ontogeny of such behaviour than does any other cross-cultural comparison, but because they imply that such a phenomenon has survival value, either during childhood or as part of the system of acquiring adult behaviour in a hunter-gatherer culture. It is then also very likely that the differences are characters of considerable antiquity.

In particular, on the subject of sex-differences, some common misconceptions about the adaptive value in pre-agricultural societies of certain characteristics of the roles of men and women in industrial societies are being corrected. Firstly, supposed differences in activity and adventurousness, based on the view that women stayed at home cooking and breeding while men went out to get the food are misleading. Lee (1968) shows how women provide at least half of the food in tropical hunter-gatherer societies. Zhun/twa women go gathering 2 - 3 times a week, each excursion being an energetic walk of up to 6 miles each way to the nut groves, carrying a child each way and 30 lb or more of nuts on the return journey. In terms of energy expenditure women probably exceed men on average in the normal life of their society. But the reverse may be true in terms of power output. We feel it may be significant that we find more vigorous activity by the Bushmen girls than by the London girls, no doubt this helps them in their active adult life no less than the London middle-class tradition of rearing sessile women helps them in their housebound adult life.

Secondly, our traditional views about the adaptiveness of males being more aggressive than females may be misleading. Although Lee (1970) has shown that the Zhun/twa have a substantial murder rate and that it is men who kill, and usually over women (married women), there is strong social pressure against aggression such that men may be banished, or even on occasion communally killed for killing people. Systematic evidence on dominance hierarchies has not been gathered on

hunter-gatherer people. Nonetheless the current concensus seems to
be that these are absent or unimportant in most such societies (Lee and
DeVore 1968). The degree of interdependence of people living as hunter-
gathers is such that a straightforward "males competing for females"
or males competing for hierarchial positions view of the survival value
of aggression is likely to be highly misleading. The comments of Trivers
(1971) on the functions of aggression in maintaining systems of reciprocal altruism provides a much better view of the adaptive value of aggression (whether over women or food or objects) within Zhun/twa society.
Ardrey's (1961) contention that hunting and inter-personal aggression
have a common motivation is belied both in carnivore (by physiological
studies) and in Bushmen by the observations of Konner (1972).

2. Significance and problems of cross-cultural comparisons

The study of differences between cultures tells us about the rules
by which cultures vary but it does not tell us about the causes of features
that do not vary across the cultures studied. Thus to study cultural features that vary along with a simple measure of the amount of behaviour
such as fighting, or frowning or crying, tells us about why some people
do more of those than others do. In our view it does not necessarily tell
us why people frown, fight or cry, nor does it necessarily tell us what
controls the development of this behaviour. The position is similar to
that discussed by Smith (this vol.) concerning temporal and individual
variations and their development. Confusion about this point lies behind
much of the controversy surrounding the importance of cross-cultural
constants, and indeed behind many of the arguments that there are no
such constants or universals. Of course one can never prove that a
feature is present in all cultures, but the extensive variation that is

known does not mean that the extensive constancy that has been demon-strated is meaningless, (e.g. Murdock 1949, Eckman et al 1969, Eibl Eibesfeldt 1972).

Our treatment of sex differences will deal, then, with cultural differences and similarities in sex differences. If, as Margaret Mead (1963) has suggested, there are virtually no cross-cultural constants in sex-differences in non-reproductive behaviour, this will clearly have implications unfavourable to certain biological arguments (e.g. Hutt, this volume). If, as we suspect, there are some constants, then we will want to know which ones they are, how they arise, but we also want to know the origins of sex differences which are not too constant from culture to culture.

Comparison of behaviour in two cultures is not as simple as might first appear. So many things differ, from situational effects like hardness of ground, temperature, sunshine, number of people available, absence or presence of traffic or predators, to traditionally cultural factors like parental beliefs about child-rearing, that it seems almost surprising that any cross-cultural constants have been found. This also implies that it is unreliable to attribute observed differences to any one particular likely cause (i.e. to other observed differences) without looking at yet other possible causes. We have attempted to do the latter, for instance by looking at choice of playmates relative to available children, at behaviour such as aggression relative to other interactions with children. We also attempted to equate features of the situation which we knew had important influences on behaviour (e.g. presence of mother, in village rather than out foraging).

3. Subjects

The subjects were two samples of children ranging in age from two to six years, one of London British children, the other of Zhun/twa (!kung) Bushmen children. The Bushman population was observed first, during August and September 1970. The 23 Bushman children observed were all of the 3-to-6 year olds in the central four villages of the population studied by Lee (1968 and elsewhere), Draper (1972), Konner (1972) and others. Ages are known, at worst to the nearest 6 months. The kin relationships of the children to other adults and children around them are known. The relationships and ages are based primarily on the demographic and census work of Richard Lee and Nancy Howell-Lee. It happened that the average age of the 13 girls available for study was rather younger than the average age of the boys. This important fact is taken into account in computing our results. The parents were all living predominantly by hunting and gathering, although many fathers may have at some time been employed temporarily at various occupations with other peoples. About half the fathers would be qualified or aspiring trance-dancers (medicine men); many would be accomplished musicians and storytellers, and most are highly scientific experts on animal behaviour. None of the parents has any formal institutionalised education. Although extremely limited in their ability to count they are highly competent at intellectual processes such as Piaget's highest stage of "concrete operations" (Inhelder and Piaget 1958). Although no formal comparison of the intellectual ability of the Bushman parents and the London parents is possible we think that a greater danger of error lies in underestimating the Bushmen than the reverse. The Bushman parents are able to maintain their families successfully (on $2\frac{1}{2}$ working days each per week, Lee 1968) in the ecological niche in

which the human brain, with all its noteworthy size, novelty and complexity, evolved.

The London sample of 21 children (10 boys, 11 girls) was observed in May 1971. They were selected to match the age composition
(for boys and girls separately) of the Bushman children. Prospective
subjects were sought among children at three playgroups and among
friends of the authors. The main criteria affecting their observation
were: availability and co-operativeness of the mother at fitting into
our very tight schedule, accessibility of children well known to the
subject, to be present as available playmates during the observations,
and fine weather (of which there was fortunately a great deal) to allow
observations out of doors. Father's occupations were in the Registrar
General's social class I and II, (the two upper classes in this largely
education-based classification). Maternal education was not recorded
but it is known to have covered a range which included grammar school
to Ph.D.

4. Observation methods

Both observers simultaneously watched the same child, and one
child only, for the period of an hour. Blurton-Jones made a detailed
account of the child's facial expressions and 'body language', including
the objects of any such non-verbal signals. The items are listed in
Appendix 1. Konner recorded a wide range of items in several categories of behaviour as listed in Appendix 2, to be defined in Konner
(in prep). It was decided to maximise the possible range of behaviour
items recorded, by observing for 30 seconds without writing, followed
by a 2 minute period for writing without observing. Twenty-four such
periods made up the hour. Observations and writing periods were

timed by a stop-watch.

The situations in which the children were observed were controlled in general aspects which we knew to affect the behaviour of the children, these were: 1) availability of mother, 2) Bushman mother and child in village not out foraging, 3) outdoors in a familiar place, 4) access to children well known to the subject.

5. Reliability of recording

The possibility of observer bias was minimised by selecting mainly detailed and objective kinds of behaviour items. In animal studies it has been traditional to rely on the replicability that is obtainable with describtion of observable behaviour. We followed this approach in the present study, in contrast to the emphasis on inter-observer reliability testing traditional in human studies. In addition, the same observers were doing the same observations in each culture. However, there were several items of behaviour which we both recorded. A detailed analysis of these items will have to be presented elsewhere, but preliminary analyses show that our two sets of data almost always gave the same culture, and sex differences. We can also demonstrate cross-individual correlations between our scores.

It is somewhat more difficult to control for the problem of observer effect. There were no sex differences in any of the reactions to observers that we measured, but there were clear cultural differences, the Bushman children showing both more "friendly" and more "fearful" responses, such as smiling and long-lasting looks (staring). This suggests that the observers were more salient stimuli for the Bushman children. The effect on our results of this cultural difference in observer effect, or of the fact that both observers were male, is impossible to specify. One can only say that this problem arises in all behaviour research by whatever method, and that it can be overcome only by measuring it and treating it as an independent variable.

TREATMENT OF THE DATA

For this paper, which is a first approximation, the data are constituted by combining several items into a few major categories. The categorisations of behaviour are based on the tendency of some behaviour items to occur frequently with certain others but rarely with yet other items. Thus Blurton-Jones (1967, 1972) found: wrestle, run, jumps, hits at, laugh, and playface to occur together but separately from hit, push, grab-tug-take, frown, fixate (equivalent to "threat" Grant 1969). He also described a cluster of cry, red face, oblique eyebrows and "pucker face" (which includes oblique brows and square upper lip). In our analysis we have tried to use these, and other empirically derived clusters. We combine them with those elements of facial expression which (as Grant 1969, Brannigan and Humphries 1972 have shown) can be regarded as correlating closely with these clusters e.g. "small mouth" (Grant 1969) and "two-lip pout" with "aggression" (hit, push, etc.).

However, the "clusters" are not true clusters, they were derived from factor analysis and, although the factors appear repeatedly, (in four groups of children in Blurton-Jones 1972, and in Smith this volume, and they are supported by other kinds of analysis, McGrew 1972) any behaviour items may load strongly on more than one factor. This means that any single occurrence of an item does not allow certain

"diagnosis" of the kind of behaviour occurring. Thus, while completed
and uncompleted hits appeared to load differentially they cannot be
taken as diagnostic of "aggression" versus "rough-and-tumble".
Indeed this result is to be expected if rough-and-tumble play is, as
Loizos (1966) suggests, a mixture of aggressive, fearful and friendly
behaviour. It happens that the highest loading on rough-and-tumble
is laugh-play face, and so we have taken this as our main diagnostic
aid for scoring the agonistic and quasi-agonistic actions. But we must
stress that this coding is highly arbitrary; a further analysis in which
we will compare results of factor analysis of the behaviour of boys and
girls in both cultures, and then compare the factor scores should provide a more sound basis for the comparisons. The results that we present here are, however, more comparable with already published data
on sex differences in European and N. American children. In future
analyses we will also look at dimensions of individual variation, and at
discriminant functions for sex differences, which may give very different categorisations of behaviour (see Smith this volume).

Histograms are presented for some results. They show the
numbers of observations that included any of the relevant items, for
boys and girls in each culture. These figures were tested by the chi-
squared procedure in 2 x 2 tables but most often individual scores were
compared, using the Mann - Whitney U-Test. Results due to the age
difference between the boys and girls were sought out by (a) looking
for correlations of the behaviour with age, and (b) looking at boy - girl
differences with the younger children omitted, giving groups of unequal
size but of balanced age. Differences showing a strong relationship to
age, such as talking to children, are omitted. More sophisticated
statistical techniques seemed to give no more clear ability to attribute

differences to age, nor to exclude this possibility. There is considerable debate about whether one should not in fact compare boys with younger girls, as we did, because of the generally more rapid development of girls on many behavioural and physical measures at this age. This could be regarded as making same-age comparisons invalid. The only ultimate answer to this problem is to look at the paths of development, and to determine whether the sex differences are the same as, or different from the developmental differences.

RESULTS

Results are described and discussed under several main headings: agonistic behaviour, rough-and-tumble play, sociable interactions, negative results, people interacted with, use of objects, sustained directed attention, activity, and differences between the girls of the two cultures.

1. Agonistic Behaviour

This category includes the facial expressions items (all directed to children): face up, two-lip pout, square lower lip (if no smile), frown while looking at another child, small mouth. The behaviour items are any from Appendix 2 Section 10, unaccompanied by smiles. "Verbal aggression" was analysed separately.

Both sets of data show that boys score significantly higher on measures of aggression than girls in both cultures, (Fig. 1a and b). There was no evidence of an age change in aggression, a result also obtained by Blurton-Jones in (1972) and Smith and Connolly (1972) for children in the same range of ages.

N. G. Blurton-Jones and M. J. Konner

Fig. 1(a) Histogram showing scores for facial expression and for actions classified as comprising "serious fights" or aggression.
Comparing London boys and London girls the histogram shows
the total number of half-minute periods in which such behaviour was recorded for all the children. Note that there are
more girls than boys.

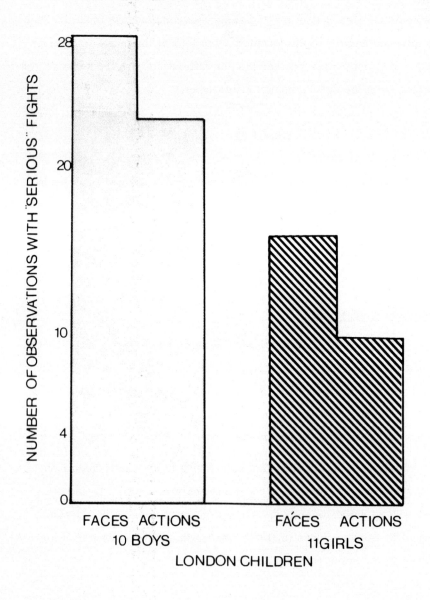

Fig. 1(b)   Same as 1(a) but for Bushman children, among whom
             there were even more girls.

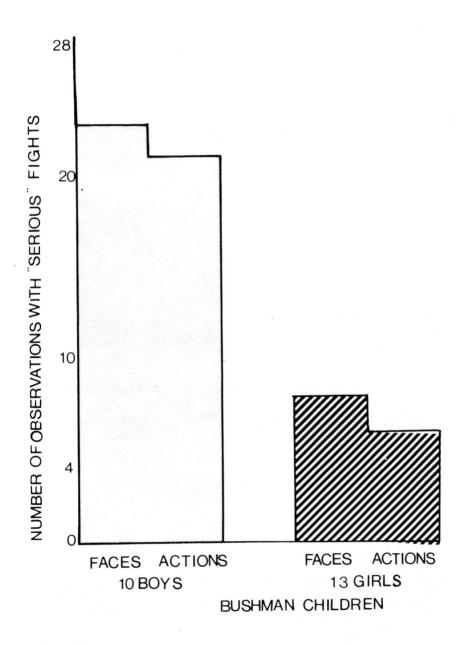

For the London children the sex difference in the facial items appear to be related to a difference in the total amount of interaction with children. The proportion of observations with aggressive faces out of observations with any face items oriented towards children is the same in the London boys and London girls. Thus although boys had more aggressive interactions than girls, the proportion of their total interactions that were aggressive was the same as for the girls. We are however suspicious that this finding results from the difference in age of the two samples since 2-3 year olds have a reputation of being rela-tively more aggressive than 4 year olds. Nonetheless this proportional measure makes the London girls' score significantly higher than the Bushman girls.

There was one difference between the London boys and the London girls which would have seemed superficial had it not been previously found in another London sample by Hall (pers. comm.). Our ten London boys showed a tendency towards a bimodal distribution of frequencies of aggression. Neither of the groups of girls nor the group of Bushman boys showed this distribution. Blurton-Jones (1972) collected data which gave the same phenomenon in a sample of boys, probably as a result of age difference in response to maternal separation in the children he ob-served (with mother absent) even though the phenomenon is not evident in his data on girls. Hall initially found this phenomenon in her larger sample of boys, where it was evident that the group of children with scores of zero were not necessarily the younger children. In our sam-ple the extreme scores at both ends were those of London boys.

Overall differences between cultures in frequency of agonistic interactions were not significant despite our impressions of reduced agg-ression in the Bushman children. It may be that this impression, gained during casual observations, resulted from the bimodal distribution of scores for London boys, and our attending most to the high scoring individuals. But when aggression is assessed by the proportion of all interactions with children that are aggressive interactions, the picture changes slightly. The Bushman boys quarrelled in a slightly smaller proportion of their total interactions with children (face data) but the difference from the London boys was not significant. Had we taken into account the effect of the number of interactions involving objects this difference may well have disappeared completely. But as described above, the proportional measure gives no sex difference for the London children. Thus the impression of a cultural difference in aggression may have been due to the lower proportion of the interactions that the Bushman girls had that included agonistic behaviour.

Vocal agonistic acts formed a higher proportion of meaningful vocalisations in London boys; there was no sex difference in this measure for the Bushman children.

2. Rough and Tumble Play

This category included the facial item open-mouthed smile, to children (results were also computed for open-mouthed smile, laugh, closed-mouthed smile, smile with squared lower lip and gave similar results except where discussed). The behavioural items were those in Table 2 Section 10 accompanied by any form of smile.

The facial expressions showed higher scores for boys in both cultures. The other items showed more rough and tumble by boys than girls in London but a non-significant difference in the Bushman children (Figs. 2a and b). In both measures Bushman girls scored very much higher than London girls.

Fig. 2(a)   Scores for "rough and tumble" play by the London children
presented as in Fig. 1.

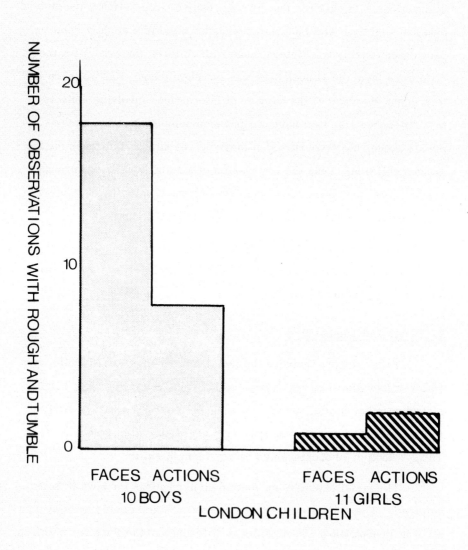

Fig. 2(b)   Scores for "rough and tumble" play by the Bushman children presented as in Fig. 1.

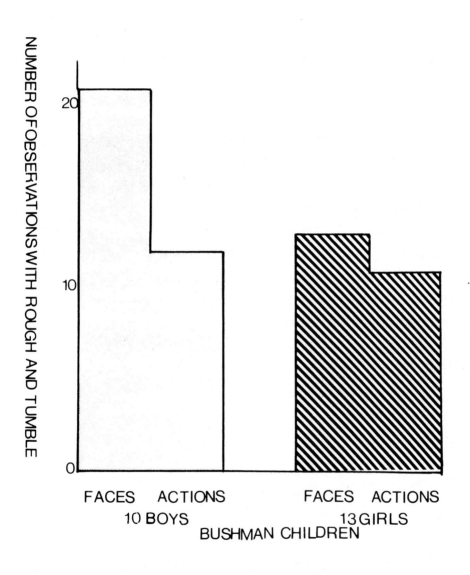

The Bushman girls differed from the London girls in showing more playfaces and laughing to children. On the other hand the London girls had many more interactions with their mother in which play-face and laughing occurred. If "playface to mother" is added to "playface to children", the sex difference is reduced in both cultures but remains highly significant in the London children and is significant at P = .05 level for the Bushman children.

The sex difference after behaviour to mother is included does not appear to be attributable to the age difference. There is a slight indication of an increase in "playface to children" with age in London (as was also found for rough-and-tumble play in the absence of mother, Blurton-Jones 1972). Measuring playface relative to sociable behaviour reveals a much smaller score for London girls even if interactions with mother and other adults are included. This is perhaps consonant with their low scores on "activity". The most vigorous activity occurs in rough and tumble and chasing.

3. Sociable Interactions

This heading includes interactions concerned with talking and exchanging objects. Facial items analysed were: (again, to children) smile, talk, lip-in-smile, pressed lips, lower lip bitten, brows up, head on side, hand on back or shoulders of other, closed mouth smile.

Sex differences in this group were not clearcut. Talking to children gave a sex difference (boys > girls) in both cultures (and in the data collected by both observers). This sex difference is the contrary to what most other workers find (e.g.: Smith and Connolly 1972). However, most other studies observe children in the absence of their mothers. Talking to children is closely related to age and we feel that this explains this apparent sex difference.

The number of observations in which any one or more of the above items of facial behaviour occurred while the child looked at another child shows a difference on the borderlines of significance for London children (U test P = .05) with boys scoring higher but there is no indication of such a difference for Bushman children. There was a nonsignificant difference (P = .10) for smiling in London. Smiling to children, and total sociable behaviour to children were constant with age. When children under three years old (mostly girls) are excluded, London boys show significantly more sociable behaviour than girls (U test P = .009). Age would seem therefore not to be the explanation of all of the London sex difference in sociability. Even if it were, this would imply a differing rate of development of social behaviour in London girls, which is also suggested by some of the data on rough and tumble play (which may anyway be the case). But it actually seems to relate more to a sex difference in who children are sociable with, which we discuss in a later section. The presence of mothers in our observations should be noted by anyone trying to compare results with other studies.

4. Sex Differences in People Interacted With

Adults versus children:

In both cultures the boys interact more often with children than adults, and the girls more often with adults than children. However, these differences were small. Using all facial items, both samples show a non-significant tendency for girls to interact in a higher proportion of interactions with adults (mother plus other adults excluding father). If the Bushman and London boys are combined and are compared with Bushman and London girls the sex difference in this proportion of interactions with adults is highly significant (U test, P = .011) For the Bushman children alone the difference is just above the 5% level on a two-tailed test, well below 10%. The London boys interact relatively more with adults than do Bushman boys (p < .05). The sex difference for the London children is just above significance whether one uses all items combined, or only looking at, or only smile. It is significant for playface and laugh but this is untestable for the Bushman children.

It is hard to determine whether these results are due to age differences. Interactions with mother are more common in the under three year old London girls, but interactions with children were lower after four years of age in London girls. If the under three year olds are excluded the sex differences in proportion of interaction with adult becomes significant for London at p < .024 (U test). If only those facial items other than "looking at" and "watching" are used then London girls interact less with children (p < .02 and proportionately more with mothers (p = .05) than do boys. The difference remains if under three year olds are excluded (p = .024 and p = .036 respectively). Studies in nursery schools do not usually produce sex differences in "sociability" but such studies are almost always in the absence of the mother.

We conclude that there is a tendency for London girls to interact relatively more with adults rather than with children as compared to boys. The difference was more marked in the Bushman children. In a study of middle class three year olds in Leicester, England, Lee, Wright and Herbert (1971) observed that in the presence of mother and another child of the same sex and its mother, the boys interact more with boys than girls do with other girls. Thus our London findings may have some generality.

(b)   Adults versus mother:

Bushman girls interacted more with adults other than the mother than did the boys (p < .05). For London the direction was the same but the figure non-significant (p < .10). When under three year olds were excluded it was again not significant (p = .077). Interaction with adults other than the mother, as a percentage of all interactions with adults, gave similar results for Bushman children (girls more to other adults, p < .02) but no difference for London regardless of age). Evidently the slightly greater interaction with adults other than mother by London girls is only proportional to their interaction with all adults, they are as selective as boys. Among the Bushman children the girls were less "selective" than the boys.

The adults available differed in the two cultures, the most familiar ones in the London sample being playgroup teachers or mothers of the child's friends. In the Bushman sample a very high proportion of available adults were close relatives. Even so it is interesting that interaction with them should involve girls more than it involves boys.

Two other measures, number of observations in which child looks at mother and number of observations in which child is face-to-face with mother, gives greater scores for Bushman girls and one shows a tendency in the same direction for London girls. These support the contention that Bushman girls interact more with mother than do boys.

The tendency for girls to interact more with adults than children thus seems likely to be true of both cultures and to be unaffected by age.

The degree of the difference differs between the cultures, and its interaction with age changes in "attachment" behaviour can be expected to be
complex. A similar result was obtained in Blurton-Jones (1972) with
regard to interactions with the (female) teacher in a playgroup. The
difference was clear in the older children and not in the younger. Girls
around four years old interacted more with the teacher than did the boys,
the proportion of their behaviour to teacher and to children being the
same as in 2 year olds whereas for boys it was less than in two year
olds. Clark, Wyon and Richards (1969) studying 3 - 4 year olds found
a similar tendency towards more interaction with teacher by girls.

Draper (in press) in a major study of Bushman childhood has
also found girls to score higher on several similar measures (staying
in the village-camp, proximity to adults etc.). This sex difference thus
seems to be replicable, and it leads to some interesting comparisons:
with non-human primates (e.g.: Japanese macaque and chimpanzee
mother-daughter relationships); with sociological studies of adults e.g.
Young and Wilmot (1957) though not of the middle-class Londoners
studied by Firth, Hubert and Forge (1970); and with psychological studies such as those of Moore (1967) and Kagan (1971) suggesting that
girls learn relatively more by verbal interaction with mother whereas
boys learn relatively more by action and experiment. However, we
must emphasise that the cultural difference in the amount of interaction
with mother was overwhelmingly greater than the sex difference.

(c)   Sex of children played with:

Sex differences in the amount children play with other children
of one or other sex have been described in English children (Clark,
Wyon and Richards 1969, Brindley et al. in press cited in Hutt, in

press, Blurton-Jones 1967) and the U.S.A. (Parten 1933) and Hawaii (McCandless and Hoyt 1961). Clark, Wyon and Richards showed the association of girls differed in two different classrooms, between playing predominantly with girls and equally with boys and girls; but all studies found boys playing predominantly with boys. In long-established groups, relationships may develop which depend on a number of variables like age and size and subtle behavioural differences. Our London sample contains some children in established groups, and some observed with long-standing friends but together with relatively strange children. The Bushman group contains long established (though not permanent) groups in a number of different villages.

At each observation the people within an estimated fifteen feet (5 metres) of the child were noted down. The people with whom the child was face to face, less than two feet away from, or touching were also recorded. The number of familiar children of each sex available in the general area (playground, village, etc.) was also extracted from our data. We have used the first and last as measures of the number of people available for interaction and the second two as a measure of with whom the child actually does interact. From this we calculated the percentage of available boys and the percentage of available girls with whom the child interacted. Siblings were excluded from these calculations. The percentages can be compared (fig. 3) and the comparison tested with the Wilcoxon matched pairs test, pairing an individual's percentage score to boys with his or her percentage score to girls.

Using this technique we find that the London boys showed the usual tendency to play more with boys than with girls ($p < .05$). The London girls do not show such a preference. The Bushman girls curiously enough played more with boys than with girls. The same result is ob-

Fig. 3   Illustration of data on choice of playmate according to sex. Results for boys and girls in both populations are shown for two measures of association between children (a) % of available children who are within two feet or are face to face with subject and (b) % of available children who are within 15 feet of subject during each half minute of observation.

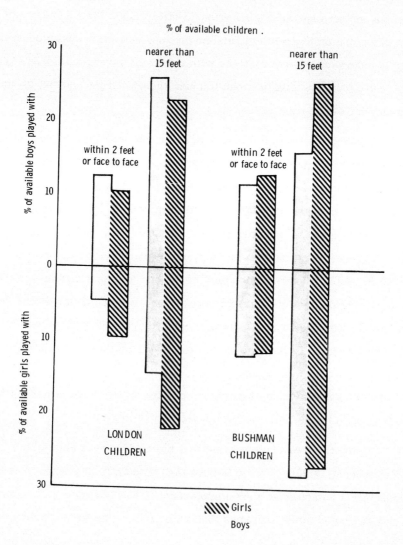

tained if the number of children within 15 feet is used as the measure of availability (fig. 3). Thus for example, London boys are within 15 feet of more of the available boys, and within 2 feet or face to face with more of those.

In seeking explanations of the cultural contrasts in these sex differences in commonest playmates we have concentrated partly on the kinds of behaviour that the two sexes perform most frequently. Blurton-Jones (1972) and Smith and Connolly (1972, see also Smith this volume) found that watching other children (looking at them but not doing anything else, or looking for a long time probably mainly at what they are doing) was inversely related to age and length of experience in nursery school and day nursery. Interacting with children (including smiling, laughing play-fighting etc.) is commoner in older and more school-experienced children. The proportion of watching to other facial items is higher in the London children aged less than four years than in the Bushman children aged less than four years (chi-squared, $P < .05$). A majority of these under-fours are girls. Thus as regards to their behaviour to other children the London children and especially the girls seem less sociably mature and on this measure interact less than do the Bushman children of either sex.

We are thus tempted to try to explain the cultural difference in preferred playmates by suggesting that the relatively unsociable (to children) London girls make unrewarding social partners for boys. The Bushman girls, besides being more sociable, also did more rough and tumble and chasing play than did the London girls which will also enable them to interact more readily with boys. (The extreme difference between the two samples of girls in amount of rough and tumble could hardly be accounted for by the lesser difference in amount of interaction with boys).

(d) Origins of cultural differences in social behaviour

Underlying this topic is a radical difference in the experience of social contacts of Bushman and London children which no doubt has far-reaching consequences. Among these consequences may be the differing patterns of interaction analysed here. Bushman children grow up with constant access to a few children of mixed ages and of sexes determined by chance. They must develop some kind of relationship to all the children that they know. The London children grow up with at the most a sibling readily available. Access to children is otherwise only by arrangement and usually with a number of close age mates, as at play-group or nursery school. However, the observation remains that the pattern of interaction of and between the sexes differs in these two environments, and that the difference is not a matter of immediate opportunity but of preferences developed in these radically different social environments. That occasionally in nursery schools one comes across devoted male-female pairs of playmates might suggest that, given a certain sort of social environment in which to develop, London children also might form patterns of interaction more resembling the Bushman pattern. Another (but not necessarily mutually exclusive) kind of explanation for this difference also merits attention. It seems that parental opinion in English cultures (as well as the opinion and example of older children) quite often favours same-sex-interactions and same-sex groups more strongly and openly than is the case for Bushman culture. Given the fact that men are more powerful and are considered superior in both cultures, and are probably perceived as such and are preferred by children (e.g. Brown, 1958, for American children), one would expect a shared tendency for <u>both</u> sexes to prefer boys. In England, where the <u>same-sex</u> trend is encouraged, boys would tend to play much more with boys, whereas girls, influenced by two conflicting tendencies (same-sex preference from training, boy preference from experience) would tend to divide their attention between the sexes. In Bushman children, where there is less same-sex preference training, girls may be influenced only by boy-preference, whereas boys' preference for boys is opposed (approximately equally?) by girls' efforts to play with them and by the fact that girls play more or less as they do. In London, boys are more active than girls, more interested in objects (longer sustained directed attention), and more engaged in rough and tumble, but these sex differences are not marked in Bushman children). Undoubtedly the culture differences in sex-differentiation of play are engaged in a cycle of mutual and cumulative interaction with the cultural differences in sex preference.

5. Use of Objects

No sex difference was significant in either culture although in the London sample, boys played a little more with objects (P just over 0.10). However, the London children played with objects much more than the Bushman children. Though our category does not distinguish uses of objects such as, on the one hand using a pencil in drawing, and on the other hand carrying an object like a security blanket, the London result is in the same direction as other workers' findings on sex differences in interest in objects. The Bushman findings show no such trend. The percentage of observations of a child with no object in which it interacted with another child was higher in boys in both cultures (Bushman $p < .002$, London $p < .02$, cf Smith and Connolly, 1972).

6. Sustained Directed Attention

The raw scores of this measure give a higher score for London boys than London girls but no significant sex difference in the Bushman children, although there is a slight tendency toward higher scores in the girls. Since a child's score on this measure was positively correlated with the number of observations in which it was holding an object we took this into account in an approximate way by calculating each child's "sustained" score as a percentage of the number of observations of that child with an object. This changes the picture in some respects. The London boys still score higher than the girls (p = .05). The Bushman girls still score about equal to Bushman boys. However, by this calculation London boys now score no higher than Bushman boys, whereas Bushman girls score higher than London girls (p < .05).

7. Negative Results

The data on the majority of these behaviour items listed in Appendices 1 and 2 but which are not discussed in the text showed no significant differences between boys and girls in either culture. Some results show differences but were not statistically significant. These were head-on-side (girls more in both cultures), lower-lip-bitten (boys more in both cultures), self-touch (girls more in both cultures, for data by both observers).

No sex differences were found in behaviour directed to the observers although, as might be expected, there was a large cross-cultural difference. We consider that the cultural differences in response to the observers is unlikely to have any effect on sex differences in the two cultures although its effect on cultural differences has to be examined.

The Bushman children looked (and smiled) at the observers much more often than did the London children. This should have effects opposite to those described as cultural differences e.g., greater interaction with children by Bushman girls. In other instances of culture difference we are able to show that the amount of looking at observer does not correlate within a culture with other culturally varying behaviour and is thus unlikely to explain the cultural differences.

8. Activity

The London boys scored significantly higher than the London girls (Fig. 4a). There was no difference between Bushman girls and boys (Fig. 4b).

Garner, Percy and Lawson (1971) have described a positive correlation between a measure of behavioural impulsivity and IQ in girls (contrary to the position with boys). These authors cite other work which suggests similar relationships between activity and IQ and discuss their measure as reflecting activity. These studies suggest that the more active an American or English girl is the more intelligent she is. It is therefore very important to investigate the cultural sources of the lower activity of girls that our results suggest before assuming that the sex differences in measures of intellectual performance which are sometimes observed are inevitably sex-linked (see also Kagan and Moss 1962).

9. Differences between Bushman Girls and London Girls

During the observations some of the London girls were notably uninvolved with other children. In analysing the data on sex differences some differences seemed smaller in the Bushman children (e.g. rough

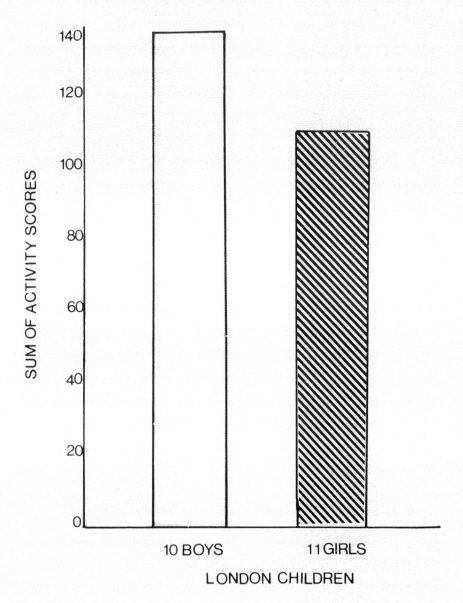

Fig. 4(a)   Histogram comparing "Activity" of the London boys and girls. The activity score is the number of half minute observations in which subject was recorded as showing vigorous physical activity.

Fig. 4(b)   Histogram comparing "Activity" of the Bushman boys and
Bushman girls. The activity score is as in Fig 4(a).

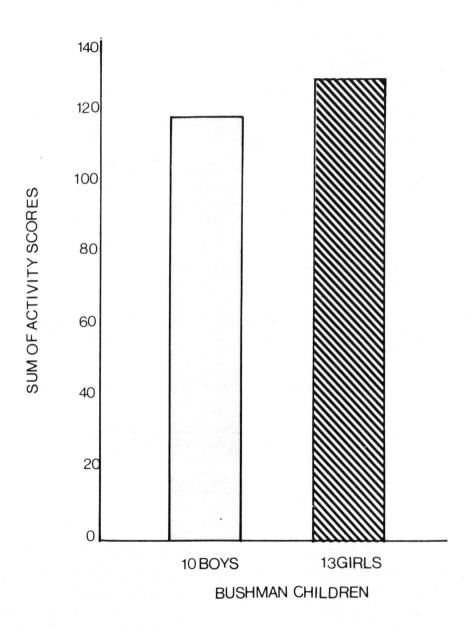

and tumble play) and this phenomenon was apparently due to differences in the scores of girls rather than boys. These differences are summarised here because they contribute important information to our discussion of sex differences in the two cultures.

(a)   Rough and tumble play:

In interactions with children Bushman girls did more playface (p < .002), play actions (p < .002) combined playful face (playface, laugh, closed lip-smiles, lower lip square smiles (p < .02). If faces to mother are also considered these differences are reduced. For playface alone it remains just significant (P = .02) for the combined playful faces (p< .10). Thus to some extent the London girls' clearly lower frequency of rough and tumble play to children is made up for by their greater interaction with their mother.

(b)   Aggression:

The raw scores for "aggressive" faces by London girls were greater than the scores for Bushman girls (p < .02), the same result was obtained for aggressive actions although girls scored clearly less than boys in both populations. Taking % of "aggressive faces"/"faces towards children" (other than "look and watch") the London girls again scored higher than the Bushman girls (p < .02), and this rendered the London sex difference non-significant.

(c)   Sociable interactions:

In London, girls scored lower than boys (p = .05) but in the Bushman children there was no difference. This difference was increased by removing the youngest girls so it was not an effect of age. The cultural difference appeared to be mainly due to a higher frequency of

interactions with children by Bushman girls, although the difference between their scores and those of the London girls was not significant
(p just over 0.10).

(d)   Total interactions with children:

Scoring all faces to children other than looking and watching gives
a sex difference for London children (boys more than girls) (p < .02) but
not for Bushman children. Again this might be due to slightly greater
interactions by Bushman girls than by London girls.

(e)   Total interactions with mother: (and relative interaction with
         mother, adults and children).

The sex differences in these measures were small compared to
the very large cultural difference. However, this implies that the difference between London and Bushman girls can be summarised as a
centering of social behaviour around the mother as opposed to other
children. The cultural difference is just as large for boys but we must
assume that this does not modify their interaction with children so much.

(d)   Sustained attention to objects

When the culture difference in amount of use of objects is taken
into account (% unbroken series with same object/number of observations with any object) the sex difference remains absent in Bushman
children apparently because the Bushman girls score higher than the
London girls, (p < .05). This difference was not obviously produced
by a differential provision of toys to boys and girls by the London mothers and teachers. The Bushman children had no toys provided, finding
their play objects for themselves in natural material or "household" articles appropriate to either sex. Conceivably the great availability of
household articles associated with food preparation in the Bushman

situations could be responsible for the difference. But this in turn implies a clear sex differentiation of interest in different kinds of objects in Bushman children of this age.

Summary of Results

We find that some measures that show the same sex differences in both cultures: agonistic behaviour, rough and tumble play, proportion of interaction with adults as opposed to children, amount of interaction with adults other than mother. Three non-significant but suggestive differences were also the same in each culture: head on side, lower lip bitten, self touch, (a significant sex difference in self touch was found in Holland by Kalverboer, pers. comm.).

Several sex differences similar to those described in the literature for North American and British children were also found in our London sample but were absent in the Bushman sample: activity, amount of play with objects, sustained directed attention, preference of boys for playing with boys. It is notable that these culturally variable sex differences include the possibly more educationally significant measures.

In our observations, differing from most others in that the mothers were present (in both cultures), there is a sex difference in several measures of the amount of social behaviour to other children in the London sample, along with a number of differences in the behaviour of girls in the cultures. These lead us to believe that those sex differences found only in N. America and Britain are a result of cultural factors which may be related to 1) differences in early maternal behaviour, 2) to the high amount of contact with mother and lower contact with chil-

dren or 3) the interaction of these factors with the greater tendency of
girls to interact more with adults than with children.

DISCUSSION: DEVELOPMENT OF SEX DIFFERENCES

Our finding that some of the commonly recorded sex differences
in North American and British children are also found in Bushman
children, while other such commonly recorded differences are not found
in the Bushman children, has some implications for the development of
sex differences, although our findings do not allow us to attribute particular differences to particular causes. First and most strongly, it implies that at most only some of the differences found in Britain and North
America can be attributed to the hormonal sex-typing of the brain. We
would do well to be cautious about which differences we assume are attributable to this process. In particular, since so much is now known
about relationships between mother-child interaction in the first year
and cognitive development and sex-differences in these measures (e.g.
Kagan 1971), it would be very unwise to readily attribute differences in
measures of intellectual performance to direct effects of hormonal sex-
typing of the brain as has been done lately in the mass media.

If as seems reasonable, one regards some of the sex differences
found in many cultures (e.g.: aggression, rough and tumble play) as
resulting from sex-typing of the brain, one must regard the sex difference found only in U.K. and U.S.A. as resulting from different mechanisms. So the second implication of our results is that there may well
be several different mechanisms of development of sex differences. We
discuss some possible examples below.

The work of social anthropologists such as Mead, stressing

differences in the behaviour of men and women between one society and another, led to the development of theories of acquisition of behaviour through parental pressures and through the child's identification with adult models of the appropriate sex. There is much strong evidence to suggest that these processes can be effective (e.g.: Maccoby 1966). However, they are processes whose measurement is very difficult to envisage.

During the current wave of interest in early hormonal influences on sex differences in behaviour we feel it is important to bear in mind that these prior theories, while certainly not proved, have also not been disproved.

More recently various other lines of work have indicated possible mechanisms for the development of sex differences in behaviour. One line concerns the effects of pre-natal and peri-natal hormones on the brain, references and an outlines are to be found in the chapter by Hutt (this volume). The other lines concern observed interactions between mother and baby during the first year of life. Moss (1967) and Bell and Costello (1964) have described differences in newborns (sleep and crying, and skin sensitivity respectively) which may, in American middle class society, lead to marked differences in maternal behaviour. Studies such as those of Ainsworth (e.g. Ainsworth, Bell and Stayton 1971) give reason to expect far reaching consequences of such differences in maternal behaviour.

Moss (1967) described an interaction whereby the more frequent early crying of boys, who are also awake more of the time and are more difficult to calm, led to higher rates of interaction with the mother but in some cases to a later decline in maternal responsiveness. Ainsworth

and Bell (in press) present data which suggest that high maternal responsiveness leads to less crying and more other vocalisations as the
baby approaches one year old. Ainsworth also has evidence that more
responsive mothers during the first year have children who at one year
explore more readily and appear in many ways more sociable. This
series of interactions although starting from differences apparently
present from birth, gives ample scope for individual and cultural variation (as in the mother's decision whether to continue increasing efforts
to calm the more irritable baby boy, or whether to give up and let it cry*)
which will have far reaching influences on differences in behaviour between boys and girls. Bushman methods of baby care (carrying in a
sling on the mother's side, see Konner 1972) are such as to lead one to
expect much smaller effects of the sex differences in crying on the
mothers' behaviour. Such interactions also make it pointless to try to
apportion responsibility between the newborn differences and the differences in the mothers' reaction to them, or to talk in terms of one culture
"suppressing" and another "producing" differences in behaviour of boys
and girls which result from such a process. Similar interaction of newborn difference and maternal differences may also apply to Moss's finding that boys were awake more and also were stimulated or aroused
more often by their mothers (even taking sleep time and irritability
into account) than were girls. If these interactions influence development of activity, they could influence IQ scores. High heritability for
IQ could in part result from congenital similarities in the babies'ability

---

*The maternal "decisions" could give rise to greater variability in the
behaviour of boys than of girls. Such differences in variability were
apparent in some of our data from each culture, and in no case was the
sex difference in the variability the same in both cultures.

to evoke behaviour in their mothers and thus not imply immutability of
the development of IQ.

Bell et al. (1971) find that a high tactile threshold in newborns
predicts "vigorous attack on barriers" at pre-school ages. He has also
described a sex difference in tactile threshold in newborns. These findings are highly suggestive of another source of developing sex differences.
However, Bell finds that vigorous attack on barriers is not related to
attacks on other children. Consequently to attribute particular measures
that we made to this newborn difference requires some caution. The developmental interaction between the sex differences in newborn thresh-
olds and cultural differences in maternal care can be expected to give
rise to cultural differences in sex differences. The Bushman baby has
almost continuous skin contact with mother, and more frequent nipple
contact. It would be hard to choose between the various possible consequences of this but they may be expected to be great. Data on mother-
infant interaction gathered by M. J. K. may be instructive in this respect.

A surprising fact lurks behind the question of sex differences in
Bushman behaviour which will be of interest to those who wonder how
much of the difference we find is racial rather than cultural. Several
investigators have now shown that adult Bushman men have very high
oestrogen levels (both in urine and blood) (see Tobias 1966). There have
been no measurements from children. It is argued by Tobias that this
is an effect of having a very low fat diet. There is little reason to expect
this endocrine phenomenon to be evident in children, nor would it account
for our observations.

Our findings do not exclude the traditional view that all sex dif-

ferences and cultural variation in them are determined by a combination of parental pressures and the child's modelling its behaviour on
selected adults. The effects of all the possible mechanisms of development that we have discussed can only be demonstrated if each is systematically measured in the same study. We have discussed to some
extent above, the differences and similarities of adult pressures in
London and Bushman culture (based on impressions rather than systematic measurements) and feel that interaction of all these processes is
likely to be needed to account for observed sex differences and their
variation from one culture to another. This has implications for the
current conflict over the role of woman and the possibilities for its
modification in industrialised society. We discuss these implications
briefly below after first discussing some problems associated with the
cross-cultural work on which the traditional (culture determined by sex
role) view was based.

Cultural Variability in Sex Differences

Margaret Mead, in two seminal works (1963, orig. 1935,
1967 orig. 1949) which still form the major literature in the cross-
cultural study of sex differences, and which have played an important
part in feminist writing (Frieden 1970, Millet 1970), advanced the view
that within each sex the possible variation of behaviour is very much
greater than one would expect from Western sex-role behaviour, and
that the differentiation (or lack of it) depends largely on specific cultural training. Of three New Guinea tribes she writes (1963, pp 6):

> In one, both men and women act as we expect women to act -
> in a mild parental responsive way; in the second, both act
> as we expect men to act - in a fierce initiating fashion; and

in a third, the men act according to our stereotype for
women - are catty, wear curls and go shopping, while
the women are energetic, managerial, unadorned partners.

Mead's point about flexibility of sex roles, exceeding the expectations of our culture is certainly made in this and the later work which
adds four more Pacific societies to the roster. But the examination of
behaviour is not systematic or exhaustive, and one wonders whether the
focus has not rested rather arbitrarily on those features in which primitive societies depart from our own cultural stereotypes. Indeed, certain consistencies seem to have been overlooked, especially in the area
of aggression. Among the "mild, parental" Arapesh men for example
(1963, p. 41)

> "... although actual warfare expeditions to plunder, conquer,
> kill or attain glory is absent, brawls and clashes between
> villages do occur, mainly over women (italics ours)"

In describing such clashes (which frequently result in wounds,
occasionally fatal wounds), Mead nowhere mentions women as participating. Similarly, Mundugomor women may be very fierce, but they
never participate in their husbands' head hunting expeditions, or in any
comparable activity. The same can be said for the Tchambuli among
whom the traditional sex roles are supposedly reversed. Competition
for women is an important source of conflict in all three societies, and
the head hunters abduct women not to eat them, but to marry them. As
might be expected, a careful reading reveals sex role consistencies which
are obscured by the emphasis on the differences.

In another cross-cultural study, this time of sex differences in
"socialisation" - parental expectation and training - based on judgements
of ethnographers' reports (Barry, Bacon and Child 1957), great consis-

tencies in sex role training were found. Of 33 societies, none were judged to train boys more than girls in "nurturance". Of 82 societies, none trained girls more than boys in "self reliance". Less, but still impressive consistency was obtained for "achievement" (boys more) and for "obedience" and "responsibility" (girls more). These are meant to be measures of training efforts by parents. They thus suggest the question, "If the sexes are so different biologically, why do all these cultures go to the trouble of doing all this training?" Barry, Bacon and Child analysed the degree of sex difference in relation to subsistence ecology and concluded that "large sex difference in socialisation is associated with an economy that places a high premium on superior strength". This included hunting of large animals. Thus before we blame industrial civilisation for sex differences, we should recognise the correlation between hunting of large animals and sex differentiation pressures since the hunting of large animals has existed in human society for some hundreds of thousands of years. It is scarcely possible that in all that time natural selection in relation to hunting, combined with the fact that it is men who engage in homicidal conflicts would have failed to maintain the biological basis for acquisition of sex differences in behaviour. The extensive sex differences in behaviour and physique of the higher primates is of course also relevant here (as Gray and Buffery 1971 also argue) although if anything, the physical differences are reduced in man.

Questions of the development of sex differences can only be settled when measures of sex differences in the child's behaviour are combined with systematic studies of both maternal behaviour and parental verbal pressures and modelling as well as consideration of the experimental physiological data. Nonetheless, the evidence strongly supports the idea that our own culture (like all cultures) burdens children with a great deal of sex role paraphernalia that goes well beyond the dictates of biology. However, our results give little comfort for those women's liberationi sts who argue that there are no differences between men and women other than those instilled by our particular sexist culture. There are differences like those in frequency of aggression which we and others find in other cultures. Along with the sex differences in rough and tumble play, there is no reason to believe that these are not (just as in other mammals) related to the pre-natal sex typing of the brain by circulating androgens. But we do have some comfort in the many culturally variable sex differences for those liberationists who believe that our culture does strange things to women. We have postulated that the low sociability, low activity, and rare rough and tumble of the middle-class London girls, combined with direct sex-preference training causes the preference of boys for other boys as playmates. This must have developmental consequences in the adult sex segregation and male grouping tendencies described by Tiger (1969). The cross-cultural difference in the girls, having no possible relationship to the known endocrine differences between the populations, and plenty of possible relationship to observed differences in infant care and opportunity for child-child interaction, could be taken as justification for those who argue that our culture makes girls unnaturally well-behaved and other than they might be.

REFERENCES

Ainsworth, Mary D. Salter, and Bell, Silvia, M. V. (in press). Infant crying and maternal responsiveness: Reinforcement reassessed. Science.

Ainsworth, Mary D. Salter, Bell, Silvia M. V. and D. J. Stayton
(1971). Individual Differences in Strange Situation Behaviour of
One-year olds. In "The Origins of Human Social Relations"
(H. R. Schaffer ed.). Academic Press, London.

Ardrey, R. (1961). African Genesis. Collins, London.

Barry, H. B., Bacon, M. K. & I. L. Child (1957). A cross-cultural
survey of some sex differences in socialisation. J. Abnorm.
Soc. Psych. 55, 337-342.

Bell, R. & Costello, N. S. (1964). "Three tests for sex differences
in tactile sensitivity in the new-born." Biol. Neonat. (Basel) 7,
335-347.

Bell, R., Weller, G. M. and M. F. Waldrop (1971). "Newborn and
Preschooler: Organisation of behaviour and relations between
periods." Monographs of the Society for Research in Child
Development, 36, 1-145.

Blurton-Jones, N. G. (1967). An Ethological Study of Some Aspects
of social behaviour of Children in Nursery School. In "Primate
Ethology." (Morris, D. ed.) Wiedenfeld & Nicholson, London.

Blurton-Jones, N. G. (1971). Criteria for use in describing Facial
Expressions of Children. Human Biology, 43, 365-413.

Blurton-Jones, N. G. (ed) (1972). "Ethological Studies of Child Behaviour". Cambridge University Press, London.

Blurton-Jones, N. G. (1972b). Categories of child-child interaction.
In "Ethological Studies of Child Behaviour" (N. Blurton-Jones
ed.) Cambridge University Press, London.

Brannigan, C. & Humphries, D. (1972). Human non-verbal behaviour:
a means of communication. In "Ethological studies of Child behaviour. (N. Blurton-Jones ed.) Cambridge University Press,
London.

Brindley, C., Clarke, P., Hutt, C., Robinson, E. & Wethli, E. (in press). Sex differences in the activities and social interactions of nursery school children. Developmental Psychology.

Brown, D. G. (1958). Sex-role development in a changing culture. Psych. Bull. 55, 232-242.

Caudill, W. & H. Weinstein (1969). Maternal Care and Infant Behaviour in Japan and America. Psychiat. 32, 12.

Clark, A. H., Wyon, S. M. & M. P. M. Richards (1969). Free-play in nursery school children. J. Child Psychol. Psychiat. 10, 205-216.

Draper, P. (1971). Paper presented at annual meeting of the American Anthropological Association, New York.

Draper, P. (in press). !kung Bushman childhood: an analysis of sex differences. Science in press.

Eibl-Eibesfeldt, I. (1972). Similarities and differences between cultures in expressive movements. In: "Non-verbal communication" (R. A. Hinde ed.) Cambridge University Press, London.

Ekman, P. (1972). Universals and Cultural differences in Facial expressions of emotion. In: "Nebraska symposium on motivation." (J. Cole ed.) Univ. of Nebraska Press.

Firth, R., Hubert, J. & A. Forge (1970). "Families and their Relatives - Kinship in a middle class sector of London: an anthropological study." Routledge & Kegan Paul, London.

Frieden, B. (1970). The Feminine Mystique. Dell, New York.

Garai, J. E. and Scheinfeld A., (1968). Sex differences in mental and behavioral traits. Genetic Psychology Monographs, 77, 169-299.

Garner, J., Percy, L. M. and T. Lawson (1971). Sex differences in behavioural impulsivity, intellectual impulsivity, and attainment in young children. J. Child Psychol. Psychiat. 12, 261-271.

Grant, E. C. (1965). The contribution of ethology to child psychiatry. In "Modern Perspectives in Child Psychiatry" (J. C. Howells ed.) Oliver and Boyd, Edinburgh.

Grant, E. C. (1969). Human Facial Expression. Man. 4. 525-536.

Gray, J. A. (1971). Sex differences in emotional behaviour in mammals including man: endocrine bases. Acta psychologica 35, 29-46.

Gray, J. A. & A. W. H. Buffery (1971). Sex differences in emotional and cognitive behaviour in mammals including man: adaptive and neural bases. Acta. Psychologica. 35, 89-111.

Howell, N. (1971). Paper presented at annual meeting of the American Anthropological Association, New York.

Hutt, C. (1972). Neuroendocrinological, behavioural, and intellectual aspects of sexual differentiation in human development. In: "Gender differences: their ontogeny and significance." (C. Ounsted & D. C. Taylor eds) Churchill, London.

Inhelder, B. & J. Piaget (1958). "The growth of logical thinking from childhood through adolescence." Basic Books, New York.

Jensen, G. D., Bobbitt, R. A. and B. N. Gordon. (1967). Sex differences in social interaction between infant monkeys and their mothers. Recent adv. biol. Psychiat., 9, 283-293.

Jensen, G. D., Bobbitt, R. A, and B. N. Gordon (1968). Sex differences in the development of independence of infant monkeys. Behaviour 30, 1-14.

Kagan, J. (1971). "Change and Continuity in Infancy." Wiley, New York.

Kagan, J. & H. A. Moss (1962). From birth to maturity. Wiley, New York.

Konner, M. J. (1972). Aspects of the Developmental Ethology of a Foraging People. In: "Ethological Studies of Child Behaviour." (N. Blurton-Jones ed.) Cambridge University Press, London.

Lee, R. B. (1968). What Hunters do for a living, or, How to make out on scarce resources. In: Man the Hunter (R. B. Lee and I. DeVore eds.) Aldine, Chicago.

Lee, R. (1970). Paper presented at annual meeting of American Anthropological Association, San Diego.

Lee, R. & I DeVore (eds) (1968). Man the Hunter. Aldine, Chicago.

Lee, S. G. M., Wright, D. S., M. Herbert (1971). Development of Social Responsiveness in young children. Report to the Social Science Research Council.

Loizos, C. (1966). Play in Mammals. Symp. zool. Soc. Lond. 18, 1-9.

Maccoby, E. E. (ed.) (1966). "The development of sex differences." Tavistock, London.

Mead, M. (1963). (orig. 1935). "Sex and temperament in three primative societies." Dell, New York.

Mead, M. (1967). (orig. 1949). "Male and female." William Morrow and Company, New York.

Millet, K. (1970). Sexual Politics. Doubleday, New York.

Moore, T. (1967). Language and Intelligence: A longitudinal study of the first eight years. Human Development, 10, 88-106.

Moss H. A. (1967). "Sex Age, and State as Determinants of Mother-Infant Interaction." Merrill - Palmer Quarterly of Behaviour and Development, 13, 19-36.

Murdock, G. P. (1949). Social Structures. The Free Press, New York.

McCandless, B. R. & J. M. Hoyt, (1961). Sex. ethnicity and play preferences of preschool children. J. Abnorm. Soc. Psychol. 62, 683-685.

McGrew, W. (1972). "An Ethological Study of Children's Behaviour." Academic Press, New York.

Parten, M. B. (1933). Social Play amongst preschool children. J. Abnorm. Soc. Psychol. 28, 136-147.

Phoenix, C. H., Goy, R. W. & J. A. Resko (1968). Psychosexual differentiation as a function of androgenic stimulation. In "Perspectives in reproduction and sexual behavior." (M. Diamond ed.) Indiana University Press, Bloomington.

Smith, P. K. & K. J. Connolly (1972). Patterns of Play and Social Interaction in Preschool children. In: "Ethological Studies of Child Behaviour." (N. Blurton-Jones ed.) Cambridge University Press, London.

Tiger, L. (1969). "Men in Groups." Nelson, London.

Tobias, P. V. (1966). The peoples of Africa south of the Sahara. In "The Biology of Human Adaptability." (P. T. Baker and J. S. Weiner eds) Clarendon Press, Oxford,

Trivers, R. L. (1971). The Evolution of Reciprocal Altruism. Qu. Rev. Biol. 46, 35-57.

Valenstein, E. S. (1968). Steroid hormones and the neuropsychology of development. In: "The neuropsychology of development." (R. L. Isaacson, ed.) John Wiley & Sons, Inc., New York.

Whiting, B. (1963). Six cultures: studies of child rearing. Wiley, New York.

Woodburn, J. (1968). An Introduction to Hadza ecology. In "Man the Hunter." (R. B. Lee & I. DeVore eds.) Aldine, Chicago.

Yellen, J. E. (in press). Ethnoarchaeology: Bushman Settlement Patterns. Paper presented at the Bushman Symposium. American
Anthropological Association meetings. New York City. November
1971.

Yellen, J. & Harpending, H. (in press). Hunter-gatherer populations
and archaeological inference. Paper presented at American Anthropological Association meetings. New York City, November
1971.

Young, M. and Wilmot, P. (1957). "Family and kinship in East London."
Penguin books, Harmondsworth.

APPENDIX

I. Faces and gestures

Facial expressions were recorded using mostly the items defined
by Blurton-Jones (1971) where small features of facial expression were
separately described from a large   number of photographs of London
children. In some cases (e.g. smile) these were combined. The list
below describes only those whose scores were counted up and it omits
definitions where these are as in Blurton-Jones (1971) or (1972) or in
Grant (1969) and Brannigan and Humphries(1972) (B&H).

Look at	Brannigan and Humphries
Watch	Blurton-Jones 1972 - Includes stare Smith and Connolly 1972
Sunface	Strong contraction of m. orbicularis occuli usually accompanied by square upper lip while looking towards or into bright sunlight, even if also looking at person.
Face up	Blurton-Jones 1971
Smile (all forms except mouth-open smiles)	i.e. from B & H: simple smile, upper smile, compressed smile, broad smile, lip-in smile.

Mouth-open smile	B & H.
Two-lip pout	lips forward, B & H.
Lower-lip pout	Lower lip out, B & H.
Lower lip square (including "grimace")	oblong-mouth B & H 1972 plus these features accompanying smiles, i.e. includes "oblong smile"B& H.
Upper lip square	Sneer B & H.
Lips pressed	Tight lips B & H.
Lower lip bitten or rolled in (exclude when smile also)	Lips in B & H.
Retract	Mouth corners back and mouth corners out B & H.
Small mouth	As Grant 1969 and B & H.
Brows oblique	Sad frown and sad raise B & H.
Brows up	Raise and Flash B & H.
Frown "general frown"	Angry frown and low frown B & H. (BJ 1972 but excluding oblique)
Narrow frown	As Grant 1969 puzzled frown
Head on side	Head to side B & H and Head tilt McGrew 1972
Hand on back or shoulder	Hand on back and shoulder hug McGrew 1972
Closed mouth smile	Simple smile B & H.
Laugh	As McGrew 1972, B & H.
Self touch when look at another child	As above regardless of gaze direction
Talk	Utter words while looking at another person (who is specified as in all the above)
Lower lip square smile	Oblong smile, B & H. Also lower lip square alone.

II. List of items of child and caretaker behaviour coded in time sample observations of two-to-five year olds, with code abbreviations used during the observations. Arranged in categories used for convenience and memonic efficiency in recording. Preceded by list of "actors" in the observations.

1. Persons emitting or receiving acts:

Mother	m
Father	f
Man	o
Woman	o_1
Older boy	c_1
Younger boy	c_3
Older girl	c_2
Younger girl	c_4
Older sister	s_2
Younger sister	s_4
Older brother	s_1
Younger brother	s_3
Slightly older girl (1 year)	P_2
Slightly younger girl	P_4
Slightly older boy	P_1
Slightly younger boy	P_3

(If more than one person of a given category appeared during the same hour-observation, these were differentiated by superscripts.)

2. Facial expressions (subjects only)

Smile	s
Frown	fr
Weak frown	w fr

Strong frown	str fr
Sunface	sun
Pucker face (fret face)	pkr
Brows up	br
Pout	pt
Lower lip pout	lle
Lower lip bite	llb
Grimace	gr
Press lips	press lips
Tongue out	to
Yawn	yawn

3. Attachment-related behaviours (usually subject; sometimes other, usually younger child; if subject, recipient indicated; if other, actor indicated).

Look at	el
Gaze fixate	fx
Vocalize	v
Talk	tlk
Approach	app
Leave	lv
Follow	flw
Give object	go ($\pm$ or $-$ indicates acceptance)
Give food	gf " " "
Touch	t
Cling	clng
Nurse	N

(for unsigned go or gf, assume $\pm$)

4. Nurturance-related behaviours (anyone; if subject, recipient specified; if other, actor specified)

(All items in 3 above except Leave, Nurse; plus the following)

Adjust	adj
Encourage	enc (± or - for compliance)
Instruct	instr " " "
Model	mod
Help	help
Entertain	ent
Sing	sng
Clap	clp
Vigorous physical stimulation	vps
Imitate, (physical, verbal)	im (p, v)
Direct	dir
Reward	rew
Nurture	nurt

(for unsigned enc, mod, no assumptions)

5. Juxtaposition to mother. Juxtaposition to other actors or nearest persons (in "other" column, individual always specified)

Face to face at least 5 sec	X
Passively touching within 2 ft	
(Distance estimated to nearest 5 ft., or best estimate)	5, 10, 25, etc.

6. Non-nurturant caretaking behaviours (specifications of persons as in 4 above.

Adjust	adj
Ignore	ign

Direct	dir (± or -)
Prohibit (physical, verbal)	vpro, ppro, v & ppro (± or -)
Punish (physical, verbal)	vpun, ppun, v & ppun (- if punished behaviour resumes)
Leave	lv
Talk	tlk
Take object	to

(plus all "Agonistic behaviours" (10 below) other than chase, wrestle, flee.)

7. Play (subject behaviour only)

Assimilative play (repetitive)	P
Exploratory play (non-repetitive, non-mobile)	(Greek letter rho)
Relating objects together	rel
Construction (building or making)	constr
Imaginitive play (pretence, make-believe)	imag
Subsistence play (food getting or food preparing behaviours, real or pretended)	subs (plus many combinations of these; plus many other described idiosyncrasies)
Rough and tumble	Agon
Gentle and tumble	gentle and tumble
Game	game
Mouth object	mth

8. Imitation, repetition.

Subject only. Person imitated indicated. Cross reference to

behaviour category column in which imitated or repeated behaviour is coded, (e.g. "Im. P. Voc").

9. People within 15 feet.

Coded as in 1 above. If many, time may not allow specification of all individuals (e.g. "5c"), but try to specify those figuring importantly for subject.

10. Agonistic behaviour (Playful, non-playful. If subject, recipient indicated; if other, actor indicated).

Hit	ht (- for miss)
Kick	kck " " "
Bite	bi
Push	push
Beat poised (threat gesture)	bt up
Object beat	obj bt
Object beat poised	obj bt up
Chase	ch
Flee	fl
Cling	clng
Wrestle	wr
Bump	bmp
Poke	poke
Direct	dir (± or - for compliance)
Adjust	adj
Gaze fixate	fx
Take object	to (± or - for success)
Snatch	snatch
Withdraw	wdraw

Pull	pull
Throw object	thro

(this column and the "non-nurturance" column are frequently cross-referenced to each other i.e. instead of recording the same behaviours twice, the code "Non-nurt" may appear in this column, and vice versa)

11. Postural communication.

Descriptive catch-all category for non-facial "body language" type postures and gestures; not systemized in advance; include the following:-

Object on head

Hand(s) at mouth

" on hip(s)

" at crotch

Pull at clothing (specified)

Arm across face

Point

Head tilt

Arms over head

Hand(s) behind head

" at neck

Hand(s) behind back

Head on hand

Arms out

Chin on hand

Present object

Hold foot

(many others; this column is often cross-referenced to the "Auto-manipulation" column, since many items in the latter column may have partial or even primary signal function)

12. Vocalisation.

Unspecified non-fretful vocalisation	V
Fret	fr
Cry	cry
One word phrase	W1
Two word phrase	W2
Three word phrase	W3
Sentence	Se
Sing	sng
Chant	chant
Hum	hum
Laugh	La
Playnoise*	plnoise
Shout	sh
Scream	scr

*(usually an imitation of something)

13. Gross motor action

Sit	Si
Stand	St
Lift (assumption) erect posture	Li
Walk	W
Run	Ru
Climb	Cl
Jump	jump

Dance	da
Bounce	Bo
Crouch	Crch
Kneel	kn
Lie	lie
Crawl	crl
Rock	rcks
Fall	falls
Extension-flexion movements	ef
Stamp	stamp
Gallop	gallop
Shuffle	shuffle

14. Automanipulation

Hand-to-mouth	hmth <u>or</u> 8
Hand-to-hand	HH
Automanipulation genital	AMG
Anal	AMA
Rock	Rcks
Extension-flexion movements	ef

Plus many others such as scratch, rub, poke, finger, pull,
hit, pick, tap, wipe, etc., with part of body speficied.
(May be cross-referenced to "Postural communication" or
"Play", e.g., hitting self with an object scored "Rel-AM"
in "Play" column).

15. State, Sunlight condition, Biological behaviours (all three coded
in same column for each observation block)

State 1-6, as in Brazelton, 1, 2, 3, increasingly active sleeping states; 4, 5, 6, increasingly active waking states; 5 and 6 appear

almost exclusively in the observations for this age period.

Biological behaviours

Nurse	N
Eat	E
Drink	Dr
Urinate	urinate
Defecate	defecate
Clean mucous, excrement	describe

16. Objects

Any object played with, handled, climbed on, thrown, carried, etc. is listed.

(Following the systematic hour-observation clinical or descriptive comments are added below it or on the reverse side of sheet).

TEMPORAL CLUSTERS AND INDIVIDUAL DIFFERENCES

IN THE BEHAVIOUR OF PRESCHOOL CHILDREN

Peter K. Smith

Department of Psychology
University of Sheffield

I. INTRODUCTION

A nursery or play group provides an ideal opportunity to watch
the relatively unconstrained behaviour of groups of 10 to 30 children,
at an age at which social, linguistic and play behaviours are rapidly developing. There is much individual variation in the behaviour of such
children, and the behaviour of a given child varies with time as his motivational state changes. This paper examines both these kinds of behavioural variation in a group of children to see if there is any relation
between them. Are individual differences related to differing strengths
of particular motivation?

This problem can be examined conveniently by using a time sampling technique. Such techniques have a considerable history in child
psychology, having been used extensively in the 1930's though much
less so in subsequent decades. The limitations of this earlier work
have been discussed by Smith & Connolly (1972). The technique is again
proving useful now that child psychology is becoming invigorated by recent work in animal and primate ethology. An individual is observed for
a specified (short) time and the occurrence or non-occurrence of particular behaviours is recorded. A large number of such time samples
are then collected for each individual in the group. Earlier psychological work of this kind generally used rather global, motivational behaviour categories, but it is possible to use finer, physically-defined categories such as are usually used in primate work, where the motivational significance of behaviours are less glibly assumed.

A traditional method of analysing time sampled data is to obtain
measures of correlation across individual totals (summing across time

samples). This gives information on individual differences, or 'per-sonality' dimensions. An alternative method of analysis is to obtain measures of correlation or contingency across time samples. This gives information on temporal relations of behaviours, or 'motivation-al' clusters. This latter method is of course only of value in so far as motivational structure is not implicit in the behaviour definitions. It has been used by a number of animal ethologists. The former method has largely been the province of psychologists studying human behaviour. The present paper applies both methods of analysis to time sampled data obtained from a group of day nursery children. Earlier work in both areas is briefly reviewed.

II. SUBJECTS AND NURSERY ENVIRONMENT

The day nursery is under the administration of the Sheffield Public Health Department. The nursery is open from 7.30 a.m. to 6.00 p.m., Monday to Friday, and provides full-day care for children of working mothers, many of whom are unmarried or divorced. Obser-vations were made between the times of 9.30 a.m. and 11.00 a.m., and 2.30 p.m. and 4.15 p.m. At these times almost all the children are present, and 'free play' activity is allowed, with very little inter-ference or direction from the nursery nurses.

Most of the children played indoors in the large 'toddlers' room of area 500 sq. ft. Those who were under three years of age played in a 'babies' room of 400 sq. ft. In fine weather all the children played together outside in an area of some 2,000 sq. ft. Available toys and apparatus included 3 steps-and-slides, climbing frame, trampoline, sandpit, mattress, doll's house, seesaw, Wendy House, scooters, balls, rubber tyres, blankets, pram, wheelbarrow, pushcarts, sleds, toy trains, toy bears and animals, dolls, comics, jigsaws, small toys, sofa, chairs and tables. Sometimes easels and chalk were present, and sometimes a water basin outdoors.

Attendance at the nursery fluctuated, the maximum possible attendance being forty-nine. Twenty-nine children were selected for observation. Twenty-three were 'toddlers' (eleven boys, twelve girls) and six were 'babies' (two boys, four girls). Ten of the children were of immigrant (Afro-Asian) origin. The majority of the children were broadly of lower middle/working class parentage. Eighteen of them had parents unmarried, divorced or separated. The mean age of the children at the commencement of observations was 38 months, range 22 to 57 months. The average length of time since admission to the nursery was $17\frac{1}{2}$ months (range 1 to 40 months). Further details of the nursery and children are available in Smith (1970).

1. Observational details. The observations took place over a period of ten weeks, from June to mid-August. Recordings were only made during periods of free play activity, and when most children were present. One hundred observation periods of half a minute were made on each child. In each half-minute period the child was observed quasi-continuously. Ticks were placed in the appropriate behavioural categories on standard record sheets, for any behaviour occurring during this period. There was thus a possible maximum of one hundred ticks for each category, per child total.

As far as possible two records were obtained for each child on each visit to the nursery, separated by at least ten minutes. Visits were usually made every weekday. Sometimes, due to lack of time or absences, three or four observations had to be made on a child during the same visit. In this case they were separated by at least five minutes, and usually ten minutes or more. One child was absent a great deal, and her total of 100 observations had to be completed in only fourteen visits.

In every visit the order of observations was randomised by shuffling up the record sheets. However, if a child had been missed on a previous visit, he was observed near the beginning of the next visit so as to allow maximum time between two observations.

A note was kept as to whether observations were indoors or outdoors. A total of 722 were made indoors and 2178 outdoors. For a given child the least number of observations made indoors was 10; the most, 37.

The standard record sheets contained 53 behavioural categories. Their use was practised for a week before commencing the study. The categories and their definitions are listed in the Appendix.

2. Inter-observer agreement. Measures of inter-observer agreement were made by a visit to the day nursery by the author and another observer, at which forty-two simultaneous half-minute records were made (not more than two on any one child). The visit took place after the termination of the main observations. The measure of agreement for a given behaviour was defined as the number of occurrences for which both observers were in agreement, divided by the total number of occurrences (estimated by taking the mean for both observers). The measure was only calculated for categories where the total number of ticks was at least ten. Values are given in the Appendix. The mean overall agreement of occurrence was 0.80.

The second observer was not especially trained in the use of the behavioural categories. He had read the written definitions previously, and practised taking records on his own, before taking simultaneous records. This is considered a more useful procedure than giving special training, since it indicates the probable level of agreement of the author's observations with those of another person who can rely only on the definitions given in this paper (Smith & Connolly, 1972).

3. Reliability. Measures of split-third reliability were obtained by splitting the data for each child into three equal parts of 33 records each. These were approximately balanced for each sample-third, and correlated across children. The three correlation coefficients obtained were averaged, and corrected by the Spearman-Brown prophecy formula to estimate the reliabilities for the whole sample. These figures represent the statistical reliability of the ordering of individual totals. Most of the reliabilities obtained were reasonably satisfactory at between 0.6 and 0.9, but were low for a number of less frequent behaviours (such as fight or dance) or for a few frequent behaviours where individual variation was small (such as walk). Values are given in the Appendix.

III. MAIN DIMENSIONS OF INDIVIDUAL DIFFERENCE: REVIEW OF EARLIER WORK.

The main approach by psychologists to the problem of 'personality' or main dimensions of individual difference, in young children has been that of teacher ratings, sometimes supplemented by parents' ratings or self reports. Factor analytic techniques have usually been employed to obtain personality factors. One difficulty in such an approach is the considerable interaction of the rater with the ratees. The factor structure is often broadly two-dimensional, representing the factors of adjustment to the social group (sociability, extraversion) and adjustment to accepted standards (conformity, stability) (Peterson 1960, Schaeffer 1961). Apparently similar factors are obtained for adults (Lorr & McNair 1965, Eysenck & Eysenck 1969). Narrow factors, on the other hand, are not readily replicable across studies, and tend to be either tautological clusters of two or three synonymous items or else statistical artifacts (Peterson 1965). The broad factor structure is replicable across teachers' reports, parents' reports and self reports on the same children; however there has been much less agreement when such factors from the same sample of children have been correlated with each other in terms of children's factor scores (Thorpe 1959, Becker 1960a, b, Hallworth 1965, Peterson 1965, Eysenck & Pickup 1968, Eysenck & Cookson 1969). In the light of such findings both Peterson (1965) and Hallworth (1965) have suggested that the broad bifactor results reflect the ubiquitous 'Osgoodian' way of verbal evaluation of other humans, but that agreement in applying these dimensions to particular subjects is likely to be poor, since the evaluations are personal to the individual and show rather limited covariance with observed behaviour tendencies.

A more promising approach is that used by Thomas et al. (1964, 1968) in their longitudinal study of behavioural individuality in early childhood, that of content analysis of data from sustained parental interview, sometimes checked by direct observation. Alternatively, behavioural differences can be classified directly in terms of differences in the frequencies of occurrence of observed behaviours. While more time-consuming than rating studies, it is reasonable, with suitable precautions, to expect considerably improved objectivity in the results.

Few previous studies have applied such an approach to the problem of personality factors.

Some half-dozen studies have previously reported time-sampled observations of a comprehensive range of behaviours in young children, and have applied some factor analytic techniques to the data, or at least presented sufficient correlational data to make such analysis possible. A few further studies (Goodenough, 1930; Koch, 1934; Gewirtz, 1956; Rafferty et al., 1960; Waldrop et al., 1968) have used rather few categories or limited themselves to particular aspects of behaviour or particular situations.

Arrington (1931) observed 20 children, aged 18 to 32 months, with at least 24 five-minute samples per child. Both observer agreements and odd-even reliabilities were reported. Inter-correlations for a number of behaviours were given; a component analysis of this data has been carried out and reported by Smith & Connolly (1972).

A study by Koch (1942) on 46 children, aged 21 to 58 months, investigated the correlations between 11 nervous habits and 20 other behavioural measures. Each child was observed over a period of eight months to obtain 400 half-minute samples. Odd-even reliabilities were given. Nine factors were obtained from centroid factor analysis. The first, called 'social extraversion' is reasonably interpreted as a factor of sociability or maturity. No evidence is given for reliability of the subsequent factors, and they are difficult to understand, as Koch herself several times admits.

Horowitz & Smith (1939) collected observational records made by trained teachers on preschool children in thirteen nursery schools. Twenty half-minute records were obtained for each child. No measures

of reliability were reported, and the total observation time of ten minutes per child does seem rather inadequate in this respect. The published correlation tables do not in fact appear very consistent across
schools.

Cattell & Peterson (1958) have published a factor analytic study
on 80 nursery school children, aged 48 to 72 months. No inter-observer
agreements between the two observers were obtained, nor were any measures of statistical reliability reported. Two forty-minute periods of
observation were made on each child, but the method of time-sampling
is not revealed. However the most frequent category ('smiles frequently') only had a mean score of 3, and this hardly seems an adequate statistical basis for the subsequent factor analysis. This was carried out
on the intercorrelation matrix between 76 categories, many of them
complex in character ('seldom rejects proferred help', 'refrains from
complaining to adult or child when expected'). Sixteen factors were
obtained after eight visual rotations. Even the first factor, called 'new
pattern', is difficult to interpret. The subsequent naming of factors,
and their identification with factors from Koch (1942) are unconvincing,
and the results do not seem to be of any value. Cattell's methods and
the validity of his findings have subsequently been criticised by Peterson
(1960, 1965) and Becker (1960a) (see also Cattell, 1961; Becker, 1961).

Martin (1964) observed 38 children, aged 31 to 42 months, for
twelve five-minute samples in the middle of each of four consecutive
semesters. Seven categories (split into 31 subcategories) were used.
These were of a complex and overtly motivational character ('securing
aid for self', 'maintain and enhance own status', 'seek mutuality through
activity') which could be considered more appropriate for a rating than
an observational study. Emmerich (1964) published a factor analysis of

the data. Observer agreements are given, referred to as 'reliability', but no measures of statistical reliability were presented. Six factors were obtained from the data from each semester; they are difficult to comprehend, and were named by showing 'significant' correlations with rather arbitrarily selected scales.

McKinney (1962) published a study on 48 boys, aged 8 to 12 years, but with an I.Q. mostly below 30, living in institutions. Twenty-four five-minute all-or-none samples were made on each child. Observer agreements and odd-even reliabilities were reported for 64 behaviours, which together with other items made up 80 categories for factor analysis. No reliabilities are given for the eight categories extracted, and their meaningfulness is difficult to estimate.

Smith & Connolly (1972) observed 40 children aged 31 to 57 months in three day nurseries. Twelve five-minute samples (sampling at ten-second intervals) were made on each child. Inter-observer agreements and split-half reliabilities were presented for the behavioural categories used, which were largely defined in physical rather than motivational terms. Principal component analysis was carried out on inter-correlations between the 35 most reliable behavioural categories (including age and nursery experience). The reliability of the components obtained was checked by running separate split-half analyses; this indicated that two to three components, accounting for 44% of the total variance, were statistically reliable. The first component was interpreted as one of social maturity, the second component reflected whether play was predominantly with or without toys and apparatus. The third component was a syndrome of crying, sucking, and submissive behaviour.

The same authors also carried out a principal component analysis on the data from Arrington (1931) as a check for validity of their results.

Two components obtained had face validity and, bearing in mind the difference in age of the children observed, showed good agreement. The first component was of social maturity, the second component amount of active contact with material objects.

Blurton-Jones (1972) observed 25 children aged about 2 years and 4 years, in a research playgroup. Fifteen five-minute samples were obtained for each child. No observer agreement or reliabilities were reported. A principal component analysis was run on 32 variables, to compare with the results of Smith & Connolly (1972). The two studies had a number of behaviour categories in common, and Blurton-Jones' first component appeared to be a similar one of social maturity. The second component contrasted active rough-and-tumble behaviours to play with objects and materials and agonistic behaviour.

Measures of reliability and validity are of great importance for factor analytic work. Reliability measures are needed to show how many factors, and how many factor loadings, can usefully be taken as simplifications of the original data. Some measure of validity is important to indicate whether generalisation to other subject samples, category lists, or methods of rotation and further analytic manipulation (if applied) is possible. In the absence of such measures the meaningful ness of the results is severely open to question. Nevertheless Armstrong and Soelberg (1968) showed that of a sample of 46 recent factor analytic studies, some two-thirds gave no report of factor reliability, and nearly half reported neither reliability or validity. These drawbacks are present in much of the previously reported work on dimensions of individual difference in preschool children. In the present research, evidence for the reliability of the findings is presented in terms of the results of split-third analyses of the data; evidence for validity in com-

parison with previous work by Arrington (1931), Smith & Connolly
(1972) and Blurton-Jones (1972).

IV. MAIN DIMENSIONS OF INDIVIDUAL DIFFERENCE:
RESULTS OF PRESENT STUDY

The 40 behaviour categories having a reliability of .45 or above,
together with the two variables of age and nursery experience, were
inter-correlated across child totals. Principal component analysis was
carried out using a standard program (ICL 1900 Statistical Analysis).
This procedure seemed preferable to cluster analysis, since it was expected to obtain a few main dimensions with high loadings for many behaviours, rather than a large number of fairly discrete clusters. This
supposition was supported by the relatively large proportion of the variance (41%) accounted for by the first three components.

No rotation of axes or subsequent factor analytic procedures have
been employed in the presentation of the results. This means that a
structure of mutually orthogonal axes is imposed on the data, but there
are compensating advantages. The solution is mathematically unique,
and does not involve any subsequent manipulation of the data by the experimenter. Subsequent rotation of axes would either involve using
'objective' mathematical criteria which might however have little validity in terms of the data involved, or else using subjective criteria and
hence introducing experimenter bias into the presentation of the results. Either might be acceptable in testing specific hypotheses, but
do not seem appropriate for an exploratory analysis of the kind carried
out here; it is not certain that later readers would approve of the criteria used for rotation, even if they were fully reported.

Instead a procedure similar to that recommended by Hope (1968) has been employed. Graphical plots are presented for the category loadings on the first three principal components. This is a completely objective procedure, but the reader can estimate visually the result of rotation of axes, at least as far as the main components are concerned.

Beside the main analysis, three split-third analyses were run to give a clear indication of the statistical reliability of the components obtained. These utilised the split-third data samples describer earlier. The first three components appeared to be reliable and to have face validity. Together they accounted for 41% of the total variance in the main analysis. The fourth component accounted for 7.5% of the total variance; this and subsequent components did not appear stable across the split-third analyses; they were also either difficult to interpret, or else highly loaded on only one or two categories. They are therefore not discussed any further.

Categories with the highest loadings on the first three components are shown in Table I, with split-third loadings in brackets. Reliability is good for the first two components. As far as the third component is concerned, the categories water, watch nurse, sand and manipulate toy are obviously unstable, and rather fewer categories have really reliable loadings. A simple measure of component reliability is obtained by correlating the split-third component loadings across categories. The mean correlations for the first three components were .85, .45 and .37 respectively. Corrected by the Spearman-Brown formula, these give reliabilities for the components of the main analysis of .94, .71 and .63 respectively.

Measures of internal validity were made by running further analyses. An analysis with the 23 toddlers only (excluding the six babies) gave component correlations with the main analysis of .90, .91 and .83 respectively. An analysis was run including the less reliable categories, and sex and immigrant status as dichotomous variables, giving a total of 59 variables; component correlations (across mutual categories) with the main analysis were 1.00, .93 and .88. A final analysis was run using only 36 variables, omitting the six categories of nature of play or activity - manipulate toy (M), with apparatus (A), neither toys or apparatus (N), both toys and apparatus (MA), hold toy (H) and wear clothes (W); here the component correlations with the main analysis were 1.00, .95 and .62 respectively.

Fig. 1 gives a graphical plot of the category loadings for the first two components of the main analysis, while Fig. 2 gives a similar plot for subject scores. Figs. 3 and 4 give analogous plots of category loadings and subject scores for the second and third components. These plots suggest clear interpretations of the components without requiring any rotation of axes.

The first component has very high loadings for social participation, talk child, and age, and is clearly a factor of sociability or social maturity, very similar to the first component obtained by Smith & Connolly (1972). The index of social participation is virtually identical in the two studies and puts this matching of the components on a very firm basis. An important difference is present in the negative loadings, however; in the present study cry and submissive behaviour have very high negative loadings, while these were only moderate in Smith & Connolly's previous result. The third component of the latter analysis - crying, sucking and submissive behaviour - has no analogue in the present analysis and the existence of such a dimension orthogonal to that of social maturity is not supported.

There is no appreciable sex difference for scores on the first component. There is also no significant overall difference between children of immigrant and non-immigrant origin on any of the three components. Sex differences are present in the second and third components however. Applying Wilcoxon's matched pairs signed ranks test to twelve pairs of boys and girls matched for age and immigrant status, the difference approaches significance for the second component $(p < .1)$. and is clearly so for the third component $(p < .01)$. These two components extract an approximately equal amount of the total variance (though the third component is appreciably less reliable) and for both there are high loadings for the categories of nature of play or activity (Table I, Fig. 3).

The second component has its highest loading for manipulate toy, and for sand, crouch, and push, pull which are all associated with manipulating toys or material. At the opposite extreme are slide, chase/flee, and swing, for which toys are not involved. The tendency is for girls to have higher negative scores on this component. This is contrary to what might be expected in comparison with the second component from Smith & Connolly (1972), where playing with toys and apparatus was opposed to playing without toys or apparatus, but with a tendency for girls to have higher positive scores. However, in the present study the greater part of the variance due to sex is taken by the third component. This opposes both toys and apparatus and hold toy to play noise, crawl/roll, and neither toys or apparatus, with boys having higher negative scores.

The second and third components provide strong confirmation of

TABLE I. Principal component analysis of correlational data. Highest category loadings for the first

three components; split-third loadings in brackets.

PRINCIPAL COMPONENT 1 : variance accounted for 21.8% (18.6%; 17.5%; 19.6%).

Social participation	+.31 (+.33; +.34; +.31)	Cry	−.24 (−.26; −.28; −.13)
Talk child	+.30 (+.30; +.30; +.30)	Submissive	−.22 (−.17; −.20; −.22)
Age	+.29 (+.31; +.33; +.28)	Touch nurse	−.21 (−.14; −.21; −.23)
Smile	+.24 (+.27; +.21; +.22)	Automanipulate	−.18 (−.06; −.08; −.26)
Run	+.23 (+.25; +.18; +.22)	React observer	−.18 (−.17; −.24; −.17)
Nursery experience	+.23 (+.26; +.26; +.21)	Stand	−.17 (−.22; −.03; −.16)
Play talk	+.20 (+.14; +.18; +.18)	Watch nurse	−.14 (−.14; −.09; −.14)
Wrestle, tumble	+.19 (+.15; +.10; +.18)		
Laugh	+.19 (+.20; +.15; +.19)		
Chase, flee	+.18 (+.14; +.13; +.20)		
Jump, hop	+.17 (+.18; +.10; +.07)		
Swing	+.15 (+.09; +.12; +.14)		
Sit	+.14 (+.13; +.13; +.13)		

PRINCIPAL COMPONENT 2 : variance accounted for 10.8% (9.3%; 10.7%; 10.5%).

Manipulate toy	+.37 (+.43; +.28; +.30)	Slide	-.25 (-.06; -.31; -.27)
Crouch	+.31 (+.35; +.24; +.19)	Chase, flee	-.21 (-.25; -.14; -.06)
Sand	+.31 (+.35; +.16; +.31)	Swing	-.17 (-.04; -.08; -.30)
Push, pull	+.29 (+.25; +.26; +.11)		
Talk self	+.27 (+.19; +.20; +.23)		
Crawl, roll	+.20 (+.19; +.09; +.06)		
Talk observer	+.20 (+.02; +.21; +.11)		

PRINCIPAL COMPONENT 3 : variance accounted for 8.6% (7.5%; 9.2%; 8.6%).

Both toys and apparatus	+.33 (+.06; +.23; +.18)	Play noise	-.38 (-.29; -.26; -.30)
Hold toy	+.24 (+.08; +.23; +.24)	Crawl, roll	-.33 (-.35; -.27; -.25)
Water	+.24 (+.04; +.00; +.06)	Neither toys or apparatus	-.25 (-.10; -.23; -.14)
Watch nurse	+.23 (+.01; +.20; -.15)	React observer	-.19 (-.10; -.14; -.04)
Sand	+.20 (+.09; +.08; -.14)	Talk observer	-.18 (-.03; -.18; -.03)
Automanipulate	+.19 (+.10; +.17; +.11)	Run	-.17 (-.03; -.11; -.13)
Manipulate toy	+.18 (+.04; +.24; -.12)		
Suck	+.17 (+.29; +.27; +.24)		

the finding from the second component of Smith & Connolly (1972), that
the amount of use of toys and apparatus accounts for a substantial part
of individual differences in behaviour. Two drawbacks of the previous
analysis are avoided by the present study. Firstly, one nursery is involved rather than three, so that the results cannot be ascribed to inter-
nursery variations. Secondly, the list of behaviours used is considerably less conducive to such a dimension or dimensions appearing than previously. Admittedly the six categories of nature of play or activity are
biased towards it, but very similar results were obtained when these
variables were omitted from the component analysis, supporting the
notion that they are acting as 'marker variables' which aid in the interpretation of the components, while not appreciably determining the component structure itself.

It can be seen from Fig. 4 that a remarkably good discrimination
between boys and girls is achieved by drawing a line through the origin
at just less than 45% to the vertical axis; only three boys and two girls
are wrongly placed (and the latter are all babies anyway). Thus a rotation of this amount gives a second component independent of sex, and
parallel to a line joining M and N in Fig. 3. Wrestle/tumble, chase/
flee, slide and swing have high negative loadings, while object oriented
behaviours together with hit/throw and dominative have positive loadings.
This is in quite good agreement with the second component of Blurton-
Jones (1972) (which also has no sex loading). The new third component
now absorbs most of the variance attributable directly to sex differences.

Comparison with other earlier research does not seem very worthwhile, for reasons already given. However, some speculations made by
Blurton-Jones (1967) should be considered. He discusses a possible
distinction between 'doers' and 'verbalizers' in nursery school children,

Fig. 1. Principal component analysis. Graphical plot of category loadings for first two components.

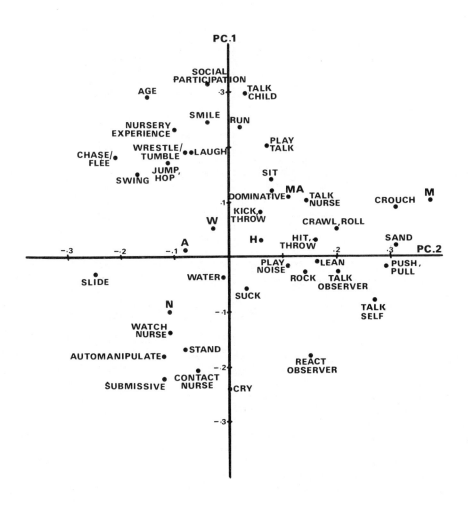

Peter K. Smith

Fig. 2. Principal component analysis. Graphical plot of subject scores for first two components.

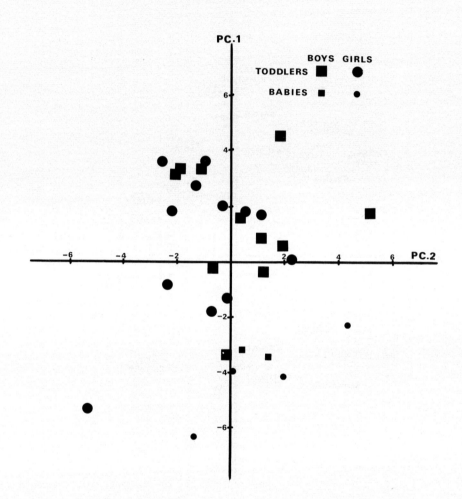

Fig. 3.   Principal component analysis. Graphical plot of category loadings for second and third components.

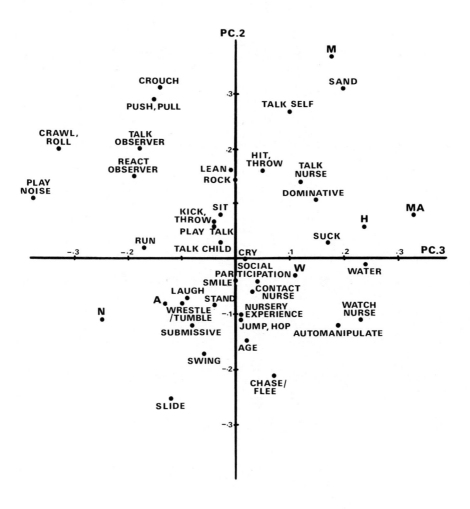

Peter K. Smith

Fig. 4.   Principal component analysis. Graphical plot of subject
scores for second and third components.

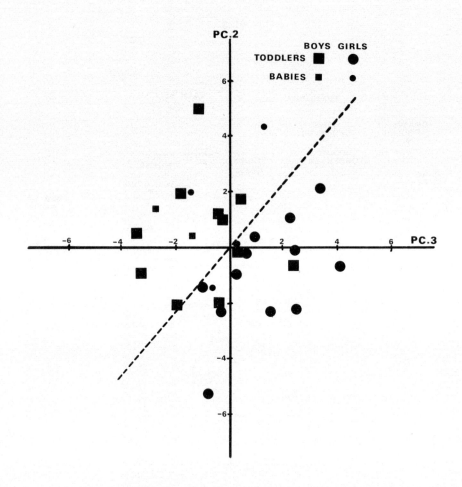

the former often making things, painting, or rough-and-tumbling, the latter often alone, looking at books, and talking a lot. As far as the present observations go, there seems no evidence for such a distinction among day nursery children.

The results of the present paper, together with those of Smith & Connolly (1972) and Blurton-Jones (1972) show a broad measure of agreement. From them two generalisations may be made concerning behavioural differences in the free play activity of preschool children:

1. The most important dimension of individual variation is social maturity; information concerning this will have the highest predictive value concerning a child's observed behaviour. It is highly correlated with age, but not so highly that the two can be equated. The amount of talking to other children appears to be a very close measure of this dimension; so is an index of social participation such as that used by Parten (1932) or by the present author.

2. A second very important source of individual variation is the degree to which the child's play behaviour involves manipulating or holding toys, as opposed to playing with immovable apparatus or indulging in general physical activity and rough-and-tumble play. Active, rough-and-tumble kinds of play are seen in most young mammals, and may have the function of preparation for aggressive and, in some species, hunting activities. Manipulative object play represents the genetic potentiality for varied tool-use and tool-making in man; while present in higher primates (e.g. Lawick-Goodall 1968), it is seen more and to a much higher level in human children than in other primate young. These two kinds of play seem to have differing degrees of appeal to otherwise equally 'sociable' children. The sex of the child may be involved here,

but there is considerable overlap between the sexes and the nature of any interaction is not fully clear. Earlier reports on sex differences in children's play (e.g. Manwell & Mengert 1934, McDowell 1937) have found boys preferring active physical play and girls finer manipulative activities. However, these findings are not always consistent, or reliable. There is also evidence that such sex differences may be affected by spatial and toy densities (Smith 1970, and in preparation), and if substantiated, this may account for some of the apparent disagreements in this area.

V. TEMPORAL CLUSTERS IN BEHAVIOUR: REVIEW OF EARLIER WORK

Temporal analysis, aided by form and situation analysis, can be considered one of the basic methods of modern ethology. Behaviours consistently occurring within brief temporal association of each other are regarded as sharing the same motivational state (Tinbergen 1959), or as sharing common causal factors (Beer 1961-63). Starting with behaviours defined largely or wholly in physical terms, it is thereby possible to arrive at motivational interpretations of the behaviours in a quite objective manner (and to put the interpretation to experimental test). This approach, now used for over a decade in the study of lower vertebrate species, is beginning to be used in the study of humans and other primates. The present paper applies it to the free play activity of preschool children. First some of the earlier work in this field will be briefly reviewed.

The work of Wiepkema (1961) on the Bitterling gives an early example of the thorough application of this technique. Wiepkema obtained sequential records of sequences of behaviour, computed ratios of observed to expected frequencies of dyad contingencies, obtained Spearman rank correlation coefficients from these, and carried out a factor analysis. He obtained three major factors, corresponding to agonistic, sexual, and miscellaneous non-reproductive behaviours.

Blurton-Jones (1968), in his work on causation of threat displays in the great tit, used a number of methods of temporal analysis, though without resorting to any factor analytic techniques. Behaviours seen at a feeding table were grouped into approaching food, attack-threat, and flight. Results from the temporal analyses agreed well with subsequent situation analysis (involving experimental manipulations) in suggesting that these groups of behaviours were controlled by separate causal factors.

Work of this kind with primates has been rare. Altmann (1968, 1965) described some 120 simple and component behaviour patterns involved in the social interactions of rhesus monkeys. The stochastic structure of interactions was analysed up to the fourth order. Linkage analysis of dyad frequencies was used to obtain eight main clusters of behaviours, labelled affinitive and mild tactile, agonistic, sexual (males), sexual (females), play, suckling and weaning, aggressing chases, and carrying infants.

Thompson (1969) obtained correlations from temporal data on the social behaviour of Macaca irus; these were apparently obtained from totals over several ten-minute periods, which seems to be rather a long period for obtaining motivational associations. Thompson claimed from his analysis that three basic motivations underlying behaviour in dyadic encounters were grooming, mounting, and spacing.

Hooff (1970, 1971) has recently carried out an analysis of social behaviour patterns of chimpanzees, using a similar procedure to that of Wiepkema (1961). Transition frequencies between fifty-three behaviours were obtained, and chi-squared statistics computed. These latter were used as the raw data for principal component analysis, and for cluster analysis. Thus behaviours showing similar patterns of sequential probabilities with other behaviours were grouped together. Hooff obtained some four or five principal groups, which he labelled as play, aggressive, affinitive, submissive, and excitement. These were checked by split-third analyses. Component and cluster analysis gave closely similar results.

The only published temporal analyses on human behaviour to date appear to be those of Swan (1938), Blurton-Jones (1967, 1972) and Grant (1968). The early report by Swan mentions temporal clusters of 'facial expressive behaviours', the main ones being smile and chuckle-laugh, frown and whimper-cry, and talk persons and laugh. Grant observed chronic schizophrenics, acute neurotics, and normal students in an interview situation, and computed chi-squared statistics for thirty-six behaviours from dyad sequential analysis. He obtained groupings which he termed flight, assertion, relaxation, and contact, as well as link elements between these clusters. The method of obtaining these groupings was not indicated.

Blurton-Jones (1967) reported chi-squared statistics between thirteen behaviours in ten nursery school children, using five-minute time samples. He obtained clusters of rough-and-tumble play, attack-threat, and crying. In his replicative study on twenty-five children (1972) he used principal component analysis. Components of rough-and-tumble play opposed to manipulative play, aggressive behaviour and social interaction were obtained.

VI. TEMPORAL CLUSTERS IN BEHAVIOUR:
RESULTS OF PRESENT STUDY

Of the 53 behaviour categories used (see Appendix), seven of them (water, book, talk observer, play beat, pushed, fight and dance) occurred in less than one per cent of the records, and were omitted from consideration. Contingency analysis was then carried out between the remaining 46 categories for simultaneous occurrence within a half-minute sample. In piloting the study, it was found that a half-minute period was usually long enough to cover most of the behaviours involved with the child's immediate activity, but not so long that the child was likely to change to another very different activity during the time sample.

Analysis was carried out using the 'Survey' program (Hope, 1968) at the Atlas Computing Laboratory, Chilton, England. Value of chi-squared, and Pearson's coefficient of contingency, were obtained for all the paired associations of variables. Due to the considerable amount of computer time required, it was only possible to carry through the analysis for one third of the total data, containing 957 time samples.

In order to simplify the presentation of the contingency data and to obtain motivational grouping, it was decided to use methods of cluster analysis. Cluster analysis seemed a more appropriate approach for a case such as this, where a large number of groupings of a few categories were expected, rather than major orthogonal dimensions embracing most categories. Two forms of cluster analysis were applied to the data, the results being shown in Figs. 5 and 6. Analyses were applied to data summed over the 29 children of the study. Such summing techniques in taxonomic studies have recently been called into question (Jardine and Sibson, 1971); see also page 785 of text.

Fig. 5 shows the result of applying Hierarchial Cluster Analysis by Reciprocal Pairs to the contingencies between the 37 definite behaviours considered. This method of analysis is described by McQuitty (1964, 1967). A reciprocal pair consists of two categories each having a highest (positive) contingency with the other. Having obtain all reciprocal pairs from the contingency matrix, new contingencies were calculated with each reciprocal pair now represented as one variable. For this purpose, McQuitty's similarity index, taking the weighted mean of the contingencies involved, was used. The process was then repeated with the new matrix. This yields a form of typal analysis, in that each member of a cluster is, on average, more related to the other members of its cluster than to members of other clusters at that level. This distinguishes dimensional from typal solutions, and as can be seen from Fig. 5 the result in this case is typal; each typal cluster may be tentatively used to define a particular motivation. Analysis proceeded up to the tenth order matrix, but for the higher connections the contingencies are small; cluster connections involving mean contingencies of less than .030 are indicated with dotted lines in Fig. 5, as they do not seem to add to the understanding of the motivational structure and are probably not reliable.

The four main typal clusters may be identified as active play behaviour not involving toys (breaking up into non-contact play, play involving apparatus, and contact play); a clustering of dependency behaviours involving crying, sucking, and behaviour oriented to the nurse or observer; stationary play; and agonistic behaviour (breaking up into aggressive and submissive components).

The method has the disadvantage of assuming a discrete cluster structure, in the sense that any category can only be attached to one cluster at the particular order of analysis considered. The advantage lies in showing the finer structure of the large clusters. An alternative method of clustering is presented in Fig. 6. This shows the results of a simple linkage analysis. Grouped around the first order reciprocal pairs are other categories having a high contingency with them. The number of lines joining two categories, and to a lesser extent the distance separating them, indicates the strength of association. This second method has the advantage of showing all the strongest contingencies in clear diagrammatic form, though obviously there are limits to which any two-dimensional representation can adequately reflect the cluster structure. Fig. 6 has the same 37 categories as Fig. 5.

Depending on the level of clustering taken, some four to nine main cluster groupings can be identified, largely though not entirely similar across the two methods of analysis. The large group of active play behaviours is fairly clearly defined; running, laughing, smiling and chasing and fleeing all group closely together and constitute a pattern of non-contact rough-and-tumble play. This has slightly looser associations with contact rough-and-tumble play, and with jumping, hopping, climbing, sliding, crawling, rolling and lying, these latter generally being associated with play involving apparatus. Of these the last three have the least clearly defined position.

The nature of the stationary play clusters is rather less clear; one group refers to crouching and talking in the sand-pit, another to sitting and talking, sometimes manipulating toys. The high association between rock and sit is tautologous and may somewhat distort the picture here. Other patterns connected with manipulating toys are kicking and throwing, and pushing and pulling. These tended to be rather solitary play patterns; their position is probably better indicated by Fig. 6 than Fig. 5.

Fig. 5.   Hierarchical cluster analysis of temporal contingencies
           between 37 behaviours.

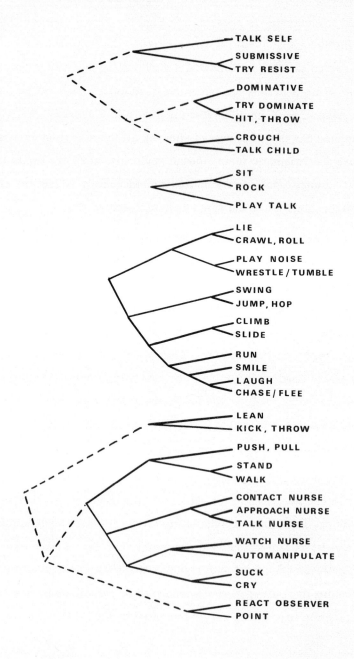

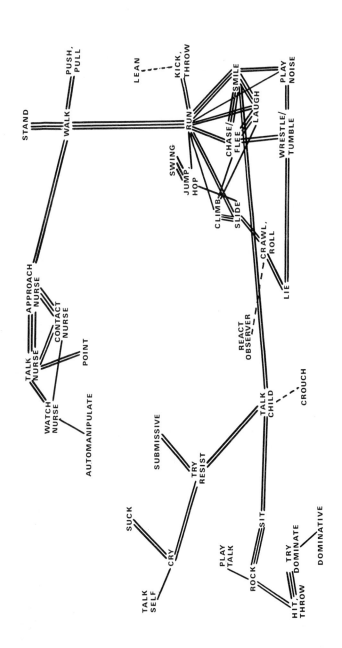

Fig. 6.   Simple linkage analysis of temporal contingencies between 37 behaviours.

The two agonistic patterns, aggressive and submissive, are fairly straightforward; the latter is associated with crying in Fig. 6, although in Fig. 5 crying and sucking join automanipulating and watching
the nurse in a pattern of isolate behaviour.

This latter has some association with the final main cluster of
what might be called dependency behaviour, mainly approaching, talking
to and making physical contact with the nurse, and to a much looser extent pointing and reacting to the observer.

The contingency analysis by Grant (1968) used a considerably finer
level of categorisation in a restricted interview situation, and his results
do not seem comparable to the present study. However a comparison is
possible with the results of Blurton-Jones (1967, 1972). His rough-and-
tumble play grouping contains laughing, running, jumping, open beat, and
wrestling (1967 and 1972). These are all present in the main active play
group here, except for the open beat, corresponding to play beat, which
occurred too infrequently for reliable analysis. His aggressive group
consists of fixate, beat and low frown, (1967), plus push and grab-tug-
pull (1972), and may be compared with the aggressive cluster here; in
this case Blurton-Jones' cluster is more valuable as his behaviours do
not involve any a priori motivational interpretation. His third (1967)
grouping of crying, red face and puckered face is fairly obvious and is
just represented by crying in the present study. His third (1972) grouping is point, give, receive, talk and smile. This does not emerge as a
very convincing cluster in the present study; talk child and smile have a
high contingency but point is elsewhere. This difference of course is
bound up with the different set of behaviour categories used. Conversely
Blurton-Jones's results lack clusters of isolate and staff-oriented behaviour, as such behaviours are absent from his list (differences in the

children and nursery environment may also be relevant here).

The best agreement is obtained for the rough-and-tumble play cluster; it is interesting that there is quite a close analogue for this in Hooff's (1970) results for adult chimpanzees. Hooff's components of aggression and submission might also be considered broadly comparable to such clusters here, but his fourth component of affinative behaviour (physical contact and grooming) does not seem to have such a direct correspondence.

One aspect of the motivational complexity in human behaviour seems to be the motivational ambiguity of a number of apparently physically defined behaviours. From Fig. 6 it can be seen that walking, sitting and talking are all very ambiguous in their clustering, and to a lesser extent this is true of other categories. Finer analysis of talking might well yield subcategories with a more clearly defined motivational context; how readily this could be done with walking and sitting is not so clear. It is perhaps an article of faith with ethologists that precise enough physical definitions will give motivationally unambiguous behaviours. However this may well be more difficult to put into practice in the case of human as opposed to infra-human species (Smith & Connolly, 1972).

As a provisional attempt at motivational analysis of general behaviour of preschool children the overall result can be considered fairly promising. Deficiencies are the non-physical definitions of a few behaviour categories (especially the agonistic ones) and over-comprehensiveness in others (such as talking and smiling). There is clearly scope for improved work in this direction. Smiling, for example, could be subdivided into 'simple smile', 'upper smile' and 'broad smile' as suggested

by Brannigan & Humphries (1969); even finer divisions are suggested
by Grant (1969).

A more powerful method of analysis might be to apply factor analysis in a hierarchial fashion; first to get main clusters, then after isolat-
ing records pertaining to a particular cluster, applying factor analysis
again to these records only. This would get at the finer motivational
structure without making the assumptions of discrete clustering usually
inherent in cluster analysis, and could help to overcome the motivational ambiguities discussed above. An equivalent procedure would be to
start by recording incidents of specific kinds of behaviour, such as aggression or rough-and-tumble play, and analyse these alone. However
the selection of appropriate incidents would in itself involve subjective
bias. It would seem to be of value to avoid subjectivity as far as possible in the selection of behaviour to record, as well as in the category
descriptions used; for this reason the more comprehensive approach
has much to recommend it.

VII. DISCUSSION: COMPARISON OF TEMPORAL CLUSTERS
AND INDIVIDUAL DIFFERENCES IN BEHAVIOUR

Blurton-Jones (1972) has previously compared individual differences in behaviour to temporal clusters and has concluded that "the
main dimensions of individual variation cut across the temporal groupings of behaviour. All the children show the same groupings but children do not differ mainly in the frequency with which they show behaviour
in each group". In this final section it is intended to examine the present
results in the light of Blurton-Jones' hypothesis and discuss further what
these results imply.

Logically, there are a number of possibilities for the relation between individual and temporal variations in behaviour. Four main distinct possibilities are summarised below:

1. there is no clear relation between individual variation and frequency of temporal clusters.

2. individual variation is mainly variation in the frequency of occurrence of single temporal clusters.

3. individual variation is mainly variation in the frequency of occurrence of several temporal clusters.

4. Individual variation is mainly selective emphasis on frequency of occurrence of certain elements within temporal clusters.

The first possibility would imply that individuals have markedly different temporal clusters of behaviour. Such an implication conflicts with direct experience; it was also checked by running a number of temporal analyses on data for particular individuals. Inspection of the contingency tables showed that in most cases broadly similar types of clusters would be present.

The second possibility would imply that there are 'rough-and-tumble' individuals, 'aggressive' individuals, 'social interactive', 'dependent' and 'isolate' individuals, for example. In such a case the principal components of individual difference would replicate the clusters or components of temporal variation. This is not the case. A principal component analysis was run on the temporal data to check that the form of data analysis was not a point at issue here. The components obtained were reasonably consistent with the results of cluster analysis (although forming it into orthogonal dimensions) and did not resemble at all the dimensions of individual variation. Furthermore, the amount of variance accounted for by the first three components was only 18%, compared with 41% for the first three components for individual variation. This suggests that (relative to the behaviours employed) temporal variation is more varied and multi-faceted than overall individual variation.

The third possibility can be checked by seeing if the components of individual variation can be made up from a differentially weighted summation of temporal clusters. This would seem to be a plausible interpretation of the results quoted by Blurton-Jones (1972). His first component of social maturity approximates a weighted sum of the rough-and-tumble, aggressive and social interactive groupings, with manipulative play and crying weighted negatively. His second component approximates a positive weighting for rough-and-tumble behaviours, negative weighting for aggressive and social interactive behaviours.

Such an interpretation seems to apply rather less accurately to the present results, (compare Figs. 1 and 3 with 5 and 6). Very broadly, component 1 of Fig. 1 contrasts social and active physical behaviours to isolate and dependent behaviours. But crawl, roll, play noise and slide, for example, do not lie close to the other behaviours in this cluster. Similar observations could be made for the two subsequent components. This leads us to the fourth possibility that individual variation may be mainly selective emphasis on certain elements in clusters.

Looking at age differences in the active physical behaviours, for example, there are positive correlations of age with all these behaviours except climb, slide, crawl, roll and lie. These last behaviours do form a subgroup or two subgroups in Figs. 5 and 6. This leads to the point that whether one considers individual variation as acting at the level of temporal clusters or behaviour elements depends on the level of behavioural integration which one is considering. Taking a hierarchial presentation such as in Fig. 6, it would seem that individual variation, as well as components of this such as age and sex, and other variables such as spatial and toy density (Smith, 1970), act at a level somewhere between the gross temporal clusters and the individual behaviour categories.

While a worthwhile objective, it does not seem feasible to make a more precise statement than this with the present results. A more comprehensive list of behaviour categories, many of them at a finer level, should be employed; hierarchical analysis can be carried out as indicated earlier (p. 784). Detailed comparisons could then be made of temporal clusters between individuals in the same environment, and for particular individuals in different environments and at different ages. Such a programme of research and analysis, while time-consuming, could lead into new insights into the nature of motivations in early childhood, their development and alternative modes of expression and the influence of environmental and background factors on social and play behaviour.

VIII. REFERENCES

Altmann, S. A. (1965). Sociobiology of rhesus monkeys. II: stochastics of social communication. J. Theoret. Biol. 8, 490–522.

Altmann, S. A. (1968). Sociobiology of rhesus monkeys. IV: Testing Mason's hypothesis of sex differences in affective behaviour. Behaviour 32, 49–69

Armstrong, J. A. & Soelberg, P. (1968). On the interpretation of factor analysis. Psychol. Bull. 70, 361-364.

Arrington, R. E. (1931). "Interrelations in the behavior of young children". Teachers College, Columbia University, New York.

Becker, W. C. (1960). The matching of behavior rating and questionnaire personality factors. Psychol. Bull. 57, 201-212.

Becker, W. C. (1960). The relation of factors in parental ratings of self and each other to the behavior of kindergarten children as rated by mothers, fathers and teachers. J. Consult. Psychol. 24, 507-527.

Becker, W. C. (1961). Comments of Cattell's paper on "perturbations" in personality structure research. Psychol. Bull.. 58, 175.

Beer, C. G. (1961-1963). Incubation and nest-building behaviour of Black-headed Gulls. Behaviour 18, 62-106; 19, 283-304; 21, 13-77; 155-176.

Blurton-Jones, N. G. (1967). An ethological study of some aspects of social behaviour of children in nursery school. In "Primate ethology" (D. Morris ed.) Weidenfeld & Nicholson, London.

Blurton-Jones, N. G. (1968). Observations and experiments on causation of threat displays of the Great Tit (Paris major). Anim. Beh. Monogr. 1, 75-158.

Blurton-Jones, N. G. (1972). Categories of child-child interaction. In "Ethological studies of child behaviour" (N. G. Blurton-Jones ed.) Cambridge University Press, Cambridge.

Brannigan, C., & Humphries, D. (1969). I see what you mean ..... New Sci. 42, 406-408.

Cattell, R. B. (1961). Theory of situational, instrument, second order and refraction factors in personality structure research. Psychol.

Bull. 58, 160-174.

Cattell, R. B. & Peterson, D. R. (1958). Personality structure in 4-5 year olds, by factoring observed, time-sampling behavior. Rass. Psi. Gen. Clin. 3, 1-12.

Emmerich, W. (1964). Continuity and stability in early social development. Child Dev. 35, 311-332.

Eysenck, H. J. & Cookson, D. (1969). Personality in primary school children. 2. Teachers ratings. Brit. J. educ. Psychol. 39, 123-130.

Eysenck, H. J. & Eysenck, S. B. G. (1969). "Personality structure and measurement". Routledge & Kegan Paul, London.

Eysenck, H. J. & Pickup, A. J. (1968). Teacher ratings of extraversion and neuroticism and children's inventory responses. Brit. J. educ. Psychol. 38, 94-96.

Gewirtz, J. L. (1956). A factor analysis of some attention-seeking behaviors of young children. Child Dev. 27, 17-36.

Goodenough, F. L. (1930). Inter-relationships in the behavior of young children. Child Dev. 1, 29-47.

Grant, E. C. (1968). An ethological description of non-verbal behaviour during interviews. Brit. J. Med. Psychol. 41, 177-184.

Grant, E. C. (1969). Human facial expression. Man 4, 525-536.

Hallworth, H. J. (1965). The dimensions of personality among children of school age. Brit. J. Math. Stat. Psychol. 18, 45-56.

Hooff, J. A. R. A. M. van (1970). A component analysis of the structure of the social behaviour of a semi-captive chimpanzee group. Experientia 26, 549-550.

Hooff, J. A. R. A. M. van (1971). "Aspecten van het sociale gedrag en de communicatie bij humane en hogere niet-humane primaten." Rotterdam.

Hope K. (1968). "Methods of multivariate analysis". University of London Press, London.

Horowitz, E. L. & Smith, R. B. (1939). Social relations and personality patterning in preschool children. J. Genet. Psychol. 54, 337-352.

Jardine, N. & Sibson, R. (1971). "Mathematical taxonomy". John Wiley, New York.

Koch, H. L. (1934). A multiple-factor analysis of certain measures of activeness in nursery school children. J. Genet. Psychol. 45, 482-487.

Koch, H. L. (1942). A factor analysis of some measures of the behavior of preschool children. J. Genet. Psychol. 27, 257-287.

Lawick-Goodall, J. van (1968). The behaviour of free-living chimpanzees in the Gombe Stream reserve. Anim. Beh. Monogr. 1, 161-311.

Lorr, M. & McNair, D. M. (1965). Expansion of the interpersonal behaviour circle. J. Pers. Soc. Psychol. 2, 823-830.

Manwell, E. M. & Mengert, I. C. (1934). A study of the development of two- and three-year old children with respect to play activities. Univ. Iowa Stud. Child Welf. 4, 69-111.

Martin, W. E. (1969). Singularity and Stability of profiles of social behavior. In "Readings in child behaviour and development" (C. B. Stendler ed.) Harcourt, Brace and World, New York.

McDowell, M. S. (1937). Frequency of choice of play materials by preschool children. Child Dev. 8, 305-310.

McKinney, J. P. (1962). A multidimensional study of the behavior of severely retarded boys. Child Dev. 33, 923-938.

McQuitty, L. L. (1964). Capabilities and improvements of linkage analysis as a clustering method. Educ. Psychol. Measur. 24, 441-456.

McQuitty, L. L. (1967). A mutual development of some typological theories and pattern-analytic methods. Educ. Psychol. Measur. 27, 21-46

Parten, M. B. (1932). Social participation among preschool children. J. Ab. Soc. Psychol. 27, 243-269.

Peterson, D. R. (1960). The age generality of personality factors derived from ratings. Educ. Psychol. Measur. 20, 461-474.

Peterson, D. R. (1965). Scope and generality of verbally defined personality factors. Psychol. Rev. 72, 48-59.

Rafferty, J. E., Tyler, B. B. and Tyler, F. B. (1960). Personality assessment from free play observations. Child Dev. 31, 691-702.

Schaeffer, E. S. (1961). Converging conceptual models for maternal behavior and for child behavior. In "Parental attitudes and child behaviour" (J. C. Glidewell ed.) C. C. Thomas, Springfield.

Smith, P. K. (1970). Social and play behaviour of preschool children. Unpublished Ph.D. thesis, University of Sheffield.

Smith, P. K. & Connolly, K. (1972). Patterns of play and social interaction in preschool children. In "Ethological studies of child behaviour" (N. G. Blurton-Jones ed.) Cambridge University Press, Cambridge.

Swan, C. (1938). Individual differences in the facial expressive behavior of preschool children: a study by the time-sampling method. Genet. Psychol. Monogr. 20, 557-650.

Thomas, A., Chess, S., Birch, H. G., Hertzig, M. E. & Korn, S. (1964). "Behavioural individuality in early childhood". University of London Press, London.

Thomas, A., Chess, S., & Birch, H. G. (1968). "Temperament and behavior disorders in children". New York University Press, New York.

Thompson, N. S. (1969). The motivations underlying social structure in Macaca irus. Anim. Behav.17, 459-467.

Thorpe, J. G. (1959). The value of teachers' ratings of the adjustment of their pupils. Brit. J. educ. Psychol., 29, 207-212.

Tinbergen, N. (1959). Comparative studies of the behaviour of gulls (Laridae): a progress report. Behaviour 15, 1-70.

Waldrop, M. F., Pedersen, F. A. & Bell, R. Q. (1968). Minor physical anomalies and behavior in preschool children. Child Dev. 39, 391-400.

Wiepkema, P. R. (1961). An ethological analysis of the reproductive behaviour of the Bitterling (Rhodeus amarus Bloch). Arch. neer. Zool. 14, 103-199.

IX. APPENDIX: DEFINITIONS OF BEHAVIOURAL CATEGORIES

(Inter-observer agreements and statistical reliabilities in brackets)

Facial expressions and vocalisations:

Smile (.53; .88): corners of mouth withdrawn and turned upwards. No distinction made as to mouth open or closed, teeth visible or not. No audible vocalisation.

Talk: any utterance containing one or more recognisable words excluding exclamations ("Oh", "Ah") or play noise. Recorded S if talking alone (-; .64), C if talking to another child, (.78; .95), N if talking to nurse (.60; .76), and O if talking to observer (-; .87).

Play talk (-; .56): repeated or stereotyped phrases made in play such as "I am a Dalek".

Play noise (.83; .88): unintelligible noises made in play, "brr-brr", "bang", etc.

Laugh (.73; .86): open-mouthed smile accompanied by audible vocalisation (rapid or staccato expulsions of breath).

Cry (-; .75): repeated, usually low-pitched vocalisations, "waaah", "aah-aah".

General posture or motor activity:

Run (.82; .75): any locomotory activity faster than walk, excluding running up steps (climb), and chase/flee.

Jump/hop (-; .56): jumping up or down, or just jumping down from apparatus; hopping on one leg or from one leg to the other; skipping.

Chase/flee (-; .45): non-contact running play in which a child pursues or is pursued by another, accompanied by laughing or smiling.

Wrestle/tumble (-; .73): play such as mock fighting or rolling around, involving gross physical contact.

Dance (-; .30): gross rhythmic movements of body, arms and legs.

Walk (.92; .40): locomotory activity on two legs, always one foot on ground, for two paces or more.

Stand (.91; .56): stands upright on both feet.

Crawl, roll (-; .63): locomotes by crawling on hands or knees, or by rolling with whole body.

Crouch (1.0; .69): crouches down with knees bent, but weight still on feet; may have hands on ground, if stationary.

Sit (1.0; .65): weight supported on buttocks which are in contact with ground or apparatus.

Lie (-; 0.0): weight supported on whole body, lying on ground or apparatus.

Lean (.55; .69): weight supported by one or both feet on ground and by whole body leaning against wall or apparatus.

Climb (-; .37): gross physical activity with three or four limbs resulting in vertical motion of whole body. Walking or running up steps is also included.

Slide (-; .69): slides down smooth surface.

Rock (-; .45): rocks in vertical or horizontal direction on horse, see-saw, or other apparatus.

Swing (-; .55): weight supported by arms only, on apparatus.

Agonistic Patterns

Try dominate (-; .40): tries to dominate another child by taking possession of toy or apparatus, but without immediate success.

Try resist (-; .32): attempts to resist another child who is trying to take over possession of toy or apparatus.

Dominative (-; .67): takes possession of toy or apparatus from another child.

Submissive (-; .85): allows another child to take possession of toy or apparatus. Being led around completely passively by another child is also included.

Hit, throw (-; .45): beats at or hits another child, or throws an object at him, in an agonistic context.

Fight (-; .20): wrestling with another child in an agonistic context.

Specific Motor Patterns and Social Interactions

Point (-; .37): arm extended outwards but not in contact with object, looks or stares in same direction.

Suck (.92; .84): digit or object in contact with one or both lips.

Play beat (-; 0.0): beat made with extended arm in play context, usually with open fist and without contact.

Kick, throw (-; .64): kicks or throws toy (not in agonistic context.

Push, pull (-; .78): pushes or pulls a toy along the ground or on apparatus. Includes riding a scooter.

Pushed (-; 0.0): in trolley or similar toy, being pushed or pulled along by someone else.

Automanipulate (.92; .58): manipulates own clothes, or part of body, in a generally repetitive and sometimes stereotyped way.

Watch nurse (.62; .69): fixates nurse (a look of 3 seconds or more), or watches nurse's activity.

Approach nurse (-; .37): direct approach to nurse from at least 3-4 feet away when apparent from context this is not just accidental.

Contact nurse (-; .79): any non-accidental physical contact with nurse.

React observer (.80; .87): fixates or makes non-accidental physical contact with observer.

Particular Activities

Sand (-; .64): child is playing with sand, earth or clay, or is in the sand pit while sand is in it.

Water (1.0; .56): child is playing with water, or toys in water (normally in bowl or basin).

Book (-; .03): child is holding or reading a book, or comic, or magazine.

Paint, chalk (-; 0.0): child is holding paintbrush, chalk, or crayon and making marks on paper, blackboard or some other surface.

Nature of Play or Activity

For each half-minute sample a tick was put in at least one of the following sex categories: manipulate toy; with apparatus; neither toys or apparatus; both toys and apparatus; hold toy; wear clothes.

A minimum duration of about ten seconds was accepted to score a category, so several (or even all six) could be scored in one sample.

Manipulate toy (M) (.90; .85): child is actively using or playing with toy or toys. A toy includes any object separate from the child, which can be moved about by him in the course of his activity. This includes sand, water paint, books, sticks, flowers, as well as the usual nursery toys. Clothes and apparatus are excluded.

With apparatus (A) (.85; .46): child is in contact with apparatus, including leaning or grasping but excluding just touching or momentary contact. Apparatus includes any object which cannot or concurrently is not being moved by the child (limited motion up and down as on a rocking horse or see-saw is not relevant). The common forms of apparatus were steps-and-slide, climbing frame, tables, chairs, rocking horse, trampoline, boxes, cupboards, see-saw. Also included is being pushed in a trolley or pram (since the child concerned is not causing the motion), lying on a blanket or mattress, swinging a door. Walls, windows, the rim of the sand-pit, and large stones lining the flower-bed were excluded.

Neither toys or apparatus (N) (.88; .64): child is neither manipulating a toy or in contact with apparatus, as defined above. H and W (see below) may also be scored.

Both toys and apparatus (MA) (.75; .67): child is both manipulating a toy and in contact with apparatus, as defined above. M was also scored but A was not.

Hold toy (H) (.72; .86): child is in contact with toy or toys (as defined above) only in a very passive sense. He may simply hold the toy while he indulges in other activity, or slowly turn it over or suck it without looking at it. His interest is elsewhere. Pulling a trolley behind him as he walks, without looking at it, is included, and so is lying with a blanket on top.

Wear clothes (W) (-; .91): child is wearing some piece of material or object other than the child's normal clothes (such as blanket over head, cowboy hat). An apron which the child is made to wear by the nurse is not counted.

Social participation

At the end of each half-minute period the social nature of the child's behaviour was recorded, as self, parallel or group; the definitions of these terms, given below, correspond closely to those of Parten (1932). If the social nature of behaviour changed during the half-minute, the most social rating which lasted for ten seconds or more was scored. A composite index of social participation was later obtained for each child by scoring self behaviour as 0, parallel as +1 and group as +2.

Self (S): the child plays alone and independently. If he is playing with toys the toys are different from those used by nearby children; if he is playing without toys then no other children nearby are engaged in similar behaviour. In either case there is no interaction with other children; a child makes no effort to keep close to or speak to other children, his interest is centred on his own behaviour which is pursued without reference to what others are doing.

Parallel (P): the child plays independently, but the behaviour he chooses naturally brings him among other children. If he is playing with toys then these are like those which nearby children are using, but he plays with the toys as he sees fit; if he is playing without toys then he uses the same apparatus or his behaviour is of a similar nature to that of other nearby children. In either case he does not attempt to influence the behaviour of nearby children and there is little or no interaction with them. He plays beside rather than with the other children.

Group (G): the child plays with other children, interacting with them in the nature of the behaviour. Interactions here include conversation, borrowing or sharing toys, following or chasing one another, physical contact, and organised play involving different roles.

SEX DIFFERENCES IN THE ACTIVITIES AND

SOCIAL INTERACTIONS OF NURSERY SCHOOL CHILDREN

C. Brindley, P. Clarke, C. Hutt, I. Robinson and E. Wethli

Department of Psychology,
University of Reading

I. INTRODUCTION

The prosaic topic of sex differences has been well documented in the psychological literature for nearly half a century. Nevertheless, an attempt by a behavioural scientist to reiterate some of these facts today occasions considerable surprise, particularly if they are placed in a biological rather than a cultural context. In other words, it is permissible to refer to sex differences if we can then proceed to dismiss them as cultural excresences, but not if we are able to postulate some biological bases for them.

More recently in this field, a singularly curious situation has arisen. We have, on the one hand, geneticists, biochemists and neuroendocrinologists striving assiduously to elucidate the genetic and hormonal control of many behavioural mechanisms in the explicit expectation of advancing our knowledge and understanding of the determinants of human behaviour. Some behavioural scientists (Jensen et al., 1967; Hamburg, 1971) have gone so far as to repudiate, by implication, the available human evidence in expressing their belief that their data on chimpanzees and monkeys will enhance our understanding of aspects of human social interaction!

On the other hand, the psychologists supposedly interested in developmental processes seem extraordinarily reluctant to acknowledge any biological bases for behavioural or psychological sex differences. For instance, one of the most regrettable changes in the new edition of what must be the developmental psychologist's vade mecum - "Carmichael's Manual of Child Psychology" (Mussen 1970) - is the substitution of a chapter on Sex-typing and Socialisation (Mischel) for an informative and exhaustive review of human Sex Differences by Terman and Tyler (1954). This is all the more lamentable since, in the time that has elapsed, there have been considerable genetic and neuroendocrinological advances which are extremely pertinent for an understanding of the process of sexual differentiation.

Referring to the reviews by Broverman et al. (1968) and Hamburg and Lunde (1966), Mischel concedes that there may be biological determinants and that "a good deal of research, chiefly conducted with lower animals, tentatively suggests some provocative links between hormonal conditions, brain functions, and behaviour". But there are biological determinants of many psychological differences and the situation regarding hormonal influences on brain and behaviour is far less equivocal than Mischel makes it appear. Research on the rat and the rhesus monkey - species which have provided us with the empirical bases for our knowledge of learning processes and attachment behaviour respectively (see Beach, 1950; Harlow, 1961) - does much more than provoke speculation.

Much of the resistance to accepting genetic or hormonal control of aspects of human behaviour appears to result from a confusion of the explication of the process with the prescription of the content. In general, the two are not wholly separable, but in principle it is possible to demonstrate, for instance, the process of genetic inheritance of a factor without having to account for every single one of its expressive forms. Similarly, in the process of sexual differentation; the hormonal influences in male and female make certain events more likely and certain experiences more salient for one sex rather than the other, but they do not prescribe the actions of males and females in all foreseeable situations.

Precisely because of the nature of early (uterine) influences,
environmental factors operate on an already differentiated organism.
The process of sexual differentiation in mammalian species involve
differentiation of the reproductive organs and tracts and of the brain
(see Harris,1964; 1970; Harris and Levine,1965; Levine,1966). The
pervasive effects of this differentiation upon the non-sexual behaviour
of mammals has been cogently reviewed by Gray (1971a, b) and by Gray
and Buffery (1971). In particular the effects upon human development
in all its manifestations have been reviewed and evaluated by Garai and
Scheinfeld (1968) and Hutt (1972a, b, c and d).

It seems remarkable then, that Mischel should state that his
review is restricted to a psychological analysis of sex differences in
social behaviour with no reference to biological determinants or physical characteristics. For surely a comprehension of the biology of
sex differences is precluded by such a procedure? In fact, rejection
of the biological bases of such differences is implicit in Mischel's
unqualified acceptance of the Money-Hampson "psychosexual-neutrality-
at-birth" theory. No other theory envisages the newborn as a tabula
rasa quite so clearly. Mischel omits to mention however, the substantial criticism that has been made of this theory, on grounds of selection, method and logic by Diamond (1965, 1968) and by Zuger (1970).
Moreover, the evidence provided by Money himself (Money and
Erhardt,1968) has been shown to be one of the strongest arguments
against his case (Hutt 1972d).

Anatomically, physiologically and psychologically, there is no
neuter sex. Male differentiation is an active process initiated by the
presence of the Y-chromosome and subsequently organised by the
testicular hormone. In the absence or failure of male differentiation,

female differentiation inevitably takes place. Thus the newborn human infant is unequivocally a girl or boy (except in rare anomolous cases) with characteristically feminine or masculine propensities, predispositions and capacities. The environment acts upon an organism which is already differentiated and organised in this manner, and it is the nature of these interactions which should be the principal concern of the developmental psychologist or biologist.

In this paper therefore, we describe a series of observational studies of nursery school children where, although not the primary objective of the studies, the analysis revealed marked and reliable sex differences. We discuss these differences in the context of other studies of children, as well as studies of infra-human primates, and attempt to evaluate the results taking cognisance of relevant experimental and neuroendocrinological work.

II. STUDY I. AGGRESSION IN NURSERY SCHOOL

The aims of this study were to record all instances of aggressive behaviour occurring in the course of everyday nursery school activity. This is an aspect of child behaviour that has interested developmental psychologists for 40 years, but as the work of these researchers has been extensively referred to and reviewed elsewhere (bibliography in Maccoby, 1966; Feshbach, 1970; Mischel, 1970) they will not be individually mentioned here.

In England, many of the nursery schools for 3 - 5 year-old children are run by the State, i.e. by City or County Education Committees. Selection for these schools is by rota, although under certain circumstances (e.g. broken home, no adequate caretaker etc.)

a child may be given priority. Since these state schools provide for
only a small proportion of preschool children, privately run nursery
or play groups operate as well. Parents pay for their children to attend
the latter. The studies described here were carried out in 3 state-run
nursery schools since in these there was a more equitable distribution
of socioeconomic status and intelligence.

Although one of the somewhat surprising features of these nursery schools is the relatively low incidence of fighting, it was supposed
that the presence of children from disturbed or disrupted backgrounds
might result in greater aggression being displayed in groups or classes
of which they were members. Furthermore, there was some evidence
that temporal fluctuations in physical activity did occur (Wright, 1970)
and we wondered whether these would in any way contribute towards
the incidence of aggression.

1. Method

(a) Subjects. 30 nursery school children, 15 boys and 15 girls
were observed. Eight were in the $3\frac{1}{2}$ - 4 year group, sixteen in the
4 - $4\frac{1}{2}$ year group and six in the $4\frac{1}{2}$ - 5 year group.

(b) Procedure. An event-sampling method of observation was
used, whereby every event that could be described as aggressive was
recorded. Feshbach (1970) has discussed in great detail the pitfalls
inherent in too casual a definition of aggression. His point is well
taken, but until our observations achieve the required degree of sophistication, we can proceed with a definition that is partly operational and
partly functional, (see Hutt and Hutt 1970, for justification of such a
procedure). Thus, any episode consisting of threatening - by gesture
or word - another child or teacher were all recorded as occurrences

of aggression; so were acts of hitting, kicking, breaking or throwing objects or toys.

In the nursery school where this study was carried out there were three activity rooms; each of the rooms was sampled for 45 minutes at a time, observations being carried out throughout a whole morning or afternoon for six days. The rooms were sampled in a different order each day. The recordings included the nature of the act, the initiator, and the person or object at which it was directed. After the observation period additional notes regarding context, preceding events etc. were made.

2. Results

Since normality of distribution could not be assumed for these data, distribution-free tests were used for evaluating the significance of results.

Friedman's analysis of variance showed no significant differences according to time of day, although there was a marked increase in aggressive encounters during the third period of the morning, i.e., the period preceding lunch.

The differences according to sex were highly significant (Wilcoxon Rank Sum test, T=308, p=0.005). The first pair of histograms in Fig. 1 shows this difference diagramatically. Dunn's multiple comparison test (Kirk, 1968), appropriate for planned nonorthogonal comparisons, showed that there was no significant difference between the persons or objects towards whom the girls directed their aggression; the boys, on the other hand, showed significantly more aggression to other boys than to girls, teachers or objects,

these latter three groups being indistinguishable (fig. 1 and Table I).
Thus, these results showed that boys were considerably more aggressive than girls, and that whereas girls did not discriminate very much
between the objects at which they directed their aggression, the boys
manifested their aggression mostly against other boys.

III. STUDY II. CO-OPERATION IN NURSERY SCHOOL

Aggressive behaviour is conventionally regarded as undesirable
or inappropriate - at any rate its valency is 'negative'. The distribution of more positively regarded behaviours was also of some concern
to us, and preliminary observations suggested that the category of 'co-
operative behaviour' was suitable for this purpose since it involved
mutual activity initiated spontaneously or at the request of one of the
participants.

1. Method

(a) Subjects. Thirty children, fifteen boys and fifteen girls were
observed in this study. Subjects were divided into older and younger
sub-group according to whether their age was above or below the median age (4 years 8 months).

(b) Procedure. An event-sampling procedure was used and
every occurrence of co-operation observed by the observer was
recorded in terms of the participants, whether spontaneuous or
requested, location and other objects involved. In those instances of
requested co-operation, it was to the person carrying out the observable act of helping that the act was attributed. Games, which usually
involved several participants, were excluded.

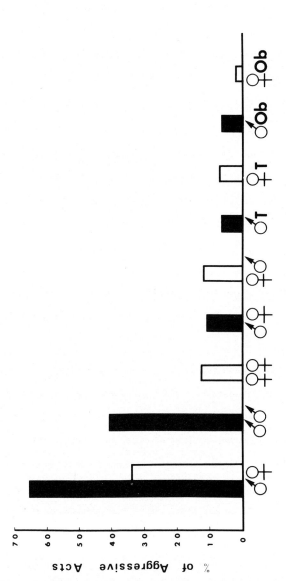

Fig. 1. Aggressive behaviour manifested by boys and girls. The first pair of histograms show the proportion of all aggressive acts committed by boys and girls respectively; subsequent histograms show to whom these acts were directed: boys to boys, girls to girls, boys to girls, girls to boys, boys to teachers, girls to teachers, boys to objects (toys, furniture, etc.) and girls to objects.

2. Results

(a) Requested and spontaneous co-operation. There were twice as many occurrences of spontaneous co-operation as of requested help (67% and 33% respectively). Acts of spontaneous and requested co-operation shown by girls are illustrated in Figs. 2 and 3 respectively.

(b) Age. Older and younger children did not differ in the total amounts of co-operation they exhibited. There was an age difference however in the frequency with which spontaneous and requested co-operative acts were engaged in: of the requested acts 77.7% were carried out by older children as compared with only 38% of the spontaneous acts. The G-test for independence (Woolf 1957) showed these differences to be highly significant (G = 11.49, d.f. = 1, p < 0.001). There was a suggestion too that the co-operative activities of the older children were longer (more frequently above the median duration of 13.5 secs) than those of the younger group, though this result was not significant.

(c) Sex. Girls exceeded boys by far in the frequency with which they exhibited these behaviours (70% and 30% respectively: Wilcoxon Rank Sum test T = 346, p = 0.005). The same trend, though not the absolute differences, was evident whether the co-operation was requested or spontaneous. Dunn's multiple comparison tests shown that girls co-operated with <u>younger girls</u> more than with older girls or with boys of whatever age; boys on the other hand attended more to <u>older boys</u> than to younger boys or to any girls. Both girls and boys engaged in hardly any mutual activity with older members of the opposite sex. (Fig. 4 and Table 2). These sex-age interactions are a result of the very different patterns of behaviour which constituted co-operation in

TABLE I. Differences between Mean% scores on Aggression

		Boys	Girls	Teacher	Objects
Boys					
To Boys	40.2	–	29.9*	35.0*	35.3*
To Girls	10.3		–	5.3	5.4
To Teacher	5.2			–	0.3
To Objects	4.9				–
Girls					
To Boys	10.8	–	0.2	4.8	7.7
To Girls	11.0		–	4.0	7.9
To Teacher	6.0			–	2.9
To Objects	3.1				–

α = 0.1;   d = 18.46;   *p<0.01

TABLE II. Differences between Mean % scores on Co-operation

		OB	YB	OG	YG
Boys					
To older Boys	19.4	–	13.1	16.6	13.1
To younger Boys	6.3		–	3.5	0.0
To older Girls	2.8			–	3.5
To younger Girls	6.3				–
Girls					
To older Boys	2.8	–	12.6	6.4	35.2*
To younger Boys	15.4		–	6.2	22.6*
To older Girls	9.2			–	28.8*
To younger Girls	38.0				–

α = 0.01;   d = 19.84;   *p<0.01

boys and girls: girls were predomonantly engaged in 'caring for' younger children (see Fig. 3), whereas boys were mostly concerned with joining in the activities of older boys (see Fig. 5).

IV. STUDY III. PLAY ACTIVITIES

A number of earlier studies have reported sex differences in play activities of children ranging from 2 years of age to 13 years (Honzik 1951; Farrell 1957; Clark, Wyon and Richards 1969; Pedersen and Bell 1970). The results of the study by Goldberg and Lewis (1969) were dramatic in the sense that they observed differences in infants of 13 months of age - differences which were completely in accord with those obtained from older children. It could of course be argued that the samples of children studied by these several authors had an unrepresentative distribution of socio-economic background, the professional classes being given greater representation. The present study therefore, carried out in 2 state nursery schools with a slight underrepresentation of the higher socio-economic classes, was an attempt to see to what extent the previous sets of results were reproducible.

1. Method

(a) Subjects. Forty children, twenty girls and twenty boys were observed altogether. Eighteen children attended one school and twenty-two the other. Although the schools differed in location and structure, the range of equipment available and activities permitted were approximately the same.

(b) Procedure. A time-sampling method of observation enabled the observers to record activity every 10 secs on a check-list. In

Fig. 2. A typical example of spontaneous co-operation by girls.

Fig. 3. A typical example of requested co-operation by girls.

general, the behaviour categories were defined by the type of motor activity involved, e.g. climbing, push/pull etc.; where however categories were infrequent, essentially similar activities were combined (e.g. sand/water play), or some given a more generic term with respect to location or posture (e.g. table play) or verbal content (e.g. fantasy). At lease 2 15-min records were obtained for each child.

2. Results

Inspection of the data from the two schools showed that the trends with respect to sex were essentially similar although the absolute values differed. The greatest difference occurred in the amount of 'rough-and-tumble-play' - this was negligible in one of the schools. The possible reasons for this are discussed later on.

The data from the two schools were pooled, and analyses carried out on the scores of all forty subjects. Since the absolute values of some categories were very small (see Fig. 6), it was considered legitimate to group the categories in terms of function or of nature of activity. Thus, the following grouping was made:

Sedentary activities:	Book
	Table-play
Physical activities:	Climbing
	Pull/push
	Running/chasing
Constructional activities:	Construction (blocks or bricks)
	Wood-work

Painting was most often done at an easel and therefore could not be classified as a sedentary activity. Similarly special considerations precluded the inclusion of Swings and Rough-and-tumble play as physical activities: swings and gliders provide a particular form of fairly

passive repetitive motion, as Pedersen and Bell (1970) found too, and
Rough-and-tumble is much a social activity. It was decided that comparisons would be made between boys and girls on four behavioural
categories - the three grouped categories noted above, and social interaction. The Nemenyi multiple comparison procedure (Nemenyi
1963) for testing all possible pairs yielded the following results:

Sedentary:	Boys vs Girls	n.s.
Physical:	Boys vs Girls	$p < 0.05$
Social:	Boys vs Girls	$p < 0.01$
Constructional:	Boys vs Girls	$p < 0.05$
Boys:	Physical vs Sedentary	$p < 0.01$
Boys:	Social vs Sedentary	n.s.
Boys:	Constructional vs Sedentary	n.s.
Boys:	Constructional vs Physical	$p < 0.05$
Boys:	Social vs Physical	n.s.
Boys:	Social vs Constructional	n.s.
Girls:	Physical vs Sedentary	n.s.
Girls:	Social vs Sedentary	$p < 0.05$
Girls:	Constructional vs Sedentary	$p < 0.01$
Girls:	Constructional vs Physical	$p < 0.01$
Girls:	Social vs Physical	$p < 0.05$
Girls:	Social vs Constructional	$p < 0.01$

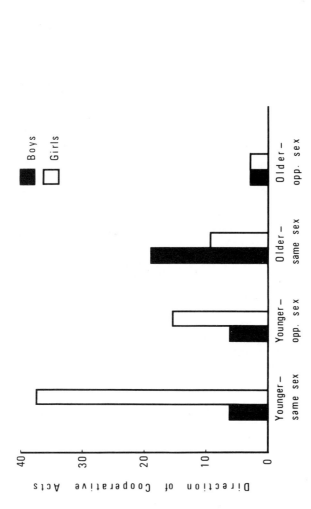

Fig. 4. Co-operative behaviour shown by boys and girls to their peers: the first pair of histograms shows the proportion of all such acts which boys directed towards younger boys and girls directed towards younger girls; the second pair shows those which boys directed to younger girls and girls towards younger boys and so on.

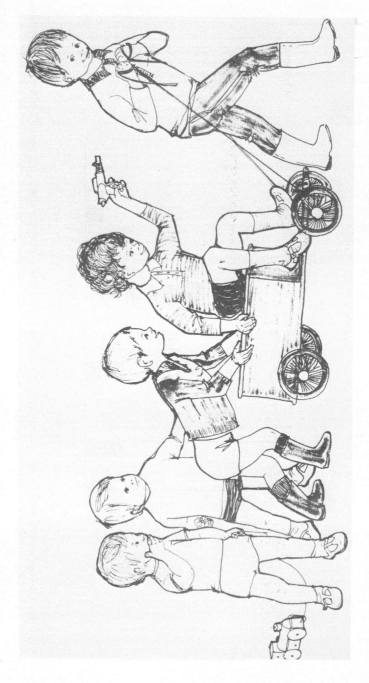

Fig. 5. A typical example of spontaneous co-operation by boys, this encounter being recorded for the second child on the left.

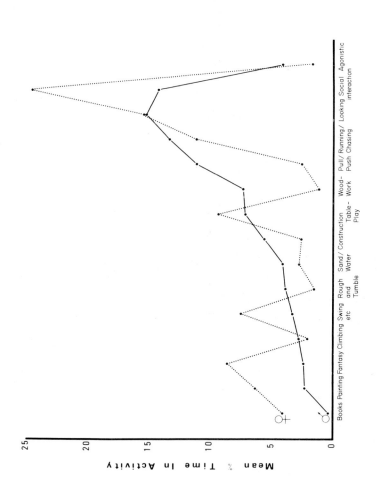

Fig. 6. Time spent in different activities by nursery school children. Fantasy consisted of 'dressing-up' and other forms of 'pretend-play'; table-play involved crayoning puzzles and plasticene-work; pull/push consisted of pulling or pushing buggies, barrows, carts, etc., social interaction consisted of all social encounters which were not aggressive or threatening.

V. DISCUSSION

The results of Study 1 showed that boys not only displayed but also elicited more aggression. Although acquisitive competition was chiefly between males, not all the disputes concerned possessions. Occasionally, there seemed to be no ostensible cause for an aggressive encounter, other than the mere confrontation of the two individuals. This kind of episode only occurred amongst boys. The greater capacity of the male to both manifest as well as elicit aggression has been demonstrated also by Buss (1963) and by Shortell and Biller (1970) in children, and by Taylor and Epstein (1967) in adults. Although there are occasional exceptions, such as the hampster, it is a general finding among mammalian species that the male is more aggressive than the female, and in particular towards other males (see reviews by Gray, 1971a; Hamburg,1971; Hutt,1972a). In fact, Lagerspatz (1969) specifically pointed out that all the experimental work on aggression in his laboratory had to be carried out on male mice, since the female animals showed little, if any, inclination to exhibit aggressive behaviour.

This behavioural dimorphism appears to be principally a function of the early (in utero in humans) differentiation of the brain according to a male or female pattern. For example, testosterone can facilitate aggression only in an animal that has differentiated as a male - it has no effect on a female animal (Beeman,1947; Conner et al., 1969; Harris, 1970). Moreover, Goy and his colleagues found that monkeys who were genetically female would show masculine levels of agonistic behaviours and rough and tumble play if they had been exposed to androgenic influences in utero (Young, Goy and Phoenix,1964; Goy,1966; 1968). Thus the greater manifestation of aggression by boys from a young age -

despite relatively low levels of circulating androgens - is comprehensible in terms of neuroendocrine function and without having to resort to wholly cultural or environmental interpretations. More recently, the dominance rank and frequency of aggression in adult male monkeys has been shown to be directly related to the plasma testosterone levels in these animals (Rose, Holaday and Bernstein, 1971) but it is unclear whether the increased androgen level is a cause or a result of the increased aggression. Nevertheless, the work of Persky and his colleagues on the neuroendocrinological control of affective states and the demonstration of a linear relationship between testosterone production rate and measures of hostility and aggression in young men (Persky et al., 1971) suggests that high levels of circulating male hormone facilitates the expression of aggression.

In terms of co-operative behaviour girls were ascendant, as in many other primate species - rhesus monkeys (Harlow, 1962; Hamburg and Lunde, 1966), squirrel monkeys (Hopf, 1971), baboons and langurs (de Vore and Jay, 1963) and chimpanzees (Goodall, 1968), as well as in adult humans (Spangler and Thomas, 1962). The predominant tendency of the older girls to care for younger children is also reflected in the fact that most of the co-operative acts of these girls were in response to requests. When boys joined together however, the initiative was apparently most often taken by the younger boy - typically running after the older boy in an attempt to be included in his game.

Both these sets of results demonstrate the tendency of boys and girls to interact with others of their own sex. Dawe (1934) described this propensity a considerable time ago, and it is a common observation that in most coeducational establishments unisex groups predominate.

In their free-play activities these children again manifested preferences characteristic of their sex. Girls generally engaged in sedentary activities or literary pursuits, like reading or phantasy-play. Boys more often took part in physical activities. The great discrepancy between girls and boys in the amount of social interaction reveals an unambiguous differentiation of feminine and masculine interests: girls are interested in people (Goodenough, 1957) and pursue these interests through verbal channels (Moore, 1967); boys are interested in objects, things and activities (Garai and Scheinfeld, 1968 ; Little, 1968).

An examination of the experimental literature reveals that many of these sex-typical patterns of behaviour are under some degree of genetic and hormonal control (Hutt 1972d). The climate of the moment militates against the recognition of the biological origins of individual differences, and the acknowledgment of the neuroendocrine bases of human sex differences appears disagreeable to many. For instance, a developmental psychologist recently pronounced that "boys may be more aggressive than girls because of 'early differentiation of the brain according to a male or female pattern' or because parents permit and encourage aggressive behaviour more in boys than in girls" (John Hill, personal communication). Notwithstanding the fact that the alternative explanation begs the question - why should parents permit aggression in boys rather than in girls ? - such an antithesis is captious. It is most improbable that the higher incidence of aggression in boys is exclusively a result of the male brain or a permissive environment. In view of such scepticism however, it seems necessary to summarise the weight of evidence in favour of the biological bases of human sex differences in general.

First, the sexual dimorphism evident in many aspects of human behaviour is also common to many other mammalian species. These sex-typical patterns of behaviour are in accordance with the reproductive roles that males and females fulfil. As Gray and Buffery (1971) state:

"If we find a sex difference which man shares with many of his mammalian relatives, if this sex difference is dependent on genetic control (as, in the case of non-human species, is almost inevitably the case), and if this sex-difference can plausibly be related to some feature of social organisation which is also shared by man with other mammalian species, then the probability is high that both the human sex-differences and this aspect of human society are of biological origin" (pg. 91).

Secondly, the degree of human structural dimorphism in many respects far exceeds that in many other primate species (Jolly, 1970). Such dimorphic features would be curious anomalies were they not accompanied by some behavioural and psychological differences.

Thirdly, many sex-typical behaviours are evident very early in ontogeny. The argument that these are learned and differentially reinforced is implausible in the face of Harlow's demonstration that such patterns of behaviour are manifest by surrogate-reared monkeys. As Harlow (1965) comments:

"It is illogical to interpret these sex differences as learned, culturally ordered patterns of behavior because there is no opportunity for acquiring a cultural heritage, let alone a sexually differentiated one, from an inanimate cloth surrogate". (pg 242).

Fourthly, exposure to androgenic influences during the critical period in development causes the behaviour of genetic females to be more like that of normal males than that of females: this is true of monkey (Goy, 1968) and man (Money and Ehrhardt, 1968), and in the latter case, even when the androgenised females are reared as females.

Finally, widely differing cultural mores and practices do nothing to obliterate these sex-typical patterns of behaviour (Whiting, 1963). Nor apparently have radical changes in child-rearing practices over the years, since the results reported in this paper confirm, in all salient respects, results obtained nearly half a century ago. The interpretations of these results nevertheless differ considerably.

Several authors have found that monkey mothers treat their male and female infants very differently, but largely as a result of the fact that male and female infants behave differently from very early infancy. Similarly, the fact that parents, teachers, or society in general, treat boys and girls differently, may be, to a large extent, because they are different.

VI. ACKNOWLEDGMENT

We are grateful to Mr. B. R. Singer, Senior Lecturer in the Department of Psychology, for his statistical advice.

VII. REFERENCES

Beach, F. A., (1950). The Snark was a Boojum. Amer. Psychol. 5, 115-124.

Beeman, E. A., (1947). The effect of male hormones on aggressive behaviour in mice. Physiol. Zool. 20, 373-404.

Broverman, D. M., Klaiber, E. L., Kobayashi, Y. and Vogel, W. (1968). Roles of activation and inhibition in sex differences in cognitive abilities. Psychol. Rev. 75, 23-50.

Buss, A. H., (1963). Physical aggression in relation to different frustrations. J. Abn. Soc. Psychol. 67, 1-7.

Clark, A. H., Wyon, S. M. and Richards, M. P. M. (1969). Free-play in nursery school children. J. of Child Psychol. Psychiat. 10, 205-216.

Conner, R. L., Levine, S., Wertheim, G. A. and Cummer, J. F. (1969). Hormonal determinants of aggressive behaviour. Ann. N.Y. Acad. Sci. 159, 760-776.

Dawe, H. C. (1934). An analysis of 200 quarrels of preschool children. Child Dev. 5, 139-156.

De Vore, I. and Jay, P. (1963). Mother-infant relations in baboons and langurs. In "Maternal behaviour in mammals". (H. Rheingold, ed.). Wiley and Sons, New York.

Diamond, M. (1965). A critical evaluation of the ontogeny of human sexual behaviour. Q. Rev. Biol. 40, 147-175.

Diamond, M. (1968). Genetic-endocrine interaction and human psycho-sexuality. In "Perspectives in Reproduction and Sexual Behaviour". (M. Diamond, ed.). Indiana University Press.

Farrell, M. (1957). Sex differences in block play in early childhood education. J. Educ. Res. 51, 279-284.

Feshbach, S. (1970). Aggression. In "Carmichael's Manual of Child Psychology", (P. Mussen, ed.), Wiley, New York.

Garai, J. E. and Scheinfeld, A. (1968). Sex differences in mental and behavioural traits. Genet. Psychol. Monogr. 77, 169-299.

Goldberg, S. and Lewis, M. (1969). Play behaviour in the year-old
    infant: early sex differences. Child Dev. 40, 21-31.

Goodall, J. van L. (1968). The behaviour of free-living chimpanzees
    in the Gombe Stream Reserve. Anim. Behav. Monogr. 1, 161-
    311.

Goodenough, E. W. (1957). Interest in persons as an aspect of sex
    differences in the early years. Genet. Psychol. Monogr. 55,
    287-323.

Goy, R. W. (1966). Role of androgens in the establishment and regu-
    lation of behavioural sex differences in mammals. J. Anim.
    Sci., 25, Suppl. 21-35.

Goy, R. W. (1968). Organising effects of androgen on the behaviour
    of rhesus monkeys. In "Endocrinology and Human Behaviour".
    (R. P. Michael, ed.) Oxford University Press, Oxford.

Gray, J. A. (1971a). Sex differences in emotional behaviour in
    mammals including man: endocrine bases. Acta Psychol. 35,
    29-46.

Gray, J. A. (1971b). "The Psychology of Fear and Stress."
    Wiedenfeld and Nicolson, London.

Gray, J. A. and Buffery, A. W. H. (1971). Sex differences in emo-
    tional and cognitive behaviour in mammals including man:
    adaptive and neural bases. Acta Psychol. 35, 89-111.

Hamburg, D. A. (1971). Psychobiological studies of aggressive
    behaviour. Nature 230, 19-23.

Hamburg, D. A. and Lunde, D. T. (1966). Sex hormones in the
    development of sex differences in human behaviour. In "The
    Development of Sex Differences". (E. Maccoby, ed.)
    Tavistock, London.

Harlow, H. F. (1961). The development of affectional patterns in infant monkeys. In "Determinants of Infant Behaviour", (B. M. Foss, ed.) Methuen, London.

Harlow, H. F. (1962). The heterosexual affectional system in monkeys. Amer. Psychol. 17, 1-9.

Harlow, H. F. (1965). Sexual behaviour of the rhesus monkey. In "Sex and Behaviour". (F. Beach, ed.) Wiley and Sons, New York.

Harris, G. W. (1964). Sex hormones, brain development and brain function. Endocrinology 75, 627-648.

Harris, G. W. (1970). Hormonal differentiation of the developing central nervous system with respect to patterns of endocrine function. Phil. Trans. Roy. Soc. London B259, 165-177.

Harris, G. W. and Levine, S. (1965). Sexual differentiation of the brain and its experimental control. J. Physiol. (London), 181, 379-400.

Honzik, M. P. (1951). Sex differences in the occurrence of materials in the play constructions of pre-adolescents. Child Dev. 22, 15-35.

Hopf, S. (1971). New findings on the ontogeny of social behaviour in the Squirrel Monkey. Psychiat.,Neurol., Neurochir., 74, 21-34

Hutt, C. (1972a). Neuroendocrinological, behavioural and intellectual aspects of sexual differentiation in human development. In "Gender Differences: Their Ontogeny and Significance". (C. Ounsted and D. C. Taylor eds.) Churchill, London.

Hutt, C. (1972b). Sex differences in human development. Human Develop. 15, 153-170.

Hutt, C. (1972c). Sexual dimorphism: its significance in human development. In "Determinants of Behavioural Development". (F. Monks, W. Hartup and J. de Wit, eds.) Academic Press, London.

Hutt, C. (1972d) Males and Females. Penguin Books.

Hutt, S. J. and Hutt, C. (1970). "Direct Observation and Measurement of Behaviour". Charles Thomas, Springfield, Illinois.

Jensen, G. D., Bobbitt, R. A. and Gordon, B. N. (1967). Sex differences in social interaction between infant monkeys and their mothers. In "Recent Advances in Biological Psychiatry", Vol. IX. (J. Wortis, ed.) Plenum Press, New York.

Jolly, C. J. (1970). The seed-eaters: a new model of hominid differentiation based on a baboon analogy. Man 5, 5-26.

Kirk, R. E. (1968). "Experimental Design: Procedures for the Behavioural Sciences." Brooks/Cole.

Lagerspatz, K. M. J. (1969). Aggression and aggressiveness in laboratory mice. In "Aggressive Behaviour". (S. Garattini and E. B. Sigg, eds.) Excerpta Medica Foundation, Amsterdam.

Levine, S. (1966). Sex differences in the brain. Scientific Amer. 214. 84-90.

Little, B. (1968). Psychospecialisation: functions of differential interest in persons and things. Bull. Brit. Psychol. Soc. 21, 113A.

Maccoby, E. E. (ed.). (1966). "The Development of Sex Differences". Tavistock, London.

Mischel, W. (1970). Sex-typing and socialisation. In "Carmichael's Manual of Child Psychology", (P. Mussen, ed.) Vol. 2, Wiley and Sons, New York.

Money, J. and Ehrhardt, A. A. (1968). Prenatal hormonal exposure: possible effects on behaviour in man. In "Endocrinology and Human Behaviour". (R. P. Michael, ed.) Oxford University Press.

Moore, T. (1967). Language and intelligence: a longitudinal study of the first eight years. Part 1: Patterns of development in boys and girls. Human Develop. 10, 88-106.

Mussen, P. (ed.) (1970). "Carmichael's Manual of Child Psychology". John Wiley, 3rd edition.

Nemenyi, P. (1963). Distribution-free multiple comparisons. New York: State University of New York, Downstate Medical Centre.

Pedersen, F. A. and Bell, R. Q. (1970). Sex differences in preschool children without histories of complications of pregnancy and delivery. Develop. Psychol. 3, 10-15.

Persky, H., Smith, K. D., and Basu, G. K. (1971). Relation of psychologic measures of aggression and hostility to testosterone production in man. Psychosom. Med. 33, 265-277

Rose, R. M., Holaday, J. W. and Bernstein, I. S. (1971). Plasma testosterone, dominance rank and aggressive behaviour in male rhesus monkeys. Nature 231, 366-368.

Shortell, J. R. and Biller, H. B. (1970). Aggression in children as a function of sex of subject and sex of opponent. Develop. Psychol. 3, 143-144.

Spangler, D. P. and Thomas, C. W. (1962). The effects of age, sex and physical disability upon manifest needs. J. Couns. Psychol. 9 313-319.

Taylor, S. P. and Epstein, S. (1967). Aggression as a function of the interaction of the sex of the aggressor and sex of the victim. J. Pers. 35, 474-486.

Terman, L. M. and Tyler, L. E. (1954). Psychological sex differ-
    ences. In "Manual of Child Psychology". (L. Carmichael, ed.)
    Wiley, New York. 2nd edition.

Whiting, B. (ed.). (1963). "Six Cultures: Studies of Child Rearing."
    Wiley and Sons, New York.

Woolf, B. (1957). The log likelihood ratio test (the G - test). Ann.
    Human Genet. 21, 397-409.

Wright, D. (1970). Periodicity in the behaviour of young children.
    Unpublished B.A. Thesis, University of Oxford.

Young, W. C., Goy, R. W. and Phoenix, C. H. (1964). Hormones
    and sexual behaviour. Science, 143, 212-218.

Zuger, B. (1970). Gender Role Determination: a critical review of
    the evidence from hermaphroditism. Psychosom. Med. 32,
    449-467.

Author Index

Page numbers which are underlined indicate pages on which the complete reference is given.